Applied Price Theory

Applied Price Theory
Cotton Mather Lindsay
Clemson University

The Dryden Press
Chicago New York Philadelphia San Francisco Montreal Toronto London
Sydney Tokyo Mexico City Rio de Janeiro Madrid

Acquisitions Editor: Elizabeth Widdicombe
Developmental Editor: Susan Meyers
Project Editor: Ruta Graff
Managing Editor: Jane Perkins
Design Director: Alan Wendt
Production Manager: Mary Jarvis

Text and Cover Designer: Margery Dole
Copyeditor: Nancy Maybloom
Indexer: Jennifer Gordon
Compositor: G&S Typesetters
Text Type: 10/12 Times Roman

Library of Congress Cataloging in Publication Data

Lindsay, Cotton M.
   Applied price theory.

   Includes index.
   1. Microeconomics.   I. Title.
HB172.L72   1982   338.5   83-20732
ISBN 0-03-056129-9

Printed in the United States of America
456-016-98765432

Copyright 1984 CBS College Publishing
All rights reserved

Address orders:
383 Madison Avenue
New York, NY 10017

Address editorial correspondence:
One Salt Creek Lane
Hinsdale, IL 60521

CBS College Publishing
The Dryden Press
Holt, Rinehart and Winston
Saunders College Publishing

*To Mather and Jefferson,
my two peanuts*

The Dryden Press Series in Economics

Breit and Elzinga
The Antitrust Casebook

Breit and Ransom
The Academic Scribblers, *Revised Edition*

Campbell and Campbell
An Introduction to Money and Banking, *Fifth Edition*

Dolan
Basic Economics, *Third Edition*

Dolan
Basic Macroeconomics, *Third Edition*

Dolan
Basic Microeconomics, *Third Edition*

Heertje, Rushing, and Skidmore
Economics

Hyman
Public Finance

Johnson and Roberts
Money and Banking: A Market Oriented Approach

Leftwich and Eckert
The Price System and Resource Allocation, *Eighth Edition*

Lindsay
Applied Price Theory

Morley
Inflation and Unemployment, *Second Edition*

Morley
Macroeconomics

Nicholson
Intermediate Microeconomics and Its Application, *Third Edition*

Nicholson
Microeconomic Theory, *Second Edition*

Pappas and Brigham
Fundamentals of Managerial Economics

Pappas, Brigham, and Hirschey
Managerial Economics, *Fourth Edition*

Poindexter
Macroeconomics, *Second Edition*

Puth
American Economic History

Richardson
Urban Economics

Welch and Welch
Economics: Theory and Practice

Preface

In the preface the author is supposed to explain why he or she wrote the book. This is a formidable task for the author of an intermediate price theory text. There are dozens of such books already on the market, and this impressive opportunity set offers a wide range of levels, coverage, and approaches. Some even contain lively prose! The reader may therefore justifiably question whether yet another book can offer anything really new. Obviously, this author believes that it can.

Topic Coverage

The most distinguishing feature of this book is its coverage. It attempts to allocate the reader's time efficiently. Most intermediate price theory books devote the lion's share of their space to the analysis of the determination of price and output in a variety of market settings. This emphasis is puzzling, since most intermediate students will have already obtained a fairly detailed understanding of demand and supply from the introductory course. Students rarely find in the more rigorous presentation of this material a justification for all the work involved—and who can blame them?

But economics can be fun and exciting. Price theory is a powerful tool that illuminates behavior in all aspects of our daily lives. It answers important and interesting questions of direct concern to all of us. Why do high- and low-income people consume different goods? Why do hotels, airlines, and restaurants offer "free" reservation service? Why are workers typically harmed by regulations aimed at improving working conditions? How do the customers and merchandise of stores that offer free parking differ from those of stores that do not? Why do different people command different wage rates? What are the links, if any, between wage disparity and education or discrimination? Surely students will better appreciate price theory if it ultimately helps them better understand their environment.

The past two decades may justifiably be called the "Golden Age of Price Theory," a period in which price theory has been used to explain such diverse phenomena as human fertility and the disappearance of the American bison. This book has shamelessly borrowed from this eclectic outpouring of scholarship to give the student a taste of the range of things modern economics can do.

This expanded coverage has not been achieved costlessly. The procession of models of market structure that typically occupies about three chapters in a price theory text has been compressed here. In its place this book offers Chapter 10, which discusses the sources of market power with a minimum of hair-splitting product differentiation among competing theories. The distinctions among monopolistic competition, oligopoly, and shared monopoly are left to the industrial organization course. In the author's view there is little reason to devote more space than this to discussions of market structure in the intermediate theory course. This is particularly true when the cost of the added detail is, as in many books, reduced attention paid to well-developed and more interesting theory.

Applications

A second distinguishing feature of this book is its format. Applications of price theory are integrated into the text, not isolated in boxes or at the ends of chapters. There are two reasons for this. If the applications are integrated into the flow of the chapter, their connections with the theory are direct and therefore easier for the reader to make. More importantly, applications are an integral part of the subject matter; to treat them separately is to invite students to regard them as a sort of gloss on the material they perceive to be important.

It is the purpose of the intermediate theory course to teach students to analyze. This differs, of course, from merely teaching them theory. Students will likely forget the various theorems they are required to memorize in this course within a fortnight of finishing the final exam. If they come away with anything more lasting, it will be the ability to pose a new question and to attack it with an open mind and the right stuff. Such skill cannot be acquired by rote memory. This book has been guided by the assumption that the best way to inculcate that ability is to provide practice with differentiated problems. The reader will therefore find in it a minimum of theory for the sake of theory, but mountains of applications. Indeed, the author once suggested to his editor that the pure theory be put in boxes!

Flexible Course Organization

As one of the applications in Chapter 3 concludes, there can be too much of a good thing. Some teachers of this course will find this to be true of any text that covers the full range of standard price theory topics. Cuts may be needed in some topics in order that others may be treated more fully. Should that be the case, instructors will find such cuts easy to make with this book. The text has been designed to permit groups of chapters to be deleted without creating problems in later sections.

The following chapter sequences are offered merely as suggestions for those who desire to make a more leisurely progress through the semester.

Sequence A: Chapters 1, 2, 3, 4, 5, 7, 8, 9, 10, 11, 12, 13, 14, 15, 16

Sequence B: Chapters 3, 4, 5, 6, 7, 8, 9, 10, 11, 12, 13, 14, 17, 18

Sequence C: Chapters 1, 2, 3, 4, 5, 6, 8, 9, 10, 11, 14, 16, 17, 18

Sequence A deletes the two chapters on welfare economics, the treatment of index numbers and risk, and the chapter on the demand for factors by price searchers. Sequence B deletes the introductory chapter and the discussion of equilibrium in markets (which contain much review material from the introductory course) and begins directly with the derivation of demand from individual constrained choice. It also deletes the chapters on capital theory and income distribution in the interest of devoting more time to welfare economics. Sequence C deletes the discussion of the choice of organization, the two chapters on derived demand, and the chapter on capital theory. Obviously there are possible alternative sequences that will be equally attractive.

Acknowledgments

The preface also offers the author the opportunity to repay some of the debts he or she has incurred along the way. In the present case these are many and large. Perhaps the largest is to this writer's former colleagues at UCLA, and especially Armen Alchian. These economists impressed on a green assistant professor many years ago the insight that the range of issues illuminated by price theory is vast and that theories need not be elaborate to be wonderfully informative. The discipline required to carry on a daily discussion over lunch with this splendid group without suffering embarrassment provided a unique and thorough preparation for the writing of this book.

A number of friends read portions of the book and offered helpful criticisms. Among the most generous with their time and effort were Chris Curran, Jerry Dwyer, and Mike Maloney. A hero's medal should be awarded to Tom Borcherding, Claremont McKenna College, who ought to list among his many talents that of being a world-class critic; Tom left red pencil on every page. Others who read all or a portion of the manuscript and made helpful comments are: Donald Bumpass, Texas Tech University; Timothy Gronberg, Texas A&M; Jessie Hartline, Rutgers University; Masanori Hashimoto, University of Washington; Thomas McCullough, University of California, Berkeley; Ernest Pasour, North Carolina State University; Sam Peltzman, University of Chicago; John Ruser, University of North Carolina at Chapel Hill; Matthew Stephenson, Wofford College; John M. Vernon, Duke University; Robert Welch, University of Kentucky; Robert Wolf, Boston University.

Two classes in intermediate price theory here at Emory used earlier versions of this text. Their patience with twenty pounds of unbound, xeroxed text was wondrous—and surprisingly, under the circumstances, they seemed to learn a great deal. Their comments and suggestions were important to the final revision and are sincerely appreciated. Beth Goldstein and Julie Perelman hung around to help with the preparation of the instructor's manual. That's real dedication!

Among the team at The Dryden Press who nursed this project along from the beginning, Susan Meyers and Liz Widdicombe deserve special mention: They know how to prod painlessly. Ruta Graff and Nancy Maybloom handled the messy business of production and copy editing with remarkable professionalism and good humor. Takako Lanier deserves special mention, not just for typing the entire manuscript and keeping it together through all the revisions, but for correcting the algebra as she typed.

Last but not least, my wife Mary deserves mention. She suffered a grumpy and disconsolate husband for far longer than it ought to take to write a book. Thank you, Mary, for your encouragement and good humor and for putting up with the typewriter and tobacco smoke in the bedroom at DeGrassi Point, Canada, every summer.

C.M.L.
Atlanta, Georgia
October 1983

Contents

Part One *Markets and Methods*

3	**Chapter 1**	**Introduction**
4	1.1	What Is a Theory?
4		*Theory as Metaphor*
6		*How Do Theories Inform?*
6		*Empty Boxes and Empty Theories*
7		*Ockham's Razor*
7		*Verification*
8	1.2	Functions and Graphs
10		*Slopes of Functions*
12		*Multivariate Functions*
13		*Maxima and Minima*
15		*Elasticity*
17	1.3	Economics as a Social Science
17		*Purposeful Choice*
18		*Equilibrium*
19	1.4	Scheme of the Book
21		Summary
22		Key Concepts
22		**Appendix**
23		Slopes of Nonlinear Functions
25		Determining Slopes

31	**Chapter 2**	**Market Equilibrium**
32	2.1	Simultaneous Systems
33	2.2	Demand with Fixed Supply
33		*First Law of Demand*
34		*Other Prices*
37		*Income and Demand*
40		*The Influence of Time*
41	2.3	The Determination of Equilibrium with Zero Price
44		*Who Gains from a Free-for-All?*
45		*Other Nonprice Rationing Systems*
46	2.4	Price as a Rationing Device
46		*Who Gains from the Price System?*
47		*How Are Prices Formed in the Market?*
49	2.5	The Supply Side of the Market
50		*Equilibrium Conditions*
52		*Cobweb Models*
53		*Arbitrage and Speculation*
56	2.6	Controlled Prices
56		*Farm Policy, 1929–1973*
58		*Rent Controls*
60		*England and the Supply of Doctors*
61		Summary
62		Key Concepts
62		Questions
65	**Chapter 3**	**The Theory of Choosing**
67	3.1	The Opportunity Set—Or When the Sky Is Not the Limit
67		*Opportunity Cost*
69	3.2	The Rank-Ordering Process
69		*People are the Same and Don't Change*
70		*Utility*
71		*Ranking with Continuous Opportunities*
72		*Properties of Indifference Curves*
75		*Marginal Rate of Substitution*
76		*Convexity*
78	3.3	Describing Choice
78		*Continuous Opportunity Sets*
79		*Solution to the Optimization Problem*
81		*Opportunity Cost with Continuous Opportunities*
82		*Corner Solutions*
83		*The Property of Consistency*
84		*Too Much of a Good Thing*
86	3.4	Social Choice
86		*The Folly of "Priorities"*
87		*Political Choice*
90		Summary

91		*Key Concepts*
91		*Questions*

Part Two   *The Choice among Goods*

95	**Chapter 4**	**Household Choices**
96	4.1	The Household Budget as an Opportunity Set
99		*The Opportunity Cost of Purchasing*
100		*The Effect of Income Changes*
101		*The Effect of Price Changes*
103	4.2	Indifference Curves in Goods Space
104	4.3	Conditions at the Optimum
105		*Interpreting Conditions at the Optimum*
105	4.4	The Value of Exchange
109		*The Puzzle of Gifts*
111	4.5	Inefficiency and Welfare Loss
112		*The Welfare Loss of Public Housing*
114	4.6	Choice Involving Bundled Goods
115		*The Time Cost of Consumption*
118		*Consumption Optima with Different Wage Rates*
120		*Compensated Changes*
122		*The Economics of Sunday Papers and Winnebagos*
123		*Bid Rent Curves*
128		*Some Observations on Rapid Transit*
130		Summary
131		*Key Concepts*
131		*Questions*
133	**Chapter 5**	**The Theory of Market Demand**
134	5.1	Deriving the Demand Function
135		*Changes in Income*
137		*Real and Nominal Income*
138		*Changes in Own Price*
141		*Income Effects of Price Changes*
143		*Substitution Effects*
144		*Combining the Effects*
144		*Compensated and Uncompensated Demand*
146		*Why Two Demand Curves?*
149		*The Giffen Paradox Examined*
151	5.2	Aggregating Demand
152		*Altering the Distribution of Goods*
153		*The Economics of Hoarding*
155	5.3	Demand Elasticities

157		*Income Elasticity*
158		*Price Elasticity*
159		*Arc Elasticity*
160		*Point Elasticity*
161		*The Linear Demand Curve*
164		*Elasticity and Nonlinear Curves*
164		*Constant Elasticity*
168		Summary
169		Key Concepts
170		Questions
171		**Appendix**
171		Constant Elasticity Demand Curves
173	**Chapter 6**	**Income Measurement and Uncertainty**
174	6.1	Index Numbers
174		*Weights and Measures*
176		*Measuring Real Income*
177		*Laspeyres and Paasche Measures*
184		*Converting Changes to Indexes*
186		*The Purchasing Power of Money*
186		*Price Indexes*
189		*Practical Considerations*
190	6.2	Choice with Imperfect Information
191		*Risk and Insurance*
192		*Ranking with Uncertainty*
195		*The Opportunity Set*
197		*Informal Markets for Insurance*
199		*Transaction Costs and Imperfect Information*
200		*The Lemon Principle*
201		*Brand Loyalty*
202		*Property Rights and Information*
203		*Advertising and Demand*
206		Summary
207		Key Concepts
207		Questions

Part Three   *Organization, Output, and Market Structure*

211	**Chapter 7**	**The Choice of Organization**
212	7.1	The Theory of Organization
212		*The Limits of Organization*
215		*Costs and Optimization*
220		*The Firm as a Metering Device*
223	7.2	Nonprofit Organization

223		*Private Nonprofit Organization*
224		*Government Organization*
227		*Government and Quality*
230	7.3	Organization and Market Structure
232		Summary
233		Key Concepts
233		Questions

235 Chapter 8 The Choice of Output: Price Taker Case

238	8.1	The Components of Profit
238		*Revenue and Output*
240	8.2	Costs and Outputs
240		*Operating and Overhead Costs*
242		*The Rate of Output*
242		*Average Costs*
244		*Positioning Cost Curves*
247		*The Shape of the Total Cost Curve*
249		*Rising Costs of Constant-Scale Operations*
249		*The Short and the Long Run*
251		*The Choice of Scale*
252		*The Envelope Curve*
254		*Economies and Diseconomies of Scale*
256	8.3	Supply for Price Takers
259		*Supply Response for a Firm of a Given Scale*
262		*Price and Scale*
263		*Supply Price Elasticity and Time*
264	8.4	Industry Supply
266		*Regulation of Entry: The Case of the CAB*
268		Summary
268		Key Concepts
269		Questions

271 Chapter 9 The Choice of Output: Price Searchers

272	9.1	Output and Price for Price Searchers
272		*Revenue for Price Searchers*
274		*Marginal Revenue and Elasticity*
276		*The Choice of Output and Scale*
278		*Price Searcher Output with Price Ceilings*
281		*Some Qualifications*
283		*Price Searcher Supply*
285	9.2	Price Discrimination
289		*Price Discrimination among Customers*
292		*Conditions for Price Discrimination*
293		*The Separation of Markets*
296		Summary
297		Key Concepts
298		Questions

301	**Chapter 10**	**The Sources of Market Power**
302	10.1	Monopoly
302		*Government-Sanctioned Monopoly*
302		*Natural Monopoly*
304		*Regulation of Natural Monopoly*
307	10.2	Location and Information
307		*Advantages of Location*
311		*Costs of Information*
311		*Equilibrium with Transportation or Information Costs*
314	10.3	Collusion
316		*The Stability of Cartels*
320		*Collusion and Entry*
322		*Augmented Collusion*
323	10.4	Tactics that Don't Work
324		*Vertical Integration*
325		Summary
326		Key Concepts
326		Questions

Part Four *The Choice of Technology*

331	**Chapter 11**	**Production Theory: The Choice of Technology**
332	11.1	The Production Function
333		*Total, Marginal, and Average Product*
337		*Diminishing Returns*
337		*Varying the Fixed Factor*
338		*Returns to Scale and Cost*
340		*An Ambiguity: Do All Factors Vary?*
341	11.2	The Other Perspective
341		*Isoquants*
341		*Fixed Proportions*
342		*Perfect Substitutes*
343		*The Rate of Technical Substitution*
346		*Isoquants and Returns to Scale*
349		*Technical Change*
350	11.3	Choosing the Technology
352		*Conditions at the Optimum*
353		*Output Expansion Path*
355		*Elasticity of Substitution*
357		*Elasticity of Substitution and Factor Income Shares*
358		*Technical Change and Employment*
360		Summary
361		Key Concepts
362		Questions

Chapter 12 The Demand for Factors: Productivity and Employment — 363

- 364   12.1   The Revenue Effect: Marginal Revenue Product (MRP)
- 369   12.2   Costs and Inputs
  - 371   *The Cost of Output in Terms of Inputs*
- 373   12.3   The Demand for Factors
  - 373   *Choosing the Level of One Factor*
  - 374   *The Demand Curve with One Variable Factor*
  - 376   *Demand with All Factors Variable*
  - 377   *Demand for a Normal Factor*
- 380   12.4   Productivity in Theory and Practice
  - 382   *Productivity Growth and Productivity Statistics*
  - 383   *The Paradox of Increasing Returns to Labor*
  - 385   *The Capital–Labor Ratio*
  - 387   *Technical Change*
- 389   12.5   The Demand for Labor and the Number of Jobs
  - 389   *Sources of Unemployment*
  - 389   *The Minimum Wage*
  - 392   *Supply Restrictions*
  - 393   *Seasonal and Cyclical Unemployment*
  - 395   *Unemployment as Job Information Search*
- 397   Summary
- 398   Key Concepts
- 398   Questions

Appendix — 400

- 400   Demand for an Inferior Factor

Chapter 13 The Demand for Factors: Other Market Structures — 403

- 404   13.1   Market Power in the Output Market
  - 406   *Profit Restrictions*
  - 408   *Isoprofit Curves*
  - 408   *The Averch-Johnson Effect*
- 414   13.2   Exploitation: Different Interpretations
  - 416   *Exploitation by Price Searchers*
- 418   13.3   Market Power in the Input Market
  - 419   *Rising and Falling Supply*
  - 421   *Marginal Factor Cost with Rising Supply*
  - 424   *Monopsony Demand*
  - 425   *Anticompetitive Arrangements*
  - 427   *Locational and Contractual Advantages*
  - 428   *Minimum Wage Restrictions with Rising Supply*
  - 431   *Difficulties of Wage Regulation*
- 433   Summary
- 434   Key Concepts
- 434   Questions

Part Five   *The Choice of Resource Supply*

439   **Chapter 14   The Supply of Labor**

440	14.1	The Opportunity Set
441		*The Time Endowment*
443		*Shifting the Opportunity Set*
444	14.2	Choosing the Quantity Supplied
446		*The Income Effect on Labor Supply*
448		*A Change in the Wage Rate*
452	14.3	The Market Supply of Labor
454		*Choosing to Supply: Labor Force Participation*
457		*Income Conditional Grants*
459		*The Negative Income Tax*
462	14.4	Direct Constraints on Supply
462		*The Employer View*
463		*The Maximum Workweek as a Supply Restriction*
464		*Union Contracts*
466		*Conditions of Employment*
469		*Regulation of Working Conditions*
471		Summary
473		Key Concepts
473		Questions

475   **Chapter 15   The Supply of Capital: Savings and Investment**

476	15.1	The Measurement Problem
477	15.2	The Supply of Capital and the Interest Rate
479		*Saving: The Supply of Loanable Funds*
482		*Preferences for Time-Specific Consumption*
483		*Changing the Interest Rate*
484		*Substitution and Income Effects*
485		*Two Supply Curves for Loanable Funds*
487	15.3	Investment Opportunities: The Demand for Loanable Funds
488		*A Change in the Income Endowment*
488		*The Decision to Invest*
491		*The Present Value Rule*
492		*Varying the Interest Rate to Demanders*
494		*The Equilibrium Interest Rate*
495	15.4	Multiperiod Analysis
497		*Investment in Multiperiod Analysis*
497		*Constant Yield Assets*
499		*Infinitely Lived Assets*
500		*The Supply of Capital Services*
502		*Declining Industries: The Case of Passenger Rail Travel*
503		*Depreciation and the Opportunity Cost*
504		*Asset Prices and Capitalization*
505		*Property Taxes and Tax Relief*
509		Summary
510		Key Concepts
511		Questions

Part Six   *The Big Picture*

517   Chapter 16   The Distribution of Income

518   16.1   The Distribution of Total Family Income
519   *The Distribution of Wealth*
522   16.2   The Distribution of Earnings
524   *Sources of Wage Variation*
524   *Coercion*
525   *Variation in Ability*
525   *Tastes for Work of Different Types*
529   *Income Growth and Relative Wages*
529   *It Pays to Be Different*
531   16.3   Human Capital
534   *Education as Human Capital*
535   *The Signaling Explanation*
540   *Some Unanswered Questions*
541   16.4   Discrimination and Wages
541   *The Tastes of Demanders*
543   *Response to Prejudice*
545   *Necessary Conditions for Wage Rate Disparity*
546   *Evidence on Wage Disparity*
548   Summary
550   Key Concepts
550   Questions

553   Chapter 17   Welfare Economics: Defining Efficiency

554   17.1   Efficiency Defined
556   *Normative Limits of Efficiency*
556   *Measuring Utility*
557   *The Weighting Problem*
558   *The Measurement Problem*
562   17.2   Conditions for Pareto Optimality
563   *Three Conditions*
564   *Technological Efficiency*
568   *Distributional Efficiency*
570   *Allocative Efficiency*
574   *The Rate of Product Transformation*
575   17.3   Pareto Optimality with Public Goods
575   *Public Goods*
576   *Allocative Efficiency with Public Goods*
579   *Pareto Optimality Again*
580   Summary
581   Key Concepts
581   Questions

583   Chapter 18   Markets, Governments, and Efficiency

584   18.1   The Competitive Model
586   18.2   Market Failure

587		*Price Searching*
589		*Price Discrimination*
590		*Price Searching for Inputs*
591	18.3	Government Failure
591		*Price Controls and Rationing*
593		*Excise Taxes*
595		*Income and Other Taxes*
596		*Regulation*
597	18.4	Transaction Costs and Property Rights
597		*The Coase Theorem*
599		*External Costs and Benefits*
602		*Market Provision of Public Goods*
603		*The Individual Adjustment Equilibrium*
604		*Transaction Costs in Public Good Allocation*
609	18.5	The Government Alternative
609		*Optimal Intervention*
610		*Which Way Is Up?*
612		*The Problem of "Second Best"*
614		*The Politics of Efficiency*
618		Summary
619		*Key Concepts*
619		*Questions*
621		**Index**

Part One

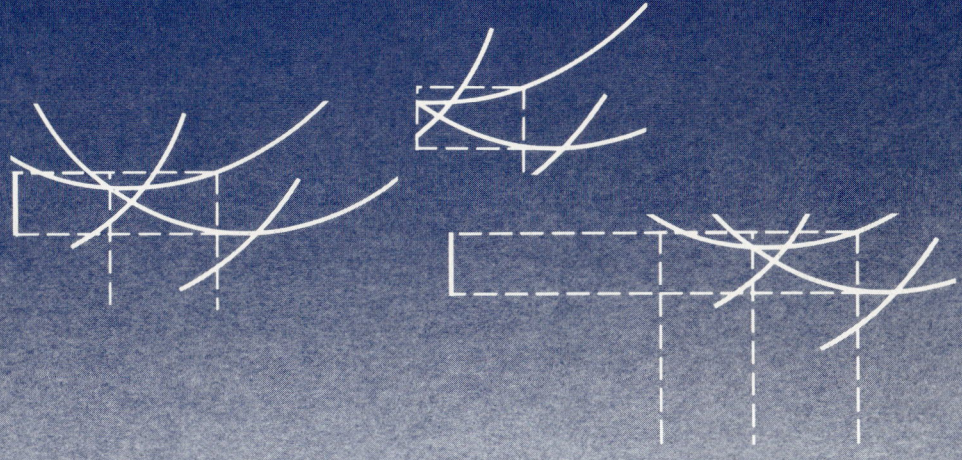

Markets and Methods

Chapter 1

Introduction

Connections *This section of each chapter will provide a survey of the tools and techniques about to be used along with references to earlier chapters where these were first introduced and developed. Economics is like mathematics in the sense that its theory develops linearly. Bits and pieces learned at one point continue to be employed at later points. Individual principles presented in early chapters return as critical elements in the derivation and development of new principles in later chapters. New forms of analysis in later chapters will often bear strong parallels in method and spirit to earlier forms.*

Readers are urged to take advantage of these introductory sections. Those who learn to recognize the recurring analytical issues in disparate theoretical topics and applications and the similarity in our approaches to each of them will find economic theory both more intelligible and more enjoyable. At the beginning, alas, we have no such fund of previously acquired knowledge on which to draw. These early chapters may thus seem odd and difficult. Persevere! By the end of Chapter 18 it will all seem routine and eminently logical.

Many of you reading these words for the first time wish fervently that you did not have to. Most of you are economics majors; few seem to enroll in intermediate price theory as an elective. And economic theory, in the popular view, is inflicted upon students as a sort of ceremonial initiation into the cult of economists, a process seemingly as void of useful learning as it is overflowing with mind-boggling diagrams and tedious algebra. The question foremost in your mind (though one to which you expect no satisfactory answer) is, "Why do I have to take a course in price theory?" Those of us who insist that it be taken might state the question differently, but the answers in each case are the same. Understanding requires theory—indeed, understanding *is* theory.

1.1 What Is a Theory?

Theory as Metaphor

A theory is a metaphor. Without these metaphors the world would appear to us as a whirlwind of unrelated objects and sensations lacking coherence and organization. We interpret all of this observation by creating in our minds images that suppress most of what we have seen and altering much of the rest, distilling some bit of the world into a **model** of what is happening. How many times have you begun an explanation with the phrase "It works *like* this . . . ?" The principles of electricity are often introduced in terms of a metaphor for water—indeed, the movement of electrons through a conductor is commonly referred to as an electric "current." Voltage is *like* water pressure; amperes are *like* the rate of water flow.

Imagine how you would respond if someone asked you to explain the flight of the Saturn rockets in the Apollo moon missions. You might send away for the plans and describe in detail the workings and interrelationships of each of the thousands of parts and components, though this procedure would certainly create more confusion than illumination in your audience. Alternatively, you might sketch certain key parts, such as fuel tanks and combustion chambers, and refer to certain essential principles, like Newton's third law of motion. This description would be a metaphor, held to be true of all rockets yet literally descriptive of none. You might stretch the metaphor further to include descriptions of gunpowder rockets and the movement of unsealed but inflated balloons released in the air. These analogies would contain many elements that are not at all true of Saturn rockets but share important principles that make them like their larger counterparts. The point is that such metaphors help us to grasp the *idea* of rocketry, which is quite distinct from being able to construct a working version of a rocket. It is this ability to abstract by metaphor that enables us to understand complex phenomena without comprehending each of their component parts in detail.

To be able to theorize is to be able to understand. But theory does more. To understand what theory does we must construct metaphors of theories. In one sense theories serve the function of filing systems. They enable us to organize knowledge into smaller and more manageable groupings. Consider the development of chemistry in the last century. By 1850 scientists had developed a considerable body of knowledge concerning the chemical nature of matter. Lavoisier had shown that fire reflects a chemical union of certain substances with oxygen, and Faraday that water could be separated into hydrogen and oxygen by electrolysis. Chemists had identified many of the basic elements and understood that most substances were chemical compounds of these elements. However, the number of these compounds seemed uncountable, and the properties of many containing similar or seemingly similar elements varied bewilderingly. This knowledge was essentially empirical and could be organized into little more than a list of known substances and corresponding properties. It lacked a unifying theory permitting the organization of elements into groups that reacted similarly when combined with others. The development of this theory was hampered by the fact that many rare elements were unknown at the time, producing gaps in the series that chemists sought to construct. Lacking this theory, however, scientists were unaware that such gaps were present.

The missing theory was ultimately supplied by the Russian chemist Mendeleev. He was the first to group the known elements on the basis of atomic weight and valence, forming what we now refer to as the Periodic Table. Chemical compounds could be described as molecules made up of atoms of elements whose specific valences provided balance. The theory provided whole new groupings of molecules whose properties shared particular traits: organic or inorganic, sulfides or bromides, acids or bases. Chemistry was converted from an assembly of ad hoc lists into a tightly organized body of knowledge that could be discussed and analyzed in meaningful parts.

Theory provides us with more than a filing system, however. It also provides a compass. It guides us toward new knowledge that is as yet undiscovered. In our chemistry example, the assembly of the Periodic Table pointed out existing gaps. Certain elements were missing from the table, and the knowledge that scientists gained from the table itself provided clues to where they might seek these missing substances. As the table was organized by atomic weight and valence, Mendeleev predicted that the missing elements would have atomic weights and valences within particular ranges. The theory suggested a shortcut to the discovery of new elements and compounds. Chemical research, aided by the new compass, exploded with unprecedented force into the twentieth century.

Economics is a social science, and economic theory concerns itself not with elements and chemistry, but with social behavior. It contains some of our knowledge of how people will respond to changes in their environment. Some of those responses are grounded in economics, and some are not. Social behavior is far more complex than chemistry. People are motivated by many more influences than are atoms, and no single theory can hope to account for all of them. Economic theory nevertheless provides a filing system and a compass for a great deal of that knowledge. With it we may organize what we know about social economic behavior and let it guide us toward a sharper and more certain understanding in areas of particular concern. Without it we would confront a bewildering beehive of human activity far too complex to be understood in detail.

How Do Theories Inform?

We have already noted that a theory is a metaphor, but what else is it? The statement "The world is my oyster" is also a metaphor, but it is not a theory. A theory must be informative; it must suggest consequences of conditions or actions, which this statement does not. A theory must imply, If A, then B. The statement "Water runs downhill" does inform us in this way. It is metaphorical in the sense that it applies to many situations in which it is not *literally* applicable—for example, water running through a pipe in a building or over the lip of a tilted jar. We understand that this theory applies to a broad range of cases that differ in detail. In those cases it is informative in the sense that it narrows the range of possible outcomes. For example, it tells us that if water is released on a slope, it will neither sit there nor flow toward the top of the hill. These possibilities are *ruled out* by the theory.

Empty Boxes and Empty Theories

If a theory is to be informative, it must rule out possible consequences. One test of a good theory, therefore, is the sharpness of its prediction. The more occurrences that are ruled out by the theory, the more informative is the theory. A theory that says that water will freeze at $0°$ C is preferred to a theory that holds that water will freeze at some temperature below $10°$ C. The former rules out the possibility that water may freeze at $5°$ while the latter does not. A completely uninformative theory rules out nothing. This sort of theory (or nontheory) is labeled a **tautology**. An example of a tautology is "A good general is worth a thousand men." Even when we restate this more concretely as "An army with one more good general and a thousand fewer men will win more battles," the statement is uninformative. What does it rule out? It does not rule out the possibility of winning fewer battles after the substitution of *any* general for a thousand men. The statement requires a *good* general, and possibly the only test of the worth of generals is whether they can win under these circumstances. We already know that by this definition good generals can win with fewer men, and the statement tells us nothing else.

Consider the old standby of the financial writer in the evening paper, "A sell-off by profit takers today leads to a decline of eight points on the closing Dow Jones average." What is a "sell-off?" Every share that was sold was bought by someone. Why not call the experience a "buy-off?" What is a "profit taker"—someone who sells during a sell-off? Implicitly the writer is offering us the following theory: Sell-offs by profit takers cause a fall in the Dow. Is that informative? Not in my book.

A tautological theory is said to be an "empty theory." A theory for which there is no application is sometimes called an "empty box." A theory that applies to the widest possible set of circumstances is a *general* theory, while a theory of more limited application is regarded as *narrow*. The "water runs downhill" theory is not completely general, as an astronaut in orbit might tell you, but it suffices for most cases. On the other hand, the theory of the behavior of water in a gravity-free environment was an empty box until two decades ago. Other things being equal, we would prefer a more general theory to a narrow one.

Desirable characteristics of theory are rarely free. Typically, generality is obtainable only at the expense of sharpness of implications. A theory relating the weights of animals to the volumes of their diets might predict reasonably well—but it would not predict as well as one that sought to identify the relationship for hogs alone.

Ockham's Razor

On purely esthetic grounds we prefer simple and elegant theories to convoluted and messy ones. Had the theories of Ptolemy and Copernicus predicted the movements of planets equally well, we would have preferred the latter on these grounds alone. Ptolemy's theory relied upon revolutions of spheres within spheres: stars in one, planets in another, and comets in yet another, all orbiting the earth in eccentric patterns. It was an untidy theory, to say the least, offering in compensation only the placement of the earth, and therefore man, at the center of things. The theory of Copernicus was majestic in contrast to its busy competitor. Even the persecution of its adherents by the Church could not secure its suppression.

A preference for simplicity unfortunately has not always been universal. In the time of William of Ockham, a fourteenth-century Franciscan theologian and philosopher, argumentation had come to be appreciated for its own sake. The monks of that period clearly had more time on their hands than we today can devote to such matters. It had become fashionable to fill pages—indeed, books—with elaborate syllogisms, including unnecessary arguments, redundant assumptions, and painstaking definitions and distinctions. In many cases it was difficult to find the woods among the trees—in fact, one could imagine a good deal of it was simply trees. Ockham understood opportunity cost. He propounded, "To employ a number of principles when it is possible to use a few is a waste of time." He would slash away at the verbiage of his contemporaries, insisting that they eliminate unnecessary argumentation and get to the point. Scientists ever since have remembered his lesson and counseled their fellows to exercise **"Ockham's razor"** when theories became excessively elaborate.

Verification

The ultimate test of a theory is its usefulness. A theory may be very general, produce sharp predictions, be a model of elegance, and yet lead us astray. While it would be presumptuous of any scientist to claim his or her theory is absolutely true, clearly all scientists hope that their new contributions will yield better predictions than the theories they seek to displace. At any time, however, there are many possible theories, and users of this knowledge must select among them. How is such a selection made? Trial and error is one method, but errors can be costly. The unfortunate consequences of the adoption of the tranquilizer thalidomide suggest just how costly learning by doing can be. For this reason, the process of **verification** of theories has become a coequal activity in the realm of scientific endeavor.

The verification process is performed differently among various branches of science. These differences are largely guided by the nature of the experiments necessary to duplicate and control the conditions to which the theories apply. Galileo is said to have verified his theory of gravity by dropping fruit from the Leaning Tower of Pisa. The testing of Einstein's theory of gravity required awaiting the solar eclipse of 1919 so that the effects of the sun's gravity on starlight passing close to it might be observed. Tests of the properties of new chemical substances can typically be performed in a laboratory.

It is the nature of much theory in economics, however, that laboratory testing is impractical.[1] For the most part we must test our theories retrospectively—that is, we must seek to verify the predictions of our theory on past behavior. This poses a number of difficulties, which the modern science of econometrics has sought to address. First, unable to control all features of these experiments in a laboratory, we must be concerned about the possibility of omitted variables. Results that seem to falsify or confirm our theories may be spurious. Second, economic theories rarely come in the form of single equations. Our models are typically **systems of equations**, raising the possibility of simultaneity bias. For example, at Christmas the number of passenger miles flown is higher than average, and the prices of airline tickets are also higher than average. On the other hand, fewer tomatoes are sold at Christmas, but these also command higher prices. Economic theories nevertheless have unambiguous things to say about the relationships between quantities and prices. The problem here is that these relationships are embedded in a system containing both demand and supply equations. Shifts in one or both must be statistically identified before the theory may be validated. This is neither the book nor the course to equip you to deal with these and the host of other statistical problems associated with the verification of economic theories. We raise them only to indicate the important complementary roles played by statistics and economics. Inadequately tested theories in economics may be the "thalidomides" of social science.

1.2 Functions and Graphs

Theories inform us about relationships. Take the statement used earlier, "Water runs downhill." This statement informs us about the relationship between free water and the direction of its movement. As stated, however, the relationship is vague. It tells us nothing about the speed of this movement or the relationship of the slope of the hill to that speed. An exact statement of these interrelationships would be quite complicated to communicate in English, as are many relationships in economics. By stating these relationships algebraically they may be made more precise, reducing ambiguity that might result from long and convoluted verbal arguments. They may also be manipulated according to the logic of mathematics in ways that are less obvious when stated verbally.

The basic building block of this mathematical language is the **function**. A function states a relationship between two variables. If a functional relationship

---

[1] This is not to say that laboratory experimentation with economic models is never done. Notable exceptions are the recent works of Vernon Smith and Charles Plott reporting the results of testing economic propositions in laboratories with human subjects and the work of Battalio and Kagel, who have tested the results of economic choice models on the behavior of laboratory animals.

exists between one variable and another, the value of one is implied by the value of the other. For example, there is a clear relationship between temperature as expressed according to the centigrade system and the corresponding temperature expressed in the Fahrenheit scale. The choice of a centigrade temperature implies one—and only one—Fahrenheit temperature. Indeed, this relationship may be expressed as the function

$$t_f = 32 + \frac{9}{5} \cdot t_c,$$

where t_c and t_f are the respective temperatures. Some sample values of t_c and the implied values of t_f are listed in the table of Figure 1.1.

It is sometimes said that a picture is worth a thousand words. This is more likely to be true of some pictures and groups of words than of others. A color photograph of a sunset in Arizona may indeed convey a better sense of the experience of seeing one than a thousand words devoted to that subject. On the other hand, it would probably require more than 45 pictures to communicate unambiguously the meaning of the First Amendment to the U. S. Constitution, which contains precisely that number of words. Indeed, men could draw long before they could write, yet the latter skill is far more closely associated with the advance of science than the former.

In spite of this, and for reasons that are difficult to understand, many economics students (and teachers!) find it easier to deal with economic relationships when depicted in graphs. This imposes some limitations. Certain economic relationships cannot be depicted graphically, and others must be simplified almost beyond recognition to represent them in two dimensions.[2] Nevertheless, we will use them here whenever we can. Let the student be warned, however, that learning economics has little to do with learning to reproduce graphs. Of far more importance is an understanding of the behavior that gives the curves in these diagrams their shapes. The subject matter of economics is social behavior, not mathematics or geometry, and unless these tools inform us about that behavior, they have nothing to contribute to social science.

In order to make the connection between the mathematics and behavior, however, it will be necessary to know a few things about the manipulation of these techniques. Economics can be taught using only a limited number of mathematical techniques, and we will introduce those here stressing the appeal to intuition rather than rigor in presentation.

Geometrically, the **vertical intercept** of a function is the point where the function crosses the vertical axis. The curve described by our temperature conversion function is depicted in Figure 1.1. For each value of centigrade temperature there is a corresponding Fahrenheit temperature. The function thus identifies combinations of values of temperatures from each scale, and these combinations may

---

[2] An example of a topic that is very difficult to deal with graphically is complementarity. Apart from shifting around demand curves for goods and inputs in response to other price changes, as we do in Chapters 2 and 5, there is little that one can do with this concept in two dimensions. This may explain the seemingly minor role played by complementarity in theory and applied economics.

Figure 1.1 *Function Relating Centigrade to Fahrenheit Temperature*

For any temperature on the centigrade scale there is one—and only one—Fahrenheit temperature. A line connecting all pairs of temperatures that satisfy the function expressing this relationship is shown in this figure as $f(t_c)$. The vertical intercept of this function is 32, and its slope is 9/5.

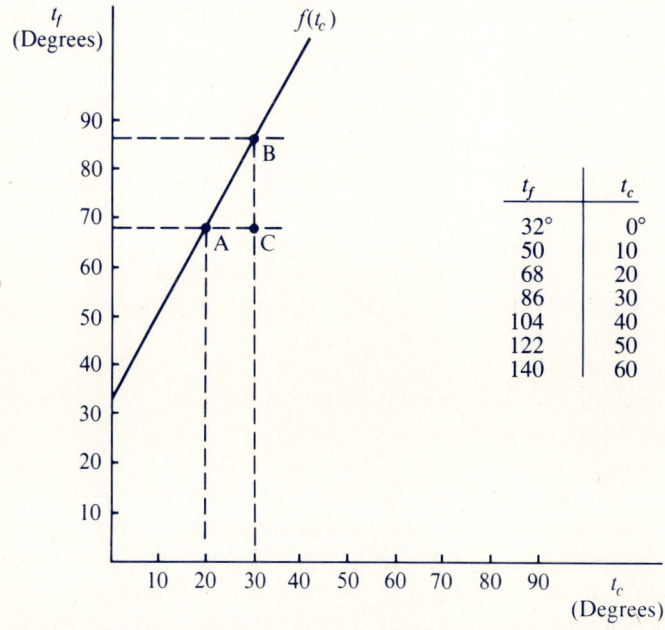

be thought of as coordinates of points in the two-dimensional space depicted in the figure. One such combination is the first entry in the table of Figure 1.1. As centigrade temperature is measured along the horizontal axis, the horizontal coordinate of this pair is zero. The function must cross the vertical axis when the horizontal coordinate is zero, so this particular combination identifies the position of that intercept. The vertical intercept of any function may thus be identified by evaluating the function where the value of the variable measured along the horizontal axis is zero.

Slopes of Functions

Probably the most important, and certainly the most frequently examined, property of functions in economics is the **slope**. The slope expresses the ratio of changes implied by a function. If the horizontal variable changes, this implies a particular change in the vertical variable. Here and throughout this book we will denote a "change in" a variable by preceding it with upper-case delta (Δ). Thus, the change in t_f is written Δt_f, and the *changed* value (original plus change) would be ($t_f + \Delta t_f$). According to our function, however, any change in t_f must be related to a change in the value of t_c. More specifically, the new value of t_f must correspond to a new value of t_c. We may therefore infer that

$$t_f + \Delta t_f = 32 + \frac{9}{5} \cdot (t_c + \Delta t_c)$$

Subtracting our original function from this expression yields a new function, which relates the *change* in the Fahrenheit temperature to the *change* in the centigrade temperature. This new function is called the **differential** of the original function:

(1.1) $$\Delta t_f = \frac{9}{5} \cdot \Delta t_c.$$

Solving this differential for the ratio of these changes gives:

$$\frac{\Delta t_f}{\Delta t_c} = \frac{9}{5}.$$

Consider the geometric interpretation of this ratio. Let us assume that the temperature ten minutes ago was 20°C. Figure 1.1 reveals that this corresponds to the Fahrenheit temperature of 68°. Now let us assume that the temperature rises to 30°C. This new temperature may be thought of as the original temperature plus the temperature change (20 + 10) and corresponds to a new Fahrenheit temperature equal to that temperature plus its change (68 + 18). The dotted lines identifying the new and old coordinates of these pairs of temperatures form the right triangle ABC in the figure. The height of this triangle is Δt_f, while its width is Δt_c. The **tangent** of the angle at A is equal to the length of the opposite side, BC (equal to 18 = Δt_f), divided by the length of the adjacent side, AC (equal to 10 = Δt_c). This ratio is therefore:

$$\frac{BC}{AC} = \frac{\Delta t_f}{\Delta t_c} = \frac{18}{10} = \frac{9}{5}.$$

The tangent of the angle at A is the slope of the curve. Note that the slope of this temperature conversion function is equal to the coefficient of the right-side variable, t_c.

Referring back to Equation 1.1, we may also note that the differential contains the slope. We might rewrite this expression as

$$\Delta t_f = \frac{\Delta t_f}{\Delta t_c} \cdot \Delta t_c,$$

which tells us that the change in Fahrenheit temperature will always be the product of two quantities: the change in centigrade temperature and the *rate of change in one per unit change in the other*. The change in total earnings might similarly be expressed as the product of the change in hours worked and the rate of change in earnings per unit change in hours. The latter rate of change is simply the wage rate.

So far we have glided past an ambiguity in the presentation. The temperature conversion function is a straight line. The slope and differential are therefore independent of both the "starting" temperature and the magnitude of the change. Experimentation with a ruler will confirm this. Unfortunately, this independence is lost with respect to both properties when our function is nonlinear. We may nevertheless meaningfully discuss the slope of a curved function and calculate that slope with precision. A brief review of these procedures is provided in the appendix to this chapter for those students who feel the need for a refresher. A student can get quite far in price theory, however, by remembering the simple relationships identified so far. For linear functions, at least, both of the following properties hold:

The constant term of the function corresponds to the vertical intercept of the graph of the function.

The coefficient of the right-side variable corresponds to the slope of the function.

Economic science has not progressed to the stage where we can derive an explicit structure for most of our functions. On the contrary, for many purposes relationships are denoted in terms of the sign of the slope alone. A relationship between two variables p and q in economics might simply be stated as

$$p = f(q), \frac{\Delta p}{\Delta q} < 0,$$

which we would interpret as "p is a function of q, and the slope of this function is negative."

Multivariate Functions

The rate of evaporation of water depends on both the temperature and the atmospheric pressure. We may therefore identify a clear correspondence between the rate of evaporation and the temperature if we hold atmospheric pressure constant. Similarly, we may identify a correspondence between evaporation and air pressure if we hold temperature constant. This more complex relationship between a single variable and *combinations* of other variables is called a **multivariate function**. In general notation this relationship is expressed as

$$e = h(t, p), \frac{\Delta e}{\Delta t} > 0, \text{ and } \frac{\Delta e}{\Delta p} < 0,$$

where e is the rate of evaporation per time period, t is the temperature, and p is the air pressure. The slope terms for this function are defined holding all other right-side variables constant.

Multivariate functions have differentials, too. For example, we might estimate the change in the rate of evaporation due to a particular change in temperature, holding constant air pressure, as the temperature change times the appropriate slope. The **total differential** is simply the sum of all such changes; that is,

$$\Delta e = \frac{\Delta e}{\Delta t} \cdot \Delta t + \frac{\Delta e}{\Delta p} \cdot \Delta p.$$

Consider the following example. We wish to express the value of the coins in our pockets as a function of the numbers of each kind. Let the total money value be denoted $ and the numbers of each kind of coin as:

p = pennies
n = nickels
d = dimes
q = quarters

This relationship might thus be expressed as:

$\$ = v(p, n, d, q).$

Clearly, the rate of change in the total value of holdings per unit change in any of the variables is positive. The total differential for this function may be expressed as:

$$\Delta\$ = \frac{\Delta\$}{\Delta p} \cdot \Delta p + \frac{\Delta\$}{\Delta n} \cdot \Delta n + \frac{\Delta\$}{\Delta d} \cdot \Delta d + \frac{\Delta\$}{\Delta q} \cdot \Delta q.$$

Now consider what this expression is telling us. At what rate does the dollar value of our pocket change increase per unit change in the number of quarters? Clearly, at a rate of ¼. The slope $\Delta\$/\Delta q$ is therefore the constant ¼, and similarly,

$$\frac{\Delta\$}{\Delta p} = \frac{1}{100}, \frac{\Delta\$}{\Delta n} = \frac{1}{20}, \frac{\Delta\$}{\Delta d} = \frac{1}{10}.$$

The explicit form of this function is given by

$$\$ = \frac{1}{100} \cdot p + \frac{1}{20} \cdot n + \frac{1}{10} \cdot d + \frac{1}{4} \cdot q,$$

and the total differential is

$$\Delta\$ = \frac{1}{100} \cdot \Delta p + \frac{1}{20} \cdot \Delta n + \frac{1}{10} \cdot \Delta d + \frac{1}{4} \cdot \Delta q.$$

Note that, as the implied relationships between $ and each of the right-side variables are themselves linear, the coefficients of these variables are constant and independent of the magnitude of the changes. Students should pay particular attention to these differential relationships for, though they are sometimes neglected in standard college mathematics courses, they play an important role in economic theory.

Maxima and Minima

In economic theory we are almost invariably attempting to discover what is true at some extreme value or other. We want to know the conditions at the profit-maximizing output. We seek to understand the nature of a cost-minimizing tech-

Figure 1.2   *Maxima and Minima*

A necessary condition for an extreme value is that the slope of the function be zero, regardless of whether it is a maximum or a minimum. The function in panel (a) reaches a maximum at x_1, where the slope falls to zero before becoming negative. The function in panel (b) reaches a minimum at x_1, where the slope rises to zero before becoming positive. However, a slope of zero is not sufficient to ensure an extreme value. In panel (c) the function has a slope of zero at x_1, which is neither a maximum nor a minimum.

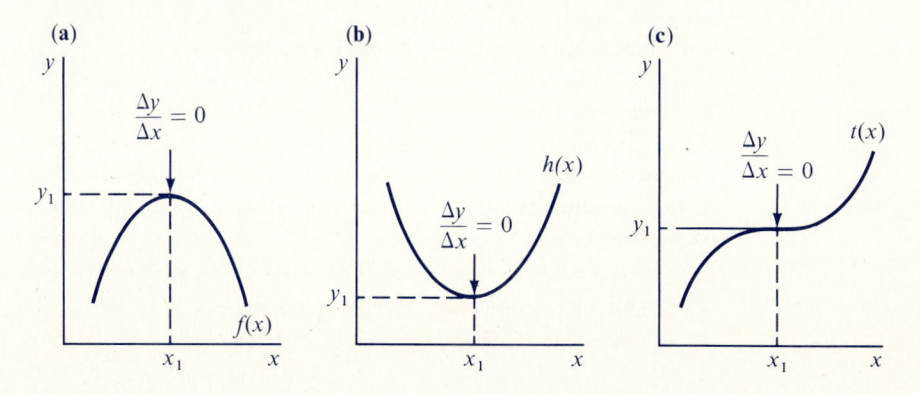

nology. Late in the book we develop necessary conditions for maximizing aggregate social welfare. Being able to evaluate the slope of a curve can be of great benefit in these types of analyses. Consider the three panels of Figure 1.2. In panel (a) quantity x_1 maximizes the value of y. In panel (b) quantity x_1 minimizes the value of y. One is a **maximum** and the other is a **minimum**. Each may be identified, however, by *finding the value of* x *at which the slope of the function is zero*.

Of course, this process will not distinguish maxima from minima; the same condition applies to both. A slope of zero may therefore be considered to be a *necessary* condition for a maximum, but not a sufficient condition. A slope of zero is also a necessary condition for a minimum. It is even possible for a function to have a slope of zero, which is neither a maximum nor a minimum. This is the case in panel (c) of Figure 1.2. Whether the function has a maximum or a minimum or neither at a point where the slope is zero can be determined by what are called "second order conditions." Although these play a vital role in more advanced expositions of economic theory, they are rarely made an integral part of the intermediate theory course, and we will ignore them here. In many cases, therefore, our theory will lead us to necessary conditions for the extreme values we are concerned with but will not inform us concerning the sufficient conditions.

An extreme value of a multivariate function is a more complicated affair. Clearly a slope of zero in a single dimension is not sufficient to guarantee a maximum value for the left-side variable. Marching in a straight line in the general direction of a hill will not guarantee that the peak will be reached, even if we come to a spot where we stop climbing up and begin going down. We may pass to the left or the right of the peak. At the top of the hill the slope must be flat from any angle. Thus, for an extreme value to be identified, the slopes of a function with more than one right-hand variable must be zero with respect to each variable.

Again this will not insure either a maximum or a minimum. The seat of a saddle is flat with respect to the axis of the horse's spine as well as side to side. This point is neither the highest point on the saddle nor the lowest. Second order conditions can be developed to discriminate maxima from minima and to discriminate either from "saddle points," but we will not concern ourselves with these in multivariate equations. As in the case of simple, single-variable functions, our theory will be limited to developing necessary conditions for these extreme values.

Before leaving the topic of slopes, we offer the reader a helpful hint. The slope of nearly every function in economics is referred to as the **marginal** property of that function. The slope of the total cost function with respect to output is referred to as *marginal cost*. The slope of the revenue function with respect to quantity sold is called *marginal revenue*. The slope of a production function with respect to one of the inputs is referred to as the *marginal product*. This information may be useful in short-answer or multiple-choice questions on examinations. More importantly, however, is the connection between slopes and extreme values that we have just surveyed. If output is to be maximized or cost is to be minimized by economic agents in our models, attention will clearly need to be directed to the slopes of these functions. Marginal cost, marginal revenue, marginal product, etc., will therefore play an important role in the analysis of economic behavior.

Elasticity

Economic theory seeks to predict the behavioral responses to changes in variables describing conditions of the environment. The various functions that make these relationships explicit typically relate the levels of two or more variables denominated in totally different units. The quantity of apples demanded is related to their price. The number of man-hours of labor supplied is related to the wage rate. The output of buttons is related to the number of hours of labor and the number of machines employed in their production. Where the left- and right-side variables are not measured in the same units, the slope of the function describing the **responsiveness** of one variable to the other will vary depending on the choice of units in which the two are measured.

Consider the following example. It is well recognized that the rate of fatal highway accidents is related to the average velocity at which automobiles are traveling. We might on occasion wish to express the responsiveness of these deaths to changes in average velocity. A reasonable guess at an expression relating these two variables might be $R = -1.6 + 0.10 \cdot S$, where R is deaths per 100 million vehicle miles and S is velocity in miles per hour. We may express exactly the same relationship of fatal accident rates to average speed in metric form; that is, $R' = -0.96 + 0.036 \cdot S'$, where R' is deaths per 100 million kilometers driven and S' is velocity in kilometers per hour. The slope of the former expression, $\Delta R/\Delta S$, is 0.10. The slope of the latter, $\Delta R'/\Delta S'$, is 0.036. Merely changing the units in which the fatality rate and speed are measured changes the slope dramatically.

Economists prefer to gauge the responsiveness of the relationships with which we deal in a way that is free of any ambiguity. If the response of demand to a change in price is unusually high, we want to recognize this instantly—not worry about the units of measure. We may do this by converting that response (or any other economic response) into an **elasticity** form. The elasticity of response is given by the ratio of the percentage change in the left-side variable to the percentage change in the right-side variable. For the function $y = f(x)$, the elasticity of the change in y to changes in x is therefore given by:

$$\varepsilon = \frac{\% \Delta \text{ in } y}{\% \Delta \text{ in } x} = \frac{\Delta y/y}{\Delta x/x} = \frac{\Delta y}{y} \cdot \frac{x}{\Delta x}.$$

By reordering the two denominators, this becomes:

$$\varepsilon = \frac{\Delta y}{\Delta x} \cdot \frac{x}{y},$$

which is instantly recognizable—it is simply the slope of the function times the ratio of the right-side variable to the left.

From this expression two things are clear. First, even if the slope of the function is constant the elasticity will not be, except in the case where the ratio x/y itself is constant for all points on the functions. Clearly, that will be possible only for functions with positive slopes—that is, where x and y increase together. Second, since the elasticity of a function typically varies along the function, elasticity describes the responsiveness of that function only at a single point.

With these two facts in mind, we may verify that elasticity is independent of the units of measurement. Consider the two functions described in the traffic mortality example just presented. We will evaluate this elasticity at a velocity of 60 miles per hour, which is roughly 100 kilometers per hour. Substituting into our respective functions at these velocities yields the following information:

$$\begin{array}{ll} S = 60 & S' = 100 \\ R = 4.40 & R' = 2.64 \\ \Delta R/\Delta S = 0.10 & \Delta R'/\Delta S' = 0.036 \end{array}$$

From this information the responsiveness of fatalities to speed may be estimated in each case:

$$\varepsilon = \frac{\Delta R}{\Delta S} \cdot \frac{S}{R} = 0.10 \cdot \frac{60}{4.40} = 1.36$$

$$\varepsilon = \frac{\Delta R'}{\Delta S'} \cdot \frac{S'}{R'} = 0.036 \cdot \frac{100}{2.64} = 1.36.$$

There are many functional relationships in economics, and most of them have an elasticity measure associated with them. As each relationship is simply a special case of this general discussion, you need learn the principle of elasticity only once.[3]

---

[3] This is not to say that special difficulties will not present themselves along the way. Because of the peculiar way demand and supply curves are drawn, for example, the elasticity formula appears upside down. Careful attention to the explanation at that point will reveal, however, that it is the diagrams rather than the formula that are inverted.

1.3 Economics as a Social Science

As a social science economics seeks to provide theories that enable us to understand and predict social behavior. However, there are many influences on individual and group behavior, and social scientists come in many colors reflecting natural groupings of these influences. Sociologists focus on the influence of tradition, custom, and institutions on that behavior. Psychologists explain individual behavior in terms of personality and the forces of the environment upon it. Anthropologists seek to develop consistent patterns of behavior across cultures rooted in both the functional and ceremonial needs of all people. These disciplines offer approaches to the understanding of social behavior that are methodologically distinct, yet complementary.

Where does economics fit into this picture? Students in an introductory course often respond to this question by pointing to the location of the behavior studied. They often claim that economics is distinct in its attention to market behavior, to the setting of prices, to the determination of the character and quantity of output, and to getting and keeping a job. While no one would deny the correctness of the relative amounts of attention devoted to market behavior by economists, this is not really a feature that distinguishes economics from its sister disciplines. Producers of consumer products pay far more attention to psychologists than they do to economists in determining the design and marketing strategy for their goods. The "organization man" has been a staple of sociological research from the very beginnings of this branch of social science. On the other hand, some topics studied by economists are a bit remote from markets as conventionally conceived. Economic models with empirically verified explanatory power are now routinely developed to predict the number and the spacing of children per family. Economic models have been shown to have predictive power in the area of criminal activity—even passionate, violent criminal activity—which psychologists would like to stake out as their own exclusive preserve. Chestnuts of sociology such as marriage and divorce have yielded some of their secrets to economists. Indeed, an interesting paper on the practice of footbinding in China informs us that even here economics has something to say.

Purposeful Choice

The distinction between economics and other social sciences concerns the particular lever with which economists probe behavior. Economists assume that behavior is based on rational choice—that individual actors consider alternatives and select that behavior which is consistent with their own interests. Sometimes we can specify those aims explicitly. At other times the objectives remain shrouded in a black box about which we may infer only broad parameters of preference. In either case, however, the key word is **purposeful**. In economic theories people are not blown one way or the other by the winds of abstract social forces. They confront a set of possible actions and *select* the action that they perceive to be best for them.

This does not mean that economists assume that people always choose to do what is in fact best for them. On the contrary, there is scope in economic theory for people to be ill informed and to make mistakes by incorrectly assessing consequences of their actions. Ultimately, whether a fully informed person will choose to do what is best for him or her is a philosophical and a theological question that cannot be answered by economists. We economists certainly do not assume a positive answer to this question. Our claims are much more modest. We assert only that actions that promote the interest of individuals as they perceive them will be favored over those that subvert those interests. Only to the extent that these perceptions are informed by the contemplation of other-worldly rewards will individual choice in economic models be influenced by this more elevated sense of best.

Equilibrium

Economics is also differentiated from other social sciences by the important role played in our theory by the concept of **equilibrium**. This powerful tool in economics may be compared to the concept of inertia in Newtonian physics. A body at rest will remain stationary unless acted upon by some force. A price will not change unless there are forces in the market that move it up or down. If a price is an equilibrium price, such forces will be absent. A disequilibrium price will be changed by market forces.

What is the source of such forces? In every market there are two sets of people—demanders and suppliers—whose behavior is influenced by price, but the plans of each must be consistent. If those plans are inconsistent, then some modification of the behavior of one or both must be made. Demanders' buying plans at a particular price must be the same as the selling plans of suppliers. If those plans are confirmed by the existing price, no modification of plans or behavior is implied. The market price will be unchanged. At a given price, if demanders seek to buy some quantity different from that offered by suppliers, either demanders will get less than they seek or suppliers will sell less than they offer. Response by one or both sets of actors to this situation will provide the force moving price toward its equilibrium level.

The concept of equilibrium is a powerful tool. It informs us, for example, that *changes* in price or quantity are likely to be the result of *changes* in the underlying factors determining the behavior of demanders or suppliers. Prices do not move about randomly; they are pushed. Explanations for price movements may therefore be sought by examining conditions of demand and supply. Moreover, if we have sufficient knowledge about the behavior of suppliers and demanders, we may *predict* the response of equilibrium market prices and quantities to specific changes on one side or the other.

Economic theory in its most general form permits us to make certain qualitative predictions of this type. We know, for example, that an expansion of supply unaccompanied by any change on the demand side of the market will result in a lower equilibrium price. More detailed information permits us to make more precise predictions. If we know the elasticity of demand for this product and the exact change in supply, we may predict the precise amount of the price change. It is in order to better understand the decisions of demanders and suppliers that economic theory is developed in the elaborate detail that characterizes intermediate theory books. A downward-sloping demand curve and a positive-sloping supply curve can take us only so far. If more precise predictions are to be obtained, more detailed analysis of the individual decisions of the actors on the demand and supply sides of the market must be done.

Chapter 1   Introduction

Figure 1.3   *The Circular Flow of Goods, Resources, and Payments*

Economic activity may be represented as a pair of concentric circles with money flowing in one direction and real goods and resources flowing in the opposite direction. The figure contains two markets, one for goods and the other for resources. Households exchange resources for income in the lower market and exchange money for goods in the upper market. Firms exchange wages and rental payments for the services of resources in the lower market and exchange goods for revenues in the upper.

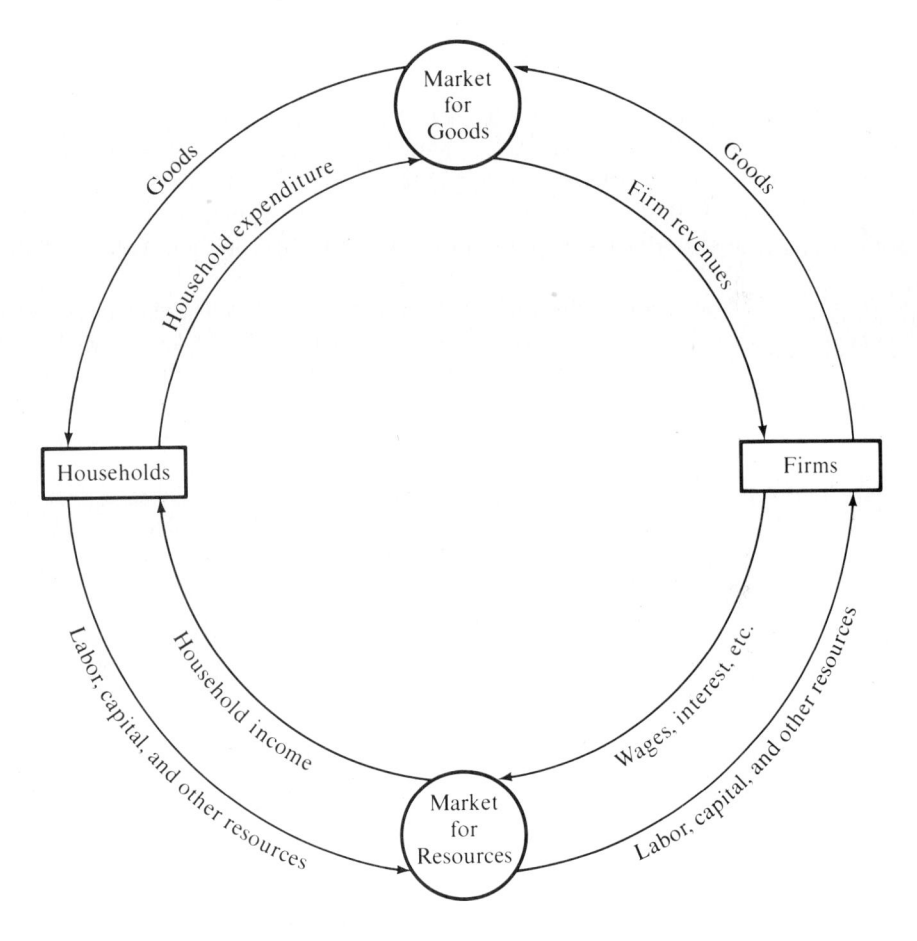

1.4   Scheme of the Book

This book is chiefly concerned with two sets of actors: households and firms. Both households and firms are suppliers and demanders. The private economy may be represented as in Figure 1.3, as a pair of concentric circles through which flow the two fundamental elements with which economics deals. Goods and resources flow counterclockwise in the outer ring, while money flows in the opposite direction in the inner ring. In the market for goods, households are demanders exchanging money for the output of firms. However, households are also suppliers. They own the productive resources that firms must employ to engage in production. Households are therefore the principle suppliers in the market for resources, exchanging the services of those resources for income.

Firms are on the opposite side of both these transactions. They supply goods that they exchange in the appropriate market for revenues. They are also demanders of resources that they require for production. In exchange for these resources they offer wages, interest, rent, and other payments to resource owners.

The essential symmetry of the economy in these respects suggests several possible organizational schemes for this book. In the course of study we must consider households as demanders of goods and suppliers of resources. We must also consider the behavior of firms as suppliers of goods and as demanders of resources. These topics might be grouped by function. We might look at both sets of demanders first and then at both sets of suppliers. Household demands for goods might be followed by firm demands for resources. Then household supply could be presented, followed by the supply of goods by firms. Alternatively, we might group topics by type of actor. Household demand might be followed by household supply and resources. Then, firm demand might be followed by the supply of goods by firms.

Neither of these groupings has been chosen, though both offer some advantages. In many ways analysis of the supply of factors by households more closely resembles the demand for goods by these households than it does the supply of goods by firms. Similarly, the theory of the supply of output and the demand for inputs by firms are more closely related than are demand and supply in either market. These considerations suggest that a grouping by type of actor might offer the student a more accessible format than either of the other groupings. Similarity in approach can make two separate topics easier to grasp. In spite of this, the format adopted is a grouping by market. We will consider factors affecting the demand for goods, then consider the theory of the supply of those goods. The demand for resources is developed next, followed by the theory of the supply of those resources.

This approach is the traditional one, but it offers advantages as well. The focus on markets directs attention toward the determination of equilibrium prices and quantities. Demanders of goods, for example, are influenced in their purchasing decisions by the prices of goods. Suppliers of these goods look to the same prices in making production decisions. Neither sets the price; rather, both react to it and accommodate their behavior to it. Price is determined, as just noted, when it reaches a level that is consistent with both sets of plans.

This focus on the determination of price is symmetrical with respect to both markets. We begin with a description of equilibrium in the goods market. The underlying theory of demand as it relates to price is then presented and followed by the theory of output. We then turn our attention to the input market. The theory of the demand for productive resources is presented and followed by the theory of the supply of two important resources, labor and capital. Equilibrium in these markets is described, and the implications of these conditions for the distribution of income among households are developed.

Science is knowledge, and knowledge is purely descriptive. Equilibrum is reached when the price stops changing, and that price may be regarded as high by some and inadequate by others. Economics as a social science does not concern itself with value judgments, just as physics does not classify the boiling point of water as dangerously high or conveniently low. A knowledge of physics suggests some methods for changing the boiling point of water. Salt may be added to lower it, and the container may be sealed to increase it. A thorough knowledge of physics will also alert us to the consequences of these changes. A saline solution is the result in the first case and high pressure and a possible explosion in the second. Similarly, knowledge of economics affords some suggestions for changing prices, though these also have consequences that are potentially important. Here, too, a little knowledge can be dangerous.

In Chapters 17 and 18 we depart from this socio-scientific posture to explore the normative implications of economics. In a limited sense economic theory does distinguish between a good price and a bad one. Some prices are consistent with an efficient allocation of economic resources and others are not. Chapter 17 is devoted to the definition of economic efficiency as well as a discussion of its theoretical and normative limitations. Chapter 18 analyzes the institutions engaged in the allocation of resources, both markets and governments, for insights into the question of the efficiency of those arrangements.

Summary

This chapter has attempted to explain what social science and economics are really all about. This is quite a heavy-duty undertaking, especially for the first reading assignment in the course. The next chapter is comfortingly down to earth; it should provide some relief for those students who like economics because of its concrete subject matter. In our brief discussion here we have had to seek answers to some very basic questions, like "What is a theory?" and "What makes theories good and bad?" First we noted that a theory is a metaphor and by its very nature abstract. It enables us to understand aspects of the world around us without detailed knowledge. In the words of the metaphors used earlier to describe theories, a theory must serve as both a filing cabinet for knowledge and as a compass leading toward new understanding.

A theory must be informative; it must imply consequences of conditions or actions. These consequences must narrow the range of possible results, or the theory is a useless tautology. A theory that rules out nothing is an empty theory. A theory that has no application is an empty box. The broader the circumstances in which a theory applies, the more general the theory. The antonym of general in this sense is narrow. Good theories should also be concise; Ockham's razor should always be honed and at hand.

A theory that is not a tautology will ultimately be confirmed or falsified by the facts implied by its prediction. A calendar containing only 365 days will eventually be rejected because of snow in July. As this sort of trial and error is costly, it is better to attempt to verify theories before their dissemination. Practitioners and students of economics are therefore expected to have a reasonable understanding of statistical methods employed in the testing of economic theories.

Economics is a social science and thus concerns itself with human behavior. It distinguishes itself from its fellow disciplines in social science through its assumptions regarding the wellsprings of behavior rather than the arena of this action. Economic theory assumes that behavior is rooted in purposeful choice. People are assumed to pursue ends, and as the environment in which that pursuit takes place is modified, behavior responds. Economic choices are not limited to the selection of goods placed in the market basket. However, the techniques introduced to analyze that selection have found a surprising and satisfying variety of uses beyond the walls of the corner A & P.

Economics is also distinct from the other social sciences in its emphasis on equilibrium. Equilibrium in economics describes a condition of models. It resembles a state of inertia in which variables in the models remain the same because they are not influenced to change. If a market price is in equilibrium, the plans of buyers and sellers are in agreement, and neither will be influenced to change it. In most economic analyses it is assumed that variables move quickly toward equilibrium levels and that at any moment observed markets are in a state approximating such levels. As it is possible to predict the direction of change in equilibrium values for a large number of events that take place in the economy, this assumption of rapid convergence is both verifiable and a highly useful aspect of economic theory.

This chapter gave a brief presentation of certain mathematical principles that will be regularly employed in subsequent chapters. No attempt will be made to summarize this material or that which follows in the appendix. It is sufficient here to reiterate that the list of principles is short, but mastery of it is essential. The final portion of the chapter was devoted to an outline of the book showing that it is organized around the circular flow diagram in Figure 1.3.

The next chapter begins our journey around that circle. It is a long trip, but that is because there is a great deal to see and take note of along the way. Travel is broadening, and the author hopes your journey will prove no exception. Bon voyage!

Key Concepts

model
tautology
Ockham's razor
verification
systems of equations
function
vertical intercept
slope
differential
tangent
multivariate function
total differential

maxima and minima
marginal
responsiveness
elasticity
purposeful choice
equilibrium
circular flow
unit change
nonlinear function
chain rule
product rule

Chapter 1   Appendix

This appendix is provided as a refresher for those students who have taken calculus and also as a sort of cookbook for those who have not. No attempt is made here to adhere to the rigorous development of the material presented that is required of formal mathematics courses. After all, you are not math students; you are here to learn economics. Nevertheless, a knowledge of certain principles will assist the reader in understanding algebraic manipulations at various points in the book. We therefore include here a very intuitive presentation of the derivation of mathematical techniques relied upon frequently in the text.

Slopes of Nonlinear Functions

Consider the function $y = 3x + 2x^2$. A change in the value of x implies a particular change in the value of y. We may write the expression for this *changed* value of the equation as:

$$y + \Delta y = 3 \cdot (x + \Delta x) + 2 \cdot (x + \Delta x)^2$$
$$= 3x + 3\Delta x + 2x^2 + 4x \cdot \Delta x + 2\Delta x^2.$$

Subtracting our original equation from both sides yields:

$$\begin{array}{rl} y + \Delta y = & 3x + 3\Delta x + 2x^2 + 4x \cdot \Delta x + 2\Delta x^2 \\ -y \quad\quad = & -3x \quad\quad\quad - 2x^2 \\ \hline \Delta y = & \quad\quad 3\Delta x \quad\quad\quad + 4x \cdot \Delta x + 2\Delta x^2, \end{array}$$

which may be solved for the slope $\Delta y / \Delta x$:

(1A.1) $$\frac{\Delta y}{\Delta x} = 3 + 4x + 2\Delta x.$$

There are two differences between this expression and that developed for the slope of a linear function presented in the text of this chapter. This expression contains *both* x and Δx. The slope therefore depends on the *level* of x at which it is evaluated and the *interval* over which it is evaluated. Functions with varying slopes are called **nonlinear functions**. Table 1A.1 presents various values for this slope for different combinations of x and Δx. In this case the value of the slope increases as we hold Δx constant and increase x. It also increases as we hold x constant and increase Δx. This need not be the case. The slopes of functions may

Table 1A.1 *Points, Slopes, and Intervals*

$\Delta y / \Delta x$	x	Δx
9	1	1
11	1	2
13	1	3
15	1	4
13	2	1
15	2	2
17	2	3
19	2	4

Figure 1A.1   *Slopes of Nonlinear Functions*

The slope of this function, $\Delta x/\Delta y$, depends both on the value of x at which the slope is evaluated and on the size of the change in x over which the slope is measured. When evaluated at x_1, the slope is greater over interval Δx_2 than over interval Δx_1. The slope is also greater at x_3 than at x_1 over interval Δx_3, which is equal to interval Δx_1.

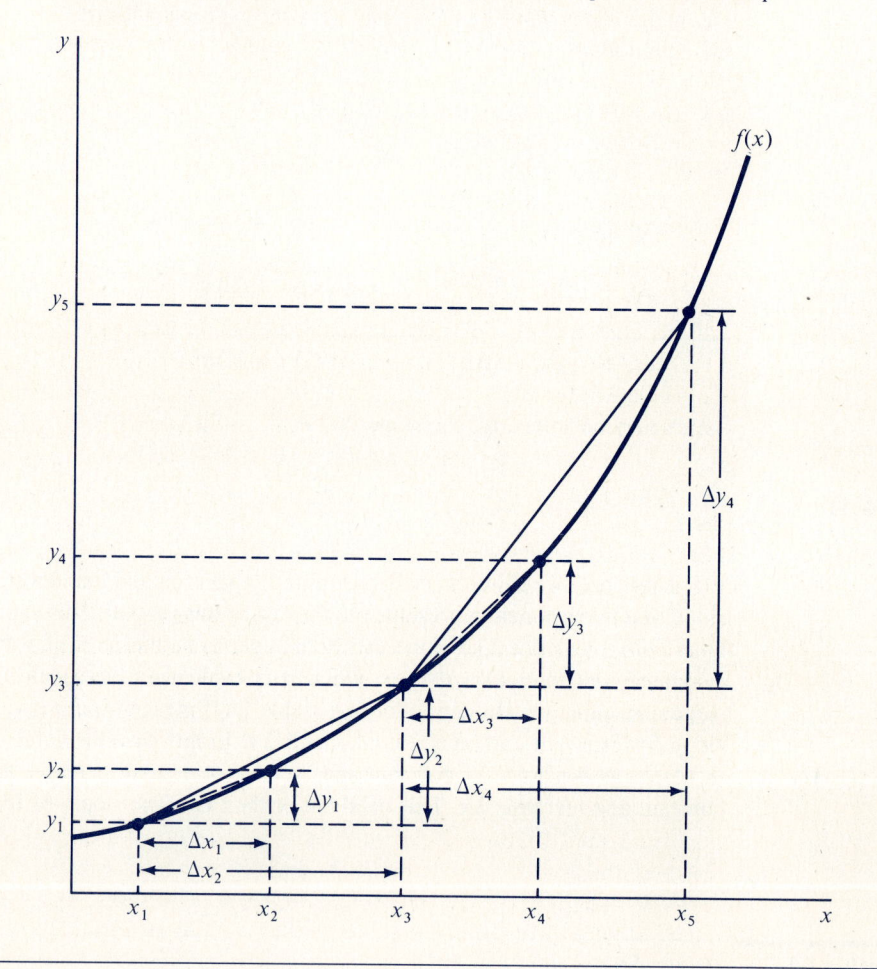

increase or decrease as either x or Δx increases. The important point to remember is that the slope is defined only for specific values of both.

    Figure 1A.1 reveals why this is true. Consider the slope at x_1. Evaluated for a change in x equal to Δx_1, the slope is $\Delta y_1/\Delta x_1$. Because the function is concave upward, however, the angle of the larger right triangle formed with the larger side, Δx_2, is wider than that formed by Δx_1. Its tangent, $\Delta y_2/\Delta x_2$, is therefore larger. Compare these slopes with those at x_3. The change in x given by Δx_3, which is equal to Δx_1, is different still. It is equal to $\Delta y_3/\Delta x_3$, which is greater than $\Delta y_1/$

Δx_1. Similarly, the slope over the larger interval Δx_4, which is equal to Δx_2, is larger than both $\Delta y_3/\Delta x_3$ and $\Delta y_2/\Delta x_2$.

Many functions employed in economic theory are nonlinear, and it is important to be consistent in our definitions of slopes. We can do this by employing the same interval of change in all applications. We might simply identify this change as a *unit increase* in the right-hand variable. Many principles of economics texts implicitly adopt this standard by defining marginal quantities as the change in the left-side variable associated with a **unit change** in the right-side variable. Marginal cost, for example, is often defined as the increase in total cost associated with a one-unit increase in output. For careful economic analysis, however, this procedure is unsatisfactory. The interval of change in this case depends on the units of measurement.

Consider the marginal cost of nails. If the unit of measurement is individual nails, the interval of change will be quite different from that identified when nail production is counted in tons. Our estimate of marginal cost will therefore differ per nail or per ton, depending upon the unit of measurement. The point here is not that the cost per nail will differ from the cost per ton at the margin. It is that marginal cost using either measure will differ depending on how a unit is defined. This can be shown by referring back to Figure 1A.1. Let Δx_1 be one nail and the conversion of nails into ounces be constant at a rate of two for one. If Δx_2 is equal to $2 \cdot x_1$, then Δx_2 will reflect a 1-ounce change. At this rate of conversion, the marginal cost per nail should equal one half of the cost of an extra ounce of nails, and the marginal cost per ounce should be twice the cost of a unit increase in nails. Clearly, this is not the case. The change in y, Δy_1, is less than half of Δy_2, and twice Δy_1 is less than Δy_2.

Economics solves this problem by defining the interval of change not as a unit change, which depends on the size of the unit, but at zero, which has the same length regardless of what is being measured. We may not actually evaluate a ratio with zero in the denominator; such a ratio is undefined in mathematics. However, we may determine a limiting value, which such a ratio approaches as the change in x approaches zero. This is illustrated in Figure 1A.2. Note that for successively smaller changes in x, the slope that we calculate as $\Delta y/\Delta x$ itself gets smaller. This is not true indefinitely, however. This slope does not go to zero as Δx approaches zero. On the contrary, in the limit, as the horizontal side of the right triangle gets very tiny—say, as small as the eye can discern—we can see that the angle in its corner would approach the slope of the line TT, which is just tangent at point t. Indeed, this is the value of the slope of a function that we use in economics. When we refer to the slope at x_1, we intend the reader to interpret that statement as referring to the slope of a tangent to the function at this value of x. Note that our expression for the slope of the function, $y = 3 \cdot x + 2 \cdot x^2$, in Equation 1A.1 is not zero but $3 + 4 \cdot x$ when Δx is equal to zero.

Determining Slopes

For many applications in economics it is sufficient to know the difference between a positive and negative slope. As the slope is a ratio, the denominator of which is always positive, the sign of the slope is determined by the sign of the change in the

Figure 1A.2   *The Slope as a Tangent to a Nonlinear Function*

As the size of the interval Δx diminishes, the value of the ratio that measures the slope of the function also diminishes. It does not diminish without limit, however. As Δx approaches zero, the slope approaches the slope of the straight line tangent to the function at t.

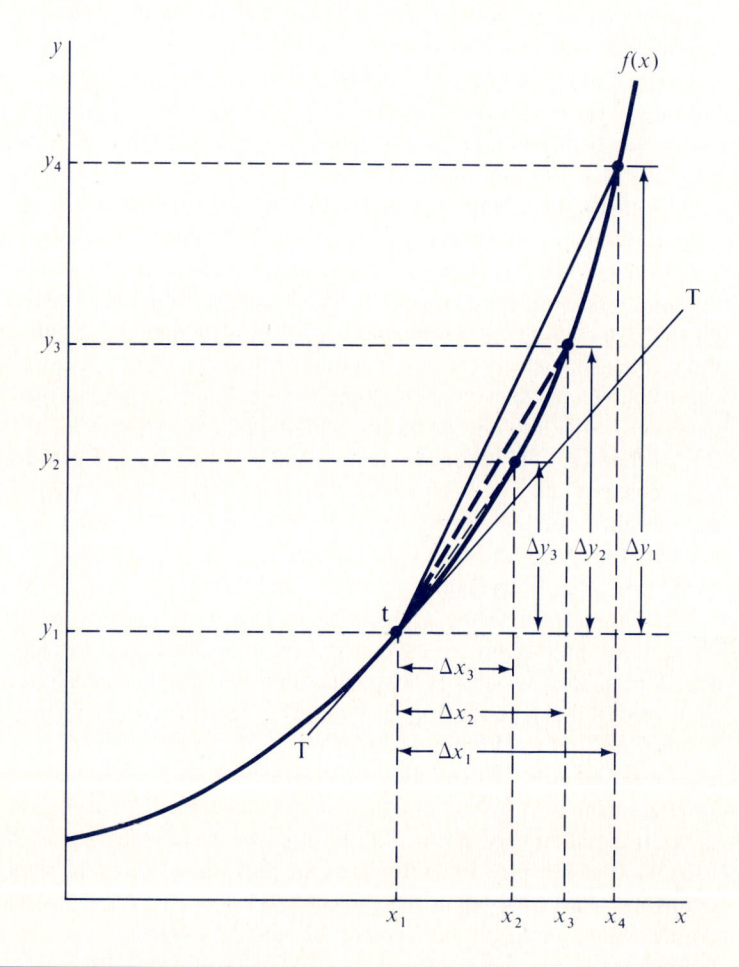

---

left-side variable. The slope of the function in panel (a) of Figure 1A.3 is therefore positive, while the slope of the function in panel (b) is negative. Calculus provides a series of shortcuts for identifying the slopes (called derivatives) of various kinds of functions. In this course it is not necessary to specifically identify slopes of the functions with which we deal, and we will therefore refrain from adding here to the anxiety and burden that you must bear by specific reference to each of these rules. However, two of these rules play an important role at several points in the development of our theory, and we will therefore sketch them here.

Chain Rule The first of these is referred to as the **chain rule**. Recall our temperature conversion function, $t_f = 32 + (9/5) \cdot t_c$. The slope of this function was shown to be simply 9/5. Let us assume that the rate of evaporation of a liquid may also be expressed as a function of temperature (holding constant air pressure); that is,

$$e = K + \alpha \cdot t_f,$$

where K and α are constant. The slope of this function, $\Delta e/\Delta t_f$, is also the coefficient of the right-side variable, in this case, α. Although the rate of evaporation function is expressed in terms of Fahrenheit temperature, we may evaluate the slope of a different function, that is, $\Delta e/\Delta t_c$. In general, if we have *two functions, the right-side variable of one of which is the left-side variable of the other, we may evaluate the slope of the implicit function relating the remaining two variables as the product of the two slopes.* For example, here we have $t_f = h(t_c)$ and $e = k(t_f)$. The slope $\Delta e/\Delta t_c$ is simply $(\Delta e/\Delta t_f) \cdot (\Delta t_f/\Delta t_C)$, or $\alpha \cdot (9/5)$.

This may be illustrated as follows. Substituting for t_f in the evaporation function, we obtain:

$$e = K + \alpha \cdot (32 + \frac{9}{5} \cdot t_c)$$

$$= k + \alpha \cdot 32 + \alpha \cdot \frac{9}{5} \cdot t_c.$$

Figure 1A.3 *The Sign of a Slope*

The function in panel (a) has a positive slope. The change in y implied by a positive change in x is positive. The function in panel (b) has a negative slope. The change in y implied by a positive change in x in this case is negative.

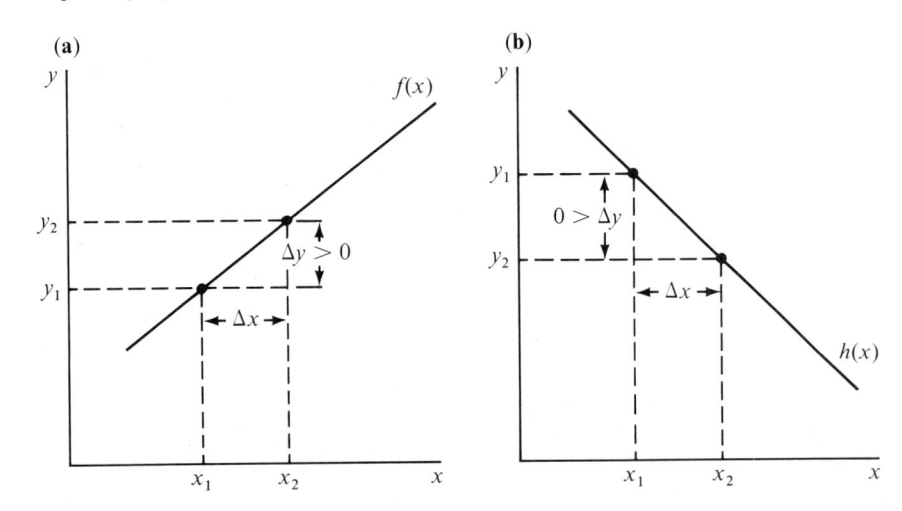

For any change in the centigrade temperature, the changed rate of evaporation is:

$$e + \Delta e = K + \alpha \cdot 32 + \alpha \cdot \frac{9}{5} \cdot t_c + \alpha \cdot \frac{9}{5} \cdot \Delta t_c.$$

Subtracting our original equation gives:

$$\begin{aligned} e + \Delta e &= K + \alpha \cdot 32 + \alpha \cdot \frac{9}{5} \cdot t_c + \alpha \cdot \frac{9}{5} \cdot \Delta t_c \\ -e &= -K - \alpha \cdot 32 - \alpha \cdot \frac{9}{5} \cdot t_c \\ \hline \Delta e &= \alpha \cdot \frac{9}{5} \cdot \Delta t_c. \end{aligned}$$

Solving for the slope $\Delta e / \Delta t_c$ gives:

$$\frac{\Delta e}{\Delta t_c} = \alpha \cdot \frac{9}{5}.$$

Although the chain rule has been illustrated here with two linear functions, the rule holds for nonlinear functions as well, when evaluated in the limit where the change in the denominator approaches zero.

Product Rule The second rule that we will have occasion to employ also involves a function composed of two other functions. In this case we have a function of two variables that may themselves be expressed as functions of a third variable. This rule is known as the **product rule**. In this case the slope we seek is $\Delta z / \Delta x$ when $z = v \cdot y$ and $v = f(x)$ and $y = h(x)$. It can be shown that this slope is equal to the sum of the first right-side variable times the slope of the second plus the second right-side variable times the slope of the first; that is,

$$\frac{\Delta z}{\Delta x} = v \cdot \frac{\Delta y}{\Delta x} + y \cdot \frac{\Delta v}{\Delta x}.$$

The changed value of z will equal the product of the changed values of v and y:

$$\begin{aligned} z + \Delta z &= (v + \Delta v) \cdot (y + \Delta y) \\ &= v \cdot y + v \cdot \Delta y + \Delta v \cdot y + \Delta v \cdot \Delta y. \end{aligned}$$

Subtracting our initial function leaves:

$$\begin{aligned} z + \Delta z &= v \cdot y + v \cdot \Delta y + \Delta v \cdot y + \Delta v \cdot \Delta y \\ -z &= -v \cdot y \\ \hline \Delta z &= v \cdot \Delta y + \Delta v \cdot y + \Delta v \cdot \Delta y. \end{aligned}$$

Dividing through by the change in the variable x gives:

$$\frac{\Delta z}{\Delta x} = v \cdot \frac{\Delta y}{\Delta x} + y \cdot \frac{\Delta v}{\Delta x} + \frac{\Delta v}{\Delta x} \cdot \Delta y.$$

From our discussion of differentials we know that $\Delta y = (\Delta y/\Delta x) \cdot \Delta x$, the right side of which may be substituted for Δy:

$$\frac{\Delta z}{\Delta x} = v \cdot \frac{\Delta y}{\Delta x} + y \cdot \frac{\Delta v}{\Delta x} + \frac{\Delta v}{\Delta x} \cdot \frac{\Delta y}{\Delta x} \cdot \Delta x.$$

As this expression for the slope $\Delta z/\Delta x$ contains Δx, we might infer, even if we did not know, that the function z is nonlinear. Evaluated in the limit, however, as Δx approaches zero, the third term on the right side itself is zero, leaving:

$$\frac{\Delta z}{\Delta x} = v \cdot \frac{\Delta y}{\Delta x} + y \cdot \frac{\Delta v}{\Delta x}.$$

Chapter 2

Market Equilibrium

Connections   This chapter presents the foundations of market analysis. Markets determine two things: how much will be produced and who will receive how much. In order to understand how these results are achieved, however, we must understand the nature of market equilibrium and the way such an equilibrium is established and maintained. The general concept of equilibrium was defined in Chapter 1 in abstract terms. Here we will develop a much more detailed application of this idea to the behavior of two sets of agents in an economy, demanders and suppliers. This will require a rather extensive development of the theory relating to the responsiveness of both sets of agents to changes in their economic environment. The quantity demanded of a good responds to changes in many things. Demander behavior is therefore presented in terms of functions for several variables. This analysis is elementary, but the reader unaccustomed to thinking in these terms is urged to reread the section on multivariate functions in Chapter 1.

One of the earliest concerns of economists, and certainly one of the most successful aspects of economic analysis, has been the determination of market prices. Rare is the person in our present-day society who does not recognize at least partially the role played in the determination of price by the two forces of demand and supply. This chapter will develop the theory of the role played by these forces and provide some insights into the way in which this ingenious model allows us to make firm predictions about the response of price to changes in one or the other of its determinants.

2.1 Simultaneous Systems

The chief difficulty of economics for the untutored (and the source of much consternation on the part of those seeking answers from economists) is rooted in the fact that many of its principles are stated in terms of simultaneous systems. You will recall from Chapter 1 that in simultaneous systems everything depends on everything else. Most people want economics to be like Newtonian physics: a series of formulae with the answers to each of their questions on the left-hand side and all the relevant data on the right (preferably involving only routine mathematics). We can easily calculate the force with which an object will strike the earth given merely its weight and the height from which it is dropped; or, the distance traveled by a projectile, in which case we need to know only the angle at which it is fired and its muzzle velocity.

We would like to be able to calculate price in a similar way. The early economists were very much preoccupied with developing formulae for price in which the various payments to factors of production played the key role. Price was made up of this much for labor and that much for capital. Rent sometimes did and sometimes did not play a role in the determination.

The point is, however, that it cannot be done like this. For price cannot be determined without our knowing how much is sold—and quantity sold is determined simultaneously with price. There are, in other words, two unknowns in economic problems. Thus, we require two equations to solve for these values; we cannot simply plug values into a single equation. The price determined in any single market depends on quantity sold, and quantity in turn depends on price.[1]

One might legitimately object at this point with the rejoinder that "If everything in economics depends on everything else, of what use is it to anyone? If you

---

[1] If the demand equation is $P = 20,000 - q$, for example, we cannot determine P without knowing q. If quantity is known to be 10,000, then the demand equation may be used to determine a price of 10,000. But price will take on other values for different quantities. A price of $5000 is implied by a quantity of 15,000, and a price of $12,000 is consistent with an output of 8,000. Nor can a supply equation by itself tell us quantity. The supply equation $q = 19 \cdot p$ does not permit us to identify quantity without specifying price. At a price of $10,000 an output of 190,000 will be produced, while at the lower price of $100 only 1900 will be supplied. With these two equations together, however, we may solve for both P and q simultaneously. The solution values for these two equations are $P = 1000$ and $q = 19,000$. Note that this pair of values—and no other—satisfies both demand and supply equations.

can't know some things without knowing everything else, and we never know everything else, we can never know anything." Economists frequently encourage this sort of objection by beginning every answer to a question with the phrase "That depends. . . ." The point is, however, that we *can* know some things without knowing everything else. This is possible because in practice as well as in theory, many factors affecting one of our equations have no influence on the other. A change in the level of one of these factors can be expected to shift only one of the equations with predictable results. This type of exercise is called **comparative statics** and employs a principle referred to as *ceteris paribus*, meaning "other things the same." Let us consider some comparative statics on the demand side of the market.

2.2 Demand with Fixed Supply

First Law of Demand

In order to focus attention on the behavior of demanders, we will proceed by assuming that quantity supplied is fixed. The only thing left to be determined in this case is market price. The factors affecting demand will determine price, and as these factors themselves change they will exert either an upward or a downward influence on price.

By **demand** we mean "ability and willingness to buy." This is, of course, different from "wishing we had it" or "planning to purchase it in the near future." When we estimate demand for a product, we use market data which, of course, refer to people's actual purchases, not their hopes and dreams. Despite the obviously whimsical nature of many of these purchases, economists have found demand for many products to be responsive to economic variables and consistent over time. Here we will examine the influence of three such variables on the quantity people are willing to buy.

The three demand variables to be considered here are (1) the price of the good itself, (2) the prices of other goods, and (3) the income of the demander. As discussed in Chapter 1, when we wish to show a relationship among variables, it is convenient to express that relationship as a function. Here we may express the relationship between the quantity people want to buy and the variables that influence that quantity as a function:

$q_i^d = f(P_i, \bar{P}_j, I)$.

q_i^d = quantity demanded of the ith good

P_i = price of the ith good

$\bar{P}_j$ = a vector of all other prices

I = income of the demanders

Consider first the relationship between the quantity demanded and the price of the good under consideration. We do this by making the assumption of ceteris paribus

Figure 2.1   *Demand Curves*

Demand curves come in all shapes and sizes. The first law of demand requires only that they slope downward to the right over their full range. Each of the curves in this figure satisfies this condition, so each is consistent with this law.

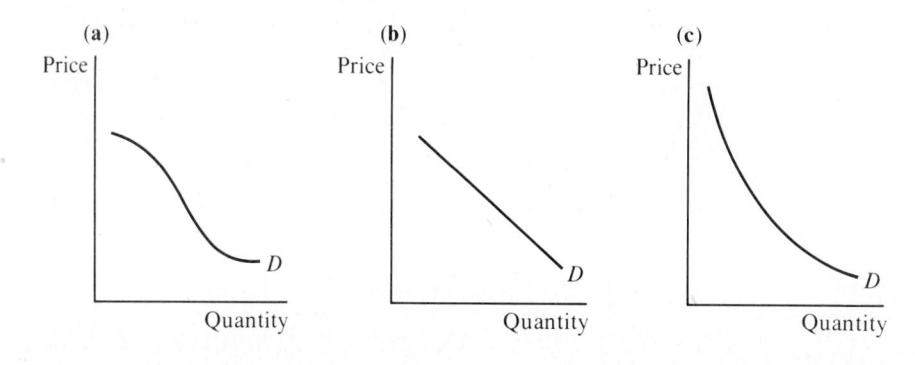

(a) (b) (c)

again. Income and all other prices remain constant; only the good's own price varies. Under this assumption the relationship between these two variables is given by the **first law of demand**:

First law of demand: Quantity demanded varies inversely with price.

By treating $\bar{P}_j$ and I as constant, we isolate the following relationship, which by the first law of demand has the sign shown:

$$\frac{\Delta q_i^d}{\Delta P_i} < 0.$$

This inequality does not place much of a restriction on the shape of demand curves. All it tells us is that, regardless of quantity, an increase in price will reduce the quantity demanded. This condition is satisfied at every quantity in each of the curves depicted in Figure 2.1. Demand curves may be curvilinear as in panels (a) and (c) or linear as in panel (b). The first law of demand states simply that demand curves slope downward to the right. They therefore have a negative slope.[2]

Other Prices

It is best to consider the effect of other prices individually. Take the everyday example of hot dogs. As hot dogs get more expensive we buy fewer, conforming to

---

[2] Mathematically punctilious readers will note that the expression $\Delta q_i^d/\Delta P_i$ is not the slope of the demand curve. That slope is expressed as $\Delta P_i/\Delta q_i^d$. The former is the expression for the slope of the inverse function to the demand curve. Economists as a group became adept at geometry before they learned much mathematics, and tradition now dictates drawing the curve backwards. However, as the slope of one function is the reciprocal of the slope of its inverse, this causes few serious problems. Both slopes must carry the same sign.

Chapter 2   Market Equilibrium

Figure 2.2   **Complements and Substitutes**

The two panels of this figure illustrate the relationship between the quantity of one good demanded and the prices of other goods. The two goods in panel (a) are complements, because price increases for sauerkraut reduce the quantity of hot dogs demanded. The opposite relationship occurs in panel (b), between the price of hamburgers and hot dogs, so those two goods are substitutes.

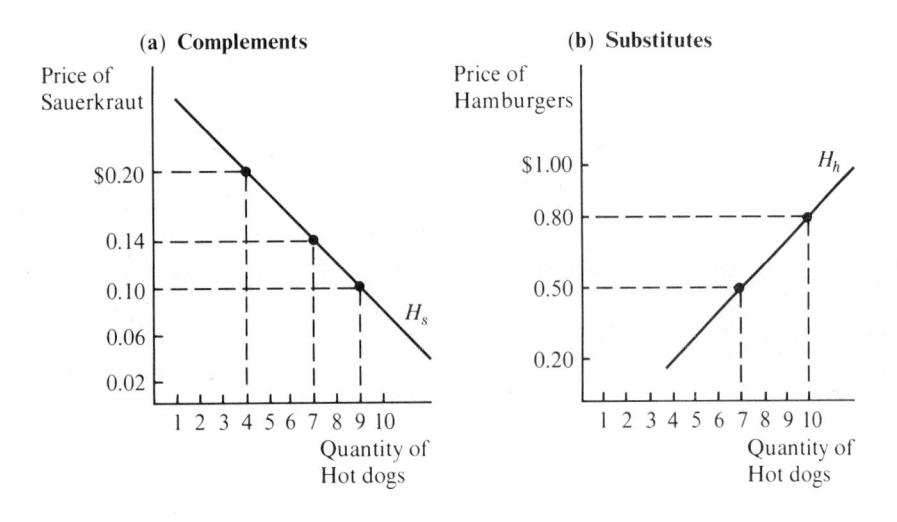

the first law of demand. But how does the demand for hot dogs behave as other goods vary in price? Clearly, that depends on the good. A fall in the price of hamburgers is likely to reduce the quantity of hot dogs we are willing to buy at a particular price. However, a fall in the price of sauerkraut is likely to have the opposite effect (at least for those of us who will buy sauerkraut at any price). The effect of a price change of another good on demand cannot be predicted a priori. There is no law of demand governing this relationship. We therefore do what all good social scientists do when they cannot predict the effect of a change in one variable on another: We categorize.

Consider Figure 2.2. Both panels depict the two cases in which demands in two markets are related by price. Here again we make the assumption of ceteris paribus—that is, we assume all other variables (in this case own price and income) are held constant. What we observe then is the effect of the price of the other goods on the demand for hot dogs. In panel (a), the curve (H_s) looks very similar to the demand curve shown in panel (b) of Figure 2.1. We must remember, however, that it is not the price of hot dogs but the price of sauerkraut that is on the vertical axis. Goods whose demands are inversely related to the price of other goods are defined as **complements** of those goods.

Complements: Those goods for which $\dfrac{\Delta q_i^d}{\Delta P_j} < 0$.

In panel (b) of Figure 2.2, the curve relating quantity of hot dogs demanded to the price of the other good, hamburgers (curve H_h), has the opposite slope. A rise in the price of hamburgers increases the quantity of hot dogs that people are willing to buy. Goods whose demands are positively related to price changes in another good are defined as **substitutes**.

Substitutes: Those goods for which $\dfrac{\Delta q_i^d}{\Delta P_j} > 0$.

We may see the effects of these price changes of other goods on the demand curve of the good being considered by incorporating the information from Figure 2.2 into the demand curve analysis. Figure 2.3 depicts the demand curves for hot

---

Figure 2.3 *Price Changes in Other Goods and Demand Curve Shifts*

Price changes in other goods shift the demand curve, implying that different quantities of hot dogs will be purchased at a constant hot dog price. A rise in the price of sauerkraut from $0.10 to $0.20 reduces the quantity of hot dogs demanded at each hot dog price. For example, at a hot dog price of $0.80 this rise in the price of sauerkraut reduces the quantity of hot dogs demanded from 7 per period to 4. The leftward shift of the demand curve in the case of a price increase in sauerkraut indicates that hot dogs and sauerkraut are complements. The rightward shift associated with the increase in the price of hamburgers indicates that hot dogs and hamburgers are substitutes.

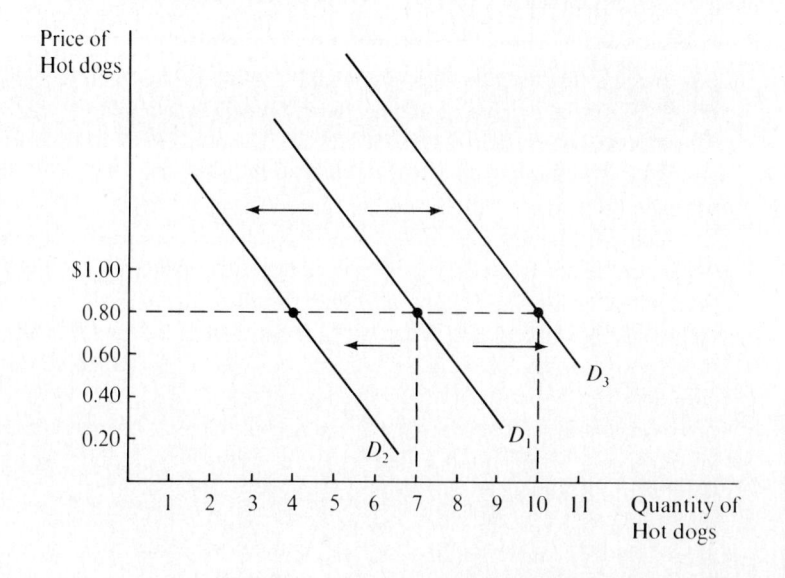

dogs themselves varying with the price of hot dogs in the appropriate way. Let us assume that the curves from Figure 2.2 were drawn for a price (held constant) of $0.80. Assume further that the price of sauerkraut is $0.10 and the price of hamburgers is $0.50. Under these assumptions the information given by the three curves is consistent: Quantity demanded is shown to be the same in each. Original demand curve D_1 tells us that at a price of $0.80 7 hot dogs will be demanded. At the prices just quoted for sauerkraut and hamburgers, the curves relating demand for hot dogs to other prices in the two panels of Figure 2.2 also inform us that this is the quantity that demanders will buy.

Now let the price of sauerkraut rise to $0.20. Panel (a) of Figure 2.2 tells us that at this higher price only 4 units of hot dogs will be demanded. The higher price of sauerkraut must therefore produce a *shift* of the demand curve for hot dogs in Figure 2.3 to the left. At a price of hot dogs of $0.80 fewer hot dogs are demanded, though at a lower price for hot dogs people will purchase the original 7. Therefore, *a rise in the price of a complement will always shift the demand curve to the left; a fall in the price of a complement will always shift the demand curve to the right.*

Next, assume that the price of a substitute good, hamburgers, rises, say from $0.50 to $0.80. Panel (b) of Figure 2.2 tells us that at this higher price for hamburgers the number of hot dogs demanded will increase from 7 to 10. In Figure 2.3, this results in a rightward shift in the demand curve to position D_3. This new demand curve indicates that at a price for hot dogs of $0.80, exactly 10 will be demanded. Price changes for substitutes thus influence demand in the opposite direction from price changes of complements. *A rise in the price of a substitute shifts the demand curve to the right; a fall in the price of a substitute shifts the demand curve to the left.*

Unfortunately, there is no hard and fast formula for determining whether any two goods are related in demand as complements, substitutes, or neither. Here we must rely for the most part on common sense and observation. We may nevertheless offer some crude rules that may be applied with caution. Components or ingredients in some final product are typically complements. Thus, pasta and tomato sauce are complements. Sewing machines and fabric, gasoline and tires, opera performances and gala dinners also qualify, being components in the final products clothing, automobile transportation, and social distinction, respectively.

On the other hand, goods that tend to be used in lieu of each other are substitutes. Thus the more specifically we identify goods, the more likely they are to be substitutes. Exxon gasoline is a substitute for Texaco gasoline. NBC programming is a substitute for CBS programming. Beef is a substitute for pork. By the same token, the more generally we identify products, the less responsive will demand for them be to changes in the prices of other broad categories of goods. Motor fuel, television, and meat are most likely completely unrelated to one another in demand.

Income and Demand

There is no law of demand governing the effect of income on demand either. A rise in income is likely to lead a person to purchase fewer hot dogs for the same reason that a rise in income is associated with more purchases of pâté de foie gras. As people's incomes rise they may substitute more expensive items for cheaper items in their shopping lists. This results in decreases in demand for cheap things and increases in demand for more luxurious items—indeed, the effect of income on demand can be very troublesome. Demand for many products probably increases over a certain range of income and then decreases. This becomes more likely as we get more specific about the type of good we are analyzing. The demand for automobiles probably rises continuously with income over the entire range of income. If we consider the demand for Cadillacs, however, the demand increases up to the point at which purchasers begin to substitute Mercedes-Benz or Rolls Royces.

In spite of these difficulties, and in the absence of theoretical reasoning leading to a clearcut result, we categorize the possible outcomes as we did with the influence of other price changes. Figure 2.4 depicts these relationships between income and quantity demanded. Here, as always, we assume ceteris paribus with respect to the price of the goods in question and the prices of all other goods.

Panel (a) depicts the relationship between income and the quantity of hot dogs demanded. As income rises, fewer hot dogs are demanded. Goods whose demands are inversely related to income are defined as **inferior goods**. This does not, of course, imply anything about the nutritional content or other measurable service-

Figure 2.4 *Income and Demand*

Quantity demanded is influenced by income. The inverse relationship shown in panel (a) indicates that hot dogs are inferior goods. A rise in income from $16,000 to $20,000 results in fewer hot dogs being consumed. In panel (b), the same income change is associated with an increase in the consumption of steak. Steak is therefore a normal good.

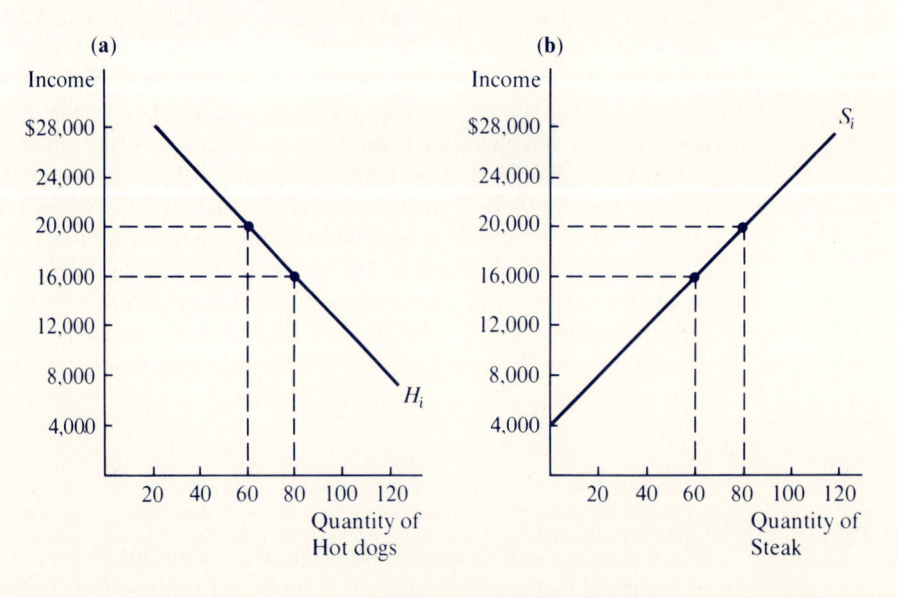

related aspects of such goods—hot dogs are, after all, more nutritious than many things that high-income people snack on, such as bonbons or pastries. The designation "inferior good" means only that high-income people regard them as inferior since they can afford to purchase more than can lower-income people but choose other goods in their place.[3]

Inferior goods: Those goods for which $\dfrac{\Delta q_i^d}{\Delta I} < 0.$

Panel (b) depicts a similar relationship for the demand for steak. As incomes rise, people choose to buy more units of steak at any quoted price than they would at lower incomes. Thus, at a given price for steak, holding other prices constant, the curve relating quantity demanded of this good to income (S_i) rises with income. Those goods whose demands rise with income are defined as **normal goods**.

Normal goods: Those goods for which $\dfrac{\Delta q_i^d}{\Delta I} > 0.$

The effect of income changes on the demand curves for these goods is shown in Figure 2.5. To make the demand curves in this figure consistent with the curves in Figure 2.4, assume that the price of hot dogs on which panel (a) of Figure 2.4 is based is $1.20 per pound and that median income of American households is $16,000 per year. In panel (a) of both figures a quantity of 80 units is demanded. Now assume that incomes rise, lifting median income to $20,000 per year, leaving price and other variables unchanged. Panel (a) of Figure 2.4 informs us that only 60 units of hot dogs will be demanded at this higher income. The demand curve for hot dogs in Figure 2.5 must therefore shift to the left. At a price of $1.20 per pound fewer hot dogs are sold, although, of course, 80 units of hot dogs can be sold at a somewhat lower price. In general, *rises in income produce leftward shifts in the demand curve for inferior goods; declines in income shift the demand curve to the right.*

Similarly, assume that the market price of steak for which S_i was constructed in Figure 2.4 is $2.80 per pound and median income is $16,000. At this combination of price and income 60 units of steak are demanded. From this we see that the same rise in income examined for the demand for hot dogs results in an *increase* in steak demanded from 60 to 80 units. Thus, in panel (b) of Figure 2.5, the demand curve for steak must now pass through the quantity 80 units at a price of $2.80 per pound. This demand curve must therefore shift to the right in response to the rise in income. *For normal goods, increases in income shift the demand curve to the right; declines in income shift it to the left.*

---

[3] In Chapter 4 we will consider a modern extension of demand theory that attempts to explain, in terms of the rational allocation of time on the part of consumers, why some goods are inferior. Neither this theory nor any other based exclusively on economic principles is likely to eliminate the need to assign many goods to one category or another on the sole basis of demanders' treatment of them in the market. Recall our discussion of the limitations of economics as a social science in Chapter 1.

Figure 2.5 *Shifts in Demand Due to Income Changes*

The position of the demand curve is also sensitive to changes in income. Panel (a) illustrates the case of an inferior good. At a higher income, fewer hot dogs are demanded at a price of $1.20; this occurs at each price level. Panel (b) reflects the opposite shift for steak, indicating that this good is a normal good.

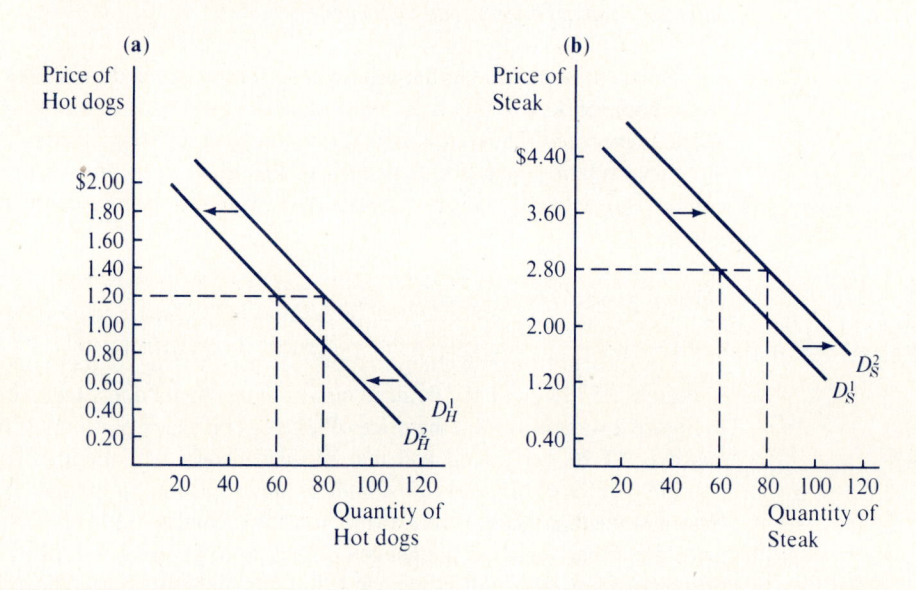

The Influence of Time

Much of the theory that will be developed in subsequent chapters will make the assumption that information is costless and that consumers are therefore fully informed. This will be done, as always, to simplify the analysis when the assumption has no bearing on the implications derived. Where imperfect information provides useful extensions of the theory, as in the discussion of investment theory in Chapter 15, the assumption of costless information will be relaxed. Such an extension can be made here in connection with the theory of demand.

Being an efficient consumer is costly. One must continuously invest in information concerning the prices of all goods, the qualities of different grades of similar goods, the properties of new goods, and alternative methods of satisfying the same wants with different combinations of goods. Consumers obtain this information by reading and watching commercial messages, by shopping and examining merchandise available and noting prices, by informal discussions with others, and by many other means. The important feature of all these methods is that they require the consumer to invest time and even money that might be used in other useful activities. Consumers will want to devote as little of their time and resources to this sort of "search" as is expedient; it is therefore rarely, if ever, efficient to become fully informed about any product or market—rather, information is generally obtained in a continuous, piecemeal fashion. The longer a person is a buyer in a market, the more information he or she is likely to accumulate.

Prices and income changes provide consumers with new consumption opportunities and constraints. Initially they have little information concerning alternatives made available by the changes; hence, they continue to purchase similar quantities of most goods. It is this lack of information concerning alternatives to their previous purchases that accounts for the appearance of "entrenched buying habits" referred to in casual discussions of consumer behavior. As time passes after such changes, however, consumers accumulate a larger fund of information. Awareness leads to different market choices. It is on this basis that we assert the **second law of demand**:

Second law of demand: Responsiveness of quantity demanded to changes in prices and income will increase with the passage of time.

This law tells us that demand curves will be flatter in the long run than in the short. Given price changes will result in larger quantity adjustments as time passes. Demand curve shifts due to income changes and other price changes will be larger after several weeks than the day after the changes are announced.

2.3   The Determination of Equilibrium with Zero Price

Demand curves tell us how much people are willing to buy at any price. The first law of demand tells us that this amount is greater at low prices than at high ones. However, as we stated earlier, demand by itself does not determine price. We will better understand how prices actually get determined if we begin our analysis of the market process at the point where there is *no* price—that is, where goods are offered free of charge. This approach has the added advantage of illustrating conditions of market equilibrium where some criterion other than willingness to pay is used to ration the available quantity.

In most cases the quantity supplied—that is, the quantity available for sale—depends on the price as well. To facilitate the development of the theory, however, we will employ ceteris paribus once again. We will assume that quantity available for sale is fixed, hence it does not vary as price varies. Consider the market for seats in the student section at home football games. (Most universities at which I have taught or that I attended have grappled at one time or another with this pressing issue.) The quantity of seats is determined by the size and design of the stadium and certainly is not variable on a week-to-week basis.[4] The question is *which* students will win the privilege of being able to occupy that fixed number of seats.

---

[4] We will ignore here the inconsiderate practice of many university athletic departments of shrinking the size of the student section for the "big game" so that tickets for those seats may be sold to alumni.

Figure 2.6   *Nonprice Rationing*

If price does not vary, markets must clear through some other rationing mechanism. With no before-game wait, the quantity of seats available, x^*, will clear the market at a price of P. If price is prevented from rising above zero, however, a quantity of x_1 will be demanded. A pre-game wait in the stadium reduces the value that students place on attendance, implying that at any given price fewer would seek to attend. This shifts demand to the left. As the waiting time increases, demand shifts further to the left. The waiting time will stop increasing when demand shifts to the point where x^* is demanded at a zero price.

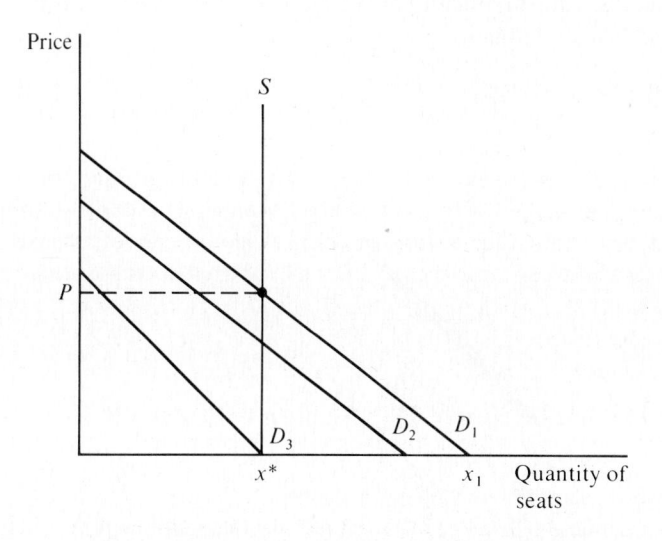

[Graph: Price on vertical axis, Quantity of seats on horizontal axis. Vertical supply curve S at x^*. Three downward-sloping demand curves D_1, D_2, D_3 (from right to left). D_1 intersects horizontal axis at x_1. Price P marked where S meets D_1.]

The problem is illuminated in Figure 2.6. The students' demand curve for seats is depicted by D_1, which obeys our laws by sloping downward to the right. The figure also contains a supply curve (S), which is perfectly vertical here, reflecting the assumption that the number of seats available for sale does not vary with price. That quantity is x^* regardless of price.

As trite as this example may appear, it presents one of the fundamental normative problems to be addressed by an economic system. More is demanded at a price of zero than is available. Some (perhaps all) demanders will not get as much as they want at this price. Let us list some obvious truths about such a situation before we proceed with the analysis:

1. The *value* of the good (in terms of what demanders are willing to give up to obtain it) may vary among demanders.

2. Someone will have to decide which demanders get more of the good and which get less (perhaps indirectly by selecting a system for allocating the supply among the competing demanders).

3. Different choosers and different systems will result in different allocations to different demanders.

4. Some demanders will be better off under (and may therefore prefer) some systems than others.

5. Under different systems demanders will "compete" by adapting their behavior in order to qualify themselves for a share of the scarce good.

The person or committee who makes the decision concerning student seating has (as does anyone under similar circumstances with respect to the allocation of a scarce good) a great deal of power. He or she may designate the best seats for friends, sometimes called the "rally committee," or use them to gain political advantage. Usually, however, the extent of such graft is limited (for reasons we explore in Chapter 7), and most of the available supply of such "free" goods is not used for such purposes. Let us then consider some of the methods that may be employed to allocate student seats designated for general use.

Perhaps the most common system for allocating such seating is the **free-for-all**. It is not a "system" at all, of course, but it does assign seats on the basis of first come–first served. This is the way that the scarce good seating is actually **rationed** among the competing demanders in this case. Returning to Figure 2.6, we see that x^* seats are available, but x_1 students might actually arrive to watch the game. If demanders did not accommodate their behavior to this condition, we might expect that the first x^* students who appeared would take the available seats and the remainder $(x_1 - x^*)$, having nowhere to sit, would return home.

This rarely happens. Some students modify their behavior so as to insure that they obtain a seat: They plan to arrive early. If everyone adopted the same tactic, however, nothing would be solved: x_1 students would arrive early, and some would still not obtain a seat. In order to get to the end of such a process, we must introduce another of the topics discussed in Chapter 1: *equilibrium*. Recall that we defined equilibrium as the state in which no element endogenous to the system is influenced to change. To get a description of the results of this method of allocation, we must determine what the nature of the equilibrium will be. For our purposes we need to determine the circumstances under which people cease modifying their behavior in adapting to the system.

In the free-for-all approach, the factor producing equilibrium is the time given up by early arrivers. The downward-sloping demand curve reflects the fact that some students who demand a seat at a low price are not willing to buy one at a high price. Another way of saying this is that some people are willing to give up more money to obtain a seat than others. Under the free-for-all system no one is required to give up money, but everyone is required to give up some of their time on Saturday morning. Those who get there earliest will get the best seats, but those who get there too late get no seat at all.

We may describe the approach to equilibrium in the following way. Demanders (students) arrive a little earlier at each game in order to be assured of a seat. Because their early arrival makes them have to sit in the stadium doing nothing before the game is finally played, going to the game will no longer be attractive to some. An expected wait at the game beforehand of, say, one hour therefore reduces demand to D_2. The longer the wait, the more demanders are discouraged and the further demand shifts to the left. Equilibrium will therefore be established when the pre-game wait discourages sufficient demanders that the demand curve for seats will shift to position D_3. A wait of this length now *clears the market* at a zero price. This is an equilibrium because students are no longer motivated to modify their behavior.

At the waiting time associated with curve D_3, everyone who arrives finds a seat; no one decides to arrive even earlier because he found none. The necessary waiting period has become widely known, and students have built this into their plans when they schedule football weekends. We therefore have derived our **first equilibrium condition**:

First equilibrium condition: Quantity demanded must equal quantity supplied.

For market equilibrium this condition must hold regardless of whether the available supply is rationed by price or any other method. This condition is often referred to as the **market-clearing condition**.

Before moving to a discussion of other approaches to the rationing problem, we must make a few observations on market clearing. For a market to clear, quantities demanded and quantities supplied must be equal. If supply is fixed, there is only one way for this equality to be achieved: Something must occur to *reduce* quantity demanded. The free-for-all method achieves this by reducing the value of the product. This can be seen in Figure 2.6. Originally, people are willing to pay a price of P for the available supply—that is, among those who want a ticket there are enough demanders to buy up the total quantity, x^*, at that price. As the wait gets longer, however, the price that people will pay for each quantity falls. Demand shifts downward, reflecting this reduced value to positions like D_2 and ultimately D_3. Finally, equilibrium is achieved by the singular result that value falls until the seat is worth exactly what students pay for it: nothing. The *value* of attendance at the game has been completely depreciated (at least to the marginal watcher) by the inconvenience and cost of having to arrive early.

There is a further result of the free-for-all method of rationing that we will mention only briefly here (further elaboration of this result must be postponed until Chapter 18): The free-for-all method is a very *wasteful* method of allocation. Resources (in this case, the students' time) are used up in merely gaining access to a product that has already been produced. If students had merely been required to *buy* tickets, no such waste would have resulted. Money is obtained in a market economy by using resources to produce something valuable—that is, that people will pay for. The resources used to gain a seat in this free-for-all system might have been used to make money—hence, to add to the total output of the economy. Instead, they have in effect been thrown away in idleness and boredom waiting for the game to begin.

Who Gains from a Free-for-All?

This is not to say that everyone is worse off under such a system of distribution. We would be quite surprised if a system as widespread as this benefited no one. Some will prefer the free-for-all method to a system of money payment. Who will this be? Clearly, those who gain friends and influence from their power to distribute "free" seats. For some students, too, game attendance under this system will ultimately cost them less than under a money price system. Those who would be doing nothing productive on Saturday mornings anyway will not care a great deal where they pass their idle time. It will be the students who work on weekends

Chapter 2   Market Equilibrium

or who are conscientious about their studies who will be disadvantaged by the free-for-all and will ultimately be unwilling to attend. The free-for-all thus benefits those whose time is less valuable and penalizes those for whom the cost of waiting is greater.

Other Nonprice Rationing Systems

Many schools with successful athletic programs have attempted to do something about the long waits and disappointments occasioned by the free-for-all system. Some schools distribute passes on campus prior to the game. However, since the number of passes cannot exceed the number of seats, tickets will run out; a market disequilibrium will occur here as well. Students will adapt in this case by arriving early at the ticket booth and forming a line. Clearly, nothing has been changed here but the location of the waiting. Such lines will grow in length until the wait discourages enough demanders to clear the market—indeed, if time during the week has roughly the same value to students as time on Saturday morning, the wait in line should take approximately the same time as the pre-game wait.

The students who benefit from the free-for-all also enjoy an advantage under the free-pass distribution system. Those whose time is less valuable will benefit since they can afford to outwait those whose time is costly. By contrast, this system penalizes those whose schedules are uncertain and who do not know early in the week whether they will be able to attend. By the time these people settle their schedules, all the passes will have been distributed. Certain unscrupulous student leaders will prefer this plan, since it is difficult to police the distribution of free passes. It is therefore far easier to exploit this system for political gain than the more cumbersome free-for-all. Recipients of the purloined passes can be expected to be more appreciative if use of them does not entail a two-hour wait prior to the game.

A third system of nonprice rationing will be mentioned briefly as it, too, is instructive concerning the results of market behavior. That is the lottery. This system is also popular as a method of rationing seating at athletic events. Students desiring tickets to the game fill out applications, and a list of those who get tickets is drawn from the applicant pool. This system has advantages and disadvantages relative to the previous variants of the free-for-all.

One advantage is that it admits little adaptive response on the part of the demanders and thus minimizes the waste associated with queuing. Once a name is drawn or passed over there is nothing to be done. This method does not promote lines before ticket booths or early arrivals, and hence leaves the student body as a whole free to devote more of its time to productive activities.

On the other hand, this system has a distinct disadvantage. The free-for-all system insured that those who ultimately got to attend the game regarded it as more valuable than those who did not—that is, those who got seats or received passes were willing to give up more of their time to get them than those who were discouraged from doing so by those rationing systems. It is true that for some the sacrifice of time imposed a greater burden than for others. However, there can be little doubt that attendance at the game means more on the average to those who see it under the free-for-all system than to those who see it under the lottery system. The lottery system is certainly the "fairest," in the sense that it gives no one an advantage in qualifying for the good. The problem here as we see it is that fairness is costly, like most goods, and we may not always find it worth the price.

2.4 Price as a Rationing Device

All rationing systems are methods of discrimination. They are employed to distinguish those who may obtain what is available from those who may not. Discrimination is necessary because more is demanded than is available. The free-for-all methods discriminate on the basis of the time people can devote to obtaining goods, while a price system discriminates on the basis of willingness and ability to pay. The lottery system, on the other hand, discriminates on the basis of pure luck. In choosing among these methods of discrimination, however, we must consider their behavioral implications as well as their distributive results.

Equilibrium is achieved under a free-for-all system through queuing or waiting, which reduces the value of the good until quantity demanded and quantity supplied are equal. Universities might employ a different mechanism to achieve equilibrium in this market: the price system. By charging a price, the university is able to discriminate between those who are willing to give up money to see the game and those who are not. By raising the price, they obtain still more information: They are able to discriminate between those who are willing to give up the higher sum to see the game and those who would give up less money. Raising price discourages some demanders from seeking admission to the game. The first law of demand tells us that there must be some price that clears the market—that is, equates the quantity demanded to that available.

Consider the advantages of a pricing equilibrium over the others just discussed. The lottery system involves little waste associated with adaptive behavior on the part of demanders at the cost of a completely whimsical distribution of the good. Recipients under the lottery system value the good no more than those who do not receive it. The free-for-all ultimately discriminates in favor of those for whom the good is valuable, but only by reducing the value of the good to zero at the margin. Market clearing through price has both of these advantages and neither of the defects.

When the price is raised to the market-clearing level, there is no way that demanders may adapt to improve their chances of obtaining some of the good. Standing in line or arriving early will not cause the price to be any lower, and because the market-clearing price has been charged, everyone willing to pay the price is assured that the goods will not run out. There is no waste associated with this market equilibrium. On the other hand, the distribution of the good is certainly more satisfactory than that determined by the lottery. Only those who are willing to pay the market-clearing price—that is, those who value it most in terms of the money they are willing to give up for it—obtain the good.

Who Gains from the Price System?

As we saw earlier, the free-for-all system provides some demanders with an advantage in competition for available goods. Those for whom time is less valuable will certainly be more willing to give it up than those for whom it is precious. A pricing system provides similar advantages. Those for whom money is less valuable (particularly those who have a great deal of it) are benefited by a pricing system. This is rarely as important an argument as noneconomists frequently think it is. As Ernest Hemingway claims to have observed to F. Scott Fitzgerald, "The rich have more money."[5] Those with more money have an advantage in the competition for everything. It rarely makes sense, therefore, to eschew the price system in some particular market in order to take away this advantage. It is sometimes argued that the price system should be abolished in certain areas like medical care to eliminate this advantage and allegedly to extend equal access to everyone. As we have seen, most nonprice rationing methods provide advantages to some group. The only system that is completely fair in the sense of offering equal access is the lottery. Few would agree that absence of advantage is worth the distributional anomaly of offering medical care randomly rather than to those willing to give up something to obtain it.

How Are Prices Formed in the Market?

Although we did not mention it at the time, the example we used to illustrate alternative rationing mechanisms is a *monopoly*. There is only one supplier of home football games for each university. Monopolists have more discretion in their pricing decisions than do competitive firms, for reasons that we will explore in Chapter 10. Thus, it made sense to discuss the determination of price in that context in terms of the supplier (in this case, the university) simply choosing a price. In the more usual market environment, there are many suppliers. Clearly, no single decision is made by anyone as to whether the *market* price will be zero or positive or the market-clearing price. This price is determined by the actions of many independent buyers and sellers in the process of adapting to disequilibrium prices.

We will consider first the behavior of demanders in this market situation, continuing to assume that market supply is fixed. These assumptions are consistent with market results in the very short run. For many agricultural and manufactured goods the quantity available for sale cannot be altered readily. Production plans must be revised, new materials must be ordered, and additional acreage planted. Thus, even when quantity supplied is not immutably fixed, it may be treated as such in the short run without sacrifice of realism.

Consider Figure 2.7, which again presents a downward-sloping demand curve with vertical (fixed) supply. Although there are many sellers, only one price may prevail, because no buyer will pay more to one seller than another. Our question is: What determines this market price? This is best answered by asking another: How do buyers and sellers adapt when their plans do not coincide?

---

[5] Hemingway's priority in making this observation has recently been disputed. See A. Scott Berg, *Maxwell Perkins: Editor of Genius* (New York: E. P. Dutton, 1978). Whether apocryphal or genuine, this conversation presents an interesting example of the competition of economic and noneconomic theories of observed behavior. Hemingway's remark was allegedly made in response to Fitzgerald's claim that "The rich are different," that is, that differences in their behavior were the result of different culture and breeding. Hemingway adopted the methodological posture of the economist. He claimed, in other words, that these differences were fully explained by the greater command over goods and services exhibited by the rich by virtue of their higher income.

Figure 2.7 *Market-Clearing Price*

This market clears at a price of P^*. At a price of p_1 more than q^* is demanded, leaving some demanders disappointed. Demanders adapt by offering higher prices. If the price is P_2, suppliers adapt by offering lower prices. Only when the price is P^* will both demanders and suppliers have no reason to modify their price offers.

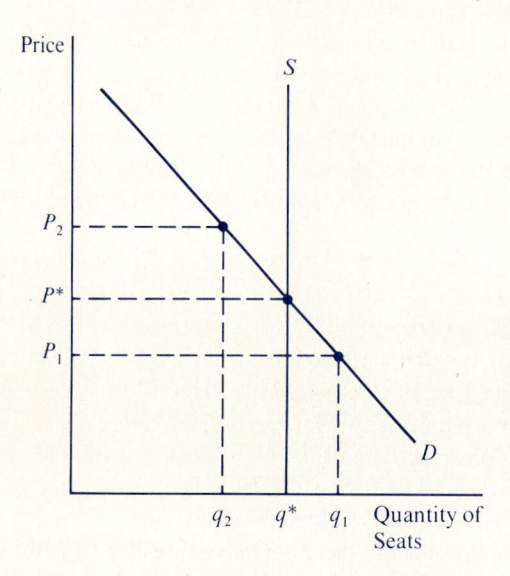

Price P_1 is not a market-clearing price. More is demanded at this price than is available. Goods available will be exhausted at this price before all demanders have obtained the quantities they seek. Some demanders will be disappointed and will adapt (just as disappointed ticket seekers did earlier) by modifying their behavior. In this case, however, the modification will take the form of *higher price offers*. Since many of the demanders will be willing to pay more rather than do without, they will offer suppliers a higher price than suppliers are currently obtaining. Suppliers can be counted upon not to resist such a tendency in the market. This upward pressure on prices will continue until the price reaches P^*, the market-clearing price. Once this price is reached, such adaptive behavior ceases. The quantity demanded at this price is precisely q^*, the quantity available. No demander is disappointed; each is able to purchase the quantity he or she desires at this price. Suppliers may hope for continued inflation in their market, but demanders have no reason to bid prices higher. The market is therefore in equilibrium at this market-clearing price.

Similarly, adaptive behavior on the parts of demanders and suppliers moves price toward the market-clearing level when price is above P^*. In this case it is suppliers who are disappointed in their market plans and who thus take the active role in modifying price. At a price of P_2, less will be sold than is available. Some (perhaps all) suppliers will find unplanned inventories accumulating on their shelves and will adapt to this result by lowering price. Demanders will not resist such a price change, and price will fall. As price falls, demanders will purchase more until price reaches P^*, the market-clearing price. No further adaptation is required by suppliers. They are able to sell all of their available stocks at this price, so no one is influenced to bid the price lower. The market-clearing price is thus an equilibrium price. It produces no further adaptation on the part of demanders or suppliers.

2.5 The Supply Side of the Market

Thus far we have considered only behavior on the demand side of the market. This has been facilitated by the assumption made earlier that the quantity available is fixed and therefore not responsive to price. This is rarely true, of course. Most things that people buy in the market are produced, and the quantity available therefore depends on choices that have been made about the level of production. The second equation in our model must therefore describe the response of quantity supplied to price. These two equations taken together are sufficient to determine the *equilibrium price and quantity*—that is, the solution values for the two variables in the two equations tell us the price at which demanders will wish to buy exactly the quantity that suppliers will be willing to produce.

Although there is a wide range of institutions that make output decisions without reference to price, this is not true of the *proprietary firm*. These organizations are privately owned and assembled for the express purpose of earning profits for their owners. As these institutions dominate the American economy, we will introduce supply-side analysis in terms of behavior implied for the proprietary firm. Discussion of the supply behavior of other types of organizations will be deferred until Chapter 7. A large part of this text is taken up with the development of the supply behavior of private firms in various dimensions in a variety of market settings. As we are more concerned here with the analysis of the determination of price than with the details of firm behavior, this supply response to price will be sketched with a very broad brush.

First, we will concern ourselves here only with competitive markets. The supply behavior in noncompetitive settings (monopoly, oligopoly, etc.) cannot be systematically related to price and will be discussed in a later chapter. Second, this response by competitive firms can be understood only in terms of the dynamic process that underlies it. The supply behavior of firms is in the long run related to the underlying cost structure of the industry involved.

In the long run, the supply curve of an industry reflects the cost of production. Entry by new firms will continue, causing prices to fall to the point where profits are eliminated. If industry costs rise with output (due, for example, to the rising costs of resources employed), then higher industry output can be obtained only at higher prices. Higher output could not be obtained at lower prices, since costs of production could not be covered and supplying firms would fail. On the other hand, it is conceivable that costs of production may actually fall as industry output expands. Where this is true, quantity available may actually increase in association with falling prices. We will restrict our discussion here to the increasing cost case.

Equilibrium Conditions

Earlier in our discussion we noted that a necessary condition for market equilibrium is that the market "clear" in the sense that quantity demanded equal the quantity available in the market. This condition by itself cannot fully describe equilibrium, since it tells us nothing about the determination of the quantity available. As long as *suppliers* are influenced to change that quantity, no equilibrium exists by definition. A full description of equilibrium must identify conditions under which producers as well as buyers are no longer influenced to modify their behavior. Those conditions are best developed by examining the dynamic process described earlier in greater detail.

As we have seen, time is an important dimension in the analysis of demand. The second law of demand states an important relationship between time and demand. Time also plays a critical role in the theory of supply. Production is a time-consuming process; hence, production and supply decisions must in most cases be made prior to the actual sale of the product. It is convenient, therefore, to describe supply behavior in terms of two phases: production and sale.

In planning for production, suppliers can rarely know with certainty what the price of their output will be; they must make these plans on the basis of *price expectations*. However, at any particular time, a certain level of output available for sale already exists. Assume for the present discussion that this output is perishable (like labor) and cannot be saved and sold the next day. The price that obtains in such a market on a particular day will simply be the market-clearing price. The various "sale" prices will, of course, influence the price expectations of those making production plans for future days. A necessary condition for market equilibrium with respect to supply, the **second equilibrium condition**, may therefore be stated:

Second equilibrium condition: Supplier expectation about price must be confirmed.

This may best be explained with the aid of Figure 2.8. This figure depicts a downward-sloping demand curve (D) and an upward-sloping supply curve (S_L) reflecting the producers' willingness to provide the product at different prices. For example, producers will be willing to produce output q_1 at a price of P_3 and a larger volume of output q_2 at the higher price P_4. Now let us assume that suppliers are led to expect that price will be P_3 when current output reaches the market. Based on this expectation concerning price, suppliers will therefore produce output q_1. Clearly this cannot be an equilibrium. When output q_1 reaches the market, price P_3 is not the market-clearing price. More is demanded at this price than is available for sale. The price will be bid up until quantity demanded equals quantity supplied, that is, to P_1. Suppliers' expectations concerning price are not confirmed.

The method and information suppliers use to modify expectations about price can have a profound effect on the path of price and output over time. We will make a very simple assumption about this process initially, then explore alternative, more complex methods. For our present purposes we will assume that when the market sale price exceeds the expected price, suppliers will revise upward their expectations about price in the next period. In Figure 2.8 this implies that because the sale price P_1 is greater than expected price P_3, suppliers now expect a some-

Figure 2.8   Equilibrium Supply

Curve S_L identifies the quantities that producers choose to sell at each price. At any time the quantity available for sale depends on how much has been produced. This depends on the price expectations of producers in earlier periods. These price expectations are modified toward the equilibrium price, leading suppliers to produce the equilibrium quantity. If producers expect a price of P_3, they will supply only q_1. This sells for the market-clearing price of P_1, leading producers to modify upward their expectations about price in future periods. These revised expectations lead to increased output toward the equilibrium level, q^*.

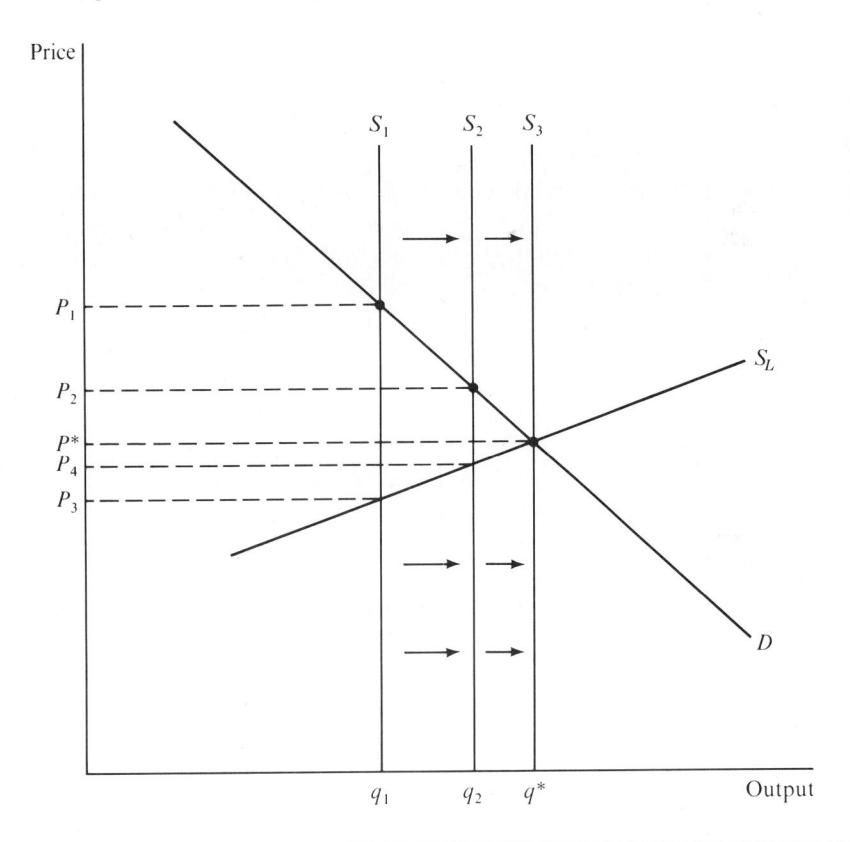

what higher price in the next period. Assume that the new expected price is P_4; hence, producers will supply output q_2 in the next sale period. Expectations will not be confirmed at this output either. The market-clearing price for this output is P_2; since this is also higher than the expected price, expectations will again be revised upward.

It is clear that such a process will eventually lead suppliers to supply output q^*. Price expectations at that output will be confirmed; the market-clearing price will be P^*, which is exactly the price upon which this production plan was based. Once this output is reached, producers will have no reason to further modify expectations concerning price. Because original expectations are confirmed, they will therefore have no reason to modify output. Such a market is in **full equilibrium**. Neither demanders nor suppliers are influenced to change their market behavior at this price and output. If, of course, initial price expectations are excessive, a similar iterative modification of price expectations and output plans from above rather than below will result in the same equilibrium being established.

Cobweb Models

Now consider a different method of modifying expectations. Let us assume that instead of raising or lowering their expectations slightly in the direction of the most recent price, suppliers simply adopt the most recent market price as their expected price for the next sale period. Results of such a process are described in Figure 2.9. Demand and supply curves are shown again as D and S_L. Assume that output in some initial period is q_1, producing a market-clearing sale price of P_2. Suppliers adopt this as their expected price in their production plans for the next period and produce q_2 accordingly. But this output has a market-clearing price of P_3; hence, suppliers must modify their expectations downward again. Based on the new expected price of P_3, producers offer output q_3 for sale, which sells for the price of P_4. This is the highest price yet, stimulating output of q_4 which, when it reaches the market, depresses price to P_5. The pattern is clear by this point. Such a method of formulating expectations can lead to increasingly violent oscillations in price and output, moving them further and further away from the equilibrium levels.

Such a result is called a **cobweb model**, for obvious reasons. This explosive outcome depends upon the relative slopes of the demand and supply curves. The readers are left to verify for themselves that the cobweb will converge *toward* the equilibrium output rather than explode away from it if the supply curve is steeper than the demand curve. The point to be stressed here, however, is that dynamics of market behavior in disequilibrium deserve careful attention. It would be of little comfort to us to know that beneficial results were obtained in market equilibrium if the actual dynamic processes of markets prevented equilibrium from ever being achieved. Fortunately, economic theory provides some reassurance on this score.

There are several reasons to expect that the type of cobweb phenomena just discussed will rarely be a problem. The first of these concerns the plausibility of the assumed behavior. It depicts suppliers as unbelievably forgetful. Consider the experience of the sellers described in Figure 2.9. In the set of market periods discussed, prices ranged from a low of P_5 to a high of P_6. Each time prices were expected to be above the equilibrium price, they turned out to be lower than expected; each time they were expected to be lower than the equilibrium price, they were higher than expected. Any method for developing predictions that uses *all* recent price information (for example, the mean of all previous prices) causes prices to converge toward the equilibrium price regardless of the slopes of the demand and supply curves. Only in the case where the single most recent price observation is adopted as the expected price do we get the cobweb result. There are few market situations in which such naive behavior seems plausible.

Figure 2.9   Cobweb Model

The path of price and output toward (or away from) equilibrium depends on the manner in which producers modify their expectations about price. The cobweb result can occur if price expectations are changed to the most recent price after each adjustment. Price increases and decreases resulting from such adjustments lead to increasingly large output modifications in each period, and the price "explodes" away from, rather than converging toward, the equilibrium level. If the supply curve is steeper than the demand curve, however, price converges toward equilibrium.

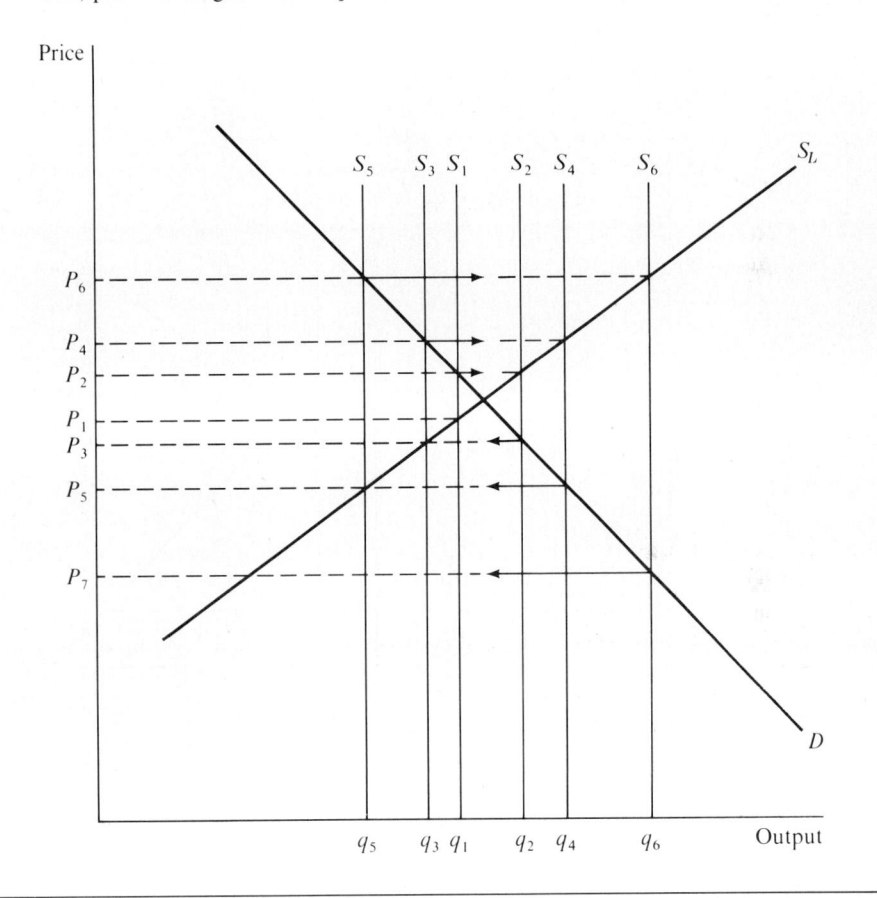

Arbitrage and Speculation

In order to discuss the second reason for discounting the possibility of widespread explosive cobwebs, we must expand our discussion of supply behavior to markets where goods are not perishable. In such markets it is not unusual to find "middlemen" who buy for the express purpose of reselling. In some markets these middlemen perform the services of distribution and transportation, but these services are not the only functions they perform. These middlemen may remain in business

Figure 2.10 *Stabilizing Effect of Speculation*

Successful speculators buy low and sell high. This requires that they add to their inventories when supply is greater than normal and reduce their inventories when supply is lower than normal. An extremely large output like S_3 might lower the price to P_6. Purchases by speculators of ΔI_2 would drive price up to P_3. Small outputs like S_1, on the other hand, would lead speculators to reduce inventories, lowering price. A reduction of ΔI_1, for example, would lower price from P_2 to P_5. This behavior can be seen to reduce the variation in quantity supplied over time and also reduce the variation in price.

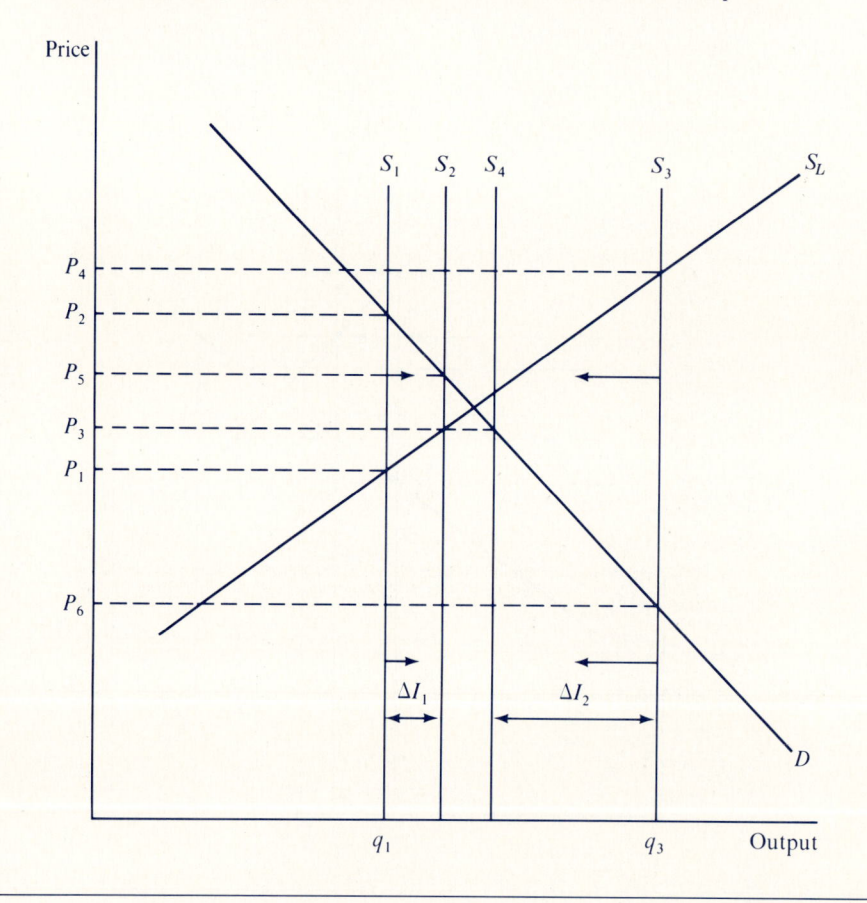

only if on average they sell at a higher price than they buy. Success in such efforts will itself stabilize prices over time.

Consider Figure 2.10, which again contains the demand and supply schedules D and S_L. Assume furthermore that producers have the same naive method of forming price expectations—that is, the last price in the market will be that which is anticipated in the next period. In this case, however, middlemen are present; their very livelihoods depend on their knowledge of prices in this market. They specialize in developing information on prices in particular markets. Indeed, these middlemen are actually known as "specialists" in certain markets (the securities markets, for example).

These middlemen hold inventories of the product, and their management of these inventories performs the stabilizing function. Assume again that due to low expectations output q_1 is initially produced. The market-clearing price for such an output is P_2, as previously noted. Middlemen with knowledge of demand and long-run supply relationships in the market will recognize an opportunity for profit in this situation and sell off a portion of their inventories. Let this change in their holdings be denoted as ΔI_1. Total supply available for sale in this period will therefore be $q_1 + \Delta I_1$, and price will therefore be P_5 rather than P_2. Suppliers will thus reckon with a lower price in forming their production plans for the next period than they would have otherwise. On the other hand, if their price expectations are unrealistically sanguine, say, P_4, and they produce output q_3, the sale price might be expected to be P_6. Here again, however, informed middlemen will be aware that such a price is not an equilibrium. In this case they will buy up some of the output, adding it to their inventories. The amount available for sale will therefore be q_3 *less the change in inventories* ΔI_2. Price will therefore be P_3 rather than P_6, again closer to the equilibrium price than in the absence of such speculative behavior.

Note that we have represented middlemen as selling at a price of P_5 and buying at P_3. This difference in the buying and selling price is referred to as the *spread*. Out of this difference the middlemen must cover the cost of storage, recordkeeping, and research into the price behavior in the relevant market. Competition among such agents will keep the spread close to the level that covers these costs. If these costs are negligible the spread will be too, and the dampening effect on price fluctuations will be complete. If they are large (for example, the storage of many commodities requires refrigeration) the spread will also be large, and price fluctuations between these extremes may be considerable.

Speculative students will have already noted that the forces that act to stabilize price fluctuations due to incorrect price expectations of producers will perform the same function for price fluctuation due to other causes as well. Year-to-year variation in output may occur due to factors beyond the control of producers. For example, agricultural output may vary because of differences in weather and outbreaks of disease. Middlemen may be counted upon to sell in bad years and buy during bountiful harvests and in so doing stabilize supplies available for sale, and thus price.

Buying and selling by middlemen shifts supplies of goods out of time periods when they are plentiful (and prices are low) to periods when they are scarce (and prices are high). This activity is called **speculation**. Buying and selling by middlemen performs a similar service among a different set of markets: those separated geographically rather than temporally. To the extent that they are able to buy a commodity in one location or community where price is low and sell it in another at a higher price, middlemen achieve a similar result. Buying in one location and selling in another is called **arbitrage**. Success by middlemen in this endeavor moves goods into the markets where they are most valuable. It is ironic that activities that stabilize supplies and prices over time are often the subject of public censure and obloquy while trade in goods geographically, which produces a similar result (that is, equalizing prices across markets differentiated geographically), is almost universally regarded as beneficial to society as a whole.

2.6 Controlled Prices

Government occasionally intervenes in the price-setting process, sometimes to "support" prices (that is, hold them above the market-clearing level) and sometimes to "control" them (that is, hold them below this level). These policies can have both *demand-side effects* and *supply-side effects*. Some price regulation will have neither.

It is therefore necessary to distinguish between **binding price regulation** and **nonbinding price regulation**. A price support set below the market-clearing level will have no economic effect; it is nonbinding. The market processes just described will invariably raise price above such a support level to the market-clearing price, rendering the support ineffective. No support will be required. Competition among demanders will insure that the price does not fall below the market-clearing level, much less the support level. Similarly, price ceilings that are set above the market-clearing price have no effect and are therefore nonbinding. Competition among suppliers insures that price does not rise above the market-clearing level. Examples of such nonbinding price regulation include usury laws in most states (which are quickly raised if the equilibrium interest rates rise above the statutory level). Whatever function is performed by such laws, they have no effect on price.

Binding price regulation, on the other hand, does interfere with normal pricing dynamics. Price supports that maintain price above the market-clearing level are binding because competition among suppliers would otherwise depress price below the support level. By the same token, price ceilings set below the market-clearing level will interfere with competition among demanders for the available supply, which would ordinarily carry price above the controlled level. Let us consider the effects of implementation of these two types of binding price regulation.

Farm Policy, 1929–1973

Agricultural prices declined sharply after World War I due to diminished demand from a rebuilding Europe and increased American output. In 1929 Congress passed the Agricultural Marketing Act, the first of a series of laws aimed at supporting agricultural prices above their then current (market-clearing) levels. The effect of this law can be analyzed in Figure 2.11. Output of grain in a typical year is fixed and is given by x^*, yielding a vertical supply curve (labeled S). A demand curve for grain is also shown, labeled D. The market-clearing price in the absence of supports would be P^*, but the intent of the law is to maintain price above this level, say, at P_1.

The most obvious demand-side effect of this law is to influence buyers to reduce their purchases of grain. At the support price P_1, demanders in the market

Figure 2.11 *Price Supports*

The market-clearing price of quantity x^* is P^*. If price is not permitted to fall below P_1, less than this full quantity will be sold. The surplus, $(x^* - x_1)$, will be left unsold.

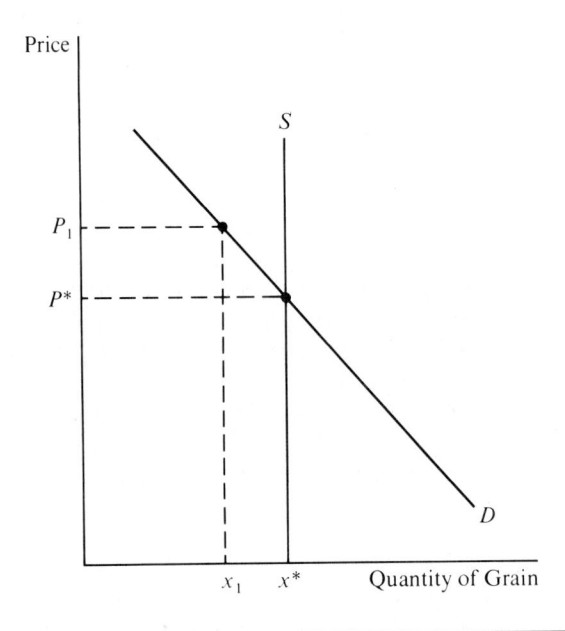

will purchase only x_1 bushels of grain. A grain **surplus** is thus created, as in each year demanders will purchase less than the full crop, and this excess above the amount bought accumulates. This is doubly unfortunate, because buyers stand ready to purchase it at lower prices. Instead, taxpayers must pay to store grain that will never be consumed so long as price is maintained above the market-clearing level. It is not surprising, therefore, that agricultural policy over the next three decades grappled with alternative approaches to reduce output of agricultural commodities and thus eliminate or reduce these surpluses. In the mid-1930s, the Agricultural Adjustment Administration was introduced and instituted acreage allotments to farmers as a means of controlling output. Marketing agreements between processors and producers, with allotments of output quotas assigned to each, were also introduced. Finally, in the 1950s, the headline-grabbing "Soil Bank" proposal of Secretary of Agriculture Ezra Taft Benson was enacted. This plan actually paid farmers to keep land out of production.

It is difficult to assess the impact of these programs, for we do not know what output of farm products might have been in the absence of crop and acreage controls. None of these controls were effective in completely eliminating surpluses, as carryovers occurred in all but the war years until the mid-1960s. Until recently growth in world demand increased more rapidly than supply. The farm "problem" became one of food shortages rather than surpluses, and support programs became nonbinding price regulations. For thirty years, however, the federal government embraced a program that fostered production of more output than consumers would buy at artificially inflated prices, then spent the taxpayers' money to store the surplus, most of which rotted because it was never used.

Rent Controls

Municipal governments occasionally enter the price regulation game. One price that frequently comes under such control is apartment rent. Consider the following scenario with the aid of Figure 2.12. Demand, originally D_1, shifts due to a rise in income and population to D_2, causing a rise in the market-clearing price of housing from R_1 to R_2. People become concerned over the shortage of low-cost housing, which is another way of saying that rents have risen. Some municipalities respond to this mandate by rolling back rents, perhaps to their former level.

Figure 2.12   *Price Ceilings*

In an earlier period demand is given by D_1, and the quantity of rental housing clears the market at a price of R_1. A rise in income causes demand to shift rightward to D_2, raising the market-clearing price to R_2. If rents are not permitted to rise above R_1, however, more rental housing will be demanded than is available. Some method other than price increases must be used to clear the market of the shortage ($q_1 - q$) produced by this price ceiling.

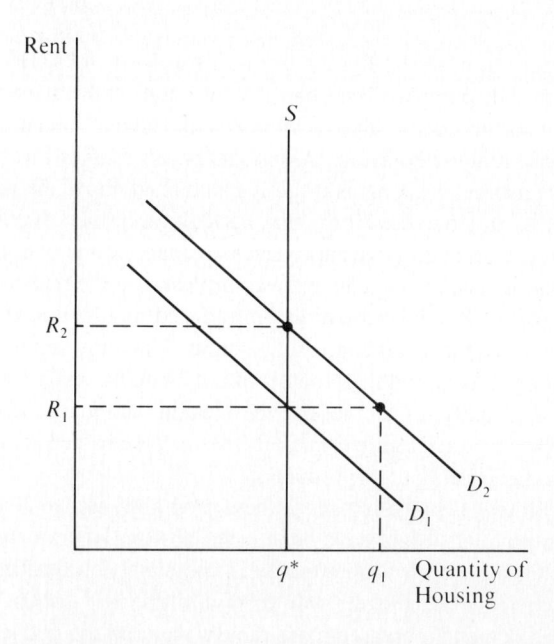

Consider the demand side results of this well-intentioned policy. Rental fee R_1 is no longer a market-clearing price and, if landlords may charge no more than this, quantity demanded q_1 will exceed the available number of rental units. Indeed, the shortage of apartments caused by rent controls can become quite severe. Santa Monica, California, adopted a rent control ordinance by referendum in 1979. Rents were reduced to their 1977 levels and allowed to increase each year after 1979 by only 7 percent per year, regardless of inflation. The prices of all residential housing were rising rapidly over this period so that the controls had a dramatic effect on rents. A colleague of mine at UCLA who was seeking an apartment at this time became most discouraged. He would pore over the listings each morning, then venture forth to examine the new units available. At every new apartment he visited, however, there were literally scores of people hovering around the landlord or manager seeking to persuade this person to accept their application. It was not uncommon to find more than fifty applications left for each available unit.

Demanders of rental units adapt as best they can. It was not uncommon to see anxious would-be renters meet the new edition of the *Evening Outlook* as soon as it left the press room in order to be first to contact new listings. They also sought among their acquaintances far and wide for the names of people leaving apartments in hopes of obtaining referrals (the above-mentioned colleague eventually moved into my apartment when I left California). And, of course, they spend days driving around the city submitting applications until someone offered them an apartment. All of this adaptive behavior is costly and, as was the case in the student seating example earlier, can be expected to dissipate the benefits of lower than market-clearing prices.

Consider also who benefits from rent controls. Those already in apartments who plan to stay put certainly benefit. Landlords and investors in rental property lose (and this surely discourages new investment in rental property). (Rent controls have supply-side effects, too.) Landlords must make the best of their situation, however, and since they are limited in the amount of rent they can charge, they attempt to select tenants who will add little to the cost of operating their units. They will therefore choose among the many competing demanders for their apartments—for example, renters without children or pets. Since landlords do not want to risk default on the rent they are allowed to charge, they will rent to high-income applicants with secure employment as opposed to those with low income or the intermittently employed (like actors). Those in mobile occupations, who must move frequently, are greatly inconvenienced by rent controls, while those who do not often move benefit. Rent control also fosters racial and religious discrimination in housing.

Rent control practiced on a large scale can severely impair the efficiency of an economy. In Great Britain nearly half of the population lives either in rent-controlled or publicly owned (and underpriced) housing and has done so since World War II. This has had a perhaps unforeseen effect on the labor force. Because the controlled and subsidized housing of the average Briton is so underpriced compared to what he or she might find in another location, labor mobility has been severely impaired. Workers are reluctant to move to new jobs in other parts of the country even though the salaries offered may greatly exceed those obtained in their present jobs. Labor has failed to move out of industries that are inefficient and should be declining and into those that should be growing. On the contrary, because workers are so attached to their present housing and thus their existing jobs, powerful political forces are brought to bear on Parliament to subsidize and shore up companies and industries that cannot compete and should (on an economic basis) be allowed to fail. Some economists have attributed to rent controls a large share of the responsibility for the low rate of economic growth in Great Britain during the postwar period.[6]

England and the Supply of Doctors

Supply-side effects of controls are observed in the following example. Physician fees in the United States are determined by a market. In the short run, that fee is the market-clearing price. In the long run, the number of physicians will adjust until earnings expectations of those choosing a medical career are confirmed. This situation prevailed in Great Britain until 1948, when the medical care industry was nationalized. The British National Health Service (NHS) made all doctors and surgeons employees of the government and thus dependent for their earnings on the pay policy of the NHS. Prior to its introduction these professionals did quite well economically. Average general practitioner earnings were more than four times the earnings of manual workers. Once dependent on the government for their incomes, however, their economic position deteriorated rapidly. By 1978 the ratio of doctor to manual worker incomes declined to only a little more than two. This policy has had a profound effect on the availability and average quality of physicians in Great Britain.

Physicians began to emigrate to other countries at an alarming rate. By the mid-1960s net emigration of trained physicians had reached 500 per year, and statistical analysis of physician emigration data confirms that the rate at which doctors leave is related to the rate of pay under the NHS.[7] Indeed, the NHS would have been severely understaffed were not the places of these doctors taken by surgeons and doctors trained in British Commonwealth countries. By the early 1970s this substitution of foreign-trained for domestically-trained doctors had taken place to the extent that one third of the NHS hospital staff had been trained overseas. Roughly half of those hospital staff in positions of registrar and below are immigrants from abroad.

These supply-side effects are observed across the board under the British NHS. The number of staff personnel of all types per hospital bed in the United States exceeded that ratio in NHS hospitals by 40 percent in 1950. By the early 1970s U. S. hospital staff outnumbered their NHS counterparts by more than 100 percent. There can be little doubt that at least a part of this disparity in numbers of health personnel in the two countries reflects the low economic rewards of those

---

[6] *The New York Times*, June 8, 1980, p. 1.

[7] C. M. Lindsay, *National Health Issues: The British Experience* (Nutley, N.J.: Roche Laboratories, 1980), p. 66.

careers where earnings are controlled by governmental wage scales rather than competitive markets. Were wages higher in Great Britain, the supply of medical practitioners would be greater as well.

Summary

The principal object in this chapter has been to establish the methods by which markets achieve equilibrium. Two values are determined in equilibrium: price and quantity. One of the features of economic theory that make it difficult to grasp is that typically both variables appear in both equations describing behavior in these markets. The price of any quantity is determined by demanders—that is, demanders determine the market-clearing price. However, we cannot know what that price will be unless we also know what quantity will be supplied. On the other hand, the quantity supplied is ultimately chosen by producers, but this choice is influenced by price. We must know both before we may determine either.

Principles governing behavior on each side of the market were developed. Markets serve two functions: (1) They ration the quantity available among competing demanders, and (2) they determine what quantity will be produced. Demand was analyzed in terms of the market's rationing function. The first and second laws of demand were defined and explained. The first states that a price increase will lead to a reduction in quantity demanded. The second states that the magnitude of this response increases with time. Increases in price reduce the amount sought in the market and therefore represent one form of rationing. For a given quantity available, price will reach an equilibrium when the quantity demanded equals the quantity supplied. This first equilibrium condition is described as a market-clearing price. Income and other prices were also shown to have an influence on quantity demanded. Unfortunately there are no laws to guide us in predicting these responses. If quantity demanded rises with income, the good is a normal good; if quantity demanded is inversely related to income, the good is inferior. If quantity demanded increases with the rise in the price of another good, the two goods are said to be substitutes. If quantity demanded falls with a rise in the price of a second good, the two goods are said to be complements.

If price is not free to vary, some other mechanism will serve this rationing function. The free-for-all and lottery methods were examined from a number of points of view, including their implicit advantages to different groups of demanders and the waste associated with these forms of rationing.

Supply behavior was introduced briefly, the important point for our discussion here being that price expectations influence producers in their choice of output and that this output will not remain stable unless these expectations are confirmed. Disappointed suppliers will modify their output plans. If prices are higher than expected, suppliers will increase their price expectations and expand their production plans, and vice versa. Equilibrium will occur on the supply side, therefore, only when realized market prices no longer generate changes in price expectations and production plans. This is the second equilibrium condition.

The manner in which producers modify their price expectations can have dramatic effects on the dynamic path of price and output over time. A simplified model in which producers look only to prices in the immediate past period was shown to lead to explosive instability in certain circumstances. This particular case is called a cobweb model. Price and output converge toward equilibrium values when a more reasonable formulation of expectations is used. The role of speculators in stabilizing prices was discussed. Demand and supply-side effects of price controls were examined in several applications.

Key Concepts

Comparative statics
ceteris paribus
demand
first law of demand
second law of demand
complements
substitutes
inferior goods
normal goods
free-for-all
ration

first equilibrium condition
market-clearing condition
binding price regulation
nonbinding price regulation
surplus
second equilibrium condition
full equilibrium
cobweb model
speculation
arbitrage

Questions

1. *Easy* Gasoline prices are higher now than they were in the 1960s and automobiles are smaller, suggesting that people are buying less automobile than they used to at lower gasoline prices. On the basis of this information alone, would you say that gasoline and automobiles are substitutes or complements? Draw a diagram illustrating your argument.

Hard Per capita income is also higher now than it was in the 1960s. What data might you consult to confirm that this observation is not simply a reflection of the influence of income on demand (that is, that automobiles are inferior goods)?

2. *Easy* An inward shift of the supply curve in a market is predicted to result in a sharp rise in price followed by a decline. This was observed in connection with OPEC's manipulations of the world oil supply in both 1973 and 1979. Explain this in terms of the second law of demand.

Hard New stores often offer impressive discounts for a brief period after opening day. Prices are typically raised to "normal" levels afterward. Explain how this observation is consistent with the second law of demand.

3. *Easy* If the student section at football games were expanded and admission continued to be offered on a free-for-all basis, what do you predict would happen to the equilibrium length of wait in the stadium by students prior to the game? What if the student section remained the same size but was moved toward the center of the field?

Hard Football tickets for the general public at campuses of powerhouse teams are often priced below market-clearing levels. Those desiring tickets are typically expected to make a "donation" to the school's athletic association in addition to paying the stated price of the tickets. Why don't these schools merely raise the stated price to the market-clearing level?
(*Hint*: Ticket revenues must often be shared with opposing teams; donations are not shared.)

4. *Easy* Assume that the demand curve for labor also slopes downward. Explain the relationship between a minimum wage and unemployment. How do employers and those seeking work adapt to this price floor?

Hard If unemployment compensation is financed by a tax on the wage earnings of workers when they are employed, under what circumstances does anyone gain from having a minimum wage?

5. *Easy* Prices of commodities that may be cheaply stored (like gravel) vary less than prices of those that are costly to store (like ripe peaches). Explain.

Hard It is sometimes maintained that speculators destabilize markets, driving prices up beyond "normal" levels only to cause them to plunge eventually to unreasonably low levels. Assume that you observe the same individuals engaged in this business year after year. Would this be consistent with the alleged destabilizing role played by speculators?

6. *Easy* At all universities some teachers and class times are more popular than others. Typically, those that meet at 10:00 AM and those offered by the "best" professors must be rationed one way or another, because the number seeking to schedule them exceeds the space in those classrooms. How does the rationing system at your school accomplish this? How do students adapt their behavior to this rationing system? Who profits and who is disadvantaged by this system in equilibrium?

Hard How would this distribution of advantages and disadvantages be modified by a change to a system that adjusted fees charged for each class to insure that no student was unable to schedule a class or professor that he or she desired? Why do you think that this practice is so rare among universities?

Chapter 3

The Theory of Choosing

Connections *This chapter presents the foundations for much of our future discussion. In later chapters we will discuss choices by households of the quantities of each good they wish to consume and the quantities of resources they wish to supply to the market. We will also discuss choices by firms of the designs of their products, the quantities of each to produce, and the quantities of the various resources they wish to employ. The theory of choosing is destined to play a large role in each of these topics. In reading this chapter, it is important to bear in mind the comments offered in Chapter 1 concerning the role of theory. A theory must be metaphorical; it cannot describe reality in absolute detail or it loses the advantage of abstraction. One important criterion of a good theory is that it predicts. The theory of choice permits us to predict the results of choices. It is therefore instrumental in scientific study of the above choices. The reader may also wish to review the discussion of evaluating slopes of curves at points in Chapter 1.*

If economic theory presupposes rational calculation, serious attention must be paid to the format in which choice is made. Choice goes on everywhere in an economy; producers, consumers, factor suppliers, and regulators all make choices. Though the subject matter of these decisions varies from context to context, there are features that all have in common. Indeed, economics students who discover this linkage early in their study of price theory have a distinct advantage over their fellows. The rules of logic do not vary from market to market. Microeconomic theory therefore consists of repeated applications of the same logical process from situation to situation. Those who understand the process see each new topic in terms of this familiar formulation. Those who do not regard price theory as a mind-boggling series of special cases that have nothing in common but a penchant for referring to curves in terms of multiple-letter acronyms.

Every choice consists of two elements: the **opportunity set** and the **rank-ordering process**. The analysis of choice may therefore be treated as a particular type of problem called **optimization**, the solution of which involves finding that quantity or group of quantities in the opportunity set which ranks highest. As economic theory is rooted in choice, every application of economic theory may be approached by identifying the relevant opportunity set and discovering the criteria that will govern the decision.

This is not meant to imply that economists believe that households and firms really make decisions in this way. On the contrary, not even economists set up their household spending decisions as optimization problems, and business students typically forget their training in operations research long before they make their first management decision. We approach the theory of choice in this way because it yields predictions of the *results* of choices, and we have reason to believe that observed behavior will be constantly modified toward conformance with those predictions. In the development of choice theory we are not interested in describing how decisions are made—we seek only to be able to predict the results of those choices.

Few sailors have ever heard of Daniel Bernoulli, much less studied his principles of hydrodynamics that explain how a sailboat moves into the wind. A few weekends of trial and error and a helpful hint or two from a friend are nevertheless sufficient to enable most interested people to move about in a small sloop with tolerable efficiency, even to windward. The typical household has had far more than a few weekends of experience in spending money. These decision makers may never have heard of optimization, but they learn sooner or later that certain spending patterns yield more satisfaction than others. Folklore is full of tales like the tortoise and the hare. If the implicit optimization problems and solutions they contain were not intuitively appreciated by most, these stories would not be told. Television "sitcoms" have for decades traded on the plight of the impulsive spender who devotes his or her entire paycheck to singing lessons or robot house-cleaners. Indeed, our enjoyment of these programs may have something to do with our own similar experiences. We would hardly regard them as funny, however, if we all budgeted so foolishly on a day-to-day basis.

Similarly, individual businesses may err greatly in selecting output, production technology, or product design. Excessive error will cause failure. Firms that conform closely to the solutions to their particular optimization problems— whether through careful planning or luck—will prosper. Those that fail to conform will fail to survive. Survival implies conformity of decisions to the solutions to optimization problems, even if the structure of these problems is unknown to all. We therefore approach economic choices as if the agents being studied did, in fact, calculate the solutions to the problems posed, because we have reasonable expectations that observed choices will approximate these results.

3.1 The Opportunity Set—Or When the Sky Is Not the Limit

The opportunity set quite simply is the group of all *possible* alternatives from which the decision maker must choose. For the motorist at a fork in the road, the opportunity set consists of the two alternative routes. For the patron at a restaurant, the opportunity set consists of those items listed on the menu (unless he or she is well known to the chef). There must be at least two alternatives, or no genuine choice may be said to take place. A person who has fallen out of a window may place a very low value on the option of reaching terra firma. As he or she has no alternatives, however, economic theory has nothing to add to the study of this person's misfortune. Beyond this formal restriction, the opportunity set may contain only a few options or be infinitely large.

Opportunity Cost

The requirement that opportunity sets contain more than one opportunity has another important aspect: Alternatives in the opportunity set not chosen are by definition foregone; they represent options foreclosed by the decision itself. Such choices are invariably mutually exclusive; if they are not, the opportunity set has not been properly defined. Those alternatives not chosen thus represent the cost of the option selected. More specifically, the most highly valued of those forgone alternatives represents the *opportunity cost* of the choice made. For example, the opportunity cost to the motorist of taking the longer but more scenic route is the time lost at the destination that would be obtained by taking the shorter route and the added expense of driving more miles. The cost to a patient of ignoring his or her doctor's advice is the longer life expectancy that would be obtained through the prescribed regimen.

At the other end of the spectrum, economic choice depends on a *limited* opportunity set. There are a few things that people can choose at zero opportunity cost, and these things are normally excluded from the opportunity set associated with economic choice. For example, people generally may breathe as much air as they desire without foreclosing other opportunities (we naturally exclude here the case of divers and astronauts). Opportunities involving costless choices such as these are called **free goods**. It is important to distinguish free goods from those discussed in the previous chapter that for one reason or another have a zero money price that does not clear the market. The acquisition of these latter goods may not reduce one's money-spending opportunities, but it will typically impose opportunity costs of some other type. As we saw in Chapter 2, goods offered for lower than equilibrium prices are typically rationed by requiring that the recipient stand

Figure 3.1 *The Opportunity Set for Resting and Working*

Combinations of working and resting time lie on the diagonal line extending from R to W. Combination R includes 24 hours of resting per day and no work. Combination W includes 24 hours of work and no rest. Combinations M and N contain some hours of both. In every case the total time included in the combination must sum to 24 hours, the total time available.

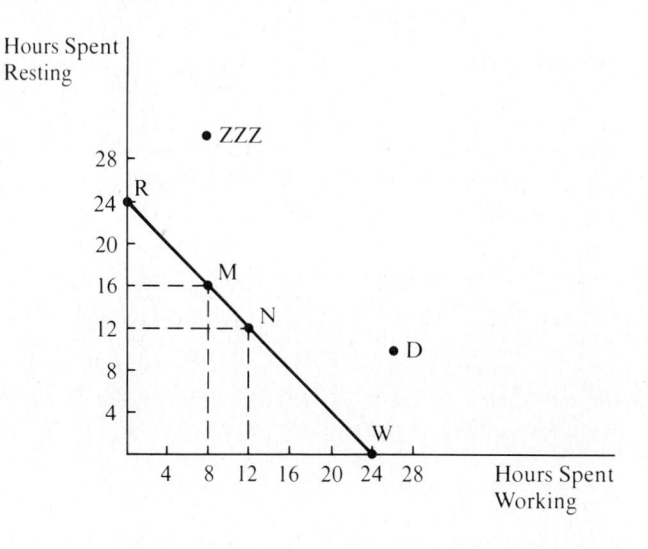

in line or arrive early; both are costly methods. Genuine free goods are those that have a zero market-clearing price. We cannot call them unimportant for, like air, they may be vital—indeed, one songsmith has asserted that "The Best Things In Life Are Free." On the other hand, for the same reason that good health occupies a small place in the curriculum of medical schools, free goods are not matters of consuming concern to economists.

An important feature of the opportunity sets we will deal with in economics is that the alternatives contained in them typically represent *combinations* of things. This is sometimes confusing to students because, as was just mentioned, choices themselves must be mutually exclusive—in choosing one option, one forgoes all others. However, this does not mean that one chooses one *item* to the exclusion of all others. In deciding how to divide our day, say, between work and rest, we are not constrained to devote all 24 hours to doing one or the other; we may divide up the day as we see fit. The opportunity set appropriate to this choice is thus the set of all possible combinations of work and rest that together add up to 24 hours.

Consider Figure 3.1. On the vertical axis we represent the number of hours spent resting and on the horizontal axis the number spent working. As there are 24 hours in each day, the maximum amount of time one might spend doing either is the whole day. Two points on the opportunity set are therefore W, where the amount of work time chosen is 24 hours, and R, where the total day is devoted to rest. As any division of the day into work and rest may be chosen, however, the complete opportunity set is represented by the diagonal line connecting these two points. Someone making such a choice must select a combination along this line. The choice of point M, for example, would mean that the individual divided his or her day into 16 hours of rest and 8 of work. Such a choice rules out the possibility of other combinations like W, R, or N. As all of these points lie within the opportunity set, however, the chooser is free to select any of them.

Rare is the person who has not lamented the fact that the opportunity set in Figure 3.1 is immutable. There are times (usually near the end of the semester) when teachers think longingly about points such as D. Then there are other times (like spring break) when one dreams of points like ZZZ. The fact of the matter is, however, that such constraints as time in this example, or resources and technology in the more typical case, limit the alternatives available. Economic choices must be made from within the opportunity set. In Figure 3.1, more rest implies less work, and more work may be done only at the expense of rest. In universities, the dashing of dreams about D and ZZZ has given economics the reputation of being a dismal science among more optimistic social sciences. A more widespread recognition of the real economic opportunities available to individuals and society as a whole would nevertheless elevate the discussion of many of today's pressing social concerns.

3.2 The Rank-Ordering Process

People Are the Same and Don't Change

Except for the obvious exceptions discussed below, economic theory treats people as if they were identical. This is not because we think they are, but because economics offers little theoretical basis for treating them differently. This is a recognized weakness. Different members of society manifest widely differing manners, customs, habits, and points of view, which doubtless influence their behavior. On the other hand, it turns out not to be as much of a disadvantage as might be suspected at first glance. For though individual behavior clearly differs from one person to the next, much of this individuality has an economic explanation. The fact that some members of society drive absurdly expensive automobiles while others drive very modest ones results at least in part from variations in the position of the opportunity set with respect to transportation and other goods that each confronts. Economic variables such as income and the cost of different alternatives have been found to be at the root of much of the variation in behavior that we observe. In the next chapter we will harness these factors into an analysis that explains some differences in consumption patterns.

Let us therefore set down the ways in which economists assume behavior to be identical. We do this in terms of the other half of the choice theory apparatus: the *rank-ordering process*. When a person chooses, he or she implicitly arranges all of the alternatives in the opportunity set from best to worst. The option chosen is the best available. For many choices we will be examining in price theory, the criteria that form the basis of such a ranking are unambiguous. For example, the choice of output by the manager of a firm is that which produces the most profit. If the relationship between output and profit is fully understood by everyone, then economists can replicate the manager's rank-ordering system. By analyzing the way in which changes in prices affect the manager's opportunity set, economists may predict the output choice. This prediction will hold regardless of the personality and tastes of the manager.

In other aspects of behavior—particularly consumer behavior—the criteria underlying the rank ordering of alternatives is far from obvious. The human mind never fails to astonish us in the way it gives importance at some times to certain things and exactly the opposite a few years later (or a few doors down). Wide ties then narrow ones, miniskirts then maxis, long, sleek cars then short, square ones—not even social psychologists have discovered a pattern.

Utility

Because of such ambiguities economists, when treating household choice, make as few limiting assumptions about these rank orderings as are required by the theory of demand. These will be detailed with the aid of the device conventionally used to represent such a household rank ordering, the **utility function**. Utility is a term borrowed from a group of idealistic nineteenth-century philosophers and has been accumulating ambiguous meanings ever since. We shall not bother ourselves about those. For our purposes utility has a simple, straightforward interpretation derived directly from the rank-ordering process itself. Utility is a measure of *preferredness*. If someone prefers baked alaska to crème caramel, we may say that the first dessert provides this person with more utility than the latter. A more elaborate choice—for example, the bundle of goods purchased on the weekly trip to the supermarket—would assign a utility value to every possible combination of foodstuffs within the means of the shopper. The utility of each combination would descend in the order in which the shopper ranked it.

It is the *order* in such a ranking that is important—not the level of utility itself. The units in which utility is measured play no role in our theory. We might double some people's utility and triple others', and it would affect none of our results. The reason for this is simple. When we rank things, we simply put them in a particular order and assign numbers corresponding to this ranking in descending order. Clearly, if we multiply every number in such a scheme by two, the order of the ranking will be unaffected. Indeed, most of the results of economic theory can be derived with utility indicated by lettered order rather than by numerical (measured) quantities. As the concepts are more intuitively approachable in a numbered format, we will follow the easier course of assuming that the utility associated with each option in the opportunity set is a number. The relationship between options and utility is therefore a function.

Many thoughtful students will rebel at the requirement that a straightforward concept like "baked alaska is preferred to crème caramel" be clothed in such awkward language and symbols. To say "baked alaska produces higher utility than crème caramel" does indeed appear to be "common sense made difficult," a not infrequent accusation hurled at economists by the uninitiated. If simple comparisons such as this one were all that economists dealt with, then such accusations would be valid—indeed, economists are often guilty of couching simple statements in their own peculiar parlance to the mystification and annoyance of their audience. The real purpose of developing such a framework for the expression of preferences is to permit us to deal with much more complicated operations. The notion of utility makes their expression much simpler. So, let us start small.

The simplest possible utility function involves a single binary choice, an example of which confronts Hamlet in his well known third-act soliloquy. Utility functions associate options in the opportunity set with levels of utility. Hamlet's choice problem may thus be represented as follows:

Opportunity set: States of being = B = 0, 1.
Utility function: Utility = U = f(B).

Having expressed Hamlet's choice function in this way, we confront a familiar problem in economics. We have expressed it in general functional notation, but doing this tells us nothing about the choice itself unless we know something about the structure of this function. This brings us to the first limiting assumption about the rank-ordering process:

Postulate 1: More is preferred to less.

This tells us that Hamlet's utility of "being" exceeds that of the alternative: that $f(1)$ is greater than $f(0)$. In the more general case this is interpreted to imply that, *in comparing combinations of goods, that combination containing more of anything and the same amount of everything else will be preferred*. In Hamlet's case, this is the only assumption needed to predict his decision. Unfortunately, few problems of household choice are as easily resolved.

Ranking with Continuous Opportunities

Hamlet's choice, though the source of great mental anguish to him, is simple to represent—too simple, in fact, to capture the nuances of most economic decisions. There are two properties of the opportunity set that must be extended to make the analysis applicable to the typical household choice problem. These are (1) quantities of goods in the opportunity set should vary continuously rather than discretely; the choice must involve **continuous opportunities**, and (2) more than one good should be available. Though the option of "half a life" is of course not very useful in depicting Hamlet's opportunity set, we frequently observe people choosing half a pound of asparagus. And with regard to the second property, the possibilities for substitution are the life's blood of economics.

The utility function needed to deal with such an extended opportunity set ranks combinations of goods over continuous quantities of these goods. We will be illustrating most of the analysis in this book with opportunity sets containing only two goods. This is because diagrams are more easily represented and understood if they contain only two dimensions. In general, of course, choices involve numerous goods. Fortunately, however, most of the properties of household choice identified in connection with a two-good opportunity set can be generalized to larger choice problems. We may therefore make this simplifying assumption without losing much of the richness of the analysis of these problems.

Let us consider one such utility function containing two goods and defined over continuous quantities of these goods. To give the choice a flavor of realism, let the choice concern selection of after-dinner music, more specifically, recordings of a Beethoven symphony versus a Mozart symphony. As the opportunity set is continuous, the units in which each of these goods is measured will be denominated in hours of performance. The utility function representing such a choice therefore has the following form:

$U = f(B, M)$,

where

B = Hours of Beethoven symphony
M = Hours of Mozart symphony

This implies that an individual described by such a function is choosing among combinations of hours of these two compositions. As expressed it represents a function of U in terms of the two right-hand variables, B and M. We may usefully explore the properties of such a function by holding one of the variables constant while allowing the remaining two to vary. Holding U constant, for example, converts this into a two-variable expression,

$M = h(B)$,

in which selection of a quantity of Beethoven determines the number of hours of Mozart.

It is important to understand that in this case it is the holding of U constant that allows B to determine M—not aspects of the opportunity set. We shall not introduce the opportunity set until later in our discussion of this choice. Here, the holding of utility constant determines M, in the same mechanical way that holding constant the number of pairs of shoes and choosing the number of right shoes determines the number of left shoes.

Assume that the combination of two hours of each produces a level of utility equal to 160; that is,

$160 = f(2, 2)$.

For convenience's sake, we will occasionally describe such combinations as producing 160 "utils," although, as already mentioned, absolute quantities of utility are not observable and never play an important role in our theory. If we hold utility constant at 160 and set B equal to 2 hours, there is only one value of M(2 hours) that will satisfy our original equality.[1]

Properties of Indifference Curves

Consider Figure 3.2 which measures hours of Mozart on the vertical axis and hours of Beethoven on the horizontal axis. For the time being we will assume that the entire quadrant is in the opportunity set. The choice combination just described is depicted in this space by point A. This combination produces a level of

---

[1] A simple form of this utility function might be $U = 40B + 40M$. If the level of utility is set at 160, then we may solve for M as a function of B alone; that is, $M = 4 - B$. Clearly, if B is given a value of 2, M must also equal 2.

Figure 3.2 The Slope of an Indifference Curve

Combination A contains 2 hours of listening to each composer and produces a utility of 160. All points in the shaded area above and to the right of A are preferred to A because each contains more Mozart, Beethoven or both and no less of either. All points below and to the left produce less utility than A because these contain less of one or both composers and no more of either. The only regions that contain combinations that can possibly be equally preferred to A are those in the unshaded areas above and to the left of A and below and to the right of A. Each of these contains more of one of the compositions and less of the other than the combination A. The indifference curve $U = 160$ must connect point A with combinations in each of the unshaded regions.

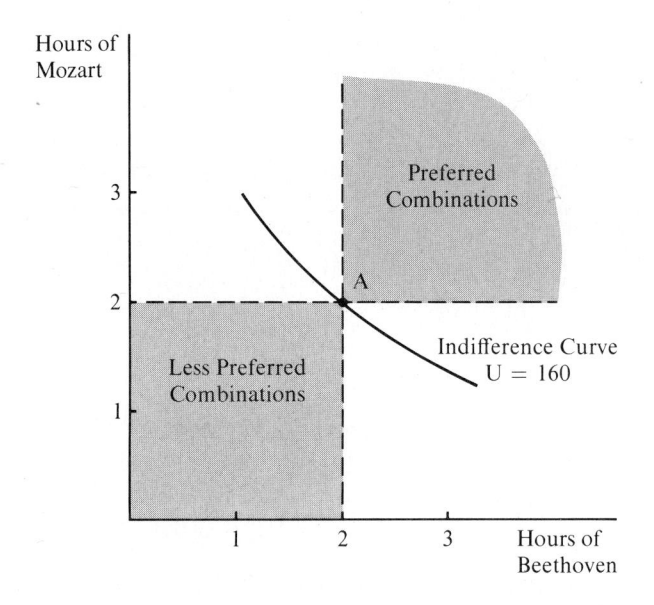

utility of 160. On the basis of our first postulate, we may infer some limited information about the preference ordering of combinations in the diagram with respect to point A. We know, for example, that all points that lie above and to the right of the dotted intersecting lines passing through A produce more than 160 utils and are therefore preferred to the combination A. This follows because all such combinations contain at least as much of Beethoven and Mozart as A and more of at least one of them. Similarly, all points below and to the left of A produce less utility and are regarded as inferior to A. The combinations producing the same utility as A can only lie in the unshaded regions northwest and southeast of A. We may therefore infer at least one property of the function $M = h(B)$ from Postulate 1: A curve connecting all points producing 160 utils must slope downward to the right.

A curve connecting all combinations of goods producing the same level of utility is called an **indifference curve**. This curve gets its name from the fact that a person with such a utility function would derive the same utility from each combination, indicating that these combinations occupied the *same* position in the ranking of all possible choices. That they must indeed slope downward to the right

Figure 3.3 Indifference Curves May Not Intersect

Combination B must be preferred to C, because B contains more hours of Beethoven and the same of Mozart. If C lies on the same indifference curve as A, both must produce the same utility. If B lies on the same indifference curve as A, both of these combinations must yield the same utility. If both B and C yield the same utility as A, the utility produced by each must be the same. This cannot be true so long as B is preferred to C.

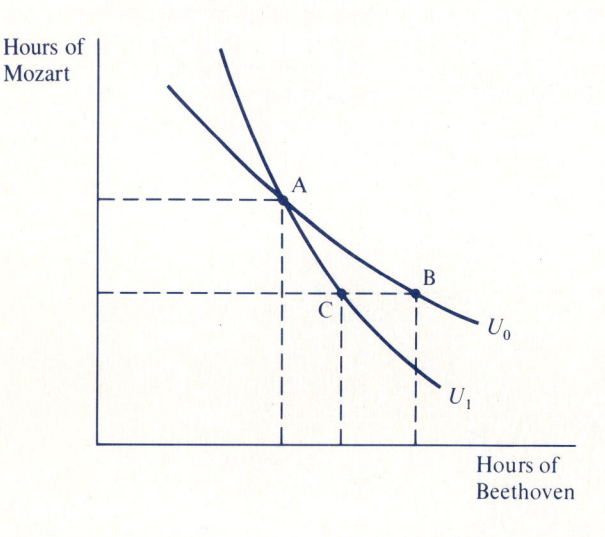

may be seen from the simple fact that points producing the same utility as A must, by process of elimination, lie above to the left and below to the right.

Thus, we derive our first property of indifference curves:

Indifference curves must slope downward to the right.

A second property of indifference curves is derived from the functional representation of utility itself. Continuing our musical example, if point B in Figure 3.3. is on the same indifference curve as point A, then it is impossible for point C to lie on the same indifference curve as A. Since point B contains the same amount of Mozart and more Beethoven then C, then B must produce more utility than C. If A produces the same utility as B, then, quite obviously, it cannot produce the same utility as point C. We may thus derive a second important property of indifference curves:

Indifference curves do not intersect.

This property is sometimes referred to as the property of **transitivity**—that is, the rank ordering of utility functions over all combinations must be transitive. If the combination represented by point B is preferred to that of point C, and A is on the same indifference curve as B, then A must also be preferred to C. Symbolically this may be expressed:

$U(B) > U(C)$, $U(B) = U(A)$

$\therefore U(A) > U(C)$.

Marginal Rate of Substitution

The slope of indifference curves at various points in the opportunity set is a matter of considerable importance to the theory of household choice. We have already noted that this slope must be negative (that is, downward to the right). The slope also bears a direct relation to the choice process itself, which must be understood. Consider two points, A and B, along the indifference curve U_0 in Figure 3.4. Point A contains more Mozart and less Beethoven than point B. As long as the two points lie along an indifference curve, however, the person whose preferences are being represented will not care which he or she hears.

We may describe such a pair of points in the following language. A person hearing combination A would be *willing to exchange* the quantity $(M_a - M_b)$ hours of Mozart for $(B_b - B_a)$ hours of Beethoven. The *ratio* of these two quan-

---

Figure 3.4   *The Marginal Rate of Substitution*

The marginal rate of substitution (MRS) expresses the per unit value of one good in terms of the amount of another good that would be given up to obtain it. An increase in hours of Beethoven equal to $(B_b - B_a)$ is worth $(M_a - M_b)$ of Mozart. This exchange of combination B for combination A keeps the chooser on the same indifference curve, U_0. The value of Beethoven *per unit* obtained is the amount of Mozart given up divided by the amount of the increase in Beethoven—that is, $(M_a - M_b)/(B_b - B_a)$. This ratio, evaluated for very small increases in Beethoven, measures the marginal rate of substitution.

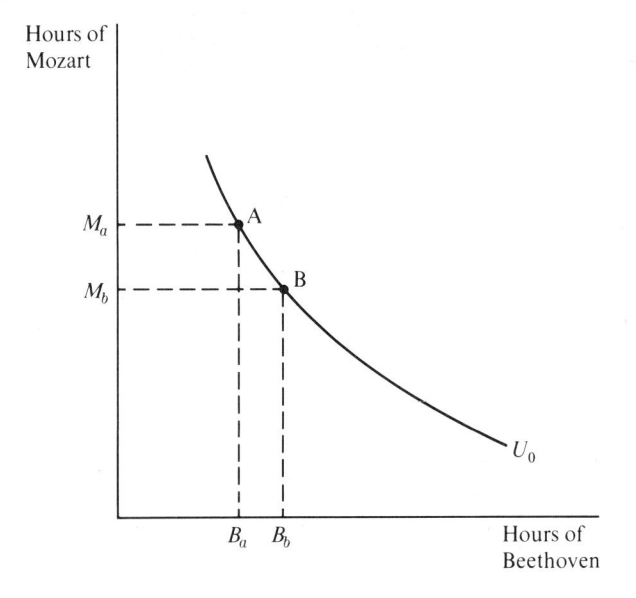

tities $(M_a - M_b)/(B_b - B_a)$ is the maximum amount of Mozart such a person would be willing to give up *per unit of additional Beethoven obtained*. If the indifference curve is not linear (and typically it will not be), this ratio will vary depending on the amount of the increase in hours of Beethoven. For that quantity of *additional* Beethoven that is as close as possible to zero (so that we may talk about such a ratio *at a single point*), this ratio is defined as the **marginal rate of substitution** between the two goods, that is, the MRS. In our example,

$$\frac{M_a - M_b}{B_b - B_a} = MRS_{BM}.$$

This ratio expresses the value of Beethoven in terms of the amount of Mozart the chooser is willing to give up per unit of Beethoven obtained. As the amounts in the denominator and the numerator of this expression are related to changes in the right- and left-hand variables of the indifference curve function $M = h(B)$, there is a close relationship between MRS_{BM} and the slope of the indifference curve linking combinations of the two goods. Indeed, by merely rearranging terms in the numerator of the above ratio (in recognition of the fact that the change in this variable is negative), we see that the slope of the indifference curve is equal to minus the marginal rate of substitution of the indifference curve:

$$\frac{M_b - M_a}{B_b - B_a} = \frac{\Delta M}{\Delta B} = -MRS_{BM}.$$

Convexity

A third property of indifference curves to be considered concerns the influence of the mix of goods being chosen on the marginal rate of substitution. It may not be derived from the assumptions made thus far and must therefore be stated in the form of a postulate.

Postulate 2: As one good is substituted for the other along an indifference curve, the marginal rate of substitution may not increase.

In the limiting case, of course, this implies that indifference curves may be straight lines. More typically we expect them to exhibit *diminishing marginal rate of substitution*, that is, to be convex downward. It is important to understand exactly what is implied by the **convexity** of indifference curves.

Consider Figure 3.5. Here again we have two points identified along an indifference curve combining combinations of hours of Mozart and Beethoven that produce a constant level of utility, U_0. The fact that the curve is convex downward implies that the slope of the indifference curve at point B is smaller than the slope at point A. We interpret this convexity to imply that a person with such a utility function would give up more Mozart for an extra hour of Beethoven at point A than at point B.

While we cannot prove this, it seems plausible to most people who reflect on it. After all, at point A the person whose utility is being represented confronts a bundle containing more of the good being given up and less of that being obtained than the bundle at B. It stands to reason that this person would be more grudging

Figure 3.5 Convexity

The assumption of convexity implies that the slope at A containing more Mozart and less Beethoven is steeper than the slope at B containing less Mozart and more Beethoven.

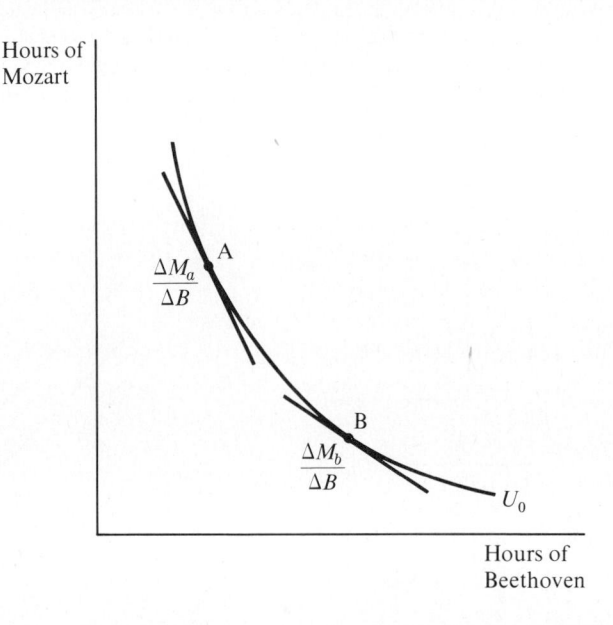

[Graph: Hours of Mozart on vertical axis, Hours of Beethoven on horizontal axis. A downward-sloping convex indifference curve U_0 with point A (upper-left, steeper slope $\frac{\Delta M_a}{\Delta B}$) and point B (lower-right, shallower slope $\frac{\Delta M_b}{\Delta B}$).]

in sacrificing additional units of the good being given up when it is scarce and that being obtained is plentiful than when the reverse is true. Imagine having heard Mozart's G minor symphony twice nightly for three months running! Clearly a listener on such a musical diet would be more anxious to exchange hours of this composition for the alternative than if it were the Beethoven that he or she had been listening to for so many nights.

For some pairs of goods the convexity of indifference curves is extreme; for others it is nonexistent. In this case the factor in the background producing the variation in curvature is the **substitutability** of the two goods. In general, the more substitutable are the two goods, the less convexity they will exhibit. The property we have in mind may be illustrated with two extreme cases. These are presented in Figure 3.6.

In panel (a) we have illustrated two indifference curves between left shoes and right shoes. Each forms a right angle at the points in the quadrant at which the quantities of each type of shoe are equal. The two goods are not substitutable at all. At point A in this panel, the "value" of additional left shoes in terms of the number of right shoes this person would give up is zero. At the kinks in these curves, representing equal quantities of left shoes and right shoes, these indifference curves therefore exhibit the "maximum" convexity.

In panel (b) we illustrate the case at the opposite extreme. Here we have represented two indifference curves identifying combinations of quantities of salt

Figure 3.6 *Extremes of Substitutability*

Panel (a) illustrates indifference curves for goods that are not at all substitutable. Utility may be only increased by increases in both left shoes and right shoes. Additional left shoes beyond the number of right shoes possessed are worthless in the sense that no number of right shoes will be exchanged for any number of left shoes. Panel (b) illustrates the case of perfect substitutes. The *MRS* along these indifference curves is equal to one at all points, implying that the chooser will willingly exchange Brand B salt for Brand A salt on a unit-for-unit basis.

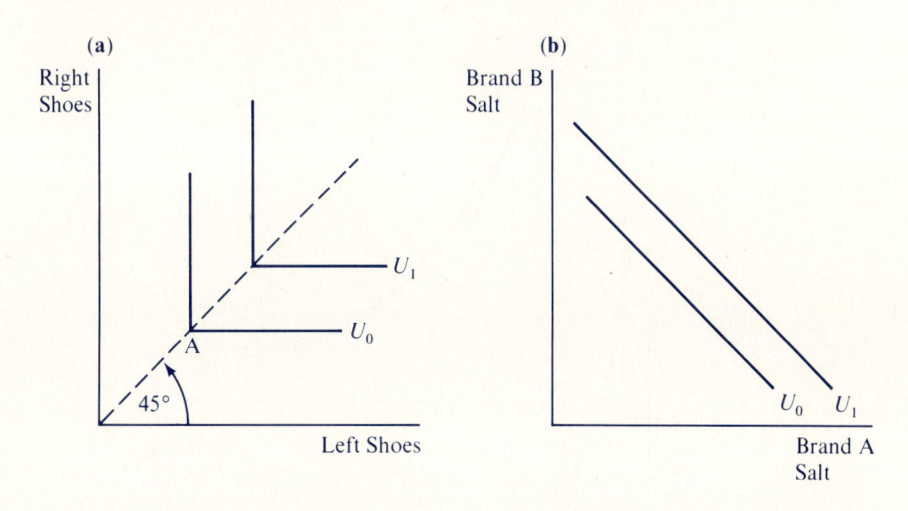

marketed by two different manufacturers that produce constant levels of utility. As salt is salt regardless of packaging and source, we would expect these two goods to be perfectly substitutable. The quantity of Brand B that a person would give up to obtain one pound of Brand A is exactly one pound, no matter how much of each brand is contained in alternative combinations. Fifteen ounces of salt produce less utility than sixteen regardless of how many came from whom. The marginal rate of substitution between these two goods is therefore exactly one at every point on the indifference curve, and the slope is exactly minus one. These indifference curves must therefore be parallel, straight lines as shown in this panel.

3.3 Describing Choice

Continuous Opportunity Sets

So far we have described the rank-ordering process of household choice. The development of this theory has provided us with a good deal of information concerning the structural characteristics of utility functions and the indifference curves derived from them. We know that indifference curves (1) slope downward to the

Chapter 3   The Theory of Choosing

right, (2) do not intersect, and (3) are convex downward. In order to describe choice, of course, we must introduce an explicit opportunity set over which such utility functions will rank alternatives. This can get very messy, as you will discover in the next chapter. However, it will make the theory of household choice more accessible to begin its description with a simpler constraint. We therefore introduce the theory of choice in the context of our musical entertainment problem.

Let us simply assume that the individual has at his or her disposal a certain number of evening leisure hours that may be allocated between the two musical compositions. This time endowment may be apportioned between Beethoven and Mozart in any way this person chooses, so long as the total time devoted to the combination adds up to the total endowment. Let this total amount of time available be T hours, to be divided between Beethoven hours (B) and Mozart hours (M). As B and M must add up to T, we may solve for the expression for the opportunity set algebraically as follows:

$M = T - B.$

We treat the time endowment T as a constant. The opportunity set expression is therefore a function identifying amounts of Mozart that may be listened to in conjunction with particular quantities of Beethoven. The geometric representation of this function is presented in Figure 3.7, with the constant term T as the vertical intercept. The slope is the rate of change in M implied per unit change in the dependent variable B. Algebraically, we know the slope of such a function is the coefficient on this latter variable, that is, minus one. Common sense reinforces our algebra, however. If one increases one's listening of Beethoven by one hour and listening time is fixed, the implied change in Mozart associated with this increase is a one-hour decrease. The rate of change in *M per unit increase* in *B* is therefore minus one.

Solution to the Optimization Problem

All combinations of M and B along the diagonal line TT in Figure 3.7 are in the opportunity set. We may identify the one to be chosen by ranking these points according to the utility function as represented by the person's indifference "map." Every point along TT has an indifference curve passing through it, though we will draw only two of these curves. Indifference curve U_0, for example, passes through two combinations of Mozart and Beethoven that lie along the opportunity set, points A and B. The solution to the optimization problem involves discovering which combination along TT produces the most utility—that is, finding the one that lies on the highest indifference curve. More important for our purposes, however, is discovering characteristics of the solution combination that are shared by all such combinations chosen. It will be shown that the most preferred combination in a broad class of cases will be that, like point C in Figure 3.7, involving a tangency between an indifference curve and the opportunity set.

First let us confirm that the tangency is an optimum. We begin this argument by showing that points that are not tangencies are less preferred as a class than those that are. The indifference curve U_0 passing through points A and B is not tangent to *TT* at either point. We know from our discussion of indifference curves that all points lying above U_0 identify combinations that are preferred to those lying directly on it. All points lying between A and B on *TT* are therefore preferred to these two combinations. Indeed, any indifference curve that intersects *TT* at any point will envelop a set of points including some on *TT* like those between A and B that are more preferred. A combination through which the indifference curve and the opportunity set have different slopes cannot be an optimum.

Consider conditions at combination C, however. All combinations that are preferred to C lie above *TT*. None of these preferred combinations is contained in the opportunity set *TT*. A shift to combinations containing more hours of Mozart and fewer of Beethoven along *TT* will make the chooser worse off; such a shift must move him or her to a lower indifference curve. A move down the opportunity set in the opposite direction will also make the chooser worse off. Only for combinations through which the slopes of the indifference curve and the opportunity set are the same is it true that a shift in either direction will make the chooser worse off. *The optimum combination—the one most preferred—must be characterized by a tangency between the indifference curve and the opportunity set.*

There remains one detail that must be disposed of. We have shown that for any combination that does not satisfy the tangency condition there is a tangency that is preferred to it. We must now consider the possibility that there can be more than a single tangency. This may occur in two possible configurations, both of

Figure 3.7   *The Optimum Combination*

Combination C will be chosen over any other in the opportunity set *TT*. All combinations preferred to C lie above the opportunity set; hence, they are unobtainable. All other combinations in the opportunity set, like A and B, lie on lower indifference curves than C.

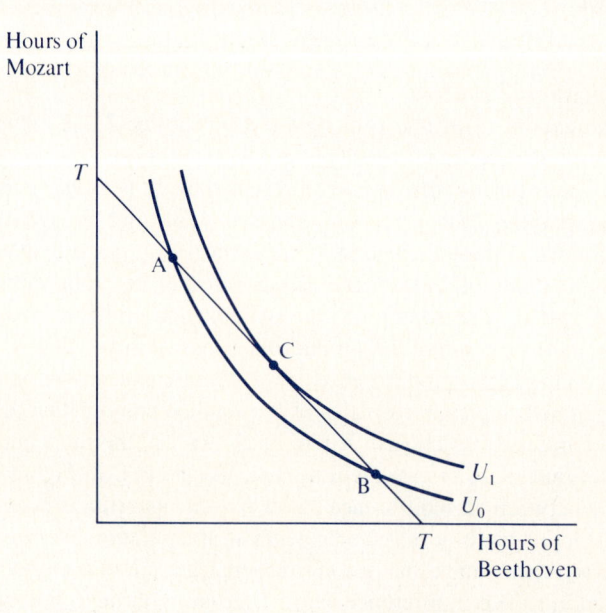

Chapter 3 *The Theory of Choosing*

Figure 3.8   *Multiple Tangencies*

Panel (a) illustrates one configuration of multiple tangencies. This case is ruled out, because indifference curves may not intersect. Panel (b) illustrates the other geometrically possible case of multiple tangencies. This case is also ruled out, because one indifference curve is not convex. Indifference curves embodying all three properties will produce unique optima.

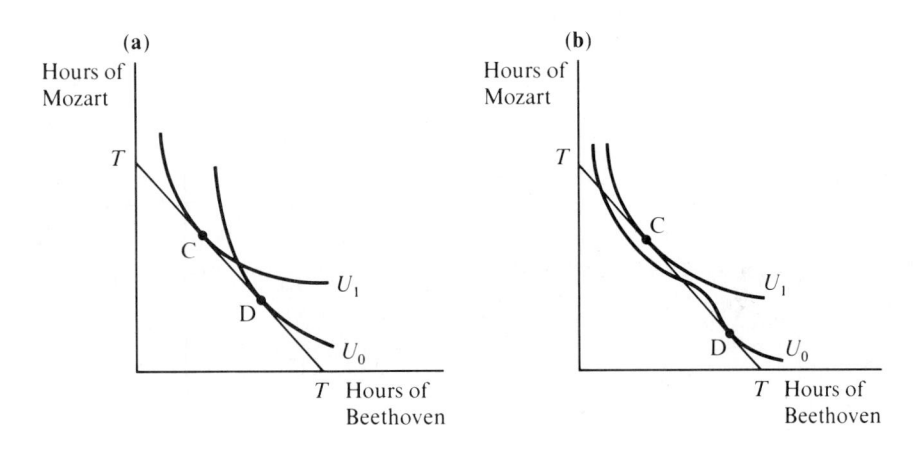

(a) Hours of Mozart vs. Hours of Beethoven, with points C and D, curves U_0 and U_1, and line TT.

(b) Hours of Mozart vs. Hours of Beethoven, with points C and D, curves U_0 and U_1, and line TT.

---

which are ruled out by the properties of indifference curves just developed. These are illustrated in Figure 3.8. Both panels of the figure contain two tangencies occurring at points C and D. Consider the portions of the two indifference curves between these points in the two panels. If both indifference curves exhibit convexity in this region *and* remain negatively sloped, they must intersect—and indifference curves may not intersect. On the other hand, if they do *not* intersect, as in panel (b), then at least one of the indifference curves fails to satisfy our assumption of convexity. Multiple tangencies are inconsistent with our three properties of indifference curves. The tangency solution to our optimization problem is unique.

As long as the chooser decides on some of both Mozart and Beethoven, the combination selected will be identified by a *tangency* between an indifference curve and the opportunity set. The slopes of both curves must be equal through the point representing the combination selected. The slope of the indifference curve, as we have noted, is minus the marginal rate of substitution. The slope of the opportunity set TT itself has an important interpretation.

Opportunity Cost with Continuous Opportunities

As we move downward to the right along TT, we in effect exchange hours of Mozart for hours of Beethoven. The rate of this exchange in this example is one for one, or minus the slope of the opportunity set. This rate of exchange of one for the other identifies the option forgone when an additional unit of Beethoven is chosen. We may think of it, therefore, as the opportunity cost of additional hours of this composition. It is in fact true, generally, that *the opportunity cost of one good in terms of the other is equal to minus the slope of the opportunity set.* The tangency depicted in Figure 3.7 therefore tells us that, for combinations chosen like C, the marginal rate of substitution will equal the opportunity cost. Minus the slope of one curve is equal to minus the slope of the other.

Chosen combinations containing positive amounts of both goods will therefore invariably be identified by tangencies between an indifference curve and the opportunity set, whatever determines the latter's configuration. This is the fundamental principle of choice upon which a great deal of price theory is based. That principle may be restated in its general form as follows:

When interior combinations are chosen from the opportunity set, the marginal rate of substitution of the chooser must equal the opportunity cost as reflected by the opportunity set.

Corner Solutions

This statement of the principle excludes from coverage a class of choices that here warrants brief discussion. These situations are defined as **corner solutions**, for obvious reasons. One such choice is depicted in Figure 3.9. In this choice the

Figure 3.9 *Corner Solution*

The second solution to the optimization problem is the corner solution. This is not a tangency. Corner solutions result when the MRS is either greater than the opportunity cost or less than the opportunity cost for all combinations in the opportunity set. In this case the chooser would devote all of his or her listening time to Mozart and none to Beethoven. The author reaches an interior solution with respect to Mozart and Beethoven but a corner solution with respect to John Cage.

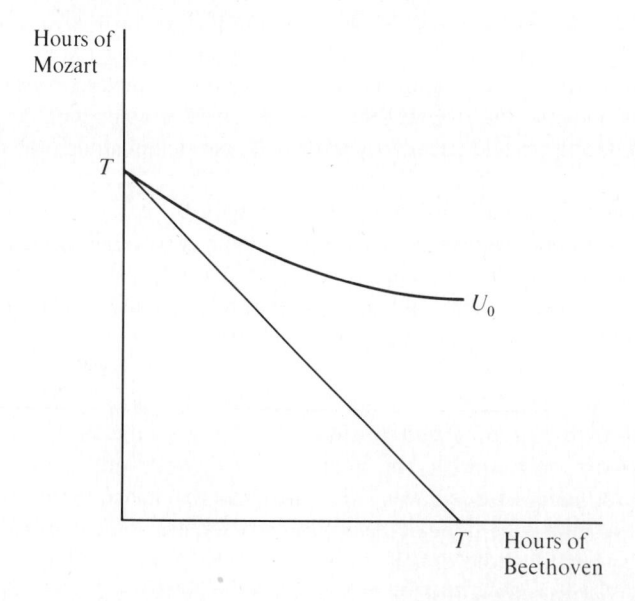

combination of Mozart and Beethoven yielding the highest utility contains no Beethoven at all. The favored combination is not an *interior* one. The reason for this result may be discerned by inspecting the opportunity set and the indifference curves in the figure. It will be noted that on no point on the indifference curve does the marginal rate of substitution (minus the slope of that curve) rise to the value of the opportunity cost (minus the slope of the other). This provides us with an important clue concerning when to expect corner solutions: They will appear most often in connection with indifference curves exhibiting little convexity—that is, those linking combinations of goods regarded as *highly substitutable*.

Consider the salt example developed earlier in Figure 3.6. In this extreme case, the goods in question are so substitutable that the chooser perceives no difference at all between them; the chooser's marginal rate of substitution is everywhere equal to one. If the slope of the opportunity set is less than one (that is, the opportunity cost of a pound of Brand A salt is less than a pound of Brand B), the person whose preferences are so represented will "specialize" in Brand A. If, alternatively, the opportunity cost of a pound of Brand A is greater than that of a pound of Brand B, no Brand A will be purchased. Contrast this with the shoes case, where the goods are not substitutable at all. Regardless of the slope of the opportunity set here (as long as it presents opportunities to exchange left shoes for right at some cost), interior combinations will invariably be chosen.

The Property of Consistency

The theory of choice enables us to infer certain things about economic behavior on the basis of changes in the opportunity set alone. As the opportunity set shifts, the properties of utility functions we have described allow us to infer changes in the choices that will be made. In the simplest case, for example, if a modification of business tax policy makes it possible for a business firm to produce higher profits by increasing output, our theory predicts that firms will expand output. Business owners prefer more to less, like everyone else.

The theory of household choice with respect to combinations of goods consumed is unfortunately less rich as a source of direct implications. Analysis of some of these will occupy us in the next two chapters. One important property of utility functions that permits a fuller use of this theory, however, must be made explicit here. This is the property of *consistency*. A theory of choice that predicts how shifts in the opportunity set affect a person's choices is not very useful if its predictions also depend on such unobservable factors as what company the person is keeping or what side of the bed he or she gets up on. Yet these factors do affect choice in important ways. On some evenings we are in the mood for Mozart and on others we prefer Beethoven. When we are in the company of others, we frequently seek their participation in such decisions. If the rank-ordering process is quixotic, choices will be quixotic, as well, in spite of the elaborate theory we have constructed to describe this process.

Economic theory gets around this quandary by merely assuming that such factors are unimportant, hence, that utility functions are stable. This is not merely a case of economists burying their heads in the sand, as it may initially appear. There are two important reasons why the influence of such "circumstantial" factors may for the purpose of most economic analysis be ignored.

The first reason results from the broadness with which most goods are defined in policy analysis. Economic policy is never concerned with hours of Mozart or Beethoven in recorded home entertainment. Thus, while mood and circumstance may affect which composition is heard on a particular night, such factors are undoubtedly less important in a person's behavior toward recorded music in general and still less important in the larger levels of aggregation, like total leisure time, with which most analysis is concerned.

The second consideration that affects the influence of circumstantial factors is the time dimension of these choices. So far we have been intentionally vague about the time element. We have not discussed whether the combination of hours devoted to evening entertainment being chosen concerns one evening or many. If the unit of time defining the choice is very small, say, one evening or part of an evening, the influence of circumstantial elements will be so large that our theory of choice will add nothing to our ability to predict the choices made. Mood will dominate such short periods; hence, preference orderings will be observed to shift and reverse themselves, confounding attempts to identify consistencies in the choices being made.

While mood and other circumstantial factors may cause rank orderings to vary from one short period to another, we can reasonably expect such influences to average out over longer periods of time. The fact that I choose Beethoven over Mozart tonight does not deny that over a longer period of time, perhaps two months, obvious consistencies will appear in my listening and that Mozart will dominate. On any particular day I may have a ham sandwich or soup for lunch. The fact remains that over a month's time, I have nothing but a salad about 80 percent of the time, and this percentage is very stable from month to month. Economic theory is not particularly useful for predicting daily or hourly behavior. However, over longer periods of time, when the influence of these circumstantial factors averages out, people's preferences exhibit greater consistency.

Too Much of a Good Thing

Postulate 1 states that more is preferred to less. This obviously applies to goods only and not to such patently undesirable items as bruises, sinus congestion, and foul aromas. Many things that economics deals with are not so easily categorized, however. A little rain can be both useful and pleasant; too much can be a disaster. Beethoven symphonies are to some among the sublimest forms of consumption ever created; by contrast, Anthony Burgess in his novel *A Clockwork Orange* depicts Beethoven's Ninth Symphony as an instrument of torture. If we are to apply Postulate 1 intelligently, we must be able to discriminate between goods and "bads," and in particular know when the one becomes the other. This can be done best with the aid of Figure 3.10.

In this figure we depict another simplified choice. We assume that the person doing the choosing must select a combination of bedrest and exercise from the opportunity set *ER*. For simplicity we will assume that these two activities together take up the day. An hour of additional bedrest costs an hour of exercise. A person free to choose from all these alternatives would select combination A, at which his MRS is just equal to the opportunity cost of an additional hour of bedrest—that is, one. This combination produces a level of utility equal to U_0 as noted on the indifference curve.

Chapter 3 *The Theory of Choosing*

Figure 3.10   *Goods-Bads*

Some items may be goods in some quantities and "bads" in others. Here both bedrest and exercise are goods in certain combinations and "bads" in others. Someone free to choose would select combination A, in which the *MRS* is positive. At combination D, however, the MRS of bedrest for exercise is negative. The slope of the indifference curve is positive. At D the chooser would actually give up some exercise (which is here a good) if he could consume less bedrest (which is a "bad" in this combination).

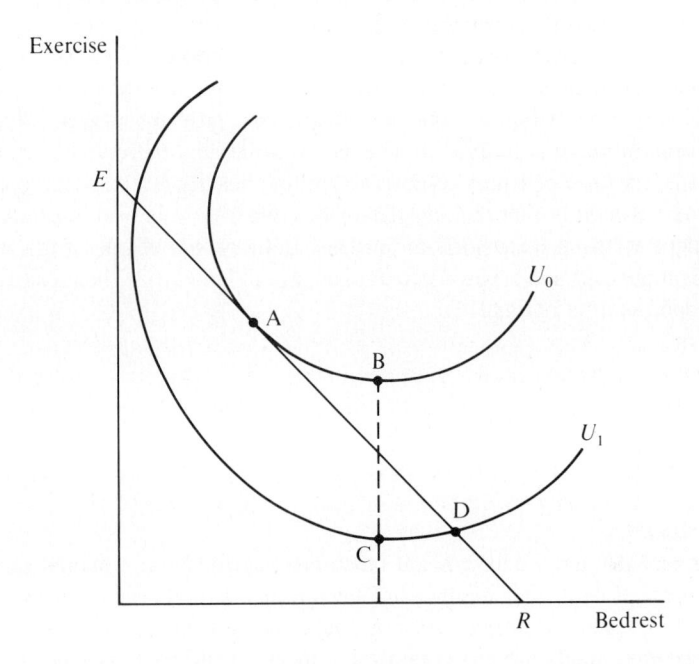

We see by observing the shape of this indifference curve that bedrest for this person is not a good over indefinitely large quantities. The value of additional bedrest beyond point B on this indifference curve is zero in terms of the amount of exercise time he or she would be willing to give up for it; the MRS at this point is therefore zero. Beyond this point bedrest is a "bad." The slope of the indifference curve beyond this point becomes positive, indicating that the MRS is *negative* (recall that the sign of the MRS is opposite that of the slope). In order to keep this person's utility at the level U_0, we would have to somehow compensate him or her for extra bedrest with additional exercise time.[2] Note that too much exercise per day can make exercise a bad as well.

No one facing a positive opportunity cost (that is, a negatively sloped opportunity set) would ever *choose* so much of something that it would become a bad. If

---

[2]Combinations other than A along U_0 are clearly not feasible given the fixed length of the day. However, combinations of things, whether they be cakes and ale or hours of alternative activities, need not be in the opportunity set to be ranked by a person's utility function. The only limits to the scope of the utility function are the boundaries of the chooser's imagination.

the cost of the chosen quantity of an item is positive, the MRS of that quantity must be too! Consider, however, a prisoner confined to a cell except for two hours per day for exercise. His opportunity set is not the whole of ER but those combinations along ER that extend from point D to the horizontal axis. Such a prisoner's MRS of bedrest for exercise is negative at every combination in his attenuated opportunity set. We may think of his situation as a type of corner solution. There is no combination among his opportunities at which his MRS is equal to the opportunity cost. He does not choose to consume bedrest in this quantity. If he could, he would certainly choose less at this cost.

When a person or a society has no choice concerning a bad, economics loses much of its analytical power and usefulness. We may tabulate the cost of a hurricane or an earthquake, but such information provides little of value but a sort of misanthropic entertainment. This is not to say that the involuntary experience of bads does not consume resources or weigh heavily on the social conscience. Our point is merely that the analysis of this experience is best left to scientists more adept at lifting these sorts of burdens. In the words of one of this century's most distinguished and revered economists, Frank Knight: "When a situation becomes hopeless, it is optimal!"

3.4 Social Choice

The Folly of "Priorities"

In recent years we have heard much rhetoric concerning **priorities**. One national administration after another has been accused of shortsighted or misguided priorities. Each has been warned by spokesmen for interest groups composed of city dwellers, small farmers, minorities, independent truckers, and illegal aliens, to name a few, to "get their priorities in order!" Although it is typically obvious what will make this or that group happy at the time the warning is delivered, the literal meaning of the declaration itself is far from clear and warrants our consideration. Having just surveyed the theory of choice in the context of individual or household decisions, it will be useful to develop extensions to choices at larger levels of aggregation. It will be observed that there are strong parallels between household choice and social or governmental choice, but there are irreconcilable divergences as well. One of the seemingly important similarities concerns the properties of choices themselves.

As we have just discussed, people may in their day-to-day choices specialize in the consumption of one good or another, but over longer periods, which permit expression of the full cycle of their taste, they tend to choose mixed bundles of goods. In more technical language, they prefer **interior combinations** to corner combinations; people prefer some Beethoven and some Mozart to a steady diet of either. If we were to ask such people to tell us their favorite composition they might name either one of these, and the one named would probably be the one they listened to most often.

However, imagine asking these people the following question: "If that is your favorite composition, why don't you listen to it all of the time? Why do you listen to the other at all?" They would probably respond to the effect that, while they enjoy listening to this piece most often, they also revere other music and would not want to go completely without hearing it. Also, their enjoyment of any composition would diminish with too-frequent repetitions. The respondents would, in other words, be giving expression to the idea of *convexity* that we asserted was present in all choice. A person's MRS diminishes as he or she considers bundles of goods containing larger and larger portions of the good being evaluated. The fact that some goods may be more important in terms of preserving life (like water or air) or providing enjoyment (like musical compositions) does not imply that rational choice requires specialization in these goods. Rational choice, given the assumption of convexity, implies that *at the margin everything is equally important*.

This can be seen quite clearly in terms of our musical example. As the cost of listening to Mozart for one hour in this example is one hour's worth of Beethoven and vice versa, the opportunity cost of either is exactly one (that is, minus the slope of this opportunity set). Such a person may regard Mozart as his or her favorite composer and devote twice as much listening time to Mozart as to Beethoven. At the margin, however, the chooser's MRS (the rate at which he or she would willingly exchange one for the other) must equal the opportunity cost. The person must therefore choose a combination at which his or her MRS is precisely one for one.

Extending this discussion to the social arena, the very word "priorities" suggests specialization—that is, *solving* one problem before moving on to another. It is not difficult to understand why interest groups use words like this. The city dweller would like very much to have the problems of air pollution and traffic congestion completely eliminated before the government moves on to what appear to be the comparatively trivial concerns of agricultural price supports or high diesel fuel prices. Farmers and truckers undoubtedly have quite different sets of priorities.

If we may for a moment consider the government to be like a household, assigning importance to many interests and activities, we can see that such a characterization of its decision process is inappropriate. Its opportunity set is limited by the resources it can command through taxation and other means. A "rational" government will therefore choose an interior combination. It will devote the resources at its command to many of these activities. In the process it will solve few of the problems completely and therefore fail to satisfy any of the interests it serves absolutely. On the other hand, from the vantage point of the people doing the budgeting and making these decisions, these choices are completely rational. At the margin they have no priorities; every problem is equally important in terms of its own opportunity cost. While national defense may consume more dollars in the aggregate than farm subsidies or space exploration, each is viewed in the neighborhood of the combination of appropriations chosen to have equal social value per dollar spent.

Political Choice

In our discussion of priorities we sought to develop an analogy between governmental choice with respect to policy options and fundamental principles concerning individual choice behavior. It was stressed that, if social decision makers' preferences exhibited the same convexity that seemed reasonable for individuals, then a "priorities" approach to issues would not be applicable. Social choices will tend to exhibit the same type of marginalist, something-for-everyone attitude that we ourselves exhibit in our own choices with respect to the goods we consume.

We must beware of anthropomorphizing the governmental decision-making process to an excessive extent. There are long-established reasons for believing that government behavior—or at least democratic, political behavior—will not abide by the sorts of rules and principles that seem reasonable for individual choice. The application of choice-theoretic analysis to government and political decisions is actively being pursued by economists in the comparatively new applied field of *public choice*. We shall present here an example of the type of problem we have in mind drawn from this new and intriguing literature.

One of the properties of individual utility functions assumed above and absolutely essential for the analysis of choice is the property of *transitivity*: that is, if alternative A is preferred to B, and B is preferred to C, then A must also be preferred to C. We shall see that majority-rule democracy can produce results that are intransitive, even when the individuals participating in the political process all possess utility functions with the properties enumerated in this chapter.

One aspect creating difficulties for political decision making is the fact that for many governmentally provided services it is necessary for everyone to consume the same (that is, the governmentally provided) quantity of those services. As we have seen, certain items when consumed in some quantities can be goods and in other quantities can be bads. This may be true for governmentally provided items as well, particularly when taxes must be levied to finance them. Consider Figure 3.11, in which we have superimposed in a single quadrant an indifference curve for each of three people referred to simply as A, B, and C. These indifference curves are closed so that they represent *all* combinations yielding the same utility, including points R and N, where bread and circuses, respectively, become bads for individual A and even combinations like T, where so much of both goods are provided that they are both bad and the MRS is positive once again. The points labeled A, B, and C in the figure represent combinations (B_A, C_A), (B_B, C_B), and (B_C, C_C), respectively. Each identifies for one individual the *most preferred* combination of any in the quadrant. For simplicity we will consider only these three alternative combinations. The point we illustrate can, however, exist for many sets of combinations.[3]

Each person is assumed to vote for that program (combination of bread and circuses) among those offered which produces the highest personal utility. The set of indifference curves depicted has been judiciously chosen so that each person's ranking of the alternatives may be ascertained. For example, person A's ranking of the three alternatives is $U_A(A) > U_A(B) > U_A(C)$. We know this because the combination A, as already stated, is A's most preferred combination. Combination B lies on indifference curve U_A, which passes between combination C and the most preferred point, A. This higher indifference curve on which point B lies indi-

---

[3] For a thorough discussion of the problem on which this presentation is based see James M. Buchanan, *The Demand and Supply of Public Goods* (Chicago: Rand McNally, 1968), Chapter 6.

Figure 3.11 *Intransitive Social Rankings*

Indifference curves of three individuals are depicted here. Tastes between bread and circuses differ among these voters, hence the positions of their indifference curves differ. Combinations A, B, and C, respectively, indicate the points of *maximum* satisfaction for each. The indifference curves are closed, illustrating in each case all combinations providing the same utility, including those like T, for which both goods are "bad." Voter A prefers B to C. Voter B prefers C to A, and Voter C prefers A to B.

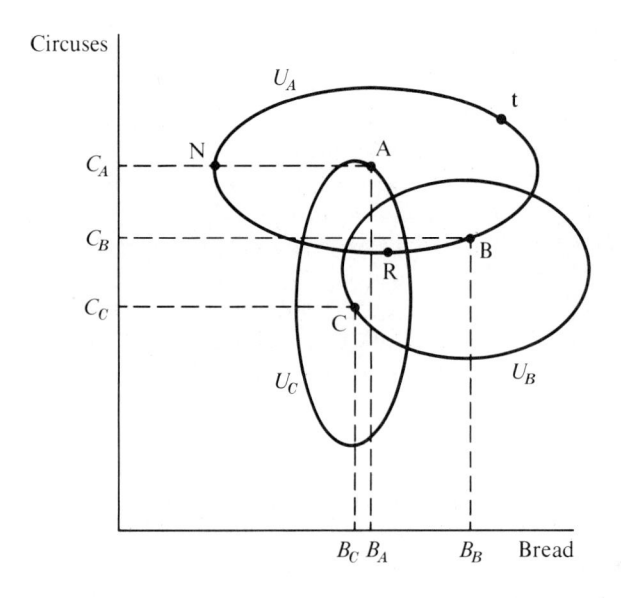

cates that it is preferred to combination C, which lies on a lower one (not shown). The rankings of individuals B and C may be similarly deduced from the indifference curves. Thus we can summarize the orderings of the alternatives as shown in the following table:

	Person A	Person B	Person C
Most Preferred	A	B	C
	B	C	A
Least Preferred	C	A	B

If the election were thrown open to all alternatives, each individual would vote for his or her most favored program, and each would therefore receive precisely one vote. None would obtain a majority, nor even a plurality. Let us therefore assume that, as is frequently done in decisions involving numerous alternative programs or candidates, a process of successive pairings is employed. Assume, for example, that voters must choose between A and B, and that the winner of this contest will then be paired with C to determine the outcome. As Person A and Person C both prefer alternative A to alternative B (A is higher than B in both rankings), the former alternative will emerge the victor in the first contest. When paired with alternative C in the second pairing, however, C receives two votes to

A's one. Both Person C and Person B rank alternative C higher than alternative A. Alternative C therefore emerges the overall victor in the election process.

Let us examine the results of this process more closely, however. So far the election results have provided the following information about the preference orderings in the alternative set: Combination A is preferred to combination B, and combination C is preferred to combination A. If the rankings of this democratic process have the property of transitivity, then we should be able to infer that combination C is *also* preferred to combination B. Surprisingly, this is not the case. Both Person A and Person B prefer alternative B to alternative C. If these two alternatives were paired in an election, the outcome would be a victory for the former.

We thus find that, although each person in the small society we have examined has preferences that obey all the rules we have established for reasonable choice, the outcome of democratic expression of these preferences can violate one of these rules. Even though all individuals have utility functions that exhibit transitivity, *majority-rule decisions by the group together can produce intransitive results.*

Another interesting result can be observed in the influence of the ordering of the pairings on the eventual outcome. In the order just described, C was the ultimate victor. If, however, B and C are paired in the initial balloting, and the winner of that pairing (C) is matched with A, combination A will be the final choice. The pairing of A and C, with the winner matched against B, results in the final choice of B. Clearly, the only factor important in the final outcome of this process is the ordering of the agenda. It is not surprising, therefore, that the majority leaders in Congress wield such power. The power to determine the agenda can be the power to determine the outcome.

Summary

This chapter has presented the basic building blocks of the theory of choice. A choice must involve more than one alternative; the group of all feasible alternatives is the opportunity set. A choice must also involve a group of criteria that are combined to evaluate the alternatives in the opportunity set. This system of criteria is the rank-ordering process. Each of these components is developed here in increasingly complex choice problems, beginning with a simple binary decision involving two alternatives. Choice with continuous opportunities is then presented, and finally the theory of choice is extended to social decisions.

The fundamental concept of opportunity cost was presented and applied to opportunity sets containing continuous amounts of two goods. Utility theory as a rank-ordering process was also introduced and applied to continuous opportunity sets to produce two important analytical concepts: the indifference curve and the marginal rate of substitution. The latter expresses the limiting rate at which a household will exchange one good for another. This limiting rate was shown to be a ratio of quantities of goods that produce the same utility. There is therefore an obvious connection between the MRS and the indifference curve through any combination of goods: The MRS has a value equal to minus the slope of the indifference curve passing through that point.

Two postulates were stated that determine the properties of indifference curves: (1) more is preferred to less, and (2) the marginal rate of substitution may not increase. From the first we inferred that indifference curves for goods must have a negative slope and may not intersect. From the second we inferred the property of convexity.

Choice was presented as being analogous to the solution of an optimization problem. Conditions identified at such solutions were held to be present in all choices, regardless of whether the chooser explicitly formulated his or her choice in these terms. Two types of optima were introduced. When interior combinations are chosen, the solution to the problem will consist of a tangency between an indifference curve and the opportunity set. This implies that at the margin, the value of one good in terms of the amount of the other that would be given up (the MRS) will be precisely equal to the opportunity cost. Corner solutions will occur when the marginal rate of substitution is either higher or lower than the opportunity cost at every combination in the opportunity set. Corner solutions were predicted to be more likely between goods that are highly substitutable.

In order for choice theory to be useful empirically—that is, useful in predicting behavior of households—it is necessary that utility functions exhibit consistency. Tastes must be stable in the face of shifting choice opportunities. The limitations of this assumption for applied work in economics were discussed. Some goods become "bads" if we consume them in excessive quantities. Indifference curve analysis was extended to include this case. For economic situations in which the household is free to choose, the ambiguity of goods becoming bads raises no problems. Choosers will never freely select combinations containing excessive quantities of these good-bad items so long as their opportunity cost is positive.

The chapter closed with a discussion of social choice, in which good-bad items play a central role. While individual rankings are expected to exhibit transitivity, social rankings may not. It was further shown that selection of the order in which alternatives are considered may determine the outcome.

Key Concepts

opportunity set
rank-ordering process
optimization
opportunity cost
free goods
utility function
continuous opportunities
indifference curve

transitivity
marginal rate of substitution (MRS)
convexity
substitutability
corner solutions
interior combinations
priorities

Questions

1. *Easy* On a given evening most of us would rather watch a full hour of one television show than 45 minutes of one and 15 minutes of another. Over one-hour intervals like these indifference curves will not conform in one of their properties to the description of indifference curves in this chapter. Which property will such indifference curves fail to exhibit? Draw such a curve.

Hard In the example illustrating the utility function for alternative combinations of symphonies of Mozart and Beethoven, no allowance was made for the fact that most people prefer to hear musical compositions from beginning to end. They get much more enjoyment from hearing a full symphony than they do from hearing only the first three movements. They also get virtually no additional enjoyment from starting over and hearing the first three minutes of the symphony a second time. What would a more accurate rendering of these indifference curves look like if they incorporated this "lumpiness" quality of preferences into this case?

2. *Easy* When we eat at a restaurant on a particular evening, we do not order some of everything on the menu. The combination of items ordered represents a corner solution with respect to pairs of certain goods and an interior solution with respect to pairs of other goods. Which is which? If we ate every night at the same place and represented our choices over a six-month period, how would this change?

Hard Recall our left shoe-right shoe example and the indifference curves drawn in Figure 3.6. The horizontal portion of these curves imply that no number of right shoes will be given up for extra left shoes. Is this absolutely true? Is it true of suit jackets and trousers? People do in fact purchase "two-pants suits." In what way are the buyers of these suits substituting trousers for jackets?

3. *Easy* The marginal rate of substitution between two goods reflects the value of one in terms of the amount of the other that would be given up per unit to obtain it at the margin. A steeper slope of an indifference curve (other things equal) therefore reflects a _____ value at the margin than a flatter one.

Hard Bill Ayers has a neighbor who helps him maintain his backyard vegetable garden "just for the fun of it." Otis Mayberry has to pay laborers to persuade them to help him farm his 600 acres. Is working for Otis less fun than working for Bill? In what sense?

4. *Easy* The following list contains events that will affect choice. Specify in each case whether choice is affected through a change in the opportunity set or a change in the rank-ordering process.
 a. Doug Banks is getting on in years and decides to give up tennis and play golf.
 b. Road construction on Highway 64 forces all traffic onto a detour.
 c. Dr. Boozer advises his patient William Throckmorton to refrain from eating foods containing saturated fats.
 d. The curriculum committee of the economics department decides to increase the number of economics courses required of its majors.
 e. Due to the annual shift from daylight saving time to standard time in October, we are permitted to sleep an extra hour one day per year.
 f. The new direct flight from Atlanta to San Antonio cuts 1½ hours off this trip.
 g. The invention of a new drug, cimetidine, has reduced the incidence of surgery for peptic ulcer in the United States by 60 percent.

Hard Hugh Stevens is laid off from his job at Canada Wire and is seeking a new one among firms in the Toronto area. What is the opportunity cost of his accepting a job that is offered to him among the first few places he visits? What is the opportunity cost of his refusing such a job offer? How is this latter opportunity cost affected by an increase in his unemployment benefits?

Part Two

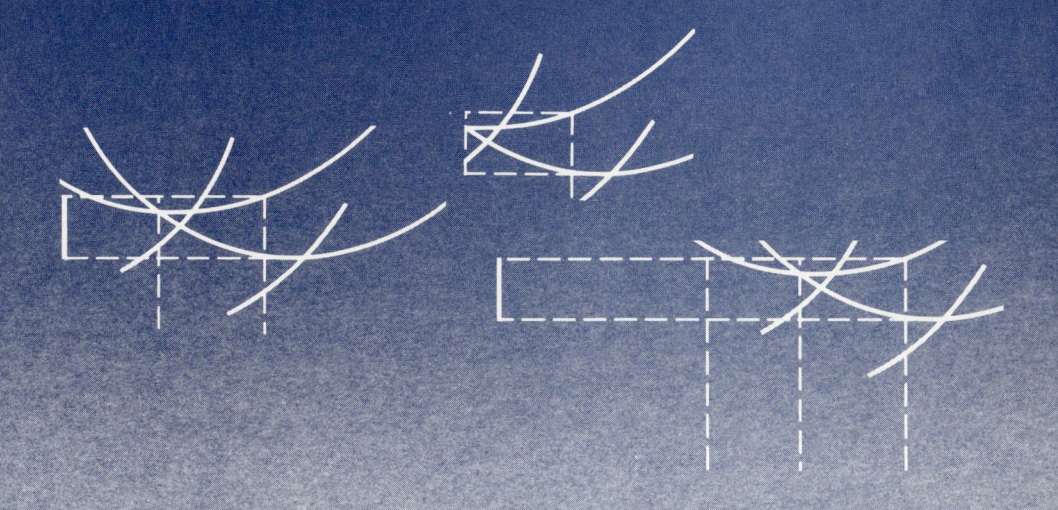

The Choice among Goods

Chapter 4

Household Choices

Connections   In this chapter the theory of household choice is applied to the selection of combinations of goods available at given prices in the market. It builds directly on the choice theory developed in Chapter 3. Utility theory and the postulates governing choice are retained in unmodified form. The chief difference is that here the opportunity sets with which we deal must be derived from the budget information of households—that is, from household income and market prices. The analysis is introduced with the simple budget constraint involving two goods. This opportunity set identifies pairs of goods that can be purchased out of household income at prevailing prices. The choice problem is then enriched by incorporating consumption time into the opportunity set. In a similar extension, time devoted to commuting is incorporated into the opportunity set to develop a theory of residential land pricing. The development in the latter half of the chapter is messy but not difficult. The student who is not fluent in algebra should prepare for the chapter by reviewing the discussion of slopes and intercepts of linear functions in Chapter 1.

The theory of choice may be usefully employed to analyze many household choices. It is particularly useful in developing an explicit theory of demand and will help us to rationalize and elaborate on our discussion of demand in Chapter 2. We may use choice theory to identify how income and prices determine the quantities of consumer goods that households seek to purchase and how the combinations chosen are influenced by changing prices and income. In addition, we may use it to identify and quantify the gains to individual households from their ability to exchange in markets. Bearing these potential gains from trade in mind, we may employ the theory to measure the loss to households from restrictions on trade.

Utility theory forms the basis for the more complex analysis of the demand for goods as collections of service components, each of which is valued in its own right. For example, automobiles provide comfort, carrying capacity, safety, and performance. Some aspects of the demand for automobiles are best understood in terms of the changing relative prices of these components. The consumption of most goods requires some time on the part of the consumer. As each household places a different value on time, this time cost element may be used to predict different choices of consumption goods across households. This last application has a broad range of uses extending from the variation in the size of daily newspapers to the variation of real estate prices between city and suburban locations.

Before we may explore these applications of utility theory, we must introduce a different form of the opportunity set. In much economic choice the opportunity set is made up of combinations of goods and services that people buy in the market. The quantities that can be bought are not unlimited, however, and the constraints on these obtainable combinations determine the shape of the opportunity set. The following section develops the theory of household choice as it concerns the buying of goods and services.

4.1   The Household Budget as an Opportunity Set

The quantities of items that people can buy are limited by their incomes and the prices of the items. Obviously, with more income a person can buy more so long as prices are unchanged. Similarly, with the same income a person can buy more if prices fall. It will be useful to develop more explicitly this relationship between prices and incomes and the set of obtainable combinations of goods that may be purchased. We do this with the aid of Figure 4.1. Again we simplify our problem by illustrating the principle with an opportunity set containing only two goods. The results are nevertheless valid for any number of goods. The vertical and horizontal axes measure the quantities of these goods, cakes and ale.

As before, we note that coordinates in this two-dimensional space identify *pairs* of quantities of the two goods. The combination K in the figure, for example, has coordinates (3, 4), indicating that it represents the combination containing 3 units of cake and 4 of ale. It is clearly possible, therefore, to represent any conceivable combination of two goods using a two-dimensional space of this type. The more circumscribed set of those combinations that someone with a given in-

Figure 4.1 The Budget Constraint

The budget constraint identifies all combinations of two goods that may be purchased from a given income. Combination K, for example, contains 3 units of cakes and 4 units of ale. Expenditure on cakes at these prices is $3 \cdot \$8 = \$24$. Expenditure on ale is $4 \cdot \$4 = \$16$. The sum of this spending exhausts the $40 income of the household. All other combinations along this budget constraint will also exhaust the $40 income.

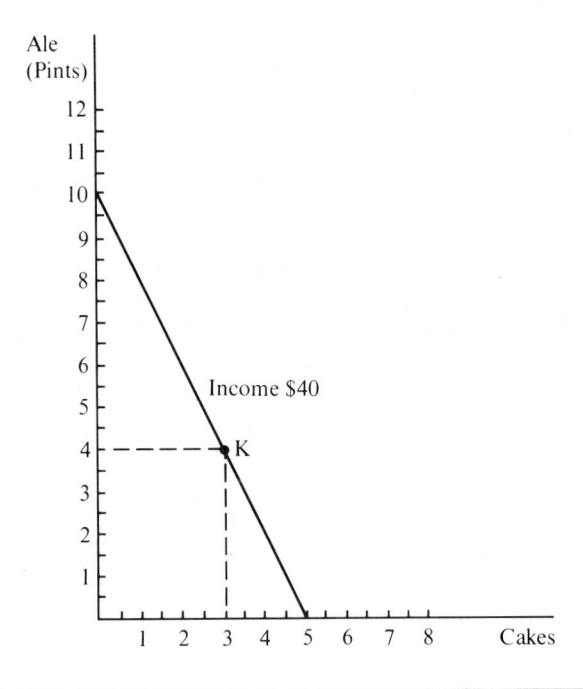

come can afford can also be represented in such a space. Let us consider how this might look in general.

Assume that a person has an income (B) and will spend this income completely on cakes (c) and ale (a), and that the prices of these two goods are P_c and P_a, respectively. As income must equal spending, we may state that equality as

$$B = P_c c + P_a a.$$

However, our coordinates are denominated in quantities of the two goods being selected, so it is more convenient to express this budget equation in a different form. In other words, we wish to express it as a function of the quantity of one good in terms of the quantity of the other. This is achieved by solving the expression for a, the quantity of ale. We will have many occasions to refer to this form of the budget equation, which we call the **budget constraint**:

$$a = \frac{B}{P_a} - \frac{P_c}{P_a} \cdot c.$$

We shall treat income for the time being as given although, as noted in Chapter 1, income itself is determined in a market. Supply and demand in that market will be discussed in Part IV.

Our budget constraint therefore identifies a simple relationship between the quantity of cakes chosen and the quantity of ale that may be consumed with each quantity of cakes. The first term on the right-hand side contains the ratio of two constants, income and the price of ale; this gives us the vertical intercept of this function. Since both income and the price of any good are positive, the vertical intercepts of all budget constraints are positive.

The second term on the right-hand side contains the variable c. The slope of the budget constraint function is the coefficient of this variable—that is, $-P_c/P_a$—minus the ratio of the prices of the goods being chosen. Since prices are always positive and constant, the slope of all budget constraints is negative and linear.

The general shape of budget constraints is therefore apparent from these two right-hand terms. Budget constraints are represented by diagonal straight lines extending downward from an intercept on the vertical axis to an intercept on the horizontal axis.

By considering the right-hand terms of this budget constraint, we can also determine how *changes* in the market parameters affect the position of the budget constraint. As income (B) appears only in the numerator of the intercept term, we know that increases in income, with prices held constant, will increase the value of this intercept and hence shift the budget constraint upward. This shift corresponds to our common-sense notion that more income gives a person greater command over goods and services. The opportunity set of someone with more income contains combinations that are not obtainable for someone with less.

The prices of the two goods appear in one or both of the right-hand terms of the budget constraint. An increase in the price of cakes increases the numerator of the slope term. If income and the other price remain constant, this will cause the budget constraint to have a steeper slope while leaving the intercept unchanged. A change in the price of ale, on the other hand, influences both the vertical intercept and the slope, appearing in the denominator of both of these terms. An increase in the price of ale, therefore, lowers *both* the vertical intercept and the slope. The horizontal intercept identifies the quantity of cakes that a person could purchase by spending his or her entire income on this good. A rise in the price of ale will not affect this quantity. Such a price rise lowers both the vertical intercept and the slope by just enough to leave the horizontal intercept unchanged.

Consider a budget constraint involving the following data:

$B = \$40$
$a = 4$
$c = 8$

The budget constraint faced by someone in this situation will thus have the following form:

$$a = \frac{40}{4} - \frac{8}{4} \cdot c.$$

Chapter 4   Household Choices   99

Table 4.1   *Cakes and Ale Purchasable with $40*

Quantity of Cakes	Quantity of Ale
0	10
1	8
2	6
3	4
4	2
5	0

This reduces to:

$$a = 10 - 2c.$$

By choosing values for the quantity of cakes, we may determine the *combinations* of cakes and ale that may be purchased with an income of $40. These obtainable combinations are listed in Table 4.1. If we apply the budget constraint to our example in Figure 4.1, we see that 3 cakes may be purchased along with 4 pints of ale—that is, $10 - (2 \cdot 3) = 4$. Other values in the table may be verified in the same way.

The Opportunity Cost of Purchasing

In Chapter 3 we pointed out that the opportunity cost of goods chosen has a geometric interpretation derived from the opportunity set. In general, the opportunity cost of purchasing one unit of a good is minus the slope of the opportunity set. This may be shown to apply to the case of goods and services purchased at market prices. The opportunity cost of purchasing an extra unit of cakes is the corresponding reduction in the quantity of ale that may be purchased. This opportunity cost may simply be read off the entries in Table 4.1. When the quantity of cakes chosen is increased from 0 to 1, the number of units of ale that may be purchased falls from 10 to 8, a reduction of two units of ale. Similarly, when the quantity of cakes is increased from 1 to 2, from 2 to 3, from 3 to 4, etc., each unit increase in cakes is accompanied by a two-unit decrease in ale. The opportunity cost of purchasing cakes does not vary along the budget constraint; it is two at every point.

Now consider the slope of the budget constraint. It has been shown to be equal to minus the ratio of the prices of cakes and ale. This price ratio is $8/$4 = 2, and the slope is therefore -2, the coefficient of c in the budget constraint expression. Since the opportunity cost is minus the slope, the opportunity cost of purchasing an extra unit of cakes—and in all cases—is therefore simply the ratio of the prices of the two goods purchased. Later in this chapter we will consider the opportunity cost of purchasing *and consuming* goods when consumption involves the use of time. There it will be shown that this opportunity cost may differ from the opportunity cost of merely purchasing the good.

The Effect of Income Changes

Examination of the pairs of quantities in Table 4.1 will confirm that they lie along the diagonal line depicted in Figure 4.1. Let us consider how the position in this figure is changed by changes in income. Assume that income rises to $48. Our expression for the budget constraint now has a higher vertical intercept, expressed as

$$a = \frac{48}{4} - \frac{8}{4} \cdot c,$$

which reduces to

$$a = 12 - 2c.$$

In Table 4.2, we compare the combinations that may be bought with this higher income with those obtainable at the lower income. In this case, selecting a quantity of cakes permits the chooser to have more ale in each combination. At an income of $40, only 4 pints of ale can be had with 3 cakes. Now we see that the higher income allows 6 pints of ale to be chosen (should thirst demand it!) with the same 3 cakes.

When the two budget constraints are plotted in a two-dimensional space, as in Figure 4.2, we find the properties that we identified algebraically to be confirmed geometrically. Income was alleged to shift the budget constraint upward (that is, to increase the vertical intercept) without changing the slope. This is precisely what has happened. The vertical intercept (the quantity of ale that might be purchased with 0 cakes) increases from 10 to 12 pints. That this slope has not been changed by this rise in income is confirmed by the fact that these two budget constraints are parallel.

A rise in income clearly expands opportunities. At the higher income, the chooser may select opportunities that were not available at the lower income. We therefore need have no more information about people's utility functions than we assumed in Chapter 3 to infer that a rise in income improves people's welfare. This rise makes possible the selection of preferred combinations, no matter what combination was previously chosen. Consider the two opportunity sets in Figure 4.2.

Table 4.2   Cakes and Ale Purchasable with Different Incomes

Quantity of Cakes (at Either Income)	Quantity of Ale (Low Income)	Quantity of Ale (High Income)
0	10	12
1	8	10
2	6	8
3	4	6
4	2	4
5	0	2
6	X	0

Figure 4.2   Income Shift of the Budget Constraint

A rise in income shifts the budget constraint outward parallel to the original. Income appears only in the vertical intercept of the budget constraint expression. That intercept, I/P_a, is 10 for a price of ale of $4 and an income of $40. An increase in income to $48 increases the vertical intercept to 12.

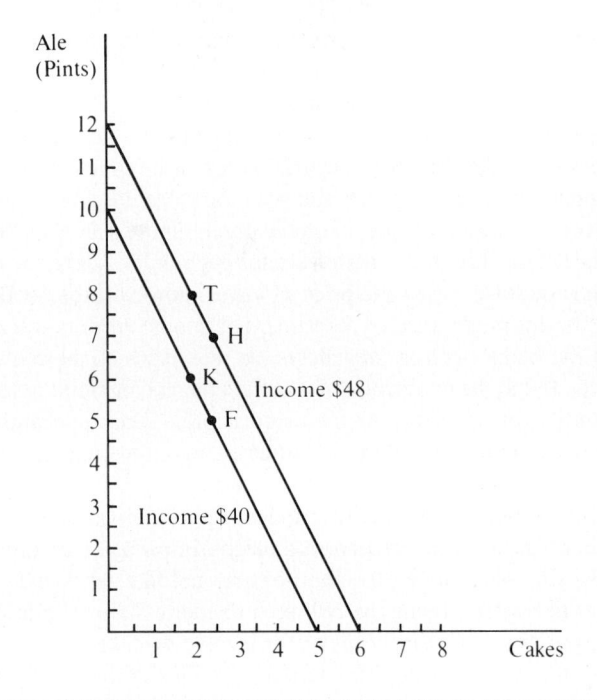

There is no point along the inner budget constraint that is not inferior to some point on the outer budget constraint. For *any* point on the inner budget constraint there is some point on the outer that contains more of at least one good and equal amounts of the other. Of course, it is not true that any point on the outer curve is always preferred to *all* points in the inner constraint. While we can confidently conclude that combination T is preferred to combination K in the diagram, we cannot know that T is preferred to combination F without more information about the chooser's utility function. On the other hand, though it is unclear whether T is preferred to F, there must be combinations that can be purchased with a higher income, like H, that are clearly preferred to F.

The Effect of Price Changes

Now let us consider the effect of a price change. Let the price of cakes fall to $4, holding income at the original $40 and the price of ale at its original level of $4. The budget constraint in this case may be expressed as

$$a = \frac{40}{4} - \frac{4}{4} \cdot c,$$

which reduces to

$$a = 10 - c.$$

When we plot this new budget constraint together with the original, we find that it has the same vertical intercept but has a flatter (less steep) slope. Combinations along the old and new budget constraints are presented in Table 4.3. The top row in this table confirms that the vertical intercept of each budget constraint is 10. The lower price of cake, however, means that for each reduction in the quantity of ale chosen more cake can be purchased with the released purchasing power. The two budget constraints are depicted graphically in Figure 4.3. This "exchange" of ale for cakes takes place at 2 pints of ale for each unit of cakes before the price change. After the lowering of the price of cakes, however, the goods may be exchanged (in the chooser's selected assortment of goods) on a one-for-one basis. As the slope of the budget constraint reflects the rate at which these exchanges may take place, the fall in the coefficient of c in the budget constraint reflects the fall in the opportunity cost of cakes. At the original price, the opportunity cost of an extra cake was 2 pints of ale. After the price change, the opportunity cost is only 1 pint of ale.

The fall in the price of cakes also expands opportunities, though the extent to which this benefits the chooser depends on the importance of this good in the choice bundle. If, for example, the chooser does not like cakes and uses all of his or her budget to buy ale, he or she will be no better off after the price change. A person who spends a large part of his or her income on cakes, however, will benefit greatly by this fall in price. This is most obvious at the southeast end of the budget constraints, where combinations containing only cakes are depicted. At the lower price, twice as many cakes may be purchased if the budget is devoted exclusively to these items.

Table 4.3 *Cakes and Ale Purchasable with Varying Ale Prices*

Quantity of Cakes (Either Income)	Quantity of Ale (Cakes' Price $8)	Quantity of Ale (Cakes' Price $4)
0	10	10
1	8	9
2	6	8
3	4	7
4	2	6
5	0	5
6	X	4
7	X	3
8	X	2
9	X	1
10	X	0

Chapter 4   Household Choices   103

| *Figure 4.3* | *Price Shift of the Budget Constraint* |

The price of cakes, P_c, appears only in the slope term $-P_c/P_a$. A change in the price of cakes, therefore, affects the slope but not the vertical intercept. A decrease in the price of cakes decreases the numerator of this slope term, making it smaller in absolute value. A decrease in P_c from \$8 to \$4 reduces the steepness of the slope by exactly half.

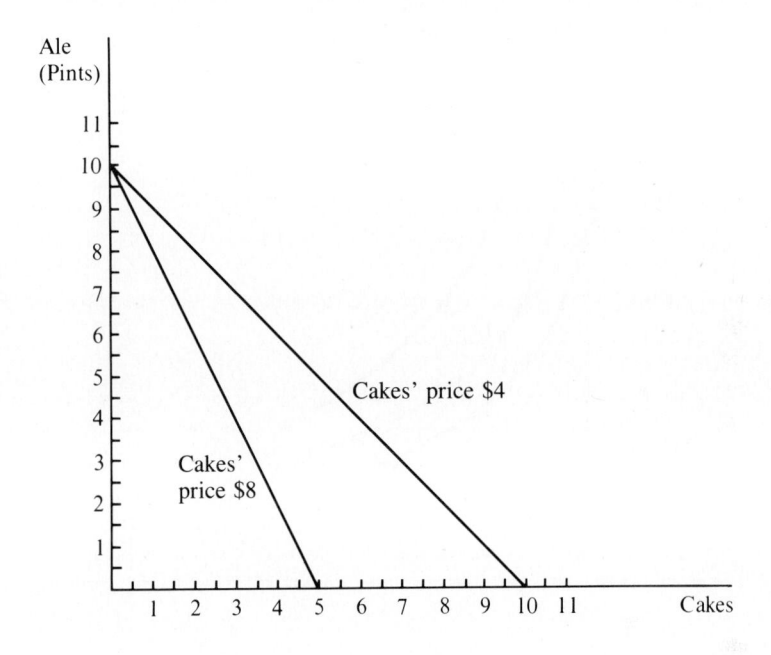

4.2   Indifference Curves in Goods Space

Assuming that income and prices are determined externally (and are thus free of the influence of the chooser's behavior) allows us to derive opportunity sets from this budget information alone. However, as we learned in Chapter 3, an opportunity set by itself gives us only half of the picture describing choice. A full description of choice requires some representation of the chooser's *rank-ordering process*. We must supply our chooser with a *utility function*, developed in Chapter 3, in order to identify which combination of goods within the opportunity set is selected.

The postulates governing the rank-ordering process and the properties of indifference curves derived from them are assumed to hold for market-purchased goods. Indifference curves for these goods will slope downward, exhibiting the property of convexity; they may not intersect. The combination chosen will therefore be identified by a tangency of the opportunity set with the highest possible indifference curve containing a point on the opportunity set. Such a **consumption optimum** is depicted in Figure 4.4.

Figure 4.4 Consumption Optimum

The consumption optimum is the combination favored by the chooser over all others in the opportunity set. Any combination, such as K, in which the indifference curve intersects the budget constraint cannot be the consumption optimum, since the intersection itself implies the availability of combinations preferred to the one at the intersection. The consumption optimum will therefore be a combination like T, at which the indifference curve and the budget constraint are tangent.

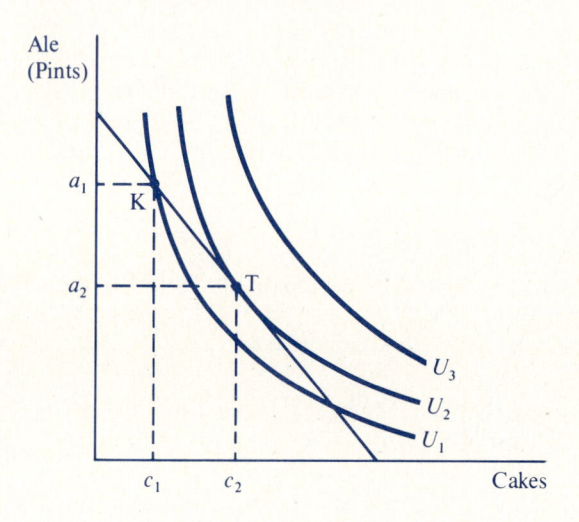

Combination K, containing c_1 cakes and a_1 pints of ale, is not a consumption optimum. It lies on indifference curve U_1, which is clearly not the highest level of utility obtainable along the opportunity set. Point T is the optimum, because the consumption combination represented by this point lies on the highest attainable indifference curve. Other combinations to the southeast along the opportunity set will lie on lower indifference curves, as will combinations to the northwest. Point T is the optimum, because this consumption combination produces more utility for the chooser than any other point on the opportunity set.

4.3 Conditions at the Optimum

The conditions of this optimum are important to much of our later discussion. We note that, as in Chapter 3, the optimum is identified by the tangency between an indifference curve and the opportunity set. It therefore follows that the slopes of these two schedules are equal. The slope of an indifference curve is *minus* the marginal rate of substitution—that is, minus the rate at which the chooser will willingly give up ale for cakes (in very small quantities). As we have seen, the slope of the opportunity set for market-purchased goods is minus the ratio of the prices, $-P_c/P_a$. Since both of these slopes have negative signs, it is convenient to express this consumption optimum after multiplying both slopes by -1. In doing so, we get:

$$MRS = \frac{P_c}{P_a}.$$

The consumption optimum for a chooser buying goods in markets is therefore characterized by the equality of the marginal rate of substitution and the price ratio. Though we have derived this condition under circumstances in which there are only two goods, it generalizes to the case of many goods—that is, at the consumption optimum the marginal rate of substitution between any pair of goods must equal the ratio of the prices of those goods.

Interpreting Conditions at the Optimum

Let us consider the economic interpretation of this result. The chooser's MRS expresses the maximum quantity of ale that he or she would give up at the margin *per unit* of cakes obtained. We may therefore think of the MRS as an expression of the chooser's *value of cakes in terms of ale*. A high MRS (associated with a steep indifference curve) suggests that the good on the horizontal axis is valuable in terms of the quantity of the other good represented. A low MRS (associated with a flatter indifference curve) suggests the opposite. The slope of the opportunity set, on the other hand, equals minus the opportunity cost of the good on the horizontal axis. In the case of market-purchased goods, the slope is equal to the ratio of the prices of the goods. The price ratio itself is therefore the opportunity cost.

The opportunity cost of consuming another cake is not money; money has no consumption value. The opportunity cost of cake is the ale that could have been purchased with the money spent on cake. If the price of cakes is P_c, then obviously the money spent on an additional cake is P_c. The amount of ale that can be purchased with D dollars is D/P_a. If P_c dollars are spent on cakes, the *reduction* in ale implied by this expenditure is therefore P_c/P_a. If, for example, the purchase price of cakes is $8 and the price of ale is $4, the opportunity cost of another cake is 2 pints of ale. One additional cake requires a reduction in spending on ale equal to the price of cake, $8. As ale can be purchased at $4 per pint, such a cut would imply a reduction in ale obtained equal to $8/$4 = 2.

4.4 The Value of Exchange

Opportunities for exchange never make anyone worse off and nearly always make people better off—at least as long as they know what they're doing! This simple concept of **gains from trade** is sometimes treated with exaggerated importance by economists who occasionally fall into the trap of inferring from this that everyone is better off with a market system than without one. (The normative statements that one may make about an economy and an exchange system will be discussed

Figure 4.5 *Trade Opportunities*

The endowment combination K, together with the prices of cakes and ale, identifies combinations obtainable from exchange. Combinations obtainable from exchange are the same as those identified by a budget constraint involving money income equal to the market value of the endowment. One measure of value of the gains from trade would be the increase in cakes from c_1 to c_3, holding ale consumption constant at a_1. This would provide a combination on indifference curve U_2 producing the same utility as combination T.

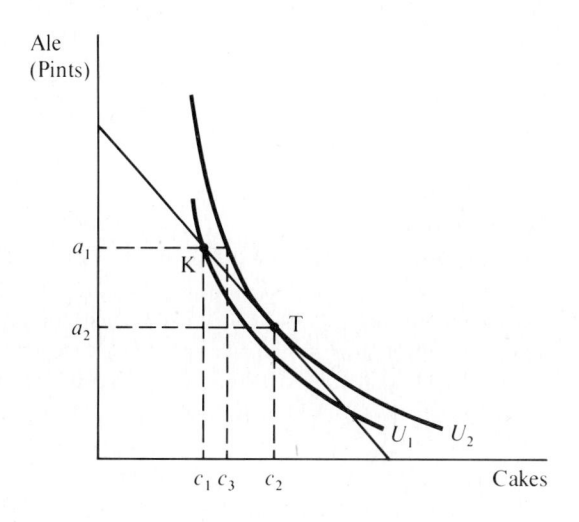

in Chapter 18. Those related to gains through trade are not trivial, but limited, as we shall see.) The opportunity to exchange in a market is nevertheless frequently quite valuable to interested parties, and the source of this value should be understood.

We can illustrate the nature of these gains from trade with the aid of Figure 4.5. Here again our two-dimensional space is defined in terms of quantities of two goods, cakes and ale. In this case, however, assume that our chooser has an **endowment** of goods rather than income. Let that original endowment of goods be combination K, that is, a_1 units of ale and c_1 units of cakes. If there is a market for these two goods, the consumption opportunities will not be limited to combination K but will contain all the possible consumption combinations that may be acquired through market activity. If there is no *spread* between the buying and selling price, these opportunities will form a diagonal line identical to the budget constraints with which we have been dealing. In Figure 4.5, such a line is shown passing through points K and T.

The opportunities indicated by this line result from the ability of a person with such an endowment to enter the market first as a seller and then as a buyer. The chooser first sells a part of his or her endowment—say, $a_1 - a_2$ pints of ale—using the revenues obtained to purchase more of the other good—in this case, $c_2 - c_1$ cakes. This pair of transactions would make available the combination T. The actual position of T in the goods space depends on three factors: the quantity of ale sold, the price of ale, and the price of cakes. For any such pair of transactions it must be true that the amount spent on the good obtained equals the amount received for the good sold. For any hypothetical quantity of ale sold, such as Δa, we may express this equality as:

$$\Delta a P_a = -\Delta c P_c.$$

The implicit exchange rate of cake for ale resulting from such transactions is therefore:

$$\frac{\Delta a}{\Delta c} = -\frac{P_c}{P_a}.$$

The slope of the opportunity set passing through any initial endowment point, such as K, is therefore the same as that of a budget constraint, that is, $-P_c/P_a$. Indeed, as a practical matter it makes no difference whether one starts with an endowment of money income or with an endowment of goods that may be exchanged for money. The *slope* of the opportunity set will reflect the opportunity cost of one good in terms of the other. In the case of all marketed goods, that opportunity cost will be the price ratio.

Now let us turn to the *value* of the gains from trade. A person initially endowed with combination K will, if he or she is free to exchange any quantity of ale and cake at the market prices, choose combination T. This is the utility-maximizing combination of the two goods. Obtaining combination T would require the sale of $a_1 - a_2$ pints of ale and the purchase of an additional $c_2 - c_1$ cakes. As is apparent from the indifference curves passing through points K and T, this trading would improve the welfare of the person making the exchange. The question confronting us is how to measure this gain.

It is clear that we cannot measure the change in utility directly. There remain a number of imperfect gauges of utility change. All of these indicators seek to express the change in welfare in terms of various changes in the chooser's portfolio that produce equivalent utility changes. We might, for example, express the value of the gains from trade in terms of an increase in the endowment of cakes that produces the same utility change. The gain from trade in this case might thus be gauged as worth a certain number of cakes ($c_3 - c_1$ in Figure 4.5). More commonly, we measure such gains in terms of money. This calculation is illustrated in Figure 4.6.

In this figure, we wish to evaluate the gains from trade that permit the chooser to consume combination T rather than the initial endowment, K. We may do this by determining what change in the money value of this endowment of goods would produce the same utility change. If the chooser must consume endowment K, his or her utility will be U_1. Exchanging that endowment for combination T produces utility U_3. Let the money value of the initial endowment be B_1, such that

$$B_1 = P_a a_1 + P_c c_1.$$

By simultaneously allowing the individual to trade and "taxing" away a certain part of the value of his or her endowment, we may influence the chooser to select a combination like F which, given such a tax, is the utility-maximizing combination of cakes and ale. We may express the value of the sum of such changes as:

$$\Delta B = P_a \Delta a + P_c \Delta c.$$

The set of changes resulting in the choice of combination F still permits the chooser to enjoy a higher level of utility than by choosing K in spite of the reduction in the value of his or her portfolio due to the tax. We may, however, calculate the value of a tax that will keep the chooser at the same level of utility as at initial endowment K. In Figure 4.6, combination H produces utility level U_1 and also represents the utility-maximizing choice for an individual with an endowment of value B_2 such that:

$$B_1 - B_2 = P_a(a_1 - a_2) + P_c(c_1 - c_2).$$

Because this change in utility is proxied by a change in income, it is referred to as an **income-compensating measure of welfare change**. The change in income compensates for the welfare-changing phenomenon we wish to evaluate, in this case, the right to trade. Later we will employ this measure to evaluate the welfare-changing effects of other phenomena, such as the effect of a change in prices or the efficiency loss of programs that inhibit trade.

Figure 4.6   *Gains from Trade*

Gains from trade are measured in money terms by identifying the change in income that produces the same change in utility as the ability to trade. Consumption of combination K rather than of T reduces utility from U_3 to U_1. Consumption of combination H rather than of T also reduces utility from U_3 to U_1. The reduction of income leading to the choice of combination H therefore measures the gain from trade.

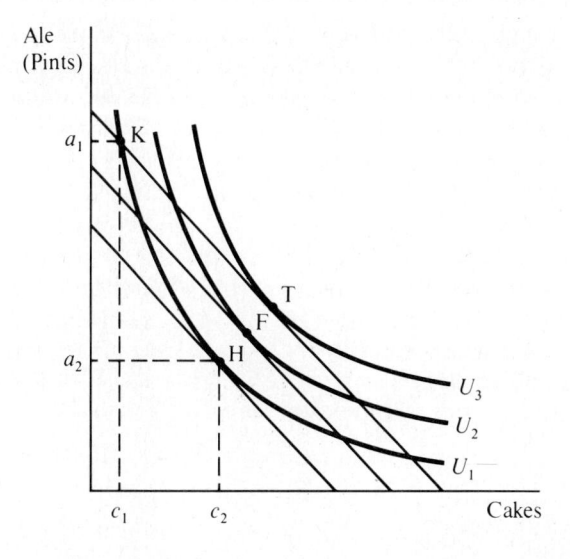

Figure 4.7   *Transaction Costs of Selling*

This household is provided with endowment K and would like to exchange some cakes for ale. Selling imposes transaction costs, represented here by the horizontal shift (representing lost purchasing power) from K to F. Once these transaction costs have been borne, cakes and ale may be exchanged at the market rate. The optimum in this case (combination G) is less preferred than endowment combination K, so no exchange will take place. Combination T would be chosen in the absence of transaction costs.

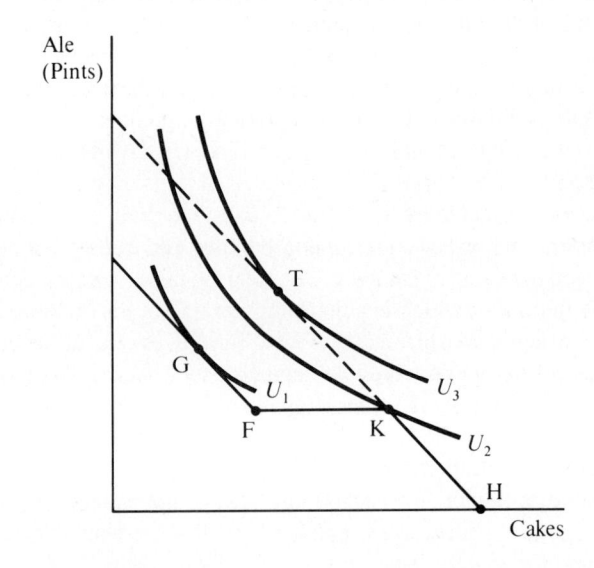

The Puzzle of Gifts

In real life, people's use of the market and exchange is limited by a number of factors. Because markets are costly to organize, it pays to use them only when the value of exchange exceeds these **transaction costs**. Households use the market as sellers only for limited sets of exchanges. Typically households are sellers of labor services and suppliers of loanable funds. Occasionally they will sell a house or a used car, but it rarely pays for households to deal in specific goods and services directly useful to other households. Transaction costs of selling require a high volume of sales to make the organization of markets worthwhile; hence, we observe firms specializing in the distribution and sale of these items.[1]

Quite frequently we find ourselves in the situation depicted by Figure 4.7. We have an endowment such as that shown by K, in which the value that we place on a

---

[1] Consumers sometimes attempt to achieve the required sales volume by accumulating unwanted goods to be disposed of at "garage sales." My experience is that the cost of these events is usually underestimated.

good (in this case, cakes) is less than its opportunity cost at market exchange rates. Let this cost be reflected in the slope of the dotted line passing through K. Had we started with enough money to purchase combination K, we would never have bought so many cakes but would have chosen the consumption optimum, T. Often, however, we find ourselves in this situation due not to our own purchases but to someone else's. (Birthday gifts from uncles usually produce this result.)

In order to dispose of the unwanted cakes, transaction costs of selling must be incurred. We represent these money costs of selling in the market as an inward horizontal shift of the budget constraint from K to F. The assumption is that once these costs have been incurred, any amount of ale may be sold at the market price. The real opportunity set concerning consumer goods, therefore, is represented in Figure 4.7 as the solid line diagonal from point H to point K, horizontal from K to F, and having the slope of minus the price ratio upward from that point to the vertical intercept.

In the case represented by this figure, a consumer with endowment K will not attempt to modify his or her consumption bundle. The transaction costs of doing so would exceed the value of exchange. By bearing these costs the consumer could acquire combination G, which is a consumption optimum. In doing so, however, the consumer would lower his or her welfare from U_2 to U_1. If the costs of transacting were zero, he or she would sell some of the cakes in the endowment and consume combination T. At the transaction costs depicted in Figure 4.7, however, sticking with the initial endowment, K, is the best that the consumer can do.

This raises a puzzle that economics cannot explain. Gifts frequently leave us in situations like combination K, where the MRS is not equal to the market–price ratio. We are given ill-fitting shirts and loud ties that we would dearly love to exchange at market prices for John Le Carre novels or a new Timex. However, the transaction costs of organizing such exchanges is usually too great—so the shirts and ties find their way into the bottom drawer. We would probably be better off in terms of our economic model of choice if all our gifts were cash money. No such dilemmas as that presented by combination K would occur if all we ever received was cash.

The custom of gifts "in kind" is strongly entrenched, however, and it seems rooted in something stronger than mere tradition. There are probably good explanations for this practice in psychology and sociology that do not involve self-serving calculation so much as ceremonial emblems of mutual caring and dependence. Gifts chosen by the giver indicate to the recipient that he or she has been thought about and mentally measured in a way that is completely unnecessary for gifts of money. For whatever reason, the practice of in-kind gifts seems unlikely to be replaced by exchanges of money on a wide scale, regardless of the latter's efficiency properties. Economics cannot and probably should not seek to explain all behavior in terms of such rational calculation. Social behavior is extremely complex and unlikely to yield all its secrets to any single interpretation, be it derived from economics or from some other social science. In a sense that economics cannot rationalize, people probably will continue to prefer receiving those ill-fitting shirts and gaudy ties to money. And in a complicated but nevertheless sincere way, they will probably exclaim upon receiving them, "This is *just* what I wanted!"

Figure 4.8   Welfare Loss from Trade Restrictions

The purchase of cakes is limited to quantity c_1. In the absence of this restriction, combination T would be chosen containing more cakes. This restriction produces a welfare loss equivalent to the reduction of income from that associated with budget constraint B_1 to that associated with B_2.

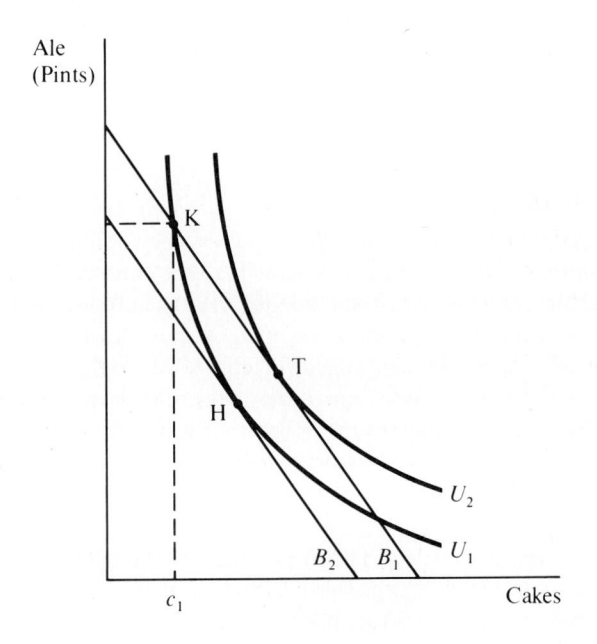

4.5 Inefficiency and Welfare Loss

While the puzzle of gifts may be explainable in terms of noneconomic considerations, we observe many occasions where exchange is inhibited for which plausible rationalizations are more difficult to construct. Governments frequently adopt policies that actually prohibit certain exchanges. Government policies restricting trade may be based on perceived benefits of this practice. It is nevertheless useful to have a measure of the cost of such restrictions so that the net benefits, or possibly the net welfare loss, associated with such restrictions may be calculated.

The cost of restrictions or prohibitions on exchange is the value of the gains from trade forgone. We may therefore calculate this cost just as we calculated the value of exchange in section 4.4. Consider Figure 4.8, in which a person has income sufficient to purchase any combination along his or her budget constraint B_1, including combinations K and T. Assume now that due to a government regulation individuals are not allowed to purchase more than c_1 units of cake. There may be good reasons for such a regulation, but restricting trade in this way is not costless.

The cost of this restriction is the welfare loss that each person would suffer by consuming combination K rather than T.

We may proxy this cost by calculating the decrease in income that produces an equivalent **welfare loss** from point T. We see here that an income reduction that shifted the budget constraint to position B_2 would produce just such a welfare loss. Given this reduced income, the consumer depicted would purchase combination H, which lies on the same indifference curve as point K, the combination available with the exchange restrictions. The difference in the two incomes associated with budget constraints B_1 and B_2 is therefore the measure of the welfare loss from this trade restriction and therefore the cost of such a policy.

The Welfare Loss of Public Housing

The federal government sponsors many programs providing goods in kind that embody features producing welfare loss of the type described. The government makes available medical care, food stamps, insurance, education, job training, and other items with the expectation (as with other uncles bearing gifts) that the items bestowed will not be exchanged for things we would rather have. As we must usually pay for these "gifts" ourselves at tax time, however, it is worthwhile in this case to inquire whether we might be better served by being left to buy these things on our own. Even if we cannot afford them ourselves, we should ask whether it is more efficient to be given money when we need it or to receive specific benefits instead.

One such program, federal public housing, provides apartments to families qualifying on income and other grounds. These apartments are typically on the site of a federal housing project and are built to standard specifications. The recipients of such a benefit therefore have limited discretion concerning the location, size, or layout of the housing they receive (at highly subsidized rates) from the government. Most in-kind programs have the result of influencing the recipients to consume more of the good in question than they would purchase at their consumer optimums. Other programs, like public housing, because of their numerous restrictions can influence recipients to consume less than they would choose.

Consider Figure 4.9, which depicts an individual's budget constraint and the combination of housing and other goods (h and y, respectively) that they would purchase given these opportunities. The alternative of moving into public housing is depicted by combination K alone. Typically some rent is charged, but since this is subsidized the reduction in income due to the rent ($y_1 - y_2$) is lower than that required to purchase h_1 units of housing on the market. If the government charged the market price for this amount of public housing, income in the amount $y_1 - y_3$ would have to be paid, and this household would choose not to live there.

Once living in public housing, one cannot add or subtract space, rearrange floorspace, or even sublet excess rooms; one must simply accept the apartment as it is. Access to the vastly larger market available in the private sector is lost and with it the ability to search for exactly the size, design, and location of housing desired. Because of the large subsidy provided with public housing, however, many (but by no means all) of those eligible take advantage of this government program; one is frequently counseled when facing such a choice "not to look a gift

Figure 4.9   *Welfare Loss of the Housing Program*

The government housing program provides H_1 units of housing at a cost in terms of other goods of $(Y_1 - Y_2)$. The opportunity cost of housing in the market is given by minus the slope of budget constraint B_1. The beneficiary of this program may not add or subtract from the housing provided H_1. Spending all remaining income on other goods provides combination K. Failing to take advantage of the program involves choice of a combination along B_1 such as H, which may contain more or less housing than K. Providing a money transfer equal to $(Y_2 - Y_3)$—the cost of the in-kind program—would permit choice of combination T rather than K.

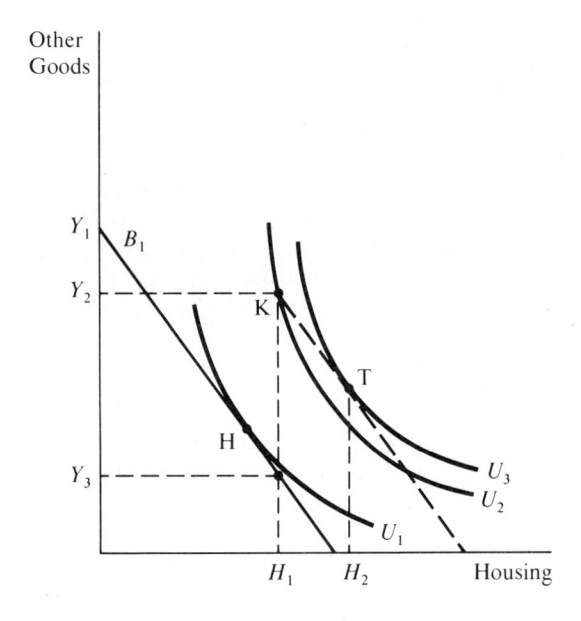

horse in the mouth." In Figure 4.9 the option of choosing combination K rather than H clearly increases the welfare of the chooser.

Combination K is not a consumption optimum, however. As depicted in Figure 4.9, the consumer's MRS would exceed the opportunity cost of additional units of housing if incremental units could be purchased in the market. Were the consumer able, he or she would supplement housing services obtained from the government by purchasing more in the market and would consume H_2 in all. Under the program described, however, this is not possible. One must consume the public housing that is available—no more and no less.

Clearly such a program involves a welfare loss for at least some of its beneficiaries. Because they cannot engage in the exchanges indicated by trading along the dotted line between K and T, recipients are prevented from reaching utility level U_3; they must consume the inferior combination K instead of the preferred bundle T.

It is easy to see from Figure 4.9 that a grant of money (like a gift of money) is superior on efficiency grounds. Assume that housing can be purchased in the market for no greater cost than it can be provided for by public housing projects. Under these circumstances, for the cost of providing this consumer with h_1 units of housing in a project, he or she might be given a cash grant worth $y_2 - y_3$ in terms of other goods. Such a grant would make possible the purchase in the market of combination K, the same combination available through public housing. With the cash grant, however, the indivdual will select the efficient combination T, *receiving more housing than would be provided through the in-kind program.*

Such a program seems demonstrably superior on every score. The cost to the government is no greater—indeed, if the market can provide better housing through its diversity of location, size, design, and other characteristics and eliminate the red tape that invariably seems to accompany administration of in-kind programs, then the cost to the government can even be lower. The target population ends up consuming even more housing services than the government sought to provide. And these beneficiaries are themselves better off in terms of their own assessment of their situation.

This example should not be dismissed as hypothetical. Kraft and Olsen[2] examined the housing choices of low-income families in an effort to discover whether in fact such "underconsumption" was actually being created by public housing. According to their findings, 49 percent of the respondents in their survey would have consumed more housing services if they had been given cash grants equal in value to the public housing they were occupying; the remainder would have chosen the same services or fewer. However, either too little or too much involves a welfare loss of corresponding dimensions. A program that provides the same goods for all people similarly circumstanced but with different tastes for the characteristics describing those goods (size, location, design, etc.) must therefore be inefficient.

4.6 Choice Involving Bundled Goods

Life for an applied economist is rarely so simple and neatly laid out as it has appeared in our presentation of choice theory thus far. The markets with which we deal rarely present straightforward choices involving more cakes and less ale. More often we deal with consumers who juggle whole menus of baked goods and alcoholic beverages whose composition may change radically from period to period. Take the automobile, for example. During the period from 1950 to 1972, automobiles grew steadily longer, faster, heavier, and more costly to operate. After 1972, however, this trend reversed itself for about a decade. An analysis that treated the automobile as a homogeneous item over this entire period would have serious problems. The typical new automobile in any one year would not have exchanged on a one-for-one basis with that in any other.

One way of dealing with the problem is simply to assert that tastes changed from year to year; that speed and comfort were more important in the 1960s while

---

[2] John Kraft and Edgar Olsen, "The Distribution of Benefits from Public Housing," in *Studies in Income and Wealth*, ed. F. Thomas Juster (Cambridge, Mass.: Ballinger, 1977), vol. 1, 51–64.

maneuverability and economy became more important in the 1970s. Tastes do change, and we must always be alert to the implications of such changes for economic analysis.

In many cases, however, what may appear to be a change in taste may in reality be a response to a change in relative prices. For example, advancing technology in the 1950s and 1960s made possible the production of reasonably compact auto engines, which delivered more power than could be achieved with earlier engines of similar size and weight. The cost of peformance and size-related comfort fell with these innovations, and car design was modified to exploit these falling costs. The sharply rising cost of gasoline during the 1970s offset these cost advantages. The higher price of fuel raised the cost of auto speed and weight, and car designs were again modified to reflect the new cost of these attributes.

It is therefore frequently useful to treat commodities as collections of items performing varying services at costs that may themselves differ over the period of analysis. Choices of apparently different items by different people, or by the same people under different circumstances, may be analyzed in terms of choice models that retain consistent tastes. One aspect affecting the choice of goods that exhibits considerable variation from person to person and that is conveniently observable for empirical analysis is the value of time. The opportunity cost of one hour of time is greater for someone who may use that hour to earn $60 than for someone who forgoes only one hour's earnings at the minimum wage. Economic theory therefore suggests that choices of goods whose use involves time will differ among high- and low-wage earners. In the remainder of this chapter we will develop two applications of this principle.

The Time Cost of Consumption

Returning to our cakes and ale example, let each good require a fixed amount of time per unit for its consumption. The total time devoted to consuming cakes will be the product of the number of cakes, c, and the unit time cost for cakes, t_c. As the household consumes only cakes and ale, the total time spent consuming all goods, t_g, may thus be expressed as:

(4.1) $$t_g = ct_c + at_a.$$

The total time available per day, week, or whatever the time frame of the choice will be represented by T. We will assume that time is spent either working or consuming. As work time is denoted by t_w, this implies:

(4.2) $$T = t_g + t_w.$$

Finally, we assume that the wage rate is given by w, so that wage income may be represented by:

(4.3) $$I_w = t_w w.$$

By solving for t_w in (4.2) and substituting in (4.3), we obtain:

$$I_w = (T - t_g) \cdot w.$$

Substituting the right side of (4.1) for t_g here, we obtain an expression for wage income in terms of the **consumption time cost** of our two goods, the wage rate and the time endowment:

$$I_w = (T - ct_c - at_a) \cdot w.$$

Total income with which the household obtains goods is the sum of wage income and nonwage income, I_0. We will assume no saving by the household so that spending on cakes and ale exhausts total income. This implies:

$$P_c c + P_a a = I_0 + I_w$$
$$= I_0 + (T - ct_c - at_a) \cdot w.$$

From this we obtain:

(4.4) $$c \cdot (P_c + wt_c) + a \cdot (P_a + wt_a) = I_0 + (wT).$$

This expression is a more elaborate version of the budget equation from which we obtained the budget constraint in prices and income at the beginning of this chapter. As before, we will solve this expression for the quantity of ale purchased, giving an opportunity set quite similar to the budget constraint in shape and interpretation:

(4.5) $$a = \frac{I_0 + wT}{P_a + wt_a} - \frac{P_c + wt_c}{P_a + wt_a} \cdot c.$$

As was true in the simpler formulation of the budget constraint, only the variable c on the right-hand side of this equality is controlled by the chooser. The remaining terms, including prices and consumption time costs, wage rate, time endowment, and nonwage income, are assumed to be fixed as far as this household's choice is concerned. This constraint therefore looks exactly like its simpler counterpart. The first ratio is the vertical intercept term. Both the numerator and denominator of this term contain only positive variables, so the vertical intercept is itself positive.

The slope of this opportunity set is linear and negative. This may be confirmed by noting that all terms in this ratio are also positive while the ratio itself carries a negative sign. The constraint in this case looks exactly like the simpler budget constraint. It slopes downward from a positive vertical intercept with a linear slope. Figure 4.10 depicts such an opportunity set.

The interpretation of this constraint is somewhat different. As in the earlier example, the vertical intercept expresses the total amount of ale that can be purchased when all income is devoted to the purchase of ale. In this case, however, that amount is given by an intercept term much richer in meaning. The numerator expresses the money value of all household assets, nonwage income and time. The household consuming no cake devotes all of these assets to ale, but here the assets must be devoted to two activities: purchasing ale and consuming it. The denominator therefore expresses the money value of both these activities per unit of a. That

Figure 4.10 *Opportunity Set with Prices and Consumption Time*

Combinations on this opportunity set reflect the assumption that all time must be exhausted earning income or consuming one of the two goods. The numerator of the vertical intercept measures the money value of all household assets, both nonwage income and time. The denominator measures the unit cost of a good, ale, in terms of both the price and consumption time cost. This ratio therefore gives the quantity of ale that might be purchased and consumed if all assets were devoted to ale. The slope is minus the ratio of the full cost of ale. As the wage rate appears in both numerator and denominator of this slope term, the opportunity cost of cakes will vary depending on the wage rate.

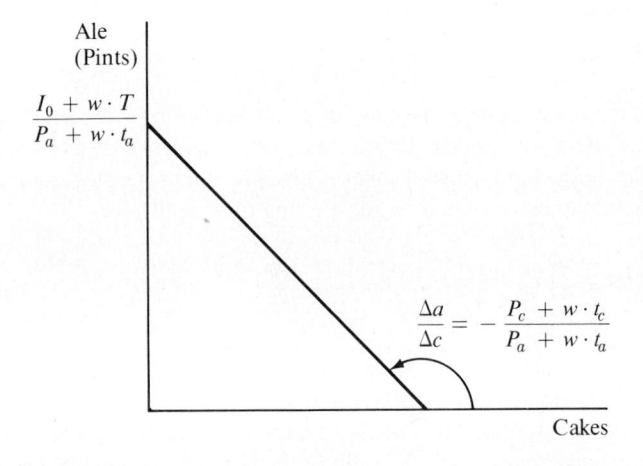

Ale (Pints)

$\dfrac{I_0 + w \cdot T}{P_a + w \cdot t_a}$

$\dfrac{\Delta a}{\Delta c} = -\dfrac{P_c + w \cdot t_c}{P_a + w \cdot t_a}$

Cakes

---

this intercept is equivalent to the result obtained with the simpler budget constraint is easily shown. Setting c equal to zero in Equation (4.4) yields:

$$aP_a + awt_a = I_0 + wT.$$

Recall that where c is zero, $T = at_a + t_w$. Thus, when we substitute for T, we obtain:

$$aP_a + awt_a = I_0 + wat_a + wt_w$$

$$aP_a = I_0 + wt_w$$

$$a = \dfrac{I_0 + wt_w}{P_a}.$$

The numerator is the total income of the household. This amount divided by the price of ale yields the total amount of ale that can be purchased with this income, the same value as the intercept of the simple budget constraint presented earlier.

While the slope of the earlier budget constraint is simply minus the ratio of the prices, the slope of this new opportunity set recognizes both the money cost and the time cost of consuming these goods. This term therefore contains the wage rate in the numerator and denominator. Unless the time costs happen to be proportional to the money prices of the two goods, the ratio, and therefore the opportunity cost of consuming cakes, will not be the same for households with different wage rates. This has important implications for household choice. In general, when the ratio of consumption time cost exceeds the ratio of money prices, an increase in the wage rate increases the opportunity cost of the relatively time-intensive good, and vice versa.

This can be shown as follows: Let $t_c = kP_c$ and $t_a = hP_a$ where h and k merely relate time to money cost per unit so that:

$$\frac{t_c}{t_a} = \frac{k}{h} \cdot \frac{P_c}{P_a}.$$

When k is greater than h, the ratio of consumption time cost exceeds the ratio of prices for these two goods. In this case, cakes are the **relatively time intensive good**. The opportunity cost of cakes is given by minus the slope of the opportunity set, which may be rewritten by substituting for t_c and t_a as:

$$\frac{P_c + wt_c}{P_a + wt_a} = \frac{P_c + wkP_c}{P_a + whP_a} = \frac{P_c}{P_a} \cdot \frac{1 + wk}{1 + wh}.$$

Consider the expression at the extreme right. In the case where k is equal to h—that is, when the ratio of the consumption time cost is equal to the price ratio—it is clear that the second term of this expression is unity. The opportunity cost of consuming cakes will equal the ratio of the prices regardless of the wage rate. In this case, wage rates have no effect on the opportunity cost of cakes. From this expression we may also see that the opportunity cost of cakes will exceed the price ratio when k is greater than h—that is, when cakes are relatively more time intensive. We may also see that when k exceeds h, an increase in the wage rate increases the numerator proportionately more than the denominator. *Increases in the wage rate therefore increase the extent by which the opportunity cost will exceed the price ratio.*

Consumption Optima with Different Wage Rates

We have seen how different wage rates yield different opportunity costs of consuming particular goods. Higher wage rates also increase the value of the vertical intercept, because they provide more wage income with which to purchase the good measured on that axis. However, as work time is not fixed, proof of this assertion is a bit more subtle than might be expected and cannot be demonstrated with the limited techniques that we are using in this text.[3]

---

[3]For the student more familiar with calculus, the proof of this point involves evaluating the derivative da/dw where a is the intercept of the opportunity set:

$$a = \frac{I_0 + wT}{P_a + wt_a}.$$

Taking the derivative of a with respect to w, we obtain:

Chapter 4 Household Choices 119

Figure 4.11   Wage Rates and Opportunity Sets

Increases in wage rates shift the opportunity set for purchase and consumption of two goods by increasing the vertical intercept and increasing the opportunity cost of the more time-intensive good. At the lower wage rate a combination along OS_1 must be chosen. The consumption optimum on OS_1 is combination F. As cakes is the more time-intensive good, an increase in the wage rate makes the slope steeper. At the higher wage rate the opportunity set is OS_2. The consumption optimum on OS_2 may be anywhere between combination G and combination Z. The increase in the wage rate may therefore result in consumption of either more or less of the time-intensive good cakes.

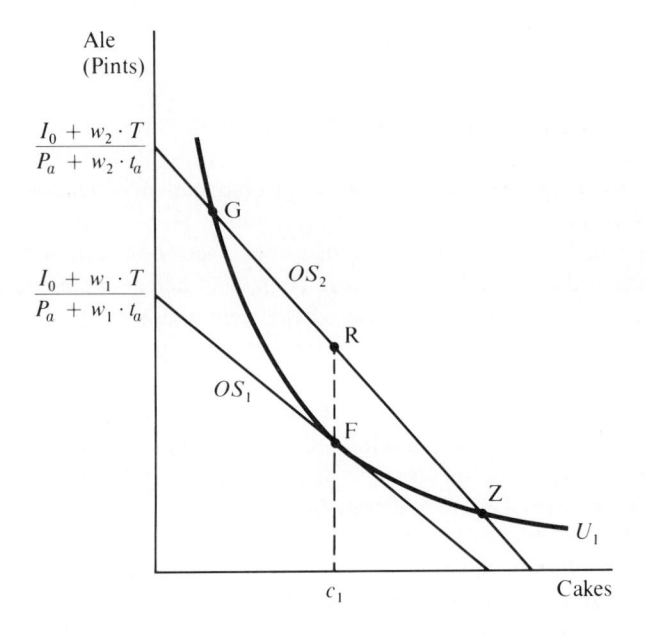

We will continue to assume that cakes are the time-intensive good—that is, t_c/t_a is greater than P_c/P_a. Observe the effect on a household's opportunity set of an increase in the wage rate in Figure 4.11. At the lower wage rate w_1 the opportunity set OS_1 has the lower vertical intercept and a flatter slope, reflecting the

---

$$\frac{da}{dw} = \frac{P_a T - I_0 t_a}{(P_a + wt_a)^2},$$

which is positive when $P_a T > I_0 t_a$—that is, when $T/t_a > I_0/P_a$. This must always be the case as long as households are constrained to consume all goods they purchase. The ratio I_0/P_a is the amount of ale purchased out of nonwage income. The ratio T/t_a is the total amount of ale that can be consumed if the total time endowment is devoted to consumption of ale. If any time is devoted to work so that total income exceeds I_0, more than I_0/P_a units of a will be purchased. Since T/t_a must equal total units of a consumed, T/t_a must in this case be greater than I_0/P_a. In the limiting case when no work is done and all time is devoted to consumption of a, the two ratios will be equal. In this case, clearly changes in the wage rate have no effect on the position of the opportunity set. No time is spent working; hence, wage changes have no effect on income.

lower opportunity cost. At the higher wage rate w_2 the intercept is increased, and the slope of this opportunity set, OS_2, is steeper. Clearly, it pays to have a higher wage rate: It makes possible consumption of larger amounts of ale with any amount of cakes chosen.

We cannot predict how this change alone will affect the amount of cakes consumed even though the opportunity cost of consuming cakes has been increased. At the lower wage rate, combination F is chosen. At the higher wage rate, any combination between points G and Z may be chosen. An indifference curve may be tangent to the higher opportunity set at any point between these two intersections of the original indifference curve and the higher opportunity set without violating our assumptions about preferences. Combinations between G and R contain less of cakes, and combinations between R and Z contain more.

Compensated Changes

A prediction can be made for a particular combination of changes. Observe the effect of an increase in the wage rate *and* a reduction of nonwage income. Nonwage income appears in our expression for the opportunity set, (4.5), only once—in the numerator of the intercept term. As I_0 does not appear in the coefficient of c, the slope of the opportunity set is independent of nonwage income. Changes in nonwage income affect the intercept but not the slope. An increase in nonwage income shifts the opportunity set outward from the origin, leaving it parallel to the original opportunity set; likewise, a decrease in nonwage income will cause a parallel inward shift of the opportunity set. In Figure 4.12, the household receives a wage rate of w_1 and faces the opportunity set labeled OS_1. The consumption optimum for this set of prices and wage rates is combination F. A wage rate increase to w_2 shifts the opportunity set in the manner just described to position OS_2. Again assume that cakes is the time-intensive good so that at the increased wage rate the opportunity cost (minus the slope of the opportunity set) is larger.

We must now identify the conditions of this particular reduction in nonwage income. Nonwage income is to be reduced so that the resulting opportunity set permits the household just sufficient time and income to purchase and consume the original combination chosen. This reduction in nonwage income is defined to be a **compensating change** in income, since it *offsets* the movement of the opportunity set due to the change in the wage rate. Such a reduction in nonwage income shifts the opportunity set to its final position, OS_3, parallel to OS_2 but shifted downward so that it passes through the original combination chosen, F. Thus, even with the higher wage rate, choice of combination F exhausts all time and income.

Compensated changes play an important role in the development of economic theory at many points in this book. In this particular case, a price (wage) change is accompanied by a compensating change in income. At other points, income changes are accompanied by compensating changes in prices. In each case, however, the purpose of the compensating change is to permit us to perform a ceteris paribus analysis of choice. Many changes that we wish to analyze affect both the choosers' command over all goods and the opportunity cost of one good in terms of another. In Figure 4.12, for example, a wage rate change expands consumption opportunities beyond those available along OS_1 as well as altering the opportunity cost of cakes in terms of ale. By making a compensating change in nonwage in-

Figure 4.12 *Opportunity Sets with a Compensated Wage Increase*

Cakes is the time-intensive good. An uncompensated wage increase shifts the opportunity set from OS_1 to OS_2. Reduction in nonwage income shifts the opportunity set downward but parallel to OS_2 through the original consumption optimum, combination F. This results in the choice of combination H, which contains less of the time-intensive good cakes than original combination F.

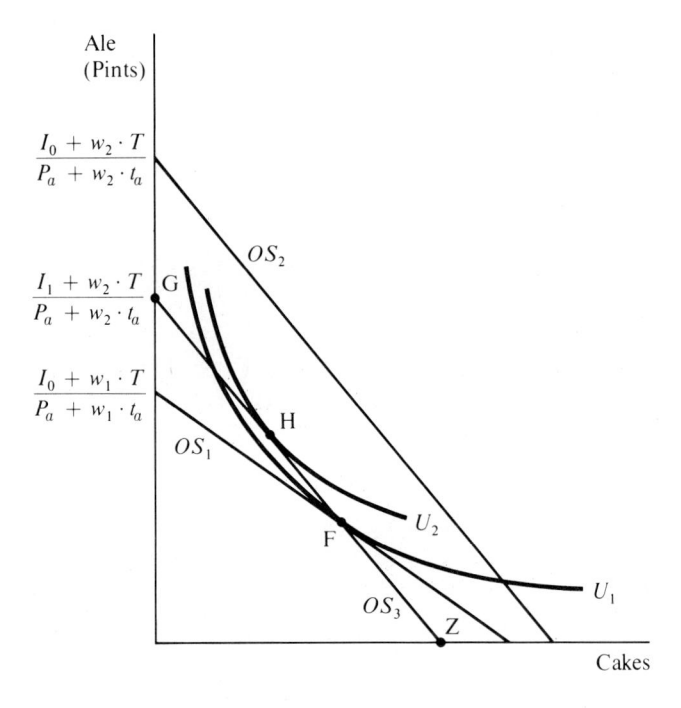

come, we are able to isolate the influence of the effect of the opportunity cost change alone. The reader is advised to give this analytical technique careful attention.

Clearly, this compensated change in the wage rate results in less of cakes being chosen at the higher wage rate. This may be confirmed through the following logic. The combination chosen at the higher wage rate and lower nonwage income must be a point somewhere on the opportunity set OS_3. But those combinations that lie between F and Z are below the original opportunity set, OS_1. In choosing combination F originally, the household expressed a preference for this combination to all others on or below OS_1. Having indicated a preference for F over any point from F to Z along OS_3, the household will not now choose any of these combinations after the shift in the opportunity set. As OS_3 intersects OS_1 from above, however, there must be some combinations between G and F that are preferred to F. Let the most preferred combination along OS_3 be combination H. All points on OS_3 between G and F contain less of cakes than combination F, and H must lie on this segment. Our theorem is therefore established: *The combination chosen at the higher wage rate with a compensated reduction in nonwage income must contain less of the relatively time-intensive good.*

The Economics of Sunday Papers and Winnebagos

In order to apply our theory of time cost and choice, it will be useful to convert our definition of relative time intensity into a more useful form. Recall that the definition of relative time intensity for cakes requires that:

$$\frac{t_c}{t_a} > \frac{P_c}{P_a}.$$

By cross-multiplying, we see that this implies that cakes will be relatively time intensive when

$$\frac{t_c}{P_c} > \frac{t_a}{P_a},$$

that is, when the ratio of the consumption time cost to the price of one good is higher than that ratio for another good. As an example, an afternoon spent flying a kite is relatively more time intensive than a night at the opera. The consumption time cost is approximately the same, but the money price of kite flying is considerably lower.

Applying this theory requires that we identify occasions in which compensated wage changes occur. Perhaps the most obvious is the change that occurs at retirement. On the date of retirement, the wage rate falls to zero. This decrease in the wage rate is compensated for by increases in nonwage income in the form of income from retirement plans and social security. We should therefore expect people to consume relatively more time-intensive goods in retirement than they did during their working years. Another way of saying this is that we should expect to see a larger number of retired people consuming relatively time-intensive goods than working people.

There are many observations that tend to confirm this implication. Compare the average age of travelers to Europe who go by steamship to those who go by airplane. The money prices are just about the same when allowance is made for the food, accommodations, and recreational activities provided on a ship. The time cost of steamer travel is greater, however, suggesting that relatively more retired people will make the passage by ship while relatively more working people will fly. The same comparison may be made with overland travel. Retired people will tend to travel more by automobile, while working people will fly—indeed, the theory suggests that disproportionately more retired households will purchase vehicles adapted to extended highway travel. This leads us to predict that retired households form an important part of the market for Winnebagos and other recreational vehicles.

Another example in which such comparative statics may be performed is within the household itself. Typically, the adults work while the children do not. One reason why this is so is that the market wage rates of the adults exceed those of the children. The lower wage rates of the children are compensated for (at least to the children) by nonwage income bestowed on them by their parents. Our theory therefore predicts that goods consumed by children will be relatively more time intensive than those consumed by their parents. Thus, it is not surprising that most kite flyers are children while most opera audiences are adults. Parents will choose several big nights on the town, while for a similar expenditure the children will be packed off to summer camp for a month. In both these cases the children, for whom the opportunity costs of the relatively time-intensive goods are lower, consume more of these goods; their parents, who face a higher opportunity cost of these goods, choose fewer. A schoolboy plays soccer on Saturday morning, while his father plays golf. Both require about the same consumption time cost, but the money price of golf (green fees, carts, and lost balls) is greater.

A similar application may be found in the allocation of weekly consumption time. During working hours, the opportunity cost of consumption time per hour is the wage rate. On the weekend, however, the opportunity cost of this time is lower. We may therefore predict that adults will consume relatively more time-intensive goods on the weekend than on workdays. This suggests that more golf and tennis will be played on weekends while recreation during business hours will be limited to a leisurely lunch or a quick glance at *Sports Illustrated*. The willingness of people to spend more time reading on weekends may explain why the Sunday paper in most cities is so large compared to its weekday counterpart.

There is reason to believe that this theory of consumption time cost may even be used to predict consumption differences among households with different wage rates. As noted earlier, such comparisons may be made only when higher wage rates are accompanied by compensating reductions in nonwage income. Thus, no predictions may be made when wages alone differ among households. However, in Chapter 16, a theory of wage differentials will be presented suggesting that higher wages are often associated with compensating income reductions. In order to earn higher wages, workers typically must undergo training to obtain the skills that command these wages. This training is usually acquired by sacrificing time that might otherwise be devoted to work. In equilibrium, the value of work forgone will equal the value of the higher wages obtained, just compensating for the higher wages.

To the extent that this is true we may use the theory presented here to compare the consumption bundles of goods chosen by accountants and bookkeepers, lawyers and clerks, or doctors and nurses. If the higher wages earned in each of these comparisons are indeed fully offset by forgone earnings during the training periods, then we should be able to predict lower consumption of time-intensive goods by the high-wage workers. Accountants will travel more by air while bookkeepers will travel by automobile; lawyers will attend plays while clerks will read them; doctors will ski in Austria while nurses will ski in Vermont. Note in each of these cases that these differences are not predicted on the basis of wealth; the value of earnings over entire careers is the same in each. It is the higher opportunity cost of time-intensive goods that leads the high-wage workers to choose fewer time-intensive consumption activities.

Bid Rent Curves

In a related application of time cost we may develop a rudimentary theory of the prices and consumption levels of residential land. This development may be used to explain two widely observed features of this market. First, we observe that the price of real estate falls as we move away from the center of the city. Second, among households with the same income we observe a relatively higher rate of land consumption as distance from the city increases. There are topographical features that make certain areas more attractive than others and architectural factors that make homes in some areas more desirable than others. A theory that seeks to explain *all* variation in residential land prices can be very complex indeed. We will restrict ourselves here to consideration of those factors producing these two general features.

In order to simplify the problem, we will assume that each wage earner has a fixed amount of time that he or she may devote to work and to commuting to and from the center of the city, where each is employed. Let the total time available be T, which is divided between work, t_w, and commuting, t_c. We may therefore express total time as $T = t_w + t_c$ and work time as $t_w = T - t_c$.

Assume further that the household consumes two goods, land (h) and all other goods (y). It must purchase these goods at their respective prices, P_h and P_y, out of the income obtained from work. Let the wage rate be w so that income available for the purchase of these goods is $w \cdot t_w = w \cdot (T - t_c)$. Now assume that all income is spent either on land or on other goods so that total income equals total spending:

$$wT - wt_c = P_h h + P_y y.$$

This expression may be solved for the quantity of other goods, y:

(4.6)
$$y = \frac{wT - wt_c}{P_y} - \frac{P_h}{P_y} \cdot h.$$

This forms another opportunity set identifying combinations of land and other goods that may be consumed at varying commuting times.

Consumption time is not incorporated in this model. The opportunity cost of land (minus the slope of the opportunity set) is therefore simply the ratio of the prices of housing and other goods. The intercept term must be positive. Commuting time t_c cannot exceed the total time endowment T; hence, the numerator is positive, as is the denominator, P_y. This intercept expresses the amount of y that might be purchased if all income net of commuting cost were devoted to y. This naturally depends on the commuting costs themselves. Assume that commuting costs are zero; that is, the residence of the household is in the city center so that t_c is zero. In this case the vertical intercept is simply $w \cdot T/P_y$. Any move from the center of town in any direction that raises commuting time will therefore reduce the vertical intercept. For any given commuting time, however, and therefore for any location, the opportunity set identifying purchasable combinations of land and other goods is given by a familiar looking diagonal line that has a positive intercept and a constant negative slope.

Now let us consider how a particular household would value land at different distances from the city center. This will be illustrated in Figure 4.13. Here we fix the rental price of land at the center of the city. Let this price be P_h^1 per year. Housing in this location involves no commuting cost, so the intercept of the opportunity set as just noted is wT/P_y, and it has a slope of P_h^1/P_y. Let the consumption op-

Figure 4.13 *Determination of Land Price Bids*

At the city center, the opportunity set for housing and other goods is given by OS_1. The vertical intercept is given by the ratio of income to the price of other goods, and the slope is minus the ratio of the housing price to the price of other goods. As commuting time increases, income net of commuting cost decreases, causing the vertical intercept to fall. With no compensating fall in the price of land, this would shift the opportunity set to OS_2. In order for land at this distance from the center to be equally attractive to land at the center, its price must fall to P_h^2, permitting the opportunity set to rotate to position OS_3. The consumption optimum on OS_3 is X, which lies on the same indifference curve as F.

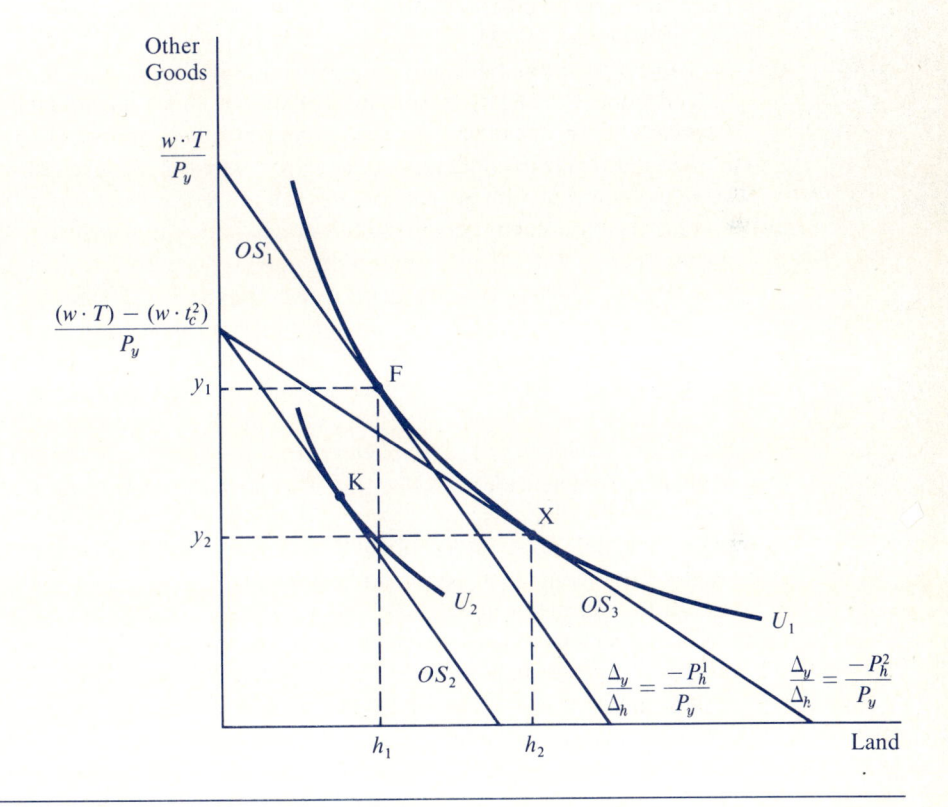

timum for this opportunity set be combination F which, when consumed, provides the household with the utility indicated by indifference curve U_1. Under these circumstances, the household will choose to consume h_1 units of land[4] and y_1 units of other goods. The rental prices for land at locations remote from the center of town may then be obtained by determining the price reduction at each location that permits the household to enjoy the same utility as from the location in the city center.

---

[4]This theory explains only the variation in the price of residential land. The price of structures will depend on construction costs.

We will assume for the moment that commuting is done at a constant velocity so that commuting time is proportional to distance traveled, d. For a given distance d_2, the commuting time will therefore be the amount t_c^2. As noted, positive commuting time lowers the vertical intercept by the amount of the commuting cost. The new intercept will be $(wT - wt_c^2)/P_y$. At unchanged land prices the opportunity set faced by this household at this location would be that indicated by OS_2. Under these circumstances this household and other similar households would decline to locate here. The consumption optimum along OS_2 is combination K, yielding lower utility U_2. At a lower price of land, however, the household could obtain a combination along the original indifference curve, U_1. The maximum land price that permits consumption of such a combination is P_h^2, associated with opportunity set OS_3.

Note the shift in the opportunity set that results from the decrease in the price of land from P_h^1 to P_h^2. The price of land appears in the opportunity set equation (4.6) only in the slope term. As it occurs in the numerator of this term, a decrease in the land rental price P_h makes the slope less steep. As changes in this price leave the intercept term unchanged, this fall in the price of land has the effect of rotating the opportunity set around its vertical intercept in a counterclockwise direction. For a fall to P_h^2 the opportunity set will rotate from position OS_2 to position OS_3, at which it is just tangent to the original indifference curve, U_1. The opportunity set OS_3 permits consumption of combination X containing h_2 units of land and y_2 units of other goods. This combination provides the same utility as combination F, since it lies on the same indifference curve.

The household would, of course, welcome even greater price decreases for land at this location, since they would permit consumption of combinations lying on higher indifference curves than U_1. This price, P_h^2, nevertheless identifies the *maximum* price that this household would offer for land at this location. At prices greater than P_h^2, no combination on U_1 could be purchased out of the income remaining after commuting costs had been borne. This household would therefore decline to offer prices in excess of P_h^2.

Readers should appreciate the similarity between the process used to develop these rental price offers and that used in the theory of time cost in the previous section. In the theory of time cost, wage rate changes caused differences in the opportunity costs of consuming two goods. In order to make predictions using that theory, it was necessary to impose the condition that the change in opportunity cost be compensated for by a change in nonwage income. In a sense, the rental price offer model reverses this theoretical process. A move from one location to another changes net income. In order to discover what rental price offer the household will make at the new location, we must inquire what price change will compensate for the income reduction implied by the higher commuting costs at the new location. In the former case, the theory was initiated by price (wage) changes requiring compensating income changes. In the present case, the theory is initiated by (net) income changes due to different commuting costs that require compensating price (offer) changes.

Figure 4.14 shows how successive rental price offers are generated for locations of increasing distance from the city center. Opportunity set OS_1 in panel (a) corresponds to OS_1 in Figure 4.13. This is the opportunity set for the household residing at the center of town and incurring no commuting cost; the distance from

Figure 4.14 Derivation of the Bid Rent Curve

Panel (a) shows the opportunity set at the city center, OS_1, and compensated opportunity sets OS_2, OS_3, and OS_4 at increasing distances from the center. The higher commuting cost at each successive distance is compensated for by an increasingly large fall in the price of land. The bid rent curve connecting distance and price at each location is shown in panel (b).

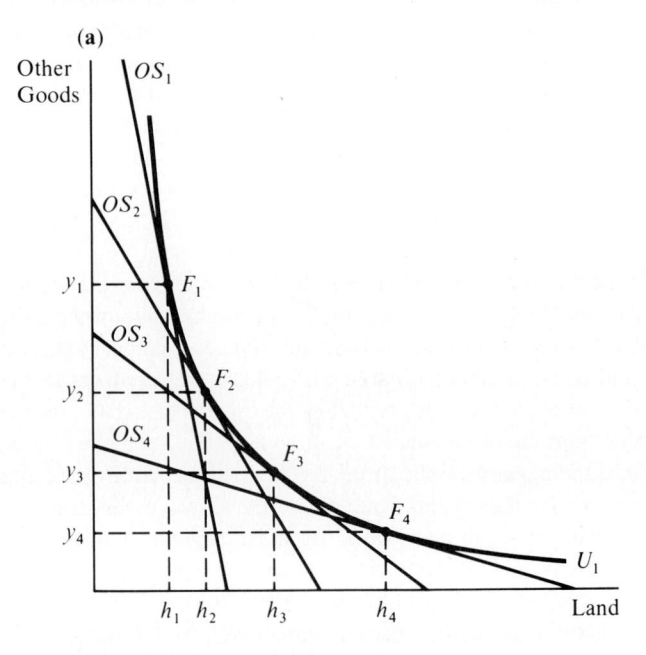

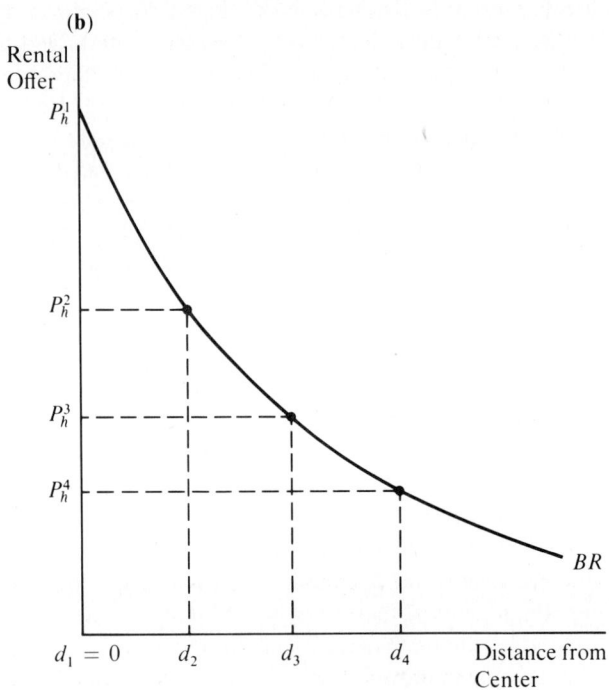

the city center d_1 is zero in this case. In panel (b), we depict the implied relationship between distance and rental price offer. Where distance (and thus commuting costs) are zero, the rental price offer is P_h^1. At positive distance d_2 commuting time costs are incurred, lowering net income and therefore the vertical intercept in panel (a). This requires a compensating reduction in rental price offer, rotating the opportunity set at this distance to position OS_2. The rental price offer corresponding to this slope is P_h^2 in panel (b). Similarly, at distance d_3 higher commuting costs are incurred, lowering net income even further. This requires a larger compensating price reduction so that the position of the opportunity set at this location will be OS_3. The rental price offer corresponding to the slope of OS_3 is P_h^3. By the same logic, a still larger distance, d_4, implies a still larger price offer reduction, to P_h^4.

The logic of the process should by now be apparent. For any given distance from the city center there is identified a maximum rental price offer for land that a household with a particular income will bid. The curve connecting all such distance and price offer combinations is called a **bid rent curve**. This curve must slope downward to the right, reflecting the lower offers that will be made at greater distances from the city center.

From the negative slope of the bid rent curve we may explain one of the general features of residential land prices noted when this topic was introduced: Rental prices must fall as distance from the city center increases. The supply of land is fixed at each location. Price at each location will therefore be that which clears the market. Competition among households at every location will raise the price to that implied by the bid rent curve (BR). No household will offer a price at any location that exceeds that indicated by the bid rent curve, since utility U_1 can always be obtained at the central point. The price offers, and therefore market rental prices, of any wage rate group will always be lower for more distant locations than for locations closer to the center of town.

Observation of panel (a) of Figure 4.14 also permits us to explain the second general feature: the tendency of households with the same income to consume greater quantities of land in more remote locations. Note that at the center combination F_1 is chosen; this contains h_1 units of land and y_1 units of other goods. As distance from the center increases, the household will choose combinations F_2, F_3, and F_4 successively, each containing more land and less of other goods. This pattern results from the fact that the opportunity cost of land relative to other goods falls as the price of land itself falls while net income reductions compensate for this decline in opportunity cost. Land is substituted for other goods, which are relatively more costly at remote locations.

Some Observations on Rapid Transit

One of the most vehemently debated urban issues of the last two decades has concerned the construction and operation of fixed-rail rapid transit systems for our major cities. Proponents of these systems maintain that the air pollution and congestion costs of relying on the automobile for intracity travel are excessive. They argue further that the improved speed of movement provided by rapid transit systems will revitalize those city centers suffering from urban decay, giving commuters more rapid access to the center and giving the poorer residents of central cities access to jobs that may be available on the periphery. Opponents argue that these advantages are exaggerated. They maintain that congestion and environmental problems are not the sources of urban decay. They hold that widespread ownership of the automobile in the postwar period has made it possible for many employers to take advantage of the relatively low cost of land in the suburbs, and that it was the earlier widespread reliance on streetcars and buses that molded cities into their "wagon spoke" shape. Possession of automobiles by the masses of working people permitted them to get to jobs located away from these major conduits. In other words, these opponents of rapid transit argue that it is the high cost of central city real estate that has influenced employers to locate outside the city, not congestion and commuting costs. They claim that the building of costly rapid transit systems will provide transportation along routes where it is no longer widely demanded and therefore cannot be cost effective.

We cannot begin to resolve these issues here. Courses in urban economics treat them in detail and present the evidence for and against each position. However, we can illuminate some aspects of the arguments employing the model of real estate prices developed earlier. We can, for example, consider some of the effects of the construction of a rapid transit system on rental prices in the city and on the periphery and some possible results of these changes on location decisions by business.

Let us assume that most employment continues to be offered in the central city giving rise to the falling rent gradient just described. Recall that commuting time lowers net income, requiring compensating rental price adjustments as distance from the center increases. A rapid transit system lowers the required commuting time at locations along the routes of the system. It therefore expands the geographical area associated with each commuting time, since area itself expands with radius from the center. This should have two predictable effects. First, it will reduce all rents. An increased supply of land at each commuting time must clear each market at lower prices. Second, it should reduce the slope of the bid rent curve. As commuting time at a given distance from the center is decreased, the differential in rent at this location relative to rent at the center will itself decrease. Thus, even if employer location decisions are made on the basis of land prices in the center versus the suburbs, this process should make location in the central city more attractive relatively as well as absolutely.

This is not to argue that the introduction of rapid transit is justified everywhere. Rapid transit is not free—indeed, it is prodigiously expensive. A proper evaluation of such a policy requires consideration of the construction and operating costs on the one hand and the reductions in commuting costs on the other. It is quite possible that the stimulus provided by lower central city rents will be inadequate to attract sufficient employers and riders to make a system self-supporting in the long run. Certainly experience with newly built systems under the federal UMTA program supports such a conclusion.[5] This experience suggests that such systems have difficulty covering operating cost alone.

---

[5]George W. Hilton, *Federal Transit Subsidies: The Urban Mass Transportation Assistance Program* (Washington, D.C.: The American Enterprise Institute, 1974).

Nor should these conclusions about falling rents due to the introduction of rapid transit systems be extended to marginal extensions of existing systems. Consider the case of Kathy Banks, who works in the banking district of Chicago. Until recently she lived in a rented apartment with no access to rapid transit. For years she drove to her job but looked forward eagerly to the extension of the rapid transit system into her neighborhood. When completed, the line reduced her commuting time from 45 to 15 minutes, and her commuting costs were reduced by her wage rate times the 30-minute savings per trip. Unfortunately for Kathy, her good fortune was short-lived. Other workers in the central city were also hoping to avail themselves of this commuting time savings. They competed with Ms. Banks for her apartment by offering higher rent, reflecting the increased value of this location. In the end it was the apartment owner who benefited from the opening of the line in Kathy's neighborhood. The market price of this location was bid up until it was equivalent to other locations offering the same commuting time.

It may well be the case that the ultimate rent charged at this location was lower than the rent previously obtained for the smaller area offering 15-minute commutes to the banking district. However, a small extension of such a system leaves the size of areas offering other commuting times unchanged. Generally it will not lower and flatten the rent gradient as will the introduction of a whole system. In such a case, it is quite possible that rents will actually increase in areas where commuting times are affected—indeed, that might prove the rule rather than the exception for marginal changes such as this.

Summary

In this chapter we used the theory of choice to explore the behavior of households in making market purchases. We developed expressions for the opportunity set in different contexts and observed how choices of combinations of goods were influenced by changes in variables that determined the position of the opportunity sets. We began with the simplest formulation, the budget constraint. This opportunity set expresses the opportunity cost of purchasing an additional unit of a good in terms of the amount of another good that must be forgone. The consumption optimum was identified and characterized by the equality of the marginal rate of substitution between each pair of goods and the ratio of the prices of those goods.

The influence of changes in income and changes in prices on the position of the budget constraint was introduced. Increases in income shift the budget constraint outward parallel to the original curve. Changes in the price ratio affect the slope. A method of evaluating gains from trade was developed consisting of calculating the income reduction necessary to return the household to its original indifference curve prior to trade. We showed that freedom to purchase in the market secures for the household the maximum possible gains from trade. Transactions costs of selling in small quantities may imply a welfare loss in the form of forfeited gains from trade when in-kind goods are received. We analyzed the welfare loss associated with public housing programs from this vantage point.

In real life, many goods are composites of attributes combined in varying proportions that may themselves reflect relative prices. The changing design of American automobiles in the postwar period was interpreted in terms of this characterization. One im-

Chapter 4 Household Choices

portant feature of nearly all goods is that their consumption requires time. A more detailed model of household choice was developed that recognized not only the opportunity cost of purchasing but the opportunity cost of using each good. This latter cost varies depending on the wage rate. Goods that are more time intensive are relatively more costly for higher-wage households. This approach was applied to a number of hypothetical choices, including the differing consumption behavior of the very young, retired people, and working households. It was also applied to the allocation of consumption behavior over a week's time by those who work a standard nine-to-five schedule.

The principle of compensated changes was introduced. Many changes in the economic environment affect both the opportunity cost of an activity and the household's command over all goods and services. Changes in income alone can lead to almost any result; compensated changes in opportunity cost, however, lead to predictable results. The compensation may take one of two forms. In the time cost application, wage changes produce both changes in opportunity cost and changes in income. Nonwage income was therefore varied to compensate for the income change produced by the wage change. In the bid rent curve application, this process was reversed. Distance from the city center lowered net income due to the time cost of commuting. In this case, it was necessary to calculate the price change that compensated for the income reduction in order to identify bid rents at each location.

The theory of bid rent curves was used to explain two general features of the residential housing market. First, housing prices decline with distance from the center of town. Second, for households of given income, consumption of land relative to other goods increases as distance from the center of town increases. A few observations were made concerning the effects of the introduction of rapid transit in large cities. If such a system is effective in reducing the commuting times from all locations, it must lower all rental prices in the city and reduce the slope of the rent gradient.

Key Concepts

budget constraint
consumption optimum
gains from trade
endowment
income-compensating measure of welfare change

transaction costs
welfare loss
consumption time cost
relatively time-intensive good
compensated change
bid rent curve

Questions

1. *Easy* The slope of the budget constraint developed in this chapter was shown to be equal to minus the ratio of the prices of the two goods purchased. It was claimed, however, that this slope reflects the opportunity cost of one good in terms of the amount of the other forgone per unit consumed. Explain how the price ratio can reflect quantities of goods forgone.

Hard The slope of the budget constraint was shown to be linear for the cases discussed. What assumption does this reflect? What would the budget constraint look like if the price paid for one of the goods increased as more of the good was purchased? Would this imply different conditions at the optimum? Before answering, remember that purchasing an extra good in this case reduces what may be spent on the other for two reasons: (a) As in the fixed price case, the amount spent on the last unit may not be spent on the alternative goods, and (b) the price of all units already purchased must also increase as the quantity is increased.

2. *Easy* Assume that purchasing some goods requires the purchaser to bear costs (like travel costs) in addition to the money price of the good. If these costs are fixed per unit of the good, how will this affect the placement of the budget constraint? How will it affect the opportunity cost of the good including these transaction costs?

Hard Assume that such transaction costs may be avoided by purchasing many goods at each transaction and storing them for future use. Show diagrammatically the gain in utility from bulk purchase of one period's entire quantity of such goods. The purchase of most goods entails some transaction costs of this type. Why do you suppose people do not make one enormous bulk purchase of all goods and services consumed over their lifetimes?

3. *Easy* Explain whether true or false: If indifference curves were concave to the origin rather than convex, as economists assume them to be, individuals would always specialize in their consumption—that is, they would never buy some of each commodity but would devote their entire budgets to a single good.

Hard Mr. Flood finds it easier to resist drinking altogether than to stop after one or two. Mrs. Sprat has the same problem with chocolates, and Bob Tollison's weakness is brownies. What does this say about the indifference curves of these individuals with respect to the goods listed? None of them specialize exclusively in the goods referred to; they each devote some portion of their income to the purchase of other goods. How do you interpret this information?

4. *Easy* The Veterans Administration provides zero-priced hospital care to qualifying veterans in VA hospitals across the country. There are only 144 of these facilities in the United States, and many are located as far as 100 miles from some of the veterans they are intended to serve. Show how this travel cost may be incorporated into the opportunity set confronting beneficiaries of this program by making appropriate modifications in Figure 4.9. Explain why fewer than 20 percent of all veteran hospitalizations occur in these facilities.

Hard What alternatives could you suggest to the Veterans Administration to the present system of providing hospital care only in VA hospitals that would improve service to veterans at no additional cost? Can you think of any reasons why these alternatives are resisted by the Veterans Administration? By veteran organizations?

5. *Easy* The relative time intensity of consumption of some goods, like jigsaw puzzles and model airplanes, differs from that of the consumption of truffles and attendance at theatrical performances. Which are the relatively more time-intensive goods? What does this suggest about the identity of consumers and timing of the consumption of each of these goods?

Hard Some people, because of their choice of leisure activities, are described as "fast livers"; many of them are labeled "high rollers." Can you give an economic interpretation to the behavior giving rise to these epithets?

6. *Easy* Assume that the imposition of the 55 mph speed limit substantially increases the commuting time for most residents of Los Angeles. What impact would this policy be predicted to have on the relative prices of suburban and central city real estate? The increased price of gasoline has also substantially increased commuting costs. Will this have the same effect on relative prices of real estate in the two locations?

Hard The bid rent curves derived in this chapter were constructed on the assumption that wage rates were uniform for all demanders of land. What difficulties are introduced when wage rates among these demanders are permitted to vary? It can be shown that in such cases different bid rent curves exist for each wage rate. Whose bid rent curve will determine land rents at each location under these circumstances?

Chapter 5

The Theory of Market Demand

Connections This chapter applies choice theory to the analysis of demand. Relationships between quantity demanded and factors that influence that quantity are rigorously developed here. The reader may wish to review section 2.2 of Chapter 2, where these demand relationships were first introduced. Most of the analysis here builds upon the basic budget constraint construction developed in Chapter 4. Again use is made of the technique of compensation, in this case to isolate two separable effects on demand of changes in price. Price changes not only influence the quantity demanded but have important implications for the distribution of goods among competing demanders. These implications are explored here. Finally, the chapter contains the first application of the standard measure of responsiveness in economics, elasticity, which was discussed in general terms in Chapter 1.

In the previous chapter we grappled with the elements of choice theory in the context of purchases from a budget-determined opportunity set. Having honed our skills to a fine edge, we are now prepared to reconcile these principles with our discussion of demand in Chapter 2. In that discussion we related the quantity of a good demanded to such factors as the prices of that and other goods and demanders' incomes. But we merely asserted those relationships; we made no attempt to derive them from a logically based theory of choice. In this chapter we will attempt such a reconciliation.

We will begin with individual choice amidst changing prices and income. We will then extend the results to derive implications about aggregate market response to such changes. The chapter ends with a discussion of demand elasticities. Demand elasticities are measures of the responsiveness of demand to changes in income and prices. As such they represent the chief means of characterizing market demand for individual goods. These measures are therefore essential tools for the analysis of real-world market behavior.

5.1 Deriving the Demand Function

In Chapter 2 we asserted that demand for a good responds in a systematic way to changes in the price of that good, the price of other goods, and income. The quantity demanded of a good may be expressed as a function of these variables. We may state this relationship in general functional notation as

$$q_i^d = f(P_i, \bar{P}_j, I),$$

where q_i^d is the quantity of the ith good demanded, P_i is the price of that good, $\bar{P}_j$ is the vector of other prices, and I is income. In Chapter 4 we examined how individuals confronting an opportunity set determined by these variables would make choices. To reconcile these approaches we must determine whether it is possible to relate *changes* in these variables to changes in the choices so that the asserted demand relationships will hold.

The most important factor to keep in mind during this analysis is that the variables in the demand function operate through their influence on the opportunity set. They do not affect the rank-ordering process. People's appreciation of goods or combinations of goods is assumed to be independent of prices and income. The utility associated with a particular combination of goods does not rise or fall because one of those goods becomes cheaper or more expensive. Similarly, a rise in income for a household does not make the margarine consumed less tasty, though newly wealthier households may purchase less of it while buying more butter. The utility associated with the bundle of goods bought at lower incomes would still be obtained if that original bundle were consumed after income rose. It is the changes in the position of the opportunity set occasioned by changes in prices and income that lead to the observed preference for goods of varying quality under differing circumstances. Consumer *tastes* may indeed change over time as fashion and tech-

Changes in Income

An increase in income expands options for consumption of goods. It makes available a range of combinations of goods that were unattainable at lower income levels. This does not imply, however, that such an income change will be associated with increased demand for all goods. Consider Figure 5.1. In panel (a) we depict two consumer optima associated with different income levels. The combination of x_1 units of x and y_1 units of y is purchased at income B_1 (associated with vertical intercept B_1/P_y). The combination containing x_2 and y_2 is purchased at income B_2, which is higher than B_1. Neither price has changed, but the increase in income influences households to choose more of both goods at their original prices. Re-

Figure 5.1 *Income Consumption Curves*

Income consumption curves (ICC) connect all combinations of two goods for which the MRS is the same. Thus, if income is increased from B_1 to B_2 in each panel and prices remain the same, the combinations chosen will lie along the same ICC. The slope of the ICC reflects the response of demand for the two goods to changes in income. The ICC in panel (a) has a positive slope, indicating that both x and y are normal goods. The negative slope of the ICC in panel (b) suggests that one of the two goods (in this case, good x) is an inferior good.

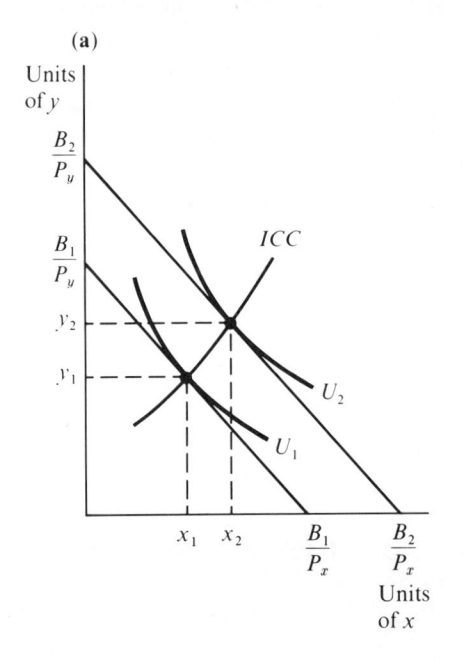

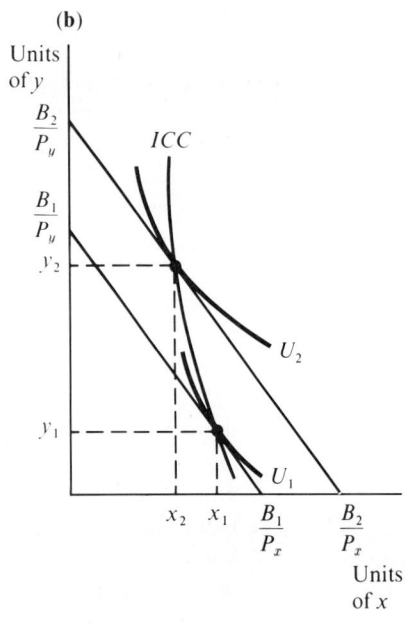

calling our definition from Chapter 2, both of these goods are *normal goods*: Demands for each are positively related to income.

Consider panel (b), however. The same income change results in less of good x being chosen. Good x in this case corresponds to our definition of an *inferior good*: Demand for x is negatively related to income. Note the lines passing through the consumer optima in the two panels. These lines identify the position of *all* such optima as income varies and prices of all goods remain constant. This curve is known as in **income consumption curve (ICC)** and will be used repeatedly in our discussions of household demand. If both goods are normal, the income consumption curve will have a positive slope. If one of the goods is inferior, the income consumption curve will slope downward to the right. The student should note that a line connecting two optima depicting y as inferior and x as normal will also have a negative slope.

Arithmetically it is impossible for all goods to be inferior though, as we note in panel (a), all may be normal. This may be demonstrated easily. Given a budget equation

$$B = xP_x + yP_y,$$

we obtain, by taking the total differential:

$$\Delta B = \Delta x P_x + \Delta y P_y.$$

By assumption the prices of the two goods do not vary. Any positive income change, ΔB, must be associated with a positive change in the right-hand sum. This can be true only if at least one quantity change, either Δx or Δy, is positive.

Income consumption curves are drawn for particular combinations of prices. It is therefore useful to note the effect of a price change on the position of an income consumption curve. There is no simple rule of thumb for such a shift, as the direction of movement for inferior goods depends upon whether x or y is the inferior good. It is therefore best to make such a determination on the basis of the properties of indifference curves.

The property of convexity states that indifference curves become less steep as they slope downward to the right. Each income consumption curve may therefore be thought of as dividing the goods space into two sections. In one section, the consumer's marginal rate of substitution will be everywhere greater than the price ratio. In the other, his or her MRS will be everywhere lower than the price ratio. Should the price ratio increase, it follows that the new income consumption curve will pass through that section of the goods space in which the MRS was greater than the previous price ratio. In Figure 5.2, for example, income consumption curve ICC_1 identifies all combinations of x and y that will be purchased by the individual depicted at any income so long as the prices remain P_x^1 and P_y^1, respectively. If the price of x rises to P_x^2, however, combinations along ICC_1 will no longer be consumption optima—the MRS at these points is P_x^1/P_y, not P_x^2/P_y. Without actually seeing the indifference curves, we cannot know exactly where the new income consumption curve will lie. However, because the new income consumption curve must connect all points at which the MRS equals the latter ratio, we know that it must lie in this case above ICC_1.

Figure 5.2   The ICC and the MRS

Any given ICC separates the combinations of goods in the two-dimensional space into two groups: those for which the household has an MRS greater than the price ratio and those for which the MRS is lower than the price ratio. A change in the price ratio alters the opportunity cost in ways that permit us to predict whether the new combination chosen lies above or below the original ICC.

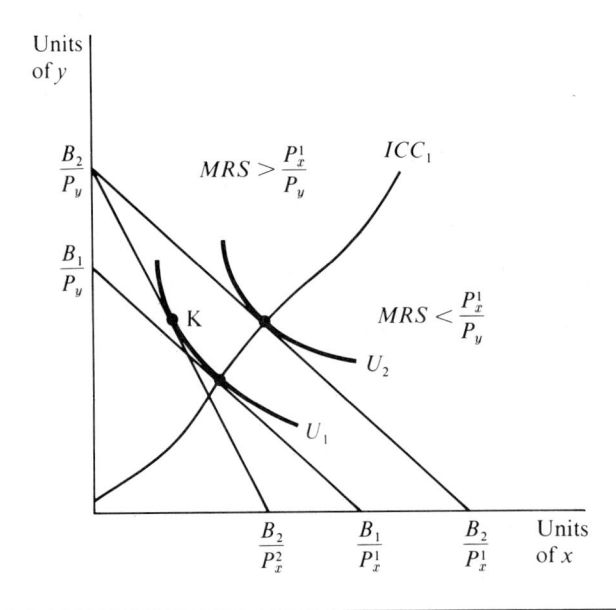

Real and Nominal Income

Another useful interpretation of the income consumption curve is that it links all combinations of the two goods for which the MRS is the same. This interpretation is important, for it permits us to identify combinations that will be chosen (that is, demanded) in terms of only two pieces of information, the opportunity cost and **real income**. If we know the market opportunity cost of good x and the level of real income enjoyed by the household, the combination chosen can be determined. In Figure 5.3, for example, only combination T produces utility U_1, with a MRS associated with the income consumption curve ICC_1. Other combinations will be chosen at the same opportunity cost that yield different real incomes; still other combinations will produce the same real income but will not be chosen at this opportunity cost. The intersection of ICC_1 and indifference curve U_1 determines T.

Each combination of real income and opportunity cost determines a different choice. For example, assume that some set of changes in prices and **nominal income** leaves the individual with the same real income but an opportunity cost equal to the MRS associated with ICC_2. The individual will choose combination K in this case. At the same time, opportunity cost and real income might change. Consider a change in real income to U_2 and the same change in opportunity cost.

Figure 5.3   *The ICC and Real Income*

The combination chosen depends on two factors: the opportunity cost and real income. All combinations chosen at the opportunity cost equal to the MRS at T are identified by ICC_1. Only combinations along U_1 provide the same real income as T. Combinations along ICC_2 will be chosen at a different and lower opportunity cost than those along ICC_1. If opportunity cost were lowered to this level and real income were simultaneously lowered to U_2, combination H would be chosen.

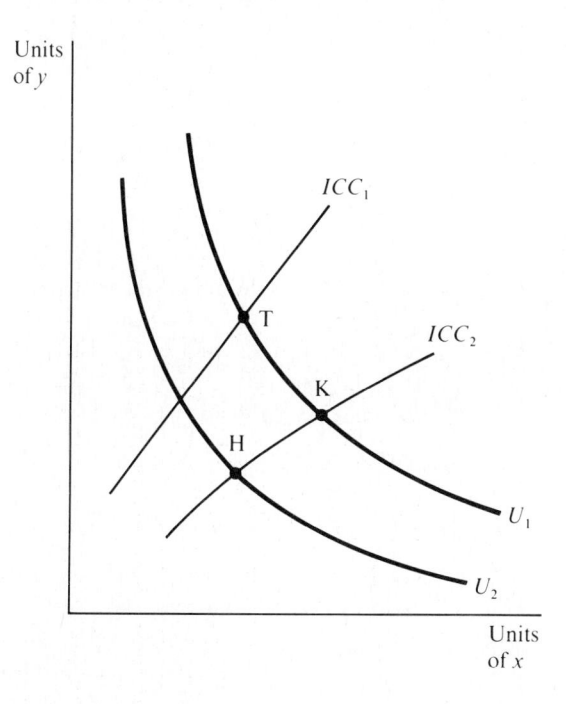

This would lead to the choice of combination H. Our ability to relate changes in these two variables to the quantities of goods chosen (and therefore to demand) permits us to predict the effect of price changes on demand. A price change can be shown to affect both opportunity cost and real income. The analysis of demand therefore involves identifying and measuring both of these influences.

Changes in Own Price

Changes in a good's own price, like changes in income, will shift the opportunity set and therefore affect the entire range of combinations of goods from which the household must choose. The combination chosen after such a price change will typically contain different amounts of all goods, including different amounts of that good whose price has affected the opportunity set. The first law of demand states that the quantity demanded is inversely related to a good's own price. Therefore, one might assume that the quantity of that good in the combination chosen

Chapter 5   The Theory of Market Demand

will be less when price rises and more when it falls. It is easy to show that this need not be the case for a single household.

Consider Figure 5.4. Here income remains constant at B per time period. At prices P_x^1 and P_y combination $x_1 y_1$ is chosen, as this is the only combination along the budget constraint at which the MRS is equal to the price ratio. Now let the price of x rise to P_x^2. Recall that the vertical intercept is given by the first term in the budget constraint, B/P_y. Neither variable in this intercept term is affected by the price change for x, so the shifted constraint will pass through this point as well. The numerator of the *slope term* of the budget constraint, $-P_x/P_y$, will be affected, however. An increase in the price of x raises the absolute value of the slope, making it steeper. An increase in the price of x therefore has the effect of *rotating* the budget constraint clockwise around a pivot point at the vertical intercept. Say this rotation shifts the budget constraint to the lower position in Figure 5.4. Clearly, it is possible for more of x to be chosen at this higher price for x. The

---

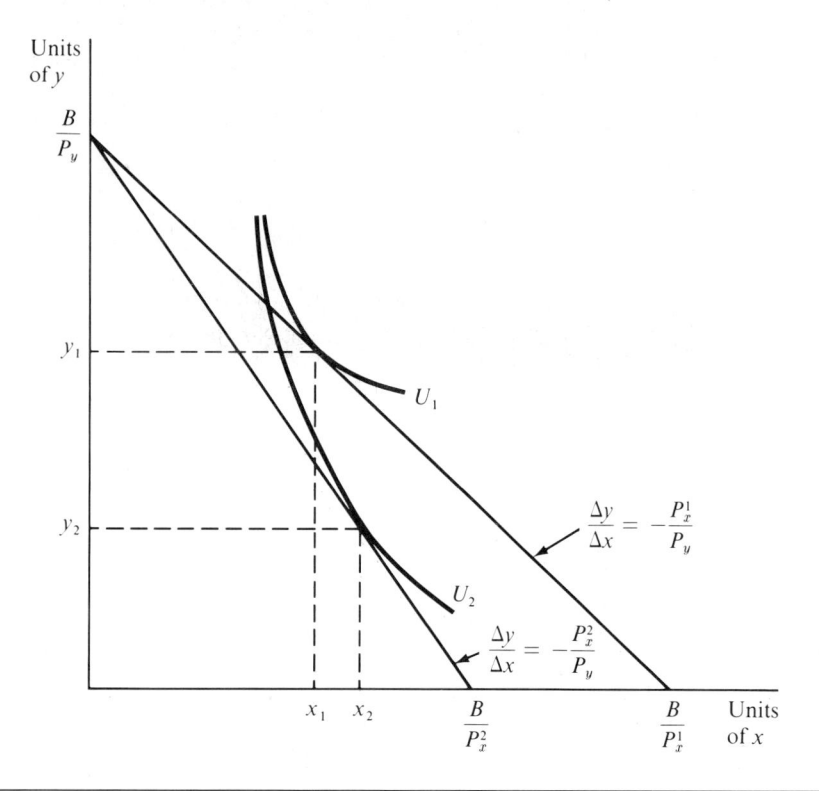

Figure 5.4   *Choice with Changing Price: The Perverse Case*

It is possible for an increase in the price of a good to lead to more of that good being chosen. An increase in the price of good x rotates the budget constraint clockwise around the vertical intercept. Here x_2 units of this good are chosen at the higher price, while a smaller number, x_1, was chosen at the original, lower price of good x.

Figure 5.5 *Choice with Changing Price: The Conventional Case*

Here less of good x is chosen at the higher price. At the original price of x, quantity x_1 is chosen. At the higher price of x associated with the steeper budget constraint, the smaller amount x_2 is chosen.

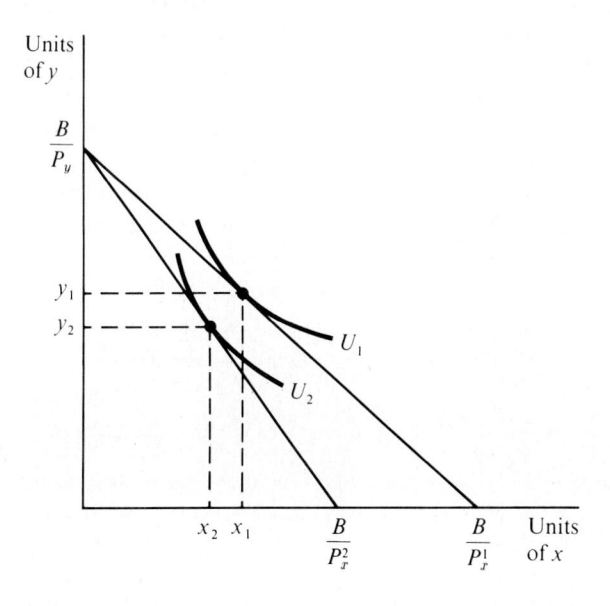

quantity x_2 selected at this higher price is larger than x_1 chosen at the lower price P_x^1.

This possibility, first described by the eminent Cambridge economist Alfred Marshall (without the aid of indifference curves), was attributed by him to another economist, Robert Giffen.[1] It has therefore come to be known as the **Giffen paradox**. As it raises at least the logical possibility of violations of the first law of demand, it warrants our close attention. We will therefore return to consider the Giffen paradox in due course.

First, let us be reassured that this result is only a possibility. *Inverse* relationships between price and quantity demanded can also be demonstrated, as may be confirmed in Figure 5.5. Here the same price increase depicted in Figure 5.4 results in less of good x being demanded at the higher price. We cannot rule out the result in either figure on the basis of admissable properties of indifferent curves. Both indifference curves in Figures 5.4 and 5.5 conform to the rules laid down in Chapter 3. Each indifference curve is downward sloping and convex to the origin, and none intersects another. The results depend solely on the positions of the curves.

---

[1] Alfred Marshall, *Principles of Economics*, 8th ed. (New York: The Macmillan Company, 1949), 132.

The first law of demand is not intended to hold only for goods for which indifference curves are favorably contoured. It is intended to apply to all goods. On the other hand, it is an empirical law meant to describe observed behavior, not a logical theorem to be proven or disproven. It does not state that upward-sloping demand curves are logically impossible; it holds that they will not be observed. We will therefore take a more detailed look at choice under conditions of changing prices. This analysis should provide a better understanding of why Murphy's law (also unprovable, by the way) does *not* hold in the case of demand curves: "Whatever can go wrong in this case does not go wrong!"

Income Effects of Price Changes

Note that the price increases in Figures 5.4 and 5.5 make both households worse off. Real income itself is reduced by the price increase. Household command over goods as a whole diminishes, and some modification in the combination chosen will be made on this basis. Note also that a change in the price of good x alone will alter its opportunity cost in terms of good y. This will also influence demand. A change in the price of a single good holding nominal income constant will therefore have two distinct effects on the ultimate combination chosen. An **income effect** results because price changes affect real income, influencing the household to choose more or less of the good. The **substitution effect**, on the other hand, is the result of the changed opportunity cost. We will consider each of these influences in detail.

We may identify the income effect of a price change by using the principle of compensation developed in Chapter 4. That is, by observing the quantities of x demanded before and after a compensating income adjustment has been made, we can isolate the influence of the real income change on demand. The income consumption curve just introduced is useful for this purpose. Panel (a) of Figure 5.6 depicts the response in combinations chosen to a price increase for a normal good. The original budget constraint extends from its y intercept, B/P_y, to the x axis at B/P_x^1. Given these opportunities, the chooser selects combination A containing x_1 units of x. The rise in the price of x rotates the budget constraint clockwise to an intercept on the x axis at B/P_x^2, and combination B is chosen containing x_2 units of x. We wish to identify the quantity of x demanded before and after an income adjustment is made that returns the chooser to his or her original real income. To do this, we need only observe the movement of the income consumption curve through indifference curves U_1 and U_2. This will give us the change in quantity demanded attributable only to the change in real income.

The same income consumption curve cannot pass through both point A and point B in panel (a). We know this because the chooser's MRS at B must be higher than at A, reflecting the different price ratios associated with these choices. The income consumption curve passing through point B must pass to the left of A on indifference curve U_1. The income consumption curve passing through A must cut indifference curve U_2 to the right of B for the reasons just discussed. This presents a methodological question: Which income consumption curve will be used to identify the income effect? Convention dictates that the curve associated with the new price of x—that is, the curve passing through point B—be used for this purpose.

Figure 5.6   *Substitution and Income Effects*

In both panels responses to price changes are decomposed into substitution and income effects. In each case the substitution effect is measured along the original indifference curve, U_1. Holding real income constant, the increase in the opportunity cost of the good causes substitution of combination C for combination A. The income effect is measured along the appropriate ICC curve. Good x in panel (a) is a normal good; hence, the reduction in real income due to the price increase of this good causes less of this good to be chosen. Good z in panel (b) is inferior; therefore, the income effect causes more of this good to be chosen.

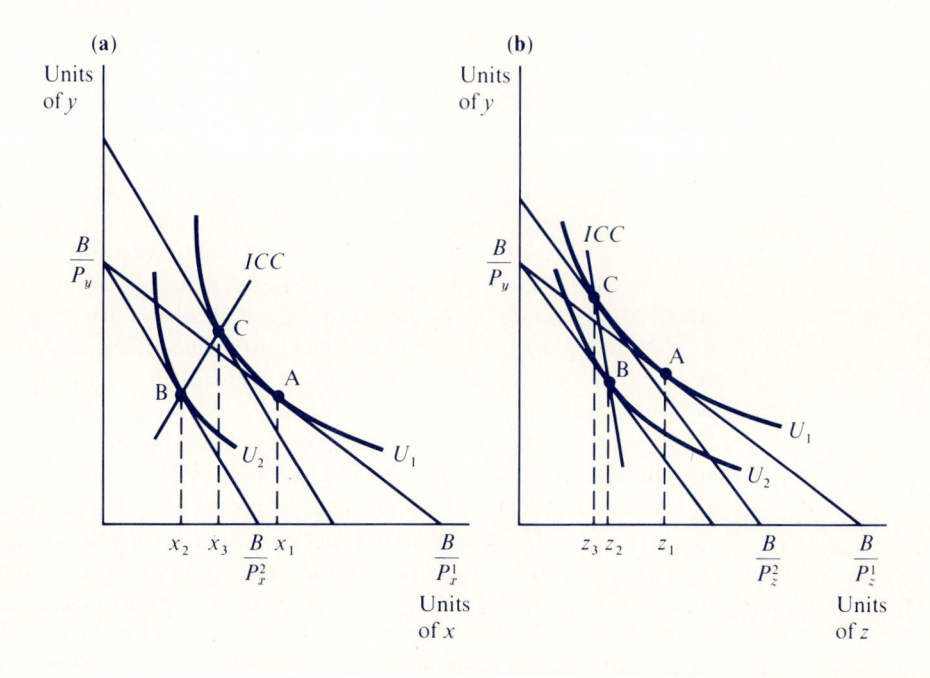

This curve cuts the original indifference curve U_1 at point C. Demand for x is thus shown to diminish from x_3 to x_2 as real income declines from U_1 to U_2.

Of the total change in the quantity demanded, $x_1 - x_2$, the income effect accounts for that part identified by the income consumption curve $x_3 - x_2$. The decline in real income produced by the price change reduces demand by this amount. Were money income increased enough to allow the chooser to purchase combination C at the new higher price of x, demand for x would increase from its level at B by precisely this amount.

Now let us apply the same logic to panel (b). This panel reflects choices of combinations of a different pair of goods, y and z. Units of good y are measured along the vertical axis again, but this time the horizontal axis measures good z. The vertical intercept B/P_y is, of course, the same, since spending of total income on y will permit purchase of the same number of units of Y (assuming that income and P_y have not changed). The horizontal intercept this time is B/P_z^1, and the slope reflects the relative prices of y and z rather than x and y. Combination A is chosen along this initial budget constraint, and a rise in the price of z to P_z^2 rotates the constraint clockwise as in panel (a). Again, the new combination chosen at the higher price is identified by point B.

An income consumption curve passing through B will cut indifference curve U_1 to the left of point A. In this case, however, the income consumption curve will have a negative slope. Recall from our previous discussion that a positively sloped income consumption curve indicates that both goods depicted are *normal* goods; a negatively sloped curve indicates that one of the goods is *inferior*. Inspection of panel (b) will reveal that the inferior good is z. A fall in real income from U_1 to U_2 in this case results in more rather than less of z being chosen. Instead of adding to the response of demand to the rise in the price of z, the income effect of this inferior good diminishes that response. In the absence of such an income effect, demand for z would decline by the amount $z_1 - z_3$. The reduction in real income due to the price increase of this inferior good *offsets* a part of that response.

Substitution Effects

Now let us consider the remainder of these responses to price changes. In each case considered, the income effects accounted for only a portion of the total change in quantity demanded. To what do we attribute the balance of this response? In each case we observe that the remainder of this response is identified by two points along the original indifference curve. The first occurs at the point at which the MRS is equal to the original price ratio. The second occurs at the point at which the MRS has risen to the new, higher ratio. Recall from Chapter 4 that consumer optimization requires consumption up to the point at which its value at the margin (given by the MRS) is equal to the opportunity cost (reflected in the price ratio). As the prices of goods rise, the opportunity cost of their consumption does also, and the opportunity cost of goods made relatively cheaper by the price change declines. Optimization therefore requires substitution away from goods whose opportunity cost rises relative to other goods. The shift from combination A to combination C in both panels of Figure 5.6 along indifference curve U_1 identifies such a substitution. It may be regarded as a pure substitution, because the change measured in this way is not "contaminated" by the influence of changes in real income. For this reason it is referred to as the substitution effect of the price change.

The direction of such substitution effects will always be in the opposite direction of the price change. This follows from the properties of indifference curve themselves. At point A in both panels the MRS must equal the original price ratio, and point C is positioned at the point where the MRS equals the new, higher price ratio. By the postulate of convexity, points along any indifference curve with higher MRSs (steeper slopes) must lie to the northwest in the goods space. Such points must reflect combinations containing less of the good whose price has risen. Substitution effects of price decreases, on the other hand, would involve substitution of more of goods whose opportunity costs had fallen relative to other goods. The chooser's MRSs at lower prices must themselves be lower, and points on indifference curves with lower MRSs (flatter slopes) must lie to the southeast of the original point. *Price increases lead to substitution effects that decrease demand for a good. Price decreases lead to substitution effects that increase demand for a good.*

Combining the Effects

Let us summarize the analysis of the effect of price changes on demand up to this point. Nominal income and prices determine real income and opportunity cost. Real income and opportunity cost themselves fully determine the combination of goods chosen. A change in a single price alters both real income and opportunity cost. The full influence of this price change on demand may therefore be broken down into the results of two separate influences: (1) the income effect, operating through the impact of a price change on real income, and (2) the substitution effect, reflecting the change in opportunity cost resulting from the price change. The full change in quantity demanded will equal the sum of these two effects. For the two panels of Figure 5.6, this implies the following relationships:

	Panel (a)	Panel (b)
Substitution Effect	x_1 to x_3	z_1 to z_3
Income Effect	x_3 to x_2	z_3 to z_2
Full Effect	x_1 to x_2	z_1 to z_2

Note that the substitution effect of the price increase depicted in both panels is negative. The substitution effect of a price *decrease*, on the other hand, is positive. Substitution effects invariably operate in the opposite direction from the change in price. The income effect of the price increase is negative in panel (a) and positive in panel (b). This is because the income effect operates through the influence of the change in price on real income, and different goods respond differently to changes in income. Thus, in panel (a) x is a normal good, and the decrease in real income due to the price change reduces demand for it. Good z in panel (b) is inferior, however, and the income effect of the price increase here results in more of z being demanded. The two effects are additive for normal goods and offsetting for inferior goods. The full effect of the price change is therefore larger than either the substitution or the income effect for normal goods. For inferior goods, however, the full effect must be smaller than the larger of the two isolated effects.

Compensated and Uncompensated Demand

Having broken down the response of households to price changes into two separate effects, we may now take advantage of this analysis to define two types of demand curves. The **uncompensated demand curve** reflects the influences of both income and substitution effects. (The analysis of demand to this point has applied to uncompensated demand curves.) The **compensated demand curve** reflects only the influence of substitution effects. The compensated curve is constructed under the assumption that real income is held constant by compensating payments that offset the income effects of price variation along it.

This distinction is illustrated in Figure 5.7. Panel (a) contains the choice analysis involving an increase in the price of good x. With the households' income and

Figure 5.7 *Compensated and Uncompensated Demand Curves for Normal Goods*

Panel (a) depicts the choices of combinations of goods both with compensated price changes and with uncompensated price changes. In panel (b) the quantities of good x chosen are related to price with a compensated price increase and with an uncompensated price increase. Good x is normal in this case; hence, the income and substitution effects are additive. The price increase therefore causes a larger quantity response with the uncompensated price increase than with the compensated price increase.

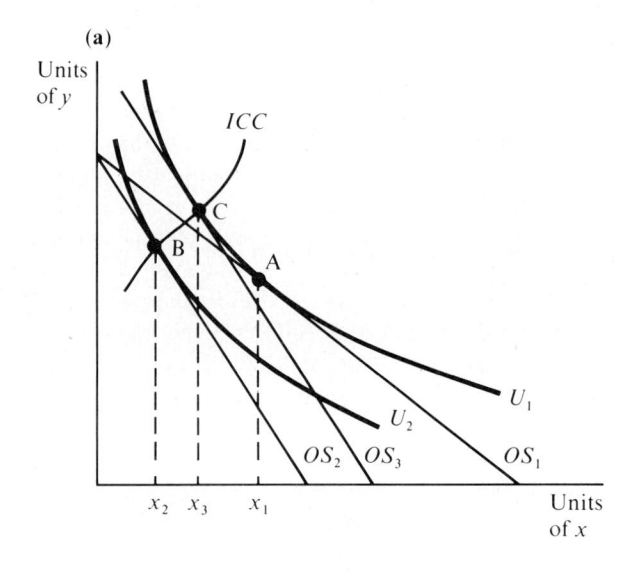

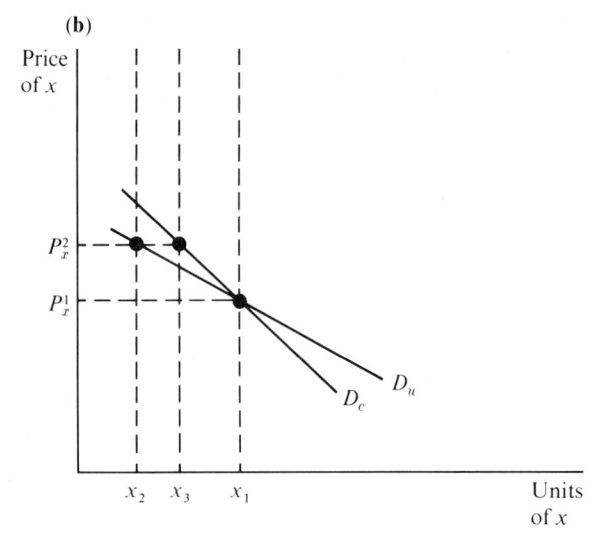

original prices determining budget constraint OS_1, combination A is chosen containing x_1 units of x. Thus, in panel (b), at the original price P_x^1, both demand curves indicate a quantity demanded of x_1 units. In panel (a) the effect of the higher price of x is to shift the budget constraint to the position OS_2, leading the household to choose combination B containing x_2 units of x. As we have confirmed, this response reflects both a substitution effect (x_1 to x_3) and an income effect (x_3 to x_2). A demand curve reflecting the combined effect of this price change on quantity demanded is an uncompensated curve. Curve D_u, which indicates that the quantity x_2 is demanded at the higher price P_x^2, is therefore an uncompensated demand curve. This curve reflects the full influence of price on demand through its effects on both real income and opportunity cost.

A compensated demand curve reflects only the influence of the change in opportunity cost—that is, it reflects only the substitution effect of such a price change. This is identified in panel (a) in the manner just established. The effect of the price change on real income is to lower utility from U_1 to U_2. Real income is therefore restored by giving the household sufficient income to shift the budget constraint to position OS_3, along which combination C can be purchased. The quantity chosen at the higher price under these circumstances is x_3. Thus, in panel (b) the compensated demand curve D_c indicates that the larger amount x_3 is demanded at price P_x^2. This curve gets its name from the fact that price variation along it is *compensated for in its derivation*. Real income is held constant at every price.

The good whose demand is analyzed in Figure 5.7 is clearly a normal good. The income consumption curve *ICC* has a positive slope. In the case of normal goods, the income effect of price changes is added to the substitution effect. The uncompensated demand curve reflecting the sum of both effects is therefore less steep than the compensated curve containing only the substitution effect. Over the same price interval, the response to any given price change is greater along an uncompensated curve than along a compensated curve for normal goods. The opposite is true for inferior goods. Figure 5.8 depicts the derivation of compensated and uncompensated demand curves for an inferior good, z. The income effect of this price increase is to increase the demand for z from z_3 to z_2. The combined response reflected in the uncompensated demand curve D_u is therefore smaller than the substitution effect alone reflected in the compensated curve D_c. The uncompensated curve D_u is therefore steeper in this case.

Why Two Demand Curves?

Economics students have been known to express resentment at this point. "Why have two types of demand curves?" they exclaim bitterly. "Isn't one enough?" Unfortunately, one is not enough. Price changes that economists must analyze are of two types. One is the result of innovation or technical change. Suppose someone invents a new fertilizer that permits twice the amount of wheat to be grown per acre, lowering the production cost and therefore the prices of bread and flour. Consumers of these products are made better off by this technical change. The lower prices have real income effects. Alternatively, suppose that, due to regulation of production processes, the costs, and therefore the prices, of textile goods

Figure 5.8   *Compensated and Uncompensated Demand Curves for Inferior Goods*

These two panels reflect the same process depicted in Figure 5.6. Good z, whose price increases in this case, is inferior. The income and substitution effects of this price change are therefore offsetting. The total response to this price increase must therefore be smaller than the substitution effect. The compensated demand curve in panel (b) therefore reflects a larger response than the uncompensated demand curve.

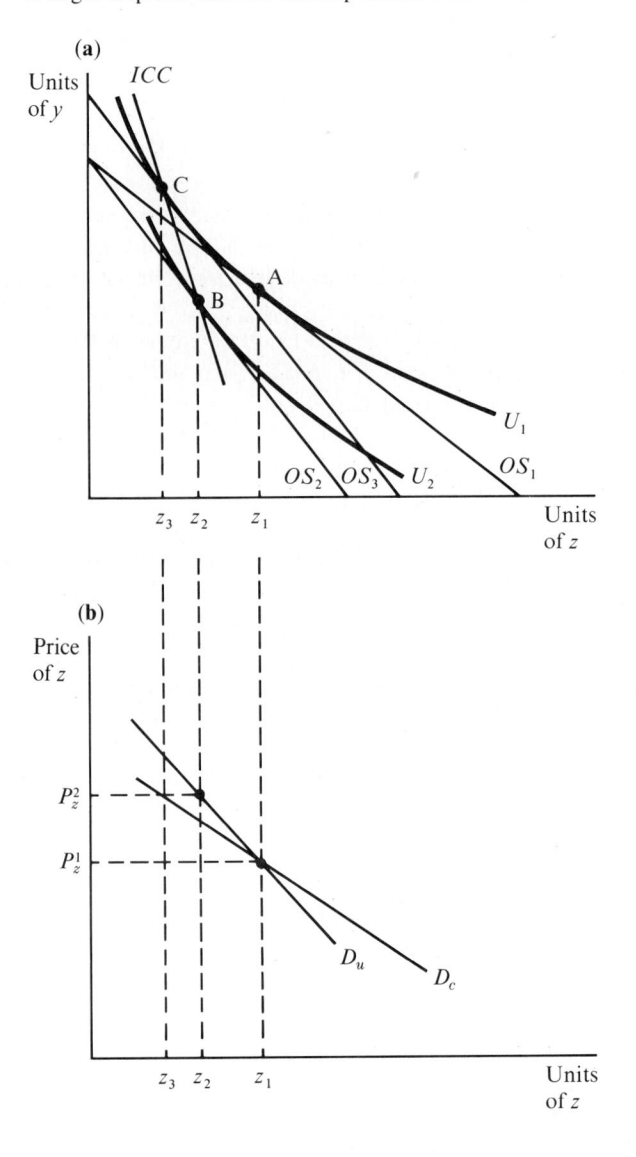

increase. Consumers of these products are harmed by this government-imposed change that increases prices. In both these cases the income effects of the price changes are experienced by consumers. These income effects should therefore be incorporated into an analysis that seeks to predict the full response of demand to this type of price change.

More commonly, however, demand analysis is used to predict responses to price changes *that are not accompanied by income effects*. This may seem implausible, but it is true. Unless technology or the resource base changes at the same time price changes, the same total productive capacity of the economy is available to provide goods to consumers. The consumers as a group may be influenced to consume different goods, but the higher price of one good does not imply that consumers are necessarily worse off. Consider the simplest case: The government places an excise tax on one good, which raises its price. Has the typical consumer been made worse off by this policy? This depends on what is done with the revenue from the tax. What if the tax is used to finance the reduction in another tax? Consumer budgets net of tax are unaffected on average by this price increase; they pay more for the good that has been newly taxed. This price increase is *compensated* for, however, by the reduced taxes from other sources. The opportunity cost of the newly taxed good is increased, but the real income of consuming households is virtually unchanged.[2]

Under these circumstances compensated demand curves are required for estimating demand. Such curves reflect the effect of changing opportunity cost alone. However, this is not their only application. Consider the case in which instead of simply reducing other taxes the government uses the tax revenue raised to finance cash transfers to everyone. Again there is no resource withdrawal from the productive sector. The same resources are there to produce goods for the consumers who are taxed, and the money is there, too. Only the opportunity cost of the taxed good is changed. As consumers are influenced to reduce their consumption of this good, resources are freed to produce other goods for these same consumers. Real income will be virtually unchanged in this case as well.

Finally, consider the case in which the government taxes a good and uses the revenues to finance something like police protection. Certainly there is a resource withdrawal from the private sector in this case. The production of police services is not costless. Resources are required for this production that cannot be used to produce substitute goods in the private economy. Even here, however, compensated demand curves may be appropriate. Police protection is valuable. It is a substitute good itself: The more we consume—other things constant—the better off we are. Goods provided by government, like police protection, national defense, roads and highways, and schools, can compensate us for the higher prices we pay for taxed goods. In estimating the response of demanders to the higher prices that

---

[2] This is not to say that individual consumers cannot be harmed by such a tax substitution. Some purchase more of certain goods than others, and they will therefore suffer more than others from the imposition of particular taxes. Likewise, some will benefit more from tax reductions than others. On average, however, the net effect of tax "reform" of this type is to leave everyone more or less on the same indifference curve.

Taxes do have an impact on aggregate welfare, though this is small relative to the full amount of the tax. This issue will be discussed in Chapter 18.

result from such taxes, it is therefore appropriate to use demand estimates that consider substitution effects alone. We must therefore use compensated demand curves in these cases.

When do we use which? This depends on the question we seek to answer. Many economists are engaged in analyzing the effect of government policy on different sectors of the economy. Clearly, here the appropriate demand curve for analysis is the compensated curve. Goods and services are taxed and occasionally subsidized, and we wish to know the effects of this fiscal activity on the affected markets—that is, if the aggregate effect of such policies is expected to leave real incomes of consumers unaffected on average, then the compensated curve is appropriate. Sometimes, however, questions arise requiring the use of the uncompensated curve. When OPEC raised the price of crude oil to the world market, this represented a withdrawal of resources from the economy. Less oil was made available for consumer use. This withdrawal had important income effects, and forecasts of demand at those higher prices should have taken these effects into account. Uncompensated demand curve estimates were appropriate in this application.

The answer to the above question therefore turns on income effects, as might be expected. The reader must determine whether the price changes contained in his or her observations are the product of changing resource commitments to the production of the good considered or whether these prices reflect some "artificial" force like a tax or a subsidy. The latter influence can alter the opportunity cost of a good without affecting real income. Sometimes taxes are levied for explicit production projects in the public sector and therefore involve resource withdrawals from the private sector. In that case compensated demand curves may be the appropriate tools for the analysis. The test there is whether the production in the government sector is likely to fully compensate for the resources withdrawn.

The Giffen Paradox Examined

The possibility of upward-sloping demand curves raised in connection with Figure 5.4 may now be considered. First, we may observe that such a possibility is ruled out for compensated demand curves. These curves contain only substitution effects of price changes, which must invariably operate in the opposite direction of the changes. When price rises, the quantity demanded along a compensated demand curve must diminish. If the Giffen paradox exists, it does so in the form of an uncompensated demand curve.

Uncompensated demand curves for normal goods must invariably slope downward as well. In this case both the substitution and income effects operate in the opposite direction from the price change. If the price rises, the uncompensated change in demand represents the sum of two reductions in quantity demanded: a negative change due to the substitution effect and another negative change due to the income effect of the price change.

A Giffen good, if one exists, must then be an inferior good. For the uncompensated demand curve to have a positive slope, the income effect of this price change must be larger in magnitude than the substitution effect so that the sum of these two effects will have the sign of the income effect. The geometry of this result is presented in Figure 5.9. Combination A is chosen along the original budget constraint at the initial price of x. As the price of x increases, the constraint

Figure 5.9 *The Giffen Paradox*

The Giffen paradox is a logical possibility only for uncompensated demand curves for inferior goods. It can be seen to occur in this case only because the income effect measured along the ICC is larger in magnitude than the substitution effect. The substitution effect of the price increase depicted decreases the quantity demanded from x_1 to x_3. The income effect of this price increase increases the quantity demanded (holding opportunity cost constant) from x_3 to x_2.

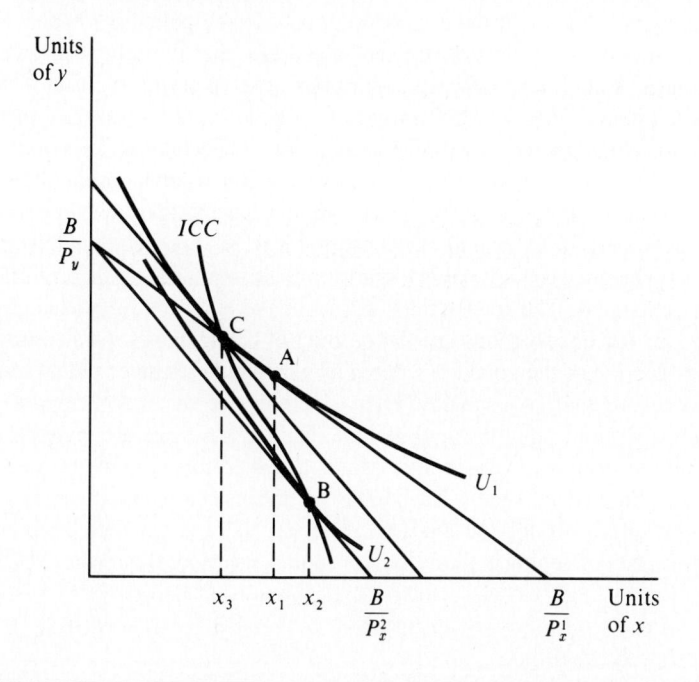

rotates clockwise around the vertical intercept, and combination B is chosen. Combination B contains more x than combination A, however, by the amount $x_2 - x_1$. Examination of the figure reveals that the substitution effect of this price has in fact reduced demand from x_1 to x_3. Good x is inferior in this case, however, so the income effect of this price increase influences the chooser to demand more. This income effect of the lowered real income from U_1 to U_2 increases quantity demanded from x_3 to x_2. As the income effect is larger in magnitude than the substitution effect, the sum of the positive and negative effects is positive. The quantity of x demanded rises with price.

Will we ever observe consumers seeking to purchase more of anything at a higher price than at a lower one? At least we know where to look. It may occur only on occasions when the price rises due to changing technology or resource endowments that produce income as well as substitution effects. It may also occur only with inferior goods—and important inferior goods, at that. The Giffen paradox depends on the income effect of the price change being more influential than the substitution effect. These conditions taken together give us some clues that help to explain the rarity of this phenomenon. The conditions taken together represent an unlikely combination.

5.2 Aggregating Demand

The analysis of choice thus far has been developed exclusively in terms of a single chooser. Typically, however, demand curves are discussed at the market level and reflect the combined choices of all demanders. The process of aggregating demand across households is an important but easily understood extension of our theory.

Figure 5.10 contains three panels. Panels (a) and (b) contain demand curves of individual households for gasoline. Studies of demand for gasoline indicate that it is a normal good. We assume that the Smith household in panel (a) has a higher income than the Brown household in panel (b) but similar tastes. Under these circumstances the Smith household will demand more gasoline at any given price per gallon than will the Brown household. The demand curves in these two panels are

Figure 5.10 *Aggregating Demand across Households*

Market demand represents the sum of the quantities that each household will seek to buy at each price. At prices above P_3 only the Smith household is willing to buy any, and their demand is the market demand. At the lower price P_1 the market demand quantity is $q_1 = q_1^S + q_1^B$. Equilibrium in the market will occur at a price of P^* and a market quantity of q^*, with q_2^S going to the Smiths and q_2^B being purchased by the Browns.

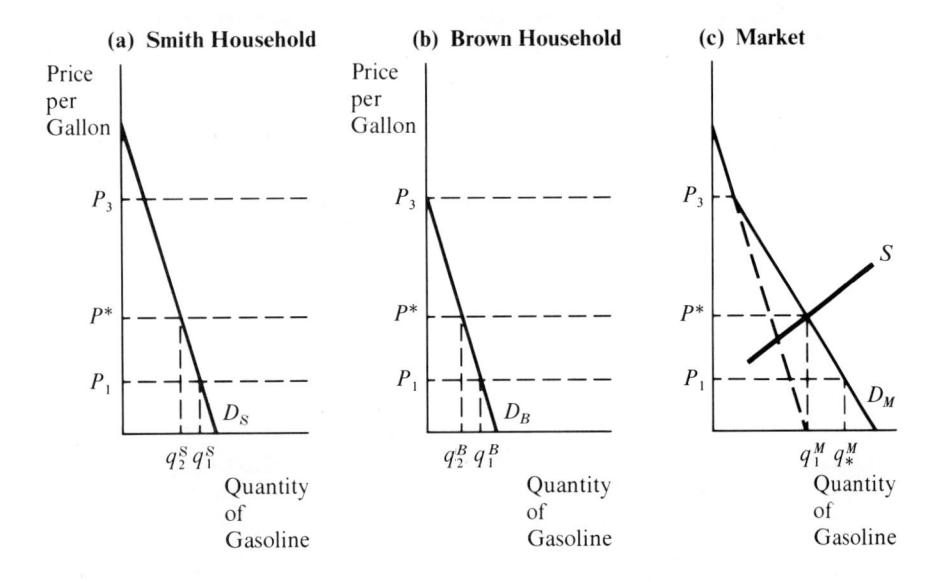

drawn to reflect this difference in demand. At price P_1, for example, the Smith household demands q_1^S while the Brown household demands the smaller quantity q_1^B.

To simplify we will assume that these two households are the only demanders of gasoline. The **market demand** for gas may be determined by simply adding up the quantity that all households demand at each price. In Figure 5.10, therefore, market demand may be obtained by adding the quantity that the Smiths demand to that demanded by the Jones in panel (c). In that panel, total quantity demanded at price P_1 is $q_1^S + q_1^B = q_1$. The point (q_1, P_1) identifies the quantity that the market will demand at price P_1 and thus represents a point on the demand curve. At price P_3, the Browns cease to demand any gasoline. The market demand at prices higher than P_3 is therefore only that quantity demanded by the Smiths—they *are* the market at these prices.

It is quite easy to construct market demand curves from individual household curves. For normal goods we simply draw the demand curve of the highest-income household into the diagram, then "lean" the remaining curves up against it in descending order of income (the order would be reversed for inferior goods). This leaning process must satisfy two conditions. First, the point of contact of the curves must occur at a price corresponding to the price intercept of each added curve. Second, the horizontal distance between the added curve and the one on which it is leaning must represent the quantity demanded by the household at each price. Market demand is illustrated by the rightmost curve at each price, shown in our diagram by the solid line.

By introducing market supply into panel (c) we may determine not only the equilibrium market price and quantity but also the distributional results. Given supply curve S, we see that the equilibrium price will be P^*. Equilibrium quantity will be q^*, with q_2^S gallons going to the Smiths and q_2^B going to the Jones. Each household gets exactly the quantity it chooses at the equilibrium price. In our example the more affluent Smiths get more gasoline, but this is because the Browns have chosen to devote less of their smaller budget to this good. The Browns could buy as much gasoline as the Smiths, but to do so would mean doing without things they would rather have.

Altering the Distribution of Goods

The government occasionally seeks to interfere with the distributional results of market exchange. In response to the manipulation of oil prices by OPEC in the 1970s, Congress gave the President power to introduce rationing of gasoline should an emergency require it. The frequent use of this term in this context requires that we make a clarification. The use of the term **rationing** to denote government nonprice constraints on the purchase of certain goods is misleading; it suggests that in the absence of such constraints no rationing will take place. Clearly, this is not true. Government rationing is merely an attempt to replace one form of rationing (that based on price) with another. Typically, the objective is to eliminate *variation* in the amounts going to households differently circumstanced. Another objective frequently advanced in defense of this practice is that it prevents *hoarding*. The ability of this policy to achieve either objective is illuminated by our analysis.

Figure 5.11 Market Demand with Price Controls

The demand curve D is a market demand curve. With supply at S_1, the market equilibrium price is P_1. If supply shifts to S_2, the equilibrium price rises to P_2. If prices are not permitted to rise above P_1, a shortage equal to $(q_1 - q_2)$ will develop.

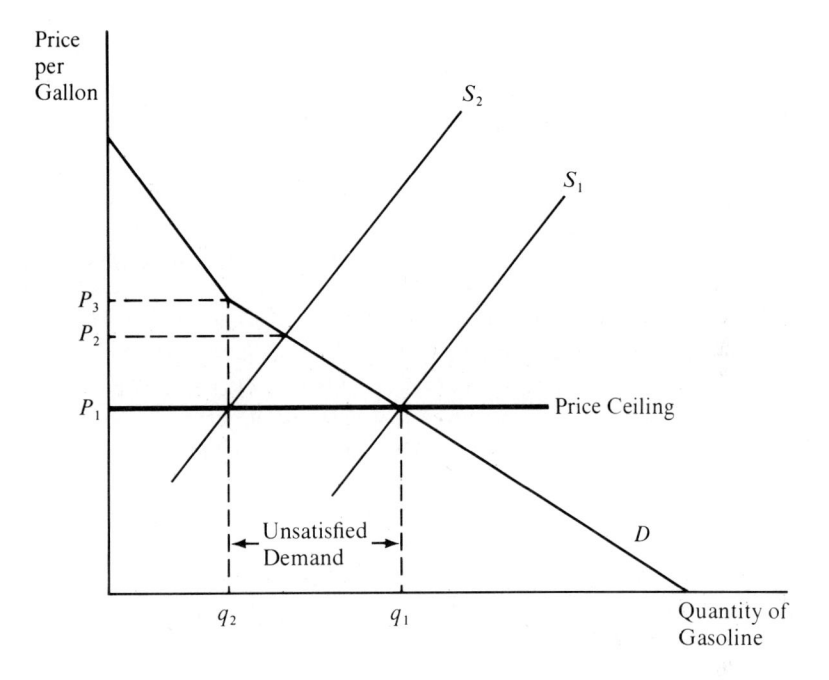

First let us set the stage. Rationing is typically discussed in connection with markets in which supply shifts dramatically leftward. This is obviously true in the case of petroleum products. Figure 5.11 contains the same information as panel (c) of Figure 5.10, except that here supply has shifted to the left. Equilibrium price should rise to P_2. Government intervenes, however, preventing price from rising. Given the new supply curve, S_2, only q_2 will be supplied at this price, but the Smiths and the Browns have no reason to alter their desired purchases; they will seek to continue to purchase their usual quantities. However, these quantities sum to q_1, which is more than is now supplied at price P_1. Shortages develop, and hoarding begins.

The Economics of Hoarding

What are people doing when they hoard? Hoarding means buying more than one intends to use right away—in other words, stockpiling. Why is this done? So far our theory has developed no role for consumer inventories of goods. Holding inventories is costly business, as anyone in retail trade will tell you. Inventories must be stored, accounted for, and rotated, and purchasing them consumes current dollars that might be deposited in banks to earn interest. Consumers who hold inventories bear these same costs. Are they being foolish to do so?

Not necessarily. In Chapter 2, we simplified our discussion of disequilibrium prices by casting it in terms of a good—student seating at a football game—that could be obtained and used only in fixed quantities. Let us return to that example for a moment. Recall that one may sit in only one seat, no matter how early one arrives. The wait for that seat is the cost that each student must bear to watch the game. Imagine what happens, however, if some students are permitted to save seats for others. Fraternity pledges are often designated to perform this role. For a wait of a particular length, the cost *per seat* is reduced as more seats are saved.

Permitting seat saving lengthens the market-clearing waits for those actually doing the waiting. The market clears only when the cost per seat rises to equal the value of a seat to the marginal student. The value of a seat to the marginal student is not affected by seat saving, only the cost per seat per waiter. If each waiter can save only two seats, for example, the cost per seat per hour waited is halved. The market will therefore clear only when the length of the wait has doubled. This will reestablish the cost per seat at its market-clearing level.

In general, when a good is rationed by waiting, the market clears only when the wait *per item* obtained has a value equal to the market-clearing price of the good. For example, if a good is underpriced due to price controls, the market will clear only when the wait per item is worth the difference in the market-clearing price and the controlled price. Thus, the more one may buy per wait, the longer one must wait to buy.

Goods whose prices are controlled are often marketed under conditions analogous to the seat-saving example. When gasoline prices were held below market-clearing levels in 1973 and 1979, lines formed to clear the market. Once purchasers arrived at the pump, however, they were free to purchase as much gasoline as they could put into their tanks at the controlled price. A substantial part of the cost that was paid for gasoline was the wait to obtain access to the pump. That wait was incurred per purchase, not per gallon. The cost per gallon could therefore be lowered *by purchasing more gallons*. Few people failed to "fill up" under these circumstances.

Clearly it makes sense to hoard gasoline when waiting is doing the rationing. The more one buys after having waited in line, the lower will be the cost per gallon. We should therefore expect people to increase the average quantity that they purchase when prices are below the market-clearing level. Let us note some important lessons from that experience:

1. One must make a distinction between gasoline purchases and gasoline use. As we saw, prices below the equilibrium level caused people to increase the size of their average purchase. Under the circumstances described, however, we know that with less available the equilibrium cost per gallon would have risen. In Figure 5.11, for example, that cost per gallon (including waiting cost) must rise to P_3 for the available quantity q_2. Gasoline use must therefore decline.

2. The hoarding described was constrained by people's ability to store gasoline. Though some people added to this capacity by purchasing cans, this way of adding to capacity is dangerous and was eschewed by most users. Most people stored only the amount they could put into their car's tank. Capacity may therefore be treated as fixed for practical purposes.

3. Although purchases and use may have diverged dramatically in the short run, this would not have been true in the long run, when several purchases would have been involved. If consumers had had a fixed capacity to store gasoline, once that capacity was filled more could have been put into their tanks only as fast as it was taken out (that is, used). Furthermore, the same reasoning leading to larger initial purchases influenced demanders to wait longer before refilling. One may, in other words, have increased the size of the average purchase by refilling when the needle reached the quarter mark rather than the half mark. Doing so had the same lowering effect on the per-gallon cost of gasoline. Once the initial hoard was purchased, inventories of gasoline in consumer hands would have been on average no larger than previously.

With this information one may construct a scenario for events in this market that seem to fit the pattern of the gasoline crises discussed. The decrease in available supplies coupled with price controls resulted in queuing to ration these stocks. People responded by increasing their purchases, a one-time phenomenon that nevertheless severely strained the inventories of gasoline distributors. Inventories of local suppliers were shifted into the tanks of demanders, and some suppliers actually ran out temporarily.

Because the cost of gasoline per gallon had risen due to the added cost of waiting, gasoline *use* diminished. In Los Angeles, where both gas crises were acute, the freeways were practically empty during periods of the day when congestion was the rule. This was true in spite of the fact that people were buying gas in unprecedented quantities. Once everyone's tanks were filled, however, gasoline purchases diminished to the rate at which it was being used (that is, less than before). Flows of gasoline to suppliers caught up with demand, and the crises were over.

5.3 Demand Elasticities

The quantity demanded by all consumers has been shown to be influenced by income of the demanding households and by market price. Theory and a priori reasoning have permitted us to predict certain aspects of the responsiveness of quantity demanded to changes in these variables. For example, we hypothesized earlier that goods defined broadly are more likely to be normal goods than goods defined narrowly. We also hypothesized that the more narrowly a good is defined, the more substitutable it is likely to be for other goods.

The extent to which we may rely on such rules and hypotheses concerning demand functions is clearly limited, however. The analysis of policy by business firms or government may require more exact information about demand functions than can be provided by these means. The impact of price controls, for example, will be quite different for goods whose demand is highly responsive to price than for goods for which quantity demanded varies little over broad price ranges. Moreover, we may hypothesize with greater confidence if our conjectures concerning these demand relationships are verified by observation of real-world market behavior. Economic analysis bolstered by facts can be counted upon to receive

Figure 5.12 *Income and Quantity Demanded*

Economists frequently must interpret relationships between two variables in the presence of such disturbing factors as measurement error and unobserved variables. The relationships identified in these cases can never be precise; it is necessary to "fit" a function to data such as these. The best fit is one that minimizes the summed squares of the errors, such as e in the figure.

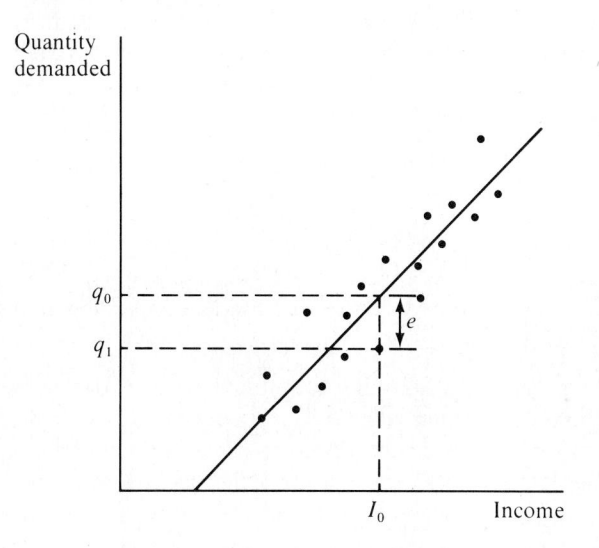

a less skeptical hearing among men of practical affairs than can presentations consisting solely of diagrams and assertions.

Both of these observations lead us directly to the need for demand measurement. Theories may be verified only by recourse to data on income, price, and quantity demanded; otherwise, they are mere conjecture. It is therefore necessary to establish methods for measuring and estimating these relationships. The balance of this chapter will be devoted to developing some basic building blocks essential to this measurement.

The central element here is the concept of elasticity discussed in Chapter 1. Responsiveness of quantity demanded to income might be measured by observing slopes—that is, we might record changes in quantity demanded associated with rising incomes over time or observe differences in purchases by households with differing incomes, taking care in both cases to insure that the price of the good was held constant. These estimates might reveal a pattern like that illustrated in Figure 5.12. One measure of the responsiveness of demand to changes in income is the slope of the curve fitted to such observations.[3] The problem with such a measure

---

[3] As noted earlier, economic theory assumes that some functional relationship exists between income and quantity demanded. Estimation of this relationship is confounded by the fact that it cannot typically be identified under laboratory conditions. Historical data on incomes and quantities demanded must be

was noted in Chapter 1: Since the slope depends on the units of measure, the measure of responsiveness will vary with changes in these units.

Income Elasticity

By measuring the responsiveness of quantity demanded to changes in income in elasticity form this ambiguity is avoided. Recall that elasticity measures the percentage change in the affected variable divided by the percentage change in the influencing variable. **Income elasticity** is therefore measured as follows:

$$\eta_I = \frac{\%\Delta x_d}{\%\Delta I} = \frac{\Delta x_d/x_d}{\Delta I/I},$$

where x_d is quantity of good x demanded and I is income. It is easily shown that this measure is unaffected by the units in which income is measured. Income must be expressed in dollars of constant purchasing power, but this leaves unsettled whether income will be measured in past, present or future dollars. The slope of the implied function varies with the dollar units; elasticity does not. Expressing income in the denominator as the product of quantities and constant prices, we see that:

$$\eta = \frac{\Delta x_d/x_d}{P_0 \Delta y/P_0 y_0} = \frac{\Delta x_d/x_d}{P_1 \Delta y/P_1 y_0} = \frac{\Delta x_d/x_d}{\Delta y/y_0}.$$

Economists have estimated income elasticities for a wide variety of goods. Some of these estimates are reported in Table 5.1. As these numbers suggest, the responsiveness of demand to changes in income varies widely. For some goods, like automobiles, demand grows more rapidly than income. The responsiveness of the demand for automobiles to changes in income was implicitly recognized in the political rhetoric of the presidential campaign of 1928. Herbert Hoover's literature maintained that "Republican prosperity has . . . put the proverbial 'chicken in every pot' and a car in every back yard, to boot." Unfortunately for the automobile industry, demand elasticities also work in reverse. Thus, the decline in economic conditions ushered in immediately after Hoover's inauguration spelled disaster for this industry. National income for the five-year period beginning in 1930 posted a

---

used that can never satisfy the conditions of ceteris paribus. Quantity demanded will be influenced by other factors whose variation has not been recorded and thus cannot be controlled in the estimates. Historical data will also contain some measurement error, and the underlying relationship may not even be linear.

These problems are assumed to produce error between individual observations and the true relationship to be estimated. Invariably there will also be error between the estimated relationship and the true relationship. Estimation must make assumptions about these unmeasured influences which may or may not be true. The process of fitting a line to these observations selects the line that minimizes in a very specific sense the deviation of the predicted path from that traced by the data. At any income I_0, the fitted line predicts quantity demanded of q_0 while the observed quantity demanded at that income is q_1. This error (e in Figure 5.12) may be computed for each observation. The procedure used, called *linear regression*, is a method of calculating the value of the vertical intercept and the slope for a line that minimizes the sum of the squared values of all such errors.

Table 5.1 Income Elasticities of Demand for Selected Goods in the United States

Good	Income Elasticity
Automobiles	2.46
Alcohol	1.54
Housing (owner occupied)	1.49
Furniture	1.48
Books	1.44
Dental services	1.42
Restaurant meals	1.40
Shoes	1.10
Clothing	1.02
Medical insurance	0.92
Physicians' services	0.75
Tobacco	0.64
Gasoline and oil	0.48
Housing (rental)	0.43

Source: H. S. Houthakker and Lester D. Taylor, *Consumer Demand in the United States: Analyses and Projections*, 2d ed. (Cambridge, Mass.: Harvard University Press, 1970).

decline of 17 percent compared to income for the previous five years. Factory sales of passenger cars over the same intervals declined by 49 percent.

Price Elasticity

The prices of goods are subject to the same ambiguity as income. Dollars change in value, and the slope of a demand curve will therefore depend on the choice of the dollar unit. Responses to changes in prices denominated in dollars of lower value will be smaller than responses in terms of more valuable dollars. A given price increase in less valuable dollars represents a smaller real change in price and leads to a smaller change in quantity demanded. As in the case of response to income change, this measure of responsiveness, **price elasticity**, depends on the units in which money is measured.

Quantity units raise a similar ambiguity. Merely changing the units in which quantity is measured can also have a profound effect on the slope of a demand curve. Consider what happens when we convert demand observations of gasoline demanded from gallons to barrels. From 1973 to 1974, the average real price of gasoline (in 1967 prices) rose in the United States from $0.35 per gallon to $0.43. This was accompanied by a decrease in quantity purchased from 100.64 billion gallons in 1973 to 96.5 billion gallons in 1974. The change in price, ΔP, was therefore $0.08, and the change in quantity demanded, Δq_d, was -4.14 billion gallons. The slope of the demand curve over this price interval may therefore be calculated as $\Delta q_d / \Delta P = -4.14 \text{ billion} / .08 = -51.75$ billion gallons per dollar.

There are 42 gallons in a barrel of gasoline. To convert each gallon price into a per-barrel price, we therefore simply multiply the former by 42. The change in the price per barrel is therefore $42 \cdot (\$0.08) = \$3.36$. To convert quantities of gallons to quantities of barrels, on the other hand, it is necessary to divide by 42.

The change in barrels demanded is −4.14 billion/42, or −98.6 million barrels. The slope of the demand curve for gasoline in terms of barrels is therefore $\Delta q_d/\Delta P$ = −98.6 million/3.36, or −29.3 million barrels per dollar. By merely changing the units we have changed the slope by more than a thousandfold.

It is clear from this example that the slope of the demand curve cannot give us a clear indicator of the responsiveness of demand to changes in price. Gasoline consumption is the same in both cases, yet a mere change in the units in which it is measured causes our indicator to vary widely. By expressing this responsiveness in elasticity terms, however, this ambiguity is eliminated. The price elasticity of response, η_P, is the same in each case:

$$\eta_P = \frac{\Delta q_d/q_d}{\Delta P/P}.$$

$$\eta_P = \frac{-4.14 \text{ billion}/100.64 \text{ billion}}{\$0.08/\$0.35} = -0.18, \text{ and}$$

$$\eta_P = \frac{-98.6 \text{ million}/2{,}395 \text{ million}}{\$3.36/\$14.70} = -0.18.$$

Arc Elasticity

The formula for price elasticity just shown contains a P and a Q leaving unresolved a remaining question. Computation of elasticity over any given price interval, including the one in the example just presented, involves two prices and two quantities. There is an initial price and a new price, an original quantity and a new quantity. Which do we use? In our example we used the initial values, as we conventionally estimate percentage changes in terms of initial values. However, in a sense this is misleading. We would like our measure of responsiveness of demand to price changes to be the same over a given price interval regardless of whether the price rises or falls over the same interval. Using initial values of P and q will yield different estimates depending on whether the price rises or falls. For example, although we computed a value for $\eta_P = -0.18$ for the price increase, an 8-cent *fall* in price from $0.43 estimated in the same way would yield a value for η_P of −0.23.

To avoid this ambiguity, economists sometimes use a measure employing the *average* price and quantity, which yields the same value whether price rises or falls. This is called **arc elasticity**. The formula for arc elasticity is as follows:

$$\text{arc elasticity} = \eta_P = \frac{\dfrac{\Delta q_d}{(q_0 + q_1)/2}}{\dfrac{\Delta P}{(P_0 + P_1)/2}} = \frac{\Delta q_d/(q_0 + q_1)}{\Delta P/(P_0 + P_1)}.$$

The arc elasticity estimate should fall between the estimates for a price increase and decrease estimate, as does that for our example:

$$\eta_P = \frac{-4.14 \text{ billion}/(100.64 \text{ billion} + 96.5 \text{ billion})}{\$0.08/(\$0.35 + \$0.43)} = -0.205.$$

Point Elasticity

It is sometimes useful, particularly in theory, to have a definition of the elasticity of demand at a single point on the demand curve. For example, we shall see in Chapter 9 that the rate at which revenue increases to a firm per unit change in output may be usefully described *for each unit of output* in terms of the elasticity of demand at given points on the firm's demand curve. For this reason we have developed an alternative definition of price elasticity of demand called **point elasticity**. This may be derived as follows. Take our original formulation of elasticity and perform the indicated division by inverting the denominator and multiplying:

$$\eta_P = \frac{\Delta q_d / q_d}{\Delta P / P} = \frac{\Delta q_d}{q_d} \cdot \frac{P}{\Delta P}.$$

By rearranging the denominator terms we obtain the following:

(5.1) $$\eta_P = \frac{\Delta q_d}{\Delta P} \cdot \frac{P}{q_d}.$$

In this expression, the first term of the product is a slope and the second term is simply the ratio of price to quantity demanded.

To evaluate this expression at a single point, we must allow ΔP to approach zero. Two things are noteworthy about the result of such an evaluation. First, as the price change approaches zero, the difference between the initial and final values of price and quantity vanish. We need not be concerned with the ambiguity for which arc elasticity was introduced; there is only a single price and quantity at a point on the demand curve. Second, the slope term is not the slope of the demand curve—it is the slope of the *inverse* of the demand curve function. The demand curve relates prices to quantities available for sale. It expresses the market-clearing price for any available quantity. This slope in the elasticity expression is the rate of change in the quantity demanded per unit change in price. The slope of the inverse of a function is equal to the inverse of the slope of that function. Thus, if the slope of a demand curve were -4, for example, the slope of the inverse of that function would be $-\frac{1}{4}$. For any given price and quantity, then, we have a convenient rule of thumb. The steeper the slope of the demand curve passing through that point, the larger its slope, hence the lower its elasticity in absolute value terms.

In Figure 5.13, for example, demand curve D_1 has a slope of -5 while demand curve D_2 has a slope of -1. Point T in this figure was chosen so that $P = q_d$ for convenience. At this point and no other on either demand curve, the elasticity will equal the slope of the inverse. Thus, the elasticity of D_1 at T is $-\frac{1}{5}$, and the elasticity at T for D_2 is -1. The steeper curve D_1 has the smaller elasticity.

A second important observation can be made here. Since the slope of the demand curve is always negative, the slope of the inverse function will also be negative. Price and quantity are invariably positive. Demand elasticity, being the product of this positive ratio and a negative slope, will always be negative.

A note of caution: Elasticity may be measured only at a point or over a price interval. One must not fall into the trap of referring to demand curves themselves as elastic or inelastic. Steep curves may be shown to have portions that are highly

Figure 5.13   *Slope and Elasticity*

At the point of intersection of demand curves D_1 and D_2, price equals quantity. The ratio of these two variables must therefore be unity. The price elasticities of demand must at this point equal the inverse of the slopes of the two curves. Elasticity at this point for D_1 is therefore $-\frac{1}{5}$, and for D_2 is -1.

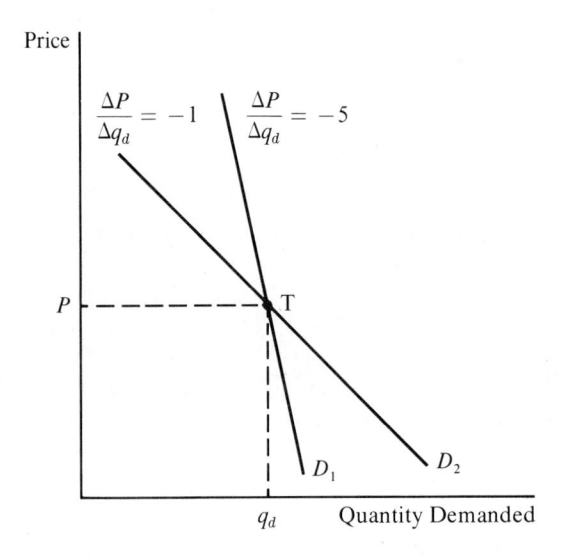

$$\frac{\Delta P}{\Delta q_d} = -1 \qquad \frac{\Delta P}{\Delta q_d} = -5$$

elastic, while very flat demand curves can have portions over which measured price elasticity is very low. Remember that the elasticity formulation contains a ratio of P and q_d. Since these curves slope downward, the numerator and denominator of this ratio change in opposite directions. It is therefore quite possible for the elasticity of demand of a single curve to vary widely. The limits of this variation are discussed in the next section.

The Linear Demand Curve

Although we have no reason to assume that any particular demand curve is linear, this curve presents a useful introduction to the way in which elasicity may vary along any given demand curve. By definition a linear demand curve has the same slope at every point. The slope of the demand curve in Figure 5.14 is equal to $-P_i/q_i$. An increase in quantity available from zero to q_i, the horizontal intercept, would reduce price from P_i to zero. Let us define this ratio of the price and quantity intercepts as s_i. The slope of the inverse of this demand curve is therefore $-1/s_i$, and the price elasticity of demand at any price–quantity combination on the curve is given by the following:

(5.2) $$\eta_P = \frac{-1}{s_i} \cdot \frac{P}{q}.$$

Figure 5.14 *Elasticity as a Ratio of Quantities*

Minus the ratio of the intercept price P_i and the intercept quantity q_i is the slope of this linear demand curve. The inverse of this amount will therefore give the slope of the inverse function. A line drawn from the origin to a point on the demand curve like K has a slope equal to the ratio of the price to the quantity *at that point*. Point K is precisely halfway down the demand curve so that it forms the top of an isosceles triangle. The ratio P_2/q_2 must therefore equal q_i/P_i. Elasticity at K must therefore equal minus unity. A point higher on the demand curve, like T, involves the same inverse demand slope but a higher ratio of p to q. The elasticity at T must therefore be more negative than at K.

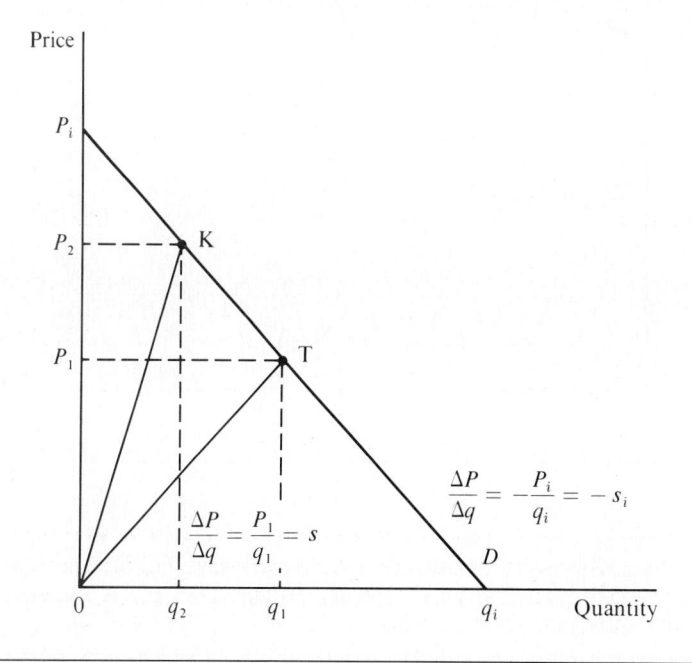

Consider how elasticity varies as we increase price along the curve. At quantity q_i the price is zero, hence elasticity itself must be zero. Increasing price increases the value of the numerator in this ratio term and diminishes the value of the denominator. The value of the ratio term must therefore increase and with it the absolute value of elasticity. As price is raised and quantity reduced along the demand curve, the elasticity must get larger. How large will it grow? The largest value of elasticity may be identified by evaluating the expression at the vertical intercept. Here q in the denominator has a value of zero; hence, the value of the ratio itself is infinite, and elasticity at this point has a value of negative infinity.

The elasticity of demand at these two endpoints is independent of the slope. We may therefore conclude two important facts about linear demand curves. (1) As we move upward along the demand curve, the elasticity becomes increasingly negative, and (2) elasticity ranges from zero to negative infinity over any linear demand curve regardless of slope.

Economists have defined ranges of demand price elasticity. Demand that is highly responsive to price change is defined as **elastic demand**, while demand that is less responsive to price change is defined as **inelastic demand**. Such a division requires a boundary, and the limit chosen in this case is -1. Elasticity at this limiting value is defined to be *unitary*. Ranges of elasticity may thus be summarized in terms of its absolute value as follows:

Elastic demand: $|\eta_P| > 1$

Unitary demand: $|\eta_P| = 1$

Inelastic demand: $0 < |\eta_P| < 1$

It is useful to be able to identify the elastic, unitary, and inelastic portions of the linear demand curve. This can easily be done. Consider point T in Figure 5.14. This point identifies combination (P_1, q_1), chosen so that q_1 is exactly half of q_i—that is, $q_i = 2 \cdot q_1$. The line from the origin to T therefore completes the isosceles triangle $0Tq_i$. The two sides formed by $0T$ and Tq_i have the same length. Note furthermore that the slope of the line $0T$ is equal to P_1/q_1, which we shall label s. Since this is an isosceles triangle, it must be the case that the slope of $0T$ is minus the slope of Tq_i. Since the slope of Tq_i is $-s_i$, it follows that $s = s_i$.

From these observations it is easily shown that the elasticity of demand at point T is unitary. Substituting s for P/q in Equation (5.2) gives the following:

(5.3)
$$\eta_P = \frac{-s}{s_i}.$$

But where $q_i = 2 \cdot q_1$ we have seen that $s = s_i$. Elasticity at this quantity is therefore $-s_i/s_i = -1$. We may therefore conclude that the point of unitary elasticity on any linear demand curve lies directly above the quantity that is precisely half the quantity indicated by the horizontal intercept of the demand curve. More simply, the point of unitary elasticity lies halfway down the demand curve. As we have already noted, movement up a linear demand curve is associated with increasingly negative elasticities. Points to the northwest of T on the demand curve therefore correspond to those defined to be elastic, while points to the southeast are inelastic.

Before leaving the topic of linear demand curves we must deal with two special cases, the *horizontal* demand curve and the *vertical* demand curve. As we have seen, elasticity must vary as one moves along linear demand curves that slope downward to the right. Price and quantity change in opposite directions, changing elasticity from point to point. These two curves are exceptions to the rule, and for obvious reasons. Although s varies in these cases the elasticity does not, due to the value of the slopes in the two cases. A horizontal demand curve has a slope of zero; hence, the slope of the inverse function is infinite. Regardless of s in this case, the price elasticity of demand is infinite. The slope of the vertical demand curve, on the other hand, is infinite. The slope of the inverse function, and therefore the price elasticity of demand, for vertical demand curves is zero.

Figure 5.15 *Elasticity of Curvilinear Demand Curves*

Elasticity depends on the slope of the demand curve at a single point. This slope may be measured as the slope of a straight line tangent to the curve at the point in question.

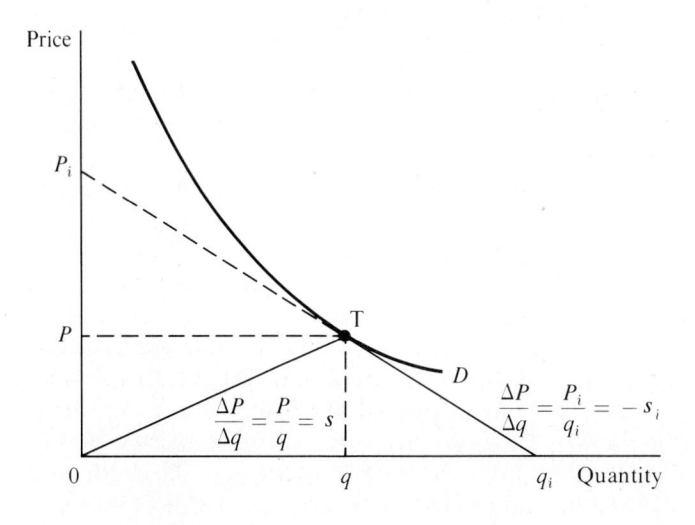

$$\frac{\Delta P}{\Delta q} = \frac{P}{q} = s \qquad \frac{\Delta P}{\Delta q} = \frac{P_i}{q_i} = -s_i$$

Elasticity and Nonlinear Curves

Since nonlinear demand curves are not so obligingly straight, it is necessary to develop a means of identifying their demand elasticity. Fortunately, our methods worked out for the case of linear demand curves transfer to this case with little modification. The slope does not remain constant, so we may not infer changes in elasticity directly from price changes. We may nevertheless easily measure the elasticity at any point on such a curve.

Consider Figure 5.15. The demand curve in this case is convex downward. Recall that the slope of a nonlinear curve at any point on the curve is the slope of a tangent to that curve. This slope reflects the rate of change in the market-clearing price per unit change in the quantity offered. At point T, therefore, the slope of the demand curve is the slope of the diagonal line tangent to the curve at T that extends to the horizontal axis at q_i. As before, let this slope be $-s_i$. The slope of a line from the origin to point T again gives us the value of the ratio P/q; let this slope be s again. Elasticity is given from Equation (5.3) as $-s/s_i$. We can see that s_i exceeds s; the slope of the line tangent to the demand curve at T is steeper than the line OT. We may therefore conclude that that demand is inelastic. Price elasticity at this point must have an absolute value less than unity.

Constant Elasticity

As just stressed, point elasticity refers to a single point on a demand curve. With the exception of vertical and horizontal demand curves, which are everywhere perfectly inelastic and elastic, respectively, straight line demand curves may not be characterized by their elasticity. However, it is possible for nonlinear demand curves to have the same elasticity at every point. One convenient form of a **constant elasticity demand curve** is the following:

(5.4)
$$q_d = \alpha \cdot P^\eta.$$

Here q_d and P are quantity and price, and α and η are constants. The exponent of price in this formulation can be shown to be price elasticity. As this demonstration requires the evaluation of a slope not developed in Chapter 1 the proof of this assertion is presented in an appendix to this chapter.

A constant elasticity demand curve must be convex to the origin. Recall that elasticity is equal to $(-1/s_i) \cdot (P/q)$ where $-s_i$ is the slope of the demand curve. As the price is increased, the quantity demanded along a demand curve must fall. The ratio of price to quantity must therefore increase along any demand curve as price increases. This has clear implications for the slope of a constant elasticity demand curve as price increases. The elasticity must remain unchanged. This can be true only if $-1/s_i$ falls in value, for the product of this ratio and P/q must equal elasticity at every price. A fall in the absolute value of $-1/s_i$ implies an increase in the absolute value of $-s_i$, the slope of the demand curve. The shape of any constant elasticity demand curve is therefore established. As prices are increased along these curves, the slope must rise in absolute value; it must become steeper.

It is, of course, a matter of conjecture whether observed responses to changes in price are more likely to resemble constant quantity reductions for given increments in price or constant *percentage* reductions in quantity associated with constant *percentage* price increases. The theory of demand developed in the preceding chapters is consistent with both. The first characterization implies a linear demand curve, while the latter implies a constant elasticity demand curve. One way to resolve this issue is to estimate the observed relationship between price and quantity using *both* formulations and determine which fits the data best.

The convenience of Equation (5.4) for fitting demand curves should be noted. Standard statistical methods for fitting curves to data require that the curves estimated themselves be linear. As the constant elasticity demand curve must be convex to the origin, this presents difficulties. These difficulties are solved for the specific formulation presented in (5.4): It has the property of being "linear in the logs." By this we mean that a simple linear expression may be obtained by taking the natural logarithm of both sides:

$$q = \alpha P^\eta.$$

$$ln(q) = ln(\alpha) + \eta ln(p).$$

A constant elasticity demand curve may therefore be estimated by simply converting price and quantity into natural logarithmic form and fitting a linear curve to the transformed data. The antilog of the intercept term from such an estimate may be interpreted as the shift parameter α, and the slope term η is the demand elasticity itself.

As an example, let us assume that a particular demand curve has this form and that the shift parameter α is 100,000 and the demand elasticity η is -1. Values for P and q may then be identified by simply substituting into the following equation:

Table 5.2 *Price, Quantity, and the Shift Parameter in Numerical and Natural Logarithmic Form*

α	P	q	lnα	ln(p)	ln(q)
100,000	1000	100	11.5	6.9	4.6
100,000	750	133	11.5	6.6	4.9
100,000	600	167	11.5	6.4	5.1
100,000	500	200	11.5	6.2	5.3
100,000	400	250	11.5	6.0	5.5
100,000	300	333	11.5	5.7	5.8
100,000	250	400	11.5	5.5	6.0
100,000	200	500	11.5	5.3	6.2
100,000	150	667	11.5	5.0	6.5
100,000	100	1000	11.5	4.6	6.9

$$q = 100{,}000/P^{-1}$$
$$q = 100{,}000/P.$$

Various pairs of price and quantity that satisfy this equation are presented in the first two columns of Table 5.2. These pairs of values identify coordinates of the demand curve presented in panel (a) of Figure 5.16. Note the convexity of this demand curve. Each price and quantity is transformed into its natural logarithm in the remaining columns of Table 5.2. When these logarithmic coordinates are plotted in panel (b) of Figure 5.16, they lie along the straight line labeled D. This demand curve is "linear in the logs." The slope is constant over all quantities for the curve in panel (b). Furthermore, the slope of this curve is equal to negative unity, the price elasticity of demand.

By taking the natural logs of prices and quantities and fitting a linear curve through these coordinates, we may estimate the two key parameters of any constant elasticity demand function. As just noted, the quantity intercept term will provide the natural log of the shift parameter, and the slope of this curve will reflect the price elasticity of demand. Some estimates of constant price elasticities for certain goods are presented in Table 5.3.

There is one final point to make before we leave demand elasticity and constant elasticity demand curves. In the case where the price elasticity is negative unity at every point along such a curve, as is the case for the hypothetical curve in Figure 5.16, we note that:

$$q = \alpha \cdot P^{-1}$$
$$q = \frac{\alpha}{P}.$$

Multiplying both sides by price gives:

$$P \cdot q = \alpha.$$

Total expenditure on the good is independent of the quantity sold. Regardless of the quantity sold or the price, total revenue will in every case equal α, the shift

Chapter 5 The Theory of Market Demand

Figure 5.16 **Constant Elasticity Demand Curves**

Coordinates from Table 5.3 are plotted in panel (a), forming the demand curve shown, which is convex to the origin. The natural logarithms of these same numbers are plotted in panel (b). The coordinates form a straight line when transformed in this way. The slope of such a curve is constant and may be interpeted as the elasticity of demand. This point elasticity will be the same at every quantity, because the slope of the curve is the same at every quantity. Note that this curve has a slope of minus unity.

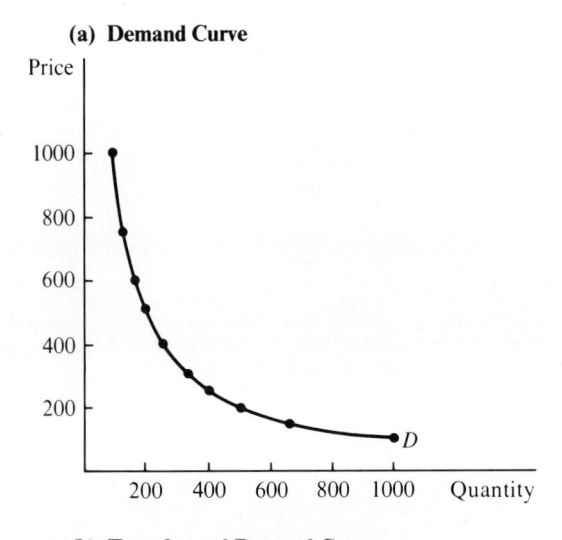

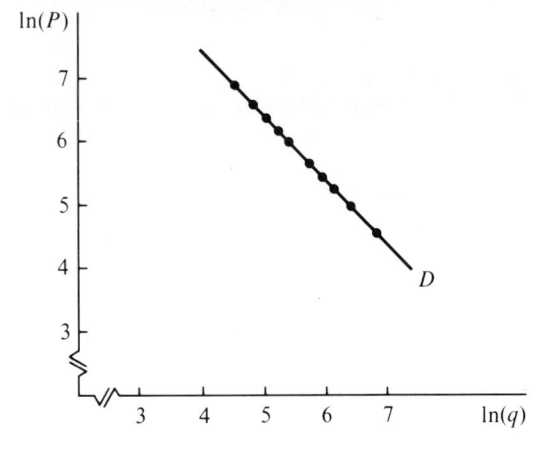

(a) Demand Curve

(b) Transformed Demand Curve

---

parameter. This holds only for demand curves that have constant unitary elasticity and will later be shown to form a dividing line between sets of demand curves in which expenditure rises and falls with quantity sold. The relationship between elasticity and expenditure will therefore play an important role in our discussions of firms and their choice of output under conditions in which output affects price.

Table 5.3 Price Elasticities of Demand* for Selected Goods in the United States

Good	Price Elasticity
Newspapers and magazines	−0.10
Electricity (residential)	−0.13
Gasoline and oil	−0.14
Natural gas (residential)	−0.15
Medical insurance	−0.31
Automobile repair	−0.36
Physicians' services	−0.58
Legal services	−0.61
Household appliances	−0.67
Shoes	−0.70
Air travel (foreign)	−0.70
Movies	−0.87
Housing	−1.00
Taxis	−1.24
Restaurant meals	−1.63

*The estimates given are short-run price elasticities. Long-run elasticities estimated over periods sufficient for full adjustment to price changes are uniformly larger, as is predicted by the second law of demand. For example, the long-run elasticity of demand for residential natural gas is −10.74.

Source: H. S. Houthakker and Lester D. Taylor, *Consumer Demand in the United States: Analysis and Projections*, 2d ed. (Cambridge, Mass.: Harvard University Press, 1970).

Summary

This chapter was concerned with two major topics. These consist of (1) a reconciliation of demand analysis with choice theory, and (2) the development of the application of the elasticity measure of response to demand. The first began with a presentation of the effects of income on the opportunity set confronting households with fixed money income. The income consumption curve (ICC) was defined and explained in terms of shifts in money income holding prices constant. The distinction between real and nominal income was refined so that the combination chosen might be identified in terms of opportunity cost and real income alone.

Price changes were shown to affect both opportunity cost and real income. The effects of price changes on the quantity of a good demanded were thus broken down into two separate results. A rise in price increases opportunity cost. Holding real income constant, we may therefore identify the substitution effect of this price change that is attributable to the change in opportunity cost alone. Similarly, a rise in price lowers real income. Holding opportunity cost constant, we may trace the income effect of this price change along a particular ICC curve. The total effect of any price change will be the sum of these two components.

We defined two types of demand curves, compensated and uncompensated demand. The uncompensated demand curve reflects the influence of both substitution and income effects. It is most useful for predicting the effects of price-lowering innovation and technical change that do in fact have an impact on total real income. Compensated demand curves, on the other hand, reflect only the influence of substitution effects. These effects are identified by making compensating income payments to households that offset the changes in real income implied by changing prices. These demand curves are useful for estimating responses to price changes due to such influences as taxes or subsidies, which by themselves may have little influence on the level of aggregate real income. Compensated demand curves for normal goods must be steeper than uncompensated demand curves for the same goods. Uncompensated demand curves for inferior goods will be steeper.

The so-called Giffen paradox was examined in detail. Giffen goods are goods that have positively sloped demand curves. This can occur only when (1) the good in question is inferior, and (2) when the income effect of the price change is larger in magnitude than the substitution effect. As substitution effects invariably operate in the opposite direction from price changes, compensated demand curves cannot be Giffen goods. No one has thus far presented evidence supporting the existence of any such good.

Market demand curves may be obtained by adding together the quantities demanded at each price by each household. As individual households respond differently to price changes, shifts in market supply that produce changes in market price may have important effects on the distribution of the goods as well. The economics of hoarding were discussed in the context of the dramatic changes in price produced by OPEC in the 1970s. It was shown that hoarding results from attempts to minimize the waiting cost per unit of a good that is price controlled.

The topic of demand elasticity was introduced as a way of characterizing the responsiveness of quantity demanded to changes in income and price that is not sensitive to the units of measurement. Although slopes of demand functions also measure response, the slope of any function is sensitive to the units of measure. Response to income change measured by slopes would vary depending on the value of money in which income was measured. Response of demand to changes in price are not comparable, because these slopes depend on the unit in which the good is measured. Elasticity is a pure number. Given responses to changes in income or changes in price will be associated with the **same** elasticities regardless of the units in which these variables are measured.

Price elasticity may be measured in a number of ways. If only one pair of points on the demand curve is identified, the best measure is arc elasticity. This measure is independent of whether the price change considered rose or fell over the interval. Point elasticity measures the elasticity at a particular point on the demand curve. The point elasticity on a linear demand curve ranges from zero to negative infinity. Points below the midpoint of a demand curve must have price elasticities of less than one in absolute value. This response is defined as inelastic. The midpoint of a demand curve will always have an elasticity of negative unity. Points above the midpoint have an elasticity greater than one in absolute value. This response is defined as elastic.

Although the elasticity varies along a linear demand curve, it is possible for nonlinear curves to have the same elasticity at every point. A simple and useful form of this constant elasticity demand curve was presented and described.

Key Concepts

income consumption curve (ICC)
real income
nominal income
Giffen paradox
income effect
substitution effect
uncompensated demand curve
compensated demand curve
market demand

rationing
hoarding
income elasticity
price elasticity
arc elasticity
point elasticity
elastic demand
inelastic demand
constant elasticity demand curve

Questions

1. *Easy* An income consumption curve for two normal goods will always be positively sloped. An income consumption curve when one good is inferior will have a negative slope. Is it possible for both goods to be inferior? What will such an ICC look like? Explain.

Hard Explain the relationship between the negative slope of the ICC involving an inferior good and the direction of the income effect of price changes.

2. *Easy* Explain why a normal good may not be a Giffen good.

Hard A compensated demand curve for a Giffen good will have a negative slope, and an uncompensated demand curve for the same good will have a positive slope. Is this true or false? Explain.

3. *Easy* A good is more likely to be inferior if it is defined narrowly than if defined broadly and more likely if it has close substitutes than if it is one of a kind. Is this true or false? Explain.

Hard Passenger travel on railroads has diminished markedly since the 1940s, and incomes have risen substantially over the same period. May we conclude from this that railroad travel is an inferior good?

4. *Easy* Using choice theory analysis, show the difference between a compensated and an uncompensated demand curve.

Hard Would a compensated or an uncompensated demand curve be the better choice for predicting the effect of a 5-cent increase in the federal gasoline excise tax on gasoline consumption? What difficulty is presented if the revenues from the tax are used to finance highway improvements and extensions?

5. *Easy* If the demand curve for a good slopes upward and a vertical supply curve shifts leftward, what happens to price? Describe the dynamics of the adjustment to the new equilibrium price. Do they make sense? Why or why not?

Hard The Irish potato famine of the 1840s is often described in the following terms. The blight struck the potatoes, reducing the supply and causing the price to rise. At these higher prices (because potatoes were Giffen goods), people ate more of them. The price increase reduced their real income to the point that they could no longer afford meat and other more luxurious foods, and they thus increased their potato consumption at the higher price. Explain why this cannot have occurred in the manner described.

6. *Easy* Price increases are sometimes thought of as driving certain demanders out of the market. Explain what is meant by this expression and how it may occur.

Hard During periods when price controls are imposed, the practice of hoarding is widely observed and universally deplored. Explain what is meant by hoarding and why people practice it. Does the fact that people are hoarding imply that they are consuming at an excessively high rate? Does the presence of hoarding have anything to do with the rate of consumption? Explain.

7. *Easy* The slope of the demand curve for tomatoes is $.0000327 per pound. The slope of the demand curve for gin is $.000298 per gallon. Is it possible to tell which demand is the more responsive to price? Why or why not?

Hard A well-known theorem in economic theory shows that the income elasticities for all goods must sum to unity. Can you give a commonsense explanation for this theoretical result?

8. *Easy* Unless the arc formulation for elasticity is used, the measured elasticity of response to a 10-cent increase in the price of pizza will be different from the measured elasticity of a 10-cent decrease over the same interval. Explain why this is true and how the problem is avoided with arc elasticity.

Hard Explain without using calculus why a constant elasticity demand curve must be convex to the origin.

Chapter 5 Appendix

Constant Elasticity Demand Curves

We wish to show that the exponent of price in the demand function $q = \alpha \cdot P^\beta$ is equal to the price elasticity of demand. Taking the derivative of q with respect to price gives:

$$q = \alpha P^\beta;$$

$$\frac{dq}{dp} = \alpha \beta P^{\beta-1}.$$

Elasticity is equal to this slope times the ratio of price to quantity:

$$\eta = \frac{dq}{dp} \cdot \frac{P}{q} = \alpha \beta P^{\beta-1} \cdot \frac{P}{q}.$$

Combining terms in the numerator and substituting for quantity in the denominator gives:

$$\eta = \frac{\alpha \beta P^\beta}{\alpha P^\beta}$$

$$\eta = \beta.$$

The exponent of price in the demand equation of the form shown above is the price elasticity of demand. This elasticity expression contains neither P nor q; hence, it is invariant with respect to either of these variables.

Chapter 6

Income Measurement and Uncertainty

Connections   This chapter contains two extensions of the theory of household choice. The first concerns income measurement. Chapter 3 introduced the notion that welfare could be measured (or at least indexed) by changes in money income under conditions of constant prices. This idea was extended in Chapter 4 to consider the case of the measurement of the income change that compensates for a price change. Chapter 5 then elaborated on the notion of compensation as a pair of corresponding price and income changes that leave the chooser's welfare unchanged. This chapter develops methods for the measurement of changes in welfare under conditions where all prices and even nominal income are changing. It also develops a method for measuring the purchasing power of money and its inverse, the price level. Next, the chapter considers choice in a world of uncertainty. Uncertainty in choice is represented by preferences for income over mutually exclusive "states of the world." Finally, the concept of risk aversion is defined and illustrated. The uncertainty model is then applied to a number of real-world phenomena. Use is made of the total differential, a technique discussed in Chapter 1.

Income is a word used very freely by economists. It is sometimes used to designate any form of money receipt. At other times its use is restricted to payments received for factor services, which is the test applied by the IRS for tax purposes. In the theory of demand, however, it is most often associated with utility or welfare. To avoid some of the confusion that must naturally result from this ambiguous usage, we shall consistently refer to income in this last sense as **real income**. A recurring theme in the two previous chapters was the relationship between changes in variables affecting the position of the opportunity set and changes in real income. Thus far, we have considered single price changes or money (nominal) income changes in isolation. In this chapter we will extend this analysis to the effects on real income of simultaneous changes in all such variables. Market prices are continuously changing; recently, they all seem to be rising at a distressing rate. Real income plays a vital role in economic analysis, and this role would be diminished if it were applicable only to changes in individual variables.

Two topics will concern us in the first part of this chapter. First, we need to extend our analysis of real income measurement to deal with simultaneous changes in prices and nominal income. The use of nominal income alone is inadequate as a measure of real income when prices change. Second, the **purchasing power of money** (and therefore *its* value) will be influenced by changing prices. We are all too familiar with the decline in the purchasing power of money due to inflation. However, knowing that it is declining is not enough. We need a measure of this decline (or rise) when it occurs.

Later in the chapter we will consider extensions of choice theory to some more specialized, but nevertheless very important, areas. We will relax the assumption of costless information in order to examine choice under uncertainty. Uncertainty emerges from two sources. On the one hand, the variability of our physical environment presents us with countless decisions that we must make without knowing for certain their outcome. On the other, the outcomes of many choices depend on the choices of others, which are equally difficult to predict.

The first of these discussions takes us into the market for insurance, then is extended to such varied areas as hotel reservations and product guarantees. The second lays down a foundation for a choice-based theory of such marketing topics as product loyalty and advertising. Many practices that seem inexplicable in the context of the simple model of fully informed consumer choice may be readily explained when we recognize that households typically function in an environment in which information, like all goods, is costly.

6.1 Index Numbers

Weights and Measures

Perhaps the most ubiquitous problem confronting applied economic analysis is the **aggregation problem**. We often talk about gross national product, the supply of labor, and the output of the steel industry as if each of these magnitudes reflected a carefully gauged quantity of homogeneous units. Clearly, this is not true. Gross national product contains amounts of every conceivable good and service, from gourmet dinners to tap dancing lessons. The supply of labor includes the services of night watchmen and astronauts. Even the output of the steel industry is comprised of many specialized products made of carbon, stainless steel, and various alloys. The aggregation problem consists of attempting to convert quantities of often completely heterogeneous items into a meaningful sum.

That aggregation is a universal problem—not even the exclusive province of market economies—is reflected in the dilemma that it presents to planners in the Soviet Union.[1] In establishing production quotas for various industries in the Soviet Union, it is clearly not feasible for central planners to itemize production targets for each plant for each and every product. Consider, for example, a product as simple as the common nail. Nails are made in a mind-boggling assortment of sizes and shapes. There are long nails and short nails and every imaginable length in between; there are thin nails and fat ones, nails with large heads and nails without heads, nails that are galvanized and case-hardened steel or made of countless other materials. How can production plans be developed by Soviet economists under these circumstances?

If quotas are established in terms of numbers of nails alone, with the decisions concerning the particulars left to individual plants or some intermediate planning level, the assortment produced is likely to be heavily biased toward short, thin, headless steel nails. These may be produced with the fewest resources *per nail*; hence, plants will be in less danger of failing to fulfill their quotas by concentrating on producing many small nails. On the other hand, if quotas are established in terms of *tons* of nails, the assortment is likely to be biased toward large nails; it takes fewer resources to produce a ton of large nails than a ton of small ones. This aggregation problem is widely acknowledged by workers and planners in the Soviet Union. The Russian humor magazine *Krokodil* published a cartoon in the 1960s depicting a group of self-satisfied workers proudly displaying their plan-fulfilling output for the month: one huge nail extending the entire length of the plant![2]

Western economists seeking to measure the growth of real income are confronted by a similar problem. The average American today consumes more meat and fewer potatoes than did his or her counterpart during the Depression. If we measured total food consumption in terms of its nutritional content then and now, we would doubtless show an increase—but probably not a large one—over this interval. If we measured food consumption in terms of calories consumed, we would probably get a smaller difference. If we measured it in terms of the physical weight of the food consumed, we might actually show a decrease. None of these measures is likely to reflect adequately the way the average person feels about having to subsist on these two diets.

Contrary to popular wisdom, we *can* add apples and oranges; economists do so daily. In doing so, however, it is important to make such a sum reflect, as best we can, the underlying economic variable we seek to measure.

---

[1] This discussion is taken from Alec Nove, *The Soviet Economy: An Introduction*, 2d ed. (New York: Praeger, 1966), Chapter 6.
[2] Ibid., pp. 163ff.

Measuring Real Income

So long as prices of goods and services do not change, the measurement of real income presents no problem. As we noted in Chapter 4, changes in nominal income will clearly index changes in economic welfare and thus real income. However, difficulties are immediately introduced when prices begin to change. Consider the simplest example: rising prices where all prices increase by the same proportion, leaving nominal income of households unchanged. This can be analyzed in Figure 6.1. Prior to the price rise the budget constraint is given by:

$$y = \frac{B}{P_y^1} - \frac{P_x^1}{P_y^1} \cdot x.$$

A typical individual will select combination H from such an opportunity set. Now let the price of both goods double such that $P_x^2 = 2P_x^1$ and $P_y^2 = 2P_y^1$. The budget constraint shifts inward to a position that can easily be placed in the two-dimensional space on the basis of two familiar rules of thumb. First, the vertical intercept of the budget constraint must shift downward to one half its original height. This follows from the fact that this intercept now has a value of B/P_y^2, which we know to be $B/2P_y^1$. Second, the slope of this budget constraint is

Figure 6.1 *Doubling Prices with Constant Money Income*

A doubling of all prices with no change in money income shifts the budget constraint downward so that the vertical intercept is halved. The slope is unaffected. The problem is to measure this fall in real income. As y is inferior, more y is chosen after the price changes than was chosen at the lower prices.

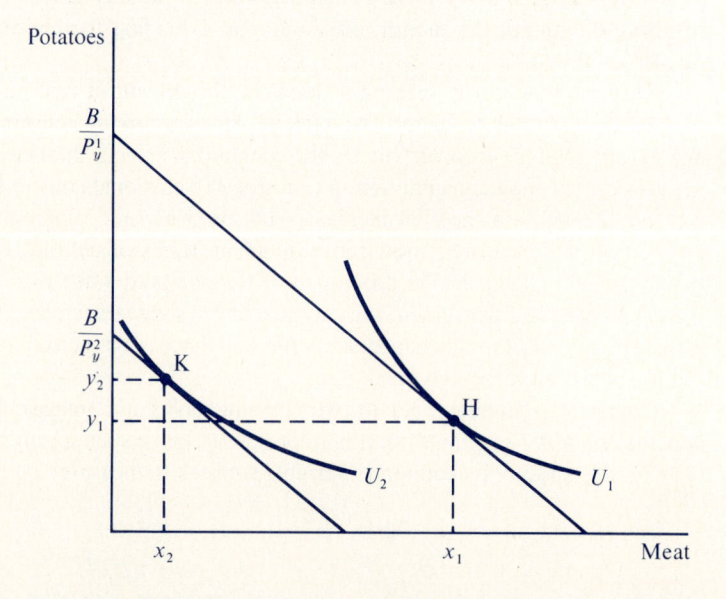

$-P_x^2/P_y^2$, equal to $-2P_x^1/2P_y^1$ and therefore to $-P_x^1/P_y^1$. The opportunity cost of a good is not affected by inflation or deflation, which is proportional in all prices. The net effect of such inflation, therefore, is to shift the budget constraint downward to a parallel position one half the height of the original budget constraint. An individual confronted with such a shift in his or her opportunity set would have no better choice than combination K. Clearly, the inflation has made this individual worse off; he or she must be on a lower indifference curve than previously.

Our problem is to measure this reduction in welfare without knowing the indifference maps of the consumers affected. **Nominal income** has not changed. Observations of nominal income are therefore inadequate to record levels of real income in a world of changing prices. Nor are we much better off observing the quantities of goods and services that are bought. The quantity of x consumed after the inflation is less than before, but the quantity of y has increased. Do we simply add quantities of x and y interchangeably to measure total quantities of all goods consumed before and after? What if x is measured in "large" units and y in "small" ones. Such a sum might easily indicate that the individual is better off with K than with H.

Figure 6.1 shows us that we do not really need to know the indifference map in order to know that combination H is preferred to K. This information can be inferred from the positions of the opportunity sets themselves. Even though we do not know the indifference map of the household affected by these price changes, we do know the properties of indifference curves, and these are sufficient to inform us that some points on the original budget constraint are preferred to combination K chosen on the new. As H is the most preferred combination on the original budget constraint, it must be preferred to K.

Laspeyres and Paasche Measures

We measure this decline in welfare by measuring the *movement* of the budget constraint itself. Recall our discussion of compensation in Chapters 4 and 5. In those examples we posed the question of which change in money income compensated for the price change under discussion. The magnitude of the compensating income change was determined by the extent of the implied shift in the budget constraint of the affected household. Here we perform essentially the same type of measurement. *We must determine the magnitude of the change in money income that will produce a change in welfare equivalent to that produced by the change in consumption bundles.* As price changes themselves affect real income, however, it is necessary to perform this measurement holding prices constant.

This poses an immediate problem. There are two sets of prices. Do we calculate the compensating income change in terms of new prices or the original prices? The answer is that we may do either. This naturally means that for any change in consumption combinations there are two, possibly different, measures of the change in real income. We define the change using the original prices as the **Laspeyres measure** and that using new prices as the **Paasche measure**. The Laspeyres measure identifies the change in income necessary to purchase the new combination at the original set of prices. The Paasche measure identifies the change in income necessary to purchase the original consumption bundle at the new prices.

As long as *relative* prices do not change, these measures may be routinely calculated. Consider the Laspeyres measure. We wish to calculate here (Figure 6.1) the reduction in spending required to buy combination K rather than H at the original prices. We know that the original budget equation is:

$$B_1 = P_x^1 x_1 + P_y^1 y_1.$$

To purchase the new combination at these same prices would require that:

$$B_2 = P_x^1 x_2 + P_y^1 y_2.$$

Our question is by how much is B_2 smaller than B_1.

First, let us recall that nominal income is assumed to be unaffected by the inflation and, therefore, combination K can be purchased with the original budget:

$$B_1 = P_x^2 x_2 + P_y^2 y_2.$$

On the basis of our previously stated relationship between the new and old prices we may rewrite this as:

$$B_1 = 2P_x^1 x_2 + 2P_y^1 y_2.$$

By factoring we obtain:

$$B_1 = 2(P_x^1 x_2 + P_y^1 y_2).$$

The expression inside the parentheses is the amount we seek, B_2, and therefore we have:

$$B_1 = 2B_2.$$

Real income has been halved as a result of the increase in prices. The reader should confirm that by using a similar procedure twice as much income is required to buy the new than the old bundle at the *new* higher prices—that is, the Paasche measure of real income change.

In more realistic cases, income as well as prices of goods and services will be influenced by inflation. Indeed, people have been known to express great bitterness over the increase in the prices of the goods they buy, though they are inconsistently uncomplaining about price increases for the things they sell (including, of course, their labor services). The impact of these combined effects on the measurement of real income is not fundamentally altered by this extension. Consider, for example, Figure 6.2, which depicts the results of the same inflation, this time associated with a rise in nominal income from B_1 to B_2. Again we calculate the change in real income by evaluating the new and old combinations of goods at either the old set of prices (Laspeyres) or the new set of prices (Paasche).

The Laspeyres measure would indicate that the income required to buy the new combination T at the old prices would be B_3, which we see is less than B_1. Alternatively, we might calculate the Paasche measure of this real income change

Figure 6.2   *Measuring Income Changes when Prices and Income Change*

In this case nominal income changes at the same time as prices. Money income rises from B_1 to B_2 at the same time that prices rise. The fact that the new combination chosen, T, lies on a lower indifference curve than H tells us that money income has risen less than prices. The fall in real income could be measured in two ways—at original prices ($B_1 - B_3$) or in terms of the new prices ($B_4 - B_2$).

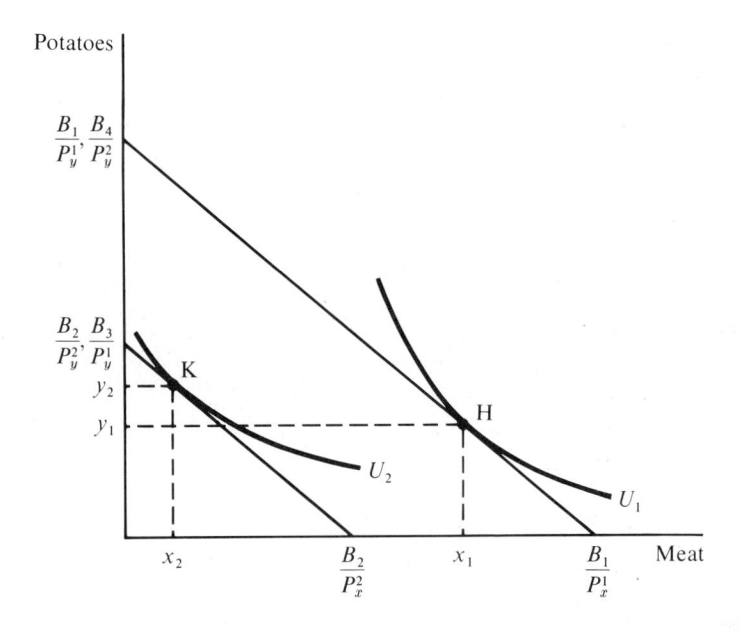

[Graph: Potatoes on vertical axis, Meat on horizontal axis. Vertical axis labels from top: $\frac{B_1}{P_y^1}, \frac{B_4}{P_y^2}$; $\frac{B_2}{P_y^2}, \frac{B_3}{P_y^1}$; y_2 (point K); y_1. Horizontal axis labels: x_2; $\frac{B_2}{P_x^2}$; x_1; $\frac{B_1}{P_x^1}$. Indifference curves U_2 (through K) and U_1 (through H).]

by computing the cost of combination H at the new set of prices and comparing that with B_2. *Both indexes will reflect a decrease in real income in spite of the fact that nominal income has risen.*

More realistic examples will also involve different changes in the prices of different goods. Where price changes are not proportional, it will be necessary to compute the level of income required to purchase the bundles of goods by actually performing the multiplication and addition indicated in our arithmetic earlier. This information is available in the market (unlike information on the positions of indifference curves) and may therefore be obtained through suitable data collection and assembly processes.

The examples presented thus far may be so simplified as to lull the unsuspecting student into believing that real income measurement is nothing more than embellished common sense. Let us therefore move directly to the more difficult but very common case of *mixed* price changes. Even in years of the worst inflation some prices fall and in periods of great prosperity some output levels decline. Unless our study of income measurement can shed light on real income changes under such circumstances, they present us with a very limited set of tools at best.

Figure 6.3 *Nonproportional Price Changes*

The price of potatoes increases while the price of meat falls. Combination K was favored under the old price regime. Combination H is favored under the new price regime. Combination H could not have been purchased at the old prices, and combination K cannot be purchased at the new. No preference for one or the other combination has been revealed by the buying patterns of the household.

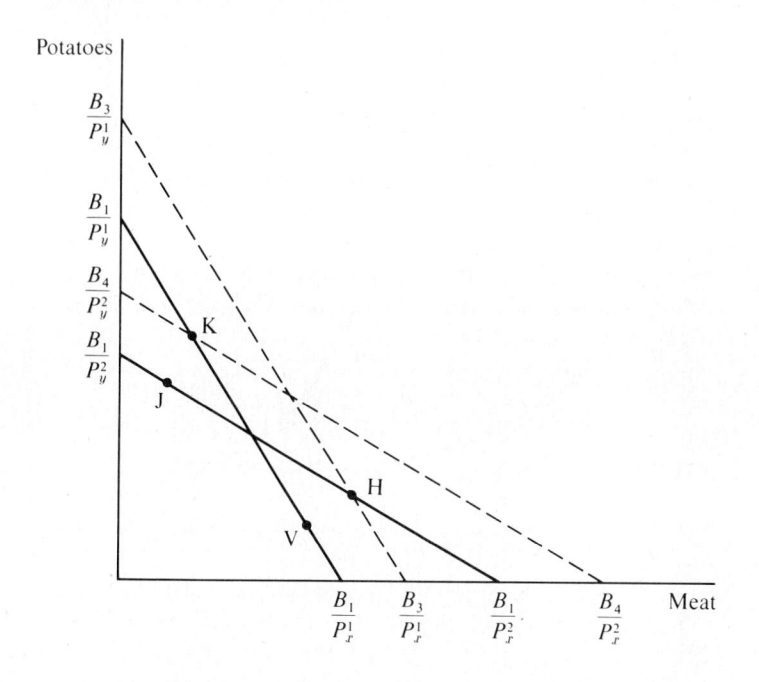

Consider Figure 6.3. Here we depict the budget constraints before and after a set of price changes that, for simplicity, are shown under conditions of constant nominal income. Prices originally are P_x^1 and P_y^1, respectively, and we shall assume that the price of x rises while that of y declines. The two intercepts of the original budget constraint are thus B_1/P_y^1 and B_1/P_x^1; those of the new budget constraint are B_1/P_y^2 and B_1/P_x^2. Because the price of x rises, the horizontal intercept of the new budget constraint lies *to the left* of the old, while the fall in the price of y implies that the new vertical intercept must lie *above* that of the original. Clearly, the two budget constraints must intersect.

We can no longer state, as we could previously when all prices rose, that for any point on the new budget constraint there must be some point on the old that is preferred to it (or the converse when all prices fell). On the contrary, some combinations on the new budget constraint are definitely preferred to some points on the old, while at the same time others on the old are definitely favored over some points on the new. Point K on the old budget constraint contains more of both goods than combination J on the new. Combination K must therefore be preferred to J. Similarly, however, combination H on the new budget constraint must be preferred to combination V on the old.

In such a case a shift in the budget constraint by itself provides insufficient information for us to gauge changes in real income. The question before us is therefore the following: Does economic theory provide us with additional information that can be used together with household budget data to assess changes in real income when prices are changing? The answer is yes—but a weak and tentative yes.

Initial trials with Figure 6.3 are not encouraging. When we evaluate the effect of these price changes on real income, we get conflicting results. According to the Laspeyres measure the new combination is preferred to the original combination. When the new and old combinations are evaluated with a Paasche measure of real income change, however, the old is favored. Not only is our *measure* of the change in doubt; we have difficulty in identifying the *direction* of change!

The reader may verify this counterintuitive result as follows. Consider combination H in relation to K in Figure 6.3. The Laspeyres measure of real income change calculates the income required to buy the new and old bundles of goods at the original prices. If more income is required to purchase one combination than the other, this is supposed to indicate expanded consumption opportunities, hence increased real income. Clearly, according to this measure, real income increases when individuals are able to purchase H instead of K. Income B_3 is required to purchase the new combination H at the original prices. We know B_3 is higher than B_1, because the intercept of this budget constraint lies above that of the original. The Laspeyres measure, therefore, suggests that the price changes have *increased* real income.

When we use the Paasche measure to calculate the incomes required to buy the two combinations at the new prices, however, we find that there is a *decline* in real income. The new combination H can be purchased with only B_1 dollars of income at the new prices. Original combination K requires higher income B_4. One index therefore indicates an increase in real income while the other indicates that welfare has declined.

Fortunately, for the purposes of national income accounting, this unhappy result need not always occur. Figure 6.4 presents all geometrically possible relationships between new and old combinations that conform to the first law of demand. In each of the three panels shown, the old budget constraint is labeled *OO* and the new constraint is labeled *NN*. In each, the initial combination chosen is labeled K and the new combination is H. As the price of *x* rises while the price of *y* declines, the first law of demand requires that the new combination must contain less *x* and more *y* than the old. Note that in each of the three panels H lies southeast of combination K. We shall see that it is possible both (1) to make unambiguous determinations of the direction of welfare change using only the information contained in such diagrams, and (2) to employ the measures of real income already developed to reveal this.

Consider Case I in panel (a). We do not need an indifference curve map to tell us that the price change has reduced the welfare of the person making these choices. At the original prices this person had an opportunity to buy combination H but chose combination K instead. By favoring K over H, the chooser reveals a

Figure 6.4 *Three Possible Cases*

In Case I shown in panel (a) combination K is favored over combination H. It would take less income at the original prices to purchase H than K. In Case II shown in panel (b) combination H is favored over combination K. It would take less income at the new prices to purchase K than H. Case III in panel (c) corresponds to the situation in Figure 6.3. No preference is revealed in this situation.

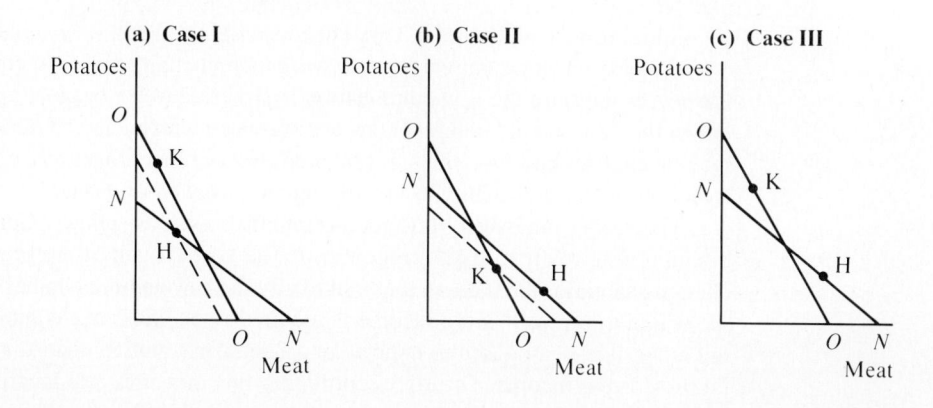

rank ordering between these two combinations. This approach to the study of index numbers is referred to as the **theory of revealed preference**.

In Case II in panel (b), the chooser reveals a preference for H over the original combination K.

Case III in panel (c) will be recognized as the set of choices depicted in Figure 6.3. We note immediately that a person who has chosen such a pair of combinations has not revealed a rank ordering between them. Combination H was not in the opportunity set when combination K was selected. Had the opportunity set included both, combination K might have been revealed as preferred to H. However, no such information is presented by the selection of K from the existing opportunity set QO. Similarly, after the price change H is selected, K cannot be purchased at this set of prices. We have inadequate information to determine whether H would have been preferred to K or whether the chooser is now settling for H because he or she can no longer afford K. Both interpretations are consistent with the revealed choices.

The function of income measurement in cases of mixed price changes, therefore, is to permit discrimination among these three cases. Sets of choices corresponding to Case I will be clearly associated with welfare declines. Those corresponding to Case II will be associated with increasing real income. Those corresponding to Case III will remain ambiguous, although the range of ambiguity has been significantly reduced by this development. To the extent that results correspond to one of the first two cases, we may know at least the direction of change of real income associated with price changes.

First, let us discriminate Case I from the remaining two cases. It is easily seen that a Laspeyres measure of real income indicates a decline only for Case I. The dotted line passing through H parallel to OO in panel (a) has a lower vertical intercept, indicating that the budget required to buy the new combination H at the old prices is lower than that required to buy the preferred bundle K. A parallel line through combination H in either of the remaining panels would have higher intercepts than the original budget constraint OO. A decline in real income indicated by a Laspeyres measure must therefore isolate an example of Case I. Real income will have truly declined in such a case.

Now consider Case II. The dotted line passing through point K in this panel identifies the constraint associated with the budget required to buy the original bundle of goods K at the new prices. That budget is clearly lower than would be required to finance the purchase of H, the combination of goods actually purchased at the new prices. A parallel line through combination K in panel (a) or (c) would reflect the opposite result. More income would be needed to purchase the original combination of goods at the new prices in those panels. A Paasche measure, which indicates increased real income, must therefore isolate an example of Case II.

In summary, then, we may note the following: Mixed price changes can either raise or lower real income. The set of all such results may be thought of as the enclosed space in Figure 6.5. This set contains income declines (the part of the enclosed space to the left of the center divide) and income increases (the remainder of the enclosed space). Some decreases in real income may be identified as belonging to Case I through the use of the Laspeyres measure of income change. Some increases may be identified as belonging to Case II employing the Paasche measure.

However, a portion of the price changes observed will fall into Case III. When the income change is estimated with the Laspeyres measure, an income increase will be indicated, ruling out Case I. But when the Paasche measure is estimated,

Figure 6.5 *The Set of All Price Changes*

Case I contains nothing but declines in real income, while Case II contains nothing but increases in real income. Those situations identified as Case III may be either.

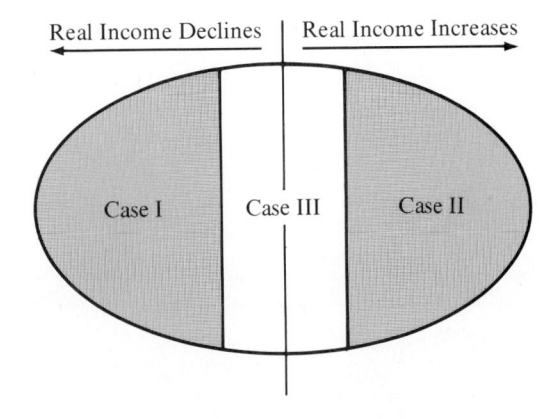

an income decrease will be indicated, ruling out Case II. This does not imply that no change has resulted. It merely informs us that the effect of these price changes on real income cannot be empirically identified.

Converting Changes to Indexes

It is often more useful to know the rate of change than the absolute change itself. This is particularly true when considering a series of income changes over an extended period of time. A $200 increase in per capita income would doubtless have been more substantial to workers in the mid-19th century than to today's labor force, even if this change were measured in constant dollars. This conversion may easily be achieved by reporting measures of real income in terms of an **index**.

An index of real income merely reflects current real income as a percentage of income in some base period. In Figure 6.6, for example, the Laspeyres measure of real income change, ΔB, may be calculated by evaluating combination K and combination H at the original prices; that is,

Figure 6.6 *Laspeyres Income Index*

The relationship between a Laspeyres measured income change is illustrated here. The income change is $\Delta B = B_1 - B_3$. The Laspeyres index measures current real income as a percentage of original real income B_3/B_1.

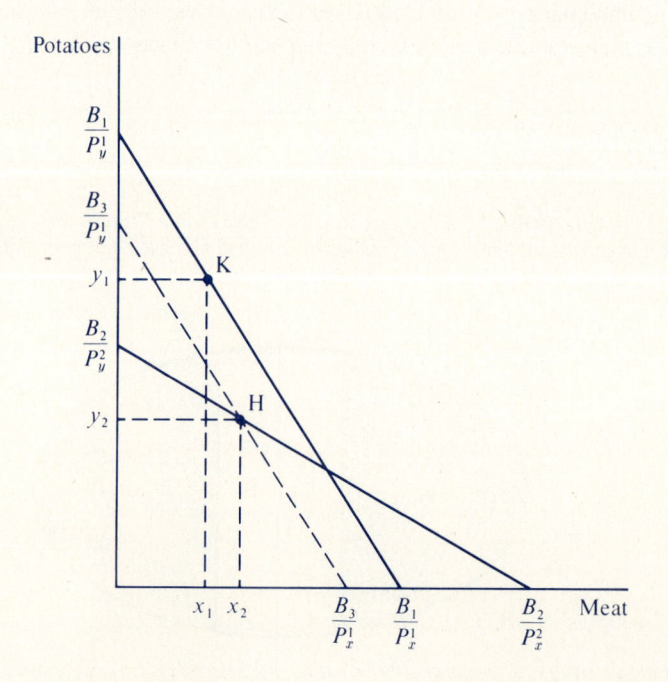

Chapter 6 Income Measurement and Uncertainty

$$\Delta B = B_1 - B_3$$
$$= P_x^1 x_1 + P_y^1 y_1 - P_x^1 x_2 - P_y^1 y_2.$$

Where there are many goods in each combination, this may be expressed more conveniently as

$$\Delta B = \Sigma P_1 q_1 - \Sigma P_1 q_2,$$

where the subscripts on the right side refer to the period in which the purchases are made and the qs refer to the quantities of each good in that combination.

The Laspeyres index of real income is expressed as the ratio of the new and original budgets:

$$Q_L = \frac{B_1 + \Delta B}{B_1} = \frac{B_3}{B_1}$$
$$= \frac{P_x^1 x_2 + P_y^1 y_2}{P_x^1 x_1 + P_y^1 y_1}.$$

Clearly, this merely expresses in terms of constant prices the real income in the new period as a percentage of expenditure in the initial or base period. In more general notation, this may be written as:

Laspeyres Index $Q_L = \dfrac{\Sigma P_1 q_2}{\Sigma P_1 q_1}.$

Using the same notation, the Paasche index may be expressed as:

Paasche Index $Q_P = \dfrac{\Sigma P_2 q_2}{\Sigma P_2 q_1}.$

We may incorporate these indexes into our measurement scheme quite straightforwardly. Real income increases may be identified by using the Paasche index. Recall that welfare increases are firmly identified by Case II, that is, when

$$\Sigma P_2 q_2 > \Sigma P_2 q_1.$$

Dividing both sides of this inequality by the positive value $\Sigma P_2 q_1$ does not change the direction of the inequality; hence:

$$\frac{\Sigma P_2 q_2}{\Sigma P_2 q_1} > \frac{\Sigma P_2 q_1}{\Sigma P_2 q_1}.$$

As the right-hand side of this inequality equals 1 and the left-hand side is the Paasche real income index, we may conclude the following:

Whenever the Paasche index has a value greater than 1, real income has increased relative to the base period.

Using a similar technique, we may identify cases of declining real income. Recall that real income falls in Case I, such that:

$$\Sigma P_1 q_1 > \Sigma P_1 q_2.$$

Dividing both sides by the positive amount $\Sigma P_1 q_2$ does not change the direction of the inequality; hence:

$$\frac{\Sigma P_1 q_1}{\Sigma P_1 q_2} > \frac{\Sigma P_1 q_2}{\Sigma P_1 q_2}.$$

However, taking the reciprocal of each side does reverse the inequality, giving:

$$\frac{\Sigma P_1 q_2}{\Sigma P_1 q_1} < \frac{\Sigma P_1 q_2}{\Sigma P_1 q_2}.$$

The left side of this inequality is the Laspeyres index of real income, and the right side has a value of 1 once again. Case I is, therefore, identified when the Laspeyres index has a value of less than unity. This provides us with a second principle of income measurement: *Whenever the Laspeyres index has a value less than 1, real income has fallen relative to the base period.*

The Purchasing Power of Money

The value of money reflects what can be purchased with it. When prices of goods rise, the amount of goods obtainable with any nominal sum declines, and vice versa. Again, however, attempts to be specific about the rate of such a decline or rise in the purchasing power of money are complicated by the aggregation problem. If some prices rise while others fall, the ability of money to purchase some goods falls while its ability to purchase others rises. Does this mean that such measures of purchasing power as the Consumer Price Index are essentially meaningless?

Certainly not. A decline in the prices of those items that we never purchase does not increase the value of money to us. Its value is determined by its ability to command those items that we *do* wish to purchase. Its value rises and falls in proportion to the importance of the given goods in our budgets. Measures of real income reflect the amount of nominal income required to produce a particular level of utility. Measures of purchasing power reflect the rate at which nominal amounts of money can be used to achieve particular levels of real income. Thus, price changes that have an insignificant impact on real income will have an insignificant impact on the purchasing power of money as well.

Price Indexes

It is convenient to express the purchasing power of money in terms of its inverse—that is, the **price level**. The higher the purchasing power of money is, the lower is the price level. It is also useful to express this measure in terms of an index, as was done with real income. The construction of a price index, therefore, involves calculating the rate of change in nominal income required to purchase a given level of real income.

Just as measures of real income may be calculated in terms of new and old sets of prices, measures of the price level may be obtained in terms of either the new or old levels of real income. This may be seen in terms of Figure 6.7, which involves the same price changes as the earlier figures. At the original prices, combination K is purchased. After a rise in the price of x and a decline in the price of y, combination H is purchased. We may use as our measure of the change in the price level either the amount of additional money required to purchase the original bundle of goods K or the reduction in the amount of money required to purchase the new combination H. As the former employs original data as the basis for comparison, it is referred to as the Laspeyres measure of price level change. The latter, using new data in this role, is referred to as the Paasche measure of price level change.

As we have already discovered, mixed price changes produce ambiguous effects on real income. Mixed price changes may similarly yield ambiguous changes in the purchasing power of money. In Figure 6.7 the nominal sum B_1

Figure 6.7   *Price Indexes*

Laspeyres price indexes are computed by identifying the ratio of the income required to purchase the original combination, K, at the new prices relative to the old prices. This identifies an increase in the price level in this case, amounting to B_3/B_1. The Paasche price index measures the percentage represented by spending required to purchase the new combination, H, at the new prices relative to the old prices; this would be B_2/B_1.

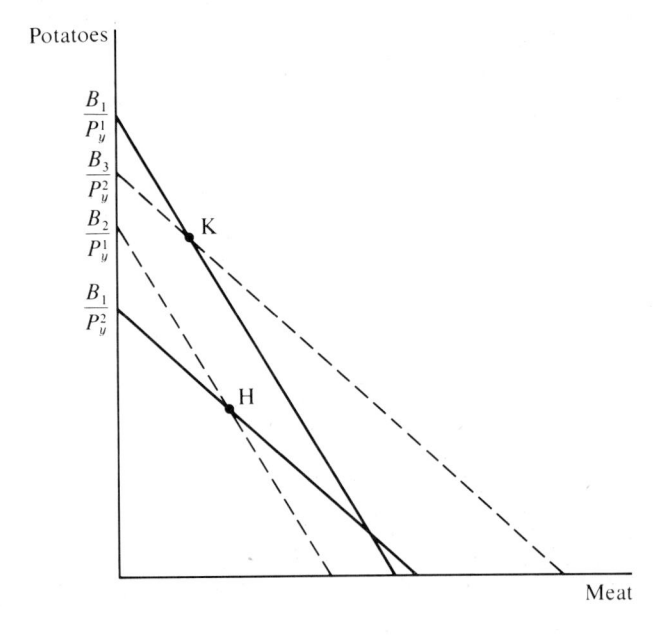

clearly falls in purchasing power, because it enables the purchaser to attain a real income that is inferior to that obtained originally. Combination K is preferred to combination H. This need not, of course, always be the result. This example corresponds to Case I in our analysis of income measurement—indeed, there is a direct correspondence between changes in real income brought about by price changes and changes in the price level produced by the same changes. A price change that reduces real income reduces the purchasing power of money, and one that increases real income has the opposite effect. We may therefore employ the three cases developed in Figure 6.4 to reduce the range of ambiguity in price level measurement.

Case I depicted in Figure 6.7 reflects a case of unambiguous price level increase. Nominal sum B_1 offers a preferred combination and, therefore, more real income before the price changes than after. From our earlier discussion we know that Case I is identified by:

$$\Sigma P_1 q_1 > \Sigma P_1 q_2.$$

Dividing both sides of this inequality by the positive quantity $\Sigma P_2 q_2$ does not change the direction of the inequality; hence:

$$\frac{\Sigma P_1 q_1}{\Sigma P_2 q_2} > \frac{\Sigma P_1 q_2}{\Sigma P_2 q_2}.$$

Inverting both sides of the inequality *does* change the direction and produces:

$$\frac{\Sigma P_2 q_2}{\Sigma P_1 q_1} < \frac{\Sigma P_2 q_2}{\Sigma P_1 q_2}.$$

The left side of this inequality measures the new period nominal income as a percentage of base period nominal income. Where total spending before and after the price change remains the same, the left side will obviously have a value of 1. The right side of the inequality now represents a Paasche index of price level change.

A Paasche price level index that has a value greater than 1 indicates that the price level has risen relative to its base period level.

The purchasing power of money therefore declines in such cases. This inequality also tells us that nominal income rises of less than the increase in the Paasche price level index clearly reduce real income relative to the base period.

Case II identifies price changes that clearly raise real income. Less nominal income is therefore required to produce the same level of real income; hence, in such a case the price level definitely falls. Recall that Case II is identified by the condition:

$$\Sigma P_2 q_2 > \Sigma P_2 q_1.$$

Dividing both sides of this inequality by the positive value $\Sigma P_1 q_1$ does not change, the direction of the inequality; hence:

$$\frac{\Sigma P_2 q_2}{\Sigma P_1 q_1} > \frac{\Sigma P_2 q_1}{\Sigma P_1 q_1}.$$

The left side of this inequality again measures the percentage change in nominal income relative to the base period. The right side in this case is a Laspeyres measure of the price index. This inequality tells us that a Laspeyres price index with a value less than 1 indicates that the real income purchasable with a fixed nominal sum increases. *Where the Laspeyres index has a value less than 1, the price level has decreased relative to its base period level.* The purchasing power of money therefore increases in these cases.

As is true with measures of real income change, a range of ambiguity remains that falls into neither Case I nor Case II. There are some sets of price changes that indicate a fall in the price level when measured with the Paasche index and that indicate a rise in the price level when measured with the Laspeyres index. These price changes correspond to Case III. As we lack enough information to assess the impact of such price changes on real income, we also cannot measure the quantity of money required to produce a given level of real income. For those sets of price changes in this category we cannot determine the direction of change in the purchasing power of money.

Practical Considerations

Most indexes of output, real income, and prices are Laspeyres measures. Gross national product, national income, and the Consumer Price Index are Laspeyres indexes, for example. The popularity of this measure is no accident. When calculating the value of any index over a series of years, one of the principal considerations will be the cost of data collection. For an index of real income, quantities of each good produced must be collected in each year. If the index is a Paasche measure of real income, using current price data in both numerator and denominator of the index, then this must be collected each year as well. If, however, the index is a Laspeyres measure, original base year prices may be used and only quantity data need be collected more than once. Similarly, Paasche price indexes require collection of both price and quantity information in each year, while Laspeyres price indexes require the collection of only one set of quantity data.

There are good economic reasons for favoring the Laspeyres index over the Paasche. Unfortunately, the Laspeyres index has some offsetting disadvantages that are not well understood in popular discussions of the various measures. For most of the period during which these indexes have been used, we might infer that measured economic activity has been growing at the same time that the purchasing power of money has been diminishing. Based on our previous discussion, however, we know that it is in precisely these instances of (1) indicated increasing real income, and (2) indicated rises in the price level that Laspeyres indexes provide ambiguous answers. Measures of economic growth and inflation are thus to be treated with caution by persons with some sophistication in economics.

Of perhaps even larger significance in the interpretation of index numbers is the problem of changing technology over time. Several decades ago, freshly squeezed orange juice was an expensive but common household beverage. The "juicer" was a popular household appliance, and greengrocers did a substantial volume in oranges expressly sold for juice. The introduction of frozen orange juice has almost completely displaced this older product not only in homes, but in most restaurants as well. A similar narrative might be told about fountain versus ballpoint pens, tailored versus ready-to-wear suits, and theater movies versus television entertainment. In each case a substantially different product (often of much lower quality) has replaced another. Changing technology, which permits the production of the new product at lower cost, is responsible for this change in buyer behavior. How are we to factor the results of these innovations into our calculations of changing real income and the price level?

Changing technology even more frequently produces *improved* products that nevertheless bear the same name. There can be little doubt that razor blades produced today are both sharper and longer lasting than those available 50 years ago. The introduction of the silicon chip has vastly improved clerical and computational devices, and the development of acrylic and other chemically produced fibers have made possible the production of more durable, comfortable, and cleanable clothing. Fixed quantities of these modern items can be expected to produce more consumer satisfaction—and therefore more real income—than their equivalents produced with earlier technologies.

Unfortunately there are no clear-cut solutions to these important problems. The emergence of new products and the disappearance of old ones clearly confounds our indexes, which require inclusion of base period quantities or prices in both numerator and denominator. A Laspeyres index will include goods that existed in earlier periods but have been displaced. The diminished importance of such goods in modern budgets need not imply diminished real income even though this would be the indication of the index number calculated. Similarly, a Paasche index will include current levels of newly developed goods and zero quantities for these goods in previous periods. This can be particularly troublesome in cases such as the one where the new good introduced is actually inferior to the good it displaced, a factor not counted in such an index.

All these problems suggest that index numbers, whether of prices or real income, are best employed over periods minimally affected by technical change—that is, short periods. While it is possible to link indexes and produce century-long estimates of per capita income or the price level, it is clear that such periods involve vast changes in technology and, therefore, consumer purchases. Economists and laymen should thus approach the interpretation of such series and empirical work employing them with appropriate skepticism.

6.2 Choice with Imperfect Information

Most of the choices analyzed up to this point have involved decisions whose outcomes were known to the chooser. Purchases in the market were assumed to make available particular quantities of goods whose characteristics were observed and understood. Two important types of transactions involve goods for which this sort of information typically is not obtainable by the chooser. The first of these concerns uncertainty arising out of the unpredictability of nature itself. Betting on red at the roulette table is one such transaction; the "good" obtained through such a "purchase" differs markedly depending on where the ivory ball happens to settle. Planting wheat is a less obvious example of the same sort of choice; the rewards to such an activity depend to a certain extent on variations in the weather during the growing season, which cannot be predicted with certainty. The second type of transaction involves uncertainty due to variability in the good obtained because of the costliness of the transaction itself. Purchasing a novel by an unknown author entails this sort of uncertainty.

Risk and Insurance

Discussion of the first type of uncertainty can best be developed in the context of resource allocation over possible "states of the world." Students should not be put off by the Buck Rogers sound of such a topic. Whenever we make choices under conditions of uncertainty, we are actually having to decide how to allocate resources over such states. When a player calls "rough" or "smooth" to decide who will serve at tennis, he or she is placing the advantage of first service in the state of the world that he or she calls. There are, of course, two possible states of the world that are relevant to this decision. In a fair spin of the racquet either is equally likely. As both are possible, however, rational choosers will wish to allocate resources so that they will not be seriously disadvantaged in either. For this reason the advantage of "choice of court" is typically given to the loser of the spin.

In this discussion we will make frequent reference to some basic principles of statistics. The first of these is the *probability* of an event. By probability we mean the proportion of the time over which a particular event would occur if the circumstances producing the event were repeated many times. The probability of the event "rough" in the tennis example is therefore 0.5. *The probabilities of all possible states of the world must sum to unity.* We will use the symbol ϕ_i to indicate the probability of the *i*th state. Thus, for *n* states,

$$\sum_{i=1}^{n} \phi_i = 1.$$

It is often important to be able to interpret the result of all possible outcomes of uncertain events. In managing the household portfolio, for example, one must choose whether to hold assets with a certain yield, like government bonds, or to hold assets whose yields are uncertain, like common stocks. In order to make such decisions rationally, it is necessary to aggregate all possible outcomes of decisions involving uncertain choices. In other words, we would like to know a way to combine all possible outcomes of holding uncertain stocks so that this investment strategy can be compared with the alternative of "riskless" investment. The proper way to do this is to weight all outcomes by the probability of their occurrence. This weighted sum is called the **expected value** of the possible outcomes. For *n* possible yields of varying value Y_i, the expected value is:

$$\overline{Y} = \sum_{i=1}^{n} \phi_i \cdot Y_i.$$

Intuitively expected value, $\overline{Y}$, is the average of returns that would be received on this investment if it were made many times.

Students should be cautioned not to interpret expected value to mean "guaranteed," for the possible outcomes of a single investment of this type may vary widely; the actual yield on such an investment may be high or low, depending on the luck of the investor. On the other hand, an investor who buys many such uncertain investments reduces the likelihood of extremely low returns (on average) as well as extremely high ones. This pooling of risks to reduce uncertainty will play an important role in the discussion that follows.

The analysis of choice under uncertainty is fundamentally no different than those of other choices we have examined. The two components of choice, the opportunity set and the rank-ordering process, must be developed. The principal difference between this choice and others examined earlier is that the chooser will ultimately enjoy only a part of the combination selected. The choices involve making provision for *all* possible outcomes only one of which will ultimately occur. The analysis of choice under conditions of unknown probabilities of various states of the world is too complex for study at this stage. We shall therefore make the simplifying assumption that the probabilities of the alternative states of the world are correctly estimated by choosers.

People typically are not indifferent concerning how their resources are allocated among states of the world any more than they are indifferent concerning how their consumption is arranged over time. Just as people budget their spending over the month so that they may eat during the final week, they will take precautions to insure that purchasing power is available to them for all possible states of the world. For example, few people will risk their life savings on one card game, because doing so would imply very much reduced consumption in the states associated with losing. To more fully understand this choice, we must develop some principles relevant to the determination of the rank-ordering process and the opportunity set.

Ranking with Uncertainty

Consider the common example of disability insurance. The two states of the world concerned with such a choice are "able to work" and "disabled." In the absence of insurance, household income will clearly be higher if the principal wage earner is healthy than if he or she is unable to work. Yet the household members are unable to predict which state will occur. Assume that there are no other income-producing assets in the household. The uninsured state in such a choice corresponds to combination K in Figure 6.8. If the wage earner is well, the household may consume income of w_1, but if he or she should become disabled, there is no income to support any consumption. The indifference curve passing through point K will connect all combinations of income in the two possible states that yield the same utility.

Let U_1 be such an indifference curve. All previously assumed properties of rank-ordering processes apply to indifference curves in this choice. Here, however, even stronger assumptions about preferences can be defended. There seems no reason to believe that income in one state is likely to yield more utility to the

Figure 6.8 *Indifference Curves over Possible States of the World*

Each combination identifies income received in two possible states: when the chooser is well and when he or she is disabled. Only one state will occur, but the chooser is uncertain about which one. Combinations lying along the 45° line provide equal income in each state. Combinations K, T, and H all provide equal utility. The property of convexity is assumed to hold for these indifference curves.

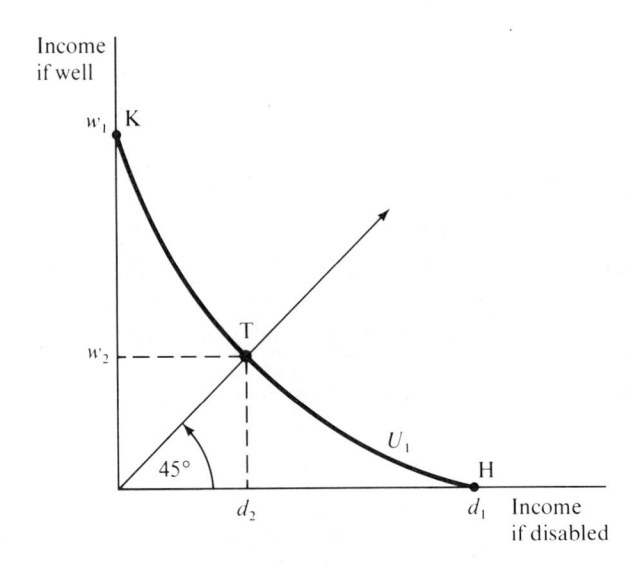

chooser than income in another. Our appreciation of a fine dinner or a good concert is not typically greater one week than another. It seems plausible to assume that consumption is equally desirable to household members regardless of whether the breadwinner is working. We therefore assume that utility associated with consumption is *independent* of which state occurs.

This assumption has important implications for the shape of indifference curves, including curve U_1 in Figure 6.8. If utility of consumption is independent of the state in which the consumption occurs, we may express this relationship between utility in the ith state and income in that state as:

$$U_i = f(Y_i).$$

Prospective utility involving the ranking of combinations of income in each state will therefore involve an aggregation of the utilities of each state. The assumption of independence implies that this aggregation will be weighted by the probabilities of the occurrence of each event. Recall our definition of *expected value* as a weighted sum of the values of possible events where the weights are the probabilities of the occurrence of each event. **Expected utility** is therefore a weighted sum of the utilities associated with each possible state in which the weights are the probabilities of the occurrence of each state. Expected utility in our disability insurance example may therefore be expressed as follows:

$$U = \phi_w U^w + \phi_d U^d$$
$$= \phi_w f(w) + \phi_d f(d).$$

In this equation ϕ_i is the probability of the ith event, w is income in the well state, and d is income in the disabled state.

Let us consider how to derive the slope of an indifference curve linking all combinations of income in these two states that produce the same expected utility. We may do this as we did in Chapter 3 by holding utility constant and observing the implied relationship between changes in income in the two states. The *total differential*[3] of the utility function is very handy for this purpose. The probabilities of the two states are constant. The total differential relating changes in income in the two states with changes in utility may thus be written as follows:

$$\Delta U = \phi_w \cdot \frac{\Delta U^w}{\Delta w} \cdot \Delta w + \phi_d \cdot \frac{\Delta U^d}{\Delta d} \cdot \Delta d.$$

As there is no change in utility along an indifference curve, the right side of this expression must sum to zero. The slope of the indifference curve expresses the ratio of the change in income in the well state, Δw, to the change in income in the disabled state, Δd, subject to the condition just stated. We may therefore derive an expression for this slope by setting ΔU equal to zero and solving for $\Delta w / \Delta d$:

$$\frac{\Delta w}{\Delta d} = - \frac{\phi_d \cdot \frac{\Delta U^d}{\Delta d}}{\phi_w \cdot \frac{\Delta U^w}{\Delta w}}.$$

We may infer an important property of indifference curves from this formulation. *At combinations containing equal amounts of income in each state, the MRS of income between states will exactly equal the ratio of the probabilities of the two states.* Recall from Chapter 3 that the MRS of any utility function must equal minus the slope of the indifference curve. The MRS will therefore equal ϕ_d / ϕ_w when $\Delta U^d / \Delta d = \Delta U^w / \Delta w$. Consider combination T in Figure 6.8, where $d_2 = w_2$. At this combination, the household receives the same income regardless of which state occurs. On the basis of our assumption of independence, the relationship between income and utility is independent of state, and therefore $\Delta U^d / \Delta d$ will in fact equal $\Delta U^w / \Delta w$ at this point. These terms will cancel in this slope expression, implying at point T and all others along the 45° line the following relationship:

---

[3] See the discussion of total differentials in Chapter 1.

Chapter 6 Income Measurement and Uncertainty

When income is equal in each state,

$$MRS = \frac{\phi_d}{\phi_w}.$$

The postulate of convexity implies that slopes along indifference curves lying above the 45° line are increasingly steeper than minus this ratio and that slopes below are increasingly flatter. For the case of equal probabilities (as in a coin toss), the MRS along the 45° line will be unity.

The Opportunity Set

Now we must consider what determines the set of alternative income combinations from which households must choose. If each household finds itself situated at a point like K in Figure 6.8, we need to determine the opportunity cost of obtaining additional dollars of income in the disabled state. While individual households will eventually experience only one of these states, all will not share the same fate; some will enjoy good health, and others will become disabled. We need to determine the cost per dollar of income of insuring against the disabled state.

Let us assume that the working population contains n people who are identical in earning capacity and in probabilities of health and disability. The number who will be well, n_w, may therefore be represented as $\phi_w n$, and the number who will be disabled, n_d, may be represented as $\phi_d n$, such that:

$$n = n_w + n_d$$
$$= \phi_w n + \phi_d n.$$

Total income of those working will be $wn_w = w\phi_w n$, and total income of those disabled will be $dn_d = d\phi_d n$, so that total income from both groups will be:

$$I = \phi_w nw + \phi_d nd.$$

The change in total income may be expressed as:

$$\Delta I = \phi_w n \Delta w + \phi_d n \Delta d.$$

A break-even insurance policy requires that all income paid out (to those who experience the disabled state) equal the income given up (by those who are well); ΔI must equal zero. Setting the right side of this expression equal to zero and solving for the implied slope of this opportunity set yields:

$$\frac{\Delta w}{\Delta d} = -\frac{\phi_d n}{\phi_w n} = -\frac{\phi_d}{\phi_w}.$$

Minus this slope gives us the opportunity cost per dollar of income in the disabled state in terms of income forgone if well.

Insurance companies, for example, may break even by offering income contingent upon disability of the wage earner at an exchange rate equal to the ratio of the probabilities of good health and disability. The amount of income received from those who are well will just offset the amount expected to be paid out. Realistically, these companies will have to charge sufficiently more for such claims to cover their costs of operation as well as to service a reserve for untypically high disability rates in particular years. We will ignore these factors and assume that prices do reflect actually fair rates for the insurance purchased.

The opportunity set available to households making these allocative decisions may be constructed in Figure 6.9. This figure is identical to Figure 6.8, except that the household opportunities are no longer limited to combination K. In this state households may exchange income for claims to income contingent upon disability at the rate just derived—that is, ϕ_d/ϕ_w. The opportunity set passing through the initial endowment K therefore slopes downward to the right at precisely minus this rate.

The *expected value* of income for every combination will be the same at every point on the opportunity set. This is true, for example, at points K, H, and F, where the expected values of income are, respectively:

Figure 6.9 *Choice under Uncertainty*

Insurance at actuarily fair rates is available at an opportunity cost equal to the ratio of the probability of the occurrence of the two states. This presents the chooser with an opportunity set extending linearly from w_1 to d_1. The chooser will select combination H, providing perfect insurance—that is, equal income—in each possible state. At this combination the chooser's MRS will just equal the opportunity cost of providing income in the disabled state.

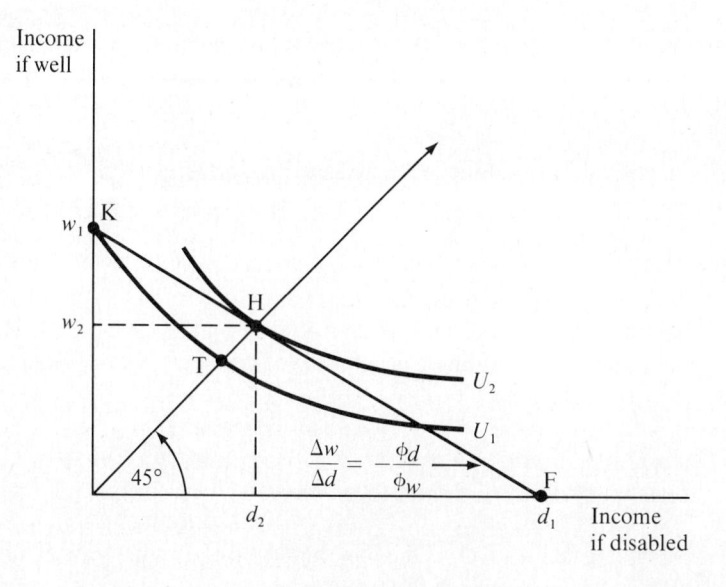

$$\overline{Y} = \phi_w \cdot w_1 + \phi_d \cdot 0 = \phi_w \cdot w_2 + \phi_d \cdot d_2 = \phi_w \cdot 0 + \phi_d \cdot d_1.$$

This does not mean that all combinations will be regarded as equivalent. Indifference curve U_1 has a slope of $-\phi_d/\phi_w$ at point T, where it crosses the 45° line and must be steeper above this line. This indifference curve must therefore lie below the upper portion of the opportunity set, indicating that combinations on the opportunity set to the southeast are preferred to K. As the opportunity set has a slope of $-\phi_d/\phi_w$ and the indifference curves have this same slope only along the 45° line, the most favored point along the opportunity set will be combination H. At this point indifference curve U_2 will just be tangent to the opportunity set.

The tangency at H has clear implications for behavior under uncertainty. People will seek to make provisions for all contingencies, and if exchange rates for claims to income among states of the world are probabilistically "fair," people will make sure to *competely eliminate* that uncertainty. Note that combination H implies that *income will not vary from state to state*. It is this preference for certainty among combinations of state contingent claims having the same market value that gives meaning to the assertion by economists that people are "risk averse."

Insurance is never offered for free, however. Insurance must be sold, funds must be invested and administered, and claims must be investigated and paid. These costs of doing business may be recovered only by charging more for the insurance than the probabilistically fair premiums. Under such conditions we might predict that less than *complete* insurance will be purchased.

Uncertainty due to the unpredictability of nature extends beyond states of health, of course. The variability of weather affects agriculture, construction, and transportation, to name a few industries, and introduces great uncertainty into the economic lives of people connected with them. Variations in the business cycle and political conditions imply uncertainty in many economic activities. Lives of household breadwinners themselves are uncertain, exposing other members to the risk of loss of the earnings they provide. The organization of markets to offer insurance in many such cases poses transaction costs that are prohibitive. These costs include not only those of administering and marketing insurance just noted but costs associated with monitoring the performance of the terms of such insurance agreements. These latter costs emerge in connection with the second type of uncertainty to be discussed here and greatly complicate insurance contracts for uncertainty due to "natural" causes. These costs inhibit the offering of universal contingent claims contracts permitting insurance of all uncertainties. This does not mean that such uncertainty fails to influence the nature of the transactions in which it occurs.

Informal Markets for Insurance

Often, in the absence of an explicit market for insurance of such uncertainty, either buyers or sellers (or sometimes both) will perform the insurance function. Consider the market for hotel accommodations. Uncertainty over the availability of accommodations could be very costly to travelers were rooms filled on a strict first-come–first-served basis. This uncertainty might easily be eliminated, however, through a system of advanced contracting for rooms. This is not exactly what we observe. Typically, prospective guests are allowed to reserve rooms in hotels at no apparent charge; when these people fail to appear to claim the rooms they have reserved, they pay nothing. This interesting practice may be explained as a type of insurance contract offered by hotels to their customers.

Travel plans themselves are often uncertain. Business meetings must often be rearranged; transportation arrangements occasionally go awry; health and weather can intervene. Requiring prospective hotel guests to contract for rooms on particular dates, regardless of whether or not they appeared to claim them, would expose these customers to uncertainty concerning a significant economic loss. Purchasing insurance to cover such uncertainty would involve significant transactions costs of the type just discussed. The bearing of these costs is unnecessary in this case because the suppliers of hotel services may themselves offer this insurance. They do this by charging a higher price for their rooms than they would be able to charge if they offered no reservations service. Hotel owners are willing to offer this arrangement because the additional revenue from the higher rates covers the cost of the increased vacancies. Hotel guests, on the other hand, are willing to pay the higher fees in order to reduce the uncertainty over the availability of rooms on the one hand and the uncertainty concerning the possible cost of contracting for unused rooms on the other.

Evidence that **risk pooling** is important to this phenomenon may be seen in another observation. We would predict that on occasions when hotel accommodations are offered on a contract basis (that is, the hotel is guaranteed revenues for rooms and thus bears none of the cost of uncertain arrivals), hotels will charge lower fees. Competition for these customers, the cost of supplying of which will be lower, will drive the price down to the level that covers the cost of the room alone. This is precisely what we observe. Rooms rented as part of packaged tours (which are not refundable) and rooms contracted for conventions (which also guarantee occupancy of certain numbers) are typically made available at substantial discounts from regular rates. Rooms offered without the reservations insurance service cost less to supply and thus are priced lower.

Insurance of this type covering the uncertainty of patronage for services is a widespread phenomenon. We observe similar arrangements in airline and restaurant reservations. We see it in appointments at the dentist and the hairdresser. The reserving of resources is costly to the supplier in each of these cases, and we can be sure that these costs are covered in the prices charged. Customers are willing to pay the higher prices because of the reduced uncertainty obtained under these arrangements.

Another important type of uncertainty concerns variation in the quality of manufactured goods. With the advent of assembly line processes, individual components of the goods assembled were designed not to fit in one particular unit but to be interchangeable within all units produced. This greatly reduced the cost of manufacture and maintenance, but at a significant cost in terms of performance in some cases. When individual parts are made to specifications within allowable tolerances, most will fit together in the manner planned. In a few predictable cases, however, the tolerated error in one part will be compounded with the errors in others, producing poor performance. Quality control procedures seek to identify these units, but perfect inspection is prohibitively costly in most cases. A certain number of units of these well designed but badly performing goods will therefore reach the market.

Goods produced in this way might simply be sold on the basis of caveat emptor. Under these circumstances, however, each purchaser would bear the risk that the unit purchased might perform badly. Such a risk can loom significant in the case of a large purchase such as an automobile, a home, or a major appliance. Even in the case of less expensive items the receipt of a bad performer[4] can be an annoying and costly experience. Consumers exposed to this uncertainty will wish to insure against these losses, but markets in such contingent claims are impractical for the same reasons as in the examples discussed earlier.

Again, however, the supplier steps into the breach. Most manufactured goods, particularly those representing a substantial outlay for the typical household, are offered with a guarantee. Those items that do not perform up to standards will usually be repaired or replaced by the manufacturer. This ubiquitous practice is not the result of sheer chance. The repair and replacement of merchandise is costly and these costs will, of course, have to be covered in the prices of the goods sold. They might clearly be sold at a lower price without such guarantees. The fact that consumers choose guaranteed goods at higher prices over unguaranteed goods at lower prices suggests that the guarantees themselves are valued by households. Clearly here, as in the hotel reservations case, households are purchasing two products: the manufactured good and a form of insurance against the uncertainty of receipt of a bad performer.

In spite of the transaction costs involved in the explicit sale of contingent claim contracts to "insure" uncertainty arising out of natural causes, we nevertheless observe efforts to arrange affairs so as to reduce exposure to such risk. Although **complete insurance**, predicted in our model of costless exchange, will not be realized where such transactions are costly, we do observe many features of market economies that are consistent with efforts to reduce uncertainty. These range from the reservation and product guarantees just discussed to the issuing of rainchecks at outdoor events and the purchase of commodity futures contracts to cover changes in the value of inventories held. The extension of choice theory into the realm of uncertainty is therefore an extremely valuable tool in the explanation of economic behavior.

Transaction Costs and Imperfect Information

Much of the uncertainty confronted by consumers in our economy has not so much to do with "luck" and "fate" as it has to do with other people. A market system is organized on an adversary basis in which each economic agent, whether a buyer or seller, is seeking to get the best deal he or she can. This poses few problems if both parties are fully informed concerning the terms of the exchange. A moment's reflection will reveal, however, just how strict a condition being *fully informed* is.

---

[4]One is tempted to refer to such well designed but badly performing items as "lemons." Unfortunately, this designation has been appropriated in the lexicon of economics to refer to another phenomenon, discussed later in the chapter.

In a sale contract, "delivery" is not legally complete until the recipient has inspected the merchandise. "Inspection" has been interpreted very narrowly by our courts, however, so that receipt itself is accepted as evidence of the buyer's full awareness of the condition of the accepted merchandise. On the other hand, when goods are purchased consumers typically make only the sketchiest inspection of what they have received. Electric toasters are purchased without verifying that they indeed brown bread satisfactorily. Tennis balls are carried away without verification that they bounce. Cans of peaches are bought at the supermarket with no thought given to opening the can beforehand to insure that the contents are indeed peaches.

Inspection might be completely performed in each of these cases. Bread might be taken along to the department store to test the toaster. Tins of balls might be opened at the tennis shop. Cans of peaches might be sampled in the market. The information obtained through such inspections would be costly to a larger or smaller degree, but unlike in the case of uncertainty discussed in the preceding section, this information is available at some cost. The feature that is important here is the fact that in so many of these transactions consumers do not find it worthwhile to engage in any but the most perfunctory inspections. Tomatos are squeezed and watermelons thumped, but tests requiring more effort are rarely performed.

Of course, consumers are protected by law to a certain extent. A supplier who grossly misrepresents his or her goods may be prosecuted for fraud. Better business bureaus bring pressure to bear on firms to supply exactly what they offer. Government agencies like the Department of Agriculture grade certain items like meat. Independent testing laboratories like the Consumer Union produce information about products that is sold to prospective customers. But even all of these activities taken together cannot give us complete confidence in the goods that we buy in most of our day-to-day transactions.

Consumer unions cannot investigate every can of peaches or tennis balls, and government grades are notoriously broad. Better business bureaus may be ignored, and the scope for misleading but still nonfraudulent claims about products is often so wide as to make legal remedies useless. As it is clearly less costly for suppliers to produce shoddy merchandise than goods of high quality, our problem is to explain why consumers so often find their expectations of high quality in goods confirmed.

The Lemon Principle

Let us attempt to formulate the problem more explicitly. Consider the case of used automobiles. For reasons already elaborated, automobiles of a particular model and vintage are not of uniform quality. Some will be very close to design specifications in all respects and perform well. Others will deviate within allowed tolerances and perform poorly. We can imagine a distribution of all such cars ranging over some quality scale. Assume that the properties of this distribution are known so that consumers are aware that a car purchased from the distribution will have an **expected quality** equal to the mean of this distribution. If no additional information about the quality of any individual car offered for sale is available to buyer or seller, then the price agreed upon by both buyer and seller will be based on this expected value.

This will not typically be the case for people who have owned their automobiles for some time. Experience alone with an automobile will provide information about its performance, giving the user a clearer idea about where this particular unit falls in the distribution. If the market price is based on the mean of all such cars, this will influence the willingness of owners to sell. Those who discover that their cars are better than average will not sell at a price based on inferior expected performance. Those with cars of below-par performance will gladly sell them at a price based on expected quality of *all* cars. Those cars actually offered at such a price therefore constitute a nonrandomly selected sample from the distribution. This sample will have a lower mean quality than that of the "population" of all cars.

Shrewd buyers will be aware of this adverse selection process. They will expect used automobiles to have a lower-than-average quality and will adjust their price offers accordingly. If such expectations do influence the market price, however, this lowering of price will further influence the quality of cars offered for sale. Owners of cars of quality in the neighborhood of the mean will now refuse to sell at a price based on lower-than-average expected quality. Lower prices, therefore, bring forth to the market a group of cars offered for sale whose quality is lower still. One can imagine this process continuing until the only used cars sold are those of the absolutely poorest quality—that is, the "lemons." Markets in which sellers have more information than buyers suffer from what is referred to in economic theory as the **lemon principle**,[5] and it is potentially a serious problem.

Clearly the scope for emergence of the lemon principle extends beyond markets for used goods. As we have just discussed, most producers have far more information about their products' quality than do purchasers of these goods. Within the government-proclaimed classification of "prime beef" are steaks of unsurpassed tenderness as well as others best suited to use as shoe leather. Good butchers can tell the difference at a glance, but many an unwary visitor to the supermarket would find the two indistinguishable. American red wines meeting government standards for sale as cabernet sauvignon can be as good as a bordeaux from a distinguished French chateau or positively undrinkable. As it is less costly to produce tough meat and awful wine, why do we not see the lemon principle in effect here? Why do not all cattle farmers and wine producers offer products that meet the letter of these standards and no more?

Brand Loyalty

At least a partial answer to this question lies in the fact that most goods are sold *in conjunction with information*. We rarely buy prime beef or cabernet sauvignon as such—we buy steaks with our favorite supermarket's label and our preferred

---

[5] This discussion is based on a well-known paper laying out the nature of information assymmetries by George Akerlof, "The Market for 'Lemons': Quality, Uncertainty and the Market Mechanism," *Quarterly Journal of Economics* 84 (August 1970): 488–500.

brand of cabernet. We rely on the reputations of these suppliers to insure the expected quality in the products we buy. The question remains, however: Why is such a reputation a reliable guide to quality? The answer is that adherence to the quality standard implicit in the name is profitable.

Consider how this information affects behavior on both sides of the market. Assume that a particular supplier of wine has a reputation for making an outstanding cabernet. Consumers who rely on this reputation will be willing to pay more for this brand of wine than they will for cabernet with an unrecognizable label. This premium in the price paid reflects the value of the information contained in the reputation. In a sense consumers in this case, as in the preceding section, purchase two products. The first is, of course, wine; the second product here may be thought of as information about that wine.

A supplier with a reputation might exploit it by misrepresenting his or her product to be of higher quality than it is. In so doing the supplier could, in the short run, obtain more for his or her output than its worth to those to whom it was sold. However, this short-run profit would be obtained at the cost of a depreciated reputation. Future buyers, wary of having been deceived once, will not buy invalid information a second time. On the other hand, customers whose expectations concerning quality are fulfilled will continue to buy this information. They will continue to attach the value of valid information to products sold by these suppliers. We cannot rule out the possibility that the potential short-term gain will always exceed the long-term cost of deception. Time alters tastes, making the sale of particular lines of products less profitable, and increases the attractiveness of "cashing out" the reputations of some products. The importance of brand names and product loyalty cannot be overestimated, however, in the fostering of orderly market processes. Even the Soviet Union, whose ideology officially regards such practices as decadent capitalism, has found it expedient to quietly permit labels identifying sources to be placed on some merchandise.[6]

Property Rights and Information

Government activities that raise the cost of supplying product-related information will reduce the extent to which it is supplied, while activities that lower that cost will have the opposite effect. Clearly, one activity that dramatically lowers this cost is protection of the exclusive rights to labels and trademarks. Consider the result if any winemaker were permitted to place on his or her product a label identical to that used by a premium table wine producer. Use of such a label would extend to this supplier's output the reputation for high quality enjoyed by the premium winemaker. Unlike the latter, however, such a producer would have little incentive to maintain the high quality standards responsible for this reputation. On the contrary, higher profits could be obtained by producing wine as cheaply as possible while attaching to it the label of the premium producer.

Consumers would find the labels on these two wines indistinguishable. Each time they inadvertently purchased the poor-quality product, the reputation of the

---

[6] Marshall I. Goldman, "Product Differentiation and Advertising: Some Lessons from Soviet Experience," *Journal of Political Economy* 68 (August 1960): 346–357.

premium firm would suffer. Such copying, if practiced on a large scale, could destroy the reputation of the brand-name producer. Customers would cease to attach information value to these labels, and premium products would eventually sell for no more than unknown wines. If the reputation of these firms did not result in higher prices being paid for their products, then they would have no reason to maintain high-quality standards. Failure to protect producers' rights to the publication of information used to identify their products increases the likelihood that the lemon principle will come into play.

Advertising and Demand

Having laid the necessary foundation, we may now construct an analysis of one of the most hotly debated topics in consumer theory: the role of advertising. First, let us consider the effects of advertising on the market for a product. There can be little doubt that the effect of spending on advertising is to shift demand for the product outward. In Figure 6.10, for example, we depict demand prior to advertising by schedule D_1. Given a fixed supply, shown by curve S, the market price for this product is P_1. By devoting resources to advertising, demand shifts rightward to some position like D_2, increasing the price of the product to P_2.

There is little disagreement concerning this effect. Critics of advertising address their attacks to the source of such shifts. Many would have us believe that "hidden persuaders" headquartered on Madison Avenue are engaged in subtle indoctrination aimed at convincing us of things about such products that are untrue.

Figure 6.10 *The Influence of Advertising on Demand*

Advertising shifts demand to the right, implying a higher market-clearing price for any quantity offered.

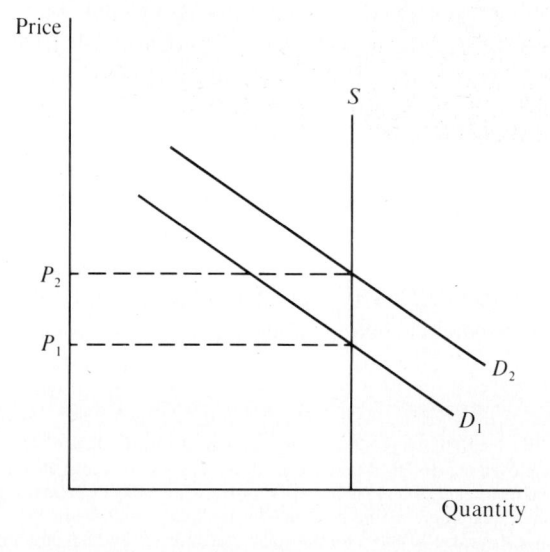

It is alleged, for example, that these messages appeal to our unconscious needs to nourish our self-images or to magnify our sex appeal. Some advertising may indeed operate through these channels, though evidence documenting the extent of this sort of influence is scant. Economics, on the other hand, provides several alternative explanations for the effectiveness of advertising rooted in logical consumer choice.

The most obvious of these holds that advertising is merely informative. It represents an effort to overcome consumers' ignorance concerning the products they seek. Consumers gain when they are able to purchase products they value in the market. If they lack information about a product's existence or performance, they may lose an opportunity for such beneficial exchange. As we have continually stressed, however, information is costly. In principle, this information may be purchased by either buyer or seller. Consumers will, of course, seek to overcome their ignorance about products in the market by investing in information themselves. They will window-shop, inquire among their friends, and study various official and "impartial" sources. However, the costs of such information need not be perfectly symmetrical between buyers and sellers. It stands to reason that some of this information can be more economically produced by sellers than buyers. The cost per unit of information distributed to a single buyer can in some cases be lower when supplied by sellers than when obtained by individual buyers.[7]

Here again we have a case of consumers purchasing more than a product. As was the case with reserved hotel rooms and automobiles sold by "reputable" dealers, sellers of advertised products offer something besides the goods themselves: They bear the cost of producing consumer information about their products. The consumer buys both the product and the information. As this combination is worth more to consumers than products about which they know little or nothing, they will pay more for them. This accounts for the shift in demand associated with the production of some advertising messages.

A great deal of advertising, however, does not seem to fall into the "informative" category. When Joe Namath climbs into a pair of Leggs, we "learn" a great deal about the strength and durability of this brand of pantyhose. When we see this same individual endorse a men's cologne or a popcorn maker, however, we may have legitimate doubts concerning the nature of the information imparted. When a famous newscaster retrieves a watch from the bowels of a concrete mixer, we are impressed with the shock and water resistance of this product. When a prizefighter endorses a household pest killer, on the other hand, our skepticism is aroused concerning his personal experience in battling the pests. If advertising is not informative in this sense, why do producers supply it and why do consumers pay for it in the form of higher prices?

It has been argued that this type of advertising provides a different and more subtle form of information about the product than mere descriptive messages. Re-

---

[7]This is not to say that such "mass produced" information necessarily benefits everyone always. Because the media employed are designed to reach as many people as possible, much of the information obtained has little value to many who read or hear it. Advertising imposes burdens in those cases (particularly when it interrupts programming in which we are keenly interested). We bear these costs, at least in part, because the value of the information in certain cases exceeds in total the cost of these interruptions.

call our earlier discussion concerning the information value of reputations of producers. It was argued there that the value that consumers place on products of reputable producers itself prevents the producers from lowering the quality of their outputs. Consideration of how such reputations might be originally established was intentionally eschewed in that discussion. We raise this problem now.

Let us assume that the only means of establishing a reputation for high-quality merchandise is through customer experience with individual producers' products. Consumers who purchase these goods for the first time will know nothing about them and therefore will pay for them only the prices of low-quality goods. As consumers gain more experience with these "bargains," their expectation of higher quality will increase and so, therefore, will the prices they are willing to pay for them. If the goods are purchased infrequently, however, the experience required for their establishing such a reputation therefore lengthens; the cost of producing such a reputation may become prohibitively high. Selling high-quality goods at low-quality prices is costly to producers. Doing so for long periods of time can more than offset the future gain of selling high quality at high-quality prices. In the absence of some other remedy, we may again be confronted with the lemon principle.

Experience is not the only way that consumers obtain information about products. Suppliers may *tell* consumers, through advertising, that their products are of high quality. The problem with such information is that "talk is cheap." The cost of merely bringing such a message before the public may be so low that it pays producers to do so even if the message is false. If the message convinces many to purchase the product at a one-time higher price, this added revenue alone may cover the cost of producing the false information. A subsequent fall in price resulting from consumers' disillusionment with the product might not be enough to deter unscrupulous producers from employing such tactics.

One way out of such a market dilemma is to make the "talk" expensive. Short-term sales at a high-quality price may be sufficient to cover the cost of "cheap talk." But a much longer experience with a high-quality price will be required to cover the cost of an expensive advertising campaign involving the paid endorsements of well-known (and therefore high-priced) celebrities. Maintenance of a high-quality price over such a long term will require many repeat sales, and this can be assured only if the information is repeatedly validated by consumers' own verification of high quality. By spending a great deal on advertising, producers therefore indirectly assure consumers that the products are as represented. Failure to produce high quality after such a campaign will result in an immediate return of price to the low-quality level, implying a loss on the advertising effort.

Such advertising, therefore, acts in the fashion of collateral on a loan. Failure to honor the terms of a borrowing agreement results in the forfeiture of the collateral. Failure to honor the terms of an advertisement of high quality results in a forfeiture of the possibility of repeat sales at the high-quality price.

It is noteworthy that this explanation relies very little on the verbal content of advertising messages. It is the *costliness* of the process itself that communicates the guarantee of high quality to consumers. Bizarre marketing activities, such as photographing automobiles on remote desert mountaintops or hiring major league athletes to engage in barroom small-talk before the camera, and sponsoring golf matches or public service programs that no one watches may be rationalized in terms of this type of effort. Marshall McLuhan, although not an economist, aptly described the nature of the information imparted in this type of advertising: "The medium is the message." Indeed!

Summary

This chapter dealt with income from two perspectives. On the one hand, we sought to develop a consistent theory of income measurement that may be applied under conditions of changing prices and nominal income. This topic was introduced in the context of the ever-present aggregation problem, the need to express in one summary measure the effect of changes in many dissimilar goods and services. Real income is measured in terms of the expenditure required to purchase different combinations of goods at a given set of prices. Where prices change proportionately, this measure will perfectly index changes in real income. If prices change by different proportions, the correspondence between measured real income and economic welfare will be imperfect. With mixed price changes it is even possible for the measured change in real income to identify incorrectly the direction of change. Only in certain cases may the direction of change be identified with confidence.

Over any set of price changes the measurement of change in real income may be performed in two ways. Expenditure may be evaluated at the "before and after" combinations using either the new or original prices of the given goods. The measure obtained with the original prices is called the Laspeyres measure; the measure employing new prices is the Paasche measure. If we desire to measure the rate of change in real income, we must calculate an index number to reflect the percentage change in measured real income. These indexes will contain the same biases present in the measured changes themselves. Only Paasche measures and indexes identify welfare increases with certainty, while only Laspeyres measures and indexes identify welfare decreases with certainty.

Economics is also concerned with changes in the purchasing power of money and its inverse, the price level. When many prices are changing at different rates, these measures are also subject to the aggregation problem. The purchasing power of money increases when a given amount permits the purchase of a combination providing more real income, and vice versa. The increase in purchasing power is measured by the reduction in the amount of money required to purchase a given combination of goods, and vice versa. Thus, the change in the price level is measured by the change in the amount of money required to purchase such a combination. Price indexes such as the Consumer Price Index reflect percentage changes relative to base level expenditure. A Laspeyres price index uses the original combination in such computation, while the Paasche measure uses the new combination. Price indexes are imprecise measures for the same reasons as are real income indexes. Only a Paasche measure of the price level identifies inflation with certainty, while a Laspeyres index identifies deflation.

The second topic in this chapter concerns household behavior in the presence of income uncertainty. A model presenting consumer attitudes toward such risk was developed, along with the opportunities arising out of risk pooling through insurance. It was shown that households will choose to insure all such risks at actuarially "fair" rates. The opportunity cost of such "fair" insurance per dollar is the ratio of the probabilities of the occurrence and nonoccurrence of the loss insured.

Due to the costs of administering insurance and the transaction costs of monitoring the terms of insurance contracts, it will not be worthwhile to insure against all uncer-

tainty. *One useful way of interpreting certain economic activities is as a form of insurance in conjunction with other market transactions. Hotel and restaurant reservation systems were examined in this light, as were product guarantees.*

Uncertainty in markets can frequently result from the unpredictability of the people with whom we transact as well as from natural events. When sellers possess more information about the goods sold than buyers, adverse selection among the goods offered for sale can severely impair the function of markets. This problem is referred to as the "lemon principle." Government and proprietary efforts to supply product information are useful but cannot completely eliminate scope for this problem. Brand names and advertising are two market institutions that may be interpreted as emerging in response to potential market failure due to the lemon principle.

Key Concepts

real income
purchasing power of money
aggregation problem
nominal income
Laspeyres measure
Paasche measure
theory of revealed preference
index numbers

price level
expected value
expected utility
risk pooling
complete insurance
expected quality
lemon principle

Questions

1. *Easy* Grades in most courses are a weighted average. Given any set of midterm exam marks, final exam marks, and other considerations, the grade given for the course will depend on the weights assigned to each. This is an example of the aggregation problem. In what ways is it similar to the problem of measuring gross national product?

Hard Grades, rather than knowledge for its own sake, seem to be the overriding objective for a few university students. For these students we would predict that changing the weights assigned to midterms and final exams will lead to a shifting of study effort. In what way is this similar to results with different success criteria for plan fulfillment in the Soviet Union? Is there any solution to this aggregation problem?

2. *Easy* The following goods were purchased in the quantities indicated before and after a set of price changes. Note that total income spent remained the same ($276).

Purchases in Period 1			Purchases in Period 2		
Good	Quantity	Price	Good	Quantity	Price
A	7	10	A	8	6
B	4	15	B	5	10
C	9	6	C	10	7
D	12	3	D	6	8
E	8	5	E	5	10
F	4	4	F	2	5

Calculate the change in real income using a Laspeyres index.

Hard Using the same information, can we say with confidence that real income has increased or decreased? Explain.

3. *Easy* Explain the difference between nominal and real income.

Hard GNP measured in 1972 dollars increased from $315.7 billion in 1929 to $1480.7 billion in 1980. In the latter year, however, consumers were able to purchase televisions, electric food processors, automobiles with power-assisted steering and brakes, automatic transmissions, air conditioning, streptomycin, and home computers. Explain the problems posed by these new products for income measurement.

4. *Easy* Insurance at actuarily "fair" rates implies that income in one state of the world may be exchanged for income in another state at a fixed opportunity cost. What is this opportunity cost? Explain.

Hard A severe problem in the marketing of insurance is the certification that a particular state of the world exists, and therefore that a claim for insurance benefits is legitimate. For example, in the purchase of health insurance, people seek to insure against the cost of unusually high medical bills in the state of the world of becoming seriously ill. Insurance companies therefore reimburse for medical bills rather than merely supplying income in that state. This does not completely solve this problem, for the purchase of medical care is not a perfect indicator of the state of serious illness for some people. Insurance companies therefore often pay only a portion of these medical bills, leaving the remainder to be paid by the insured person. Using demand and supply analysis, explain the problem and the nature of this (partial) solution.

5. *Easy* Our theory implies that if transaction costs are zero, risk-averse households will insure all risk, providing for equal income in all possible states. What is the meaning of risk aversion in this statement, and what part of the theory would have to be modified so as to describe choice without risk aversion?

Hard A key element of the theory permitting us to derive our conclusions is the assumption of the independence of income enjoyment with respect to states of the world. This assumption seems to make better sense in some cases than in others. Many people purchase life insurance to provide income to the surviving household in the event of their death. An argument could be made that some people value income less after death than during life. What would such a modification in our assumptions imply about the market for life insurance?

6. *Easy* Dentists and hairdressers permit their customers to make appointments to insure their availability at a particular time. However, they charge nothing if the appointments are not kept. Explain these phenomena in terms of the risk and insurance model described in this chapter.

Hard Airlines occasionally offer reduced fares to passengers willing to fly on a space-available basis—that is, they charge a lower ticket price to those who will take a chance on a seat being available at the time of departure they seek. Explain the reasoning behind this marketing technique.

Part Three

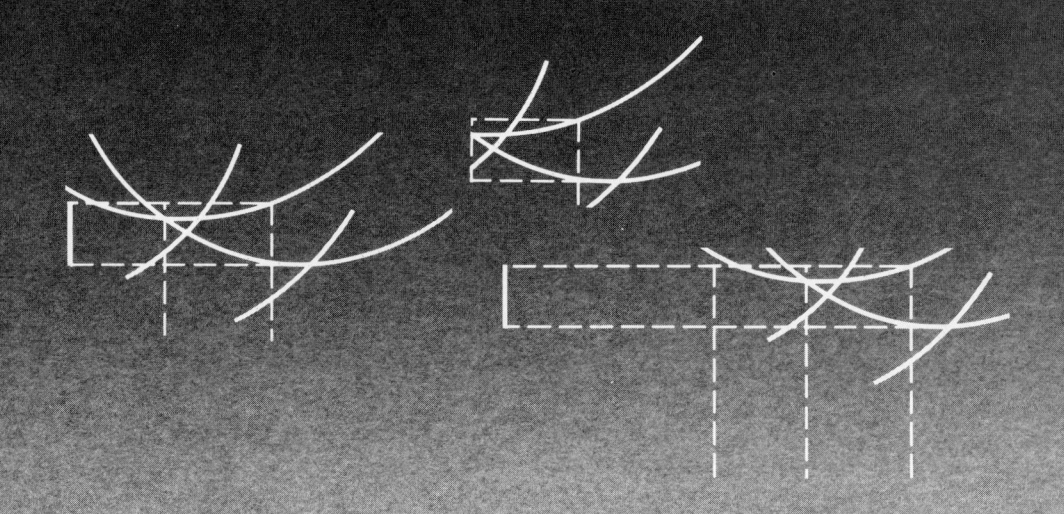

Organization, Output and Market Structure

Chapter 7

The Choice of Organization

Connections   *Most people take business firms pretty much for granted. Firms have owners, managers, and workers. The owners employ everyone else, and they can get rid of individual workers or even the manager without disbanding the whole enterprise. Economic theory recognizes, however, that a firm is an institution performing economic functions and that competition among firms requires that features they adopt be well adapted to those functions. This chapter seeks answers to several questions. What economic functions are performed by firms? Can we explain the salient features of business organization in terms of survival characteristics in competition? Some business activity is channeled into organizations such as nonprofit enterprises and government bureaus. Can economic theory shed any light on the results of choosing these forms of organization?*

The form of organization is a choice, like those explored in Chapters 2 through 6. However, the environment in which choice is made for the decisions analyzed here differs radically from those discussed previously. In this and the following six chapters we leave the utility function as a rank-ordering process. Profits are all that matter to the single-minded proprietary firm within which most of these choices will be centered. The opportunity sets will henceforth contain the range of options concerning the variable whose choice occupies us at the moment. These will range from the rate of output to the technology with which the product itself is produced.

The theory of supply is quite naturally concerned with decisions of suppliers involving what they will offer for sale. Of primary concern, of course, is the relationship between the market price and the quantity that suppliers will offer. A complete theory of supply must concern itself with other decisions as well, however. It must inform us about factors influencing product design. It should illuminate the choice of production technology. In today's world of rapid technical change, it should have useful things to say about such issues as obsolescence and modernization. It should explain decisions of firms to enter or leave an industry. And at a very fundamental level it should give us a better understanding of the organization of industry itself.

A great deal of production takes place within the household. Meals are prepared, shelter and transportation are provided, and clothing is laundered, mended, and sometimes homemade; a great deal of entertainment is organized by consumers themselves. A complete theory of supply should explain why more—indeed, why all—productive activity is not organized by households in this fashion. At the other extreme we observe some supply activity being organized by corporate giants with hundreds of thousands of employees engaged in diverse and specialized activities. Yet the production of few products is completely integrated within one organization. Even the broadest-ranging conglomerates purchase from other firms many of the components and services necessary to produce and market their products. Some productive activity is explicitly "managed" within organizations, while other aspects are coordinated by markets. The theory of supply should help us understand the limits of organization. It should tell us which decisions will be internalized within the organization and which will be left to determination by market activity.

Finally, when we turn our gaze toward the nature itself of these organizing entities, additional questions arise. Although many of these organizations are firms dedicated to earning profits for their owners, an increasingly large share of the output in this country is organized by nonprofit entities. Sixteen percent of our national income arises from government organizations, and an even larger share is produced by churches and other nonprofit groups. How does the behavior of these diverse organizations differ, and what factors influence the choice of organizational format? The theory of supply should illuminate these questions, and this chapter will attempt to introduce the reader to some of the answers being explored by economists.

7.1 The Theory of Organization

The Limits of Organization

The critical question posed by the theory of organization is a choice between two systems that perform essentially the same functions. On the one hand, we have organizations that internally assign tasks, establish rewards, monitor performance, and coordinate related activities. On the other hand, we have a market system that through variations in price guides people and resources into certain activities, rewards (or punishes), and coordinates production and distribution. In a world with no firms, individual workers, acting on their own, would rely solely on markets for the supply of those items required to perform their chosen tasks as well as for the sale of what they produced. The advantages of large-scale production would pose no problems in this regard, at least in principle. One can imagine an elaborate assembly line in which those workers performing a given task would purchase the partially assembled parts from an "upstream" worker and sell them with additional completed work to a member of a "downstream" group. Each would presumably lease space from the factory building owner along with power and whatever support services were required.

Note that in such a factory there would be no "management" per se. No one would set production targets for the factory or assign output quotas for individual workers. The prices of "upstream" components and "downstream" assemblies would determine the rate at which work moved through each point in the production process. Increased output upstream would increase supply to those at the next stage of production, lowering the price of the product at that stage and increasing the profitability of performing the next stage. A fall in the price of the final product would decrease the value of each successive stage, shifting demand leftward and leading to lower levels of activity all along the line. Thus we see that the market conceivably can control and coordinate activity even within a single factory.

Note also that the distributive function of management might also be performed by market organization within such a managerless factory. Management devotes a great deal of its time to the negotiation of pay scales, to the monitoring of workers' performance, to the promotion of some and the dismissal of others. These functions could be taken care of as a by-product of the activity just described. Wages at each level would consist of what was left over from the sale of each worker's output after rent and upstream components had been paid for. Individuals could promote or demote themselves to assignment to any task along the production line. Failure to perform any chosen task with the requisite skills would lead to lower economic rewards, discouraging "premature" self-advancement.

If credulity is strained by this example, let us focus our imagination on economies at the other extreme. Several of the world's most powerful nations have adopted the doctrine that market influences "alienate" workers from the task of production, hence must be banished from the economy. Market forces are held to exert a pernicious influence on what is produced, as well as on the distribution of that output. By removing the veil of prices and profits, it is alleged that workers themselves can manage and plan the economy to the greater satisfaction and well-being of all. We might think of the Soviet Union, for example, as one large firm in which *all* allocative decisions are made by managers and planners.

Ideology is, of course, responsible for this state of affairs in the Soviet Union. And even in communist bloc countries, markets are used to distribute output, and market conditions have been employed by planners to make investment and allocative decisions. In economies where ideology and politics have less influence on the day-to-day operation of the economy, however, we typically observe a mixed system. Firms exist to organize certain allocative functions—yet these firms have limits. A construction firm may decide to purchase its heavy equipment rather than lease it on a daily basis, but it will never decide to manufacture that equipment. A telephone company may manufacture its own wire and cable, but it will not produce its own electricity. Beyond these limits firms *choose* to allow markets to organize activity rather than to integrate the coordination of these functions into their decision-making process.

In order to understand the structure of these economies (at least those in which the structure is not determined by ideology) we must explore the determinants of these limits. What deters the firm as it considers expanding the degree of vertical integration over upstream and downstream functions? What limits the scope of market activity in organizing and coordinating production so that it is displaced in some functions by firms?

Ronald Coase, in a now classic paper,[1] answered these questions in the following way. He pointed out that use of *either* a market system or explicit organization to allocate resources imposes costs. Both of these costs are now referred to as **transaction costs**. Use of the market, for example, requires that buyers and sellers themselves be responsible for exploring the options available. Buyers must survey prices and properties of the goods offered for sale, and sellers must ascertain the tastes and needs of buyers. Both parties may reduce their investment in acquiring this information by contracting to buy and sell over extended periods, but the institution of contracts can itself be costly. Long-term contracts impose costs by binding one or both parties to terms that later developments may render unfavorable. Short-term contracts, on the other hand, impose on buyer and seller high negotiating costs and require that each invest heavily in exactly the sort of market information they seek to economize on through these contracts.

Coase concludes that a cost-effective solution to this problem is the formation of firms. Workers agree to forgo most of their market activity. They no longer buy and sell with upstream and downstream producers. Instead, they agree to become members of an organization that supplies them with a workplace, a regulated flow of materials, tools, and guidelines. Instead of taking home the residuals from his or her buying and selling, each worker receives a *wage* from the firm. If conditions worsen or improve, the terms of employment may be revised—or severed completely. The firm nevertheless remains an entity whose major function, according to Coase, is to economize on the transaction costs associated with organizing economic activity through markets.

The alternative to market coordination is not free, however. Coase identified three costs of planning and organization that limit the scope of this activity. First, he argued that costs of planning rise with the extent of the organization. The more remote are the things planned from the planner (in both a spatial and conceptual sense), the more costly will be the formulation of the plan. Advice and references must be sought; on-site inspections and conferences must be attended. Second, as the scope of the plan expands, more mistakes will be made by the organization, reducing its efficiency and viability. In other words, an organization may grow so large that the mistakes it makes in allocating resources internally may cost more than the alternative of using markets to coordinate these allocations. Competing groups of smaller, nonintegrated firms using markets will outperform larger, inte-

---

[1] Ronald Coase, "The Nature of the Firm," *Economica* (November 1937): 386–405. Reprinted in G. J. Stigler and K. Boulding, eds., *Readings in Price Theory* (Homewood, Ill.: Richard D. Irwin Inc., 1952), 331–351.

grated firms at these junctures. Third, Coase pointed to the fact that resources employed in the planning process are scarce. As the economy uses more of them, their prices, and thus the costs of planning, will rise. At some point, as the scope of planning is increased throughout the economy, these rising resource prices will make further displacement of market coordination by firms economically inefficient.

Coase's discussion suggests the possibility of a mixed economy similar to the one we observe. Firms organize a great deal of activity in most economies, but they are limited in size. Beyond some point, the advantages of avoiding the collection of market information are offset by the disadvantage of mistakes and increasing resource costs of planning. Firms, therefore, exist within a market environment where prices and competition coordinate those functions that are too costly for the firms to internalize.

Costs and Optimization

A diagrammatic and algebraic presentation of Coase's argument will serve two functions at this juncture. It will clarify the points we have sought to make and will at the same time allow us to introduce a few of the techniques that form the core of the analysis of the theory of supply. Optimization on the supply side is a simpler and more useful technique than optimization on the demand side of the market. The objectives of suppliers are less ambiguous than are those of demanders, and this permits sharper descriptions of individual optima and responses to changing market phenomena.

We will assume that the objective of suppliers is to obtain *maximum wealth*. The attainment of this objective gives suppliers the largest possible command over goods and services in their role as consumers; hence this maximand is logically implied by the theory of the household developed in Part I. Unless otherwise stated, we will also assume that suppliers operate in a *competitive setting*; they behave as rivals in seeking wealth. Greater wealth is obtained by earning larger profits, and it is the study of the various margins on which suppliers seek to increase profits that fills out the theory of supply. This study provides the rich menu of policy implications concerning the level of output, factor employment, and product design on which economists so frequently expound.

In seeking maximum profits, suppliers will naturally attempt to arrange their affairs so as to produce at lowest cost. This will afford them a larger margin and allow them to expand sales by underbidding their rival suppliers. Taking advantage once again of the convenient assumption of ceteris paribus, we may state that profit maximization therefore implies **cost minimization**. Consider how we may use this assumption of cost minimization to illuminate Coase's discussion of the limits of the firm.

Let us assume that there is a given number of allocative decisions related to the production and distribution of a single good in an economy. Each component of the final good must be produced with resources and materials, energy and imagination. Quantities of each of these items must be selected, obtained, and directed to the appropriate task. The final product must be transported to a destination and displayed. In principle, these various decisions must be made in one of two ways.

The decision may be internalized within the firm engaged in making the product, or the decision may be left to the market. This choice is commonly referred to as the decision to **buy or make**—that is, the firm may simply purchase the component item or service from the market, or it may organize that portion of the production and distribution within the organization. The decision to "make" is often described in the industrial organization literature as **vertical integration** of the production process.

Coase points out that both methods involve costs. We will refer to this form of cost as *transaction costs*. Let the number of decisions made internally be indicated by a_i. The making of decisions internally imposes costs in the form of mistakes and planning costs themselves. We may thus represent transaction costs from this source by the function $c_i = c_i(a_i)$. Increasing the number of decisions made in this way increases the transaction costs from this source; thus, we may also state that the slope of this function is positive: $(\Delta c_i / \Delta a_i) > 0$. We will call this slope the marginal transaction cost from this source, MTC_i.

Leaving decisions to the market is also costly. As was pointed out earlier, the use of markets requires either investment in information about prices and quantities or the bearing of costs due to loss of flexibility associated with long-term contracts. Let the number of decisions left to the market be indicated by a_m. The function relating these types of transaction costs to the number of decisions made by the market may thus be written $c_m = c_m(a_m)$. The marginal transaction costs from this source, $MTC_m = \Delta c_m / \Delta a_m$, are also positive. Total transaction costs from both sources, TTC, is simply the sum of both:

(7.1) $\qquad TTC = c_i(a_i) + c_m(a_m).$

We wish to find the combination of a_i and a_m that minimizes the total transaction cost, TTC.

Consider panel (a) of Figure 7.1. The horizontal axis measures numbers of decisions, while the vertical axis measures costs. The function relating the extent of vertical integration to transaction costs, $c_i = c_i(a_i)$, may thus be represented in this diagram as curve c_i. Note its positive slope. We have assumed that the total number of decisions that must be made one way or the other is fixed. Let that number be D. As each decision must be either planned or left to the market, it must be true that $D = a_i + a_m$. This permits us to construct a curve relating transaction costs to the number of market-made decisions in the same diagram. Solving for a_m gives $a_m = D - a_i$. The quantity of market-made decisions associated with any quantity made internally may simply be read off the diagram from right to left starting at D. For example, at $a_i = D$, the quantity of decisions made in the market, a_m, is zero. At a_i^2, a_m is equal to the horizontal distance from a_i^2 to D, and so on. Curve c_m therefore relates transaction costs of using the market to the number of decisions as measured from right to left from D.

Now note the relationship of the two curves in panel (a) to the single curve in panel (b). The height of curve TTC in panel (b) must equal the sum of the heights of the two curves in panel (a). This curve represents the total transaction costs of each combination of a_i and a_m. Consider the combination associated with a_i^1. Only one quantity of market-made decisions is associated with a_i^1—that is the quantity

Figure 7.1 *Optimum Vertical Integration*

In panel (a) curve c_i relates the number of allocative decisions made internally to transaction costs from this source. A decision made internally cannot be made by the market. For each value of a_i, therefore, there is implied another value of a_m, which increases from right to left. The transaction costs of using the market are thus reflected in the height of curve c_m. The curve TTC in panel (b) represents the sum of the heights of the curves c_i and c_m for every value of a_i. The cost-minimizing combination of decisions is therefore a_i^* and a_m^*, which is equal to $D - a_i^*$. At this point the slopes of c_i and c_m in panel (a) are equal in magnitude but opposite in sign.

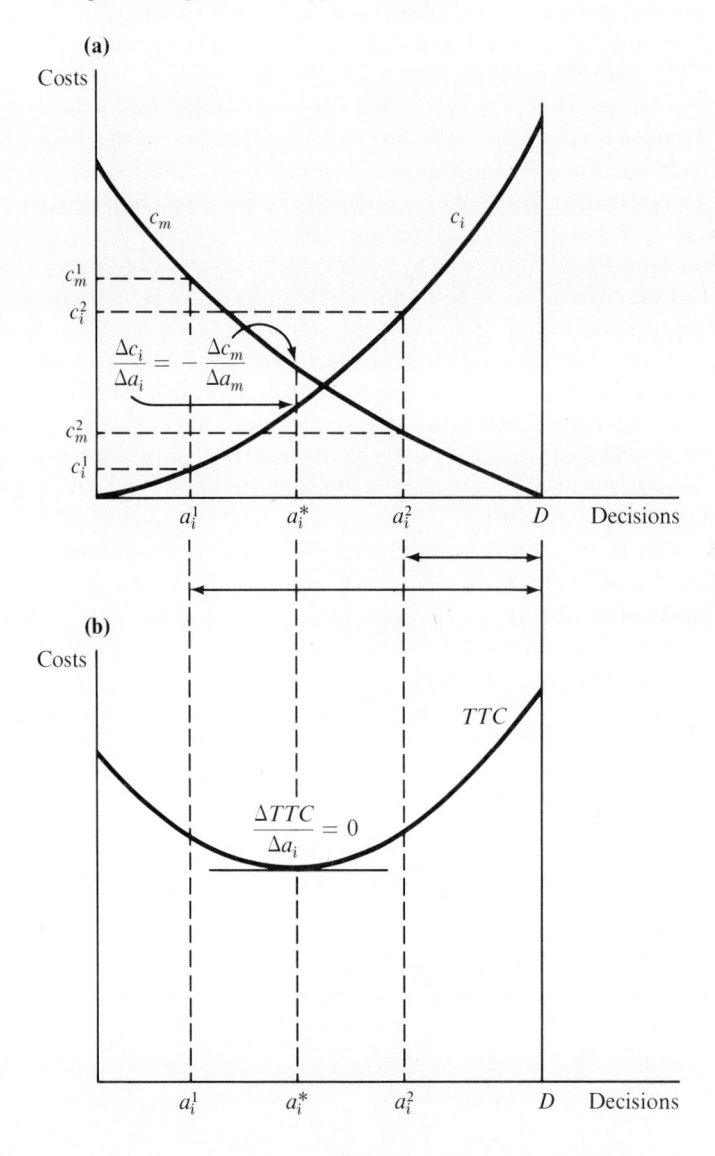

$D - a_i^1$, whose cost is represented by the height of c_m at that quantity. The height of curve TTC in panel (b) is therefore c_1, which is equal to $c_i^1 + c_m^1$. The height of TTC at a_i^2 is likewise equal to $c_i^2 + c_m^2$.

The firm under consideration seeks to minimize the total transaction costs of production and distribution. If it can lower total cost by using the market rather than vertically integrating, it will do so. If it can lower these costs by organizing certain aspects of production internally rather than relying on the market, it will likewise do so. The firm therefore seeks to identify the proper mix of decision making for the product it produces and distributes. That combination will be the one that minimizes total transaction costs. It is identified by the value of a_i (and thus, implicitly, the value of a_m), which is associated with the lowest point on the TTC curve. In panel (b), that value is clearly a_i^*.

The problem posed is to identify conditions that must hold at a_i^*. We will show that total transaction cost minimization requires that the mix of decision making be that which equates the marginal transaction costs due to each method. This is a general finding that applies not only to minimization of transaction costs, as in this example, but to cost minimization problems in general. We begin by recalling the relationship between a_i and a_m. One additional decision internalized implies one less decision to be made by the market. As $a_m = D - a_i$, it must be true that $\Delta a_m / \Delta a_i = -1$.

This discussion suggests that total transaction costs are related to the number of decisions planned, a_i, in the manner depicted in panel (b) of Figure 7.1—that is, the sum of all transaction costs declines over some initial range, reaches a minimum, and then rises beyond the point where the optimal mix has been reached. A necessary condition for the optimal mix of decisions, therefore, is that the slope of the TTC curve be zero.

First, we express changes in total transaction costs in relation to change in the number of decisions made in each mode by employing the total differential of equation (7.1):

$$\Delta TTC = \frac{\Delta c_i}{\Delta a_i} \cdot \Delta a_i + \frac{\Delta c_m}{\Delta a_m} \cdot \Delta a_m.$$

Dividing through by the change in decisions made via planning, Δa_i gives us an expression for the slope of the TTC curve:

$$\frac{\Delta TTC}{\Delta a_i} = \frac{\Delta c_i}{\Delta a_i} \cdot \frac{\Delta a_i}{\Delta a_i} + \frac{\Delta c_m}{\Delta a_m} \cdot \frac{\Delta a_m}{\Delta a_i}.$$

The slope $\Delta a_i / \Delta a_i$ has a value of unity, and $\Delta a_m / \Delta a_i$ is equal to -1. Constraining the slope of the TTC curve to be zero therefore yields the predicted conclusion:

$$\frac{\Delta TTC}{\Delta a_i} = 0 = \frac{\Delta c_i}{\Delta a_i} - \frac{\Delta c_m}{\Delta a_m}$$

$$\frac{\Delta c_i}{\Delta a_i} = \frac{\Delta c_m}{\Delta a_m}.$$

Costs are minimized at a combination of vertical integration and market-made decisions at which the marginal transaction costs of both are exactly equal.

Readers should not be put off by the extreme abstraction that characterizes Coase's analysis. The problem is not just a make-work project that economists have invested in to keep themselves busy. It is an issue that confronts businessmen daily. General Motors must decide whether they will make their own car radios or buy radios from Motorola or some other producer. They must make the same decision about tires, paint, fabric for interiors, and glass for windshields. In making these choices about whether to make or buy, they will weigh exactly the same types of considerations that we have raised here. Only when the advantages of reduced transaction costs from market-made decisions are outweighed by the offsetting costs of keeping the left hand informed of what the right is doing will the firm stop growing. Only when total transaction costs stop falling and start rising will firms stop making and start buying. Growth up to that point reduces costs and increases the profits of the affected firms. Growth will not extend beyond that point, however, for to become too large is to increase costs and reduce profits, exposing the firm to competition from optimally sized, and therefore lower-cost, organizations.

What the ice age did to the dinosaurs the market does for firms that grow too large. In a world of competitive markets, like that of the evolving animal kingdom described by Darwin, **survival** itself tells us a great deal. The firms that survive in this environment are those that have adopted the correct policies and strategies. Those that fail have erred in important ways. It is not necessary that these decisions be made purposefully and for the correct reasons. (Mammals did not consciously adopt the characteristics that helped them to survive the upheavals that doomed the giant reptiles of the Mesozoic age.) The point is that decisions that lower cost do promote survival in the competitive world, while those that result in higher costs lead to extinction. Theories that assume purposeful and informed cost minimization on the part of firms will therefore be useful predictors of the results of competitive market processes in any case. Surviving firms will appear to have consciously done so.[2]

Coase poses the question of why economists are typically critical of state intervention in planning resource allocation but do not object when a new firm is formed. He answers his own question in the following way: When individual firms err by becoming too large—by vertically integrating over sets of decisions best left to markets—competition of competing organizations of appropriate scale will force these firms to abandon this posture. When government chooses to make allocative decisions in some area, the decision is not self-correcting. Government may perform less well than free markets could in organizing resource use in many areas of present federal or state involvement. Unfortunately, government involvement almost invariably precludes competition from market institutions that could otherwise be counted upon to displace inefficient planning.

---

[2] See Armen A. Alchian, "Uncertainty, Evolution and Economic Theory," *Journal of Political Economy* 58 (June 1950): 211–221.

The Firm as a Metering Device

Recent contributions have extended Coase's development in the theory of organizations. Alchian and Demsetz,[3] for example, note that there are many features of the classical firm that are not illuminated by Coase's focus on the costs of using the market. Most firms have owners who typically supply some or all of the capital used in the enterprises and who hire labor. The owners are then reimbursed for the use of their capital, as well as for whatever managerial services they provide out of the residual from revenues after all other non-owned factors (including labor) have been paid. Why do firms typically take this form? Cooperatives of workers might be formed to "own" firms. Capital and other resources would then be rented, and workers would be left to claim residuals. This type of organization is sometimes seen, but Coase offers little guidance in predicting where such cooperative organization is likely to emerge and why it is not more prevalent.

Two central features of economic organization emerge from the Alchian and Demsetz discussion. (1) Some productive activity is more economically carried out by **teams** than by individuals, and (2) the *contribution* of individual team members to output is costly to discover. Ten men pulling a barge for one hour can move it farther than one man pulling it for ten hours. A team of ten men is therefore a more cost-effective method of pulling barges than one man pulling alone for the longer period. As pulling on a rope is tiring—the more so if one pulls strenuously rather than halfheartedly—each member of such a team will **shirk** if he can get away with it. Each will merely tag along holding the rope and let someone else do the pulling while giving the appearance of doing his part. This desire to shirk creates an organizational problem for the team. If all team members shirk, total team output will be lower than otherwise, and all will be worse off. On the other hand, each member will be better off if his performance is closely watched, preventing him from shirking. Organizational responses to this information problem explain many of the features of the modern firm. Before making this link, however, let us examine the phenomenon of shirking graphically.

Figure 7.2 presents the choice confronted by a member of the team just described. He must choose between exerting himself to a greater or lesser degree and enjoying more or fewer of the benefits of less exertion (let us call these benefits *leisure*). Assume that total team output is divided equally among the team members. If all ten members exerted themselves fully, each would therefore enjoy one tenth of the maximum team output; let that share for each be y_4 in Figure 7.2. If each team member exerted absolutely no effort, on the other hand, nothing would be produced—and one tenth of nothing is, of course, nothing. Each person in such a situation would consume the maximum amount of leisure (say, x_3 units) and no output. The diagonal line connecting points y_4 and x_3 identifies the combinations of leisure that can be consumed together with shares of output for as long as all team members exert the same effort.

So far the problem seems to be yet another example of standard choice theory. This appearance is deceiving. For although the diagonal line y_4, x_3 is in a sense the

---

[3] Armen A. Alchian and Harold Demsetz, "Production, Information Costs and Economic Organization," *American Economic Review* 65 (December 1972): 777–795.

Figure 7.2 **The Choice to Shirk**

Opportunity set y_4, x_3 represents the combinations of output and leisure that all members of the team may consume in common. The best that each can do together with the team is combination T, providing a utility of U_2. However, the slope of this curve does not reflect the opportunity cost of leisure. If all others continue to choose only x_1 hours of leisure, any single chooser bears only a portion of the total reduction in output due to his own leisure. The opportunity cost of leisure is therefore given by minus the slope of the line passing through points T and K. If each attempts to obtain combination K, total output will fall to y_1 per person. All would be better off if shirking were not possible.

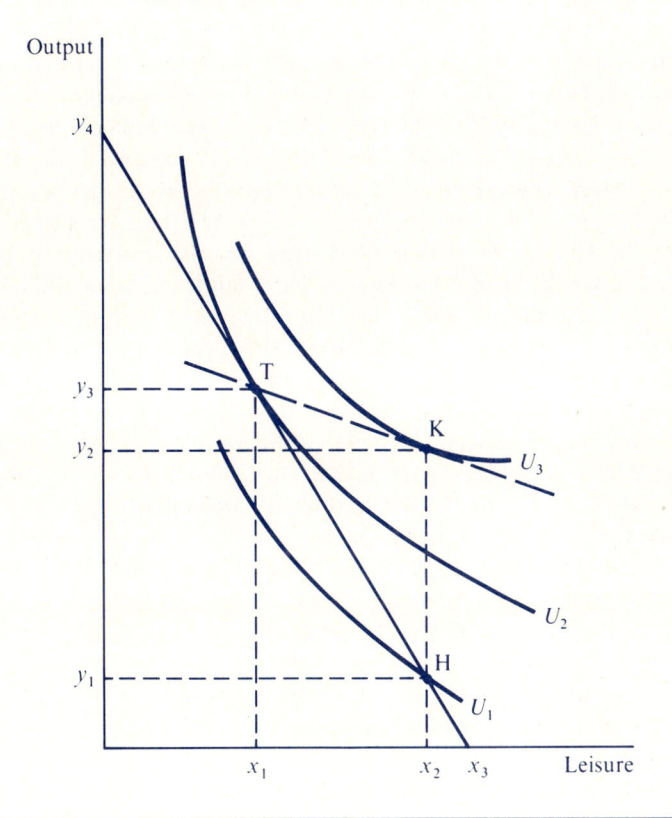

opportunity set for each team member, *the slope of this line, $\Delta y / \Delta x$, is not the opportunity cost of less exertion*. Combination T, containing x_1 units of leisure and y_3 units of output, is preferred by each team member. Assume that the team members agree to strive at this level so that each will take home y_3 units of output as his share. Changes in effort made by *all* will make available other combinations along y_4, x_3 that are less preferred. The slope of this line reflects the cost *to the team* of less effort. A team member contemplating *shirking*, however, hopes to achieve a unilateral reduction in his own effort while others make no change in their efforts. Assuming other team members continue to choose only x_1 units of leisure, a single member may reduce his effort at considerably lower cost than this *to himself*. As the reduction in total output is shared by all team members, his own share falls by only one tenth of the reduction occasioned by his choice of less effort. Under these circumstances it appears that he may achieve a combination like K, in which he chooses x_2 units of leisure while his share of total output falls only to y_2. His own opportunity cost of leisure is only one tenth of the cost of his leisure to the team.

Successful shirking by all is not feasible, however. Although each faces essentially the same opportunity cost of leisure, all cannot simultaneously consume combination K. If all choose x_2 units of leisure, total output will fall so that the share of output available for each is only y_1. Shirking by all, therefore, results in everyone consuming combination H, which is inferior to the agreed-upon combination, T. However, as long as it is impossible to monitor the level of effort put forth by each member, the best anyone can do is continue to shirk! For if all others do not shirk, anyone who does not does worse than combination H.

Now let us consider the organizational problem in this situation. One cannot shirk on oneself; if one works alone, there is no one to shift the cost of shirking onto. However, working alone means forgoing the advantages of team production. If shirking is accomplished by putting forth less than the agreed-upon effort, however, shirking can be reduced by having someone specialize in observing and metering the effort of each team member. But hiring a **monitor** does not completely eliminate the shirking problem, because monitors themselves may shirk—and who will watch the performance of the watcher?

The proprietary firm provides a unique solution to this information cost problem. Instead of the team hiring the monitor, the monitor hires the team. He or she contracts with each team member to perform whatever tasks are required with a stipulated level of effort. In exchange, the monitor agrees to pay each employee a share equal to that employee's expected contribution to output. The monitor, whom we shall now refer to as the *owner*, thus becomes the **residual claimant**. He or she keeps all output not owed by contract to the remaining team members. The larger the output, the greater will be the owner's residual share. If he or she exerts little effort to meter the efforts of others, output will be small, as will be his or her residual. If the owner observes others carefully and keeps shirking to a minimum, his or her rewards will be correspondingly large.

As the owner in such circumstances bears the full cost of shirking by others, he or she must have the authority to punish shirkers by altering or terminating employment contracts. As employees often must, as a matter of administrative convenience, supply considerable labor in advance of payment, owners must present security against these debts. The capital invested in plant and equipment conveniently serve as such a guarantee. This may explain why the residual claimant typically owns, rather than rents, many of these nonlabor inputs.

Finally, we note that many management decisions have importance for the operations of teams far into the future. If owners obtained rights to residuals only for specified periods of time, after which they relinquished them to others, decisions would necessarily be shortsighted. Owners would shirk in monitoring preparations of the team for periods after their own rights had terminated. If ownership rights to residuals are bought and sold in the market, the effects of current decisions on future profits will be reflected in *current* share prices. Free markets in ownership rights to the residual status of firms, therefore, promote efficient long-run decisions by managers.

This information cost approach, therefore, suggests as implications five features of economic organization commonly observed in a **proprietary firm**:

1. The firm has a residual claimant.
2. The residual claimant monitors and observes input behavior.
3. The residual claimant is the central party to all contracts with other inputs.
4. The residual claimant has authority to alter or terminate these contracts.
5. The residual claimant has authority to sell these rights.

7.2 Nonprofit Organization

Private Nonprofit Organization

If team production and information costs explain the structure of the classical firm, why do not all economic organizations have this character? If the economic forces we have described shape some organizations into firms, what factors exempt others from the influence of these forces, giving them the character of partnerships, private nonprofit organizations, government bureaus, or even cooperatives? The material needed to find a complete answer to these questions is typically covered in an industrial organization course. We shall nevertheless present here a few of the approaches used in that material. Let us consider first the private **nonprofit organization**.

The most conspicuous feature of this organization is the lack of a residual claimant—indeed, one is hard pressed to identify the "owner" of many such organizations. Although most of the functions performed by the residual claimant in the classical firm are vested in a chief executive, neither this person nor the governing board to which he or she answers has the right to claim the profits of the enterprise, nor can either sell in the market the rights that they do exercise. The executive or board does monitor the performance of other team members and may, within limits, hire and fire and contract for the supply of nonlabor inputs. Unlike the residual claimant in the classical firm, however, either one also typically receives a fixed salary.

This arrangement imposes a cost in the form of the inefficiencies discussed earlier. Since other team members experience difficulty in monitoring the chief executive's performance in this role, he or she may be encouraged to shirk. Shirking among the managers of private nonprofit organizations has in fact been extensively documented. Clarkson, for example, has found considerable evidence of this behavior in the management of private, nonproprietary hospitals.[4] He found that for-profit hospitals devoted more resources to supervisory control than did nonprofit hospitals. Nonprofit managers tended to be less concerned with the price and productivity of equipment and materials purchased and more concerned with

---

[4] Kenneth W. Clarkson, "Some Implications of Property Rights in Hospital Management," *Journal of Law and Economics* (October 1972): 363–384.

their quality. Nonprofits were also observed to rely more on opinion polls and less on market information such as queues or quit rates for demand and supply data. Automatic salary increases were granted far more frequently by nonprofit than by for-profit hospitals.

If private nonprofit organization imposes transaction costs such as these, how do such agencies survive? Are they merely aberrations of the market due to be displaced eventually by competition from more efficient firms organized along conventional lines? The vitality and vigor of this sector of the economy through most of its recorded history suggest that they are not. There must, therefore, be some advantage to this style of organization that offsets costs due to shirking. One such explanation has been offered by Earl Thompson.[5] Thompson notes that most nonprofit organizations deal in charity and most charities are administered through nonprofit organizations. He therefore asks whether there is some feature of the market for charity that makes it more suited to organization by nonprofit than by for-profit residual-claimant–style firms.

Thompson finds at least a partial answer in another metering problem. Consider the difficulties encountered by a "customer" of a for-profit charity seeking to "buy" paternalistic aid for a particular client group. The "product" that this customer (more commonly referred to here as "contributor") purchases is typically remote from his or her normal economic and social orbit. Customers would have to devote considerable time and effort to observing the provision of services by for-profit charities to insure that the owners did not simply retain as residual most of the revenues of the firm. One way to avoid this large investment in information is for the owner-manager to stipulate contractually that he or she will take only a fixed sum (that is, a salary) out of the operation. Observance of such a stipulation would itself have to be monitored, but failure to abide by such an arrangement would be punishable as fraud. Although the threat of criminal sanctions will not prevent all abuse of this type, we can nevertheless be confident that policing the distribution of benefits by nonprofit firms costs less than similar monitoring by customers of for-profit charities.

This is not to say that the transaction costs of manager shirking where the manager is not the residual claimant are not present in charitable organizations. On the contrary, many of the hospitals studied by Clarkson were originally financed and continue to be operated by churches and civic groups; hence, they fall into this category. Thompson's point is that the reduced efficiency due to these incentives is often offset by the increased efficiency of nonprofits in satisfying contributors that their contributions are being put to good use.

Government Organization

The other form of nonprofit organization that we will consider in this chapter is the government bureau. A great deal of government activity is concerned with protection of property on both a local and an international scale. Regulation of economic

---

[5] Earl Thompson, "Charity and Nonprofit Organizations," in *Research in Law and Economics*, supplement 1, in K. W. Clarkson and D. L. Martin, eds., *The Economics of Nonproprietary Organizations* (Greenwich: JAI Press, 1980), 125–138.

and social activity also occupies an important place in the role of most governments. Discussion of these activities will be deferred to Chapter 18. Here we wish to focus on a different sort of government activity: that of supplying goods and services in competition with, or in place of, other private agencies. We wish to consider here, in other words, the organization of nominally nongovernmental activity by governments.

Examples of such activity are postal services, parks, the provision of health services and facilities, the organization of education, the support of scientific research, and the provision of public utilities and transportation. There seems little reason why these activities could not be coordinated and planned by private sector organizations and markets—indeed, many of these government bureaus operate side by side with private agencies, producing virtually identical products or services. Various economic and sociological arguments may be marshalled in support of government involvement in these areas. (As these arguments are not essentially organizational in character, they are deferred to a later section of this text.) Here we are chiefly concerned with observing the implications of governmental organization of resource allocation.

Let us consider how these agencies differ from the classical firm. First, and most obvious, they have no residual claimant owner-manager. The chief executive of a city bus system is typically responsible to the city government and, of course—in democratic countries—ultimately to the people. This person has no rights to residuals and may not sell whatever rights he or she does have over the enterprise.

Second, he or she typically has no control over the price of the service provided; in fact, such prices are often set directly by the political process itself. Typically they are below the operating cost of the enterprise, so that substantial subsidies from tax funds are required to keep them afloat. Not uncommonly, the price is set at zero.

Third, customers have more channels through which to influence the behavior of these organizations. Customers typically influence the character of the output of firms exclusively "over the counter." If they like what is offered, they buy; otherwise, they look to competing firms to supply their needs. Ordinarily there is only one bus company, so one must "take it or leave it" as far as the market for bus service is concerned. If bus patrons are unhappy with what is provided, however, they may vote for a competing politician who promises more satisfactory service. If sufficient voters are made unhappy by the quality of the service provided, the political process offers an opportunity for expression of concern unavailable to customers of private firms.[6] It is far from obvious, however, whether or not government agencies are more responsive to customer wishes even with this additional channel for their expression.

Government agency managers are influenced to shirk just as are the managers of private nonprofit organizations. Being unable to fully capture the benefits of careful attention to the costs of production and the success of their products in the

---

[6] Unhappy customers of either type of organization may, of course, write letters to management detailing their grievances. A sufficient number of letters of this kind is likely to impress the recipient that election reverses (if a bureaucrat) or business losses (if an owner) are in the offing.

market, they will devote less effort to management in these areas. The problems of government management extend beyond mere shirking, however. In this sense the operation of government organizations is predicted to be the least efficient of those we have considered.

Government managers do compete with one another for advancement and higher wages. However, the manner in which they compete itself introduces biases in the allocation of resources within these bureaus. As we shall see, these biases in allocation lead to the production of products of lower quality than demanded by the client group served.

In order to discuss product quality from an analytical point of view, we must first define it more precisely. For most of our discussion it has sufficed to treat goods as extremely simplified objects that people possess and use in larger or smaller quantities. We must now complicate this view. Recall our discussion of goods as bundles of characteristics or attributes in Chapter 4. A meal at a restaurant means different things to different people and, more importantly, different things to the *same* person. It may contain nothing more than a beer and a pizza, or it may embrace an entire table d'hôte ranging from soup to nuts. Economic theory recognizes this ambiguity by treating each good as a **collection of attributes**. A single good such as a restaurant meal contains more or less hors d'oeuvre, entrée, beverage, dessert, table space, and service, to name only a few of its important attributes. To be absolutely precise, we would have to go into even more detail, listing the components of each of these items.

Recognizing this property of goods, we may therefore treat quality straightforwardly as an extension of choice theory. A good is of higher quality if it is preferred to another good. More of any attribute is preferred to less. A good with the same amount of each attribute but one, and more of that remaining attribute, will be preferred. In general, goods with more of each attribute are therefore regarded to be of higher quality.

As the inclusion of more attributes per good will typically add to the cost of a good, choices must be made concerning the optimal qualities to impart to products. Managers will, of course, be influenced in these choices by the incentives provided by the organizational environment in which they operate.

Incentives within a for-profit firm are explicitly linked to profit. Managers are rewarded for earning profits, and profits are directly influenced by the choice of quality. Increasing quality will increase the price that people will pay for a product. If the marginal increment to price is less than the cost of the added attributes, however, profits will be adversely affected by upgrading the product. Managers of for-profit firms are therefore very attentive to consumers, including only those amounts of attributes that consumers are willing to "buy." Products with the optimal combination of attributes will be more profitable than products of insufficient or excessive quality. The concern of customers for "bargains" in their purchases leads managers of for-profit firms to produce the appropriate qualities of their products.

Indeed, the owners of for-profit firms need engage in no quality control of their firms' output at all. Customers monitor quality and report back their assessments to the firm owners via the prices they are willing to pay. It is the subversion of this information network that produces the bias in product quality in government organizations. Government bureaus typically price their output below cost and therefore well below the prices of competing private organizations. Those people entitled to obtain government-produced output will select it because of its low price even though they would prefer the output of competing private producers. When the market price is fixed below what people are willing to pay, consumers are unable to signal variations in the quality of bureau output to government officials who must monitor government managers.

Government and Quality

This may be made clearer with the aid of Figure 7.3. Assume that the good offered for sale is hospital care, which is, of course, a varied product made up of different attributes such as nursing care and doctoring, as well as basic hotel services such as feeding and sheltering. For simplicity, we will collect all of these varied attributes into two groups that we will call *health* and *comfort*. Let the output of health be measured along the horizontal axis, z_1, and the output of comfort be measured along the vertical axis, z_2. Production of both these attributes is costly. If expenditure is limited to a fixed sum, then more of one can be produced only by reducing expenditure on the other. For any budget of the hospital we may therefore derive a curve such as $t(z)$, which connects all combinations of the two attributes that can be produced by the agency. By devoting the entire budget to health, for

Figure 7.3   *Determination of Product Characteristics*

Every combination of characteristics along $t(z)$ from K to H can be produced with a given expenditure per unit. Profits are maximized by choosing that combination which produces the most revenue per unit—that is, which sells for the highest price. Curves P_z^1 and P_z^2 each connect combinations of product attributes that will sell for the same price per unit. The firm will therefore choose combination B, which produces the most revenue per unit.

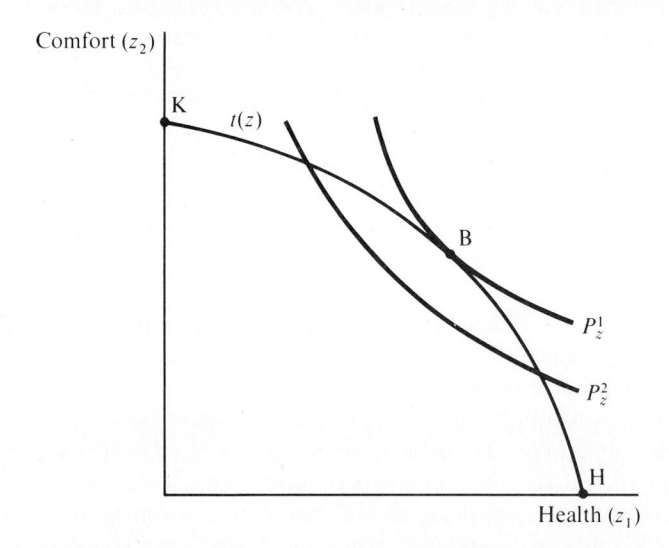

example, combination H can be produced, which contains no comfort. By devoting the entire budget to comfort, on the other hand, combination K will be produced, which contains no health.

We cannot see directly from the diagram the number of hospital stays actually produced, but assume that this number is already determined and is independent of the position selected along $t(z)$. Hospital stays that contain more of each attribute, health and comfort, are of higher quality than those that contain less of each. However, managers choosing from among combinations along $t(z)$ must give up some of one attribute if they are to provide more of the other. As noted earlier, managers of for-profit firms will be guided in this selection by the market value of attributes, including in every hospital stay only that quality of each for which customers are willing to pay.

We may illustrate this choice by observing isorevenue curves linking combinations of attributes that yield a constant revenue when sold in the market. These curves look like indifference curves, and for many purposes they serve the same function in the managerial choices depicted. Combinations that lie on higher isorevenue curves yield more revenue and thus will be preferred by managers. These are shown to be convex downward, reflecting the assumed preference of consumers for hospital stays containing some of each attribute to stays devoted exclusively to either health or comfort. Two such curves are P_z^1 and P_z^2. In selecting a combination along $t(z)$, a manager of a for-profit firm will therefore choose combination B, which yields the maximum possible revenue for the expenditure indicated.

Now let us contrast this choice with that made by the manager of a government hospital. Customers (patients) entitled to use a government-provided low-cost hospital will do so in preference to a higher-priced private hospital regardless of which combination the former offers along $t(z)$. Government officials charged with monitoring the performance of hospital managers will seek to influence them to produce the correct combination of health and comfort. However, they lack the information regarding output quality that is provided to private firm owners by market prices. These officials must therefore themselves engage in quality control activities. In order to assess the quality of government enterprise output, officials must monitor the level of each of the attributes produced. (The reporting of such information is undoubtedly responsible for the morass of paperwork and red tape often deplored by public officials who do not really understand its function.)

Of course, if the levels of both attributes in Figure 7.3 were closely observed, then government could influence these bureaus to produce combination B—or any other combination desired, for that matter. It might simply pay managers more for producing the preferred combination than for producing any other. Presumably, government does distribute its favors and rewards so as to influence its managers to produce the quality of product and service desired.

However, the inability of government to monitor all features of the bureau's output radically alters the incentives these managers face. Assume, for example, that the attribute *health* can be inexpensively observed while the attribute *comfort* cannot. Potentially important aspects of product quality will go unmonitored. Consider the situation depicted in Figure 7.4. Government officials may seek to offer the same quality product offered by private hospitals—that is, combination

Figure 7.4   Selection of Product Characteristics by Government

If this product were sold at a market-clearing price combination B would be produced, because this combination produces the most revenue per unit for a given expenditure. Since attribute z_2 cannot be effectively monitored, it is impossible for those supervising this agency to determine whether combination B or D is produced. As combination D, containing no z_2, can be produced for less, agencies will choose this combination over combinations containing any of the unmonitorable attributes.

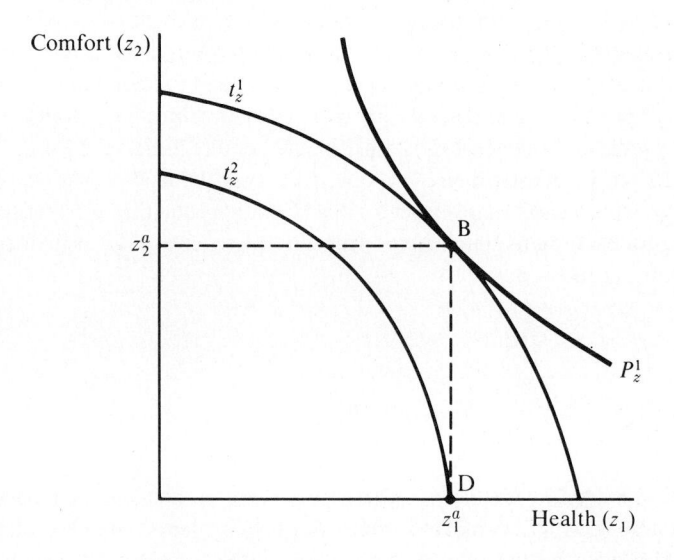

[Figure: axes Comfort (z_2) vertical, Health (z_1) horizontal; two budget curves t_z^1 and t_z^2; price line P_z^1 tangent at point B = (z_1^a, z_2^a); point D on horizontal axis at z_1^a.]

B, containing z_1^a units of health and z_2^a units of comfort. Because they are unable to observe the level of attribute z_2, however, they are unable to determine whether a particular hospital is offering combination B or combination D. Combination D lies on budget curve t_z^2, which involves lower expenditure than t_z^1 required to produce combination B. By offering D rather than B, any particular manager appears to be producing the same output at lower cost. Competition among managers may thus influence all managers of government hospitals to offer lower-quality output than patients would choose and government would have them produce. Managers of these hospitals (and of government bureaus in general) may indeed realize that production of combinations like D are less preferred by their customers than are other combinations like B producible at greater cost. However, to act on such information is to give the appearance of less management effectiveness. The increase in the quality of bureau output may not be apparent to the elected officials to whom these managers report, but the increase in cost almost certainly will be.

The ability of this model to predict differences between the character of government bureau and private firm output has been tested. In a recent study of Veterans Administration hospitals (whose services are available free to qualifying veterans), the prediction of lower quality was examined from a number of viewpoints.[7] Lower costs for VA hospitals than for private for-profit ones were predicted and observed. Most nursing and other hotel services above a minimal level are directed toward patient comfort rather than health. As services themselves are very difficult to monitor, it was predicted that fewer personnel would be employed to supply them than are found in private for-profit hospitals. This was confirmed in comparisons of staff/patient ratios for VA and for private for-profit hospitals, which indicated 70–75 percent more staff in the latter. As it costs less to supply hotel services alone than hotel services plus extensive health care, it was also predicted that VA hospital managers would seek to provide more of the former product and less of the latter product. One way to accomplish this was to admit patients well in advance of surgery or other treatment and to keep them longer after treatment has been completed. By pursuing such an admissions policy, many patients occupying beds in these hospitals would require little or no care and could be treated at lower cost than very sick patients. Evidence on patient stays confirms this prediction. When adjusted for age of patients and disease or surgical category, VA patients remained in hospitals for roughly twice as long as their counterparts in private for-profit hospitals.

7.3 Organization and Market Structure

In this chapter, as well as in others, frequent reference has been made to **competition** among suppliers. As the reader may have gathered from this discussion, competition plays a vital role in an economic system. Few of the beneficial results of market organization can be fully realized without it. It is therefore important that we make clear the nature of the activities that economists call competitive and their implications for the markets we will be addressing.

Readers of this text are undoubtedly familiar with many forms of competition. As children we competed with our siblings for our parents' attention. Later, many of us competed in athletics, academics, and romance. In most of these contests our objective was to win, and the fruits of victory were obvious, immediate, and frequently sweet. Business firms occasionally seem to compete in this same fashion. In economic theory, however, there is no scope for winning and losing. Firms have one purpose: to earn profits for their owners. The rivalrous behavior observed among competing firms must therefore emerge not from a desire for conquest and its favors but as a by-product of profit seeking. Being number one is important, in other words, only if achieving that status produces larger profits for the individual firm.

This fact is sometimes misunderstood by laymen who regard bigness in business as intrinsically anticompetitive. Any firm can become bigger, expanding its sales and therefore its share of the market relative to other firms by simply produc-

---

[7] See C. M. Lindsay, "A Theory of Government Enterprise," *Journal of Political Economy* 84 (October 1976): 1061–1077.

ing more output. The constraint on such behavior is, of course, that this additional output must be produced and sold. Firms are constrained by the demand for their products and will not increase output if that additional output will raise less revenue than it costs to produce. The size advantage that some firms enjoy in various industries is thus attributable to one of two factors: (1) The demand for the products of these firms is larger than that of their competitors, implying that they can sell any particular level of output at a higher price, or (2) they may produce that output at lower cost.

These two factors therefore determine the scope and form of economic competition in an industry. On the one hand, firms seek to modify their products in ways that make them more attractive to buyers. This will increase the demand for their product and hence raise the price that they may obtain for any chosen level of output. Firms that are successful in discovering ways to better satisfy the wants of consumers will be able to expand output profitably. Doing so will increase their market share. On the other hand, firms also seek to discover ways to lower the cost of producing their products. By lowering production costs, firms also gain the ability to expand output profitably. Doing so again increases their sales relative to other firms in the industry.

Large size in a firm presents problems for competition in only three cases. The first and most obvious is the case where a single firm is able to produce at such low cost that other firms cannot cover their costs at the price they obtain in such a market. This case is called "natural monopoly," and it will be discussed in detail in Chapter 10. Here we need only note for the record that such firms obtain this monopoly advantage by keeping price *below* the level at which competing firms can cover costs. It is therefore at worst a mixed blessing. The second case concerns an empirically more important category of industry, that in which a few firms account for most of the sales in an industry. If all firms in an industry agree to restrict output, prices—and therefore profits—will rise for each. Firms are inhibited from entering into such collusive arrangements by the costs of doing so, including the severe criminal and civil penalties assessed when such cases are successfully prosecuted. Another component of these collusion costs is the cost of negotiating the agreements (necessarily under the cloak of secrecy). An important determinant of such costs clearly is the number of firms present in an industry. The costs of collusion will be lower when the number of firms that must be brought into the agreement is reduced.

Concentration of sales among a small number of firms in an industry is therefore regarded as symptomatic of collusion. Observation of higher profits among firms in concentrated industries has bolstered this view. This interpretation has led to vigorous anticoncentration efforts by the Federal Trade Commission and the Justice Department. The connection between concentration and profits has another interpretation, however. Some firms may grow large for exactly the reason just given: Their products are regarded as better buys than those of their competitors. Collusion may be regarded as too costly even for concentrated industries and avoided on this basis. The high profits that these large firms earn may themselves reflect efficiencies rather than the fruits of collusive arrangements. These important issues and some evidence bearing on them will also be discussed in Chapter 10.

The most troublesome problem arising out of economic size has more to do with political science than with price theory. That problem emerges when a firm becomes so large that it has political, as opposed to market, power. When firms are able to gain the support of government to suppress competition or obtain other favors, the consumer is powerless to protect himself. When steel and automobile companies obtain tariffs or import quotas on the products of foreign competitors, or when truckers and airlines persuade regulators to mandate collusively determined prices, the forces of market competition are neutralized. When any firm is regarded as too large to be allowed to suffer the consequences of its own poor stewardship, then the fruits of other firms' good management are to that extent canceled. The best defense against the exercise of this size-related political advantage is a watchful and informed electorate—not the dissolution of large firms, however.

Summary

In this chapter we surveyed the theory of economic organization. The activity of production in market economies is typically carried on by teams rather than individual households, and this theory has provided us with some understanding of the forces that shape these institutions. The use of markets for the organization of economic activity is costly, but so is the use of central direction and control. Neither should be employed to the absolute exclusion of the other. Voluntary adoption of one method or the other by rival firms within a market setting minimizes total transaction costs. Errors in one direction or the other provide profit opportunities for firms that choose correctly. Competition among rival firms will insure that only the fittest (that is, the low-cost firms) will survive.

An additional feature of production activity important to the shaping of economic organization is the possibility of economies of teamwork. Groups of factors can produce more than single factors individually. However, team activity quite often presents individual workers with the opportunity to shirk. Organizations that adopt features that minimize this shirking cost will operate more efficiently and hence survive in the competition of rival organization forms. Adoption of the following characteristics reduces shirking, and such features are thus predicted to be widely observed among firms that must compete to survive:

1. The firm has a residual claimant.

2. The residual claimant monitors and observes input behavior.

3. The residual claimant is the central party to all team contracts.

4. The residual claimant may alter or terminate individual contracts without disbanding the team.

5. The residual claimant may sell his or her rights.

The classical firm, which incorporates all these features, is not the only form of organization observed. A large amount of economic activity has always been organized in nonprofit, charitable organizations. These have survived in spite of the potential for high shirking costs made possible by their lack of a residual claimant to perform the functions just listed. That survival was explained in terms of the peculiar information costs associated with the product charity. Another organizational form, the government enterprise,

Chapter 7   The Choice of Organization

has also demonstrated a marked ability to survive. The continued presence of government bureaucracies seems related more to the shelter and protection afforded them by parent governments than to any intrinsic economies of transaction costs. Private firms are often prohibited from actively competing with government enterprises like the postal service and sanitation departments. When these agencies do compete, they often are able to protect themselves by offering their output at heavily subsidized prices. This is not the place to consider the advisability of such protection and subsidies.

Finally, this chapter sketched an agenda for the subsequent analysis of firm choices. Firms are assumed to seek profits above all else. This objective governs choices ranging from the level of output to the choice of production technology. It also has implications for market structure. Firms that are successful in lowering costs and designing attractive products will find it profitable to expand. Firms that adopt more costly technologies and less attractive designs will suffer in the competitive arena. Size by itself is often an indicator of successful competition; only rarely is it the by-product of anticompetitive behavior.

Key Concepts

transaction costs
cost minimization
buy or make
vertical integration
survival
teams
shirk

monitor
residual claimant
proprietary firm
nonprofit organization
collection of attributes
competition

Questions

1. *Easy* In most markets there are no admission charges. One does not have to pay a fee to purchase and sell. In what sense, then, can one say that there are costs of relying on the market for organizing certain activities?

Hard Apply Coase's theory of the firm to household activity. Why don't households rent land and employ farmers to raise cattle and grow vegetables for their consumption rather than buying food in supermarkets? Why don't we hire electricians to assemble televisions, radios, and other appliances under our supervision rather than buying these items off the shelf?

2. *Easy* Explain why total transaction costs are minimized at the combination of market and vertically integrated decisions at which the marginal cost of these two types of decision making are equal.

Hard What would be the effect on the curve in panel (b) of Figure 7.1 and on the optimal mix of decision making of advances in computer and telecommunications technology that provide managers with more information about what is going on in the field?

3. *Easy* Player-coaches are not unheard of in professional sports, but they are very rare. Many professional athletes move directly from playing into coaching, belying the possibility that wisdom and coaching skills are exclusively acquired with age. What aspect of the theory of organization may explain the rarity of player-coaches?

Hard In Yugoslavia, workers in various enterprises act collectively as residual claimants. They hire a manager and lease capital equipment from the state. Casual empiricism suggests, however, that this form of organization fails to completely eliminate the shirking problem. Can you explain this failure?

4. *Easy* Of the five features of business firms suggested by the theory of Alchian and Demsetz, which are not characteristics of nonprofit organizations?

Hard Corporations often include incentive bonuses in the salary arrangements of their chief executives. The executives are rewarded with shares of the corporation profits and bonuses for exceeding sales projections. This introduces risk into their earnings that presumably they would prefer to avoid. Can you explain what is going on?

5. *Easy* Describe the problems likely to be encountered if a proprietary organization with a residual claimant attempted to enter the charity industry—that is, sought to collect money from donors with which it would produce benefits for the poor.

Hard Nonprofit organizations seem to invite shirking. They have no residual claimant, so that managers themselves have little incentive to monitor other workers. Yet this form of organization passes the survival test; a large portion of American output is organized within nonprofit firms. Can you explain this seeming paradox?

6. *Easy* One of the sources of continuing complaint about government bureaucracy is the burden of "red tape" that entangles all decisions and activities. Reports must be submitted and circulated on all aspects of bureau performance. Proposals for new endeavors must be submitted in triplicate and receive countless approvals. However, these burdensome practices survive in the face of all this hostility. Can you explain the economic function performed by this red tape in government enterprises? Why do we see less of this formal reporting in proprietary firms?

Hard In many states highway patrolmen are often observed concealing themselves along lonely stretches of straight highway in order to catch speeders. They might be more useful in the promotion of safety, however, monitoring driving in other locations offering less concealment but presenting real safety hazards. What feature of the theory of government organization explains this observation? Discuss fully.

Chapter 8

The Choice of Output: Price Taker Case

Connections   *This is the first of three chapters concerned with the choice of output by firms. This choice will be shown to depend on the relationship of output price to the rate of output. This in turn depends on the structure of the market in which output is sold. Two market structures are identified for which output choice differs. These are price taker and price searcher markets. While the relationship between the revenue function and market structure is sketched here, detailed treatment of this topic is postponed until Chapter 10. The principal focus of this chapter is the relationship of output to cost, a relationship that is independent of market structure. It is explored in terms of the output choice of price taker firms. Total cost is influenced by two considerations, the rate of output and the scale of operations. Both are influenced by price. Two laws of supply for price-taking firms are introduced, and the price elasticity of supply is defined. Marginal revenue for a firm is defined and derived by taking the slope of the total revenue function with respect to output. The reader may wish to refresh his or her memory concerning the product rule formula for slopes in Chapter 1.*

The relationship we seek to explore in this and the following chapter is that of output to profits. In the discussion of supply in Chapter 2, we assumed that quantity supplied rises with price. In Chapter 7, however, we argued that profit was the objective of firm organization. The hypothesized connection between supply and price must therefore operate through profit. The choice of output may be viewed as an application of the choice theory developed in Chapter 3. Owner-managers of firms confront an opportunity set from which they must select an output level. That selection involves a rank ordering of the alternatives available in that set in which the highest-ranking output is the most preferred, and hence the one chosen. Both the determinants of the opportunity set and the factors important to ranking differ from those presented in connection with the choice of goods.

A firm is necessarily self-financing. The production of output is not constrained, as are household consumption bundles, by a particular budget. A firm may finance an output increase with revenues obtained through the sale of that output. This is not to say that total expenditure on materials, labor, and capital is unlimited. Firms cannot expand output indefinitely. Revenues will be sufficient to offset these expenditures only for a certain range of output. This choice is therefore ultimately constrained by a firm's ability to cover those costs out of revenues. The limits of the output opportunity set are defined in terms of this bookkeeping condition. In this sense, the determinants of the output opportunity set are somewhat more complex than those of the opportunity set of household choice.

If identifying the opportunity set is more complicated for the selection of output by firms, the rank-ordering process is a much simpler procedure than its household counterpart. Owners—who are, in a sense, households—prefer more wealth to less. Profits increase the net worth of firms and therefore the wealth of their owners. These owners therefore seek maximum possible profits. The objective of profit maximization is thus perfectly consistent with utility maximization— indeed, it is derivable from it. As profits themselves are far less subjective than utility, however, our task of rank ordering alternative outputs in the eyes of owners can be approached with far greater precision than the previous task of comparing alternative consumption bundles.

Consider Figure 8.1. Assume that given prevailing market conditions, the current relationship between output and profit is represented by curve $\pi(q)$. As we have stated, firms must cover costs; they may not operate at a loss. The opportunity set for the firm depicted thus contains all outputs between q_1 and q_2. However, owner-managers will not be indifferent among all outputs in this opportunity set. Seeking maximum profits they will choose output q^*, at which profits reach the highest possible level. If we can derive the underlying components determining the shape of this curve, we may predict which output level will be selected by the firm.

In Figure 8.2, for example, we have two such curves, $\pi_1(q)$ and $\pi_2(q)$, reflecting alternative sets of market conditions. If we have enough information to plot these curves under these differing conditions, we may predict that a change in these conditions from those producing curve $\pi_1(q)$ to those producing curve $\pi_2(q)$ will be accompanied by an increase in output from q_1^* to q_2^*.

In many cases we may not have sufficient information to accurately plot exact curves such as these for firms in an industry. We may nevertheless be able to con-

Chapter 8 *The Choice of Output: Price Taker Case* 237

Figure 8.1 **Output and Profit**

Optimization with respect to the choice of output by the firm involves an opportunity set containing all outputs over which the firm may cover costs (those between q_1 and q_2) and a rank-ordering process concerned with the profit at each output (indicated by the curve $\pi[q]$). The output chosen will be that which produces the highest profit—that is, q^*, yielding profits of π^*.

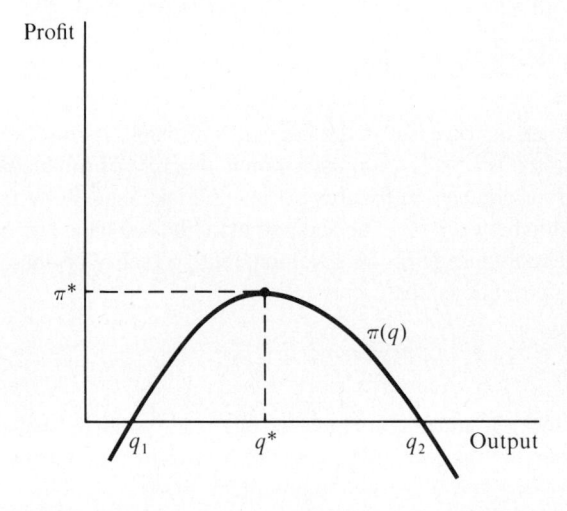

Figure 8.2 **Comparative Statics for the Firm**

Changes in the economic environment in which the firm operates may change the profit-maximizing output in predictable fashion. A shift in demand for the firm's product or a change in factor prices might shift the profit function from position $\pi_1(q)$ to position $\pi_2(q)$, allowing us to predict an increase in output.

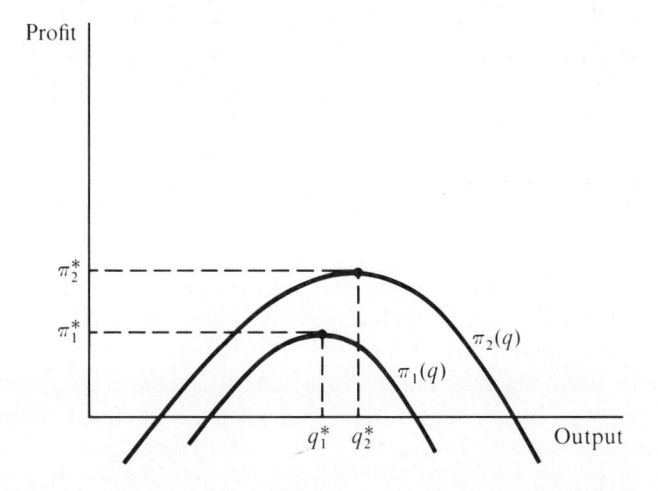

clude on the basis of theory that a change in market conditions will shift the peak of the profit curve in predictable directions. The economic theory of the firm permits a broad range of such predictions. It is therefore possible to predict the response of output to changes in market conditions such as prices without detailed information on the underlying profit relationships of individual firms.

8.1 The Components of Profit

Profits are defined as increases in the net worth of firms. Profits on current operations are therefore *revenues* from sales minus the *cost* of producing that output. The profits curves depicted in Figures 8.1 and 8.2 take their shape from the underlying relationship between revenue and output on the one hand and cost and output on the other. The first stage in the development of a theory of output is to specify these underlying relationships in more detail.

Revenue and Output

A curve relating output to revenue may take two possible shapes. These two shapes correspond to the two basic market structures in which firms operate. Total revenue for any output is given by the product of price and output. The distinction between these two cases therefore concerns the influence of output *on* price. If a firm may sell more output only by lowering its price, it is defined to be a **price searcher**. Output choice for a price searching firm will be examined in the next chapter. Here we will introduce the choice of output in the context of a less complicated model in which the firm regards the price as fixed. In this case total revenue as a function of output is expressed quite simply as

$$r(q) = Pq$$

where P is the constant price and q is quantity produced. The slope of such a total revenue curve is defined as **marginal revenue**. In this case, therefore, marginal revenue is simply:

$$\frac{\Delta r}{\Delta q} = P.$$

For each additional unit of output sold, the firm's revenues increase by exactly the price of that unit. As marginal revenue is constant, such a total revenue curve will be linear, as Figure 8.3.

Such a firm is a **price taker**. It may sell any amount at the given market price, but it may *not* charge a higher price for any amount of output. Several conditions may produce such an environment, or at least approximate it. Public utilities, whose prices are controlled by regulation, are price takers. Firms that supply a market that is also served by many rivals face a similar situation. Such firms must sell at a price that clears the market of the supply offered by all the firms together.

Chapter 8   The Choice of Output: Price Taker Case   239

Figure 8.3   Total revenue for a Price Taker

The function $r(q)$ reflects the total revenue from the sale of output q. The slope of the curve is linear and equal to price. This implies that the firm is a price taker. Marginal revenue does not vary with output in this case.

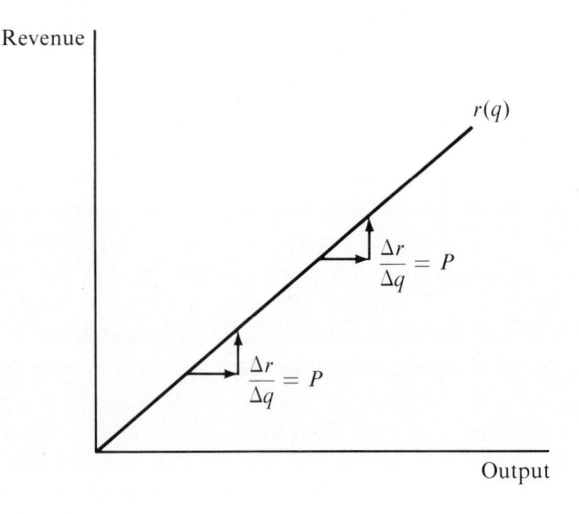

(Graph: Revenue vs Output showing linear function $r(q)$ with slope $\frac{\Delta r}{\Delta q} = P$ at two points)

Figure 8.4   Demand for a Price Taker Firm

The demand curve for the output of a price taker is horizontal. Changes in output by this firm have no influence on the price at which it can be sold.

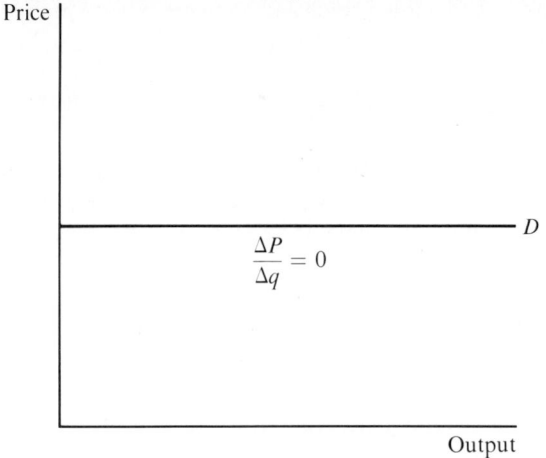

(Graph: Price vs Output showing horizontal demand curve D with $\frac{\Delta P}{\Delta q} = 0$)

If one such firm attempts to sell its output at a price above that of its rivals, it will lose its customers and therefore sell nothing.

This latter case is described as the **competitive model**. Demand for the output of such a competitive firm may be said to be perfectly elastic at the market price: It may sell *any amount* at this price. Demand curves for the output of these firms are completely horizontal, as in Figure 8.4.

8.2 Costs and Outputs

Many economists (and many textbooks) state that the relationship between costs and output varies between the long run and the short run. The short run, according to this view, is a period during which some features of the production process cannot be changed. The costs of those unchangeable features are designated *fixed* costs, reflecting the fact that they are beyond the control of the firm. Costs associated with those aspects of production over which the firm has discretion are designated *variable* costs, reflecting that they may be varied. Total cost of any output is the sum of such fixed and variable costs.

Since this view can be misleading, we will avoid it here. Certainly, nearly all features of the production process may be modified at some cost. New premises may be acquired and old ones vacated and sold at some cost. Existing arrangements with suppliers of materials may be renegotiated at any time, if the firm is willing to bear the cost of doing so. Whether in fact firms regard costs as fixed or variable in the sense just used depends on the costs and benefits of changing particular features of the production process. These will in turn depend on market conditions.

Fixed costs cannot be truly fixed in the sense of being beyond the control of the firm. Those costs that are literally fixed in this sense are not really economic costs at all, according to our definition of cost. Cost must reflect the value of an opportunity forgone. When something cannot be altered, nothing is forgone; hence, the value of that nonexistent alternative is zero. Those costs that are fixed in this sense are more correctly called **sunk costs**. This designation was coined by economists to indicate the bad consequences of former decisions that have no bearing on any current economic choice and are therefore not really economic costs. All costs must therefore be variable in that sense.

Operating and Overhead Costs

A more useful categorization identifies costs by the types of decisions to which they are relevant. We make a distinction between **operating costs**, which are relevant to the rate of output decision, and **overhead costs**, which are relevant to the choice of scale of operations. Such a distinction calls for further definition of the terms *rate of output* and *scale*. By rate of output we simply mean the number of units of output produced per accounting period. Scale, on the other hand, is a design concept. Many production processes are designed for specific rates of output in the sense that unit costs are minimized at particular output levels. Many output rates are producible with a given scale, but scale itself is measured by the rate of output at which cost per unit is minimized.

Of course, if it were economically feasible to change the use of every resource each time the rate of output changed, the distinction between operating and overhead costs would be meaningless. Each change of output would be accompanied by a change of scale as the design of the process itself was accommodated to the new output. For most production, however, it is not economical to vary output by varying the use of every resource employed in production. Firms may, and typically do, vary output over broad ranges without varying their use of buildings and equipment, top management, or marketing activity. In doing so, they implicitly choose not to vary scale. Such a choice is presumably based on the expectation that these changes in output are temporary and that the existing scale is suitable for expected output in the future. Overhead costs are therefore costs that vary as scale varies but do not vary with the rate of output when scale remains the same.

For any chosen scale, changes in the rate of output do not affect overhead costs. Overhead costs are therefore irrelevant to the choice of output but are important to the scale decision. Examples of overhead costs are administrative and marketing costs, research and development, property taxes, and insurance, all of which do not vary with day-to-day variation in the firm's level of output. Another important source of overhead costs is the cost of holding real assets, such as buildings, land, and equipment. The opportunity costs of holding such assets will include the rent that might be obtained from leasing them to other users or the interest that might be earned on their resale value. These costs also include any depreciation associated with technological obsolescence should new, better-designed equipment be introduced while the assets are held by the firm.

Operating costs are those that vary as the rate of output by itself varies; they bear directly on the output decision. Examples of operating costs are expenditures for materials, wages for production workers, and depreciation related to the actual wear and tear suffered by equipment during use.

Consider the following example. The ideal automobile for city driving is one that is small, maneuverable in traffic, and easy to park. Such a car is less suited to intercity driving on the highway, where interior comfort, "top M," and resistance to impact are more important. Someone who does little highway driving is nevertheless unlikely to purchase or even rent a different car for an occasional long trip. The gain from obtaining a more suitable vehicle for such an occasion is less than the cost of changing. Were the driving needs of our city driver to change so that highway driving was the dominant use to which his or her automobile was put, however, he or she might seriously consider exchanging a small car for a larger one.

We may interpret this example in terms of our new vocabulary. The driver in the first instance elects to vary his or her output (number of miles driven) without varying the scale of his or her production process (automobile). Certain costs increase as a result of this larger output rate: gasoline, maintenance, and depreciation on the car. These costs of resources whose use varies with output are operating costs; they will influence the decision as to how many miles are driven. The driver will consider them in deciding whether to drive or use another form of transportation, or whether to make the trip alone or to carpool.

Other costs are not affected by the decision concerning number or length of car trips. The liability insurance on a car is not affected by the decision to make an additional trip. The depreciation on the car due to the introduction of new models is not affected by increased use, nor is the amount of interest forgone on the resale value of the car. These costs are therefore overhead costs. As they are not affected by output, they will not influence the output choice.

However, when the driver recognizes that the expected output has permanently increased, he or she must explicitly consider the costs of overhead. The use of a larger-scale automobile may economize on some operating costs, but it will increase overhead costs. Depreciation costs per year and forgone interest will both increase with a larger and more expensive car, as will collision insurance. The optimal scale is that which minimizes the sum of overhead and operating costs for the chosen level of output.

Each firm is continuously reconsidering both its scale and its rate of output. It may choose at any time to (1) vary its output while holding scale, and therefore overhead cost, constant, (2) vary scale, and thus overhead cost, while holding output constant, or (3) vary both scale and output. The two decisions concerning scale and output rate are interdependent, however. The level of operating cost at any rate of output depends on the firm's scale. The decision concerning scale, on the other hand, depends on the firm's expected rate of output. In the interest of clarity in presentation, we will initially discuss these decisions separately.

The Rate of Output

If scale is held constant as output varies, overhead costs do not vary—they are themselves constant. Total overhead costs in Figure 8.5 are thus c_k regardless of whether the firm chooses to produce output q_1 or q_2. Operating costs generally increase as output increases. Operating costs at output q_1 are thus less than at output q_2 ($c_2^a < c_2^b$). We shall assume that the path of such an operating cost function is that given by panel (b) of Figure 8.5. This curve rises with output first at a diminishing rate and then at an increasing rate. Thus, the curve is initially concave downward, then becomes concave upward. (We will discuss the factors giving rise to this shape later.) Total cost at any output is merely the sum of overhead costs and operating costs at that output. The total cost of producing no output (while maintaining the original scale) is thus c_1. Since operating costs at this rate of output are zero, total cost is merely the overhead cost of that scale. At output q_1, total cost is therefore $c_t^1 = c_k + c_0^1$. At the higher output, q_2, total cost is greater by the increase in operating cost over this interval—that is, $c_t^2 = c_k + c_0^2$.

Just as marginal revenue is the rate of change in total revenue per unit change in output, the rate of change in total cost per unit change in output is defined as **marginal cost**. The marginal cost of a particular output may therefore be thought of as the slope of the total cost curve at that output. Operating cost is the only part of total cost that varies with output. The total cost curve, as we have seen, is merely the total operating cost curve shifted upward by the constant overhead cost. These curves are therefore parallel, having the same slope at each output. Marginal cost may thus also be thought of as the slope of the total operating cost curve. In Figure 8.5, the marginal cost of output q_2 is shown both as the slope of the total operating cost curve, $\Delta OC/\Delta q$, in panel (b) and as the slope of the total cost curve, $\Delta TC/\Delta q$, in panel (c).

Average Costs

It is occasionally useful to deal with another set of relationships between output and cost. If we express total cost, overhead cost, and operating cost as functions of the rate of output, we may express the relationship among these functions respectively as:

$TC(q) = KC(q) + OC(q).$

Figure 8.5   *Total Costs and Output*

The total cost at any output consists of the sum of overhead and operating costs. Total overhead cost does not vary with output. Total operating cost does vary with output. Total operating cost is generally assumed to have the shape indicated in panel (b), which gives the total cost curve itself the shape indicated in panel (c). The slope of both the total operating cost curve and the total cost curve at each output is the marginal cost, MC.

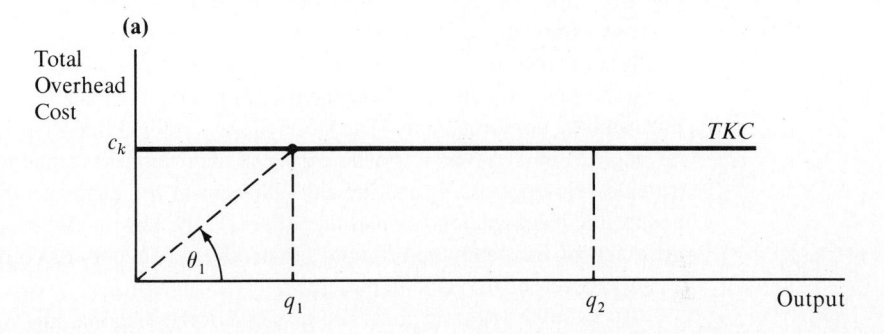

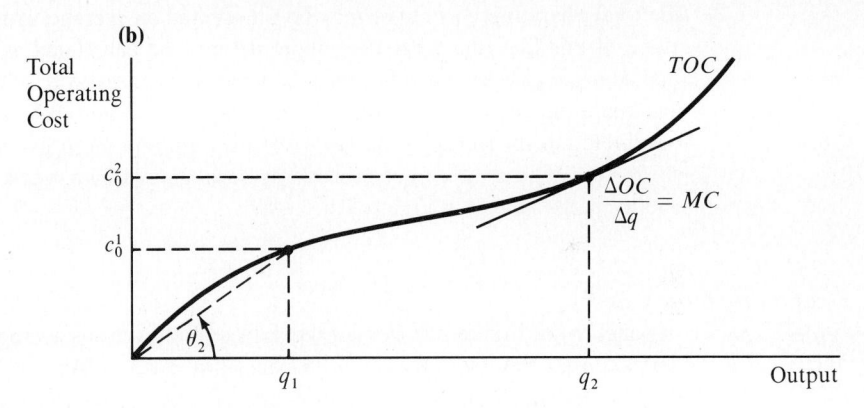

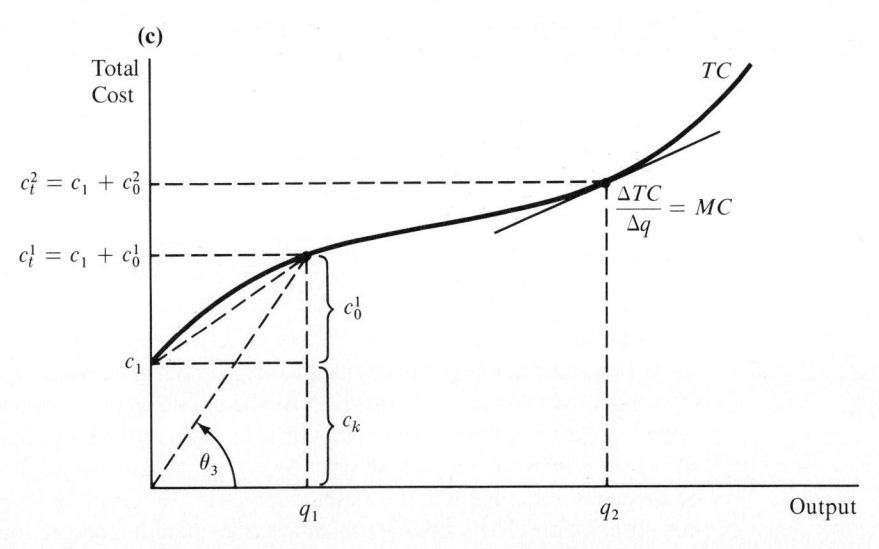

(a) Total Overhead Cost vs Output: horizontal line TKC at c_k, with angle θ_1, points q_1, q_2.

(b) Total Operating Cost vs Output: curve TOC through c_0^1 at q_1 and c_0^2 at q_2; slope $\dfrac{\Delta OC}{\Delta q} = MC$; angle θ_2.

(c) Total Cost vs Output: curve TC; $c_t^2 = c_1 + c_0^2$ at q_2, $c_t^1 = c_1 + c_0^1$ at q_1; c_1 and c_k indicated with braces; slope $\dfrac{\Delta TC}{\Delta q} = MC$; angle θ_3.

By dividing through this expression by output, we have another set of relationships; that is:

$$\frac{TC(q)}{q} = \frac{KC(q)}{q} + \frac{OC(q)}{q}.$$

Economists refer to the ratio on the left side of the equality as **average total cost**. The two ratios on the right side are referred to as **average overhead cost** and **average operating cost**, respectively.

It is interesting to note that there are geometrical equivalents of these average cost concepts in Figure 8.5. Note the triangle formed in panel (a) by the two dotted lines and the horizontal axis. The slope of the diagonal line (that is, the tangent of the angle θ_1 in the lower left-hand corner of the triangle) is equal to the ratio of the triangle side opposite θ_1 and the side adjacent to the angle. In this case, the opposite side has a value of c_k and the adjacent side has a value of q_1. The slope of the diagonal line from the origin to the overhead cost curve at q_1 is thus the average overhead cost for this output, c_k/q_1.

By a similar logic, in panel (b) the slope of the diagonal line from the origin to the total operating cost curve may be interpreted as average operating cost. The slope of this line (the tangent of angle θ_2) may be calculated as the ratio of the opposite side, c_0^1, and the adjacent side, again q_1. This ratio is, of course, the average operating cost of the quantity q_1. In panel (c) of Figure 8.5, tangent θ_3 has the interpretation of average total cost. We may employ these geometrical relationships from Figure 8.5 to position average cost *curves* with respect to one another and to marginal cost in Figure 8.6.

Positioning Cost Curves

In panel (b) of Figure 8.6 we plot the values of the various average cost measures derived from the total cost curve in panel (a). The relative positions and slopes may be derived from the information provided by the total cost curve. Recalling from our previous discussion that the tangents of angles θ_1 and θ_2 measure average total cost, the average total cost curve may be drawn with a downward slope between outputs q_1 and q_4. Since the tangent of θ_1 is greater than the tangent of θ_2, average total cost must be higher at output q_1 than at q_2, and the curve itself must slope downward in this interval.

The same relationships may be inferred concerning the slope of the average operating cost curve. Since the tangent of θ_3 exceeds that of θ_4, we may conclude that average operating cost at output q_1 exceeds average operating cost at q_3. The average operating cost curve in panel (b) must therefore slope downward in this interval.

Note further that in panel (a) a line drawn from the origin to the total cost curve *cannot* have a slope lower than the tangent of θ_2. At output q_4, such a line is just tangent to the total cost curve. Any line drawn from the origin with a lower slope than tangent θ_2 will completely miss the total cost curve. There is therefore no output with an *average* total cost lower than that of output q_4. Average total cost reaches a minimum at this output; curve ATC in panel (b) is drawn to reflect this observation. The output at which average operating cost reaches a minimum may be located in the same way. At output q_3, a line from the intercept is just

Chapter 8 *The Choice of Output: Price Taker Case*

Figure 8.6 *Total Costs and Average Costs*

The paths of the average cost curves in panel (b) can be read off of various slopes in panel (a). The slope of a ray from the origin to the total cost curve at any output is a measure of the ATC of that output. The slope of this angle declines from q_1 to q_4, where it reaches a minimum. The slope of a line from the TC intercept in panel (a) to the total cost curve at each output gives the average operating cost of that output. This declines from q_1 to q_3, where it reaches a minimum. The minimum value of marginal cost occurs at the point at which curve TC in panel (a) has the lowest slope—that is, output q_2. The curves in panel (b) are drawn to correspond to these relationships.

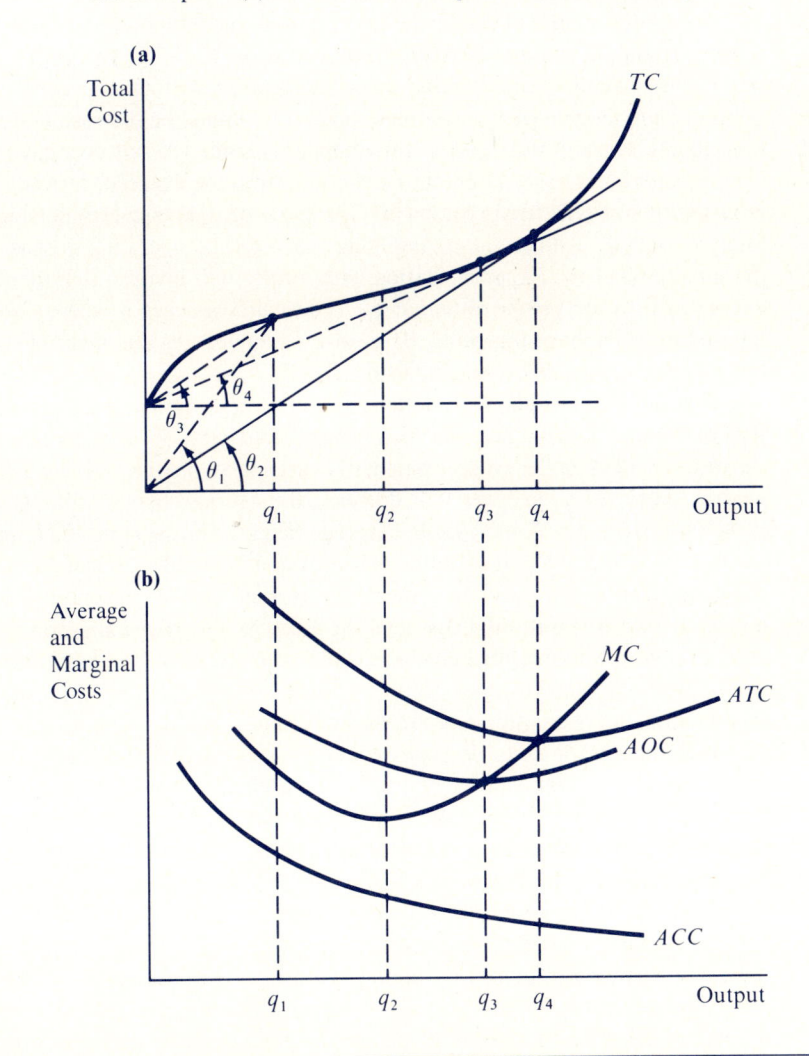

tangent to the total cost curve. Any line from this point that has a lower slope will not touch any part of the total cost curve. Hence, there is no output with a lower average operating cost than output q_3.

Consider now the relationship between these two average cost curves. At output q_1, the slope of the line forming θ_1 clearly must exceed the slope of the line forming θ_3. Average total cost must therefore exceed average operating cost at this output. A little experimentation with a ruler will be sufficient to convince us that the tangent of the angle forming average total cost will always exceed the tangent of the angle forming average operating cost for any given output. The average total cost curve must lie everywhere above the average operating cost curve. Additional experimentation with a ruler should convince us that minimum average total cost must occur at a higher output than minimum average operating cost. A more intuitive explanation for this result will be provided as we discuss the relationship between these curves and marginal cost.

Recall that marginal cost is the slope of both the total cost and operating cost curves. At output q_4, the line from the origin in panel (a) is just tangent to the total cost curve. This line therefore has the same slope as the total cost curve at output q_4. Since the tangent of θ_2 is average total cost, it must be the case that marginal cost equals average total cost at this output. A similar result occurs concerning average operating cost. At output q_3, the line from the intercept forming angle θ_4 is just tangent to the total cost curve. The slope of θ_4 is equal to the slope of the total cost curve at this output, implying that average operating cost is equal to marginal cost at q_3. Experimentation with a ruler will confirm that the total cost curve has its lowest slope at output q_2. The total cost curve is steeper both to the left and to the right of this point. This observation tells us that marginal cost, like both average cost curves, is U shaped.

Now let us consider the relationship between marginal and average cost in general. Imagine arranging the members of your class in a line from tallest to shortest to calculate the average height of everyone in the line. Adding a classmate who is shorter than average will decrease the average height; adding someone taller than average will increase the average height. The same principle applies to costs. Production of a unit of output that adds more to total cost than the average of those units previously produced increases average cost. Production of a unit of output that adds less to total cost than the average of earlier units lowers average cost. In Figure 8.6, marginal cost is less than average total cost at outputs q_1, q_2, and q_3. Average total cost thus declines at each of these outputs, as the addition to total cost associated with the production of each unit is less than the average cost of producing earlier units. Beyond output q_4, however, marginal cost lies above average total cost. The incremental cost from each extra unit beyond q_4 adds more than the average amount of cost, causing the average total cost curve to rise beyond this point. Marginal cost must therefore intersect average total cost at the minimum point on the latter curve.

Since operating cost is the only part of total cost that varies with output, the same relationship will hold between marginal and average operating cost. Marginal cost must intersect average operating cost at the minimum point of the latter curve. However, the minimum point on the average operating cost curve will be to the left of the minimum point on the average total cost curve. Total cost includes overhead cost, which is not included in the computation of average variable cost. Returning to our classroom example, imagine that the average height of the class is calculated twice, each time in a different way. In the first case, average height is computed with one class member standing on a box; in the second case, all members stand on the floor. The number of those whose height is below average will be greater in the former case than in the latter.

It will still be true that *in each case* adding someone of below-average height reduces the average height of those who remain, and vice versa. However, some added class members will be above-average height in one case and below-average height in the other. Adding new students who are between these average heights therefore increases average height in the first case but lowers it in the second case. We may therefore interpret the first case as analogous to the computation of average operating cost and the latter case as analogous to the computation of average total cost. Production of units between outputs q_3 and q_4 will increase average operating cost while decreasing average total cost.

All cost curves based upon a total cost curve like that in Figure 8.6 have the following features in common:

1. Marginal cost, average total cost, and average operating cost will each form a U-shaped curve as output varies.

2. Minimum points of these curves will occur at the lowest output for the marginal cost curve, at the next lowest for the average operating cost curve, and at the highest output for the average total cost curve.

3. Average operating cost is lower than average total cost at every output.

4. The marginal cost curve rises to the right from its minimum point, intersecting average operating cost at its minimum, then intersecting average total cost at its minimum.

5. Average overhead cost is not U shaped but declines over the entire range of output.

The Shape of the Total Cost Curve

As the shapes of all average and marginal curves are derived from the assumed shape of the total cost curve, some discussion of the underlying rationale for these assumptions is warranted. These curves rise over some interval at a diminishing rate, then begin rising at an increasing rate. For constant-scale operations, the assumed shape is explained in terms of production design. Certain features of the production process do not vary in the short run; they typically *embody* in their design some optimal level of output that minimizes unit operating cost. As output varies above or below this designed optimum, average operating cost increases.

Marginal cost declines over the lower-than-designed optimal range of output for two reasons: (1) Less time is wasted moving labor and other resources from position to position through the production process, and (2) such designs typically exploit scope for specialization in particular tasks. Costly labor required for highly skilled tasks is not used to perform tasks requiring little skill. At low levels of production, these advantages of specialization cannot be fully exploited. We will illustrate only the former of these two reasons for declining marginal and average operating cost.

Consider the very simplified example presented in Table 8.1. This table presents information concerning the labor requirements and costs for an assembly line containing two stations, one to perform Task A and the other to perform Task B. Each position is designed with access to the particular tools necessary to perform a separate part of the assembly line process. The costs of such equipment, as

Table 8.1 Marginal and Average Operating Costs for Assembly Line with Two Positions

Output per Day	Time Required to Perform Task A	Time Required to Change Positions	Time Required to Perform Task B	Total Time	Total Operating Cost	Marginal Cost	Average Operating Cost
1	10 min.	15 min.	10 min.	35 min.	$ 3.50	$3.50	$3.50
2	20	15	20	55	5.50	2.00	2.75
24	240	150	240	530	53.00	2.16	2.21
48	480	0	480	960	96.00	1.79	2.00
72	864	0	864	1728	172.80	3.20	2.40

well as the costs of the building, will not vary with output; these are overhead costs. We shall simply ignore materials and other operating costs in order to focus our attention on the varying factor, labor.

Assume that each operation requires ten minutes of labor time and that 15 minutes are required to move from one position to the other. The total labor required to produce one unit is therefore 35 minutes. If labor costs $0.10 per minute, then the marginal cost of the first unit (as well as the total operating and average operating cost) is $3.50. If two units are produced, however, the worker may perform Task A on two pieces (devoting 20 minutes to this labor), then move to the second position, where an additional 20 minutes is spent performing Task B. As only one trip is required between stations, total time to produce two units is 55 minutes, and the marginal cost of the second unit is $5.50 - $3.50 = $2.00. Total operating cost of two units is $5.50, and average operating cost is $5.50/2 = $2.75.

As output expands only a limited amount of work may be allowed to pile up at each station while the worker continues to perform one task or the other. Let us assume that in the production of 24 units, ten trips from one position to the other must be made, requiring a total of 150 minutes. Twenty-four units will require 240 minutes' worth of labor at each position. A total operating cost of $53.00 is thus incurred in the production of this output, and average operating cost thus falls to $53.00/24 = $2.21. For this interval of output marginal cost, $\Delta TC/\Delta q$ may be determined as ($53.00 - $5.50)/(24 - 2) = $2.16.

If, however, output is expanded from 24 to 48 units, two workers may be hired. With a worker at each position, no trips between stations need be made at all. Ten minutes per unit at each position is all that is required to produce at this rate of output. Total labor time required to produce 48 units is therefore 960 minutes. Total operating cost at this output is therefore $96.00, and average operating cost falls further to $2.00.

If we calculate marginal cost over this interval, however, we find that it is lower still. Recall that marginal cost is the change in total operating cost *per unit* change in output. The change in total operating cost from 24 to 48 units is $96.00

− $53.00 = $43.00. The change in output is 24 units. Marginal cost is therefore $43.00/24 = $1.79. Marginal cost at 48 units may have a different value over a smaller interval than that which we have calculated here—indeed, the "lumpiness" incorporated in this example in order to simplify it would yield some odd results were we to develop detailed cost information for each level of output. This simple example is nevertheless sufficient to demonstrate how marginal and average operating costs may behave over low ranges of output. If marginal cost declines over this range, average operating cost will also decline. Under these conditions, however, average operating cost will inevitably have a larger value than marginal cost at each rate of output.

Rising Costs of Constant-Scale Operations

For a given plant design, average and marginal costs will not continue to decline indefinitely. Once the assembly line reaches the output for which it is designed and all equipment is fully employed, economies of the type just described will have been exhausted. This does not mean that no additional output may be obtained at any cost. Additional workers may be employed to "double up" at each position so as to move work through the process more rapidly than it was designed for. Such a strategy would involve crowding at the various work stations and under such circumstances would likely involve more time per unit by each worker at each station than the 10 minutes taken under uncrowded conditions. Assume that this is true for the output of 72 units per day in Table 8.1. Because of crowding, tasks at both stations A and B require 12 minutes each rather than 10. A total of 864 minutes of labor is required at each station to produce 72 units of output for a total of 1728 minutes of labor per day. At $0.10 per minute, total labor costs are $172.80 for this output, raising average operating cost to $2.40 per unit.

Marginal cost again may be determined by calculating the rate of change in total operating cost per unit change in output. Again this involves making such an estimate over a larger discrete change than might be desirable had we a need for an estimate of the precise slope of the total operating cost curve at output 72. For our purposes, however, this crude estimate is sufficient. The *change* in total operating cost from 48 to 72 units is $76.80 ($172.80 − $96.00). Output has again increased by 24 units. The value of this ratio, and therefore marginal cost, is $3.20.

Another property of our cost curves is illustrated by this calculation at an output of 72 units. Average operating cost has increased over the range of output from 48 to 72. This should imply that marginal cost exceeds average operating cost over this range. Thankfully, this may be confirmed by comparing the information for these two outputs.

The Short and the Long Run

For the reasons just discussed, economists frequently refer to the cost curve derived under constant-scale conditions as "short-run" costs, while curves relating output to cost under changing-scale conditions are referred to as "long-run" costs. Certainly, the idea that timing has some bearing on the cost of producing particular outputs cannot be denied. Were a plant manager to decide to increase output by 20 percent tomorrow, he or she might understandably choose a different production technology than if making plans for next year's output. The changes this manager might make in plant layout and equipment would cost more to effect overnight than over a longer period. Similarly, the idea that beyond some point the passage of time exhausts all such potential "economies of delay" is appealing. In this sense, no great harm is done by labeling as "long-run costs" those that are associated with output changes sufficiently remote in the future that any changes in production design can be made at minimum cost.

These observations should not obscure a more important underlying principle: Changing the scale of operations itself is costly. It will therefore be done only if the gain from doing so exceeds those costs. In making this decision, time enters the calculations of the owner-manager in ways that make the conventional reliance on short-run versus long-run calculations very misleading. The plausibility in this example of differing scales being chosen over alternative time horizons emerges chiefly because it costs less to make changes in scale slowly than rapidly—not because the changes are made next year rather than this year. Were the choice to be made that of changing scale overnight today or overnight a year from now, the argument that different scales would be adopted over different time horizons would be less appealing.

A second influence of time on the decision to change scale operates through the benefits side of this calculation rather than through changing costs. A change in scale is more likely to be adopted if that scale is desired for long rather than short periods. The advantage of a different scale might be the lower cost of producing the desired output. This benefit will be larger if more units are produced at the higher contemplated rate of output.

Consider the hypothetical firm depicted in Table 8.2. This firm can produce 100 units per day at $25 per unit, but with the same scale it can produce 200 units at $30 per unit. It may change its scale at a cost of $5000, permitting it to produce a rate of output of 200 units at an average cost of $25. The gain in reduced cost from making this change is $1000 per day. If, however, the firm ordinarily *sells* only 100 units and receives an unusually large order for 600 units, it may not pay to invest in the larger scale. Whether it does so depends on how it interprets the increased orders for its product. If it regards this large order as portending a per-

Table 8.2   *Output and Cost at Different Scales of Operations*

	Output Rate per Day	Cost per Unit	Total Cost
Scale 1	100	$25	$2500
	200	30	6000
Scale 2	100	$30	$3000
	200	25	5000
Cost Advantage of Scale 2 per Day	100	−$5	−$500
	200	+5	+1000

Figure 8.7 *Costs and Scale*

The two average cost curves drawn here reflect alternative scales of operation. Output q_1 can be produced with the smaller-scale plant at average cost c_2, while the same output may be produced with the larger-scale plant only at higher cost c_1. The higher rate of output q_2 can be more cheaply produced with the larger-scale facility. Profit maximization requires that that scale be adopted which minimizes the average cost of production.

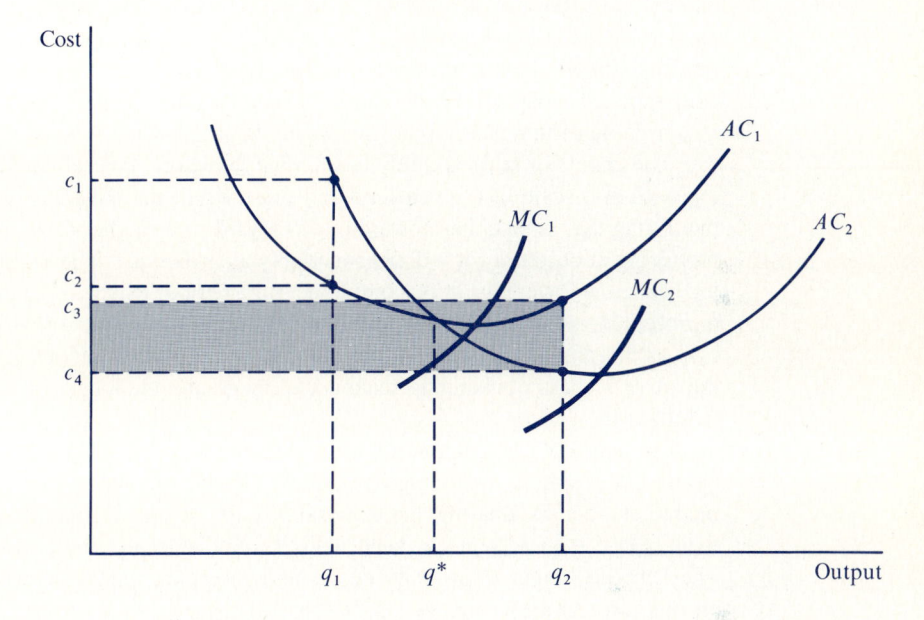

manent increase in demand for its product, the firm is more likely to regard the change as profitable than if it regards the large order as a one-time windfall. The additional 600 units by themselves will not cover the cost of the change in scale.

It is therefore misleading, at the least, to say that "long-run average cost is less than short-run average cost for plant A at an output of q." It is more correct to say that "average cost for plant A at a continuous output q is lower with scale 1 than with scale 2." Whether such a change in scale will be considered favorable by the firm depends on (1) how rapidly the change must be made, and (2) how long output q will be the favored output.

The Choice of Scale

Let us now consider in detail decisions of the firm concerning scale. In Figure 8.7 we depict two sets of cost curves, each associated with a different scale of operations. Each is drawn in conformity with our earlier discussion of costs and outputs. As the rate of output varies, average operating cost declines over some range, then rises. Marginal cost (MC) intersects average cost (AC) at its minimum point for each curve. The minimum point on AC_2 lies to the right of the minimum point on AC_1, reflecting the fact that the former is designed to produce a higher range of outputs than the latter. In general, the former will employ more of those inputs associated with overhead costs than the latter and is thus considered a larger scale of operations.

Assume that a firm's options with respect to scale are limited to the two curves shown. Clearly, that choice will be influenced by the expected rate of output. If q_1 is the preferred output, the lower scale will be preferred. Average cost of producing this output at the lower scale is c_2, while average cost of the larger-scale production is c_1. On the other hand, if the firm produces output q_2, costs are lower employing the larger scale by the difference $c_3 - c_4$. A firm that is newly entering this industry will have a reasonably uncomplicated choice. If outputs below q^* are contemplated, costs are lower using the smaller scale, while outputs greater than q^* are more economically produced using the larger scale.

The choice of scale is rarely this simple, however. Typically a firm is operating with one scale at a given time and must weigh the advantages and costs of modifying that scale either upward or downward. If a smaller-scale firm considers producing at output q_2, it will not invariably alter its scale. The advantages of doing so are the lower cost of this output per time period, which in Figure 8.7 may be represented geometrically by the area of the shaded rectangle—that is, $q_2 \cdot (c_3 - c_4)$. As this amount is saved in each future period in which output q_2 is produced, the attractiveness of changing scale is clearly greater the longer the contemplated output at this level.

The costs of changing scale are not shown in Figure 8.7. These costs arise from the disruption of existing operations, the development of new work assignments, and the dismantling and disposal of parts of the original plant and equipment. Once the decision has been made to modify scale, these costs are sunk. They are no longer relevant to decisions concerning output or even future decisions concerning scale. Firms will weigh these costs in considering current changes in scale, however, and will make such changes only if the advantages in cost savings offset the costs of changing scale.

It is not inconsistent with economic theory to observe firms of varying scale operating in a single industry, even where such scale differences seem to result in cost differences for some. Even if the smaller firm in Figure 8.8 expected to produce q_2 indefinitely, it is possible that the costs of increasing its scale would exceed the benefits of such a change. As we shall see in Chapter 15, the value of a benefit stream extending into the future indefinitely is not infinite. The advantages of making a change in scale in contemplation of a permanent change in output may therefore be more than offset by the current costs of making that change. It is quite possible, therefore, for firms to produce rates of output employing scales that do not minimize their apparent average cost for that output—even in the longest possible run.

The Envelope Curve

In Figure 8.7 a firm was depicted choosing between two possible scales of operations. More generally, scale may be treated as a continuous variable that increases as expenditure for overhead factors increases. Once the level of these overhead factors is determined, scale is fixed. In panel (a) of Figure 8.8, for example, we have three representative average cost curves, each of which reaches a minimum

Chapter 8 The Choice of Output: Price Taker Case

Figure 8.8 *Envelope Curves*

The envelope curve (*E*) identifies the minimum average cost of producing each output. In general it is identified by a series of tangencies with ATC curves, and this tangency in turn identifies the optimal scale for each output. If the envelope curve is horizontal, as in panel (a), these tangencies will occur at the minimum point on each ATC curve. If the envelope curve is U shaped, as in panel (b), these tangencies will occur on the downward- and upward-sloping portions of the ATC curves.

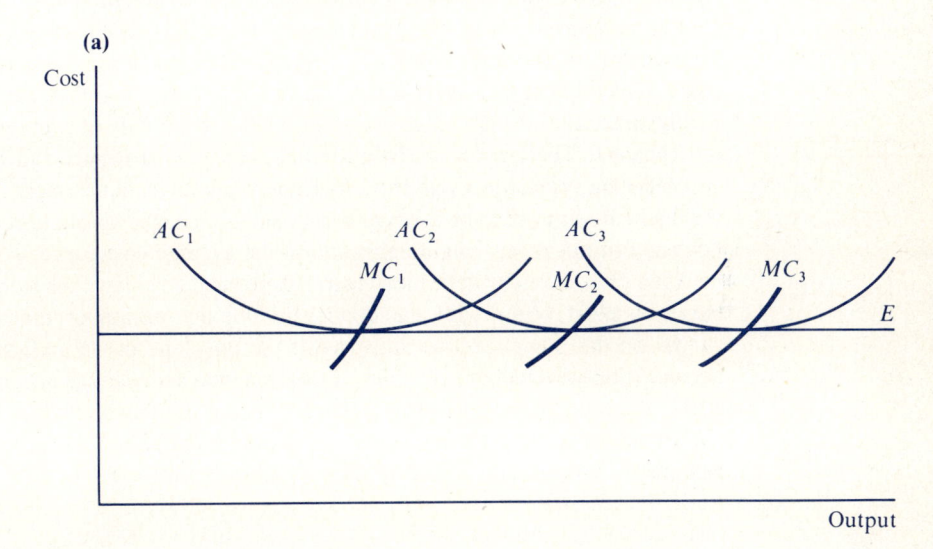

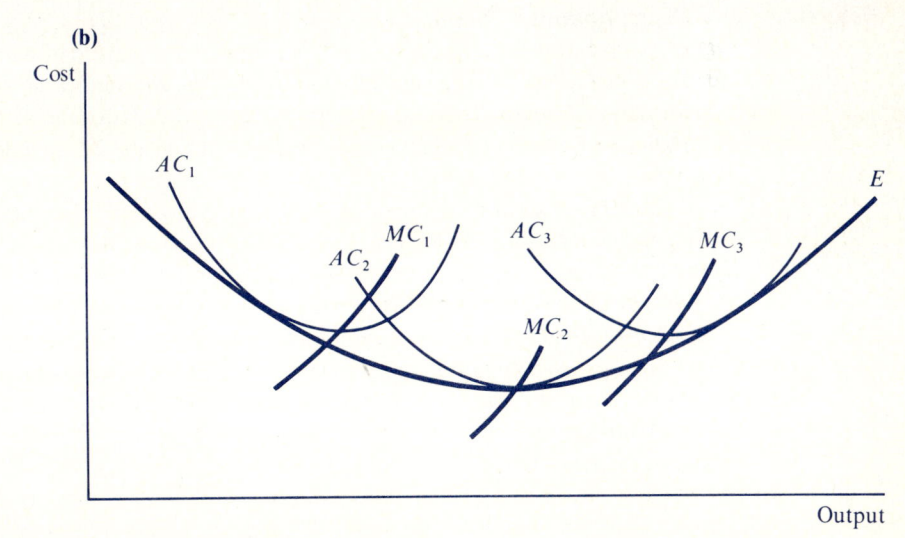

level at the same cost, c. We can imagine an infinite number of such curves filling the space between the three shown, each reaching a minimum at an average cost of c. A curve relating output to the lowest average cost of producing that output at any scale is defined here as the **envelope curve**. The envelope curve (E) in panel (a) is a horizontal line tangent to each average cost curve at its minimum point. There is no optimal scale under such conditions that lowers the average cost of production below that of any other scale.

There are good reasons to believe that at least some production processes do exhibit an optimum scale. The envelope curve for this case resembles that shown in panel (b). As the scale of the firm expands, the minimum points on the average cost curves fall progressively lower, reach a minimum, and then begin to rise. It will be noted that the envelope curve formed by this family of average cost curves is U shaped. The tangencies between the average cost curves and the envelope curve do not typically occur at the minimum points of the former. Only for that scale which minimizes the average cost at any output (the optimum scale) does the tangency occur at this minimum point on the average cost curve. As a tangency between two curves by definition exists where the curves have the same slope, this tangency must occur with the downward-sloping portion of the average cost curves on the downward-sloping part of the envelope curve and, similarly, between the upward-sloping portions of the envelope and average cost curves. Only at the point where the envelope curve reaches a minimum and has a slope of zero will it be tangent to an average cost curve where the slope of that curve is also zero.

Economies and Diseconomies of Scale

The downward- and upward-sloping portions of the envelope curve signal the presence of what are referred to, respectively, as **economies of scale** and **diseconomies of scale**. There are several reasons why costs rise with output over certain portions of the envelope curve and fall over others. These will be discussed in turn.

Diseconomies of scale (sometimes described as *rising costs*) are present over the entire range of scale. They do not suddenly become effective at the minimum point on the envelope curve, causing it to turn upward. This curve reaches a minimum when the advantages of larger scale are just offset by the increased costs of larger operations. At the minimum point on the envelope curve, in other words, the effect of factors tending to increase costs with scale becomes equal to the effect of factors reducing costs with scale. At lower outputs the effect of factors reducing costs is greater, and the envelope curve slopes downward. At higher outputs the reverse is true.

Costs rise with the scale of operations for a number of reasons. Here we may recall some of our discussion from Chapter 7. Larger size implies that those decision-making executives are more remote from the situations they control than executives of smaller firms. More costs are incurred in transmitting information and directions back and forth as scale increases. Large size provides more opportunities for that information to be edited and biased by those who gain from misinformation within organizations. Large scale implies large mistakes, and the costs of such mistakes will thus increase with scale. Finally, large scale requires a layering of management. As any one person's ability to monitor the performance of others is limited, additional people must be hired to monitor monitors. As scale increases, administrative cost increases more than proportionately because of this layering of supervisory personnel.

Costs do not increase continuously with scale, because there are important sources of cost advantage in scale as well. We may consider only a few of these here.[1] Perhaps the first to be noted by an economist (Adam Smith) is the division of labor. Large-scale production permits each worker to specialize in the performance of a small number of tasks in which he or she may develop greater skill. Specialized workers avoid the loss of time moving from one task to another, and the time of highly skilled workers is not consumed performing menial activities.

In addition to economies of large-scale production due to the division of labor, there are economies due to cost advantages of large machines. Robinson cites the case of ships as an example of this type of economy of scale.[2] While the capacity of a ship increases with the cube of its dimensions, the friction retarding its movement increases with the drag of the ship's hull as it moves through the water. As the size of the ship increases, however, this surface increases in area only by the square of the dimensions. A large ship therefore requires less power per ton of cargo than does a smaller one. As it takes a less than proportionately larger crew to man a large ship than a small one, economies of scale in labor are also possible with large machines.

Other sources of possible economies of scale are those associated with product standardization and those arising from reduced levels of required inventories. A cutter in a modern garment factory can cut out 50 dresses as rapidly as he or she can cut out one, so long as the dresses are of the same pattern. The advantages of this ability are lost if only a few dresses are made per day.

On the other hand, certain advantages of scale operate through the logic of statistics. Firms routinely hold inventories, because there are economies of scale in shipments and orders by customers that cannot be predicted accurately. A firm might wish to have a sufficient inventory to meet all orders received at least 95 percent of the time. Assume that a firm sells 100 units per week on average, and that an inventory of 120 permits it to fill all its orders this percentage of the time. Ten such firms would thus have to maintain collective inventories of 1200 to meet this sales target. If these ten firms merged, however, an inventory of only 1063 would satisfy the same sales objective of filling all orders 95 percent of the time.[3] Investment in inventories is costly, and consolidation of inventories, by exploiting this "law of large numbers," makes possible these economies of scale.

---

[1] For a splendid discussion of the theory of firm scale see E. A. G. Robinson, *The Structure of Competitive Industry* (Chicago: The University of Chicago Press, 1931).

[2] Ibid., p. 23.

[3] This may be calculated as follows. Assume that orders to each firm are randomly distributed over time. The inventory I_i that each must hold to meet all orders 95 percent of the time is given by the following:

$$I_i = \mu + 1.645\sigma_i,$$

The envelope curve is often referred to as the *long-run average cost curve*. It has this name because of the assumption that all firms in the industry will eventually adopt that scale of operations which minimizes the cost of producing their chosen output. The scale selected in the long run is thus seen to be that which is tangent to the envelope curve at the chosen output. As we have discussed, this assumption is valid only where the cost of changing scale is negligible. Bearing this reservation in mind, it will nevertheless be useful to think of the envelope curve as an average cost frontier toward which firms adjust their scale increasingly over time. In this sense, the envelope curve may indeed be usefully thought of as the long-run average cost curve.

8.3 Supply for Price Takers

We have developed the analytical devices required to trace the supply response of firms to changing demand conditions. We will do this by putting the two components of profit together. This is done in Figure 8.9. In panel (b) of this figure we have superimposed the total cost curve of the firm on top of its total revenue curve. Profit, shown in panel (a), is the difference in total revenue and total cost at any output. At any output the profit in panel (a) corresponds geometrically to the vertical distance between the two curves in panel (b). At outputs below q_1 and above q_2, profit is negative. At the output at which this distance is greatest (in a positive direction), the maximum profit is earned. This will occur at the output at which the total cost curve stops moving away from the total revenue curve and begins to move toward it again—that is, where the two curves are parallel. This may easily be shown algebraically. Let profit $\pi(q)$ be a function of total revenue, $r(q)$, and total cost, $c(q)$:

$$\pi(q) = r(q) - c(q).$$

Profits are maximized at the output at which the rate of change in profit per unit change in output, $\Delta\pi/\Delta q$, becomes zero. In panel (a) of Figure 8.9 this corre-

---

where μ_i is the mean number of orders for the ith firm and σ_i is the standard deviation around this mean. In our example, we assume that μ_i is 100 for each firm and σ_i is 12.16. Each must therefore hold an inventory of 120, and the ten firms together must hold 1200 units.

Now assume that the firms combine and may fill orders from a single inventory. The combined firm wishes to hold inventories that *on average* are equal to or greater than orders 95 percent of the time. This average inventory, $\bar{I}$, is given by the expression

$$\bar{I} = \mu + 1.645\sigma/\sqrt{n}$$

where n is the number of firms involved in the combination. For the same mean and standard deviation, this average inventory that must be held per firm is only 106.3, which for ten firms implies a total inventory of 1063.

Figure 8.9   *Output and Profit Reconsidered*

In panel (a) we reproduce the profit function from Figure 8.1. In panel (b) total revenue and total cost are both related to output, so that the vertical difference between the two curves corresponds to profit in panel (a). Profit is maximized at output q^*, at which the two curves in panel (b) have identical slopes.

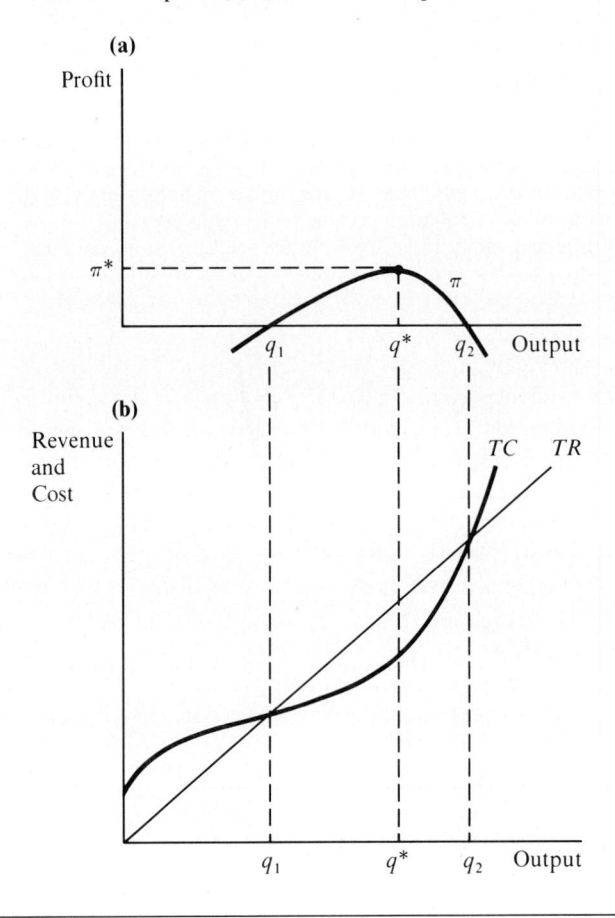

sponds to the condition that the slope of the profit function be horizontal. Algebraically, this requires the following:

$$\frac{\Delta \pi}{\Delta q} = 0 = \frac{\Delta r}{\Delta q} - \frac{\Delta c}{\Delta q}.$$

This may be written:

$$\frac{\Delta r}{\Delta q} = \frac{\Delta c}{\Delta q}$$

The slope of the total revenue curve equals the slope of the total cost curve at the output at which profits are maximized.

The slopes of these two curves have identities of their own, as we have discussed. The slope of the total revenue curve is called *marginal revenue*, and the slope of the total cost curve is *marginal cost*. Figure 8.10 shows this relationship

Figure 8.10   *Total and Average Revenue and Cost*

The vertical difference between TR and TC in panel (a) is profit. In panel (b) marginal revenue is constant and equal to price. Marginal cost is the slope of TC in panel (a). Profit is maximized when the slopes in panel (a) are identical, implying the intersection of MC and P in panel (b). Total profit is equal to the profit per unit $(P - AC_1)$ times output (q^*)—the height and width, respectively, of the shaded area in panel (b).

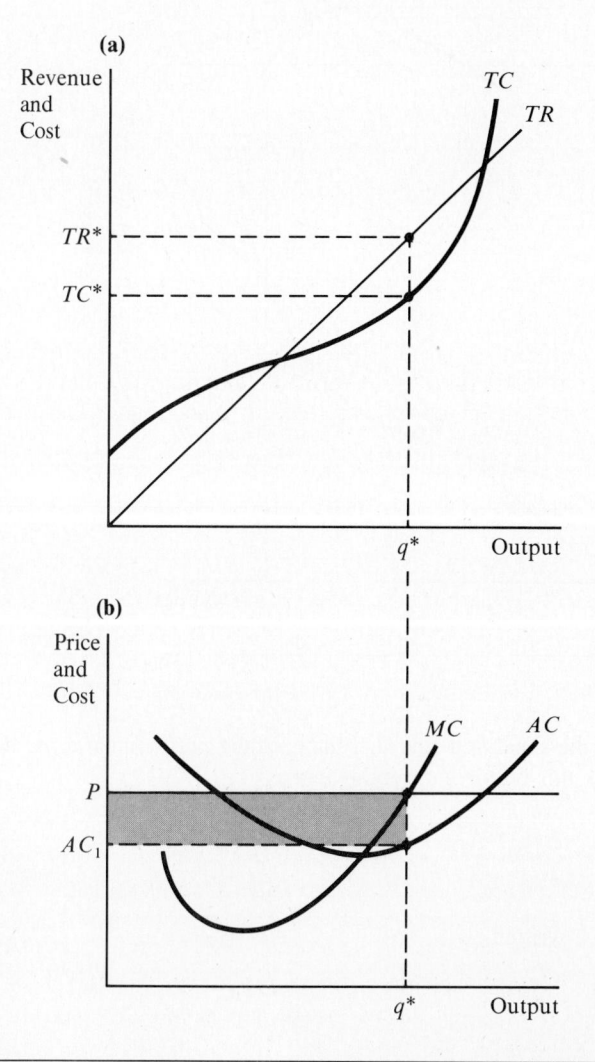

in terms of the alternative representations of the revenue and cost functions. For the price taker marginal revenue is simply price, regardless of output. In panel (b), marginal revenue is therefore a horizontal line at the vertical value P. As discussed earlier, this horizontal line may also be thought of as the demand curve of the firm.

Marginal cost has the U shape noted in our example and rises until it intersects marginal revenue at output q^*. This point of intersection corresponds to the condition of parallelism in panel (a). Profits, reflected by a vertical distance in panel (a), are represented geometrically in panel (b) by the area of the shaded rectangle. This may easily be shown with some additional algebraic manipulation. Recall that price is also average revenue; that is:

$$\frac{Pq}{q} = P.$$

Average revenue minus average cost is therefore profit *per unit*:

$$\frac{Pq}{q} - \frac{c(q)}{q} = \frac{Pq - c(q)}{q} = \frac{\pi}{q}.$$

The vertical distance between P and average cost for output q^* is therefore profit per unit and corresponds to this ratio. By merely multiplying this difference by q^*, we therefore obtain the value of profits for this output. As the length of this rectangle is q^* and its height is P minus average cost, the area of the rectangle equals profit.

Note that profits need not be greatest at the output at which average cost of production is lowest. In panel (b) of Figure 8.10, for example, we know that the minimum point on the average cost curve is at the intersection of average and marginal cost. The profit-maximizing output for the price shown is greater than the output of that intersection.

Supply Response for a Firm of a Given Scale

For the price-taking firm, the market price is not influenced by its output. Price is given as far as its own internal decisions are concerned. Our question is thus to trace its output response to changes in this market price. We will do this in two stages, considering first the choice of output given scale, then considering the effect of market price changes on firm decisions concerning scale.

The supply curve for a single firm relates the market price to the quantity that the firm chooses to make available at that price. In the foregoing discussion we identified a condition that prevails at the profit-maximizing output for any price: that marginal cost of the chosen output equal marginal revenue, which for price takers equals market price. In Figure 8.10 we were therefore able to identify one point on the firm's supply curve. At the price shown, the firm supplied quantity q^*.

Consider Figure 8.11. In panel (b) we depict the output choice at three successively lower prices. In panel (a) we have plotted the profit levels associated with output for each of the three prices. Assume that the initial price is P_1. Positive

Figure 8.11 *Output Choice with Changing Price*

Panel (a) recalls the profit curves shown in Figure 8.2. A falling output price shifts the profit curve in panel (a) downward and influences its peak in a predictable direction. As profit is maximized at the output at which *MC* equals price and *MC* itself is upward sloping, this intersection with price must occur at lower outputs with lower prices. At price P_3, for example, maximum profit is a zero profit earned by producing output q_3^*.

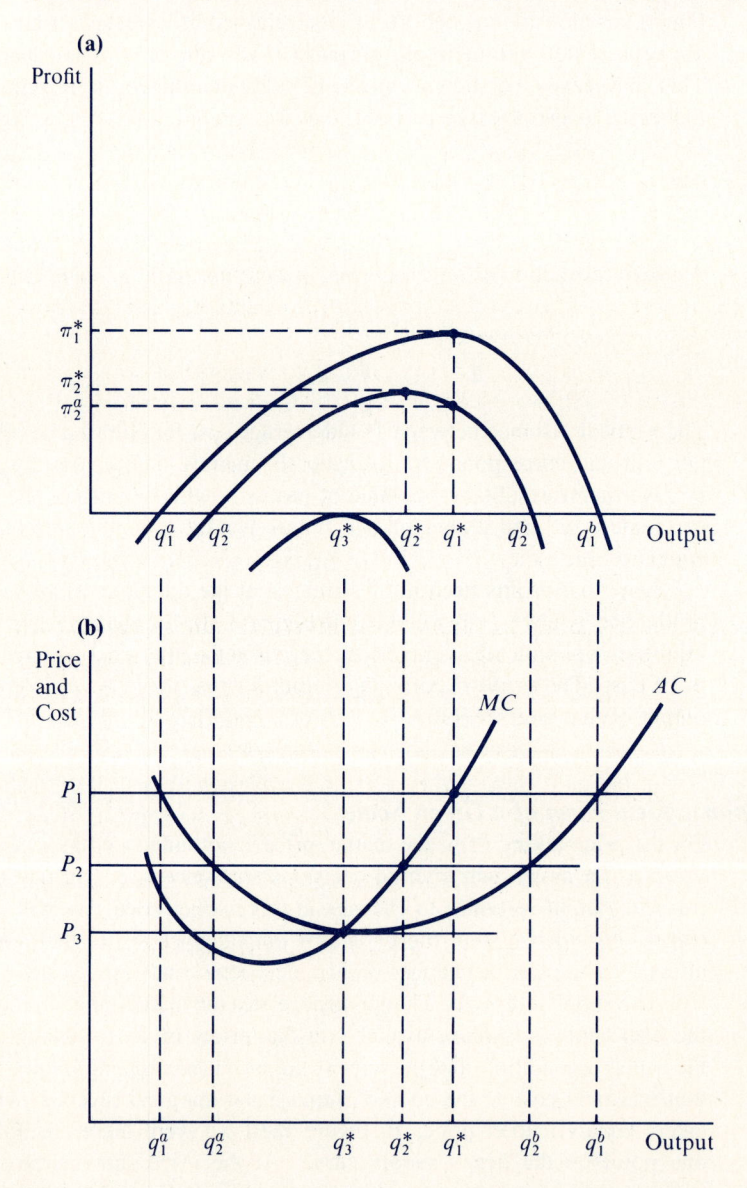

profits are possible at this price for any output between q_1^a and q_1^b. Marginal cost is equal to this price at output q_1^*, and thus the profit curve in panel (a) reaches its maximum at this output.

A fall in price has two effects in our figure: (1) It shifts the profit curve in panel (a) downward for every output, and (2) it leads the firm to modify its output. Assume that because of a shift in market demand, price falls from P_1 to P_2. A firm that continues to produce q_1 units of output under these circumstances will experience a fall in profit from π_1^* to π_2^q. The firm will also observe that it is not earning the maximum possible profit at this price. The cost of the marginal units produced at output q_1^* are in the neighborhood of P_1. We know this from the height of the marginal cost curve at this output, which is not influenced by the changed demand conditions. These changed conditions do imply, however, that the firm now receives only P_2 for each unit produced. The contribution to profit from production and sale of these last units is therefore negative. Total profit can be increased by reducing output to the point at which marginal cost equals price once again. That point is output q_2^*. This reduction in output increases profit in panel (a) from π_2^q earned at output q_1^* to π_2^*, which is the maximum profit that may be earned at this price at any output.

Finally, note the profit opportunities when the price falls to P_3. Continued operation at output q_2^* produces negative profits—indeed, production at any output other than q_3^* yields negative profits. In this case, maximum profits are obtained again at the output at which marginal cost equals price. Here that equality happens to occur at the minimum point on the average cost curve. The maximum profit that may be obtained at this price is zero. Clearly, no firm will produce any output at a price lower than P_3. Production of any output would yield negative profits, reducing the net worth of the firm.[4]

As stated earlier, the supply curve of the firm identifies quantities of output that the firm will make available for sale at different market prices. We have seen that profit considerations lead firms to supply q_1^* at price P_1, q_2^* at price P_2, and q_3^* at price P_3. We may thus construct a line connecting all quantities that the firm will supply at intermediate prices, and by manipulation with a ruler we may confirm an important fact for the theory of supply: *The supply curve of the price taker firm of a given scale is merely the marginal cost curve above its intersection with the average cost curve.*

This observation has important implications for normative economics, to be discussed in Chapter 18. Moreover, it has important positive implications for the theory of supply. Marginal cost curves are upward sloping in this range above the average total cost curve. This tells us that individual firms will supply larger quantities at higher prices. This fact, together with observations on the scale response of firms to price changes, will allow us to develop *laws of supply* for the firm and the industry.

---

[4] Recall here our earlier discussion of the fallacy of variable and fixed costs. It is sometimes incorrectly stated that firms will produce "in the short run" at prices that cover variable costs but that fail to cover fixed costs. Our definition of overhead costs includes only those costs that represent some opportunity cost of production. If costs are truly sunk costs, in the sense that they are borne whether the firm produces anything or not, they do not enter into our computation of total and therefore average cost.

Figure 8.12 *Price and the Choice of Scale*

At price P_1 the optimal rate of output is q_1 and the optimal scale is that associated with AC_1. The rate of output is optimal because using this scale, marginal cost is equal to marginal revenue at this output. The scale is optimal because at this rate of output the average cost of production is as low as it can be. Both scale and output rate must satisfy profit-maximizing conditions. If, for example, price were to rise from P_1 to P_2, the output condition would suggest an output of q_1' with scale AC_1. At this output, however, average cost is not minimized with AC_1. A change to scale AC_2 is required by this price increase, yielding $MC = MR$ at output q_2.

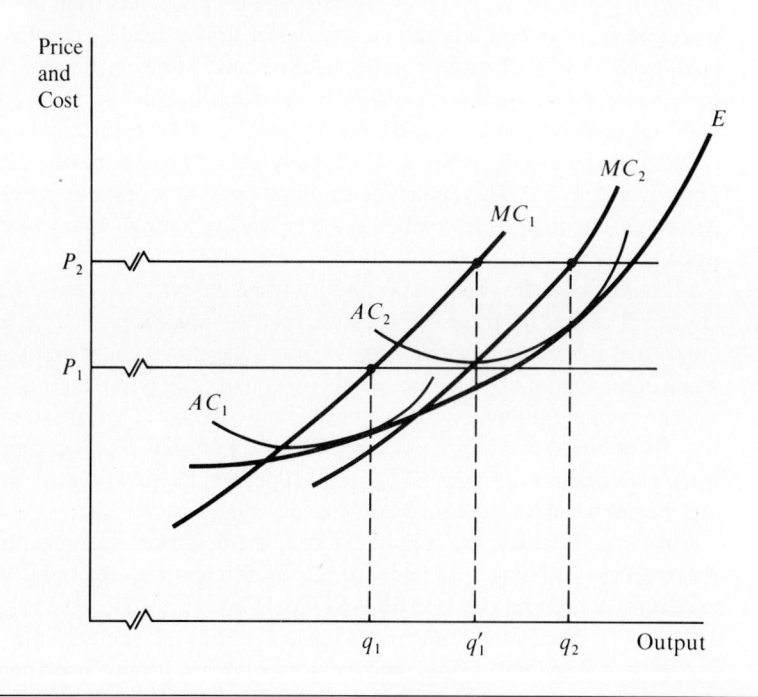

Price and Scale

The effect of price on scale is illustrated with the aid of Figure 8.12. The horizontal scale is truncated so that we see only the upward-sloping portion of the envelope curve, E. Assume that a market price of P_1 prevails initially and that a typical firm has chosen the scale associated with average cost curve AC_1. Marginal cost is equal to price P_1 at output q_1, at which the average cost curve is just tangent to the envelope curve. Now assume that due to a shift in demand, market price rises to P_2. If changing scale instantly is prohibitively costly, the firm will respond to this price change by increasing output to q_1'. The marginal cost curve of the firm's original scale intersects the firm's new demand curve at this output. This is the response discussed in connection with Figure 8.11.

It was asserted earlier in our discussion of the choice of scale that the cost of changing scale increases with the speed of the adjustment. Thus, firms that have found it prohibitively costly to adjust scale instantly will find it feasible to modify scale after the passage of some time. If, as in Figure 8.12, price P_2 is expected to prevail indefinitely, firms who find it economical to do so will adopt a larger scale. This decision involves a simultaneous choice of both the new output to be produced and the optimal scale for the production of that output. Two conditions determine these choices: (1) Marginal cost must equal price, and (2) average cost must be tangent to the envelope curve at the chosen output. In Figure 8.12, output q_2 satisfies both of these conditions.

The scale response to a price change must occur in the same direction as the output response. Both will be in the same direction as the price change itself. A rise in price leads firms to increase output for a given scale and to increase scale itself. In Figure 8.12, the output response to the increase in price from P_1 to P_2 is the output change from q_1 to q'_1. The passage of time will permit firms to expand scale, hence expand output further from q'_1 to q_2. A reduction in price would cause both output and scale reductions.

Supply Price Elasticity and Time

Responsiveness of supply to price changes is measured by an elasticity. Recall that elasticity always measures responsiveness in terms of the ratio of the percentage response to the percentage stimulus. In the very short run, in which it is uneconomical to change scale, a firm's response to the price increase shown in Figure 8.13 is the output increase $q'_1 - q_1$; the price change is $P_2 - P_1$. The **supply elasticity** (ε) of this response is therefore given from the following computation:

$$\text{Supply Elasticity } \varepsilon = \frac{\%\Delta q}{\%\Delta P} = \frac{\dfrac{q'_1 - q_1}{q_1}}{\dfrac{P_2 - P_1}{P_1}}.$$

After the passage of time, as the firm has had the opportunity to make changes in scale, its response is no longer limited to that adjustment along a single marginal cost curve. Price will again equal marginal cost at the new output, but that marginal cost curve is associated with an operation of larger scale. As time passes, therefore, the response will approach $q_2 - q_1$, and the elasticity of supply over this time interval will be larger:

$$\varepsilon = \frac{\dfrac{q_2 - q_1}{q_1}}{\dfrac{P_2 - P_1}{P_1}}.$$

We may therefore draw two conclusions from our discussion of the single firm: **the first law of supply** and the **second law of supply**.

First Law of Supply: Quantity supplied by a firm varies directly with price.

Second Law of Supply: Responsiveness of quantity supplied to change in price will increase with the passage of time.

These two laws may be paraphrased in terms of elasticity to read that the elasticity of supply (1) is positive, and (2) increases with the time over which the response is measured.

8.4 Industry Supply

An industry is a collection of all firms that produce a particular product. Industry supply is therefore the collective response of all individual producers to market prices for that product. There may be many firms in an industry or few. There are, for example, only about 20 makers of chewing gum in the United States, four of the largest of which produce 90 percent of that product sold. At the other extreme, there are roughly 2500 makers of ready-to-wear dresses, the largest 50 of which account for less than one fourth of all dresses sold in this country. Regardless of the number (so long as the firms are price takers), their supply behavior may be aggregated quite simply. Industry supply is the sum of quantities that all firms are willing to supply at each price. The process that we will illustrate in Figure 8.13 with two firms may therefore be generalized to the case of the many-firm industry.

Figure 8.13 presents supply for a two-firm industry. Firm A is willing to supply q_1^A units of this product at a price of P_1 and will increase its supply to q_2^A when the price rises to P_2. Firm B will supply q_1^B and q_2^B, respectively, at market prices P_1 and P_2. Industry supply is the sum of the quantities supplied by all firms at each price. The industry supply curve in panel (c) is therefore constructed so that at

Figure 8.13 *Industry Supply*

The industry supply is simply the sum of the quantities that each firm will supply at each price. At a price of P_1 firm A supplies q_1^A and firm B supplies q_1^B, which sum to equal the industry supply q_1^I in panel (c). At the higher price, each supplier produces more.

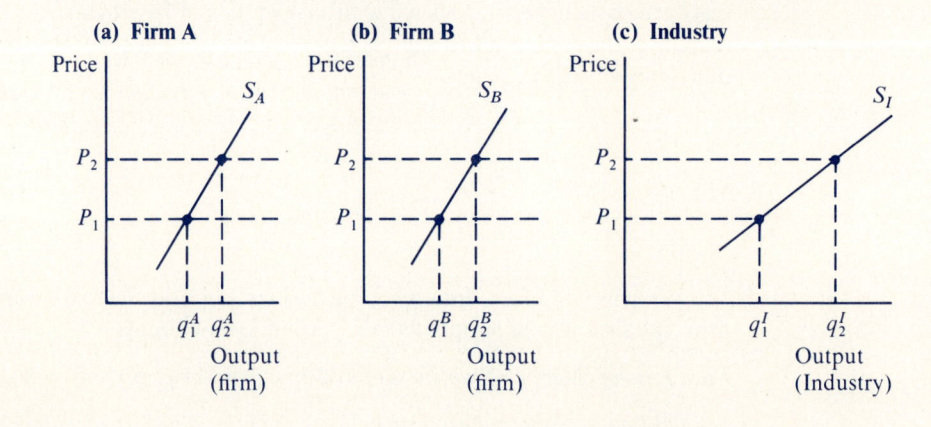

Figure 8.14 *Tracing Industry Response to an Increase in Demand*

Each firm earns zero profits at a price of P_1. This price occurs with demand curve D_1 and supply curve S_1 associated with n firms in the industry. If demand shifts to D_2, existing firms will adjust the rate of output and scale to produce output q_2 so that industry output is nq_2. Profits are earned by each firm under these circumstances. This will attract entry by new firms, shifting the supply curve to position S_2 (associated with $n + \Delta n$ firms). This returns each firm to the zero profit condition, with each producing output q_1 again with scale AC_1.

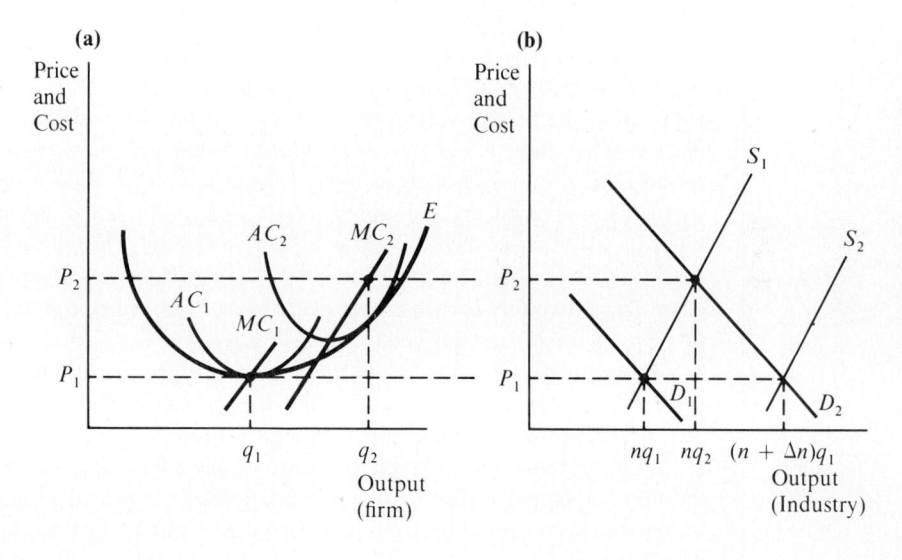

price P_1 the total industry supply is shown to be $q_1^I = q_1^A + q_1^B$ and at a higher price, P_2, industry supply increases to $q_2^I = q_2^A + q_2^B$.

So far in our discussion, industry supply has expanded for the simple reason that individual firm choices lead to increased output at higher prices. These responses followed in turn from the output and scale decisions of firms. However, this individual firm expansion and contraction does not tell the full story of industry supply. A complete theory of industry supply must also account for the entry of new firms into the supply of given products as well as for the exit from the industry of existing firms.

In panel (a) of Figure 8.14, we show the envelope curve of a representative firm in the industry to be examined. In panel (b), we depict conditions in the total market for this industry. Assume that initial demand is given by D_1 and the supply *for the existing firms* is given by S_1. The market-clearing price is that at which the quantity demanded equals the quantity supplied, that is, P_1. At this price each firm supplies q_1 units. For an industry of n firms, industry supply will be nq_1, as shown in panel (b). Average cost is just equal to price in this situation, so each firm earns zero profits.

Now let demand shift upward in panel (b) to D_2. Even after all firms have had the opportunity to modify scale, quantity supplied by each firm will expand only to q_2, where market supply clears the market at the higher price P_2. If each firm is subject to the diseconomies of scale depicted in the U-shaped envelope curve, output expansion by existing firms will cease at this point. Each is producing an output at which (1) marginal cost equals price, and (2) average cost for this output is at a minimum. Both output and scale are optimal for this price; the conditions describe an equilibrium for an industry with a given number of firms. This is true in spite of the fact that price exceeds average cost for these firms, and they are therefore earning profits.

However, this situation does not describe an equilibrium for an industry that is open to the **entry** of new suppliers. If new firms enter the industry, total quantity supplied in the market will increase even if existing firms choose not to expand output. What influences the willingness of firms to enter is the opportunity to earn profits. The profits earned by existing firms at price P_2 will therefore attract new suppliers. As this occurs, the supply curve reflecting the sum of the quantities supplied by all firms in the industry will shift rightward. This entry will not cease until profits are eliminated—for both new suppliers and existing firms. That will occur (assuming this entry has not affected costs) only when supply shifts to position S_2 and price is established once again at P_1.

Interestingly, output by each firm at the post-entry equilibrium is q_1 again. As price falls in response to entry, all firms modify scale downward and reduce output. If price returns to its original level each firm will, in long-run equilibrium, always produce the same output. Short-run supply adjustment may operate chiefly through output and scale changes by existing firms. In the long run, however, industry expansion resulting from demand growth will occur through the entry of new firms.

The student is left to run through this analysis in reverse to examine decreases in industry demand. He or she should conclude that reductions in supply occasioned by such a demand shift will also be due solely to the exit of firms earning negative profits. When exit of sufficient firms has shifted supply to a position where price P_1 clears the market, long-run equilibrium will be reestablished.

Regulation of Entry: The Case of the CAB

The foregoing analysis is useful in interpreting results of a common form of regulation: the control of price and entry. A federal regulatory agency is charged to approve changes in price as well as applications by firms to enter particular markets. The Interstate Commerce Commission, for example, establishes rates for both railroads and motor carriers and approves entry into rail or motor freight service for particular routes. The Federal Communications Commission and state agencies control rates, entry, and service conditions. The Civil Aeronautics Board until recently set fares and entry conditions for airlines seeking to offer commercial airline service between cities. In 1978, however, Congress passed the Airline Deregulation Act (PL 95–504), which for the first time in 40 years permitted airlines to reduce rates and offer new service between cities without prior CAB approval.

Summary

The output choice of firms is governed by profit considerations. Profits in turn are determined by revenues and costs. The relationship between revenue and output is determined by market structure. Marginal revenue for a price taker firm is price and is insensitive to output.

Costs may or may not vary as output varies. Those that do are operating costs; those that do not are overhead costs. Costs that cannot be avoided are not really costs but are referred to as "sunk costs." Operating costs are important to output decisions of the firm; overhead costs are relevant to scale decisions. Total cost is the sum of overhead and operating costs. Optimal scale minimizes the sum of overhead and operating costs for the chosen level of output. Marginal cost measures the rate of change in total (and operating) cost per unit change in output.

For firms of a given scale, average operating costs decline over some range, reflecting (1) a saving of labor time moving from process to process, and (2) gains through specialization of labor. For firms of a given scale average operating cost will eventually reach a minimum and begin to rise due to crowding of facilities.

Changing scale is costly and will be done only if the advantages of change exceed the costs. This is more likely (1) the longer the firm may take making the change, and (2) the longer the new scale will be employed. The curve relating output to the lowest average cost of producing each output at any scale is the envelope curve. The U shape of the envelope curve reflects economies and diseconomies of scale. Economies of scale (also called "declining or decreasing costs") result from such factors as cost savings due to labor specialization and the advantages of large machines.

Profits are maximized with respect to the rate of output decision at the output at which marginal revenue equals marginal cost. The supply curve for a firm with constant scale is its marginal cost curve. Responsiveness to an increase in price will have positive output and scale effects. The elasticity of supply for a single firm is positive and will increase with time. Entry of firms will occur if profits are positive; exit will occur if profits are negative.

Short-run adjustment to industry demand shifts will typically occur chiefly through changes in output and scale; long-run response will occur chiefly through entry of new firms. Barriers to entry can successfully secure profits to firms operating in the region of diseconomies of scale even if they compete (that is, price in a noncollusive manner). Regulation of entry can be an effective barrier, limiting industry supply expansion in the long run and protecting profits of existing firms.

Key Concepts

Marginal revenue
price taker
price searcher
competitive model
market power
sunk costs
operating costs
overhead costs
marginal cost
average total cost

average overhead cost
average operating cost
envelope curve
economies of scale
diseconomies of scale
supply elasticity
first law of supply
second law of supply
entry
exit

It is instructive to note that this form of regulation typically control price and entry. It is difficult to make a convincing case for controls on entr ticularly, if price is itself regulated. The report issued to accompany the Aeronautics Act of 1938 provides some language typical of these rationaliz The CAB was established to prevent air fares from rising too high or falli low. Concerning the latter, the CAB would prevent "competing carriers fro gaging in rate wars which would be disastrous to all concerned." This rec mind the discussion of cobweb cycles in prices and output introduced in C 2. There we learned that incorrect expectations about future prices can lea pliers to increase and decrease output, overshooting the equilibrium output i case by increasing amounts and producing in the process increasingly viol cillations in price. A necessary condition for this result, however, is formula incorrect price expectations by suppliers.

In an industry where rates are determined on the basis of a strict form airline fares have been since the inception of the CAB, there is little scope sort of dynamic instability depicted in the cobweb discussion. On the co rate changes have been permitted only after extensive investigation by th and then allowed to take effect only after a lengthy announcement period. or entry controls would appear redundant and unnecessary to maintain stab such a market.

Consider another possibility, however. Recall from the discussion in this ter that it is possible for an industry to reach a competitive equilibrium in each firm continues to earn profits. That possibility was discussed in conr with Figure 8.14. It requires existing firms to be in the region of increasin and, more importantly, that the number of firms be controlled. Under these tions, the representative firm will be influenced neither to modify its output marginal cost equals price) nor to change its scale of operations (since a cost of producing this output cannot be lowered through a scale change).

It is difficult to imagine a better method of protecting established profit tunities. Assume that existing market conditions along a particular airline approximate those depicted in Figure 8.14. Several airlines may service thi so that the elasticity of demand for any one of them is very high. Howev outputs of each are such that none can add to the profits earned by changing or scale. At price P_2 each airline supplies the quantity q_2, and none are infli to lower their price or expand output. No airline gains from submission to the for lower fares. As long as the CAB refuses to approve entry of new airl service this route, the situation will remain stable and profits of the existin servicing the route will be maintained.

The passage of the Airline Deregulation Act of 1978 provides for a fiv transition period during which the industry will move to completely dow flexible prices and freedom of entry. Competition among carriers over rout already expanded greatly and prices have declined, as predicted. The succ this deregulation has encouraged Congress to examine carefully the role ICC and other price- and entry-regulating agencies. Evidence developed CAB case suggests that this regulation is unnecessary to prevent "disastrou wars" and can be used by the firms in the regulated industry to protect profi maintain prices above their long-run equilibrium level.

Questions

1. *Easy* The marginal revenue curve for a price taker firm is horizontal at the prevailing market price. Explain.

Hard This line is also the demand curve faced by the firm. Recalling the definition of a demand curve from Chapter 2, explain how this curve is a demand curve.

2. *Easy* If a firm with many rivals producing a homogeneous product attempts to increase its price above that charged by other firms, what will happen to quantity demanded? Will such a firm gain by lowering its price below that charged by other firms?

Hard Demand faced by such a competitive firm is said to be perfectly (infinitely) elastic. This will never be literally true, but the firm's elasticity of demand rises rapidly as the number of firms increases. Explain.

3. *Easy* Categorize the following expense items as (1) overhead costs, (2) operating costs, or (3) sunk costs:
   a. Electric power for machinery
   b. The company president's salary
   c. Overtime wages
   d. Clay for a brick factory
   e. Rental payments on a five-year lease
   f. Property taxes
   g. Contributions to political campaigns
   h. Interest payments on already issued bonds
   g. Flood damage repairs

Hard In an introductory economics course many students are taught that in the very short run all costs are fixed and in the long run all costs are variable. What is wrong with this statement, and what is right?

4. *Easy* Explain the geometry of the marginal cost curve rising to intersect the average operating cost curve from below at its minimum point.

Hard What are the economic factors giving rise to the downward- and upward-sloping portions of the average operating cost curve? A more flexible plant design might have less steeply falling and rising sides on its ATC curve but a higher minimum. What types of changes in design might accomplish this? What considerations would be important in the decision to adopt a more flexible plant design?

5. *Easy* A test grade that is above the average of one's previous grades in a course is said to bring up the average. A test grade that is below one's existing average is said to bring down the average. Relate this idea to the relationship between marginal and average cost.

Hard Explain why the minimum point on the average total cost curve occurs at a higher output than the minimum point on the average operating cost curve.

6. *Easy* Explain whether the following is true or false: A firm should always produce the output at which average total costs are at a minimum. This is the lowest-cost output and therefore the most profitable for the firm.

Hard Explain whether the following is true or false: A price taker firm will never produce an output at which the average operating cost curve is downward sloping.

7. *Easy* What are the sources of economies and diseconomies of scale? Which of the following potentially qualify as one or the other?
    a. Assembly line production
    b. Losses due to incorrect forecasts of demand by the firm's staff economist
    c. Students doing poorly because they are unable to see the blackboard clearly from the rear of a crowded classroom
    d. Long-distance telephone costs due to the need to communicate with the home office
    e. Overtime pay
    f. One large pipeline being less costly to lay than several smaller ones carrying the same capacity

Hard Explain why a firm producing output on the upward-sloping portion of the envelope curve may always reduce average total cost without changing scale by producing less than the profit-maximizing output. Why are profits reduced by producing the quantity that minimizes costs with this scale?

8. *Easy* Government regulation that restricts entry of new firms into an industry or market can be a source of profits to existing firms even if there are several firms supplying these industries or markets. Explain how.

Hard Can you think of any economically sound reasons for such restrictions?

Chapter 9

The Choice of Output: Price Searchers

Connections This chapter concerns the output choice of firms that face downward-sloping demand curves. The characteristic that distinguishes this choice from the same choice made by price taker firms is that marginal revenue for price searchers is less than price at every output. Marginal revenue is related to elasticity of demand. (The reader may wish to review the discussion of price elasticity of demand in Chapter 5.) Firms that have some market power have additional decisions to make with important consequences. As the demand for their outputs is not perfectly price elastic, they have discretion over how to price that output. They may charge individual demanders different prices for different units, and they may charge different prices to different demanders. These pricing tactics are explored for their implications concerning quantity of output, price, and distribution of output. The process of aggregating demand across households for the purposes of analyzing distribution of the quantity supplied is employed for this last topic. (The reader may wish to refer to this discussion in Chapter 5 as well.)

The competitive model, for all its elegance and simplicity, at best describes only one of several market settings in which a firm may operate. In the previous chapter two forms of market structure were identified: the *price taker* case, where marginal revenue equals price, and the *price searcher* case, where marginal revenue is less than price. There we discussed the price taker case in detail. In this chapter, we turn our attention to the output decisions of price searchers.

Before confronting these issues directly, let us ask ourselves a more fundamental question: Why do we adopt such an awkward-sounding name for this market structure? As we scrutinize the sources of downward slope in demand curves in Chapter 10, it will become apparent that there are many different causes for this condition. The most obvious, but certainly not the most prevalent, is the case of monopoly. Demand curves may also slope downward for firms that operate in an industry with many vigorously competing rivals. The terms used to designate these conditions leave much to be desired. What is one to make of the terms *monopolistic competition*, *open monopoly*, or *imperfect competition*? Monopoly means, quite simply, one seller. A market with several competing sellers cannot therefore be monopolistic. Nor is it very useful to describe such conditions as imperfect competition. The rivalry for sales in such a market may be just as intense as that observed in price taker markets.

The single feature that all these markets have in common is that the price of goods sold is expressly chosen by the seller. In selecting an output, the seller must weigh the effect of his or her output choice on price and in this sense searches for the correct price. Regardless of the reasons for this condition, the selection of output and price by such sellers follows the same logical development. We will therefore develop the theory of this choice under the general heading of output choice for price searchers, then move to a discussion of the various market conditions producing this result.

9.1 Output and Price for Price Searchers

It will be useful initially to assume that the cost of producing particular levels of output is independent of demand-side conditions. Certainly, under some conditions price-searching firms will seek profits just as ardently as price-taking firms. Profits for a given output are greatest if costs are minimized, regardless of the price that the output commands in the market. In these cases input combinations, and therefore costs, will *not* be affected by market structure. Market structure will affect output alone, leaving costs to follow the same rules developed in Chapter 8. Special cases where this is not true will be considered in Chapter 13.

Revenue for Price Searchers

Demand conditions for price searcher firms differ markedly from those of price taker firms. The market price of the firm's output itself depends on output, and marginal revenue will thus differ from price. Total revenue is given by the following expression:

$TR = r(q) = p(q) \cdot q.$

It follows that the marginal revenue for any output is:

$$MR = \frac{\Delta r}{\Delta q} = P(q) + q \cdot \frac{\Delta P}{\Delta q}.$$

An increase in output thus can be seen to have two offsetting effects whose values are given by the two terms on the right-hand side of this expression. Consider the first term on the right-hand side. This is simply the price obtainable for that extra output; revenue is increased by the sale price of a marginal change in output. The second term is the product of output, which is positive, and the term $\Delta p/\Delta q$, which is the slope of the demand curve and therefore negative. This tells us that total revenue is reduced by the depressing effect of the sale of additional output on the price of the output previously sold. Marginal revenue is thus the sum of these positive and negative effects.

We can make several observations about demand for the output of these firms from this expression. First, marginal revenue must be less than price for any output. Marginal revenue is the sum of price and some negative amount given by the second term. Second, marginal revenue may actually be negative. This will be true if the absolute value of the second term exceeds that of the first. Finally, marginal revenue must decline for linear demand curves. We note this by observing that *both* terms on the right side decline in value as output increases. Price must decline because demand curves have a negative slope. The second term becomes more negative as increasing output is multiplied by a constant negative slope.

As we will have many occasions to call upon demand and marginal revenue curves, it will be useful to develop an explicit relationship between these two curves. This is most easily done for linear demand curves. Consider the curve implied by the following expression:

$P = a - bq.$

This demand curve has a vertical intercept of a and a slope of $-b$. Total revenue is given by multiplying price by output, that is:

$TR = r(q) = Pq = aq - bq^2.$

Marginal revenue is simply:

$MR = \dfrac{\Delta r}{\Delta q} = a - 2bq.$[1]

---

[1] The derivation of slopes of this type was not discussed in Chapter 1. However, we may derive it here using the same technique used for deriving slopes there. The "changed" value of the total revenue function is given by:

$r(q + \Delta q) = P \cdot (q + \Delta q) = a \cdot (q + \Delta q) - b \cdot (q + \Delta q)^2$
$= aq + a\Delta q - bq^2 - 2bq\Delta q - b\Delta q^2.$

Observation of this expression for marginal revenue reveals that this curve has the same vertical intercept, a, as the demand curve and that the slope is twice as steep ($-2b$ instead of $-b$).

An even more useful way to position the marginal revenue curve relative to the demand curve is to solve for the quantities along each curve at which marginal revenue is equal to price. Let q_{MR} represent quantity along the marginal revenue curve and q_D be quantity along the demand curve so that the expressions for these curves are, respectively:

Marginal Revenue Curve $MR = a - 2bq_{MR}$.

Demand Curve $P = a - bq_D$.

Setting price equal to marginal revenue yields:

$$a - bq_D = a - 2bq_{MR}.$$

This reduces to:

$$q_D = 2 \cdot q_{MR}.$$

This result may be interpreted with the aid of Figure 9.1. This figure tells us that the quantities associated with equal heights along these two curves will be related as shown. The demand quantity will be twice the value of the marginal revenue quantity—or, since we start with the demand curve and seek to place the marginal revenue curve appropriate to that demand, we may state that the marginal revenue curve lies exactly halfway between the demand curve and the vertical axis at any price.

Marginal Revenue and Elasticity

The demand curves of price taker firms are horizontal; they are perfectly elastic at the market price. Demand curves for price searchers are negatively sloped, reflecting their **market power**—that is, their control over price. A measure of their market power is the elasticity of that demand. It will be useful to derive an explicit relationship between marginal revenue and elasticity of demand for a price searcher firm.

Recall that marginal revenue may be expressed in the following form:

Subtracting our original total revenue from this expression yields the change in total revenue, Δr:

$\Delta r = a\Delta q - 2bq\Delta q - b\Delta q^2$.

Dividing through by Δq leaves:

$\dfrac{\Delta r}{\Delta q} = a - 2bq - b\Delta q$.

As Δq approaches zero, the term $-b\Delta q$ itself approaches zero. Evaluating this slope over an interval of close to zero gives:

$\dfrac{\Delta r}{\Delta q} = a - 2bq$.

Figure 9.1   The Marginal Revenue Curve

The marginal revenue curve identifies the marginal revenue associated with each output. For a linear demand curve, marginal revenue can be shown to lie exactly halfway between the demand curve and the vertical axis. For example, quantity q_{MR} is exactly one half of quantity q_D.

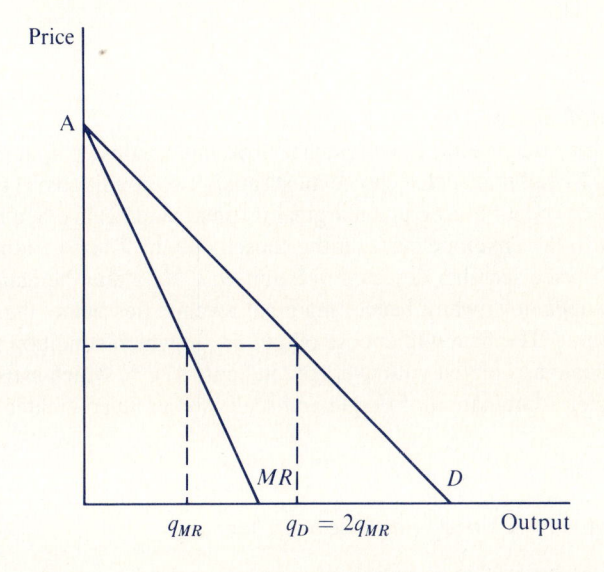

$$MR = \frac{\Delta r}{\Delta q} = P(q) + q \cdot \frac{\Delta P}{\Delta q}.$$

If we multiply the entire expression by price and divide each term by price at the same time, we will not change the value of the right side; that will still equal marginal revenue. Marginal revenue is therefore equal to the right side of this expression where such simultaneous multiplication and division have been performed:

$$MR = P(q)\left[\frac{P(q)}{P(q)} + \frac{q}{P(q)} \cdot \frac{\Delta P}{\Delta q}\right].$$

Examine the terms inside the brackets. The first term reduces, of course, to unity. Recalling that price elasticity of demand is given by

$$\eta = \frac{\Delta q}{\Delta P} \cdot \frac{P}{q},$$

we recognize the second term in the brackets as the inverse of demand elasticity. We may thus rewrite this expression for marginal revenue as

$$MR = P(q)\left[1 + \frac{1}{\eta}\right] = P(q) + \frac{P(q)}{\eta}.$$

Using this expression we may determine the sign of marginal revenue for all ranges of elasticity. For η equal to exactly -1, marginal revenue must be exactly zero. The terms inside the brackets sum to zero in that case. For demand elasticities greater than 1 in absolute value, marginal revenue will be positive. When demand elasticity is less than 1 in absolute value, marginal revenue must be negative.

The Choice of Output and Scale

As is true for price takers, price searcher firms must choose output simultaneously with scale. Recall that such a choice must satisfy two conditions: (1) Marginal cost of the chosen output must equal marginal revenue, and (2) average total cost must be tangent to the envelope curve at the chosen output. These conditions are satisfied for the price searcher depicted in Figure 9.2. Note that the demand curve for this firm slopes downward; hence, marginal revenue lies below the demand price at each output. The firm will choose output q^*, at which condition (1) is satisfied using the scale associated with average total cost ATC^*, which satisfies condition (2). No other combination of output and scale will produce greater profits for the

Figure 9.2   *Output and Scale Choice by a Price Searcher*

The price searcher maximizes profit by choosing the output for which marginal revenue is equal to marginal cost and selecting the scale that produces that output at the lowest average cost. This is the same pair of criteria as that developed for the price taker firm. For the price searcher, however, price is greater than marginal revenue at every output.

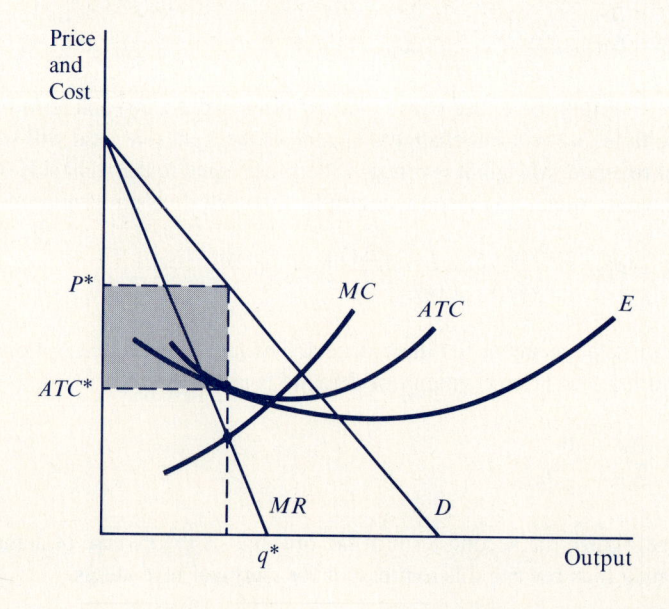

firm. These profits correspond geometrically to the area of the rectangle whose vertical dimension is $P^* - ATC^*$ and whose width is q^*.

Recall that for the price searcher, output is determined by the intersection of marginal cost with marginal revenue, but that output must be priced at P^* to clear the market. This creates a significant allocative anomaly. Price searchers will produce less than would price takers with identical cost functions facing the same market demand. This occurs because the net revenue obtained from the sale of a marginal unit is less than price. Output at the margin gains producers less than it is worth to demanders. Buyers would willingly pay producers more than they gained from the sale of extra output to make more units available. Producers decline to do so, however, because increased output lowers the price of the inframarginal units that would have sold regardless.

Price takers do not consider the effect of their output on price. They assume by definition that any amount of output may be sold at the market price—in other words, that marginal revenue *is* price. Price takers will therefore produce the output at which marginal cost equals the market-clearing price. In Figure 9.2 that output must exceed q^*, because MC intersects demand curve D to the right of output q^*. This "underproduction" argument may be stated more elegantly in terms of welfare economics and will be considered again for that purpose in Chapter 18. It is sufficient for our purposes now to note that this allocative issue is one of the important bases for government antimonopoly policy.

Another basis for government antimonopoly policy concerns the distributional results of such an output choice for price searchers. Profits earned by price takers are typically obtained only temporarily. As we saw in Chapter 8, profits are normally earned only during disequilibrium as new firms are attracted into the industry.

For certain types of price searcher markets, we cannot depend upon "normal" profit-seeking behavior to stimulate entry until a similar equilibrium has been achieved. Where this is true profits fail to serve the useful function of attracting resources, *and* they continue to be earned indefinitely. In Chapter 10 we will consider the sources of market power and their implications for the possibility of entry. At this point, suffice it to say that profits of price searchers are not self-eliminating in all cases. In those cases where they are not, a portion of the profits represents a continuing transfer of income from demanders to suppliers.

This process is illustrated in Figure 9.3. Conditions presented here are essentially the same as those in Figure 9.2. In this figure we have deleted the envelope curve, since our chief concern in this discussion is the relationship between price and profit. The price searcher chooses output q^*. Profit again corresponds to the area of the rectangle whose height is $P^* - ATC^*$ and whose width is q^*. As just noted, were this firm a price taker it would produce the output at which marginal cost equals price, that is, q_1.

The market-clearing price of that output, P_1, conveniently divides the profit rectangle into two segments. That part which lies below this price would have been received by suppliers in any event. That portion of the profit rectangle which lies above P_1, however, would not have been received by price taker suppliers. This amount, $q^* \cdot (P^* - P_1)$, represents a direct transfer of income from demanders to these price-searching firms.

Figure 9.3 *Consequences of Price Searcher Output Choice*

There are two consequences of the price searcher's output choice. First, output is less than would be supplied at a price equal to marginal cost. The price searcher will select output q^*, while a price taker would supply output q_1. Second, supply of this output results in an income transfer from buyer to seller. The market-clearing price of the smaller quantity is P^* rather than P_1. For each of the q^* units actually supplied, the firm receives more money ($P^* - P_1$) from demanders.

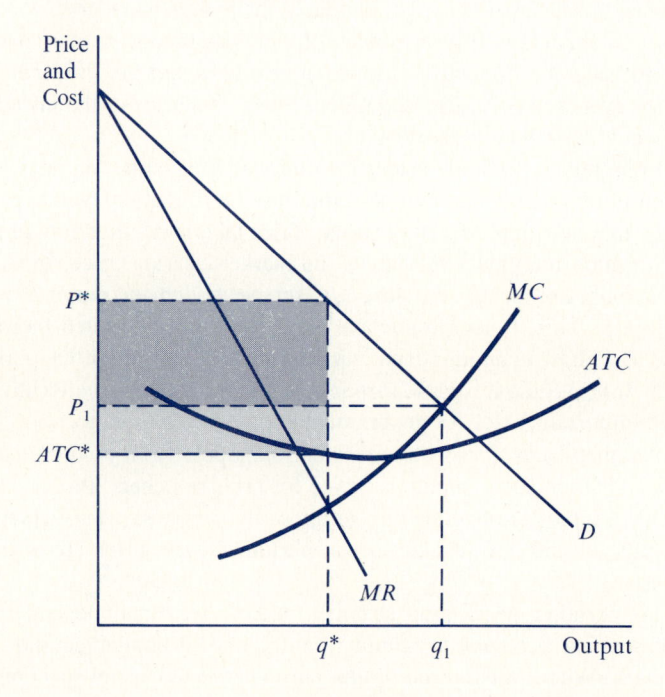

Price Searcher Output with Price Ceilings

Let us assume for purposes of analysis that the government has chosen to pursue an active policy with respect to firms enjoying substantial market power. It seeks to influence these firms to produce an output at which price equals marginal cost. How can it best achieve this goal? A regulating agency might determine the optimal output through analysis of the firm's demand and cost functions and simply instruct the firm to produce at this level. Output and sales are costly to monitor, however, making this approach to regulation vulnerable to circumvention. Production statistics can be exaggerated, and goods produced under supervision do not all have to be sold.

An alternative method of regulation that may achieve the same goal and be less costly to implement is price regulation. By placing a price ceiling on the output of a price searcher firm, regulators can influence the firm to increase output. A properly chosen price ceiling can therefore influence a firm to expand output to precisely that level at which marginal cost equals price. This result is somewhat paradoxical, since price ceilings have exactly the opposite effect for price takers. In that case, recall from Chapter 2 that a price ceiling below the market price influences firms to *reduce* output and causes excess demand in the market. The reason for the expansion of output in the price searcher case is the impact of this regulation on marginal revenue to the firm.

Consider Figure 9.4. If unregulated, the firm will produce the profit-maximizing output q^*, which sells for P^*, at which marginal revenue is just equal to marginal cost. A maximum price of P_r changes the profit-maximizing output in the following way. The firm must now sell any output it produces at a price that may not legally exceed this regulated price regardless of the fact that demanders are willing to pay more. The increase in revenue per unit increase in output is therefore simply the regulated price (at least for as long as it may obtain this price for its output). For quantities in excess of q_r, the market-clearing price is lower than P_r and the regulation is ineffective. Marginal revenue is therefore shifted by this regulation in the following way. It becomes a horizontal line at the regulated

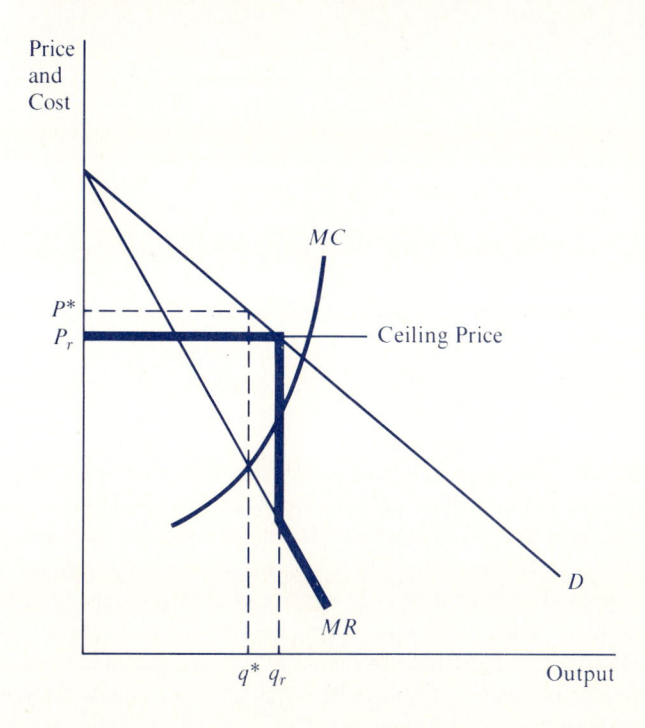

Figure 9.4 *Output Choice with Price Ceiling*

Without a price ceiling the firm will choose the output at which the declining MR curve intersects the MC curve. With a price ceiling set at P_r, marginal revenue no longer is less than price for the first q_r units supplied. Each unit sold adds P_r to total revenue. Price P_r is therefore equal to marginal revenue for these units. More than q_r units cannot be sold for a price of P_r, so for output beyond this amount the price ceiling becomes nonbinding. Marginal revenue drops to its unregulated level for outputs in excess of q_r.

Figure 9.5 *Output Choice with Different Price Ceilings*

The profit-maximizing output with price ceilings varies with the ceiling chosen. At a ceiling price of P_2, output q_2 is chosen. At the lower ceiling P_1, the larger output q_1 is selected. At prices below the intersection of the marginal cost curve with the demand curve, the chosen output is less than the amount chosen at this intersection. Thus, q_3 chosen at P_3 is less than q_1 chosen at the intersection price P_1.

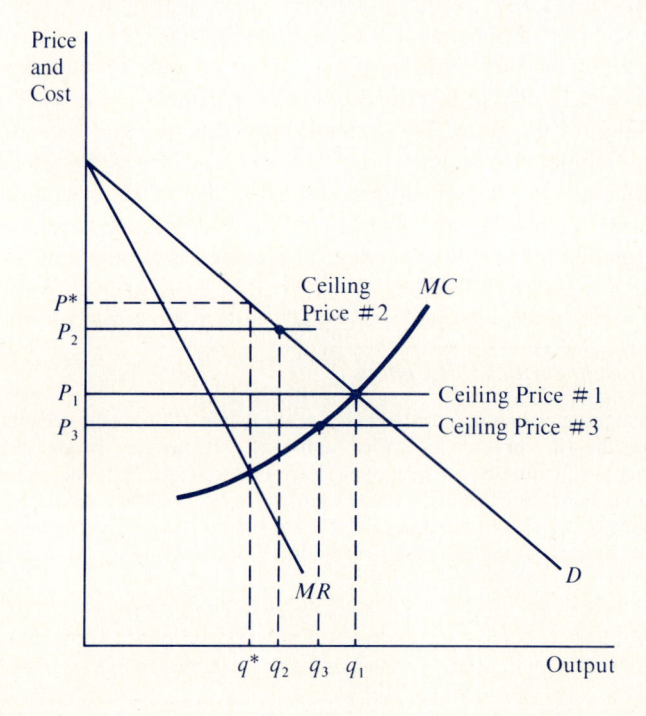

price out to the demand curve, then drops to its original position for outputs in excess of q_r.

Recall that marginal revenue is given by the following expression:

$$MR = \frac{\Delta r}{\Delta q} = P(q) + q \cdot \frac{\Delta P}{\Delta q}.$$

Where price is controlled, $\Delta P/\Delta q$ (the change in price per unit change in output) is zero up to output q_r. Marginal revenue for this range of output is therefore simply P_r, the regulated price. Beyond this output, however, increased output may be sold only by lowering price. The term $\Delta p/\Delta q$ becomes negative in this range; hence, marginal revenue drops below price as in the unregulated case.

Conditions at the profit-maximizing output depend on the price chosen by the regulators. This is elaborated in Figure 9.5. If regulators choose price P_1, firms produce exactly the quantity at which market price equals marginal cost. At a price greater than P_1, the firm will produce less than q_1 but more than the unregulated output. For example, a regulated price of P_2 yields an output of q_2. To produce less than this output does not maximize profits, because marginal revenue for these outputs (P_2) is greater than marginal cost. Producing more than q_2 also reduces profits, because marginal revenue for these outputs (as indicated along the original, unregulated MR curve) is lower than marginal cost.

At a regulated price of less than P_1, the firm will choose to produce more than it would if unregulated but less than is demanded at that price. At price P_3, for example, marginal revenue P_3 is equal to marginal cost at output q_3, which is less than the quantity demanded at this price. Excess demand will occur under these circumstances, with the unhappy results detailed in Chapter 2.

This analysis suggests that appropriately chosen price ceilings can influence price-searching firms to expand output. These price ceilings shift marginal revenue to the affected firms in ways that dramatically modify the relationship of output to profit. However, it is easy to overestimate the importance of this finding. Effective use of this policy requires detailed information concerning the demand conditions and cost structure of each firm, which may be beyond the capability of regulating agencies to assemble, much less to interpret. Moreover, agencies with price-setting power frequently seem more sensitive to political advantage than to considerations of the economic properties of the markets in which their power is exercised.

Some Qualifications

Before leaving our discussion of the arguments favoring an active antimonopoly policy by government, we must consider some of its disadvantages. In the first place, the potential benefits of such a policy are often small and therefore likely to be offset by the costs of administering and complying with its provisions. Note in Figure 9.3 that the difference between the competitive price, P_1, and the price actually charged by the price searcher, P^*, must be less than the difference between price and marginal revenue at the chosen output. That difference will be equal to:

$$P^* - P^*\left(1 + \frac{1}{\eta}\right).$$

Hence, the percentage difference is given by:

$$\frac{P^* - P^*\left(1 + \frac{1}{\eta}\right)}{P^*} = -\frac{1}{\eta}.$$

For demands that are quite responsive to price, though not perfectly elastic, this difference between the competitive price and that charged by price searcher firms will therefore not be large. The benefits of such a price change must be weighed against the administrative costs of identifying such excessive prices where they occur and securing the desired changes. Not to be ignored as an offsetting cost of such a policy is also the cost of deterring firms from proceeding with ventures that, though innocent, give the appearance of being anticompetitive.

In the second place, the exercise of market power itself can be defended in principle as beneficial. We implicitly recognize this in the granting of patents, which are government-protected rights to monopoly in the sale of the patented item. The higher profits earned by these price searchers are extended as a reward to innovative activity in the area of product development. In the absence of such protection we may be sure that fewer resources would be devoted to research and development. The granting of monopoly power is not the only way that resources may be channeled into these activities. Increasingly in recent years, the government has involved itself in the financing and organization of research. On the other hand, the highly visible lags in technology observed between market economies and centralized economies, such as China and the Soviet Union, do not inspire confidence in the efficacy of relying exclusively on this latter method.

Some economists would argue that a certain amount of market power on the part of firms holds advantages that extend far beyond the stimulation of research and product development. Joseph Schumpeter is the economist whose name is most closely associated with this view. He argued that without the protection of such a buffer against the shocks of business cycles and what he colorfully referred to as the "perennial gale of creative destruction" associated with competitive markets, entrepreneurial activity cannot perform up to its potential.[2] Entrepreneurial activity is by definition risky, and without the protection afforded by the advantageous position that some firms hold, they may be deterred from introducing new products and technology, seen by Schumpeter to be the most important aspect of the competitive system. He argues that in essence an economy produces more and grows faster *because* its firms are not subjected to the potentially violent upheavals occasioned by "perfect competition." Schumpeter sees in this "no more of a paradox . . . than there is in saying that motorcars are traveling faster than they otherwise would *because* they are provided with brakes."

These views contain not only theory but assertions about the relevant empirical magnitudes of the various effects involved. They also contain implicit judgments about appropriate levels of innovative activity. To be sure, innovation in a competitive market involves substantial risk. A measure of market power can conceivably act as a buffer to protect firms from the consequences of innovations that go awry. On the other hand, the stability of the market environment advanced by Schumpeter may foster excessive conservatism and complacency rather than increased willingness to take risk. Many successful innovators have had to establish new enterprises because existing firms in those markets were uninterested in the new products they had developed.

Tolerance of market power in an industry is not the only way that risk can be alleviated. Suppliers of capital may reduce their risk through the purchase of equity in other firms and industries. This diversification of holdings permits individual firms to engage in extensive risk taking without exposing stockholders to great losses. From these points of view, the advantages of permissive attitudes to

---

[2] Joseph A. Schumpeter, *Capitalism, Socialism and Democracy*, 3d ed. (New York: Harper and Row, 1950), 87–92.

the exercise of market power are less obvious. Both suggest that such a policy may do little to stimulate innovation.

In the nearly four decades since the original publication of Schumpeter's book there has been surprisingly little empirical analysis of these issues. Until such studies are undertaken, we must remain agnostic concerning the care and feeding of entrepreneurs. All that the theory in this chapter tells us for certain is that the "brakes" referred to by Schumpeter do, without doubt, "slow the motorcar."

Price Searcher Supply

The relationships derived earlier between marginal revenue and demand elasticity allow us to narrow the range of output that a price searcher firm will select along its demand curve. Recall that these relationships may be stated as follows:

1. $MR = P(q)\left[1 + \frac{1}{\eta}\right] > 0$ where $|\eta| > 1$.

2. $MR = P(q)\left[1 + \frac{1}{\eta}\right] < 0$ where $|\eta| < 1$.

A price searcher will therefore never select an output for which demand elasticity has an absolute value less than 1, that is, falling into case (1) above. Marginal revenue in this case is negative, implying that total revenue is decreased as output expands. The profit-maximizing output invariably is that which equates marginal revenue with marginal cost. As long as marginal cost is positive (and it is difficult to imagine circumstances where that is not the case), marginal revenue must also be positive at such an optimum. Demand elasticity must therefore be greater than 1 in absolute value at the chosen output.

Although we have little difficulty in depicting the optimum output for a price searcher, deriving useful results from comparative statics presents some problems that are not encountered in markets supplied by price takers. The response of price takers to shifts in market demand may be neatly catalogued into output, scale, and entry effects. In the short run, supply response merely traces out the marginal cost curves of these firms. In the longer run, supply curves contain this response as well as output adjustments due to modifications in scale. In the longest run, the effect of firms entering or exiting will also be felt. These effects combine to produce a positive response to changes in demand that increase over time. This useful supply curve relationship between price and output does not hold absolutely for price searchers. Increases in demand can result in higher *or* lower prices and in increased *or* diminished output.

This difficulty can be illustrated with the aid of Figure 9.6. Assume that the original quantity supplied by the price searcher depicted is q^* and that this sells for a price of P^*. The demand and marginal revenue curves associated with this initial equilibrium have been left out so that readers will be more easily able to discern two alternative subsequent demand curves, D_1 and D_2, and their respective marginal revenue curves, MR_1 and MR_2. Note that both of these curves represent increases in demand; that is, the demand curves D_1 and D_2 both pass to the northeast of point q^*, P^*. These two demand curves have been drawn so that they result in the same market price at the chosen $MR-MC$ output. In the first case,

Figure 9.6 *Output Choice with Shifting Demand*

An unrestricted demand shift can produce any combination of price and output changes. The original output chosen is q^*, which sells for a market-clearing price along the original demand curve (not shown) of P^*. Both D_1 and D_2 may be considered increases in demand, since each curve passes to the "northeast" of this original price–quantity combination. If demand shifts to D_2, output supplied increases to q_2 and price rises to P_1. If, however, demand shifts to D_1, quantity q_1 will be supplied, which sells for the same price. In the first case output increases, but in the second case it decreases over the same price interval.

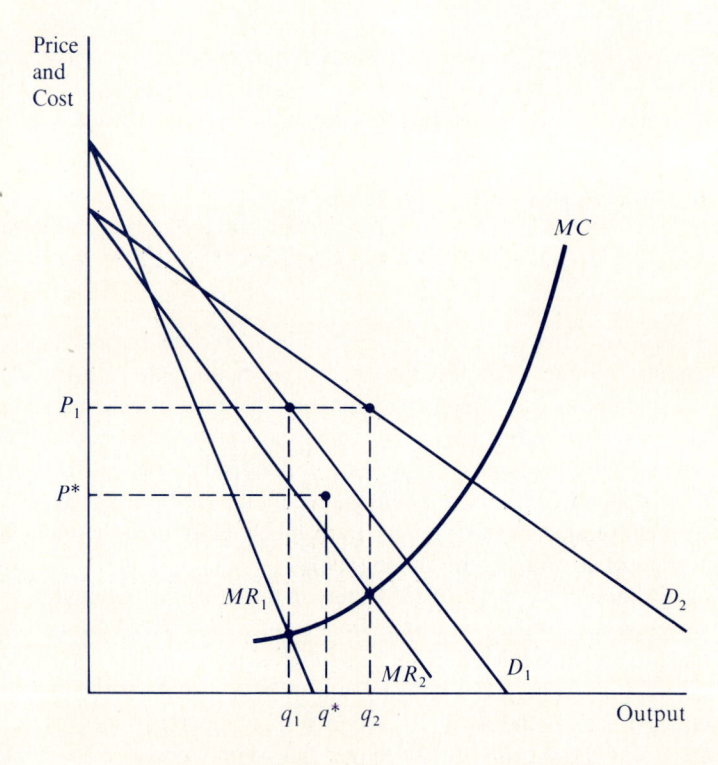

however, the firm chooses to produce *less* at the higher price P_1, while in the latter case the firm produces *more* output as price rises to P_1.

The point of this demonstration is simply to indicate that the supply response of price searchers (unlike that of price takers) is influenced by the *character* of the demand shifts. Certain shifts producing a particular change in price may lead to an *increase* in output, while other shifts producing the same price change may lead to a *decrease* in output. As long as demand is free to change in any fashion, we cannot predict the output response of these firms. It would be misleading to leave the popular impression that output response of price searchers' changing demand conditions is completely unpredictable. Changes in demand-side conditions have predictable effects on the demand curves themselves, and we can typically predict the effect of such changes on price searcher output.

9.2 Price Discrimination

Thus far we have assumed that the price searcher firm must sell all of its output at a single price. However, under certain circumstances it is not only possible to sell some of this output at different prices, but it pays to do so. This practice is called **price discrimination**. It may be done in two distinct ways: (1) There may be price discrimination among buyers or groups of buyers, or (2) there may be discrimination in the sale of output to a single buyer. In the first case different prices are charged to different customers, and in the second different prices are charged to the same buyer for different units of the same good. Let us refer to these two types as (1) **interperson price discrimination**, and (2) **interunit price discrimination**.

We encounter examples of both practices daily. Examples of interperson discrimination include different utility rates between households and industrial users, different airfares between advance booking and same-day travelers, and different long-distance telephone rates between daytime and nighttime callers. Varying prices are often linked to quantity purchased, as in subscription versus newsstand prices for newspapers and magazines or beer by the pitcher versus beer by the glass. Different prices can even be charged to riders sharing the same taxicab.

Interunit price discrimination is somewhat less common. The essential feature of this type of price discrimination is that the price paid by the buyer for *marginal increments* is less than the average price paid for *all units* of a good. The first unit might cost $0.10 and the next two $0.07 each. In this case the marginal price is $0.07, but the average price would be ($0.10 + $0.07 + $0.07)/3 = $0.08. One must make the distinction between this sort of pricing and the simple quantity discounts just mentioned. Quantity discounts do not qualify, because such a buyer's average price and marginal price are the same.[3] Examples of this type of price discrimination are tennis club fees, which typically involve payment of monthly or annual dues plus fees for court time, car rental contracts, which combine a daily rental fee with an additional charge per mile, and charges for repairmen, who add charges for parts and labor provided to a flat-rate service call charge for appearing in the first place. A special case of this type of price discrimination is the "all-you-can-eat for $5.95" restaurant, where the marginal price for the last ounce consumed is zero but the average price is, of course, higher.

A price-searching seller may increase the total revenue received for any quantity supplied through interunit price discrimination. The quantity purchased (if any is purchased) is determined by the price at the *margin*. It is not necessary to charge the same price for each unit, however. By charging more for all but this last unit, the total revenue per units may be increased. Consider the way that banks price for supplying checking services to depositors in Figure 9.7. Let D be the demand curve of a household for checking. At a price of $0.50 per check the household would write only 14 checks per month, but at a price of $0.24 per check they might write 40. At the higher price the bank obtains $7.00 from the account, while at the lower price it obtains $9.60. The bank may obtain more than either of these amounts if it price discriminates on the basis of units.

---

[3] Quantity discounts are really examples of the first type of price discrimination. They represent a method of lowering price to a particular class of customer.

Figure 9.7 *Demand and Total Revenue*

At a price of $0.50 per check, this household will write 14 checks for a total revenue of $7.00. At the lower price of $0.24 per check the household will write 40 checks for a total revenue of $9.60. However, if the bank can charge a different price for each check written, it can collect more total revenue than either of these amounts.

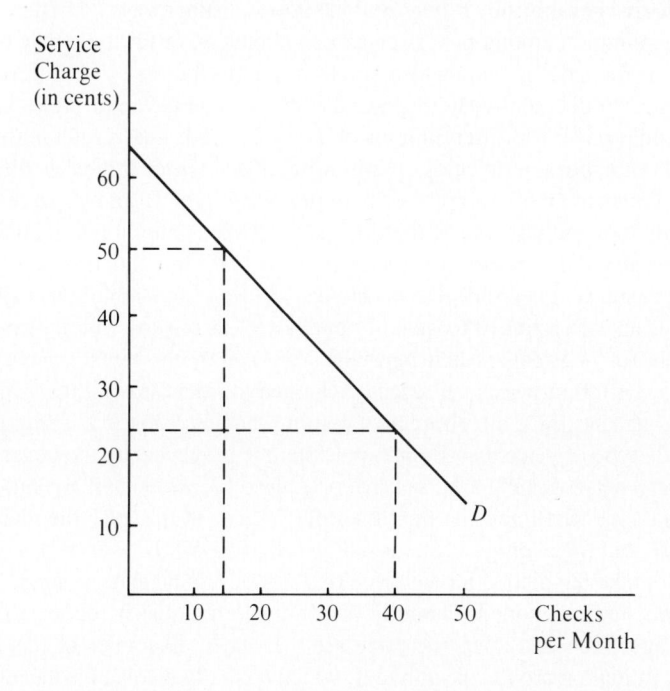

The demand price of a good or service measures its value *at the margin*—that is, the demand price reveals the household's marginal rate of substitution of that good for other things its price might buy for a particular quantity of the good. It does not tell us the maximum amount that the household would be willing to pay per unit for all of the units that it demands at that price. In some cases checks are written to reduce the overall cost of buying some items, while in other cases checks are written in transactions for which cash might be an almost perfect substitute. For example, the first four checks might be drawn to pay utility bills that would otherwise have to be paid in person at some inconvenient location. Later checks might be written for over-the-counter purchases that could otherwise be easily covered out of a somewhat larger inventory of cash. Whether or not the last checks are written will not affect the convenience, and therefore the value, of being able to write the first four. A shrewd bank will attempt to charge its customers a higher price for those checks that are valuable and a lower price for those that are not. Ideally, a supplier would wish to collect for each check written exactly the maximum amount that it is worth to the depositor.

This amount can be simply read off the demand curve, as is shown in Figure 9.8. The amount that would be paid for the first unit is $0.63. However, the first

Figure 9.8 *Maximum Total Revenue with Interunit Price Discrimination*

The maximum total revenue that can be obtained from the sale of 40 units is given by the sum of the demand prices of each of these units. That amount is given by the shaded area in the figure.

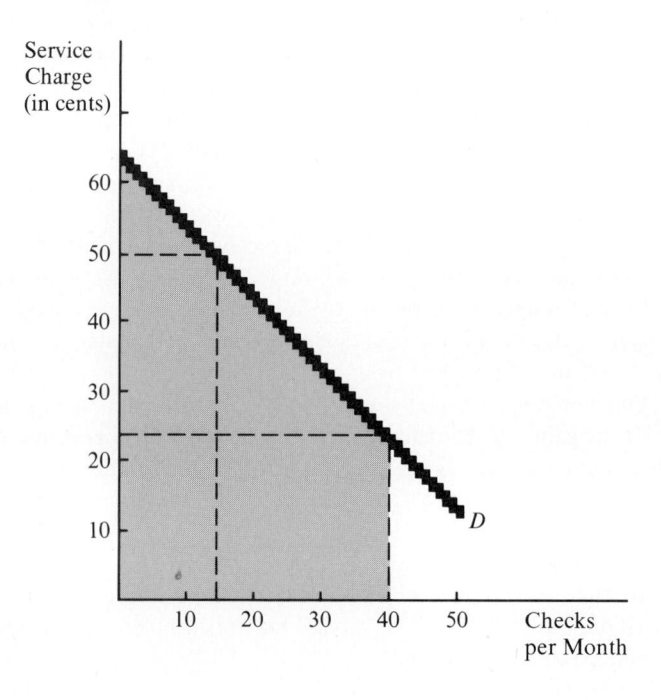

unit is no less valuable if a second one is purchased; the second one would sell for $0.62, a third one for $0.61, and so on. We already know that 14 units would sell for $0.50 each and 40 for $0.24. To determine the maximum amount that might be paid for the writing of 40 checks, we simply add up the amounts that would be paid for each check. That sum will equal the shaded area in Figure 9.8. Of course, if the demand curve is continuous over fractions of checks (as it clearly is for goods sold by weight or volume), this amount will simply be the area under the demand curve from zero to 40 checks.

That maximum amount is $17.40, which is larger than $9.60 and much larger than $7.00—indeed, it is a good deal larger than $10.24, the maximum total revenue that can be obtained from the sale of any quantity at a single price. This is obtained by pricing checking at a flat rate of $0.32 per check, in which case the household would write 32.[4] Clearly, interunit price discrimination raises more

---

[4] Recall that total revenue is maximized for constant per-unit prices at the quantity at which marginal revenue is zero. This demand curve has the form $P = 64 - x$; hence, marginal revenue is $MR = 64 - 2x$. Marginal revenue for this demand curve is therefore zero at $x = 32$, where P is also 32.

revenue per unit sold than does charging a single price. Note that the average revenue paid for these 40 units is $17.40/40 = \$0.435$ per check, which is higher than the marginal price of \$0.24 charged for the last check. If the bank attempted to raise the price of all checks to \$0.435, this household would write only 20 checks, and total revenue would fall to \$8.70.

This sort of unit pricing at a different price to each customer is cumbersome and complicated. Luckily for those price searchers seeking to obtain maximum revenue from their customers, a much easier method can be employed that achieves the same results. If all customers are similar in demand to the household we have considered here, the bank might simply announce a monthly service charge of \$7.80 and a charge per check of \$0.24. Under these conditions each depositor would also write 40 checks, for which he or she would pay a total bill of \$17.40. This would include the service charge and the \$9.60 received as payment for the checks used.

This method of pricing permits us to focus on the source of this extra revenue. Recall from Chapter 4 that the ability to purchase a good in the market confers on the buyer a *gain from trade*. That gain was measured as the maximum amount of income that might be taken from a household purchasing a good at a particular price that would leave it no better off than if it were unable to buy the good at that price. That gain will be defined here as the household's **consumer surplus**. We see now that it may be measured in two ways: (1) the compensating income change described in Chapter 4, and (2) the area above the price charged per unit and below the demand curve over the units purchased. Were the household depicted in Figure 9.8 permitted to write 40 checks at a flat price of \$0.24, it would enjoy gains from trade (that is, a consumer surplus) of \$7.80. By engaging in interunit price discrimination, the bank is able to capture for itself the consumer surplus that would otherwise go to the household.

This analysis also permits us to identify the limiting value of the fee charged by the bank over and above its price per check. That fee may not exceed the value of the consumer surplus at any price. A service charge in excess of this amount would leave the household worse off than being unable to write any checks at the \$0.24 price; hence, we can predict that the bank would be unable to do any business at all with this customer under those arrangements. Gains from trade for the household would be negative in this case. So long as the service charge is less than the full consumer surplus, however, the bank—and any price-searching supplier—may add to its revenues by such interunit price discrimination.

How will the firm select the quantity to supply under these arrangements? As before, it will select the quantity at which marginal revenue equals marginal cost. In this case, however, marginal revenue for the firm will be given by the demand price at each quantity, that is, by the height of the demand curve at every quantity. For the firm engaged in interunit price discrimination, the price must be lowered to sell an additional unit. However, only the price of the last unit is lowered. Revenue already obtained by selling earlier units at higher prices is not affected by the lowering of the price of the marginal unit. Total revenue therefore increases with the sale of a marginal unit by the full amount of the sale price of that unit.

The output and maximum possible profit for a firm engaged in interunit price discrimination is shown in Figure 9.9. The firm will select output q^*, at which marginal cost is exactly equal to marginal revenue, given by the height of the demand curve as just described. Average cost of this quantity is given by the height

Figure 9.9 *Output Choice and Profit with Interunit Price Discrimination*

Where each unit is priced at the maximum the demander will pay, the demand curve becomes the firm's marginal revenue curve. The output chosen will thus be that at which the demand curve and the marginal cost curve intersect. Total revenue is the area $OKTq^*$; total cost is area $OHFq^*$. Profit will therefore be represented by area $HKTF$. If the same quantity were sold at a single market-clearing price, that price would be P^*, and profit would be limited to HP^*TF.

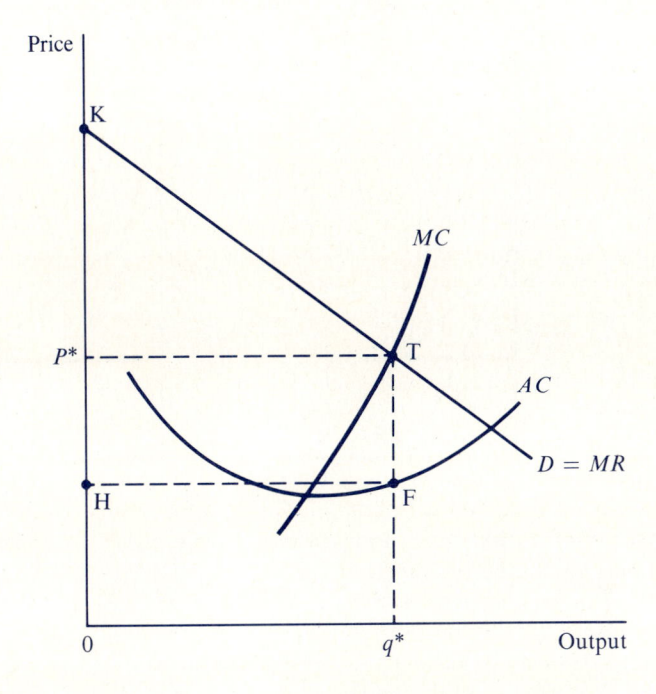

of curve AC. Total cost is therefore the rectangle $OHFq^*$. The maximum total revenue that may be obtained is the area under demand curve D from zero to q^* units—that is, area $OKTq^*$. Maximum profits for this firm will therefore be the difference between the maximum possible total revenue area and the total cost area. This maximum profit area is thus the area $HKTF$.

Price Discrimination among Customers

Price searchers may also increase their revenue for a given output by price discriminating among customers. This is illustrated in Figure 9.10, which depicts the demand curves of two individual buyers in panels (a) and (b) and their combined demand in panel (c). Marginal cost is shown to be horizontal, so we may focus our attention on the demand-side aspects of this problem. Recall that the combined demand curve in panel (c) indicates the total quantity that both buyer A and buyer B will purchase at each price. This firm therefore maximizes its profits from sale

Figure 9.10   *Combined Marginal Revenue and Household Marginal Revenue*

The demand curves in panels (a) and (b) combine to form the demand curve in panel (c). A firm that sells at a single price to both will select output q, which it sells to both at a price of p. Total revenue can be increased by reducing the quantity supplied to household A and increasing the quantity sold to household B. Marginal revenue of the chosen quantity in panel (a) is MR_A^1, which is less than the marginal revenue in panel (b) of MR_B^1.

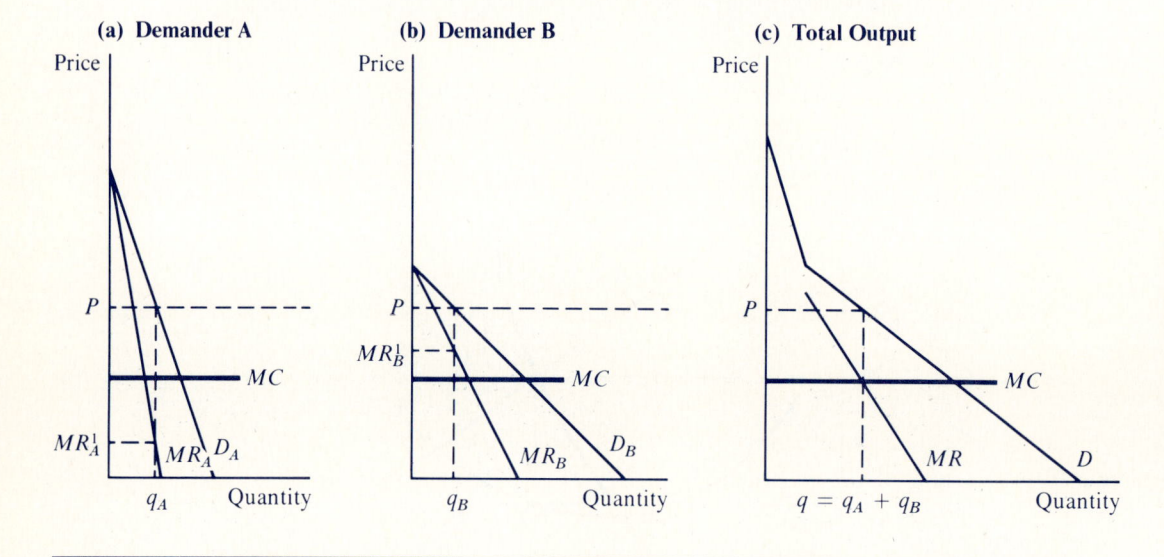

(a) Demander A   **(b) Demander B**   **(c) Total Output**

at a single price by producing the output that equates marginal cost with marginal revenue associated with this combined demand curve. It will therefore choose to produce output q and sell it at the market-clearing price, P.

Demander A will purchase q_A units at this price and demander B will purchase q_B units at this price. If we examine the level of marginal revenue for each of the individual demand curves at these quantities, however, we find that A's marginal revenue, MR_A^1, is lower than B's marginal revenue, MR_B^1, at this resulting distribution of output. Indeed, marginal revenue MR_B^1 exceeds the marginal cost of output, MC, while MR_A^1 is less than marginal cost. Total revenue could be increased *without changing output* by merely selling some of the units presently sold to demander A to demander B instead. However, doing this would necessitate selling to the two individuals at different prices. Additional units may be sold to B only at a lower price, and if fewer units are sold to A, A's demand price for these units will be higher than P.

This change will nevertheless increase total revenue. We know this from simply applying the definition of marginal revenue to this example. Marginal revenue is the change in total revenue per unit change in the amount sold. A reduction in units sold to A will therefore reduce total revenue by MR_A^1 per unit. An increase in the number of units sold to B will increase total revenue by MR_B^1 per unit. Shifting one unit from A to B therefore increases total revenue by the difference in marginal revenues in the two markets. Maximum revenue from the sale of output q is therefore obtained by selling the quantity in each market that just equates marginal revenue to each buyer.

We may derive this result algebraically as follows. Let the expression for profit for such a firm depend on revenues from Demander A and Demander B and total cost depend on total output (the sum of output sold to A and B):

$$\pi(q) = r_A(q_A) + r_B(q_B) - c(q_A + q_B).$$

Profits will be maximized when the change in profits per unit produced and sold in each market is simultaneously equal to zero; that is,

$$\frac{\Delta \pi}{\Delta q_A} = 0 = \frac{\Delta r_A}{\Delta q_A} - \frac{\Delta c}{\Delta q_A}$$

$$\frac{\Delta \pi}{\Delta q_B} = 0 = \frac{\Delta r_B}{\Delta q_B} - \frac{\Delta c}{\Delta q_B}.$$

The first term on the right side of each of these expressions, $\Delta r/\Delta q$, is marginal revenue. The second term on the right side, $\Delta c/\Delta q$, is the marginal cost of producing a unit for each market. As the cost of producing a unit for sale to either demander is the same, these two expressions may be combined into one profit-maximizing condition:

$$\frac{\Delta r_A}{\Delta q_A} = \frac{\Delta c}{\Delta q} = \frac{\Delta r_B}{\Delta q_B}.$$

This may be rewritten as:

$$MR_A = MC = MR_B.$$

A firm that is selling in two separate markets maximizes profits by choosing the output where marginal cost is equal to marginal revenue *and* dividing that output so as to equate marginal revenue in each market.

Recall that marginal revenue for any demand curve may be expressed as

$$P\left(1 + \frac{1}{\eta}\right).$$

We may therefore derive an expression relating the optimum price charged to each demander to the demander's elasticity of demand at that price. As the marginal revenues of demanders A and B must be equal at the optimal quantities sold to each, we may state this equality as follows:

$$MR_A = MR_B$$

$$P_A\left(1 + \frac{1}{\eta_A}\right) = P_B\left(1 + \frac{1}{\eta_B}\right).$$

Solving this expression for the price ratio gives:

$$\frac{P_A}{P_B} = \frac{1 + \frac{1}{\eta_B}}{1 + \frac{1}{\eta_A}}.$$

This expression tells us that at equal elasticities the prices charged in these two markets must also be equal. If, however, the elasticity of demand of buyer A is less than that of buyer B, the price to A must exceed the price to B. If this is not intuitively obvious, consider the following example. Let η_A be -2 and η_B be -4. The numerator of the right side will therefore be 0.75 and the denominator will be 0.5. Given these elasticities, the price ratio will have a value of 1.5; hence, P_A must be larger than P_B. We may conclude, therefore, that in general the profit-maximizing distribution of output between two such markets is that which results in a price ratio that varies *inversely* to the ratio of the demand elasticities.

Conditions for Price Discrimination

Being able to sell a product at different prices depends quite naturally on high-price buyers being unable to obtain the product from other sellers at lower prices. Even for a pure monopolist this is not an altogether foregone conclusion. Even where one firm is the only producer of the product, the fact that it sells some units at a higher price than others means that it faces potential competition in the high-price market from those buyers who obtain the goods at its lower prices. Buyers who obtain the good at a low price value their marginal purchases less than those who buy it at a higher price. We might expect those in this situation to seek to *resell* some of the output that they obtain. Two qualities of goods impede this resale. To the extent that neither of these qualities is present, we predict a greater tendency toward price discrimination by price-searching sellers.

We shall refer to the first of these qualities as the **transferability** of the good in question. A restaurant meal cannot very easily be resold, because it deteriorates rapidly when being transported or stored. Thus, restaurants have little difficulty charging more for evening meals than for the same meal prepared at lunchtime. Services represent the ultimate case of limited transferability, for they cannot be transferred at all. A physical examination by a doctor cannot be resold to another patient, nor can a shoeshine or legal defense in a criminal case. We are therefore led to expect a greater incidence of price discrimination in the prices charged by suppliers of services than by suppliers of goods.

The second quality affecting the resale of goods and thus the incidence of price discrimination is referred to as the **price spread**. By this we mean the difference between the price the seller receives and the cost to the purchaser. Typically, this difference exists because of the relative costs of transactions. The greater the cost of finding buyers and sellers and negotiating the terms of a transaction, the larger will be this spread. Either the buyer or the seller must bear these transaction costs; hence, the greater these costs, the greater will be the difference between the seller's net proceeds and the cost to the buyer. Clearly, if the spread is large relative to the producer's prices, arbitrage between the two markets will be more difficult. Buyers at the producer's low price will have to absorb one full transaction cost per sale (that is, one buyer's share plus one seller's share) in order to compete with the producer for sales in the high-price market. The larger this spread relative to the value of the good sold, the less attractive will be transactions for resale in this market. Price discrimination should therefore be observed less frequently in markets where the spread is high relative to the value of the items sold.

The market for original works of art is characterized by a very high spread, due to the special and difficult to communicate demands made by individual patrons and the largely unpredictable progress of the artistic development of suppliers. A great deal of search goes into the pairing of buyer and seller in such a market, often undertaken by middlemen known here as *galleries*. The nature of the product in this case strongly suggests that its demand is less than perfectly elastic. The combination of these factors implies that price discrimination will flourish here. Knowledgeable buyers—collectors—will be charged one price for an artist's work, while whimsical buyers (sometimes deprecatingly called *marks*) pay top dollar. Yet sale by a collector to a mark is virtually unknown. When collectors wish to dispose of certain pieces in their collections, they typically resell to galleries or to other collectors.

The Separation of Markets

Essential to successful price discrimination is the separation of markets, that is, the identification and separation of demanders with differing demand elasticities. As noted, the firm will seek to charge a lower price to the demander with the higher demand elasticity. Doing so naturally involves discovering which demanders have which elasticity and finding ways to charge them different prices. Many seemingly idiosyncratic marketing practices of firms can be explained in these terms.

Price discrimination is most easily accomplished if the markets are separated geographically. The infamous practice of "dumping" in international markets is neither more nor less than simple price discrimination. Producers sell in their native country at one price and sell in others at a lower one. Domestic producers in the country where the product is "dumped" are understandably bitter; it costs them money. The Japanese are noted for their dumping of steel, automobiles, and televisions in the American market. Domestic producers of these items have argued vehemently that the Japanese are selling in our market at prices that are "below cost," thus driving American businesses out of these markets. Whether these prices are in fact below *our* costs to produce is another matter. As we have seen, however, it clearly is not the case that these prices are below the costs of the Japanese producers. Even in the low-price market, price-discriminating suppliers sell quantities at which marginal cost equals marginal revenue. Marginal cost therefore must necessarily be lower than price.

Price discrimination is not limited to markets separated by international boundaries. Some of the examples cited earlier in this discussion illustrate that price discrimination is often practiced in a single location. In these cases the supplier's chief concern is to distinguish high demand elasticity buyers from low demand elasticity buyers. Consider the case of airfares. Assume for the sake of argument that there are two types of travelers: business travelers and vacationers. If, as seems quite plausible, the former have a much less elastic demand for air travel than the latter, airlines will wish to charge higher prices to businessmen than to vacationers. The question is *how* to sort these demanders into two price categories.

Perhaps the most straightforward way to do this is for airlines simply to announce two fares, one for businessmen and a lower one for vacationers. Some businessmen—but probably not very successful ones—might actually pay the higher fares. Unfortunately for the airlines, however, most would probably declare the purpose of their travel to be vacations, even if this were not true, in order to qualify for the lower fares. What is an airline to do about the announced intentions of an offshore drilling expert to visit Galveston, Texas, for some sun and surf? Doubts about the authenticity of such an itinerary would be costly to prove.

Airlines have found it more expedient to develop pricing schedules tailored to the differing travel patterns of these two sets of demanders. By setting a separate price for each travel pattern, they effectively establish different prices to different types of customer. This can be illustrated in terms of two important differences in travel patterns that figure prominently in commercial airline fares. First, business travel is typically of short duration and rarely includes weekends. Second, business travel is difficult to plan in detail far in advance of the dates of departure. Vacations, on the other hand, are more lengthy and include weekends whenever possible; they are also planned far in advance of the actual travel. Not surprisingly, therefore, airlines charge higher prices for trips of short duration, for trips not extending over weekends, and for trips arranged on short notice.

Even producers of ordinary household items price discriminate. As these items are regularly sold from supermarket shelves, it might be thought that charging different prices to different patrons of these stores would be difficult. In practice, producers have developed several ways to accomplish this. Let us assume that demanders may be divided again into two groups: (1) one group whose time is more valuable and who therefore finds it uneconomical to invest time in following prices and seeking bargains, and (2) a second group who finds this search activity more cost effective. It seems reasonable to assume that the demand elasticity of the former group will be lower than that of the latter group. Producers will therefore seek to offer their products at lower prices to the latter group than the former.

One way to accomplish this is to distribute coupons through newspaper advertisements and direct mail. These coupons entitle purchasers to a discount on the merchandise offered. As reading, clipping, storing, and redeeming these coupons require considerable time and inconvenience on the part of buyers, fewer buyers in the low-elasticity group will take advantage of them than those in the high-elasticity group. In effect, the coupons have the effect of lowering the price to the desired group. It will not work perfectly, of course, but to the extent that it does it will increase revenues to producers for any given output.

Suppliers often justify issuing coupons on the basis of "introducing" their products to demanders. Can we discount this explanation in favor of our own hypothesis of price discrimination? Yes, we can. As we have just pointed out, taking advantage of coupons to obtain a lower price for products involves a considerable investment of time on the part of buyers. This "busywork" represents a deadweight loss to both demanders and suppliers if the intent of the coupons is merely

Figure 9.11 Price Reductions versus Coupons

Handling coupons is costly and shifts the price that demanders will pay for each quantity downward from the money demand price $D(q)$ by the amount of this transaction cost. If the transaction cost is c per unit, this will shift the money price that demanders will pay downward by this amount to position $P_D(q)$. A firm originally selling quantity q_1 can therefore increase units sold from q_1 to q_2 either by lowering the money price from P^* to P_1 or by offering a coupon discount of the difference between P^* and P_2. The same increase in sales with a smaller decrease in revenue to the firm may therefore be better achieved by lowering the selling price than by offering coupons.

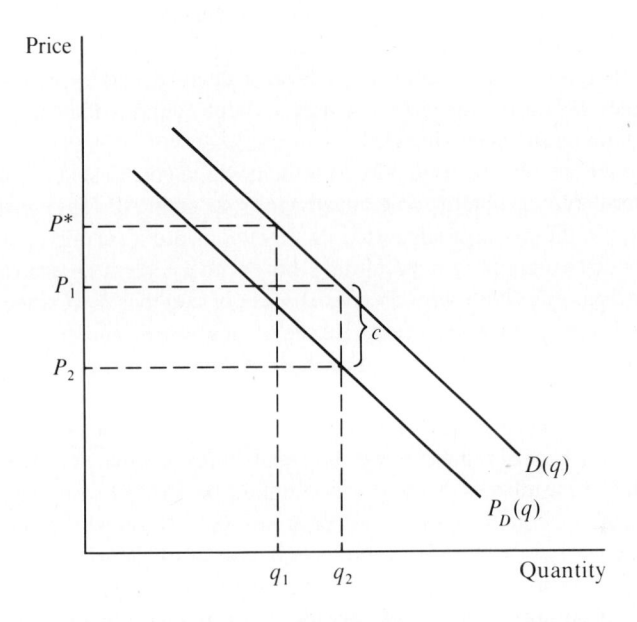

to increase sales by lowering price. Suppliers might accomplish the same increase in volume with a simple price decrease *of less than the coupon discount*. If the objective is merely to increase volume over some period, it is better from the point of view of suppliers merely to lower prices than to offer coupons.

This is demonstrated in Figure 9.11. Let market demand be as indicated by curve $D(q)$. Assume further that the costs associated with handling and using coupons are some fixed amount, c, per unit. The value that demanders place on each quantity of the product is indicated by the height of the demand curve at that quantity. Buyers would therefore be unwilling to bear a cost in excess of that amount per unit to obtain the good, and this holds regardless of the form of that cost. For users of coupons the cost of obtaining the good takes two forms: the money price paid, $P_D(q)$, and the transaction costs of handling the coupons, c. For any quantity these must therefore add up to the demand price of the good; that is:

$$D(q) = P_D(q) + c.$$

Solving for the money price the demander will pay gives:

$P_D(q) = D(q) - c.$

The use of coupons therefore shifts the demand curve faced by the seller downward by the amount of the cost of handling them.

Now assume that the seller does not use coupons and is currently offering quantity q_1 for sale at the market-clearing price of P^*. If the seller wishes to expand sales to q_2 using coupons, he or she must offer a coupon discount of $P^* - P_2$ per unit. This lowers the money price to demanders to P_2, which is the most that they will be willing to pay for this quantity. If, however, the producer merely lowers the price without coupons, the same quantity can be sold for P_1 per unit. The seller gets a higher price per unit without coupons than with them for any quantity he or she wants to sell.

If coupons may be used only at some positive cost to sellers, then we may be sure that they will obtain some advantage from their use. The most plausible explanation is the one just suggested: that coupons are a sorting device, separating buyers into two groups and permitting those who use them to receive a discount on the price paid by those who do not. The use of coupons lowers the net price that users will pay compared to the price they would pay in money alone. The sellers bear this cost, however, in expectation of the increased revenues they will obtain by charging different prices to the two groups with different demand elasticities.

Coupons are only one way of achieving this market separation. A similar argument may be made that "sales" by retail stores achieve the same result. These lower the price of merchandise for a limited period, allowing those who watch vigilantly for bargains to buy at lower prices while those who do not, pay the normal higher prices. Quantity discounts may also be explained in terms of price discrimination. Those purchasing in larger quantities have an economic incentive to search more intensively for low prices. A lower price yields a larger saving per transaction to those who buy in larger quantities. Such buyers are therefore likely to have more elastic demands than buyers of small quantities. Quantity discounts are a straightforward way of lowering the price to buyers with higher demand elasticities.

Summary

The distinction between price taker suppliers and price searcher suppliers lies in the demand curves faced by each. The demand curve of the price taker is perfectly elastic at the market price. The demand curve of the price searcher slopes downward to the right. For the price searcher this implies that marginal revenue will be less than price at every output. The relationship between marginal revenue and demand elasticity for the firm was developed in this chapter. For demand elasticities with absolute values greater than 1, marginal revenue is positive; for demand elasticities with absolute values less than 1, marginal revenue is negative.

The price-searching firm chooses output on the basis of marginal revenue and marginal cost, just as does its price-taking counterpart. However, as marginal revenue is less than price in this case, price must be higher than marginal cost at the chosen output. The difference between price and marginal cost as a percentage of price is $1/\eta$. The output choice of a price searcher may be influenced by price regulation. Typically, a price searcher firm will expand output for a range of prices below its chosen price. This range expressed as a percentage of price is also equal to $1/\eta$.

The fact that price exceeds marginal cost for the price searcher's chosen output clearly implies that the marginal cost curve is not the supply curve for this firm. Strictly speaking, there is no clear relationship between price and output for the price-searching firm. Quantity supplied depends on both price and demand elasticity at that price.

Price searcher firms will find it profitable to price discriminate. Firms may increase total revenue from the sale of a given output by charging different prices to different customers and different prices to the same customer for marginal and inframarginal units of the goods purchased. The first of these techniques is called **interperson price discrimination**; the second is called **interunit price discrimination**. As quantity purchased is influenced only by the price of marginal units, a pricing scheme that raises average revenue above marginal price will increase total revenue without affecting quantity sold. For demanders with differing demand elasticities, marginal revenue will differ at a common price. Revenue maximization for a given output requires that marginal revenues be equated in all markets. This will require charging different prices to demanders with differing demand elasticities. Those with low elasticity of demand should pay higher prices than demanders with more elastic demand.

Price discrimination may be practiced successfully only in the absence of competition from other sellers. This exclusion of competition must extend to potential competition from purchasers of the product. For this reason the ability to price discriminate is influenced by the transferability of goods and the price spread. If the transferability of a product is limited, the ability of purchasers to resell the product in competition with the original producer will be discouraged, as it also will if the price spread is large relative to the price itself. The spread typically reflects the transaction costs of matching buyer with seller. A buyer wishing to compete with the producer in such a market will have to bear both the buyer's and the seller's share of these transaction costs of the sale.

Price discrimination also requires that demanders with differing demand elasticities be identified and correctly assessed as to prices charged them. When markets are geographically dispersed, this poses no problem. When sellers seek to price discriminate in a single market, however, the costs of discovering and effectively "pricing" different demanders can themselves explain some aspects of market behavior. Varying airline fares for such travel characteristics as length of stay, inclusion of weekends, and advance purchase of tickets (all of which are unrelated to the cost of supplying the service) can be explained as a means of price discrimination. Other marketing techniques, such as offering coupons, trading stamps, and periodic "sales," may be interpreted as ways of lowering prices to those demanders with more market information and greater sensitivity to price—that is, higher elasticity of demand.

Key Concepts

marginal revenue = $P(q)\left[1 + \dfrac{1}{\eta}\right]$
market power
price discrimination
interperson price discrimination

interunit price discrimination
consumer surplus
transferability
price spread
separation of markets

Questions

1. *Easy* A price-searching seller who cannot price discriminate will select an output at which the cost of producing an extra unit is less than demanders are willing to pay for that unit. Explain the reason for this paradox.

Hard The underproduction result described above applies only to firms that cannot engage in interunit price discrimination. Sellers who can price discriminate in this way will produce exactly the output at which value at the margin is just equal to the marginal cost of production. What difference does being able to interunit price discriminate make?

2. *Easy* Show that for the price-searching firm the difference between price and marginal cost as a percentage of price will, at the chosen output, be equal to the inverse of the demand elasticity for the firm's output.

Hard Price ceilings imposed on price-taking firms lower price but invariably result in less output being produced. For a price-searching seller, it is possible for a price ceiling to result in the choice of a higher output. Explain how this can occur. The price ceiling may not reduce price by more than the percentage given by $1/\eta$, or the firm will reduce output as in the price taker case. Why is this true? What implications does this have for using price ceilings on a day-to-day basis to control firms?

3. *Easy* A price-searching seller who may not price discriminate selects the output at which marginal cost is equal to marginal revenue (less than price). What is the relationship between demand elasticity and marginal revenue?

Hard Explain why the demand elasticity at this chosen output will never be less than unity in absolute value. What would be the output of a price-searching seller who faced a demand curve that had a constant elasticity of negative unity?

4. *Easy* For a price-searching seller who may not price discriminate, price will invariably be above marginal cost. This fact informs us that this firm's supply curve is not its marginal cost curve. Explain why.

Hard Even in the above situation, price-searching firms may respond in systematic ways to changes in demand due to such influences as population or income growth. Explain why. (Hint: What effect will systematic shifts in the demand curve have on the position of the marginal revenue curve?)

5. *Easy* Which of the following is likely to represent interunit price discrimination and which interperson price discrimination? Explain.
    a. Coupons in packaged flour offering $0.15 off on the next purchase
    b. Car rental discounts over weekends
    c. A Eurail pass offering unlimited train travel in Europe for a fixed amount
    d. A television serviceman who charges $35 for coming to your home and telling you that he must take your set to the shop for repairs, which are separately billed
    e. Long-distance telephone rates that are lower in the evenings and on weekends
    f. Magazine subscription rates below newsstand prices
    g. Complete restaurant dinners priced below the cost of ordering each of the items "a la carte"
    h. City shops offering "free" parking, and hotels offering "free" limousine service to and from the airport
    i. A hospital charging a daily rate plus individual charges for each test and service provided
    j. A movie theater charging less to children and less for the 6:00 PM showing.

Hard Ben Klein owns a supermarket in Seattle. He has two groups of customers. One group drives station wagons, buys at least $200 worth of goods per trip, and shops mainly on Thursday mornings. The other drives sport cars, buys fewer than 20 items per trip, and shops on the way home from work two or three times per week. Klein guesses that the demand elasticity of the former group is much higher than that of the latter. He would like to price discriminate by lowering the price to the former group but doubts that he can get away with putting two price tags on each item. How will offering trading stamps allow Klein to achieve this objective?

6. *Easy* Which of the following are likely to be able to price discriminate?
   a. A corn farmer in Indiana
   b. A physician
   c. An electric power company
   d. A seller of premium beer
   e. A restaurant
   f. A seller of life insurance

Hard Individual state governments can be thought of as being in the business of selling locations to businesses and workers on the basis of government services and prices charged in the form of taxes. In many states the progressivity of personal income taxes has been interpreted by economists as a form of price discrimination by the states in the "sale" of their services. What does this imply about the relationship of income to the elasticity of demand for government services?

Chapter 10

Sources of Market Power

Connections In the previous chapter we explored the output and pricing behavior of price-searching firms. That model applies to a number of market environments. This chapter will survey the sources of market power as well as the equilibrium conditions in such markets and the scope for policy aimed at modifying choices. While the earlier chapters dealt more generally with the theory of the firm, this chapter builds into some of its models individual demander behavior. A review of Chapter 2 and Chapter 4 will prove helpful in reacquainting us with basic principles of demander behavior. The topic of vertical integration reappears here and plays a central role in the last section of this chapter. Those who do not feel completely comfortable with this topic and the factors that limit its extension into voluntary markets are urged to review the material in Chapter 7.

So far we have discussed the output and sales strategies of price-searching firms without concerning ourselves with the sources of market power, even though these are numerous and varied. This has been done intentionally, to dramatize the fact that all price-searching firms behave alike in their output choices. In each case profits are maximized by producing the output at which marginal cost equals marginal revenue. Where resale is uneconomical and separate markets with differing elasticities may be distinguished, firms will seek to price discriminate by selling the output that equates marginal cost to marginal revenue in each market.

Let us now turn our attention to the determinants of market environment. Recall that the distinction between price-taking firms and price-searching firms lies in their respective beliefs about price and output. The former believe that changes in output have an effect on price; the latter recognize that increased output may be sold only by lowering price. There are several reasons for demand curves of firms to slope downward, and we will consider each of them in a separate section.

10.1 Monopoly

If a firm is the only seller of a good, its demand curve is the market demand curve. This curve slopes downward on the basis of the first law of demand. A full explanation of **monopoly** must therefore identify the reasons why the equilibrium number of firms in such a market is one. There are two principal causes of this result: state intervention and the phenomenon of decreasing costs.

Government-Sanctioned Monopoly

If the government protects a firm's position as the only seller in a market, that firm will clearly enjoy a measure of monopoly power. The most obvious case of government protection is the granting of patents to developers of new products. Patents extend the protection of government to the rights of inventors as the sole sellers of their products for a period of seventeen years.

There can be little doubt that government protection is an important determinant of market structure in many industries. The granting of broadcasting licenses by the FCC effectively establishes a monopoly over network material transmitted by license holders. The granting of exclusive rights to operate concessions at airports and sports events and the awarding of all intercity bus transportation to a single transit company or all taxi business to a single cab company all establish monopoly. If the favored companies are then free to determine their own output and prices, they will behave in the manner typical of price searchers.

Natural Monopoly

The establishment of monopolies is often justified on cost grounds. It is argued that these markets are characterized by declining costs and that establishment of monopolies is efficient. Consideration of such an argument requires close examination of the second source of monopoly, declining costs.

Declining-cost industries are those in which scale economies extend over the full range of output that the market will buy. A supplier who alone produces the entire industry output can do so at lower average total cost than can a combination of firms. Such cost conditions will lead to the emergence of the single producer as a monopolist in the industry. Rival firms that attempt to enter this industry will be unable to produce at these low costs and will fail. As this type of monopoly has emerged through the conventional competitive rivalry of firms rather than by government fiat, it is referred to as a **natural monopoly**.

Figure 10.1 depicts such a market graphically. Here we have the market demand curve, D, as well as a portion of the envelope curve, E. Assume that there are two firms in the industry, each of which produces output q_1, which sells in the market at price P_1. Assume further that both firms take this market price as given; they are price takers. The market is just willing to purchase the output of both firms, $2q_1$, at this price. If we examine the cost position of each firm in this situation, however, we see that neither can be in equilibrium. Although marginal cost equals marginal revenue (price in this case), the average cost of this output lies above the envelope curve. Scale is not optimal for this output. If one firm expands scale to that shown by ATC_2, it may now produce the entire output previously offered by both firms at a price that is less than average cost at the original output.

Figure 10.1 *Natural Monopoly*

This industry initially contains two price-taking firms, each of which produces output q_1 for which it receives price P_1. Price P_1 clears the market, because total output is $2q_1$. This is not an equilibrium, because at output q_1 the ATC curve is not tangent to the envelope curve. If one firm expands, the other must leave the industry. If one expands scale to ATC_2 and produces output $2q_1$, market output will expand to $3q_1$. At this output both firms earn losses, but the losses for the small firm are greater. Neither expansion nor contraction solves the problem for the smaller firm.

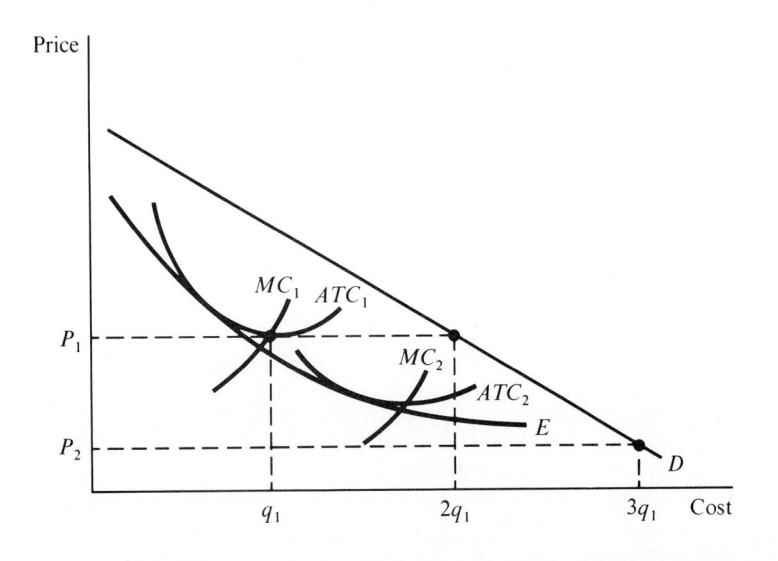

The second firm must leave the industry. If it continues to produce its original output, industry output will expand to $3q_1$ and price will fall to P_2. As its average costs are inevitably higher than those of the larger firm, however, its losses in such a situation will be correspondingly greater. There is literally nothing that the smaller firm can do in this dilemma. If it reduces scale, average costs rise, and if it expands scale, price falls. It must exit, leaving the larger firm a monopoly in the industry.

Regulation of Natural Monopoly

If monopoly is the natural result of competition in such an industry, the resulting equilibrium will be characterized by underproduction. The firm will produce too little output, in the sense that output at the margin is worth more to demanders than it costs the supplier to produce. Price regulation is often recommended on these grounds. It is possible, as we have seen, to influence price searchers to expand output and lower price. This theory of "how to" influence firms to produce the desired output must be modified slightly for the case of true natural monopoly.

In Figure 10.2 we present the relevant cost and demand curves for such a natural monopoly. The demand curve, D, and its marginal revenue curve,

Figure 10.2 *Optimum Output and Scale for a Monopolist*

Output and scale are both optimal for this monopolist. The firm's marginal cost for this scale intersects its marginal revenue at output q_1. At this output scale is optimal, because the ATC curve is tangent to the envelope curve at output q_1.

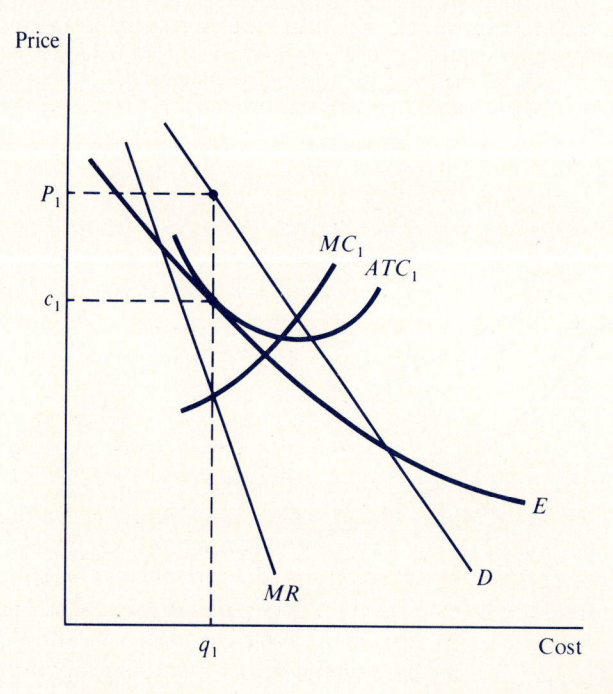

Figure 10.3 Price Regulation with a Natural Monopolist

The profit-maximizing output and scale are given by output q_1 and the scale associated with ATC_1. Price regulations can influence the firm to expand both output and scale. The optimum output and scale are q_2 and ATC_2, at which marginal cost equals the market-clearing price and the ATC is tangent to the envelope curve at the chosen output. A price ceiling at P_2 would *not* result in the choice of this optimum, because price would be less than average cost under those circumstances.

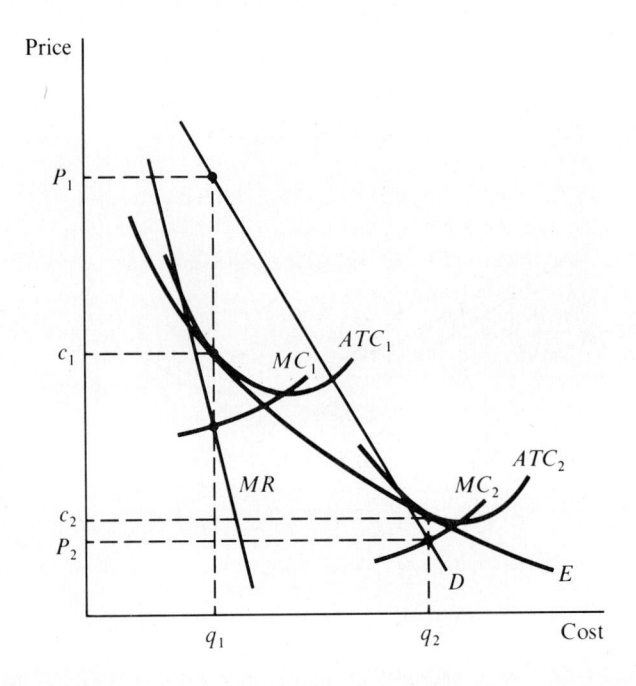

MR, slope downward to the right as usual. An unregulated monopolist would produce output q_1 using the scale associated with ATC_1. This satisfies both profit-maximizing conditions. Marginal revenue equals marginal cost, and the average total cost of this output is lower using this scale than any other. The market-clearing price of this output is P_1, and profit per unit is the difference between P_1 and c_1.

In Chapter 9 it was shown that a price ceiling can influence a price searcher to expand output at the lower price. However, a more complicated regulatory pricing formula is required to influence natural monopolists to produce the *optimum* output and scale. The specific difficulty posed by natural monopoly is that the firm's marginal cost will always lie below average cost where average cost is tangent to the envelope curve. The joint objectives of (1) price equal to marginal cost and (2) average cost tangent to the envelope curve can therefore be satisfied only where price is less than average cost. Under these circumstances such a firm must earn net losses. In the case depicted in Figure 10.3, for example, these objectives are satisfied at output q_2. The optimal scale for the production of this output is that

Figure 10.4 *Interunit Price Discrimination for a Monopolist*

Output q_2 is the rate at which marginal cost is equal to the market-clearing price. As in Figure 10.3, attempting to impose this result by price regulation will be ineffective, because the firm cannot cover costs at this price and output. If the firm is permitted to charge the higher price P_1 for the first q_1 units and the lower price P_2 for the remainder (to price-discriminate over units), the average costs of this output will be just covered by the revenues collected.

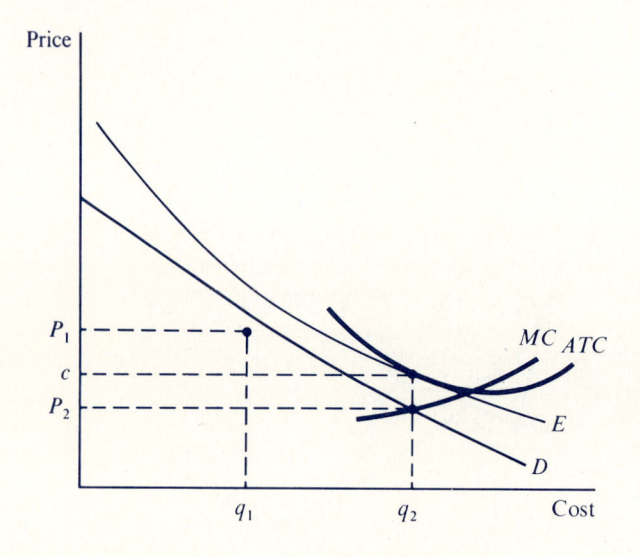

associated with ATC_2, which is tangent to the envelope curve at this output. Furthermore, the market-clearing price of this output is P_2, which is just equal to marginal cost at output q_2. However, we clearly observe that revenues will not cover costs in this situation. Hence, a policy of controlling price at P_2 will not influence such a firm to produce this output. The firm will go out of business rather than remain and earn the losses associated with this output and price.

One solution to this dilemma is to let natural monopolists engage in interunit price discrimination. As we noted in Chapter 9, by charging a higher price for inframarginal units than for the last units purchased, a supplier may raise average revenue above price. In Figure 10.4, for example, average cost, c, exceeds price P_2 at the optimum scale and output q_2. Total revenue is therefore $P_2 q_2$, and total cost is cq_2. A loss equal to $q_2(c - P_2)$ would be suffered by a firm operating at this price and output. However, such a firm may be permitted to price discriminate in such a way that total revenues cover costs. Suppose that it were permitted to charge a higher price,

$$P_1 = P_2 + 2(c - P_2) = 2c - P_2,$$

for the first q_1 (equal to $q_2/2$) units but were required to charge only P_2 for the remainder. Total revenue in this case would be as follows:

$$TR = q_1(2c - P_2) + (q_2 - q_1)P_2$$
$$= 2q_1 \cdot c$$
$$= q_2 \cdot c$$
$$TR = TC.$$

By permitting such a pricing scheme, the costs of producing the optimal output are covered while price at the margin equals marginal cost. Furthermore, a monopolist restricted to charging P_1 for the first q_1 units and P_2 for all outputs above this level will *choose* to produce q_2 units and adopt the optimal scale.

Students are cautioned against too readily adopting this view of the regulatory process. There are two serious obstacles to achievement of the regulatory solution presented here. First, this solution assumes that regulators are fully informed concerning the underlying cost function of the firms they regulate. This is hardly likely in a situation in which the regulators must obtain this information from the firms whose profits they seek to limit. Second, it assumes a benign role for the regulators themselves. Our analysis here has been exclusively normative. We have not as yet turned our attention to the behavior of regulators as economic agents and therefore cannot at this point discuss how regulators might be *predicted* to behave. At this point students should no longer have to be cautioned that developing a list of things regulators can do to benefit society is no assurance that these things will be done.

10.2 Location and Information

Even more important sources of market power than decreasing costs are the advantages of **location** and the **costs of information**. As the analysis of these two market conditions is quite similar, we will consider them together.

Advantages of Location

The customers of many firms are geographically dispersed. Firms themselves will often find it profitable to disperse so as to make patronage more convenient (that is, lower the transportation costs) to their demanders. These demanders consider the cost of transporting goods to the site of their use a part of the **full price** of those goods. A firm may therefore increase its revenues by selecting a location that minimizes its customers' transportation costs. The fact that some dispersed firms are closer to some customers than others implies that each firm will have some market power.

This will be shown in stages. Consider first a single firm and an individual demander. Let the demand curve of this customer be shown by $D(q)$ in Figure 10.5. Assume that transportation costs are constant per unit but vary with location, being T_1 at a close location and T_2 at a more distant one. The *full price* of the good purchased is the sum of the money price paid by demanders, $D_m(q)$, and the transportation cost per unit; that is,

Figure 10.5 *Full Price and Money Price with Transportation Costs*

The demand curve $D(q)$ expresses the full price that a consumer is willing to pay for each quantity, including the money prices and transportation costs. For a quantity of q_1 the consumer is willing to pay per unit a full price of P_f. Transportation costs shift the money demand curve faced by the firm downward. Higher transportation costs imply a lower money price. For transportation costs equal to T_1 per unit the consumer will pay a money price for q_1 units of P_1. For the higher transportation costs the T_2 price falls to P_2.

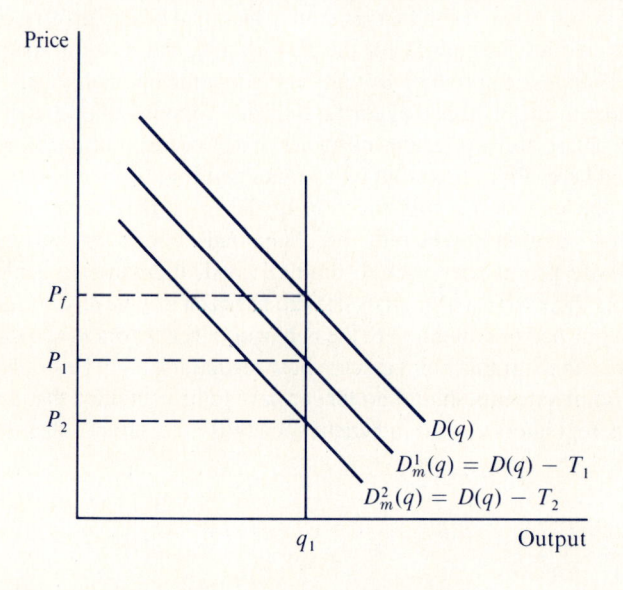

$$D(q) = D_m(q) + T.$$

The demand curve faced by the firm is, of course, the money demand curve $D_m(q)$. Solving for this value we obtain:

$$D_m(q) = D(q) - T.$$

Transportation costs merely have the effect of shifting the demand curve faced by the firm downward from its full price position by the amount of the transportation costs per unit. For a given quantity such as q_1, price per unit is therefore maximized by minimizing transportation costs. Price P_1 is greater than P_2 because transportation cost T_1 is less than T_2.

However, if there are many customers, transportation costs are reduced to some (by locating closer) only at the cost of getting farther away from others. We need not concern ourselves here with the messy problem of spatial equilibrium to develop the points we wish to make concerning transportation costs and market power. Those points follow from two observations that should be clear from this superficial discussion of the economics of location. The first is that transportation

Figure 10.6 *Full Price and Distance with Transportation Costs*

The horizontal axis here is a two-dimensional map. One seller is located at S_1 and the other is located at S_2. Transportation costs are constant per unit per mile. Full prices to customers therefore rise at a constant rate per mile as distance from the supplier increases. If both sellers supply their output at a price of P_m^1, a customer at B will face a lower full price from the seller at S_2. All customers to the right of A will find the full price lower from S_2, and all to the left of A will find a lower full price from S_1. If S_2 raises price to P_m^2, will no longer be able to sell to those customers between A and B.

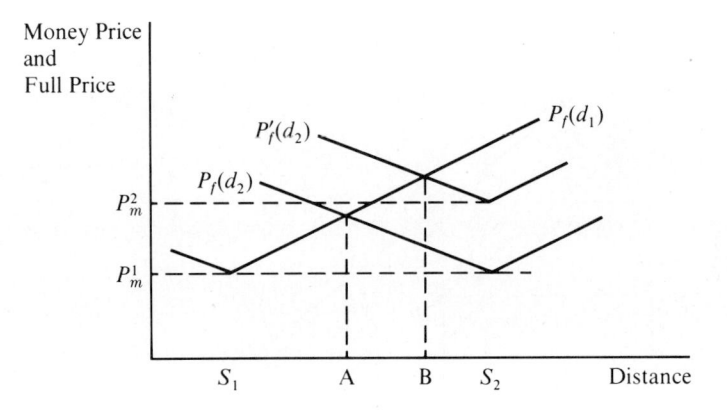

costs are regarded by customers as part of the full price of goods. The second is that wherever firms locate they will be closer to some customers than others.

Consider Figure 10.6. The horizontal axis of this figure is assumed to be a linear map—that is, S_1 and S_2 are the locations of two suppliers, and A and B are the locations of two customers. Transportation cost is assumed to be constant per mile. If each supplier charges a money price of P_m^1 for the good, the full price of this good will rise from this price linearly with the distance from the supplier. Curves $P_f(d_1)$ and $P_f(d_2)$ depict the full prices under these conditions to demanders at locations along the horizontal axis from each of the two suppliers. All demanders to the left of A will find the full price of the good lower if purchased from supplier S_1 than from supplier S_2, while those to the right of A will find the full price lower from supplier S_2.

Now consider the effect of an increase in the money price by supplier S_2. Although customer A and some of those to the right now find the full cost of purchasing from S_1 lower than from S_2, clearly all customers do not find this to be true. Even though S_2 charges a higher money price than S_1 (P_m^2 rather than P_m^1), those customers sufficiently close to supplier S_2 will continue to find the full price from S_2 lower than the full price from S_1. In fact, all demanders to the right of B find that although the full price from S_2 is higher than it was, it is still lower than the full price of obtaining the good from S_1.

The demand curve of such a firm will have a negative slope resulting from two effects. First, an increase in the money price will raise the full price to all its

Figure 10.7 *The Firm's Demand Curve with Transportation Costs*

Prices of rival producers are such that this firm may sell quantity q_1 at a price of P_1. If other producers hold price constant, the demand curve for this firm slopes downward. If this firm raises its price, some customers will no longer find its full price to be lower than that of other sellers, and will switch. Of those customers who remain, each will purchase less. Therefore, at the higher price this supplier will sell less. If, however, another firm raises its price, then the demand curve faced by this firm will shift rightward, as to $D_m^2(q)$.

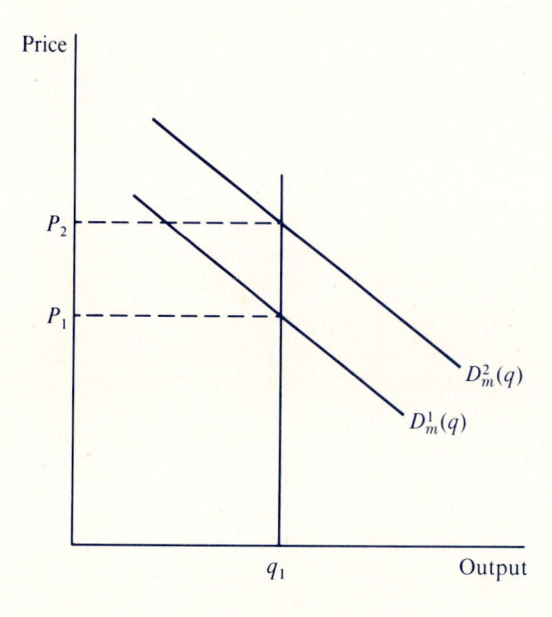

customers. Those more distant (and therefore closer to other suppliers) will thus be influenced to shift their commerce to the firm's rivals. Second, for those customers who remain, the full price of the firm's goods will have increased. They will purchase less than they did at the lower full price. A price increase therefore results in less being demanded from the firm due to (1) fewer customers, and (2) each customer buying less.

The position of a firm's demand curve therefore depends on the prices charged by rival firms. In Figure 10.7, for example, demand curve $D_m^1(q)$ identifies the prices that may be charged for varying quantities of output for a single firm at a particular location given the prices charged by rival firms. A quantity of q_1 will command price P_1 under these circumstances. At higher prices some of this firm's customers will find it worthwhile to pay the transportation costs of dealing with its rivals; hence, it will sell less. At higher prices, those who continue to trade with this firm will also purchase less. Its demand curve, $D_m^1(q)$, slopes downward to the right for this reason. If, however, its rivals increase their prices, then more of the marginal demanders will find it economical to trade with this firm at each price than formerly. Its own demand curve will shift rightward under these circumstances, say, to $D_m^2(q)$. If it continues to supply q_1, the price will rise to P_2.

Costs of Information

Information costs operate in a similar way. In Chapter 6 we discussed how demanders faced with uncertainty concerning the quality of the merchandise they are considering will rely upon supplier reputations for this information. They will be willing to pay a somewhat higher price for a good whose quality they have confidence in than for a good about which they know little. This **brand loyalty** is the result of rational economic choice. Information concerning quality is costly to obtain, and reliance on the reputation of certain suppliers economizes on these costs.

However, as the price of a known good rises relative to the prices of its rival suppliers, the premium paid for this information increases. More customers will find it worthwhile to bear the costs of investigating the qualities of goods offered by other firms. The cost of this information will vary among customers, however, just as does transportation cost in the previous case. Some will regard the risk of unsuccessful experience in trials with alternative suppliers to be extremely costly. Others (perhaps of a more adventurous bent) will take it in stride.

Demanders may thus be arrayed along a continuum of knowledge concerning various competing products in the same way that they may be arrayed along a continuum of geography. For any constellation of prices charged by alternative suppliers, there will therefore likely be demanders close to the margin of experimenting with their products. If one supplier increases its price it will sell less but will not lose all of its customers. Some customers who were willing to pay a limited premium for the quality assured by this firm's reputation at the lower price will now experiment with alternative suppliers. Of these, some will be pleased with their experiments and will shift permanently to the rival brands. Even those who remain loyal to the original brand will purchase less due to the higher price.

Both of these market characteristics imply positive market power for suppliers. To the extent that transportation costs (locational convenience) or information costs (concerning product quality) are features of these environments, supplying firms will behave as price searchers. This discussion suggests the following implications concerning the market power of firms:

The more important the transportation costs relative to the money price of a good, the less elastic will be the demand for that good faced by supplying firms.

The greater the cost of determining the quality of a particular good relative to its money price through inspection or trial purchases, the less elastic will be the demand for that good faced by supplying firms.

Equilibrium with Transportation or Information Costs

The ultimate position of the demand curve faced by price-searching firms depends on the prices of rival firms. To determine an equilibrium for these firms we must therefore consider other prices and outputs. We may do this indirectly through refer-

Figure 10.8 *Equilibrium with Transportation Costs*

The firm originally faces demand curve D_1, which slopes downward; hence, marginal revenue lies below the demand curve at MR_1. The profit-maximizing output and scale for this firm are q_1 and ATC_1, which satisfy the output and scale criteria. Profits are earned in this situation equal to $q_1(P_1 - ATC_1)$. These profits will attract entry.

Entry of new firms must shift the demand curve leftward. As this occurs, profits to existing firms will diminish. In equilibrium the demand curve will shift leftward until it is just tangent to both the envelope and the ATC curves. Demand curve D_2 is such an equilibrium. Marginal cost equals marginal revenue at output q_2, and ATC_2 is tangent to the envelope curve at this output. Since there are no profits, entry will cease when this condition occurs.

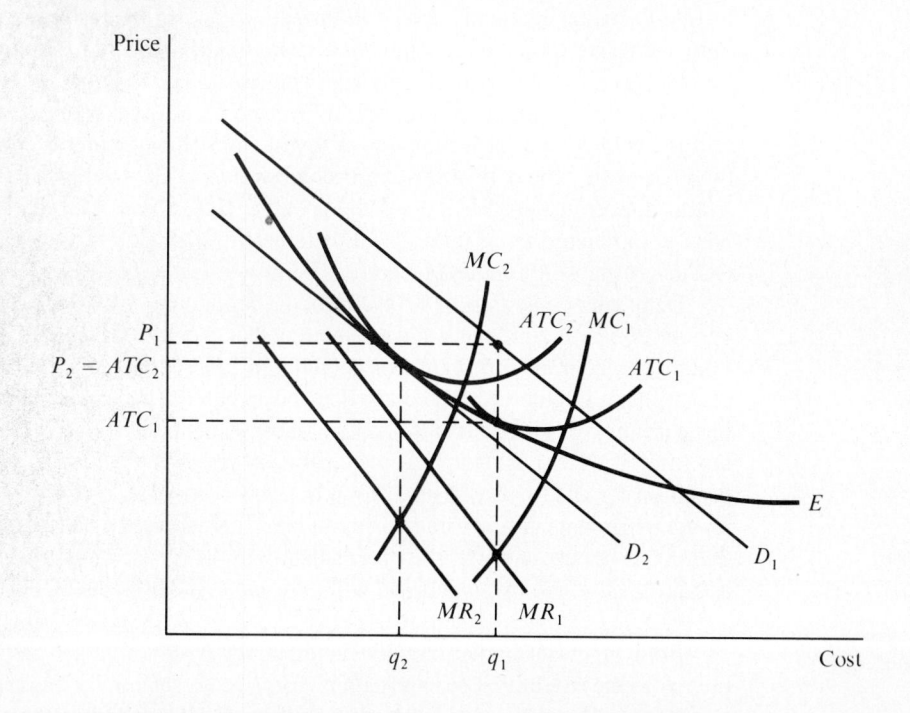

ence to the profit position of a single firm. Consider Figure 10.8, which depicts a portion of the envelope curve for a firm together with cost curves for two scales of operation. Assume initially that the demand curve for such a firm is D_1, with marginal revenue curve MR_1. This firm maximizes its profits by choosing the scale associated with ATC_1 and producing output q_1, at which marginal revenue is equal to marginal cost and the ATC is tangent to the envelope curve. Assume that demand curve D_1 has this slope due to its locational advantages relative to its customers. The situation depicted is not likely to be a long-run equilibrium, because there the firm earns positive profits. The market-clearing price of this output is P_1, while the average cost of that output is ATC_1. If this firm may earn profits at this price, other firms located elsewhere may be earning profits, too. New entrants will

Figure 10.9 *Entry with Transportation Costs*

Initially firms exist only at S_1 and S_2. Full price rises with distance from each supplier at a constant amount per unit per mile. If S_1 charges P_m^1 and S_2 charges P_m^2, then all customers to the left of location B will trade with S_1 and those to the right of B will buy from S_2. If a new firm, S_3, enters and charges P_m^1, both S_1 and S_2 will sell less at their original prices. Customers between C and D will now buy from S_3 if S_1 and S_2 continue to charge their original prices. If firms S_1 and S_2 both lower their prices, they will gain customers from S_3. Their demand curves therefore still slope downward, but each is shifted leftward.

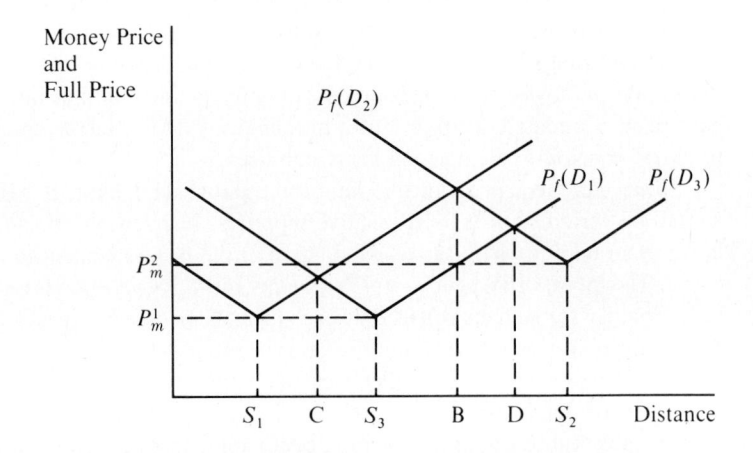

(Graph: Money Price and Full Price on vertical axis; Distance on horizontal axis with points S_1, C, S_3, B, D, S_2. Curves labeled $P_f(D_2)$, $P_f(D_1)$, $P_f(D_3)$. Horizontal dashed lines at P_m^2 and P_m^1.)

be enticed to locate among existing firms, lowering the transportation costs to some customers and drawing them away.

In Figure 10.9, for example, we show the effect of the entry of a new firm, S_3, between suppliers S_1 and S_2. Assume that the new supplier also charges price P_m^1.[1] Both original suppliers will now sell less at the prices formerly charged. Prior to the entry of firm S_3, supplier S_1 sold to all customers to the left of B and supplier S_2 sold to all customers to the right of B. Now, however, the full price to customers between C and D is less from S_3 than from either S_1 or S_2, and the quantities demanded of these firms at their original prices is now less. The reader will confirm that both S_1 and S_2 will sell less at every price than they might have prior to the entry of the new firm.

This loss of customers will shift demand to the left, as described above. In Figure 10.8 demand shifts to position D_2, and marginal revenue shifts to position MR_2. The firm must reduce scale, for at no output is the demand price along D_2 greater than the average cost of production with scale ATC_1. The best that it can do is select scale ATC_2 producing output q_2, where marginal revenue equals marginal

---

[1] Experimentation with a ruler will confirm that the point made here is valid for a range of prices. The equilibrium price will depend on the output and scale decisions of the three suppliers.

cost and the average cost curve is again tangent to the envelope curve. The firm earns neither profits nor losses in this situation, for the new market-clearing price of this output, P_2, is just equal to the average cost of producing it, ATC_2. Zero profits for existing firms will discourage further entry; hence, demand will likely become stable at position D_2, and long-run equilibrium will be achieved.

A similar narrative could be constructed based on information costs. Observation of firms earning profits through investing in reputations will encourage rival firms to adopt similar marketing procedures. This will lower the cost of determining the qualities of alternative suppliers, and erstwhile loyal customers will choose to try the new and highly advertised alternatives. This will shift the demand curves of the original firms leftward, with results similar to those depicted for the locationally advantaged firm. Confronted with shrinking demand, these firms must reduce scale and lower price. This process of entry should continue until their profits have been eliminated. Zero profits to the activity will discourage entry, and as entry stops demand to the original firms stabilizes.

What can we say about this long-run equilibrium? First, it will be characterized by varied pricing by alternative suppliers. The zero profit equilibrium will occur at an output where the demand curve of the firm is tangent to the envelope curve. This point of tangency (which also identifies price) depends on the shape of the particular demand curve faced by each firm. As demand curves will differ from firm to firm, so too will the equilibrium price differ.

More importantly, each seller faces an array of buyers with widely varying elasticities of demand. Those customers who are relatively close to a single seller or who face high costs of information concerning product quality will have relatively inelastic demand—they would "rather fight than switch." Those customers who are equidistant from many sellers or who are knowledgeable about the qualities of several competing products will have more elastic demands. Under these conditions, sellers will have strong profit motives to develop means of charging their customers different prices—that is, to price discriminate. Methods of price discrimination were discussed in Chapter 9. Our discussion here suggests two additional implications concerning the behavior of price searcher firms:

The more important the transportation costs relative to the money prices of goods, the more likely are we to observe price discrimination in their sale.

The greater the cost of determining the quality of particular goods relative to their money prices through inspection or trial purchases, the more likely are we to observe price discrimination in their sale.

10.3 Collusion

The final source of market power to a firm is not so much the product of its market environment as it is the result of the firm's efforts to change that environment in cooperation with other firms—a process called **collusion**. A single firm operating in a competitive environment will eventually reach the price taker's long-run equilibrium. A firm in this situation earns no profits; its demand curve is horizontal and tangent to the envelope curve, as described in Chapter 8. No firm will seek to alter its scale or level of output under these circumstances. To do so unilaterally would reduce profits. The reason for this is that the marginal revenue to a single price taker firm is the price itself, and changes in the level of output for a single firm have no effect on price.

If, however, all firms reduced output in concert, total industry supply would clearly be affected and price would rise. Furthermore, such a reduction would produce positive profits for all colluding firms. Firms that explicitly coordinate output changes in order to increase price are called **cartels**. Consider the effect of a cartel on prices and profits in Figure 10.10. Assume initially that each firm in the industry competes, producing the by-now familiar long-run equilibrium output, q_1, for each firm and employing the scale ATC_1, which produces this output at lowest cost. Although industry demand slopes downward to the right, this firm by itself has no influence on price; therefore, its demand curve, D_1, is horizontal at P_1, equal at all outputs to marginal revenue.

Figure 10.10 *Output and Price with and without Collusion*

If all firms in an industry act independently, none can have an appreciable effect on price—each is a price taker. Under these circumstances the demand curve for each firm will be D_1, and each firm will choose output q and scale ATC_1. Curve D_2, on the other hand, identifies market price if all firms modify output in unison. If *every* firm reduces output from q_1 to q_2, price will increase from P_1 to P_2. If firms can coordinate output changes in this way, the optimal output and scale will be q_2 and ATC_2, respectively.

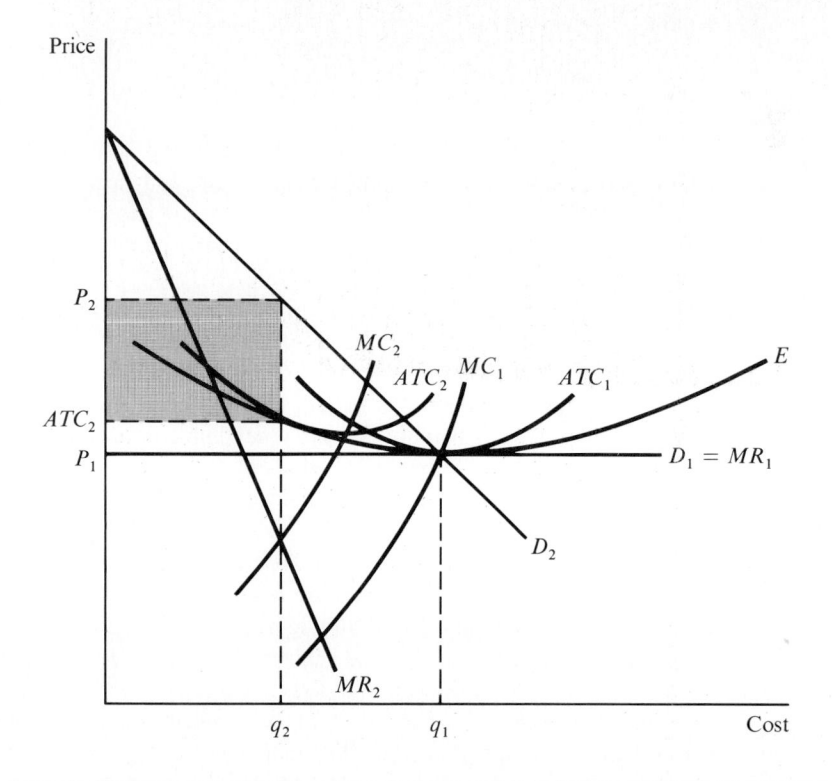

However, if all firms reduce their output together, price does not remain constant but rises as demanders bid up the market price of the diminishing supply. This rising price associated with lower outputs for colluding producers is traced out by curve D_2. It is important to note the distinction between curve D_2 and the demand curve faced by one of these colluding firms. The price–quantity path traced by D_2 will be observed *only if all firms produce identical output*. Once that market price is determined, any single firm may sell as much as it can produce without materially affecting price. In a sense, then, once the price is determined by the collusive reduction of output by all firms in the industry, the demand curve to a single firm is perfectly elastic at that price. We shall return to this point in our later discussion of the stability of a collusive equilibrium.

Does the possibility of higher prices for lower outputs actually *imply* greater profits through output restrictions for such firms? The answer to this question is an unambiguous yes. If each firm produces output q_1 price equals the average cost of production, and profits are zero. If each firm restricts its output to q_2, however, price rises to P_2 while average cost rises only to ATC_2. Profits for each firm are equal to the shaded area in the figure. The firm may continue to earn them only so long as each produces no more than q_2 units of output per time period.

So long as all cartel members cooperate, such an optimum is an equilibrium. For an industry with n firms, market output will be $n \cdot q_2$. There are reasons to believe, however, that such an equilibrium will be unstable in the long run. Expansion of industry output beyond this equilibrium level is predicted. Factors influencing the stability of such a collusive equilibrium will be discussed in the next section.

The Stability of Cartels

Two factors affect the stability of such an equilibrium: Individual cartel members are influenced to **chisel** on the collusive agreement, and the profits earned by cartel members will attract entry of additional firms. Both factors will have the effect of expanding supply and eroding the high prices produced through output restrictions of the colluding parties.

Consider the first of these factors. Each cartel member may either cooperate with other firms in the industry or chisel on the agreement. Each has only two options, but faces four possible outcomes. This ambiguity results from the fact that the outcome of either choice also depends on the choices made by the other members. Any single firm's output will have a negligible effect on price; hence, price will be determined by the output decisions of everyone else. Yet results for each firm depend not only on that price but on the output chosen in ignorance of what that price will be.

A description of these four possible outcomes is explained with the aid of Figure 10.11. As considerations of scale are not important to this discussion, we have deleted the envelope curve from this figure. The average cost curve depicted is that which corresponds to ATC_2 in Figure 10.10. The downward-sloping curve, D_c, corresponds to curve D_2 in that figure and identifies the prices obtainable if each firm cooperates. The curve MR_c likewise reflects the change in total revenue per unit change in the outputs of all colluding firms.

Figure 10.11 *Collusion from a Different Perspective*

This figure explains why price must rise above average total cost as firms collude. In Figure 10.10, at output q_1 marginal revenue was equal to average revenue, marginal cost, and average cost in the price taker case. That implies in this figure a tangency between the total cost and total revenue curves at q_1 at which the slopes of both curves reflect this magnitude. With collusion, however, price rises as output is restricted. Thus, the tangent of angle A, which is equal to price (average revenue) at q_3, must be higher than average cost at this output.

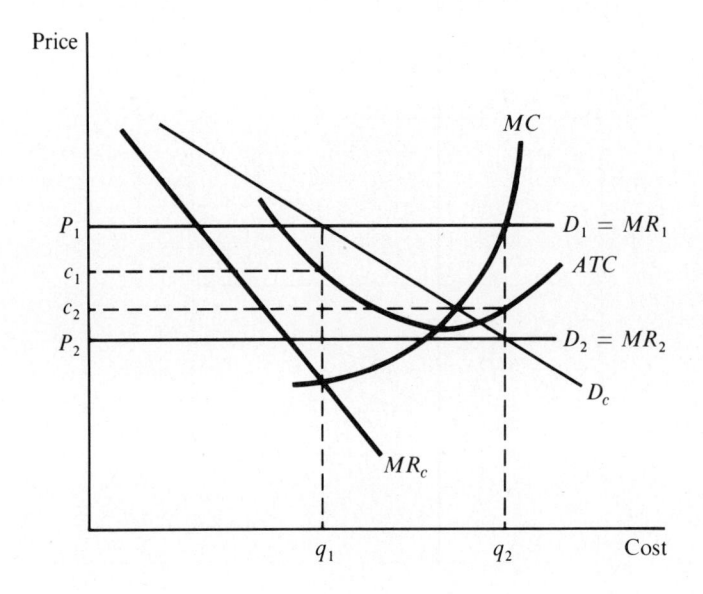

However, the actual demand curve faced by the cartel members is not D_c. As no cartel member alone influences price by changing its own output, the price is either P_1 or P_2, depending on whether all others cooperate and produce q_1 or chisel and produce q_2. The demand curve faced by each firm will be one of the horizontal lines at prices P_1 and P_2, and since these prices depend on the actions of others each firm will be uncertain which one it will face. Let us examine the results of a single firm cooperating and not cooperating in each case.

Case 1: If all other firms cooperate and restrict output while this firm does not, price will be P_1 and the lone firm's most profitable output will be q_2. Profits will be $q_2 \cdot (P_1 - c_2)$.

Case 2: If all other firms cooperate and this firm also cooperates by restricting output to q_1, price will also be P_1. Profits in this case will be $q_1 \cdot (P_1 - c_1)$.

Case 3: If all other firms chisel and produce q_2 and this firm also chisels, price will be P_2. Profits in this case will be negative, that is, $q_2 \cdot (P_2 - c_2)$.

Figure 10.12 *The Perils of Collusion*

This figure illustrates the possible outcomes of collusive arrangements. The individual firm has no control over price. If all restrict output, price will be P_1; if all chisel, price will be P_2. The firm may choose to produce only output q_1 or q_2, but the consequences of this choice depend on the behavior of others. Assume that all collude and price P_1 prevails. If the firm chooses to produce q_1, it will earn profits equal to $q_1 \cdot (P_1 - C_1)$. But if the firm chisels, it will earn the larger profits equal to $q_2 \cdot (P_1 - c_2)$. Now assume that others choose not to cooperate and price P_2 prevails. In both cases the firm will earn losses, but they will be smaller if the firm produces q_2 rather than q_1.

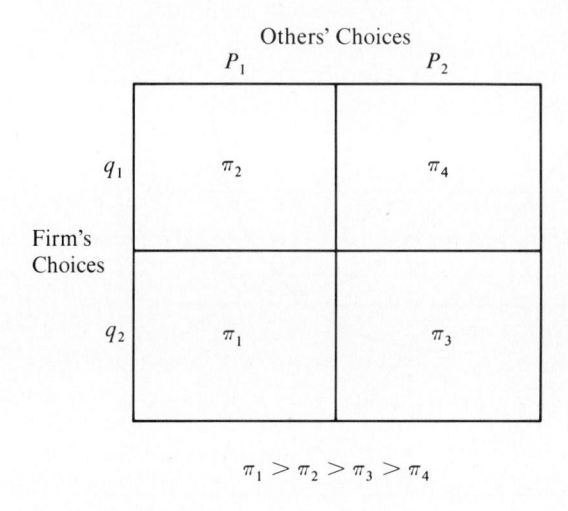

	Others' Choices	
	P_1	P_2
q_1 (Firm's Choices)	π_2	π_4
q_2	π_1	π_3

$\pi_1 > \pi_2 > \pi_3 > \pi_4$

Case 4: If all other firms chisel and produce q_2 while this firm cooperates and produces only q_1, price will still be P_2, but profits (losses) will total $q_1 \cdot (P_2 - c_1)$.

As Figure 10.12 shows, an examination of the individual profits (π_i) in each of these four cases reveals that profits diminish from Case 1 to Case 4; that is:

$$\pi_1 > \pi_2 > \pi_3 > \pi_4.$$

We may arrange this set of possible outcomes in a matrix as shown in the figure. The options available to the firm itself may be characterized as a choice of rows, while the effects of choices by other cartel members determine the column. Consider the results conditional upon each choice by the others. If the others cooperate and price P_1 prevails, the firm obtains π_2 if it cooperates and π_1 if it does not. If, on the other hand, the others chisel and price P_2 prevails, the firm will earn π_4 if it cooperates and π_3 if it does not. Regardless of what other firms do, each cartel member enjoys higher profits by chiseling and producing output q_2. If each firm rationally considers its options and behaves accordingly, cartels to restrict output should break down. The equilibrium resulting from this **game theory** approach to interdependent choice is not the collusive optimum of the upper left-hand corner of the matrix but the noncooperative result of the lower right.

We must qualify this result, however. Cartel members with any experience at attempting to form such collusive arrangements will be aware of this instability and attempt to build in policing mechanisms and **sanctions** to raise the cost of chiseling to each firm. All should willingly agree to such arrangements, since their failure to do so will insure that each receives only π_3 when the cartel breaks down, while uniform sanctions will foster the cooperative result of π_2 to each. Cartels are therefore more likely to flourish in industries in which information concerning the output of each firm is not costly to obtain and in which costs may be more readily imposed by one firm on another.

Certainly one of the most visible cartels in the world today is OPEC, the Organization of Petroleum Exporting Countries. United by opposition to Israel in the 1973 war with Egypt and Syria, OPEC declared an embargo of oil exports to the United States, perceived to be a supporter of Israel in this conflict. Out of this unity emerged agreements among OPEC members to dramatically reduce output and increase price. Reinforced by the overthrow of the Shah of Iran in 1979 and the ensuing upheavals in this major OPEC country, the high prices for crude persisted into the 1980s.

In 1973 few professional economists predicted such stability for the OPEC cartel. The potential gains from chiseling on this arrangement involved billions of dollars, and many of the cartel's member countries were desperately poor. Economists who predicted early failure of this cartel overlooked two decisive features of this particular collusion. First, oil shipments are easily monitored—indeed, they have been routinely reported for decades prior to the formation of OPEC. Chiseling by a member country is therefore easily detected. Second, the OPEC agreement was entered into by member *governments*. Unlike private firms, which may not even rely on the existing legal structure to exact sanctions against other firms that chisel, governments literally make their own rules. Failure to abide by international agreements may invoke far more serious penalties than possible with cartels of firms. A cynical economist would not be surprised, in retrospect, that a significant portion of the profits produced by the OPEC cartel have thus been devoted by member countries to the purchase of military hardware.

Monitoring the output of individual producers of many goods is far more costly than monitoring crude oil production. For some products it is so costly that chiseling by suppliers would ordinarily be impossible for a cartel to police. One method of dealing with this monitoring problem is to divide the market geographically, assigning each cartel member an exclusive territory into which it, and only it, may sell the product in question. This technique establishes each cartel member as an effective monopolist in its own territory and permits it to sell a restricted output in this market without fear that other producers will enter.

One cartel that successfully employs territorial divisions to accomplish monitoring of output exists in the markets for illegal gambling and narcotics. This cartel has been organized under the auspices of a group of suppliers known to the public as the "Mafia." We implicitly acknowledge the cartel structure of these markets by referring to these suppliers as "organized crime." The organized structure that we observe has as one of its chief objectives the restriction of output into these markets. The supplying of these illicit activities must be carried on beyond the surveillance of the police; hence, potential chiseling into a single market is far more difficult to detect than that of a "legitimate" cartel. For this reason, the Mafia has divided up its various markets into territories, awarded to individual "families." Each family has the exclusive right to sell drugs and gambling services in its own territory. It is therefore free to restrict its own output of these "goods" there without fear that it will be undercut by expanded output of other producers. Like OPEC, the Mafia has recourse to the use of violence to police observance of these arrangements.

Recognition of organized crime as a cartel poses a painful dilemma for Justice Department policymakers. Its very existence paradoxically serves to *reduce* the extent of this criminal activity. In its role as an effective monopolist over its territory, each family sells fewer narcotics and gambling services than it would were these activities organized competitively. Successful prosecution of Mafia leaders, which ultimately destroys these territorial arrangements, may therefore have the unfortunate effect of *increasing* the level of criminal activity.

Now consider the case of private firms. The outputs of firms engaged in the production of many products will be very difficult to monitor. Opportunities for undetected chiseling will be the more plentiful, and collusive agreements to restrict output will be more likely to break down. Lacking more forceful means of imposing sanctions, the firms' ability to police their agreements will be attenuated further. Also, such collusive arrangements to restrict output are illegal and subject to both criminal and civil action. Both monitoring and sanctions must therefore be carried on, like drug dealings, beyond the observation of others. In such an environment, even with lackadaisical enforcement, long-run prospects for collusive arrangements are not encouraging.

Collusion and Entry

Another source of instability to collusive equilibrium is entry by other firms into the cartelized industry. Output restrictions by cartel members will increase price above average cost. Firms that are not cartel members will perceive the possibility of earning profits by entering this industry, and some will do so. Unless a cartel can successfully prevent entry by outside firms into their industry, collusive output restrictions will be defeated by expansion of supply from this outside source. Industries that for one reason or another are less attractive for entry by outsiders than others will therefore be more likely to be successfully cartelized.

The critical role that entry conditions play in the competitive process has received widespread attention from economists. Some have argued that in many industries existing firms are protected by **barriers to entry**, which secure above-normal profits for them. Joe S. Bain, a leading proponent of this view, identifies three sources of such entry barriers: product differentiation, absolute cost advantages, and scale-based advantages.[2]

---

[2]Joe S. Bain, *Essays on Price Theory and Industrial Organization* (Boston: Little, Brown and Company, 1972), Chapter 7.

By **product differentiation** Bain means the preference that certain consumers have for the products of one supplier over equivalent products of new entrants. Bain notes that frequently such preferences are engendered by heavy expenditures on marketing by existing firms over extended periods of time. A measure of such product differentiation is the price elasticity of demand for a new seller's product. Certainly, if the price elasticity of demand for a new entrant's product is very low, entry to compete with existing firms will be less attractive than otherwise. Such a new entrant would have to charge very low prices to attract customers away from the established firms. These prices may be so low that potential profits would be eliminated. Collusive arrangements are therefore more likely to remain in effect in industries with heavy marketing expenditures and significant brand loyalty.

The second important barrier to entry, according to Bain, is **absolute cost advantage**. This may be due to superior productive technology being protected by patent or merely kept secret. It may be due to a few firms' exclusive access to key minerals or other resources used in the production process. Absolute cost advantage to a firm may result from convenient geographical location or from the exceptional talents of its managerial staff. Any of these characteristics may imply that the existing firm or firms in an industry may operate at lower cost (at any level of output) than may new entrants. Thus, even if existing firms had no marketing advantage and new entrants could sell their output competitively at the existing price, the latter would be at a cost disadvantage. Entry under such circumstances would be less attractive, even if existing firms were earning substantial profits. The higher costs of production predicted for new firms would diminish their profit opportunities. Collusive arrangements are therefore likely to be more stable in industries where existing firms enjoy such cost advantages.

The third barrier to entry noted by Bain is **cost advantages due to scale**. If scale economies are present over an extensive range of output, the capital requirements for entry may make it difficult for new firms to enter on a competitive basis. The risk of such a large-scale endeavor in an industry in which both management and workers lack firsthand knowledge may be so great that capital costs are prohibitively high. Many firms that are already large have grown with their industries and developed their skilled workforces and managers over an extended period of time. This extensive learning period may be indulged in by new entrants only at great cost. Were scale economies less important, new entrants could start small and assemble larger and larger teams over extended periods. The presence of significant economies of scale preclude this approach and can be expected to discourage entry.

However, one might easily exaggerate the importance of this barrier. Many skills and techniques are transferable from one industry to another, closely related industry at low cost. Firms that are already large stand ready to enter related industries offering profit opportunities and have the capital resources necessary to finance large-scale production. The persistent dominance of certain industries by a small number of very large firms cannot therefore be accepted as prima facie evidence of collusion supported by scale-related entry barriers. An alternative hypothesis is that existing firms are competing vigorously, and that the resulting absence of profits itself discourages entry (even by large firms in related industries that might be expected to survive). The empirical resolution between these competing hypotheses in particular cases is always difficult.

Augmented Collusion

So far we have seen that collusive arrangements to restrict output are vulnerable on two margins. On the one hand, individual cartel members have an incentive to chisel on these agreements and covertly expand output. Even if policing of output restrictions among colluding firms is perfect, however, output may be expanded from a second source. The profits earned by cartel members will attract entry of additional firms into the industry. This is not to say that collusion can never be successfully practiced. Many civil and criminal antitrust cases are prosecuted each year, and some result in findings of collusion. One purpose of the emphasis given to the features producing instability in collusive arrangements is to give the reader a proper appreciation of *demand by firms for additional stabilizing mechanisms*. As instability can result from chiseling by cartel members or from the entry of new firms, would-be colluders will value arrangements that police output and restrict entry.

We will discuss two such arrangements. Both involve support for the cartel from an unexpected ally. One of these is labor unions. Labor unions are exempt from antitrust legislation and hence may deal with an entire industry without fear of prosecution. They control both the supply of labor and work rules governing conditions of employment. If labor is limited to that industry and working conditions are controlled to prevent substitution of capital for labor, then the union effectively controls industry output. If demand diminishes or is incorrectly predicted so that excessive supply is available, industry output may be dramatically reduced through strikes. The union may therefore act to police the output of individual cartel members in the industry and has the power (through walkouts and other disciplinary tactics) to impose sanctions on those who seek to chisel on these agreements.

Consider the case of the coal mining industry. Explicit agreement among operators to restrict the output of coal is dangerous (since such arrangements always involve the risk of prosecution) and difficult to police. The United Mine Workers may indirectly limit this output, however, by controlling the number of miners in the mines, the hours they work, the length of vacations, and so on. When coal stocks grow excessive, causing price to fall below the desired level, a strike may be called, stopping production altogether. Why would a union participate in such an arrangement? Union cooperation may be purchased through higher wages paid out of the cartel profits. A convincing case has been made by Maloney, McCormick, and Tollison that unions can and have played a cartelizing role in successfully organized industries.[3]

The second type of arrangement for policing cartel output is government regulation. As we saw in Chapter 8, regulation of price and output can be an effective method of controlling industry output and restricting entry. There we discussed the role played by the Civil Aeronautics Board in protecting the profit positions of the commercial airlines it regulates. A recent study of Interstate Commerce Commission regulation of the trucking industry comes to a similar conclusion.[4]

---

[3] M. T. Maloney, R. E. McCormick, and R. D. Tollison, "Achieving Cartel Profits through Unionization," *Southern Economic Journal* 46 (October 1979): 628–634.

[4] Kenneth D. Boyer, "Equalizing Discrimination and Cartel Pricing in Transport Regulation," *Journal of Political Economy* 80, no. 2 (April 1981): 270–286.

10.4   Tactics That Don't Work

There are two strategies for consolidating market power that, though ineffective, are vigorously monitored and prosecuted by the Justice Department. The first of these is referred to as **predatory pricing**. In this scenario a single dominant firm or conspiracy of large firms lowers its price below average cost. Smaller firms in the industry must lower theirs in response and suffer losses. As large firms are perceived to be better able to sustain such losses and survive, the end result of this activity is to leave the large firm or group of firms as sole supplier in the industry. It is widely believed that John D. Rockefeller used this tactic to gain a very large market share of the petroleum industry for Standard Oil, driving smaller oil companies out of business, then expanding his own operations to fill the void.

There are both theoretical and empirical problems with this interpretation of the rise of Standard Oil. At the theoretical level we question the superior survivability of large firms engaged in such predatory pricing. In the absence of economies of scale, losses of large firms and of small firms will be proportional to output. Thus, although larger firms have more assets on which to draw to finance losses, those losses will be proportionately larger. There is no theoretical basis for the argument that ability to sustain business losses increases more than proportionately with the size of the business. Furthermore, even if the large firms are successful in driving out the smaller firms at substantial cost, what is to be gained from their doing so? As soon as price rises to the cartel optimum, entry of new firms can be counted upon to undo this result—and some of the new entrants may not be small.

This interpretation of the growth of Standard Oil has also been challenged on historical grounds. John McGee has examined this case in detail and found no evidence that predatory pricing was practiced by Rockefeller's company. On the contrary, Standard Oil's growth came principally through its purchase of smaller oil concerns, many of which were in sound financial condition on the date of purchase.[5] Purchase of and merger with rivals are clearly to the advantage of all the firms involved and will be preferred over the tactic of predatory pricing, which involves large losses for all in order for the large firm to gain even a short-run market advantage. A purchase or merger saves both large and small firms the sacrificed revenues of predatory pricing.

Such combinations for the purpose of restricting output have subsequently been made illegal. Firms today cannot employ the same technique used by Standard Oil to secure its market position. This does not imply, however, that predatory pricing will be adopted as a "second best" technique. In the absence of scale economies, lowering price below average cost is just as likely to jeopardize the fortunes of the large company practicing it as it is to drive out a small one. The advantages secured will be transitory; they will be dissipated by the entry of new firms as soon as price is increased to take advantage of the market power obtained. And, if the industry is characterized by economies of scale, predatory pricing will

---

[5] John S. McGee, "Predatory Price Cutting: The Standard Oil Case," *The Journal of Law and Economics* 1 (October 1958): 137–169.

not even be necessary to achieve the desired result. Normal competitive practice by large firms will force out smaller firms in the manner described earlier in connection with natural monopoly.

Vertical Integration

While merger of existing firms in an industry can lead to effective cartelization, this practice is now illegal and closely monitored by the Justice Department. Antitrust law has also been extended to apply to a second type of merger, which seems to offer little or no market advantage to the merging firms. This is a merger between firms performing upstream and downstream functions in the production of the same final product. This process is called **vertical integration** (the factors influencing this choice were discussed in Chapter 7). Examples of vertical integration are the purchase of a vineyard by a wine bottler, the purchase of a service station by an oil company, or the hiring of staff writers by a magazine. In each case, the two functions can be and quite frequently are performed by separate entities. Vintners quite often purchase grapes from independent growers, oil companies sell gasoline to independent service stations, and magazines purchase articles from free-lance writers.

How is this vertical integration perceived by the courts to impair competition? The courts have maintained that this process results in **foreclosure** of part of the market to rival firms. If an oil company purchases a service station, rival oil companies will no longer be able to sell to this station; their market is diminished by the loss of this potential purchaser. While one cannot deny the logic of this statement, good economics students will respond by asking "So what?" Will market output be restricted or market price of the final good be raised by the foreclosure of part of such a market by vertical integration? Economic analysis suggests that the answer to this question is no.

If vertical integration has any effect on output and price, theory suggests that output will expand and price will fall. Output, and therefore price, in the market for the final good produced and sold to consumers depends on cost and demand conditions in that market. Vertical integration cannot affect demand conditions and will, if anything, lower costs. The net effect of vertical integration therefore cannot lead to lower output and higher prices; it may, in fact, have the opposite result.

To question the appropriateness of vertical integration in markets is to raise the issue posed by Coase that we discussed in Chapter 7. After all, a firm is merely a collection of upstream and downstream functions coordinated through a single organization. Firms will seek to undertake further integration when the gains from displacing the market as a coordinator exceed the transaction costs. Firms that correctly perceive the opportunity to economize on these costs may actually *lower* the marginal cost of the process. Vertical integration may therefore have the effect of expanding output and lowering prices. An incorrect decision to merge, which increases cost, will, of course, have the opposite effect. However, in this connection it seems plausible to assume that the firms are in a better position to make these determinations than the courts. There seems little basis in economic analysis for the hostility of the courts to vertical integration.

Summary

In Chapter 9 we studied the output behavior of price searcher firms, noting two salient characteristics. First, price searchers will typically choose to produce an output at which price exceeds marginal cost. Second, where the market environment is conducive they will seek to charge different prices to different buyers—in other words, price discriminate. In this chapter we studied the underlying market conditions that make this behavior possible. We found that there are four basic sources of market power to individual firms: monopoly, location advantages, information costs, and collusion.

Monopoly is the easiest to deal with analytically. The demand curve of a monopolist slopes downward, because a monopolist is by definition the only supplier in the market. The demand curve of the monopolist is therefore the market demand curve. A firm's position as a monopolist derives either from government support and protection or from economies of scale. In some cases of monopoly, government protection is rationalized as being in the interest of promoting research and product development, as in the case of patents. In other cases, such as the delivery of first-class mail by the U. S. Postal Service, there seems to be no convincing economic rationale. Monopoly in the first case would not exist without some intervention by government. Monopoly in the second case is called natural monopoly and is the normal result of rivalrous behavior among firms in an industry. A natural monopoly may be influenced by an appropriately calculated price regulatory scheme to produce an output at which price equals marginal cost (which is less than average cost).

Location and information costs can both produce market conditions that influence the demand curves of firms. Excessive transportation costs (due to disadvantageous location of suppliers) and information costs can cause firms' demand curves to slope downward, even if there are many firms in the industry. This can best be understood by recalling the source of the perfect elasticity of demand faced by price taker firms. That elasticity occurs when any price increase above the market-clearing price for the industry causes a firm to lose all of its customers to rival firms. Obviously, this will occur only when shifting from one supplier to another is costless to buyers. Our treatment of both transportation and information costs explicitly introduced into the analysis ways in which such a shift may involve substantial costs. In such cases shifting from one supplier to another in response to a price increase clearly will not be undertaken universally. The fact that not all buyers will abandon a firm that increases its price implies some market power for that supplier.

Members of cartels may be thought of as price searchers only when they behave cooperatively. If each firm restricts output in conjunction with the others, total quantity available in the market will be reduced, and price will rise. A single member of a cartel has no influence over price, however, and thus must choose whether to behave as a price searcher or a price taker. When we examined the consequences of each option, we found that regardless of the choice of the others each firm is influenced to behave uncooperatively as a member of the cartel. In the absence of explicit monitoring of member output and some means of imposing sanctions on those who chisel, such collusive arrangements should break down. Cartels that lack forceful means of monitoring and sanctioning therefore survive best when these arrangements are augmented by some outside assistance. Two sources of such assistance are labor unions and government regulators. Both have the power to restrict output and punish chiselers.

We also discussed in this chapter two types of activity that, though regarded by the courts and by policymakers as anticompetitive, appear in our eyes to be perfectly harmless. These are predatory pricing and vertical integration. Predatory pricing has allegedly been used by large firms to drive small ones out of business. It involves charging prices that are lower than average costs, resulting in losses for all the firms involved. Large firms allegedly are better able to survive such losses. This strategy is questionable on theoretical grounds, and few convincing examples of successful price predation have been documented. Intuition suggests that most complaints of predatory pricing originate when an aggressive, efficient, and growing company begins to undercut its more complacent rivals. Prices offered by the former may indeed be lower than the average cost of the latter. If the costs of the challenging firm are lower than the other firms', however, the practice is not predatory pricing—it is merely good business.

The second seemingly innocent practice branded as anticompetitive by the courts is vertical integration. While it cannot be denied that this practice may foreclose markets for other, nonintegrated firms, the importance of such foreclosure to final product price and output is difficult to discern. Vertical integration has no effect on demand conditions in the market for final products and may quite plausibly lower marginal cost in that stage. If it has this salutary effect on cost, output of final goods will expand and price will fall. If the vertically integrated firm has incorrectly judged the gains and losses of this move and costs rise, profits will fall. We predict that firms will need no prodding by the Justice Department to correct such mistakes.

Key Concepts

monopoly
natural monopoly
location
information
full price
brand loyalty
collusion
cartels
chisel
policing cartel output

game theory
sanctions
barriers to entry
product differentiation
absolute cost advantage
cost advantages due to scale
predatory pricing
vertical integration
foreclosure

Questions

1. *Easy* A natural monopoly is a market in which the long-run equilibrium is characterized by the presence of a single firm. In one sense this is alleged to result from economies of scale. Explain this connection.

Hard Explain the method used to protect the market power of the following products or services:

    a. Telephone service
    b. Public schools
    c. Patents on pharmaceutical products
    d. Fire departments
    e. Concessions at sports events and in public buildings
    f. Public libraries
    g. Copyrights to textbooks

2. *Easy* Most cities have a single symphony orchestra. This means that each orchestra has a monopoly in the supply of live symphony music in its home town. Why don't the city fathers adopt a policy of supporting two orchestras, each of which might presumably play roughly half as often? Wouldn't this competition be beneficial?

Hard Most cities began to be wired for cable television on a large scale in the early 1980s. Typically, a single company was chosen to supply the cable service in each community. The argument for this granting of monopoly was that it was wasteful to have more than one cable strung down every residential street in town. (Presumably, all cable companies would provide identical programming.) In College Station, Texas, no monopoly was granted, and two companies wired the town. Charges for cable are roughly half as much there as they are in Atlanta, Georgia, which has a monopoly. What lessons can you draw from this? Can you draw parallels to this experience with other protected monopoly services?

3. *Easy* Explain how transportation costs can produce downward-sloping demand curves for rival firms in an industry even when there are many firms.

Hard Advocates of an extreme governmental antimonopoly policy argue that General Motors has too much market power by virtue of its dominant position in the American automobile industry. Defenders of General Motors, on the other hand, argue that it competes, not only with American producers, but with European and Japanese automakers as well. The transportation costs for automobiles from Europe and Japan are not trivial. Explain the relevance of this point to the argument concerning General Motors' market power.

4. *Easy* Explain how in a market in which transportation costs are important the entry of a single firm between two existing firms can shift the demand curve for each firm.

Hard It can be shown that under the simple assumptions made in connection with Figure 10.9, the entry of a new firm will affect the height of the demand curve but not the slope. Why is this true? What factors would influence the slopes of the demand curves of suppliers in this market?

5. *Easy* If profits of colluding firms are higher for all if everyone cooperates and restricts output than if they don't cooperate and each produces the output it prefers, why is it necessary to police the agreement and impose costly sanctions on those firms that don't cooperate? Won't they all cooperate without the threat of such sanctions?

Hard There are close parallels between the theory of cartel behavior and the theory of shirking discussed in Chapter 7. In what way is chiseling related to shirking? Why are we not disturbed when we imagine firms being formed to control shirking yet are troubled by the possibility that firms may successfully overcome the chiseling problem and successfully collude?

6. *Easy* Perfect policing of chiseling by a cartel will not ensure its indefinite enjoyment of monopoly profits. Explain why.

Hard Some American companies have greatly benefited from the restriction of output by OPEC and will not be pleased to see that cartel break up as it seems to be doing at the time of this writing. Who are these firms, and how have they benefited?

Part Four

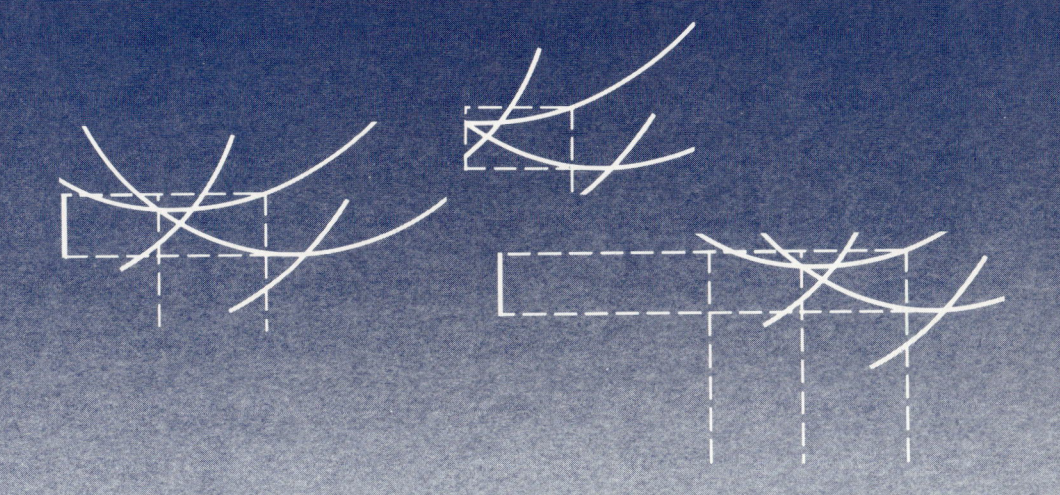

The Choice of Technology

Chapter 11

Production Theory: The Choice of Technology

Connections   This is the first of three chapters concerned with the choice of technology. In addition to choosing the rate of output, firms must adopt a technology of production. Profitability remains the yardstick by which alternatives in the opportunity set are ranked. In this chapter we develop most of the analytical tools with which this choice may be explored. In Chapters 12 and 13 these tools are applied to that choice in alternative market settings to develop the theory of the demand for factors of production.

There are many analogies between the theory of production and the theory of consumer choice. Firms choose combinations of inputs in ways that resemble the choice of combinations of goods by households. Inputs, like goods in the earlier theory, may be either normal or inferior. Conditions at chosen factor combinations are identified by the tangency of two curves. (A review of Chapters 4 and 5 may prove helpful in approaching this analysis.) There is also a close connection between production theory and cost theory; in fact, it is possible to derive the shapes of total cost curves and envelope curves from properties of the production function. As these connections form an important part of this chapter, the reader is urged to review the discussion of cost curves in Chapter 8.

In Part III of this text we were chiefly concerned with the responses of firms to changing conditions in the market for their output. We saw there that profit is the guiding consideration in these responses and that output influences choices through its effect on the two components of profit: revenue and cost. The centerpiece of this theory is the set of propositions concerning the relation of cost to output. Unless cost and output can be related in a systematic and unambiguous way, the entire apparatus of the theory of supply collapses in a heap. Without a theory of cost, no output can be shown to yield higher profits than another.

This presents a new set of problems for price theory, because for most production processes there are many different technologies that may be employed to produce a single output. The pyramids of Egypt were built with a great deal of labor and a few crude implements. Were we to reproduce them today we could use the same methods, or we might choose to use less labor together with pneumatic drills for quarrying the stone, heavy earth-moving equipment to prepare the foundation, and large cranes for placing the stones. The newer method would undoubtedly cost less than the old. In every case, where alternative technologies exist for producing a single quantity, the cost of producing that quantity will depend on the technology. How are we able to identify a specific cost of production for a particular output when that cost itself depends on the technology used? This chapter seeks to provide the answer to this question.

A second consideration of productive technology is the behavior in markets for the resources used. One of the principal concerns of classical economists was the determination of the prices paid to labor, capital, and land. This question of the distribution of income—that is, the share going to each group of suppliers—motivated the principal writings of Malthus, Ricardo, Senior, and, of course, Marx. Today we understand that the answer to these questions is inextricably linked to the previous question. The firm will seek to employ that quantity of each factor of production that minimizes the cost of the output produced. The determination of the price paid to each therefore involves the supplies and the demands by firms for cost-minimizing combinations of these resources.

11.1 The Production Function

Before we can address these concerns directly, we must introduce a new piece of analytical hardware that will allow us to deal with alternative technologies. This device is called a **production function**. It expresses the level of output in terms of varying quantities of the resources used. Most of the important properties of production functions may be illustrated using only two inputs, so we will assume that only two are employed despite the fact that most production involves the use of many. Let these resources remain anonymous for the time being; we will simply identify the quantity of one used as a and the quantity of the other used as b. Output (which we shall continue to designate q) may therefore be expressed as a function of the quantities of these two resources employed together; that is:

$$q = f(a, b).$$

Of course, we do not assume that the firm simply puts these resources into a box and shakes them up. If it did, output—and therefore the cost of output—would again be subject to precisely the sort of ambiguity we seek to eliminate in this chapter. On the contrary, we assume that the prevailing knowledge in any industry identifies some **maximum feasible output** with each combination of resources. Profit considerations influence managers of firms to produce that output with the resources at their disposal. The determination of this maximum is often condescendingly referred to by economists as "the engineering problem," which is another way of saying that we are glad that it isn't ours. This assumption permits us to assert that particular combinations of inputs imply a unique level of output, so that this relationship may be expressed as a function.

Total, Marginal, and Average Product

Functions with three variables pose some difficulty for economists who prefer to present their ideas in two-dimensional diagrams. This difficulty is typically surmounted by holding one of the three variables constant and observing the implied relationship between the remaining two. In production theory this is done in two different ways.

Total Product The first of these approaches holds the level of one input constant so that the relationship between the use of a single input and output may be analyzed. Fixing the level of input b converts our production function into a simpler expression involving only input a and output q; that is:

$$q = h(a).$$

The curve depicting this relationship is defined to be the **total product curve** for factor a.

The shape assumed for this total product curve is shown in panel (a) of Figure 11.1. The curve rises first at an increasing rate, so that it is concave upward. Then, at some point, the curve begins to rise at a decreasing rate. The slope here remains positive, but the curve becomes concave downward at this point. Finally, the total product curve reaches a maximum and turns downward.

Economists rationalize this shape in terms of precisely the same argument used to explain the shape of the marginal cost curve in Chapter 8. Assume that labor is the variable factor and that plant and equipment are held constant. For a plant of a given size, output from a small number of workers will be limited due to the requirement that workers must waste time moving from position to position. As the number of workers increases, each spends less time moving and more time performing a single task. Output will increase over this range at an increasing rate, due to two factors: (1) Each worker will spend more time producing and less time moving, and (2) each worker will perform better once permitted to specialize in his or her assigned task.

At some point in the employment of additional units of labor, gains from this source will cease. There will be little or no requirement for workers to move around, and each will have taken full advantage of the economies of specialization. Output will continue to increase as additional workers are employed by the

Figure 11.1 *Total Product and Marginal Physical Product Curves*

The total product curve (*TP*) in panel (a) slopes upward, first at an increasing rate, then at a decreasing rate, and finally reaches a peak. Use of additional units of factor *a* beyond that peak amount actually lowers output. The marginal physical product curve in panel (b) reflects the slope in panel (a). At quantity a_1 the slope of the total product curve reaches its steepest point. Curve MPP_a in panel (b) therefore has a peak at quantity a_1. At quantity a_2 the slope of the total product curve is zero; hence, curve MPP_a crosses the horizontal axis at this quantity.

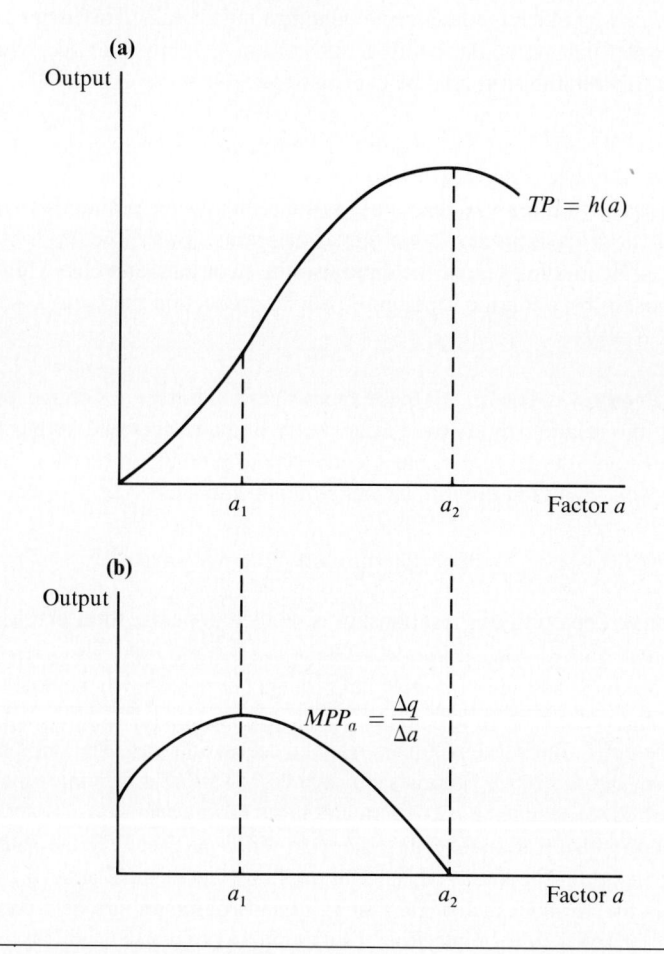

(a) Output

$TP = h(a)$

a_1, a_2, Factor *a*

(b) Output

$MPP_a = \dfrac{\Delta q}{\Delta a}$

a_1, a_2, Factor *a*

firm, but some crowding in workplaces will inhibit productivity. Each additional unit of labor will therefore add to total output, but each will add less than the previous increment. The total product curve will be concave downward over this range.

Finally, the point will be reached at which workplaces are so overcrowded that total output is actually diminished. Workers crowded into these stations will merely get in the way of those already there, deterring their performance of assigned tasks. This is not to say that firms would ever choose to employ such a quantity of labor with the fixed plant and equipment assumed. The point of this exercise is merely to describe the relationship between quantities of a factor and output over the full range of employment levels for that factor. Just as we recognize that "too many cooks spoil the broth," or that too much fertilizer may actually impair the productivity of a garden, we see that the inevitable turning downward of the total product curve merely expresses a relationship between inputs and outputs. It does not suggest that such technologies will ever be employed.

Marginal Product The rate of change in output per unit change in the level of a factor employed ($\Delta q/\Delta a$) is defined to be the **marginal physical product** (MPP_a) of the factor a. This ratio of changes in outputs and inputs will itself depend on the quantity of the variable factor used. It will thus be a function of that quantity, and the shape of that function is depicted in panel (b) of Figure 11.1. Its relationship to the total product curve is exactly that between total and marginal curves describing output and cost and output and revenue. As the total product curve relates the *level* of output to the quantity of the variable factor used, the *slope* of this curve will itself measure MPP_a, that is, $\Delta q/\Delta a$. Where the total product curve is concave upward, this slope is positive and increasing. The value of MPP_a and therefore the height of this curve in panel (b) will therefore be positive and increase over this range. At quantity a_1, the slope of the total product curve ceases to get steeper and begins to get flatter. Over the range of input from a_1 to a_2, this slope is positive but decreasing. Thus, curve MPP_a in panel (b) is shown to be positive but decreasing. Finally, at the peak of the total product curve this slope reaches zero and becomes negative. In panel (b) MPP_a intersects the a axis at a_2 and becomes increasingly negative beyond that point.

Average Product Just as it is useful to develop a notion of average cost and revenue, economists have found it useful to analyze the behavior of **average product** (AP_a) as the level of one input changes. Average product of factor a is simply total product divided by the quantity of the variable input employed, that is, $h(a)/a$. It will vary with the level of input a and may therefore itself be expressed as a function of the quantity of factor a employed. The shape of this function is depicted in panel (b) of Figure 11.2.

We may derive its shape and relationship to MPP_a by observing the geometrical counterparts of these two curves in panel (a). Average product, being the ratio of output to input, may be thought of as the slope of a ray from the origin to the total product curve. For example, the average product of input a_1 is equal to the tangent of angle ϕ, the lower left-hand corner of a right triangle whose sides are q_1 and a_1. As the ray from the origin to the total product curve at a_1 intersects the total product curve from above, we know that the slope of this ray is less than the slope of the total product curve at this input quantity. Average product must therefore be less than marginal physical product at a_1.

Marginal physical product reaches a maximum at input quantity a_2, at which the total product curve ceases to become concave upward and becomes concave downward. Readers may confirm with a ruler that although average product at a_2

Figure 11.2 *Marginal Physical Product and Average Product*

Average product is geometrically represented as the slope of a ray from the origin to the point on the total product curve associated with the quantity of the variable factor employed. The average product of quantity a_1 is therefore the tangent of ϕ equal to q_1/a_1. At quantities a_1 and a_2 the slopes of the total product curve exceed the slopes of rays from the origin; marginal physical product therefore exceeds average product at these two quantities. The slope of the ray and the slope of TP are equal at quantity a_3 indicating that the average and marginal physical products are equal at this quantity. The average product and marginal physical product curves in panel (b) reflect these observations.

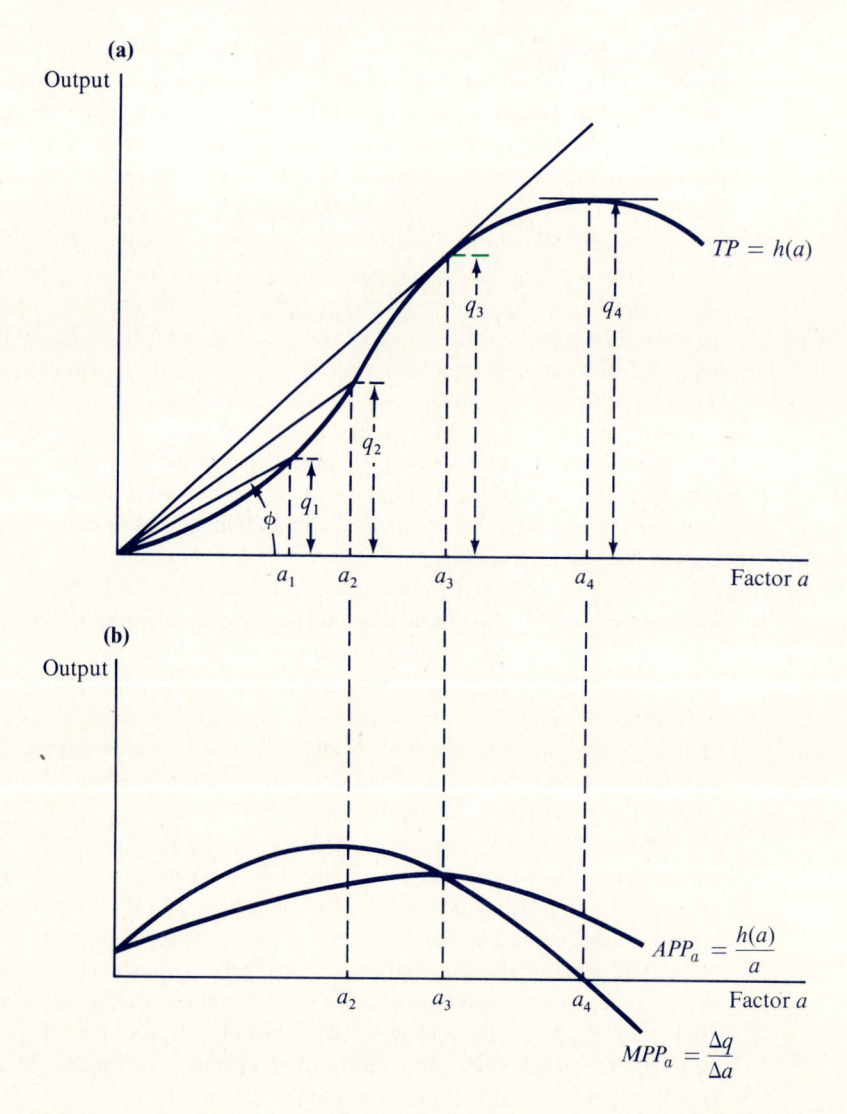

has grown larger compared to its value at a_1 so has MPP_a, with the result that MPP_a must exceed AP_a at the maximum value for the former. Beyond this input level, however, AP_a continues to increase while MPP_a falls. At the input quantity at which a ray from the origin is just tangent to the total product curve, AP_a will just equal MPP_a. The slope of the ray will just equal the slope of the total product curve at this quantity. Beyond that level, AP_a will exceed MPP_a. Average product of a factor will be zero only when the total product curve itself falls to zero.

Diminishing Returns

We may summarize the foregoing discussion in terms of the following statement frequently characterized by economists as the **law of diminishing returns**.

Law of Diminishing Returns: As the quantity of a single factor employed in production is expanded while the quantities of all others do not vary, marginal, average, and total products will each eventually diminish in that order.

As is true of the laws of demand and supply, the law of diminishing returns cannot be proven. It is merely a summary statement of the assumptions embodied in the shape of the total product curve that are based on the perceptions of economists concerning real-world productive relationships. Although it may not be logically proven, it may be refuted by empirical observation. That no evidence inconsistent with this law has come to light suggests that exceptions are rare, if not altogether nonexistent.

Varying the Fixed Factor

A somewhat fuller picture of productive relationships between inputs and outputs may be obtained by depicting simultaneously several members of the family of total product curves. Recall that there is a different total product curve for each level of factor b held constant. If b is held constant at a larger value, the output obtainable with a given quantity of factor a will itself be larger so long as factor b has a positive MPP over the range of the increase. Thus, in Figure 11.3 total product curve TP_2, employing more b than TP_1, is associated with a higher output for the use of each quantity of factor a than TP_1. Curve TP_2 lies above TP_1.

Let us be more specific about the levels of b employed in each curve in Figure 11.3. Assume that TP_2 identifies the level of output associated with the use of a for 1.5 times the quantity of b employed in TP_1. Assume further that curve TP_3 is associated with twice the factor b used in TP_1. Note the height of each curve as the use of factor a is increased by the same multiples. Use of a_1 units of this factor is associated with q_1 units of output along TP_1. By expanding its use by a factor of 1.5 and observing the height of TP_2, we may identify the level of output associated with an increase in both factors of this same proportion. That output is shown to be $1.5q_1$, an increase of the same proportion as the increase in inputs. Similarly, the height of curve TP_3 at twice the level of factor a indicates exactly twice the output produced along TP_1 at a_1. *A line connecting all such points on successively higher total product curves involving proportional increases in both factors reveals the response of changes in output to changes in scale.* This relationship has important implications for long-run cost and supply.

Figure 11.3   *Constant Returns to Scale*

The three total product curves depicted here reflect a production function with constant returns to scale. Curve TP_2 is associated with 1.5 times the amount of fixed factor b as TP_1. At quantity $1.5a$ both factors are therefore increased by 50 percent of the quantity employed along TP_1 at quantity a. Output associated with quantity $1.5a$ along TP_2 is 1.5 times the output associated with quantity a_1 along TP_1. Curve TP_3 is associated with twice the quantity of factor b as TP_1, and likewise yields $2q_1$ at quantity $2a_1$.

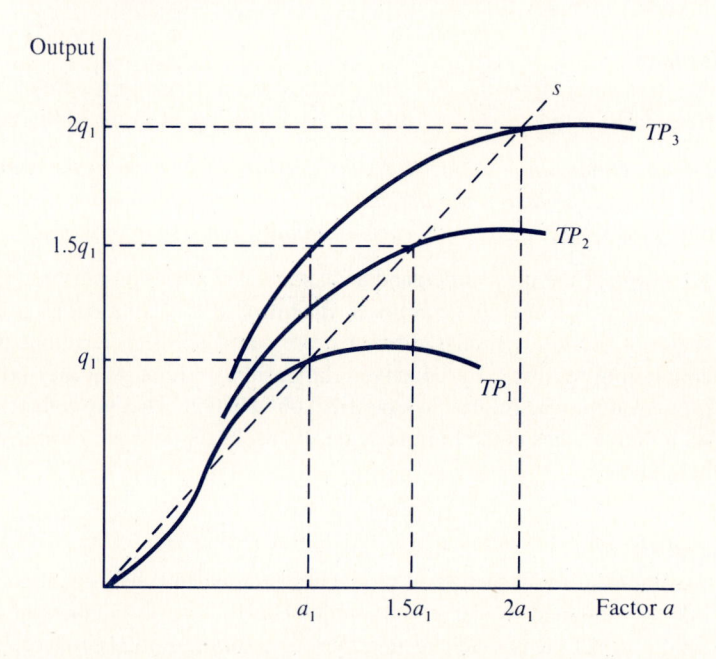

Returns to Scale and Cost

Let us be more specific. If the relationship between combinations of input and output is given by the function $q = f(a, b)$, the effect of a proportional change in input use by a factor of s to output is thus given by the following expression:

$$s_1 f(a, b) = f(s_2 a, s_2 b).$$

We may categorize the response of changes in output to proportional changes in inputs using this expression. Returns to scale may be either increasing, decreasing, or constant according to the following relationships between s_1 and s_2.

$s_1 > s_2$: Increasing returns to scale
$s_1 < s_2$: Decreasing returns to scale
$s_1 = s_2$: Constant returns to scale

A proportional increase in inputs that produces an increase in output of a larger proportion is said to reflect **increasing returns to scale**, while the opposite result reflects **decreasing returns to scale**. Where inputs and outputs change in exactly the same proportion, the production function is said to exhibit **constant returns to scale**.

Now let us consider the implications of returns to scale for the cost functions of firms. Let there be decreasing returns to scale. Assume that the firm is a price-taking demander of resources a and b, so that total cost may be expressed as

$$c = P_a a + P_b b,$$

that is, the sum of spending on each resource. Assume also that the combination chosen minimizes the cost of producing a particular output. Now let the use of each factor be increased by the same proportion, s, such that:

$$s = \frac{\Delta a}{a} = \frac{\Delta b}{b}.$$

The change in expenditure for each of the factors is given by

$$\Delta c_a = P_a \Delta a$$

and

$$\Delta c_b = P_b \Delta b.$$

Hence, the percentage change for each is given by:

$$\frac{\Delta c_a}{c_a} = \frac{P_a \Delta a}{P_a a} = \frac{\Delta c_b}{c_b} = \frac{P_b \Delta b}{P_b b} = s.$$

As each component of total cost c increases by a given factor s, the sum itself is increased by s, so that:

$$\frac{\Delta c}{c} = s.$$

For production under decreasing returns to scale, output q must expand by less than the rate of increase in factor use; that is:

$$\frac{\Delta q}{q} < s.$$

Hence, substituting for the change in scale s gives:

$$\frac{\Delta q}{q} < \frac{\Delta c}{c}.$$

Output increases by a smaller percentage than cost; cost *per unit* must therefore increase. This may be seen another way by simply cross-multiplying, obtaining:

$$\frac{c}{q} < \frac{\Delta c}{\Delta q}.$$

The left-hand side of this expression is total cost divided by output—that is, average cost. The right-hand side is the rate of change in cost per unit change in output—marginal cost. The expression therefore tells us that, under conditions of decreasing returns to scale, average cost is less than marginal cost. As we saw in Chapter 8, average costs must be rising with output where this is true.

Of course, where returns to scale are constant, output will increase in the same proportion as cost. Average cost will equal marginal cost; it neither rises nor falls. In the case of increasing returns to scale, output increases more rapidly than cost, and average cost declines with output.

There is a direct correspondence between production functions and cost functions. Economists have used this **duality** property of the theory of the firm to great advantage. In Chapter 8 we discussed at great length the importance of the choice of scale to the theory of the supply of the firm. Here those factors influencing the shape of the envelope curve have been shown to be describable as well in terms of properties of the production function. When the envelope curve has a negative slope, production exhibits increasing returns; when it turns upward, production is characterized by decreasing returns. With this new vantage point, it will prove helpful to return to our discussion of the choice of scale.

An Ambiguity: Do All Factors Vary?

When viewed in one light, the assumption of almost universal constant returns to scale has great appeal. If output is merely the product of combining given quantities of resources in a certain way, how can returns to scale ever be anything but constant? If doubling the quantities of all resources fails to double output when put together one way, it must be possible (or so it would seem) to construct two identical factories and obtain twice the output that way.

One response to this argument is to note that in some cases, at least, there are factors influencing output that are beyond the control of firm management, and hence may not be increased along with other factors in the same proportion. Factors like morale, teamwork, and imagination exist for certain organizations within firms but are difficult to transfer to others. The owner of the Philadelphia Seventy-Sixers might (NBA rules permitting) purchase another franchise and staff it with 11 players who are, man for man, as good as each player on his present team. However, we cannot be sure that such a team would enjoy nearly the success of Doctor J and company. The film *Rocky* was an enormously profitable enterprise. However, when Sylvester Stallone attempted to combine many of the same actors, situations, and settings in subsequent films, the results were far less satisfying and financially successful. We should thus expect there to be decreasing returns to scale in such enterprises and therefore increasing costs.

Similarly, certain features of the production process change when scale is expanded, even when new facilities are simply cloned from existing ones. In Chapter 8 we discussed the informational problems of management as the organization expands. Doubling the number of managers will not in itself guarantee sufficient management, because a new layer of management will be needed to manage the managers. Production must be planned and coordinated within a firm. These tasks are not merely enlarged as firms themselves grow; they are transformed into more remote, more abstract, and riskier undertakings. If information were costless (and management were therefore valueless), constant returns to scale might be a reasonable characterization of the representative firm. The fact that information is not costless suggests that firms eventually experience increasing costs.

11.2 The Other Perspective

Isoquants

Earlier we noted that there are two approaches to a two-dimensional diagrammatic presentation of production functions. One of these approaches is the total product curve. To use the second approach, we must hold output itself constant and observe the implied relationship between the quantity of one factor and the quantity of the other necessary to produce a given level of output. Holding output in our original production function constant at $\bar{q}$ gives:

$$\bar{q} = f(a, b).$$

This may be expressed as:

$$b = j(a).$$

The name given to this function is the **isoquant**. It identifies pairs of quantities each of which may be employed to produce a given level of output.

Unlike with the indifference curves developed in Chapter 3, we cannot in this case precisely derive uniform slopes and shapes from fundamental assumptions. Isoquants may be either positively or negatively sloped and may be concave or convex. Fortunately for economics students, these ambiguities are nevertheless resolved for all cases with which we commonly deal. Before proceeding to a discussion of these complications and their solution, let us consider some special cases of isoquants for production functions with particular properties.

Fixed Proportions

Some production processes exhibit very little substitutability among factors. Reductions in the use of one input are difficult to compensate for with increases in others. The limiting case of this lack of substitutability is the case of **fixed proportions**. Output is increased only when *both* factors are increased; increased use of only one does not increase output. An example of such a production process is the quantity of musical performance on a clarinet. Giving each musician two or more clarinets is not likely to increase the amount of music played in a single sitting, nor will crowding several musicians around a single instrument.

Isoquants for the fixed-proportions case are shown in Figure 11.4. The same level of output, q_2, is produced by combining b_2 units of factor b with either a_2 or

Figure 11.4   Isoquants for Fixed Proportions Production

At factor combination (a_1, b_1), increasing use of one factor without increasing use of the other leaves output unchanged. A higher isoquant may be reached only by increasing use of both factors.

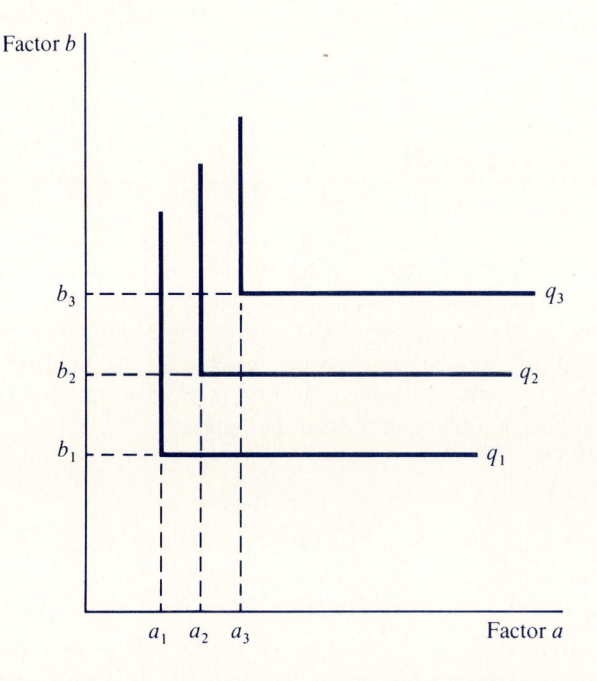

[Figure: L-shaped isoquants q_1, q_2, q_3 with corners at (a_1, b_1), (a_2, b_2), (a_3, b_3) on axes Factor a (horizontal) and Factor b (vertical).]

a_3 units of factor a. Combining b_2 units of b with only a_1 units of a reduces output to q_1, because at least a_2 units of a are required to produce output q_2. Similarly, the same output, q_2, can be produced by combining a_2 with either b_2 or b_3 units of factor b. Reducing the use of factor b to b_1 would reduce output to q_1 in this case. The isoquant derived by holding output constant at q_2 is therefore L shaped, being vertical at a_2 and horizontal at b_2. Each combination of factors a and b along this curve produces the same output, q_2. All combinations that lie closer to at least one axis are associated with a lower output and lie on a "lower" isoquant. Combinations that lie further from both axes are associated with larger outputs and lie on "higher" isoquants.

Perfect Substitutes

At the opposite extreme from the case of fixed proportions is the case of **perfect substitutes**. In these production processes the productive capabilities of the two resources are identical; hence, they may be used interchangeably without effect on production. Examples of such substitutes are solid gold hammers and steel hammers. They do not have to cost the same; it is enough that they may be used inter-

Figure 11.5   *Isoquants for Perfect Substitutes*

Isoquants for perfect substitutes are linear, reflecting that replacement of any quantity of one input with the other in the same proportions always has the same influence on output.

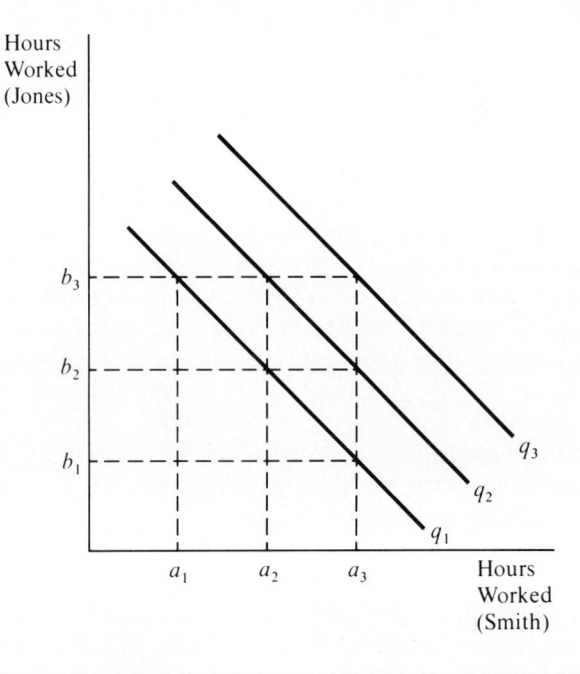

changeably without affecting production. Another example is workers named Smith and workers named Jones. (Some might regard this division of factors as excessively fine, but it illustrates our point.) When we substitute a typical Smith for a typical Jones, we do not affect the level of output. Isoquants for perfect substitutes are diagonal lines with a slope of -1.

Three such isoquants are depicted in Figure 11.5. Let b measure the hours worked by Jones and a measure the hours worked by Smith. Note that along isoquants like q_1 the total number of hours worked by both remains the same. The quantity $a_1 + b_3$ is equal to the quantity $a_2 + b_2$, which in turn is equal to the quantity $a_3 + b_1$. If Smith and Jones are truly interchangeable, then output will remain constant over each combination. Each combination will lie on the same isoquant.

The Rate of Technical Substitution

The slope of isoquants plays a very important role in the theory of production and factor demand. It is therefore very important to fully understand the interpretation given to this slope. Literally, it measures the change in the use of one factor per unit change in the use of the other—that is, $\Delta b/\Delta a$ as output is held constant.

Consider *why* there is an implied change in the use of factor b as factor a is increased: An increase in the use of one factor will increase output. As the isoquant function holds output constant, some decrease in the use of b is made necessary by the increase in the use of a.

A common-sense explanation will be offered first. The expression for this slope, $\Delta b/\Delta a$, has a quantity of b in the numerator, Δb, and a quantity of a in the denominator, Δa. It is a ratio of implied changes, and we may approach the interpretation of the slope by determining the values of these two changes themselves.

We begin with the numerator. Let us assume that we wish to make a particular reduction in output by reducing the use of factor b only. At this point the exact reduction in output is arbitrary, so let that desired change, Δq, be 6 units of output. How are we to know by how much to reduce the use of b to produce the desired reduction of 6 units? We divide Δq by the marginal physical product of factor b. If a single unit reduction in b reduces output at a rate equal to MPP_b, then the change in b necessary to reduce output by Δq units is $\Delta q/MPP_b$. If MPP_b happens to be 2, for example, then a reduction of 3 units of b would yield the desired output reduction of 6 units; that is, $6/2 = 3$. For the Δb in the numerator we may substitute $\Delta q/MPP_b$.

Now let us consider the change in the use of a in the denominator. Here again we are concerned with the relationship between a change in the use of this factor and the implied change in output. A given increase in output of Δq requires an increase in the use of a equal to $\Delta q/MPP_a$. We may therefore substitute this expression for Δa in the denominator.

The isoquant function $b = j(a)$ requires that output be held constant as a and b vary. We may interpret this as requiring that the Δqs in the numerator and denominator be equal in value but opposite in sign. Making the implied substitutions, inverting, and multiplying therefore yield the following:

$$\frac{\Delta b}{\Delta a} = \frac{\frac{\Delta q_b}{MPP_b}}{\frac{\Delta q_a}{MPP_a}} = \frac{\Delta q_b}{\Delta q_a} \cdot \frac{MPP_a}{MPP_b} = -\frac{MPP_a}{MPP_b},$$

where

$$\Delta q_a = -\Delta q_b.$$

The slope of the isoquant must therefore equal minus the ratio of the marginal physical products of factors a and b.

This may be shown more directly with reference to the production function itself, $q = f(a, b)$. The total differential of this function is given by:

$$\Delta q = \frac{\Delta q}{\Delta a} \cdot \Delta a + \frac{\Delta q}{\Delta b} \cdot \Delta b.$$

Noting that the change in output is held constant along an isoquant, we may set the right-hand side of this expression equal to zero. Solving for the slope $\Delta b/\Delta a$ therefore gives:

$$\frac{\Delta b}{\Delta a} = -\frac{\dfrac{\Delta q}{\Delta a}}{\dfrac{\Delta q}{\Delta b}} = -\frac{MPP_a}{MPP_b}$$

Again, the slope of the isoquant must equal the ratio of the marginal physical products of the two factors.

The ratio of the marginal physical products of factors of production is referred to with such frequency in economic theory that it has been given a name. It is called the **rate of technical substitution (RTS)**. In general, the slope of an isoquant will be equal to minus the rate of technical substitution. Consider the two extreme cases of production functions just considered. Rates of technical substitution for those characterized by fixed proportions are either zero (when MPP_a is zero) or infinite (when MPP_b is zero). In the case of perfect substitutability, the rate of technical substitution is constant and equal to 1. This is consistent with our understanding that the factors are perfectly substitutable; hence, the marginal physical products will always be the same in the denominator and numerator.

Most cases that we will wish to analyze fall somewhere in between these two extremes. Factors may be substituted for each other in production, but this substitution is not perfect. The nature of the productive features of these resources varies so that they are used in different ways. In agriculture, for example, the same output can be obtained with fewer workers and more land or with less land and more workers. However, the rate at which these resources can be substituted for each other will not remain constant. As one resource becomes scarcer relative to the other, constant increments of one will take the place of decreasing increments of the other. For dissimilar factors such as labor and land, the slope of the isoquant (and therefore the rate of technical substitution) will not remain constant but will vary predictably as one factor becomes scarcer and the other more plentiful. This argument provides the intuitive basis for another law governing the nature of production functions: the **law of diminishing RTS**:

Law of Diminishing RTS: As the quantity of any factor increases along a given isoquant, the RTS of that factor for the other will diminish so long as the marginal physical product of both factors is positive.

Figure 11.6 depicts isoquants exhibiting this property.

Now we may consider some of the complications regarding the shapes of isoquants whose existence was noted at the beginning of our discussion. As was pointed out in connection with total product curves, the marginal physical product of a factor eventually becomes negative as its use is expanded. At some point along an isoquant the slope must therefore turn positive. In Figure 11.6, for example, if factor *a* continues to be added to production along isoquant q_1, its marginal physical product will eventually become negative. At this point increased use of *a* no longer substitutes for factor *b*. Increased use of factor *a* by itself will reduce output. It must therefore be introduced *with more of factor b* if output is to be held constant. Positive changes in *b* are required with increases in the use of *a* in this region. The slope of the isoquant must be positive here. This may be confirmed by noting that the slope of an isoquant is $-MPP_a/MPP_b$; if either marginal physical product is negative, this implies a positively sloped isoquant.

Figure 11.6 *Isoquants with Diminishing RTS*

Combinations (a_1, b_1) and (a_2, b_2) both lie on isoquant q_1. As the latter combination contains more of factor a, the law of diminishing RTS states that the rate of technical substitution of a for b must be lower here. The slope of an isoquant is equal to minus the RTS of the factor combination at that point. The slope of isoquant q_1 must therefore be less steep at (a_2, b_2). Isoquants must therefore be convex downward.

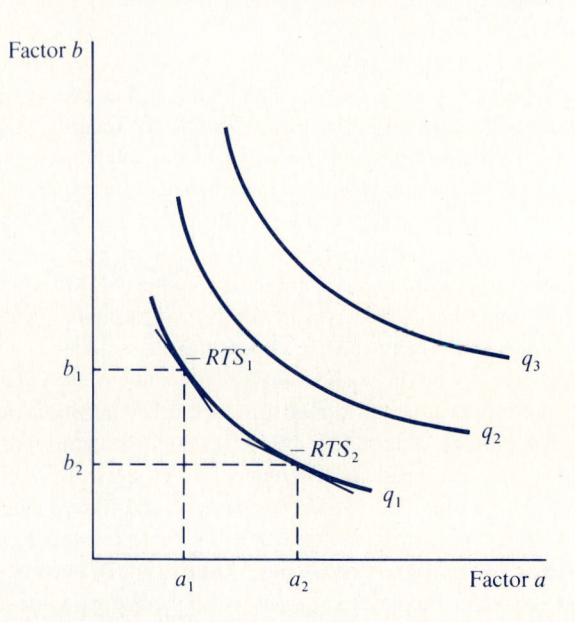

Isoquants can also become concave downward in a region in which one factor has a negative marginal physical product. Fortunately, we need not concern ourselves with the details of these portions of isoquants. We are developing our theory to explain the choice of technology by firms—and no firm will knowingly employ so much of any factor that its marginal physical product is negative. To do so would involve paying for additional inputs that would reduce output. Clearly this is not a profit-maximizing strategy. We will therefore concern ourselves only with the positively sloped portions of isoquants where both marginal physical products are positive. The law of diminishing RTS will apply to the full length of isoquants in this range.

Isoquants and Returns to Scale

Recall that returns to scale identify the relationship between proportional changes in input and output. Returns to scale therefore have important implications for the shape and position of isoquants. These are illustrated in Figure 11.7. Each panel contains two rays from the origin, each of which connects all possible combinations of the two factors in the same proportions. Along r_1 in each panel, for example, we find combination (a_1, b_1) and combination $(2a_1, 2b_1)$. The ratio of a to b

Figure 11.7 Isoquants and Returns to Scale

The three panels of this figure illustrate the three possible cases for returns to scale. Panel (a) contains the increasing returns case. Doubling the quantities of inputs along r_1 and r_2 results in more than double the output. Constant returns is shown in panel (b). Doubling the inputs results in precisely double the output, regardless of the ratio of quantities used. Panel (c) illustrates the decreasing returns case. Doubling the inputs results in output q_3, which is less than twice the original output.

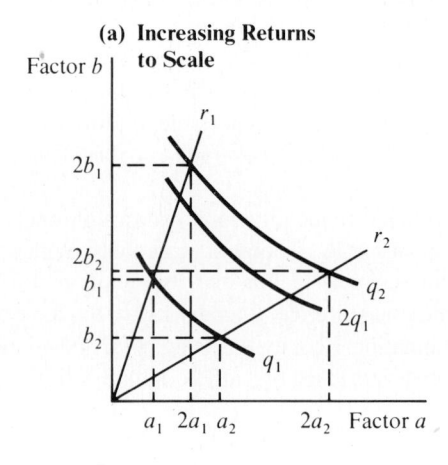

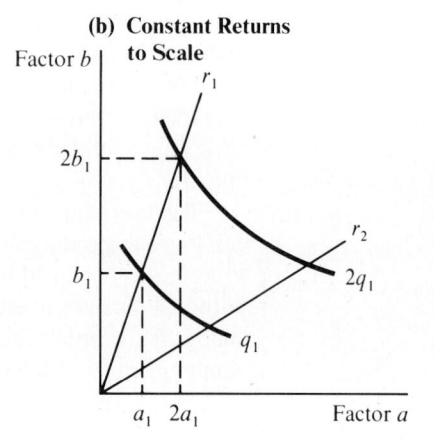

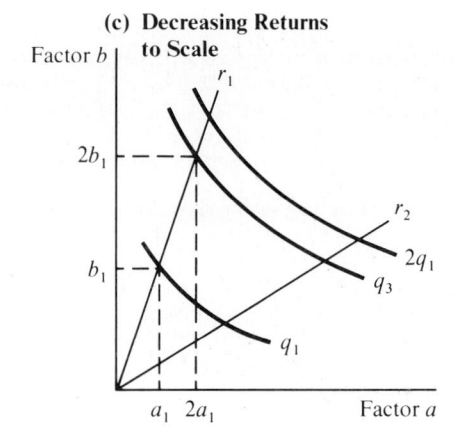

is clearly the same at both points in the input space. The same is true along the second ray, r_2, which connects point (a_2, b_2) and point $(2a_2, 2b_2)$.

As we examine input combinations and the output they produce, we observe that panel (a) exhibits increasing returns to scale, panel (b) exhibits constant returns to scale, and panel (c) exhibits decreasing returns to scale. Consider panel (a). Doubling the level of all inputs along r_1 or r_2 increases output from q_1 to q_2. Since q_2 is greater than $2q_1$, output has increased by more than a factor of 2. Output increases in this panel by a greater proportion than factor use has increased, regardless of the initial ratio of inputs. Panel (c) illustrates the opposite relationship. Doubling all inputs here produces only q_3, which is clearly less than $2q_1$. Output in this case therefore increases by less than the proportion by which inputs were changed. Panel (b) represents the constant returns to scale case. A doubling of inputs here increases output by precisely that proportion.

Economists frequently find it convenient to assume that production functions have constant returns to scale. One of the useful properties of such production functions is that the RTS depends only on the *ratio* of inputs. For any combinations of two factors in the same ratio, the RTS will have the same value. A formal proof of this theorem would require more knowledge of the properties of functions than many economics students possess. It is possible to illustrate its validity, however, using only the geometry we have developed so far. This is done in Figure 11.8.

The two isoquants in the figure identify combinations of inputs which may be employed to produce 10 and 15 units of output respectively. With constant returns to scale, proportional increases in all factors increase output proportionately. Proportional changes in employment are identified by rays from the origin such as r_1 and r_2. For example, combination T contains 32 units of a and 44 units of b. If the employment of both factors is increased by half, combination H is used containing

Figure 11.8 *Scale and the RTS*

For a constant returns to scale production function the RTS depends only on the ratio of the quantities of the factors used. This is illustrated here using discrete changes along the two isoquants shown. The slope of $q = 10$ is $(40 - 44)/(48 - 32)$ which is equal to $-1/4$. The slope of $q = 15$ is $(60 - 66)/(72 - 48)$ which is equal to $-1/4$, also. As the RTS is equal to minus the slope of the isoquant, the RTS must be the same over this interval when all inputs were increased by half.

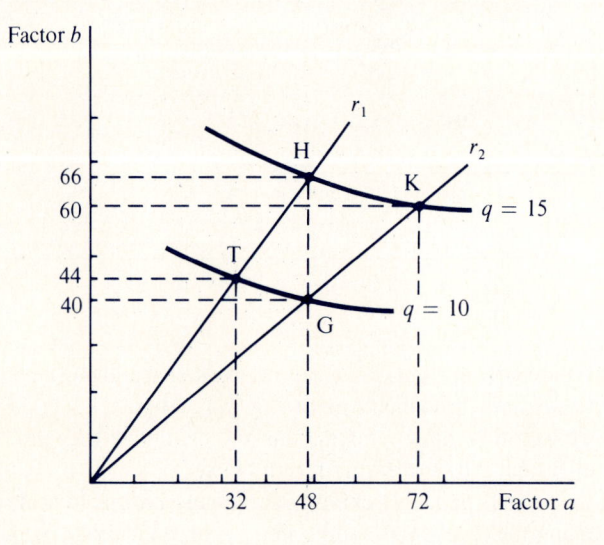

48 units of a and 66 of b, and output should also increase by this proportion. Combination H must therefore lie on the isoquant for 15 units. Similarly, combination K contains 50 percent more of each factor than combination G.

We wish to show that the RTS for this production function depends only on the ratio of the inputs. That will be true, if the slopes of the two isoquants are the same across the intervals identified by r_1 and r_2. Recall that the slope of an isoquant is ratio of the change in the quantity of b employed to the change in the quantity of a employed along the isoquant. Since the RTS is minus the slope of the isoquant, these values may be read off the isoquants and the RTSs computed:

$$\text{RTS}_{10} = -\frac{40-44}{48-32} = -\frac{-4}{16} = \frac{1}{4}$$

$$\text{RTS}_{15} = -\frac{60-66}{72-48} = -\frac{-6}{24} = \frac{1}{4}$$

This has been shown for proportional discrete changes in factor a to permit geometric treatment. However, the same argument could be made with smaller changes as the slope of r_2 approaches that of r_1.

Technical Change

It bears repeating at this stage that in order to use production functions we must assume a given "state of the art" in production. Technological progress may make it possible to increase output for a given combination of factors. If our production functions are intended to map input combinations into particular levels of output, we must hold constant such change. We must therefore make a careful distinction in our language between **technical change**, which involves a shift in production functions due to technological progress (or, as in the Middle Ages, technological retrogression) and the less complicated concept of a **change in technology**, involving merely a substitution of one factor for the other.

This distinction is illustrated in Figure 11.9. In panel (a) we have an example of technical change. Prior to the innovation producing the change, the isoquant associated with output q lay in the position indicated by the solid line. This output could be produced with combination (a_1, b_1), combination (a_2, b_2), or any other combination identified by the unbroken isoquant. Development of new knowledge and production techniques may imply that the same output can be obtained with fewer inputs. Such a change will shift all isoquants inward. For example, technical change may shift isoquant q to a position like that indicated by the broken isoquant, q'. This same level of output can now be produced with a combination of factors like (a_3, b_3), containing less of both than either of the former combinations.

In panel (b) we have an example of a change in technology. Output q was formerly produced using combination (a_1, b_1). The economic environment may influence a firm to alter the combination of factors used to produce this output. It may, for example, decide to switch to combination (a_2, b_2). A change in relative prices may influence the firm to make such a substitution. The firm is now using a different technology. It now employs more of factor a and less of factor b to pro-

Figure 11.9   *Technical Change and a Change in Technology*

Panel (a) illustrates technical change. Originally quantity q could be produced with any combination along isoquant q, including combinations (a_1, b_1) and (a_2, b_2). Technical change shifts the isoquant associated with this output inward to the position of the broken line, isoquant q'. This output can now be produced with combination (a_3, b_3), which contains less of both inputs than either combination noted before the technical change.

Panel (b) illustrates a change in technology. With any "state of the art," a firm may choose any factor combination along a given isoquant to produce that output.

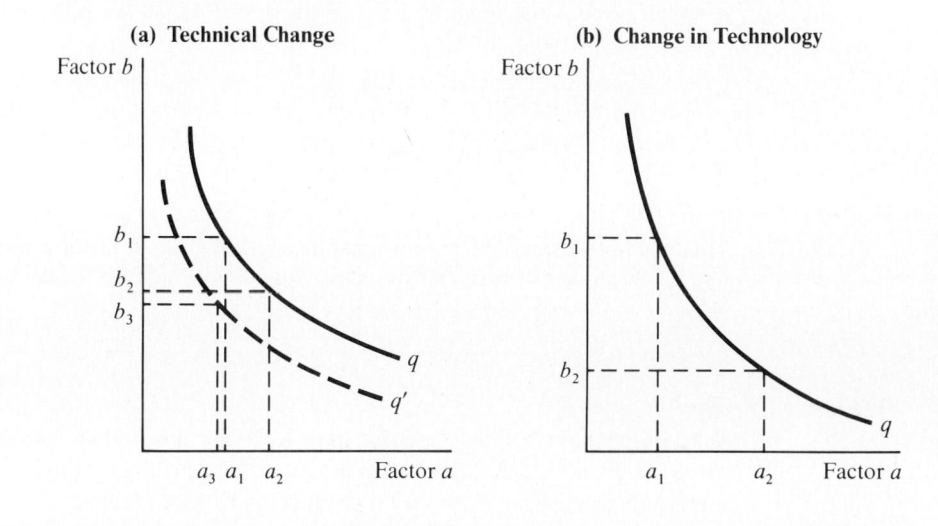

duce the same output that it produced formerly with a different technology. In spite of this change in technology, there has been no technical change. The underlying relationships between input combinations and output have not been affected.

11.3 Choosing the Technology

We can now develop the theory of the choice of technology. At any point in time the "state of the art" is given. The production function identifies the level of output that may be produced with any factor combination. Our problem therefore reduces to a completely straightforward application of choice theory to the selection of the most preferred technology. To do this we must again identify the two components of such a choice, the rank-ordering process and the opportunity set.

As in the theory of output, the rank-ordering process assumed is profit maximization. Owners seek to increase their wealth and thus direct the management of their firms to pursue policies consistent with this aim. Identification of the opportunity set for this choice is more complex. In essence, the opportunity set consists of all input combinations that permit the firm to break even. We shall simplify this decision, however, by recognizing that factors influencing the choice of output have already been treated. We can therefore analyze the choice of technology under the assumption that output has already been chosen.

In Chapter 8 we noted that these two decisions cannot really be made independently. The choice of output depends on cost—which depends, of course, on technology. The choice of technology similarly depends on output. It is nevertheless useful to separate the two components of this decision, recognizing that neither can be decided in isolation.

If output has already been chosen, the opportunity set of factor combinations reduces to those combinations identified by a single isoquant. Each combination may be employed to produce the chosen output, but only one is presumably associated with the maximum achievable profit. Our task is to discover which combination in this opportunity set maximizes profit and, more importantly, to identify necessary conditions for the employment of that technology. This identification is facilitated by the use of another curve in the input space, the isocost curve.

The **isocost curve**, like the isoquant, is a way of representing a three-variable relationship in two dimensions. In this case the variables are related to *cost* rather than output. Total expenditure on a particular input combination is determined by factor prices P_a and P_b and the quantities of each employed as follows:

$$c = P_a a + P_b b.$$

Solving this expression for the quantity of factor b used gives this familiar-looking expression:

$$b = \frac{c}{P_b} - \frac{P_a}{P_b} \cdot a.$$

This looks very much like a budget constraint, but we should not let appearances deceive us. The firm has no budget. This expression merely tells us what combinations of factors a and b can be purchased for the same expenditure, c. However, we have not yet determined finally what c is to be. For any particular value of c, this expression gives us an isocost curve that is linear and slopes downward to the right. The lower the total expenditure, the lower will be the vertical intercept of the appropriate isocost curve. The slopes of all such isocost curves are everywhere equal to $-P_a/P_b$.

Recall that profit is the difference between total revenue and total cost. If output has already been determined, then so has total revenue (that is, $P_q q$). To maximize profits, the firm must simply find the input combination along isoquant q that produces this output most economically. Since the costs of all input combinations on the isoquant are ranked by the isocost curve on which they lie, the problem reduces *to finding the combination of inputs on this isoquant that lies on the lowest isocost curve*. Such a combination is depicted in Figure 11.10.

In this figure we depict three isocost curves, each of which differs only to the extent of the expenditure on factors a and b. The highest curve is associated with the largest expenditure, since its vertical intercept, c_1/P_b, differs from the others only by the cost term in the numerator. Combination T, which lies on this isoquant, is therefore more costly than combination K, which lies on a lower isocost

Figure 11.10 *Cost Minimization*

Three isocost curves are shown here, identifying in each case combinations of the two factors that can be purchased at the same cost. Expenditure is indexed by the vertical intercept, whose numerator contains total expenditure c_i. Combination H is therefore the lowest-cost combination on isoquant q; no other combination lying on q can be purchased at a lower cost. Combination H is identified by a tangency between the isoquant and the isocost curve. At this point the slope of the isoquant $-RTS$ must be equal to the slope of the isocost curve, $-P_a/P_b$.

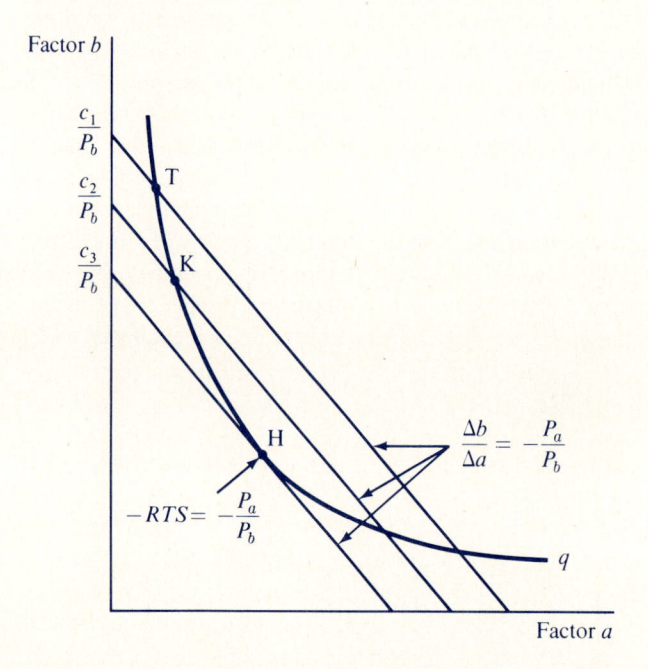

curve. However, combination K is not the lowest-cost combination along isoquant q, for other combinations containing less of factor b and more of factor a lie below the isocost curve passing through K. Clearly, the lowest-cost combination of resources that can produce output q is that indicated by combination H. No other combination in the opportunity set lies on a lower isocost curve.

Conditions at the Optimum

Note that the lowest-cost combination must involve a tangency between the isoquant q and an isocost curve. An intersection of the isoquant and isocost curve implies that some points on the isoquant lie below the isocost curve that is intersected. Only when the combination chosen lies at a point of tangency will this not be the case. From this tangency we may derive a necessary condition for profit maximization concerning the choice of technology. Only at such a tangency will the slopes of the two curves be equal. The slope of an isoquant is minus the rate of technical substitution. The slope of the isocost curve is minus the price ratio. **Cost minimization** for production of any level of output therefore requires the following:

(11.1) $$\frac{MPP_a}{MPP_b} = RTS = \frac{P_a}{P_b}.$$

By cross-multiplying this expression, we obtain:

$$\frac{MPP_a}{P_a} = \frac{MPP_b}{P_b}.$$

This has a common-sense interpretation. It tells us that costs of production are minimized only if the gain in output per dollar spent is equal for every factor at the margin.

Output Expansion Path

A firm will seek to minimize cost regardless of the output it chooses. It will therefore choose combinations of inputs that satisfy condition (11.1) on whatever isoquant reflects its output. We may identify a curve that connects all such combinations that will be chosen for a given price ratio. This curve is called an **output expansion path (OEP)**. There is an infinite number of output expansion paths, one for each price ratio. Two pairs are illustrated in Figure 11.11.

Geometrically the OEP curves are identical to the ICCs of consumer choice theory. They connect all points on a family of convex curves that have the same slope. The similarity extends to the slopes of the OEPs themselves. Just as in consumer choice theory we had to make provision for the possibility of normal and inferior goods, here we must note that it is possible for individual inputs to be normal or inferior. A normal good is one whose use expands with income, holding prices constant. A normal input is one whose employment expands with output, holding input prices constant. Similarly, an input is inferior if its use in production diminishes as output expands, holding prices constant.

Recall that the slopes of the ICC curves reflected the responsiveness of demand to changes in income. The slopes of the OEPs here reflect the responsiveness of employment of the two factors to changes in output. If both inputs are normal, the OEP must be positively sloped. If one of the inputs is inferior, the slope of the OEP must be negative. Panel (a) of Figure 11.11 identifies two output expansion paths for two normal inputs. Let the prices of inputs *a* and *b* be P_a^1 and P_b^1. A firm minimizes the cost of producing output q_1 by choosing combination T, at which the rate of technical substitution is the ratio of these prices. The higher output q_2 is produced using combination K with these prices. Combinations T and K therefore lie on the same output expansion path, OEP_1. This OEP connects all combinations of inputs for which the RTS is equal to P_a^1/P_b^1. Note that combination K contains more *a* and more *b* than does combination T. Both factors are therefore normal inputs.

Assume now that factor prices change so that the ratio P_a^2/P_b^2 is larger than the previous price ratio. The cost-minimizing combination of the two factors for the

Figure 11.11 Output Expansion Paths

Output expansion paths (OEP) identify the cost-minimizing input combination for producing each level of output holding the input price ratio constant. Cost minimization implies that $RTS = P_a/P_b$. The output expansion path therefore connects all combinations of inputs for which the RTS is the same. Panel (a) illustrates two examples of OEPs for normal inputs. Panel (b) depicts a pair of OEPs in which factor a is an inferior input. Both inputs cannot be inferior.

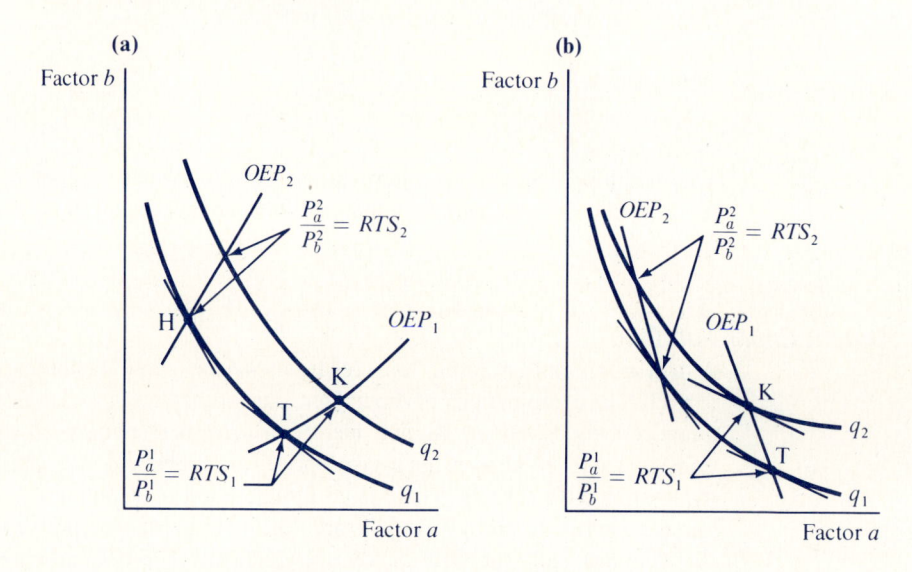

production of output q_1 is no longer combination T. The RTS for this combination is smaller than the new price ratio, for it is equal to P_a^1/P_b^1. A combination on the steeper portion of the isoquant will be chosen at these prices. Assume that it is H. Combination H therefore lies on a different output expansion path, OEP_2, along which all combinations of inputs have the higher rate of technical substitution equal to P_a^2/P_b^2. The slope of this OEP is also positive, indicating that both a and b are normal inputs at this price ratio as well.

Panel (b) depicts a pair of output expansion paths involving an inferior input. The expansion path associated with the lower price ratio P_a^1/P_b^1 is labeled OEP_1. Clearly, as output expands in this case more of factor b is employed, *but less of factor a is used*. Factor a is therefore an inferior input, giving the OEP its negative slope in this case. At a higher price ratio, combinations of inputs along OEP_2 in panel (b) would be chosen. Factor a would also be inferior along this output expansion path.

Many of the same rules apply to the identification of inferior inputs that worked for inferior goods in Chapter 4. An input defined broadly is likely to be normal; an input defined narrowly is more likely to be inferior. Carpentry equipment is certainly a normal input in the building of houses. Building houses at a more rapid rate requires more carpenters and more equipment, but individual tools may be inferior. Hand saws probably dominate in the construction of dog and bird houses. As the rate of output expands, however, such hand tools are abandoned in favor of high-powered electric rotary saws. Any designation of an input as being of a particular *scale* is almost certain to imply that it will be inferior over some range of output. Small buildings are inferior for enterprises whose output expands to require greater room than they offer; medium-size buildings are inferior over a somewhat larger range of output, and so on. On the other hand, buildings broadly defined are certainly normal inputs in almost every production process.

Elasticity of Substitution

Earlier in this chapter we introduced the possibility of substitution of factors of production by examining two polar cases: fixed proportions and perfect substitutes. In the first case, factors are not substitutable at all; in the second case, they are continuously interchangeable. Most production functions of concern to us lie somewhere between the two, yet some will exhibit greater substitutability than others. Having described the choice of factors by a profit-maximizing firm, we can now be more explicit about the interpretation of "substitutability" and develop a precise measurement of this characteristic.

Consider Figure 11.12. In this figure we depict isoquants for two different production functions. Rates of technical substitution are equal on these two isoquants at points T and G and at points K and H. Let the former be RTS_t and the latter be RTS_k. Assume that initial prices of factors a and b are such that the price ratio P_a/P_b is equal to RTS_t. A firm producing q_i units of good i will minimize its costs by using input combination (a_1, b_1). The ratio of these inputs, b_1/a_1, is equal to the slope of ray r_1. Now let this factor price ratio change so that it is equal to RTS_k. This price change will lead the firm to substitute factor b for factor a, employing the new cost-minimizing combination, (a_2, b_2). The new factor ratio, b_2/a_2, is equal to the slope of ray r_2. Note that the same change in factor prices would result in a smaller change in the proportions of factors employed along isoquant q_j. This is readily observable, because the slope of ray r_3 is smaller than the slope of ray r_2.

The degree of substitutability of two factors is therefore measured by the implied change in the ratio in which they are used to a change in rates of technical substitution, or factor prices. It is convenient to express this change in percentage terms so that the resulting expression will be an elasticity. The formal definition of this **elasticity of substitution** is given by:

$$\sigma = \frac{\dfrac{\Delta(b/a)}{b/a}}{\dfrac{\Delta RTS}{RTS}}$$

Note first that the elasticity of substitution will always be positive. An increase in the RTS implies a move to a point on the isoquant with a steeper slope. Given our assumption of convexity of isoquants (that is, diminishing RTS), this move must be to a combination containing a *higher* ratio of factor b to factor a.

Second, note that as the rates of technical substitution before and after the change are the same for the two isoquants in Figure 11.12, the percentage change in the denominator of the expression for σ is the same for both isoquants. It differs

Figure 11.12 *Elasticity of Substitution*

The elasticity of substitution expresses the ratio of the percentage change in the factor employment ratio and the percentage change in the RTS. The factor employment ratio is the slope of a ray from the origin to the combination of factors employed. The percentage change in the slope of such a ray is the numerator of this ratio. The denominator of this ratio is the percentage change in the slopes of the isoquants at two points. The "before" and "after" slopes of the two isoquants depicted here are the same. The percentage change in the denominator of the elasticity of substitution will be the same in each case. The change in the slope of the ray from r_1 to r_2 is greater than the change in the slope to r_3. Isoquant q_i therefore has a greater elasticity of substitution.

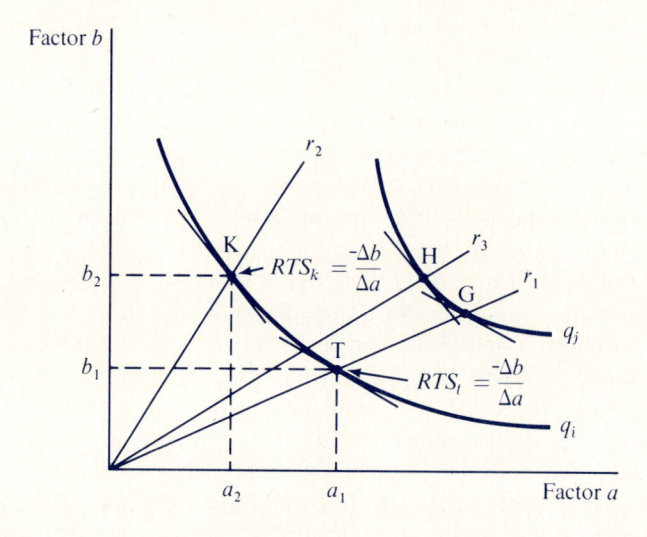

between them only in terms of the percentage change in the factor use ratio. The original factor ratio is the same for both at combination T and combination G. The change along isoquant q_i is larger than the change along q_j. It must therefore be the case that the elasticity of substitution along the former is greater than along the latter.

Third, for constant returns to scale production functions the elasticity of substitution depends only on the factor price ratio. Earlier in this chapter it was shown that for production functions that exhibit constant returns to scale, the RTS depends only on the ratio of inputs. For these production functions any factor ratio in the numerator of the expression for σ is associated with a particular RTS in the denominator, *regardless of output*. As this will be true for any combination of a and b producing a given ratio, we see that the elasticity of substitution is independent of the level of output and will be the same when evaluated along any isoquant intersecting a particular ray such as r_1. Just as it is often convenient to assume that demand functions have constant price elasticity at every quantity, it is often assumed for empirical purposes that production functions have constant elasticity of substitution at every factor ratio.

Elasticity of Substitution and Factor Income Shares

Now let us turn to an important application of the elasticity of substitution: changes in the relative **factor income shares**. Let factor b measure the quantity of capital in the economy and factor a measure the quantity of labor. If total output is evaluated by Y, then capital's share is bP_b/Y and labor's share is aP_a/Y. The ratio of capital's share to labor's share is:

(11.2) $$\frac{\dfrac{aP_b}{Y}}{\dfrac{aP_a}{Y}} = \frac{bP_b}{aP_a} = \frac{\dfrac{b}{a}}{\dfrac{P_a}{P_b}}$$

From the elasticity of substitution it is possible to determine the effect of a change in the relative quantities of the two factors on their relative shares of income—that is, if capital expands more rapidly than labor so that the relative quantity of capital to labor increases, the elasticity of substitution determines whether capital's share of income also increases. Recall that firms will use the factor combination at which the RTS equals the price ratio. The elasticity of substitution may therefore be rewritten:

(11.3) $$\sigma = \frac{\dfrac{\Delta(b/a)}{b/a}}{\dfrac{\Delta(P_a/P_b)}{P_a/P_b}}$$

Note the similarity of this form of the elasticity of substitution and equation (11.2), which is equal to the ratio of income shares. *The elasticity of substitution is merely the ratio of percentage changes in the numerator and denominator of (11.2).* From this it is possible to predict the effect of changes in the relative amounts of capital and labor on the share of income going to these two factors.

Consider, for example, the effect of "unbalanced" growth in which capital has grown more rapidly than labor in an economy whose elasticity of substitution has been less than 1. Such a value of σ implies that this increase in the capital–labor ratio would be accompanied by a *larger* than proportional increase in the price ratio. A 10-percent increase in the capital–labor ratio must be accompanied by an increase in the price ratio in the denominator of *more than 10 percent* if σ is less than 1. This value of σ also implies that the numerator on the right side of equation (11.2) grows slower than the denominator. As (11.2) must equal the ratio of shares, this implies that such an increase in the capital-labor ratio would *decrease* the relative share of income going to capital. This is true in spite of the fact that after the change there is relatively more capital earning income than formerly.

The opposite would hold, of course, were the elasticity of substitution greater than unity. Where σ has a value in this range, the percentage change in relative factor quantities will be larger than the percentage change in factor prices. In this case the numerator in the right side of equation (11.2) will increase by more than the denominator, suggesting that capital's share will increase. Where the elasticity of substitution is exactly equal to 1, change in the relative quantities of factors will

Table 11.1 *Response of Income Shares Going to Capital and Labor with Changing Factor Ratios and Different Elasticities of Substitution*

	K/L **Increases**	*K/L* **Decreases**
$\sigma < 1$	Capital's share falls	Capital's share increases
$\sigma > 1$	Capital's share increases	Capital's share falls
$\sigma = 1$	No change in shares	No change in shares

still imply changes in relative prices, but the price changes will just offset the quantity changes, leaving relative income shares constant. The possible results of such growth are given in Table 11.1.

The elasticity of substitution may also be used to predict changes in relative prices. Solving equation (11.3) for the percentage change in prices yields:

$$\frac{\Delta(P_a/P_b)}{P_a/P_b} = \frac{1}{\sigma} \cdot \frac{\Delta(b/a)}{b/a}.$$

For economies in which labor and capital are not very substitutable (where σ is comparatively low), large changes in the relative quantities of capital and labor can be predicted to have disruptive effects on the economy. For example, a large influx of capital into such an economy will require substantial changes in the relative prices of these two factors. On the other hand, economies characterized by more flexible production (where σ is higher) can accommodate large changes in the relative supplies of resources without precipitating major factor price changes.

There is some evidence that the elasticity of substitution for the American economy is less than unity. The growth of capital has led the growth of the labor force for most of this century, yet labor's share and the price of labor relative to capital have increased during this period. We must interpret these observations with caution, however, for this period has also witnessed remarkable technical change. To some extent, changing relative shares of income will be due to changing technology rather than to factor substitution involving a given production function.

Technical Change and Employment

Earlier we pointed out the distinction between what is referred to as *technical change* on the one hand and *changes in technology* on the other. For our purposes the former refers to a change in the production function while the latter involves factor substitution along stationary isoquants. Our discussion of the elasticity of substitution is pertinent to the analysis of two types of issues, both in the context of a given state of the art: (1) the analysis of factor substitution within firms and industries due to an economywide change in factor prices, and (2) the analysis of factor price changes resulting from economywide changes in the relative supply of factors. Complicating the study of production is the fact that technical change may also provoke factor substitution within firms and industries *and* produce economy-

Figure 11.13   Technical Change

Technical change is depicted here as isoquant q shifts inward to position q'. This implies that after the change the same output can be produced with less of each factor. It does not imply that the firm will necessarily choose to produce it with less of each factor. It is quite possible that the cost-minimizing combination of inputs to produce this output is now K, which contains more of factor a and less of factor b. This type of technical change is called factor a using (or factor b saving). It is possible that the cost reduction resulting from the technical change will permit expansion of the quantity produced to the point at which more of *both* factors will be employed.

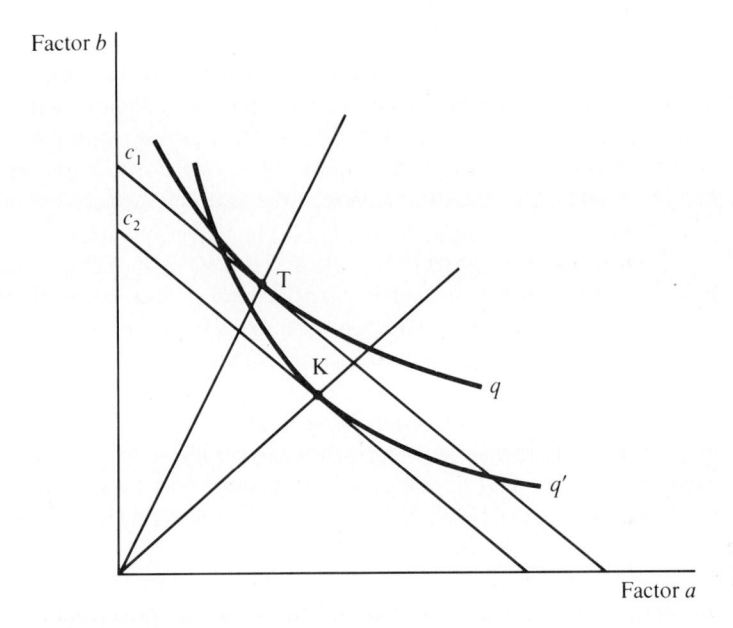

wide changes in factor prices. Let us therefore reconsider these two phenomena from the standpoint of technical change.

Figure 11.13 can be used to illustrate the case of factor substitution due to technical change. This figure depicts two isoquants for production of the same output of the same good before and after some change in the technology of production is introduced. Let isoquant q represent the possible combinations of factors a and b that can be used to produce output q prior to the innovation. Given market prices of these resources, a cost-minimizing firm would employ combination T, at which isoquant q is just tangent to isocost curve c_1. After the innovation is introduced, however, combination T no longer produces this output at lowest cost. The isoquant associated with this output is now q', and the rate of technical substitution no longer is equal to the price ratio at T. Note that the factor combination that now minimizes the cost of output q along the new isoquant q' is K, which is producible at a lower cost, c_2. Note also that because combination K lies on a ray with a lower slope than that passing through T, the factor ratio has been modified by this change. As relatively more *a* is now employed, we may describe this technical change as being **factor *a* using technical change** or, alternatively, **factor *b* saving technical change**. Technical change, which merely shifted all isoquants inward so that cost-minimizing combinations employed all factors in the same ratio, is designated as **factor neutral technical change**.

Whether technical change is labor using or capital using will clearly affect the ratio in which these two factors are employed in a particular industry. On this basis it is inappropriate to jump to the conclusion, as many noneconomists do, that such change necessarily results in the displacing of one factor by the other. Technical change must lower cost if firms are to introduce it. This lowering of cost, and the consequent increase in output implied, may result in *more* employment of labor after labor-saving technical change has taken place! In fact, the rapid growth of many industries—involving substantial growth in employment of labor—has been made possible by the introduction of labor-saving innovations. The experience of the cotton industry after the invention of the cotton gin and of the automobile industry after the introduction of the assembly line are only two examples of labor-saving technology that led to vast increases in the employment of labor.

Typically it is the absence of technical change in an industry that leads to diminishing employment in that industry. Where it does occur, technical change lowers costs. This lowers prices relative to industries that lack such change. Consumers substitute goods whose prices are falling for those whose prices are not. Labor in these static industries will therefore tend to experience declining demand in spite of the fact that cost-minimizing factor ratios remain unchanged. Consider the services of barbers and waiters. Both are employed in industries that have experienced little technical change in this century. The capital and labor requirements for a haircut or a well-served meal differ little today from what they were 50 years ago. These services have therefore become relatively more costly than goods whose production has been characterized by greater innovation. It is not surprising, therefore, that today there are far fewer barbers per capita than in 1930 and that the traditional family restaurant has given way to serviceless alternatives like fast-food emporiums.

Summary

In this chapter we introduced the production function, which relates combinations of quantities of the various inputs to production to the level of output. By holding all quantities of factors but one constant and observing the relationship between that factor's use and output we may identify total, average, and marginal product curves. The law of diminishing returns states that marginal product, average product, and total product reach peaks and diminish, in that order. Returns to scale is a method of categorizing production functions according to their response to proportional changes in the use of inputs. Returns to scale are increasing, constant, or decreasing, depending on whether the percentage change in output is greater than, equal to, or less than the percentage change in factor use.

Another useful way of looking at production functions is to hold output constant and observe the implied relationship between two inputs under these conditions. The curve describing that relationship is called an **isoquant**. Observation of the shape of isoquants informs us concerning the substitutability of the two factors. Factors that are not substitutable at all form isoquants that are right angles to each other in the input space. Factors that are perfectly substitutable in production have linear isoquants. The slope of an isoquant is equal to minus the ratio of the marginal physical products of the two inputs. This ratio itself is defined as the rate of technical substitution (RTS). The law of diminishing RTS states that the slope of an isoquant will diminish as the quantity of one factor is increased along the isoquant—in other words, isoquants are convex downward.

Firms seeking to maximize profits will be led to choose the combination of factors that produces the given output at a minimum cost. That combination may be found by observing the isocost curves on which the various combinations of factors along the isoquant lie. The combination on the lowest isocost curve will be the lowest-cost combination of factors that will produce the output identified by the isoquant. This combination will identify a point of tangency between isoquants and isocost curves, implying that equality of slopes is a necessary condition for cost minimization. From this we may conclude that cost minimization requires that the factor combination employed be one that satisfies the following property: RTS = factor price ratio.

The elasticity of substitution measures the substitutability of two factors of production. The higher the elasticity of substitution, the more substitutable are the factors. This elasticity is defined as the percentage change in the factor ratio divided by the percentage change in the RTS (or the factor price ratio). The elasticity of substitution is useful in predicting price and income share responses to changing factor supplies. One can also infer the degree to which factors will be substituted in production due to changes in relative prices.

Technical change can be represented in production theory as a shift in isoquants. Technical change is to be distinguished from changes in technology, which involve substitution of one factor for another along stationary isoquants. A technical change that leads to the employment of more of factor a relative to factor b at given prices is said to be "factor a using" or "factor b saving." A technical change that has no effect on the factor ratio is called **factor neutral technical change**. Technical change that is factor saving does not imply overt displacement of that factor in production. Technical change also lowers cost, which can be more important than factor use ratios in determining the level of employment in an industry. Those industries in which there has been little technical change typically grow relatively more costly and decline in economic importance compared to those that have experienced rapid technical change.

Key Concepts

production function
maximum feasible output
total product curve
marginal physical product
average product
law of diminishing returns
increasing returns to scale
decreasing returns to scale
constant returns to scale
duality
isoquants
fixed proportions
perfect substitutes

rate of technical substitution (RTS)
law of diminishing RTS
technical change
change in technology
isocost curve
cost minimization
output expansion path (OEP)
elasticity of substitution
factor income shares
factor a using technical change
factor b saving technical change
factor neutral technical change

Questions

1. *Easy* An increase in the use of factor *b* will have what effect on the total product curve for factor *a*? What implications does this have for the average product of factor *a* at each quantity?

Hard What assumption about the total product curve will insure that an increase in the quantity of factor *b* will increase the marginal physical product of factor *a*?

2. *Easy* At the quantity of the variable input at which the average product curve reaches its peak, this curve must be intersected from above by the marginal physical product curve for that input. Explain.

Hard Total product curves for some production functions widely used in economics have no convex-downward portion (for example, $q = ga^e b^{1-e}$, where g and e are constant). These curves are convex upward over their entire range. What is the relationship between the average product curve and the marginal physical product curve for such production functions? (*Hint*: You should be able to answer this without attempting to derive expressions for the two curves from the sample production function given.)

3. *Easy* Explain the differences between the following three principles:

   a. Diminishing returns to the use of a factor
   b. Decreasing returns to scale
   c. Diminishing rate of technical substitution

Hard Explain the relationship between the law of diminishing returns and an upward-sloping marginal cost curve. Explain the relationship between decreasing returns to scale and the upward-sloping portion of the envelope curve.

4. *Easy* What conditions must hold for a firm to minimize the cost of producing a given output? Explain.

Hard Assume that the price of one factor increases while the price of the other remains constant. What change will the firm make in the combination of factors used if it is constrained to produce the same level of output? Illustrate this diagrammatically.

5. *Easy* The elasticity of substitution describes a property of a production function's isoquants. What is that property?

Hard A large symphony orchestra in which the number of instruments playing each part is increased is not only louder but is said to produce a "richer" sound. Production might be characterized as exhibiting increasing returns to scale over this range. Explain.

6. *Easy* Assume that the elasticity of substitution for a production function is less than unity. An increase in the ratio of capital to labor employed will have what effect on the share of income going to capital?

Hard The elasticity of substitution of production is often used to describe the flexibility of the production process. In what sense is the production process more flexible if its elasticity of substitution is higher?

7. *Easy* The cost-minimizing combination of labor and capital after capital-using (labor-saving) technical change will typically contain some labor and some capital. Both factors will continue to be "used." What is meant by this expression?

Hard It is quite possible for labor-saving (capital-using) technical change to result in expanded use of labor. How is this possible?

Chapter 12

The Demand for Factors: Productivity and Employment

Connections This chapter uses the tools of production theory developed in Chapter 11 to derive the demand by firms for factors of production. The theory is general. Factors influencing the demand for capital are no different from those affecting the demand for labor. The value of these factors to the firm is the contribution that each makes to production. Firms will use both up to the point at which profits are maximized, and no further. Conditions may differ, however, depending on the power of a firm to control a factor's price. This chapter focuses on demand by a price taker in the input market. Price searching in the input market will be discussed in Chapter 13. Individual firm demand for a factor must be aggregated across all demanders to determine market demand. This process is identical to the aggregation of household demand for goods discussed in Chapter 5. The topic of productivity is raised and discussed, as is the puzzling question of unemployment. As a great deal of silliness is ventilated daily on both of these topics, the reader is especially cautioned to gird himself or herself against misleading nostrums by careful attention to this material.

In Chapter 11 we were primarily concerned with developing the theoretical conditions that must exist for optimal (that is, cost-minimizing) factor use. That discussion yielded the condition requiring that the RTS equal the factor price ratio. We also saw how changes in factor prices may lead to substitution of one factor for another, at least to the extent of requiring that the new optimum contain a different factor combination. Response by firms to such changes could not be more fully developed there because that analysis was carried on under the assumption that output was held constant. In this chapter, we shall relax that assumption.

A change in the price of a factor will have an impact on several decisions made by firms. Of these we will concern ourselves in detail with two. A change in factor prices may, as we saw previously, influence firms to substitute toward the factor that has become relatively less costly. However, as costs of production are influenced by the prices of the resources used, changes in factor prices will also affect costs and therefore output. The effect of factor price changes on the demand for a single factor is therefore the combined result of these two influences. We will analyze these underlying determinants of factor demand in detail in this chapter.

A closely related topic of great policy concern today is productivity and its rate of growth. The marked decline in the rate of growth of labor productivity during the 1970s spurred a serious reconsideration of federal tax policy as well as major reevaluation of regulatory interventions introduced during this period. In this chapter we will give careful consideration to the interpretation of productivity statistics with an eye toward analysis of some of these policy discussions.

Finally, we shall consider the topic of jobs. Politicians point with pride to the number of jobs created under their jurisdictions during their tenure in office. There can be little doubt that finding a job can be a matter of serious concern to someone lacking one; at times it has appeared that there were not enough for all those actively seeking them. In this chapter we will examine carefully the factors determining the number of jobs as well as the causes of unemployment.

Recall that profits are defined as the difference in revenues and costs. Varying the quantity of a single factor of production affects both these components of profit. A change in the use of a resource changes output, and therefore revenue, at the same time that it influences total cost. It will therefore be useful to express total revenue and total cost in terms of the use of inputs. We will do this for the general case in which output and input prices may or may not vary. We will then sort out the implications of our results for all possible structures in the input and output markets.

12.1 The Revenue Effect: Marginal Revenue Product (MRP)

Output may be expressed as a function of the combination of inputs used. This is simply the production function relationship developed in Chapter 11. The price of output may itself vary with output if the firm is a price searcher in this market. Output price may therefore be expressed as a different function of the combination of inputs used. Let these two relationships be denoted as follows:

Chapter 12 The Demand for Factors: Productivity and Employment

Output $= q = q(a, b)$.

Price $= P = P(a, b)$.

Total revenue for any combination of inputs used is therefore price times output, or:

Total revenue $= R = P(a, b) \cdot q(a, b)$.

We now define the **marginal revenue product** of a factor as the change in total revenue per unit change in the use of that factor. For example, $\Delta R/\Delta a$ is the marginal revenue product of factor a (MRP_a). As both price and output may change due to an increase in the use of a, we must use the product rule to determine the MRP_a:

(12.1) $\quad MRP_a = \dfrac{\Delta R}{\Delta a} = P(a, b) \cdot \dfrac{\Delta q}{\Delta a} + q(a, b) \cdot \dfrac{\Delta P}{\Delta a}$.

Consider the term $\Delta P/\Delta a$. The rate at which price varies with the use of a factor may itself be broken down into two effects: the change in output occasioned by the use of more of the factor $\Delta q/\Delta a$ and the change in price due to the offering of more output for sale, $\Delta P/\Delta q$.[1] We may therefore substitute for $\Delta P/\Delta a$ the following product:

$$\dfrac{\Delta P}{\Delta a} = \dfrac{\Delta P}{\Delta q} \cdot \dfrac{\Delta q}{\Delta a}.$$

This, when substituted into equation (12.1), yields:

$$MRP_a = P(a, b) \cdot \dfrac{\Delta q}{\Delta a} + q(a, b) \cdot \dfrac{\Delta P}{\Delta q} \cdot \dfrac{\Delta q}{\Delta a}.$$

Examining this expression for MRP_a reveals that $\Delta q/\Delta a$ appears in both terms. Factoring out this common term gives:

$$MRP_a = \dfrac{\Delta q}{\Delta a}\left[P(a, b) + q(a, b) \cdot \dfrac{\Delta P}{\Delta q}\right].$$

You may recognize the expression inside the brackets. We encountered it in Chapter 9. The term inside the brackets is the firm's marginal revenue. The reader will recognize that marginal revenue product is simply $\Delta q/\Delta a$ times *marginal revenue* itself. The change in output per unit change in the use of a factor $\Delta q/\Delta a$ is the marginal physical product of that factor. Marginal revenue product is therefore

---

[1] The output price P is a function of output $P = P(q)$, and output depends on the inputs used, $q(a, b)$. To determine $\Delta P/\Delta a$, we must use the chain rule from Chapter 1.

simply the marginal physical product of the factor times marginal revenue. Recalling that marginal revenue may be expressed as $P[1 + 1/\eta]$,

$$MRP_a = \frac{\Delta q}{\Delta a} \cdot P(a, b)\left[1 + \frac{1}{\eta}\right] = MPP_a MR.$$

Though the derivation of this expression is somewhat messy, it has a very common-sense interpretation. An increase in the use of a factor of production will increase revenue in the following way. It will increase output at a rate equal to MPP_a. The effect of this output change on total revenue is reflected by marginal revenue. Marginal revenue gives us the rate of change in revenue *per unit* change in output. Marginal revenue product is therefore the marginal physical product times marginal revenue. If, for example, a unit increase in factor a produces a five-unit increment in output ($MPP_a = 5$) and total revenue increases at $2.00 per unit of output ($MR = \$2.00$), then this unit increase in the use of factor a will increase revenue by $5 \cdot \$2 = \$10$. In the limiting case where the firm faces a perfectly elastic demand curve for its output ($\eta = -\infty$), marginal revenue is simply price and marginal revenue product reduces to $MPP_a P_q$.

Holding constant the use of all other factors, we may identify a MRP_a curve. This curve relates the use of the varying factor, a, to the value of MRP_a. Marginal revenue product must eventually decrease with the expansion of factor a. We know this because MPP_a must eventually decrease due to the law of diminishing returns. Marginal revenue either diminishes with output or remains constant, depending on the elasticity of demand. The product of a diminishing value and a constant or diminishing value must itself decrease. Figure 12.1 depicts such a MRP_a curve.

Figure 12.1   The Marginal Revenue Product Curve

A marginal revenue product curve identifies the marginal revenue product of a factor at different use levels holding constant the quantities of all other inputs. It must slope downward due to the law of diminishing returns.

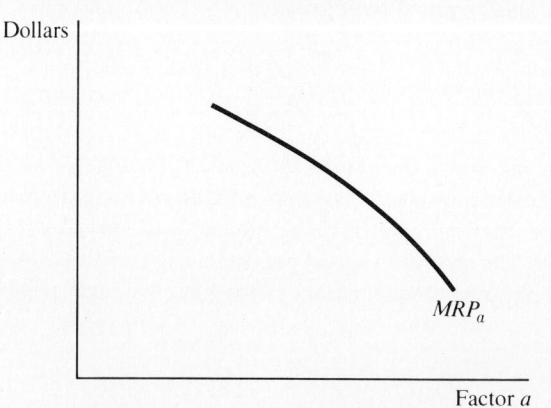

Figure 12.2   MRP$_a$ *with Different Amounts of the Fixed Factor*

Increasing the amount of the fixed factor increases the marginal physical product of factor a at given quantities of a. Thus an increase in factor b shifts curve MRP_a upward at every quantity of a.

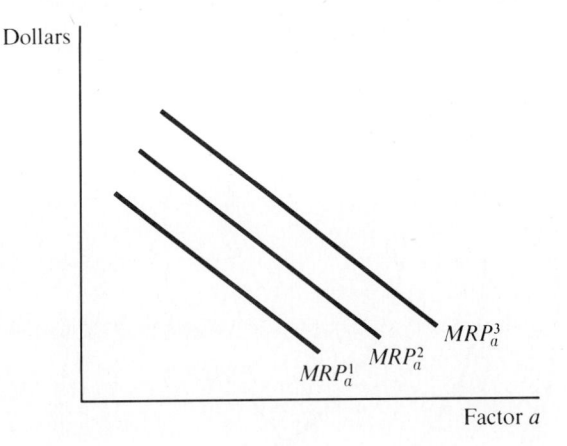

[Graph: Dollars on vertical axis, Factor a on horizontal axis, showing three downward-sloping parallel curves labeled MRP_a^1, MRP_a^2, and MRP_a^3 from left to right.]

Increases in the use of factor b will typically increase MPP_a and therefore shift curve MRP_a upward at each quantity of factor a. Similarly, a decrease in the use of factor b will lower the MPP_a at every quantity of a. In Figure 12.2, the marginal revenue product curves MRP_a^1, MRP_a^2, and MRP_a^3 are thus associated with increasing quantities of factor b.

We shall have occasion to use another curve depicting the relationship between the use of a factor and its marginal revenue product. The MRP_a curve just shown indicates the level of the marginal revenue product as factor a is varied and the quantity of b is held constant. However, as we pointed out in the previous chapter, the level of the marginal *physical* product will vary predictably as both factors increase and decrease along a given output expansion path. If the firm's production function exhibits constant returns to scale, then MPP_a will itself be constant at each combination along such a path. If the production function exhibits decreasing returns, MPP_a will diminish, and vice versa. To be consistent with our discussion of the theory of output in Chapters 8 through 10, we shall assume here that decreasing returns prevail. The reader is assured that the results developed here do not depend in any critical way on this assumption.

We define the **expansion revenue product curve (MRP_{exp})** as identifying the marginal revenue product of a factor as its use is expanded along a particular output expansion path. Obviously, as there is a different expansion path for every possible RTS, there will be an infinite number of expansion revenue product curves. Figure 12.3 depicts one such output expansion curve in panel (a) and its related expansion revenue product curve in panel (b). Curve MRP_{exp} must slope downward to the right for two reasons. First, recall that the marginal revenue product of a factor is merely the MPP of that factor times marginal revenue. As just pointed

Figure 12.3 *The Expansion Revenue Product Curve*

An output expansion path identifying all input combinations with the same RTS is presented in panel (a). This production function exhibits decreasing returns to scale, implying that the marginal physical product of factor a decreases as the use of this factor and factor b expands along RTS_1. Curve MRP_{exp} in panel (b) identifies the marginal revenue product associated with quantities of a employed at each combination along RTS_1. Since MPP_a decreases in each combination in panel (a), MRP_{exp} in panel (b) must also decrease.

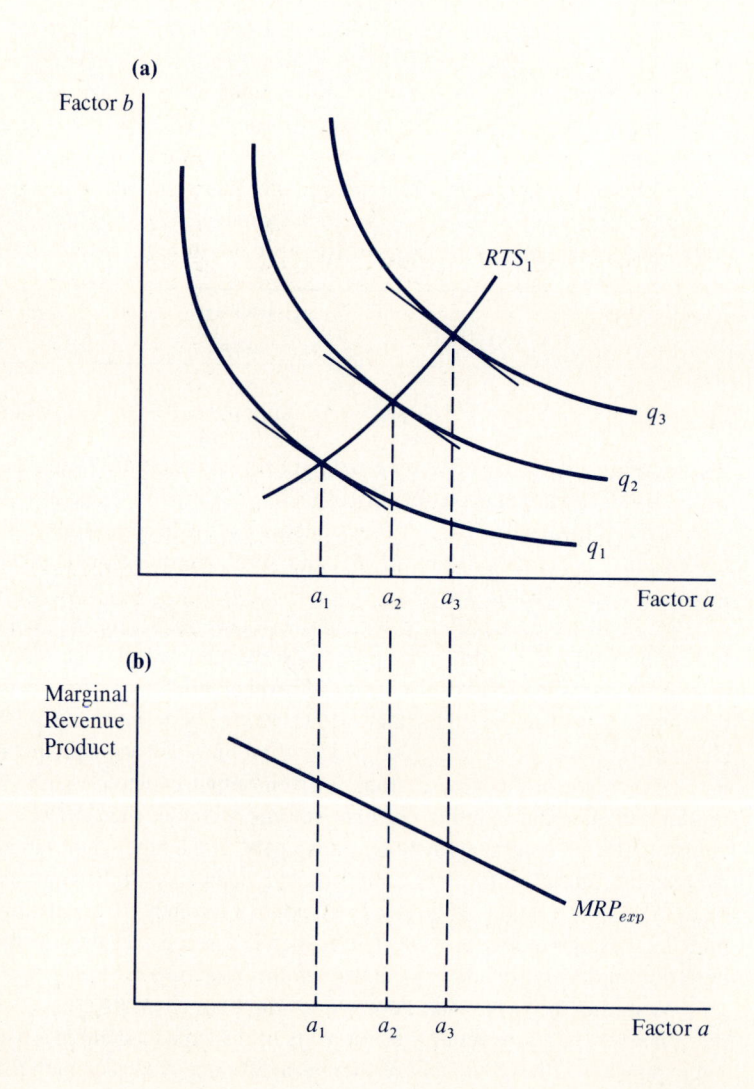

out, for production exhibiting decreasing returns to scale the MPP diminishes along an output expansion path, lowering the first term in the marginal revenue product expression. Second, marginal revenue itself diminishes with output for firms that are price searchers. In this case, the second term in the marginal revenue product expression also diminishes as we move to higher levels of a (used at higher outputs).[2]

The relationship between the marginal revenue product curve MRP_a and the expansion revenue product curve MRP_{exp} is illustrated in Figure 12.4 for the case where both inputs are normal. Curve MRP_a will always intersect MRP_{exp} from above in this case. This may be explained as follows. Consider the combination (a_1, b_1) in panel (a). Curve MRP_a in panel (b) identifies the marginal revenue product of factor a at successive combinations along a horizontal line extending from b_1 on the vertical axis of panel (a) through (a_1, b_1). Curve MRP_{exp} identifies the marginal revenue product of a as we move upward along the output expansion path RTS_1 through the same combination. There is a unique marginal revenue product of factor a at (a_1, b_1); hence, in panel (a) these two curves must intersect at a_1. Let the value of the marginal revenue product of a be MRP_1 at this quantity of a. For the reasons just discussed, curve MRP_{exp} will be higher at a_2 units of this factor than at a_1. Let the value of the marginal revenue product at this point be MRP_2 in panel (b). This corresponds to the marginal revenue product of a at combination (a_2, b_2) in panel (a).

However, the height of curve MRP_a at a_2 measures the marginal revenue product of a at a different combination, (a_2, b_1). This combination contains the same amount of factor a but *more* of factor b. The marginal physical product of a will therefore be higher at this combination than at (a_2, b_2). This in turn implies a higher marginal revenue product along curve MRP_a than along curve MRP_{exp}—say, MRP_3, compared to MRP_2. For quantities of factor a greater than a_1, the opposite will be true. Combinations along MRP_a will contain less of factor b than those along MRP_{exp}, and the marginal revenue product will be less along the former than the latter for each quantity of factor a.

12.2 Cost and Inputs

Increased use of a factor of production will affect cost in a more straightforward way. The cost of a resource is typically merely the total spending for its use. Total spending will be related to use as follows. Spending on any quantity of factor a is simply that quantity times its price. As the price of a may be influenced by the quantity purchased (where the firm is a price searcher in this market), we will express the price of factor a as a function of the amount used, that is, $P_a(a)$. Total spending on a is therefore given by the following expression:

Spending on $a = c_a = P_a(a) \cdot a$.

---

[2] The case of inferior inputs is somewhat more complex and will be discussed separately.

Figure 12.4 *The MRP_a Curve and the MRP_{exp} Curve*

Both a marginal revenue product curve and an expansion revenue product curve are associated with each point in panel (b). The curve MRP_a in this panel is associated with b_1 units of this factor in panel (a). The curve MRP_{exp} is associated with output expansion path RTS_1 in panel (a). These two curves therefore intersect at a_1 in panel (b), because combination (a_1, b_1) in panel (a) lies on RTS_1. Combination (a_2, b_2) on RTS_1 contains fewer than b_1 units of this factor. The MRP_{exp} curve must therefore lie below the MRP_a curve at a_2.

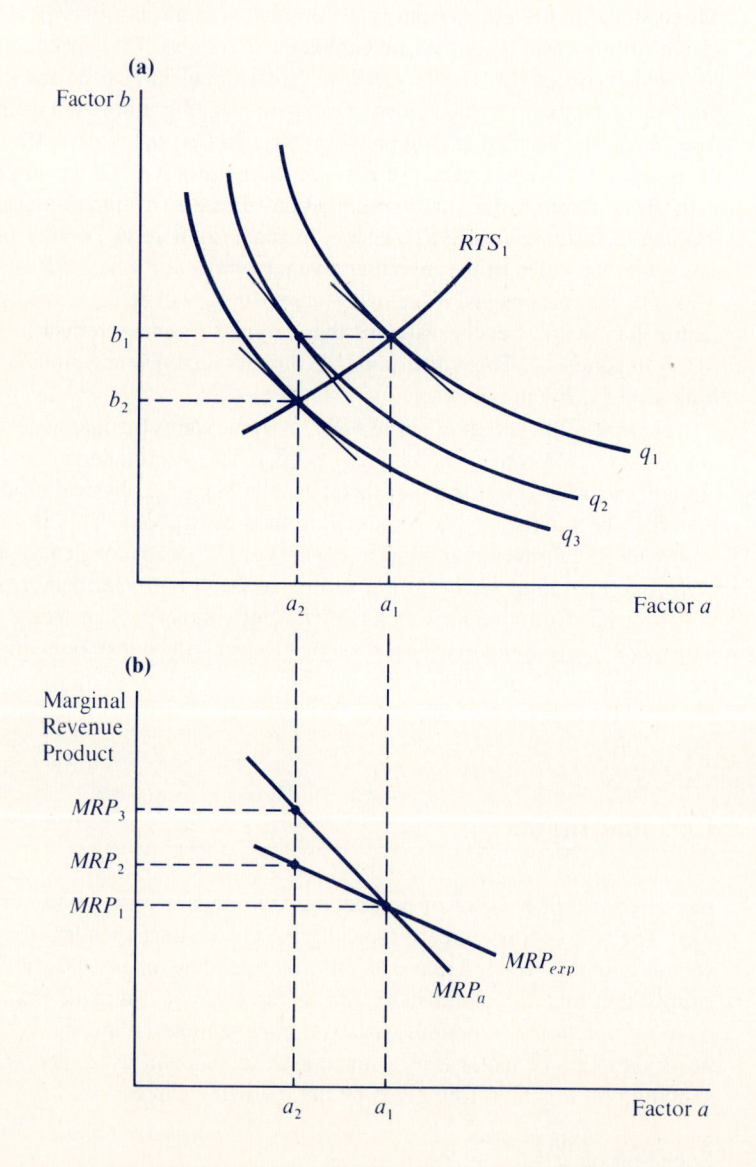

Increased use of factor a will therefore increase spending at the following rate per unit change in a using the product formula:

$$\frac{\Delta c_a}{\Delta a} = P_a(a) + a \cdot \frac{\Delta P_a}{\Delta a}.$$

This rate of change in spending on factor a per unit of its use is defined as the **marginal factor cost** of a (MFC_a). We may also relate this expression to an elasticity. Dividing each term by the price of a, then multiplying the entire expression by $P_a(a)$, does not affect its value. This yields:

$$\frac{\Delta c_a}{\Delta a} = MFC_a = P_a(a) \left[\frac{P_a a}{P_a(a)} + \frac{a}{P_a(a)} \cdot \frac{\Delta P_a}{\Delta a} \right].$$

Note now that the second term inside the brackets is equal to the reciprocal of the elasticity of supply of factor a. Let that be denoted ε. Marginal factor cost may therefore be expressed simply as:

$$MFC_a = P_a(a) \left[1 + \frac{1}{\varepsilon} \right].$$

The marginal factor cost curve will have a slope equal to or greater than zero. Consider the limiting case where the elasticity of supply of factor a to the firm is infinite; the supply curve is horizontal. In this case MFC_a can be expressed as simply:

$$MFC_a = P_a(a) \left[1 + \frac{1}{\infty} \right] = P_a(a).$$

Marginal factor cost will simply be the constant factor price, $P_a(a)$. In all other cases supply curves will slope upward; hence, the elasticity of supply ε will be positive but less than infinity. Marginal factor cost will in these cases equal the factor price plus something equal to $P_a(a)/\varepsilon$. Two MFC_a curves are shown in Figure 12.5 depicting these two cases.

The Cost of Output in Terms of Inputs

It will prove useful to have a way of gauging the marginal cost of output in the input space in which we are dealing. This is accomplished with reference to isocost curves introduced in Chapter 11. Assume that factor b is supplied to the firm at a constant price per unit. We may define the size of these units any way we like; small-size units will therefore cost less *per unit* than large-size units. Let us therefore choose the size unit that yields a price per unit of factor b of exactly $1.00.

Recall from our previous discussion that the expression for an isocost curve relating quantities of factor a that may be purchased with factor b for a given expenditure, c, is the following:

$$b = \frac{c}{P_b} - \frac{P_a}{P_b} \cdot a.$$

Figure 12.5 Marginal Factor Cost and the Elasticity of Supply

When the price of a factor is insensitive to the quantity employed, the marginal factor cost is simply the factor price. The marginal factor cost curve MFC_a in panel (a) illustrates this case. When the price rises with the quantity employed, however, marginal factor cost is greater than supply price. At any quantity this difference is the ratio of the factor price and the price elasticity of supply at that quantity.

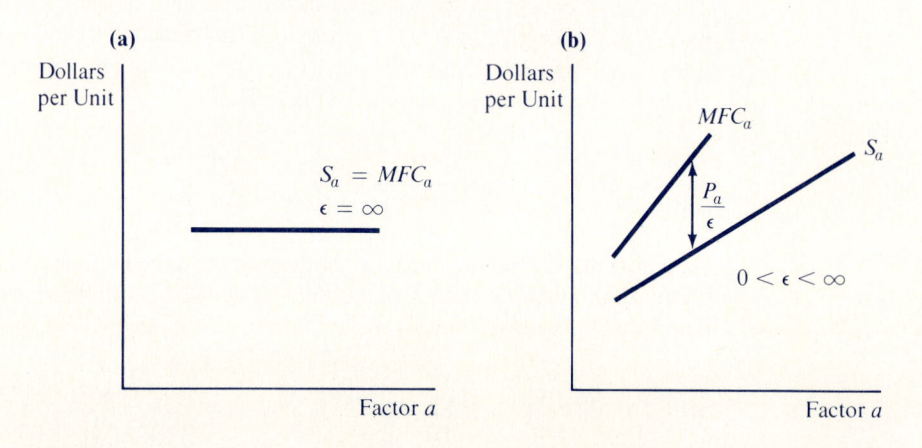

(a) Dollars per Unit vs Factor a: $S_a = MFC_a$, $\epsilon = \infty$

(b) Dollars per Unit vs Factor a: MFC_a, S_a, with $\frac{P_a}{\epsilon}$, $0 < \epsilon < \infty$

The vertical intercept of this expression may be obtained by evaluating it where none of factor a is purchased—that is, where $a = 0$—giving:

$$b = \frac{c}{P_b}.$$

Having chosen units of b such that the price of this factor is $1.00, we observe an interesting result. The height of the vertical intercept of the isocost curve is equal to total cost; that is:

$$b = \frac{c}{1} = c.$$

As output is expanded, the output expansion curve links combinations of a and b along successively higher isocost curves, each with the same slope. The distance between the vertical intercepts of these curves will thus measure the increase in cost associated with the successively higher outputs. Marginal cost, being $\Delta c/\Delta q$, is therefore indicated by the ratio of the upward change in the vertical intercept to the change in output. For constant changes in output we may determine whether marginal cost is rising or falling by observing whether the vertical intercepts of the relevant isocost curves are getting farther apart or closer together.

In Figure 12.6, for example, three isocost curves are shown associated with three outputs. Let each isoquant represent a constant interval of output (for exam-

Chapter 12 *The Demand for Factors: Productivity and Employment* 373

Figure 12.6 **Isocost Curves and Cost**

Defining units of factor b so that one unit costs $1.00, the vertical intercept measures total cost of producing the chosen output. The total cost of q_1 is b_1, the total cost of q_2 is b_2, and the total cost of q_3 is b_3. As the difference between b_2 and b_3 exceeds the distance between b_1 and b_2, and output changes are by definition equal, marginal cost is rising.

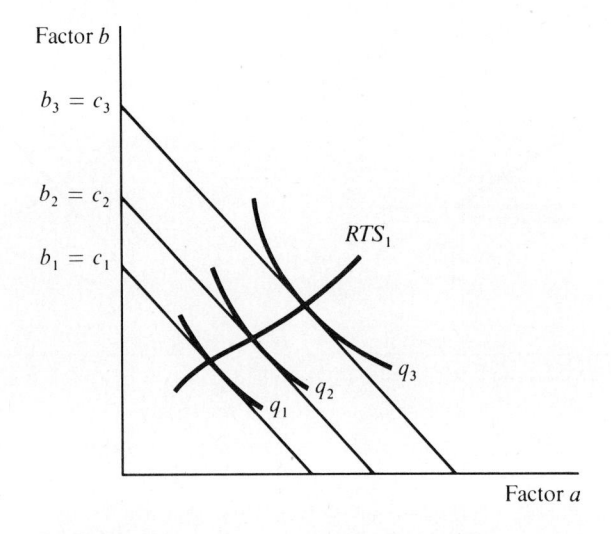

[Graph: Factor b on vertical axis with $b_3 = c_3$, $b_2 = c_2$, $b_1 = c_1$ marked; Factor a on horizontal axis; isoquants q_1, q_2, q_3 shown with RTS_1 expansion path]

---

ple, let $q_1 = 40$, $q_2 = 50$, and $q_3 = 60$) so that the output *change* is constant. As the vertical increase from b_2 to b_3 exceeds that of b_1 to b_2, it must be the case that marginal cost has risen over this interval. This may be expressed as

$$\text{Marginal cost} = \frac{\Delta c}{\Delta q} = \frac{\Delta b}{\Delta q},$$

and

$$\frac{b_3 - b_2}{\Delta q} > \frac{b_2 - b_1}{\Delta q}.$$

12.3   The Demand for Factors

Choosing the Level of One Factor

Let us now consider a firm choosing the quantity of one factor, holding others constant. Varying the level of a factor has been shown to affect both sides of the profit ledger, revenues and costs. If a factor contributes more to revenue than cost at the

Figure 12.7 *The Profit-Maximizing Level of a Factor*

For profits to be maximized, marginal revenue product must equal marginal factor cost. Thus, at the optimum quantity of a factor, curve MRP_a must intersect curve MFC_a. This is shown in panel (a) for the case in which the firm is a price taker in the input market and in panel (b) for the case in which the firm is a price searcher in the input market.

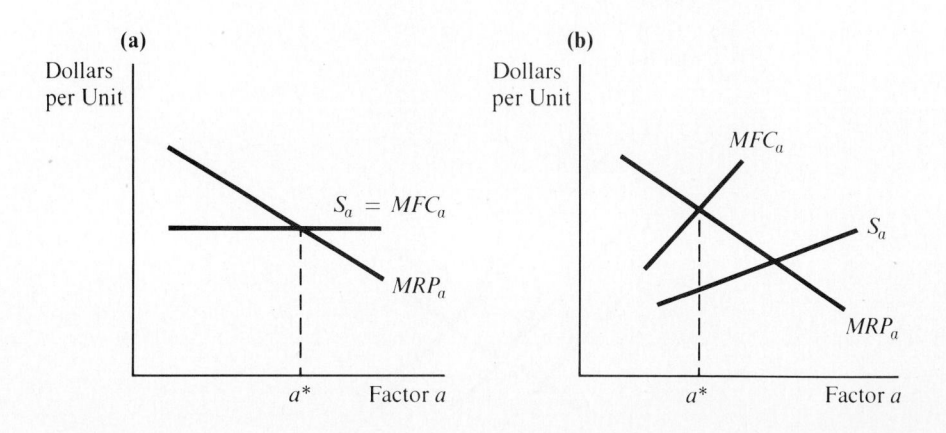

margin, increasing its use will increase profits. If hiring an extra unit of a factor increases costs more than it adds to revenue, then obviously its use should be curtailed. Profits from the use of a factor will be maximized when the gain from its employment at the margin is just equal to its cost. That will be at the point where $MRP_a = MFC_a$. Figure 12.7 depicts the profit-maximizing use of factor a under the two possible supply conditions, given that the quantities of other factors have already been determined.

What is true for the use of one factor will be true for all. In choosing the quantity of any factor, firms seeking the greatest possible profits will hire that amount which equates the marginal revenue product of each factor to its marginal factor cost.

The Demand Curve with One Variable Factor

Note that the determinants of the profit-maximizing level of factor employment are the production function for the firm, the demand function for its output, and the supply function of the factor itself. Given this information, we may determine the optimal quantity of each factor that the firm will employ.

However, it is rare that economists will have at their disposal such rich data resources in their analyses of factor markets. In many cases, they will have to fall back on theory alone for analyzing particular markets at particular times. It is therefore useful to know that the theory of the firm provides unambiguous qualitative guidance with respect to the demand for factors of production by firms that are price takers in both input and output markets. In that case the quantity demanded will invariably be inversely related to price. Demand for factors in the cases in

Figure 12.8   *Demand with One Variable Factor*

If the firm is a price taker in the input market, the marginal factor cost curve will be horizontal at the input market price. The quantity demanded will thus be the quantity at which this horizontal MFC_a curve intersects the MRP_a curve.

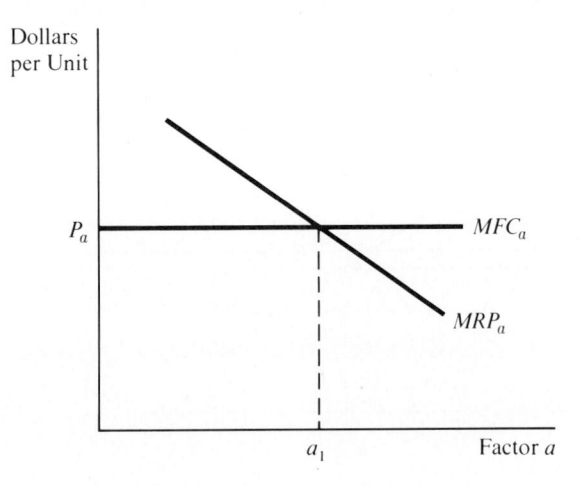

which the firm has some market power in one or both of these markets will be considered in Chapter 13. We shall begin this discussion with a special case of demand—one in which there is a single variable factor.

Where the firm is a price taker in the output market, marginal revenue product is equal to $MPP_a \cdot P_a(1 + 1/\infty)$, which reduces to simply $MPP_a P_a$. Such a MRP_a curve is shown in Figure 12.8. As a is the only variable factor here, this is the only possible MRP_a curve. Now let us also assume that the firm is a price taker in the market for factor a. The MFC_a in this case is simply the constant factor price, P_a, so this curve is horizontal at this level. The profit-maximizing use of factor a is the quantity that equates MRP_a and MFC_a—that is, a_1.

The firm's demand curve for a factor is the set of price–quantity combinations identifying the firm's chosen quantity at each price offered. The intersection of MRP_a and MFC_a in Figure 12.8 depicts one such price–quantity combination. At a price of P_a the firm seeks to obtain a_1 units of a. Figure 12.9 depicts the quantities that this firm would seek under a variety of supply conditions. At each hypothesized supply price, P_1, P_2, and P_3, the quantities demanded by the firm are a_1, a_2, and a_3, respectively. These combinations merely trace out the position of curve MRP_a at every price. In this case, therefore, curve MRP_a itself *is* the firm's demand curve for factor a. Since curve MRP_a must slope downward toward this intersection, the demand curve itself must by definition slope downward. As the price of the factor is increased to the firm, the quantity it demands will necessarily diminish.

Unfortunately, this straightforward result holds only for the simple case of a firm that may vary only one factor of production. It may, at best, reflect results in

Figure 12.9 *Factor Demand with Changing Supply Price*

As the supply price changes to a price-taking demander of factor a, the intersection of the marginal revenue product curve and the marginal factor cost curve traces out the MRP_a curve. Where only factor a is variable, the MRP_a curve is the firm's demand curve for factor a.

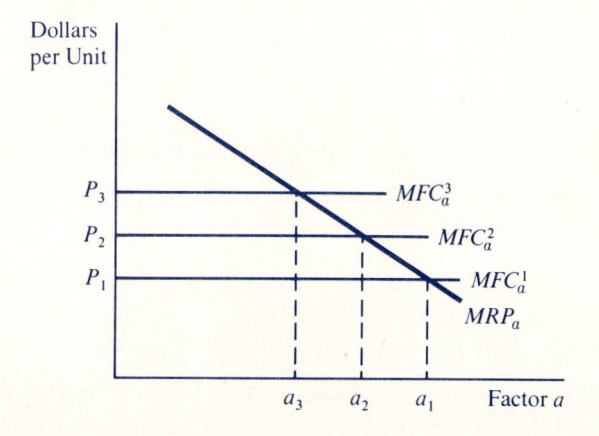

the very short run, when it is uneconomical to vary any but a single resource. We have difficulty imagining a production process in which only one factor is variable over an extended period. Even the simplest production process requires the use of several resources, and most of these are available for purchase in varying quantities by all users. A more useful theory of the demand for these resources must therefore take into account the response of a factor price change, not only on the use of that factor but on the employment of others as well. Incorporating these effects complicates the analysis but does not alter the result. Quantity demanded will be negatively affected by a factor price increase even when all factors may be freely varied.

Demand with All Factors Variable

If factor price changes influence firms to adjust the use of all factors, we may no longer count on the law of diminishing returns and a single downward-sloping MRP_a curve to produce a negative relationship between price and quantity demanded. Recognizing that a change in the quantity of factor b employed itself shifts the MRP_a curve, we seem to leave open the possibility depicted in Figure 12.10. This *impossible* result can be made to *seem* plausible in terms of the curves in this figure alone. Assume that factor a is initially supplied at a price P_1 and that the quantity chosen is a_1, where marginal revenue product MRP_a^1 is just equal to MFC_a. The rise in the price of a to P_2 will not only influence demand for a but will typically result in the firm choosing more of factor b than formerly. Increasing the quantity of factor b shifts curve MRP_a upward. If this increase shifts curve MRP_a sufficiently, it seems possible that more a will be demanded at the higher price P_2

Figure 12.10 Upward-Sloping Factor Demand—the Impossible Case

This plausible result is impossible—demand for a factor cannot slope upward. It seems that a price rise from P_1 to P_2 will cause more of factor b to be used. This will imply an upward shift of the MRP_a curve and seems to leave open the possibility of an intersection at a_2, a higher quantity of this factor than was used at the lower price.

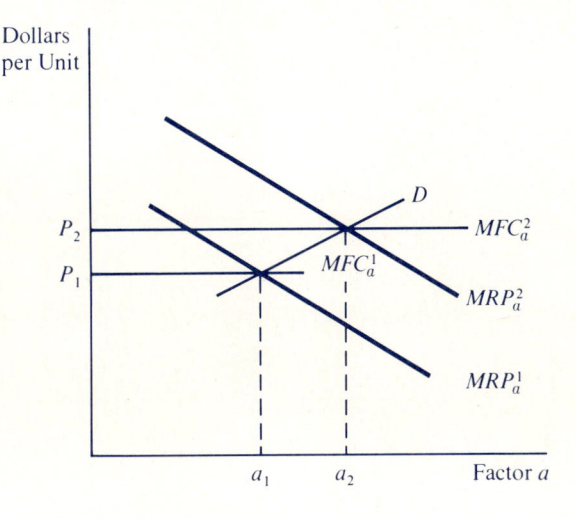

than at the original lower price P_1. Although an upward-sloping demand curve for a factor seems possible within this context, *this result cannot occur*.

Demand curves for factors of production must be negatively sloped. To prove this, however, we must employ isoquant analysis and the theory of output. We will show that factor price changes affect both the level of output and the optimal technology for producing that output. A change in the quantity demanded of a factor may thus be broken down into two effects: the **output effect of factor price change** and the **substitution effect of factor price change**. Ironically, unlike similar results in the theory of household demand for goods, it does not matter whether the input being considered is a normal or inferior input. In both cases, both output and substitution effects operate in the opposite direction of the price change. The case for a normal factor will be considered here. Demand for inferior factors is presented in the appendix to this chapter.

Demand for a Normal Factor

Two conditions must hold for both output and technology to be optimized: (1) Marginal cost must equal marginal revenue, and (2) the rate of technical substitution must equal the factor price ratio. Both conditions are assumed to prevail at combination (a_1, b_1) in panel (a) of Figure 12.11. Output q_1 has been chosen based on the first condition, and the tangency of this isoquant with isocost curve c_1 (incompletely drawn) reveals that the second condition is also satisfied. An increase in the price of factor a will disturb both of these conditions.

Figure 12.11 *Demand for a Normal Factor*

A rise in the price of factor a implies that the cost-minimizing technology for the production of output q_1 in panel (a) is no longer (a_1, b_1) but (a_2, b_2). The change in technology in response to this factor price change is called *the substitution effect*. As this latter combination lies on output expansion path RTS_2, marginal revenue product at this combination is identified by point K on MRP^2_{exp} in panel (b). This curve is higher than MRP^1_{exp} associated with RTS_1 in panel (a). This increase in the factor price also increases marginal cost in this case, influencing the firm to reduce output to q_2. The cost-minimizing technology for the production of q_2 at the new price ratio is (a_3, b_3), which must contain less of factor a, since a is a normal input. This part of the response to the price change is called *the output effect*. Both effects must be in the opposite direction to the price change, ruling out the possibility of the case presented in Figure 12.10.

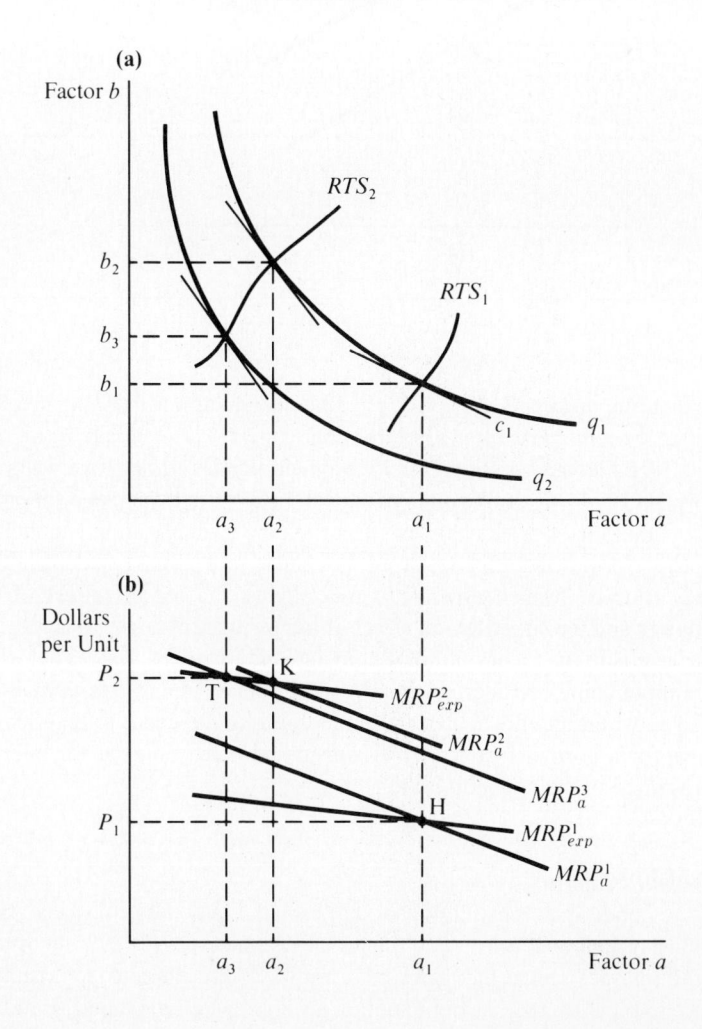

Consider first the *substitution effect* of this price change. Combination (a_1, b_1) cannot now be the cost-minimizing technology for producing output q_1, because the RTS at this combination is equal to the previous, lower price ratio. As the price ratio P_a/P_b has been increased, the new cost-minimizing technology must be one associated with a higher RTS. On the basis of the law of diminishing RTS, we may conclude that this new optimal combination must lie to the northwest along isoquant q_1. Assume that this combination is (a_2, b_2). The change in the quantity demanded holding output constant is the substitution effect of this factor price change. As we have just shown, an increase in the factor price must lead to a decrease in the quantity demanded due to the substitution effect. By the same logic, a decrease in the factor price would result in more of the factor being employed to produce a given output. Substitution effects, therefore, invariably operate in the opposite direction of the price change.

Note the influence of the substitution effect on results in panel (b) of Figure 12.11. This influence may be followed by observing the implied shifts of the marginal revenue product curve and the expansion revenue product curve. Marginal revenue product curve MRP_a^1 is associated with b_1 units of factor b. It therefore reaches a level equal to the original marginal factor cost, P_1, at a_1 units of factor a. The expansion revenue product curve MRP_{exp}^1 is associated with the original rate of technical substitution, RTS_1, and therefore intersects MRP_a^1 at this same quantity, a_1. The substitution effect not only changes the quantity of factor b employed, shifting MRP_a upward; it also produces a shift to a different output expansion curve, RTS_2, in panel (a). This implies a shift to a higher expansion revenue product curve, MRP_{exp}^2 in panel (b). The net result of the substitution effect, therefore, is to increase marginal revenue product to the height of point K in panel (b). Point K is identified by the height of MRP_{exp}^2 at quantity a_2 of this factor. It also lies on a higher marginal revenue product curve MPP_a^2.

The *output effect* of a factor price change wields its influence solely through the impact of factor prices on marginal cost. Factor price changes not only affect the choice of technology, they affect the output decision as well. As this effect is concerned only with output, it is measured along a given output expansion path where the RTS is held constant. Output effects may therefore be represented as movement along a given expansion revenue product curve. This is also depicted in Figure 12.11.

For normal inputs this effect is straightforward. An increase in a factor price will clearly increase the marginal cost of producing every level of output. The impact of a factor price increase on output may therefore be simply traced. A price increase shifts the marginal cost curve upward, forcing it to intersect marginal revenue at a lower output. Assume that this new optimal output is q_2, whose isoquant is depicted in panel (a) of Figure 12.11. As long as factor a is a normal factor, this lower level of output will employ fewer units of the input than were used to produce q_1 with RTS_2. Combination (a_3, b_3) must therefore contain less of factor a than combination (a_2, b_2). The output effect of the factor price increase on the demand for a is therefore the reduction in the quantity demanded from a_2 to a_3. Clearly, lowering the price of a would have the opposite effect; it would shift marginal cost downward, increasing output and therefore the use of a. *The output effect of a factor price change, like the substitution effect, will invariably operate in the opposite direction of the price change itself.*

This effect may be observed in panel (b) by following the expansion revenue product curve associated with output expansion path RTS_2 from a_2 to a_3 units of this factor. Marginal revenue product for factor a rises as a (together with other factors) is taken from production. This withdrawal will be stopped when marginal revenue product has increased to the point at which it is equal to the new marginal factor cost, P_2. Note that the figure is drawn so that in this position of full adjustment to the factor price change more of factor b is employed than was initially. The resulting point, T, therefore lies on a higher marginal revenue product curve, MRP_a^3, than the original point, H. This need not be the case. We cannot predict the effect of a factor price change on the use of other factors. Thus, the final position T may in principle lie on a higher, a lower, or the same marginal revenue product curve as that identified by the initial position H.

The total effect of a factor price change on the quantity of the factor demanded by a firm will be the sum of these two effects. As each effect is inversely related to price changes, so too must be their sum. The firm's demand curve for a factor must therefore be negatively sloped. As such a demand curve links factor prices with the quantity that the firms will seek to employ at those prices, the demand curve would pass through points H and T in panel (b) of Figure 12.11. This curve has been omitted from the figure to avoid cluttering, but let us repeat nevertheless why these two points would lie on it.

At the original price of factor a (P_1), marginal revenue product was equal to marginal factor cost at the point at which MRP_a^1 (associated with b_1 units of factor b) fell to the level of that price. The substitution effect of this price change led to the employment of b_2 units, shifting MRP_a upward and at the same time increasing the RTS. This latter effect is shown by the move to expansion revenue product curve MRP_{exp}^2. However, the output effect led to a reduction in both factors. As factor b was reduced from b_2 to b_3, this shifted MRP_a again, this time in a downward direction to the position shown by MRP_a^3. The reduction of factor a along the expansion revenue product curve MRP_{exp}^2 continues to a_3 units, at which point it is just equal to the new marginal factor cost, P_2. That this position, T, corresponds to combination (a_3, b_3) in panel (a) can be discerned by noting that T lies on (1) MRP_{exp}^2, associated with points on output expansion path RTS_2, and (2) MRP_a^2, associated with b_3 units of factor b. This will be true of no other point in panel (b).

12.4 Productivity in Theory and Practice

The market demand for a factor of production identifies the quantities that all users of the factor together will employ at every price. We may obtain this by determining how much each individual user seeks and adding them up. Since each individual firm must demand less at high prices than at low ones, the sum of all quantities demanded at high prices will be correspondingly lower than the sum of all quantities demanded at low prices. For a given supply of a factor the market price will thus be determined by the intersection of that demand curve with supply, as shown in Figure 12.12.

Figure 12.12   Market Demand

Market demand for factors is aggregated from individual firm demand by adding up the quantities demanded by each firm at each price. This is done in panels (a) and (b) to obtain the demand curve for the market in panel (c). The equilibrium price is P^*, which clears the market. A lower price such as P_1 fails to clear the market. Price also determines the distribution of the factor among competing users in the market.

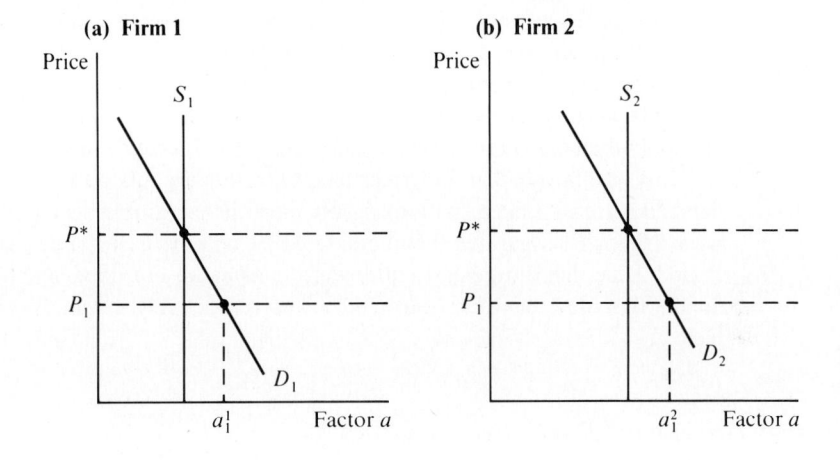

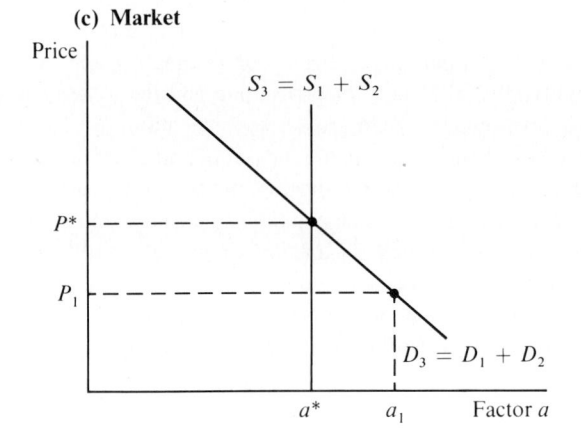

(a) Firm 1

(b) Firm 2

(c) Market

In panels (a) and (b) we depict the demand curves of two individual firms for factor a. Assume that these have been derived in the manner just described. For expositional purposes, assume further that these two firms are the only demanders of this factor but that they behave as price takers in the market for factor a. The total quantity demanded at each price by all purchasers of this input will be the quantity firm 1 demands at this price plus the quantity firm 2 demands at this price. At price P_1, for example, firm 1 demands a_1^1 units and firm 2 demands a_1^2 units of factor a. The market demand curve in panel (c) therefore indicates that a total of a_1 units (equal to $a_1^1 + a_1^2$) will be demanded at this price. Now let the total quantity available for sale be unresponsive to price and equal to a^*. Clearly the equilibrium price under such circumstances is P^*, at which the quantity sought in the market is just equal to the quantity available. If the price were lower than this, the two firms together would seek to purchase more than a^*; being frustrated in this attempt, each would be led to increase its wage offer toward the equilibrium price, P^*. If, on the other hand, the market price were greater than P^*, the two firms together would employ less than the total quantity available for sale. Unemployed factor owners would seek to obtain employment for their factors by offering to supply them at lower prices, causing the price to change toward P^* again.

It is in this way that the prices paid to factors are related to productivity. The demand price of a factor will invariably equal its marginal revenue product—that is, $MPP_a \cdot MR$. Measures that increase MPP_a will increase the demand for factor a, and those that diminish it will lower the demand. For fixed quantities of these factors this must therefore raise and lower, respectively, the market price of this factor.

Productivity Growth and Productivity Statistics

The 1970s saw a growing concern over the topic of labor **productivity**. It was noted with alarm that after growing at rates of 2 to 3 percent per year for the two previous decades U. S. output per man-hour leveled off and in some industries declined dramatically. The study of production and factor demand permits us to interpret these developments with greater sophistication.

First, let us ascertain what is being measured and discussed in this context. In casual conversation and reports in the press, the term "productivity" is often used as if it were synonymous with per capita output and income. In this context it seems that increases in productivity are invariably good and that policies that increase productivity should be adopted unquestioningly. However, conventional measures of productivity may not be interpreted in this way, and policy based on increasing productivity regardless of cost can have undesirable consequences. Output per man-hour worked is an *average* concept; the reader at this stage should need no reminder that few economic objectives are successfully optimized through attention to averages.

Consider Figure 12.13. Panel (a) depicts a total product curve for "output" of the economy as a whole under the assumption that the quantity of capital is fixed in the short run so that only labor may be varied. In this case output per man-hour worked is simply the height of this curve at a given quantity of labor divided by the quantity employed. For example, at a_1 units of labor employed this measure of productivity yields q_1/a_1—that is, ϕ, the slope of the ray from the origin to the total product curve at labor quantity a_1. As we saw in Chapter 11, this is simply the average product of the variable factor.

Panel (b) reflects the average and marginal physical product curves derived from the total product curve above. Clearly, average product (and therefore output per man-hour worked) can be increased by the simple expedient of reducing the amount of labor employed. Does it follow that policies leading to a reduction in

Figure 12.13 *Measured Productivity*

Measured productivity statistics report total output per man-hour employed. This is equivalent to measuring the average product of labor (letting labor be factor a) in panels (a) and (b) of this figure. This measure is obviously sensitive to the amount of labor used. One way to increase productivity is to simply employ less labor. This would reduce output per capita but would achieve the objective of increasing measured productivity.

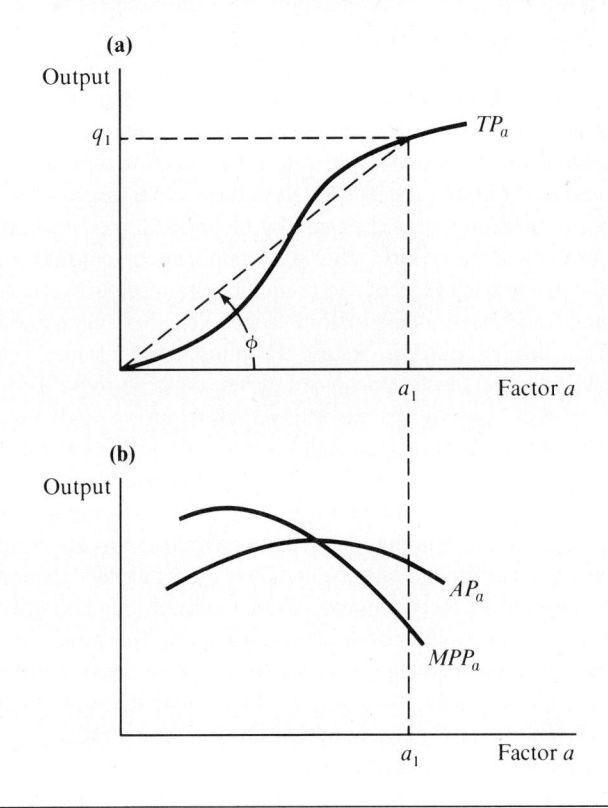

(a) Output vs Factor a: curve TP_a with q_1 at a_1, angle ϕ shown.

(b) Output vs Factor a: curves AP_a and MPP_a, evaluated at a_1.

employment should be implemented simply because they "increase productivity?" Of course not! Total output (and therefore per capita output) is increased at a_1 by expanding, rather than contracting, employment.

The Paradox of Increasing Returns to Labor

A straightforward implication of this discussion would seem to be that productivity will move countercyclically with the business cycle. In other words, during recessions, as more and more workers are laid off, the remaining workers will be employed with the same capital resources used during periods of higher economic activity. This would in turn suggest that the productivity of these workers and (given the linkage between productivity and factor demand) wages would be higher during recessions than during booms. Many studies of productivity trends over the past two decades seem to suggest the opposite result—as does casual observation. Output per man-hour in the comparatively prosperous years of 1972 and 1977 increased 3.5 and 2.4 percent, respectively; productivity increased in the recession years of 1974 and 1982 by −2.4 and 0.4, respectively. More systematic statistical correlations of output and employment seem to confirm this suggestion of increasing returns to labor. Some economists have even maintained that this observed relationship between productivity and employment of labor has "exploded" the marginal productivity theory of labor demand.[3]

Abandonment of our theory of the demand for factors of production would seem an excessively harsh sentence to impose on the basis of the reported evidence. There are a number of explanations to which we may appeal to resolve this paradox that are not inconsistent with standard production theory.

First, measured output may incorrectly reflect actual output. Reported output for the economy measures only the quantity of finished goods produced. During recessions, firms will have little reason to build up inventories of completed goods, but they may use some of the retained employees to work on unfinished assemblies and to do postponable maintenance. The work performed will not be included in measured output. Reported total output, and therefore reported output per worker, will thus be biased downward during these periods.

Second, workers themselves exert more effort during good times than bad. One can think of this in terms of an analogy with businesses for which demand is seasonal. College professors have an implicit contract with their university to read exams in enough time to get their final grades in on time. Sometimes this requires them to work late into the evenings—but these peaks of effort are compensated for at other times by a certain amount of sanctioned "goofing off" during the regular sessions. Agricultural workers could tell similar tales of long hours worked during harvest time and other months of well-paid idleness. The same thing can occur with employers over the business cycle. When orders are backing up, workers may be persuaded to put out extra effort with the knowledge that when things slack off they will be allowed to slow down the pace. Output per man-hour would therefore be greater during the busy periods than slack periods.

This does not really suggest that our production theory of derived demand is defective. It merely recognizes that there are at least two important dimensions that must be considered in measuring labor input: the quantity of man-hours and the quantity of effort. According to this interpretation, workers are paid wages equal to their typical, or average, marginal revenue products. It also suggests that an increase in the number of workers employed *over the cycle* would be associated with lower average productivity and with lower wages.

In a recent paper[4] John Tatom proposes yet another interesting explanation for the observed procyclical behavior of productivity and wages. He maintains that rising productivity is observed over the business cycle not because of increasing returns to labor but because capital employment itself varies over the cycle as

---

[3] See, for example, Arthur M. Okun, "Inflation: Its Mechanics and Welfare Cost," *Brookings Papers on Economic Activity*, no. 2 (1975): 378.

[4] John A. Tatom, "The 'Problem' of Procyclical Real Wages and Productivity," *Journal of Political Economy*, 88 (April 1980): 385–399.

well. By statistically estimating a production function using man-hours employed and the capital stock, Tatom finds the usual result of increasing returns to labor. When he employs data on "utilized capital" instead of existing capital, however, he observes diminishing returns. This is not surprising, as his utilized capital quantity falls sharply relative to man-hours employed in each downturn. However, Tatom leaves unexplained the dramatic cycles in capital employment, which until now economists have treated as much more stable than labor employment.[5]

At any rate, few economists are ready to abandon the theory of derived demand at present. There is far more evidence that is consistent with the theory than is inconsistent with it. Moreover, no one has proposed a competing theory that is superior. Let us therefore turn to a different set of topics concerned with productivity, one that considers productivity under conditions of full employment. The aspect of productivity that dominates most popular discussion is not the movement along a total product curve but an upward shift in that curve that increases output per worker at every level of employment. This discussion is concerned with obtaining greater output from a given workforce, rather than increased output per worker from a shrinking workforce. Let us therefore turn our attention in the remainder of this chapter toward factors that influence productivity in this dimension.

The Capital–Labor Ratio

It is fruitful to view changes in factor productivity in the context of an underlying production function for economywide output. Changes in this output are thus related to changes in the use of inputs, scale effects, and technical change in the manner described in this and the preceding chapter. The primary source of such change, particularly in the short run, is change in the use of inputs. A seemingly irrepressible feature of the American economy is that population, and therefore the supply of labor, is continuously growing. The effects of a growing labor force on a static production function are easily traced.

Assume that a constant proportion of the population is employed so that productivity and per capita income move together. An increase in the quantity of labor supplied through population growth, coupled with a fixed quantity of capital, must diminish both productivity and per capita income—indeed, productivity will decline even with positive net investment and a growing capital stock. If there are constant returns to scale in the production function, then capital must increase in proportion to population growth *merely to maintain productivity at a constant level*. As the demand for labor is directly related to productivity, population growth, which proceeds faster than the growth of the capital stock, will also produce declining wages.

---

[5] The interested and technically equipped reader may also wish to consider Christopher A. Sims, "Output and Labor Input in Manufacturing," *Brookings Papers on Economic Activity*, no. 3 (1974): 695–728. Sims makes a novel and convincing case that the appearance of increasing returns to labor is merely a statistical artifact resulting from the fact that employers are making continuous changes in their workforces toward optima that are themselves moving. As this dynamic process unfolds, the resulting path of output and employment leaves the deceptive appearance noted. When Sims reestimates the relationship by employing a procedure that purges the results of this bias, no increasing returns are observed.

In the long run, of course, technical change may produce offsetting shifts in the production function so that productivity may rise even with less than proportional growth in capital. However, recent studies on the sources of U. S. growth in the postwar period cast doubt on the importance of technical change as a contributor to that expansion. While earlier work[6] has maintained that the contribution of advances in knowledge has accounted for as much as one third of the growth in output, a more recent study by Berndt and Khaled[7] found no evidence to support any measurable effect. On the contrary, these writers attributed most of the growth in per capita output to economies of scale in American production. This suggests that we cannot expect technical change to rescue an economy from lagging capital accumulation.

If capital accumulation is essential to maintain and expand productivity in the face of continuing population growth, it is important to weigh carefully the impact of policies that are inimical to savings and investment. Federal policy in the income security and tax areas have created an environment that is seriously inhospitable to both in the postwar period.

Consider the social security system. In the absence of such a system, people will save during their working years to finance consumption during retirement. These savings will free current resources for the purposes of investment and capital formation. With the introduction of a social security system, workers perceive that a substantial share of their retirement needs is provided for and will engage in less saving on their own. They are, of course, taxed under this system, but these taxes are not accumulated in a fund, as are contributions to private pension plans, but are directly distributed to current beneficiaries, who promptly spend them. Private savings are reduced with no offsetting government savings to replace them. One widely cited study estimates that the social security system has produced a net deficit of 38 percent in the American capital stock.[8]

Furthermore, the income from capital has been singled out for special treatment in a number of ways that retard savings and thus diminish the available stock of capital. We have a separate corporate income tax that must be paid on capital income originating in the corporate sector. Until recently the personal income tax on unearned (capital) income rose to a higher marginal rate than did the rate for earned (labor) income. In addition, there are property taxes levied by state and local governments on capital equipment and buildings, as well as "intangibles," which are taxes on corporate stock held by residents of the corporation's state. Finally, there is the impact of inflation on all these taxes, which exaggerates the income earned and causes the taxes to be even more burdensome.

Consider, for example, the impact of inflation on holding real estate assets. In considering whether to construct a building, a firm must consider that should it decide to sell the building ten years later, its price will be higher due to inflation. The firm will have to pay a tax on this "capital gain" even though on the date of

---

[6] See, for example, Edward F. Denison, *Accounting for United States Economic Growth, 1929–1969* (Washington: The Brookings Institute, 1974), 131.

[7] Ernst R. Berndt and Mohammed S. Khaled, "Parametric Productivity Measurement and Choice Among Flexible Functional Forms," *Journal of Political Economy* 87 (December 1979): 1220–1245.

[8] See Martin Feldstein, "Social Security, Induced Retirement and Aggregate Capital Accumulation," *Journal of Political Economy* 82 (September/October 1974): 905–926.

sale it is no more valuable (in terms of its exchange value for other goods) than it was on the day it was purchased.

A recent study concluded that the effect of the present tax treatment of capital income is a net reduction of personal savings of nearly $60 billion per year.[9] In another study, the same author states:

In the 1973 through 1977 period the average rate of personal saving in the United States was 6.7 percent. By 1978 it had fallen to 5.3 percent. The first quarter of 1980 it fell to a thirty-year low of 3.3 percent. This compares to personal saving rates in the same period of almost 25 percent in Japan, over 15 percent in France, and almost 18 percent in West Germany.[10]

This treatment of capital income is undoubtedly responsible for some part of these savings deficits. The impact of these reductions in capital available for use on American productivity must therefore be substantial.

Technical Change

There is considerable disagreement among economists on the role played by technical change in postwar growth. The vastly improved efficiency of transportation and communications, along with the technological advances imbedded in the modern industrial complex, have had an impact on output per man-hour that could not have been achieved 100 years ago with a tenfold increase in the capital stock. Technological progress has not only made possible substantial advances in the quality of life—it has influenced the quantity as well. Due to recent scientific and medical advances, life expectancy in the United States has increased from 54 years in 1920 to well over 70 today.

Although we cannot measure technical change with the precision that we would like, we can easily observe the influence of factors that either foster or inhibit technological progress. Rarely is such progress spontaneous. For every "bolt out of the blue" discovery there are dozens that are the result of years of painstaking trial and error. Innovation responds to economic incentives. The greater the rewards, the more individuals and companies will make the necessary investments in trial and error; hence, the more rapid will be the progress.

Technical progress is manifest not only in the development of new products but in the production of existing products at lower cost. The chief advantage to the investor in this innovation is profit. Factors that inhibit or depreciate profits of firms can be expected to have a discouraging effect on innovative activity, hence, will retard progress. The tax policies discussed in the previous section will therefore not only reduce the rate of capital formation but can be expected to diminish the rate of technological advance as well. However, taxation is not the only feature of the economic environment to discourage research and development. Regulation of business can also inhibit innovative activity.

---

[9]Michael J. Boskin, "Taxation, Saving, and the Rate of Interest," *Journal of Political Economy* 86 (April 1978): S19.

[10]———, "U. S. Economy at the Crossroads," in *The Economy in the 1980s: A Program for Growth and Stability*, ed. M. J. Boskin (San Francisco: Institute for Contemporary Studies, 1980), 3–20.

Peltzman observed this effect in his widely cited study of the impact of the 1962 "proof of efficacy" amendments to the Food and Drug Act.[11] This act sought to limit the introduction of inefficacious drugs by mandating a much more stringent testing and drug approval process. The results apparently have not been what the authors of this legislation intended. Peltzman found that compliance with the regulations roughly doubled the cost of drug development, with obvious effect on its economic attractiveness. He also established a direct statistical link between profitability and the rate of drug development. As a consequence, he was able to attribute virtually the full reduction in the introduction of new chemical entities since 1962 (a reduction of 51 percent) to this regulation. No reduction in the proportion of inefficacious drugs among those that were introduced after 1962 was observed.

Regulation can also directly affect productivity. Much of the new "social regulation" introduced during the 1970s had as a direct consequence the lowering of output per man-hour of labor employed. Environmental legislation requires firms to modify production processes by mandating diversion of labor and capital away from producing output and into cleaning up waste products. Product safety regulation requires the addition of safety features to products (at a cost in terms of the labor, materials, and capital involved). Occupational safety and health regulation requires the implementation of work rules and process design that may be safer but undoubtedly are more costly.

To be sure, a cleaner environment is appreciated by all, and such improvements should be, but are not, included in measurements of national income. To date, however, there is little evidence that this regulation has had a substantial effect on the environment; hence, there may be little that is overlooked in these accounts. By the same token, safer products should sell for higher prices. If the safer products meet such a market test, firms ought to be willing to supply them without regulation. With respect to safety in the workplace, it might also be pointed out that worker productivity is detrimentally affected by this type of regulation. As wages are likely to bear some part of this cost, workers themselves might be better positioned than regulators to determine whether or not a particular safety measure is worth this cost.

We cannot resolve the questions raised here concerning the desirability of such regulatory activity. Our point in raising them is to indicate the general link between this type of regulation and productivity. To the extent that productivity is adversely affected, wage rates of affected workers will—indeed, do—reflect it. Denison has in fact estimated the effect of this change in the regulatory environment since 1967 and finds it substantial.[12] He finds that in 1975 output per unit of input was a full percentage point below the level that could have been achieved had pollution abatement restrictions remained unchanged from the earlier date. A similar deficit of roughly half this magnitude was attributed to employee safety and health regulation.

---

[11] Sam Peltzman, *Regulation of Pharmaceutical Innovation: The 1962 Amendments* (Washington: The American Enterprise Institute, 1974).

[12] Edward F. Denison, *Accounting for Slower Economic Growth: The United States in the 1970s* (Washington: The Brookings Institution, 1979), 68.

12.5 The Demand for Labor and the Number of Jobs

Next to inflation and productivity, perhaps the most talked-about economic topic among laymen is the **number of jobs**. Civic groups work diligently to bring new employers to their communities, and politicians proudly keep scorecards on the number of jobs "created" during their administrations. Certainly, not having a job is a source of great anxiety to a person without one, and finding a job can be just about the most important thing on such a person's mind. However, one of the most difficult tasks an economist has is to explain to anyone, much less the job seeker referred to, that this sort of thinking cannot be extended to the labor market as a whole. There is no finite number of jobs to be sought out, and a job can no more be "created" than can a worker.

Sources of Unemployment

The number of jobs cannot be fixed, for the demand for labor depends on its price. More labor is demanded at low wages than at high wages. Thus, assuming each worker supplies a fixed quantity of labor, the number of jobs available at a particular time is itself dependent on the wage rate. The concept of "full employment" used in macroeconomics therefore corresponds to our notion of an equilibrium wage rate. When the wage rate paid to labor is below this equilibrium rate, more jobs exist than there are workers willing to fill them. This condition produces rising wages. On the other hand, when wages exceed the equilibrium wage rate, more workers will seek jobs than there are jobs available. This is the principal source of unemployment. Our understanding of this phenomenon may be enhanced through a more detailed discussion of the reasons for discrepancies between wage rates paid and the equilibrium wage.

The Minimum Wage

The most obvious source of such a discrepancy is a restriction on wage rates that prevents them from falling to equilibrium levels. Minimum wage legislation is one such restriction. For some members of the labor force, particularly the young and inexperienced, the market-clearing wage is quite low. Not only are these workers relatively unproductive due to their lack of skills, but their lack of experience implies that the employers may wish to spend some of their firms' own resources training them. The expenditure on training will further lower wages for the following reason. Let the marginal revenue product of these workers be given as MRP_a. The marginal factor cost, on the other hand, will include not only the wages paid, w_a, but the expenditure on training, c_t. These workers will therefore be hired under the condition that marginal revenue product equal marginal factor cost; that is:

$$MRP_a = w_a + c_t.$$

Solving this expression for the wage rate gives:

$$w_a = MRP_a - c_t.$$

Clearly, the higher these training costs, the lower will be the money wage the employer will be willing to pay.

This is not to say that the workers are taken advantage of by their employer. They may be receiving very valuable training, which will greatly improve their productivity in future years. In fact, the acceptance of wages below a worker's marginal revenue product in exchange for training may be usefully thought of as an investment by the worker in his or her future earning ability. This topic will be more thoroughly explored in Chapter 16.

Our point here is to suggest that the imposition of a minimum wage will have two adverse effects. First, it will reduce the number of untrained workers that employers will seek to hire. Second, it will influence those workers remaining employed to accept less training, hence adversely affecting their future productivity. These effects are briefly indicated in Figure 12.14. Let the number of workers in this category be a^*, and assume that the quantity of labor that they will supply is unresponsive to wage rate changes so that the supply of labor is the vertical line above a^* labeled S_a. The demand curve for these workers in the absence of training is given by D. As previously discussed, this curve indicates the marginal revenue product for each quantity of labor along the horizontal axis. Workers who re-

Figure 12.14 *The Minimum Wage and Employer-Provided Training*

Curve D is the firm's demand curve for labor identifying the marginal revenue product for labor at each quantity on the assumption that no training is provided. The firm will provide training if it may reduce wages by an amount that covers the training cost. It will therefore offer the training and continue to hire a^* units of labor if it may reduce the wage paid from w_{nt} to w_a^* and in so doing recoup training costs c_1. The minimum wage of w_m prevents the firm from paying a wage as low as w_a^*. It may reduce employment to a_1 or reduce expenditure on training to some amount like c_2, at which it will hire a_2 units of labor. The minimum wage therefore causes a reduction in training and leaves some workers (the difference between a^* and a_2) unemployed.

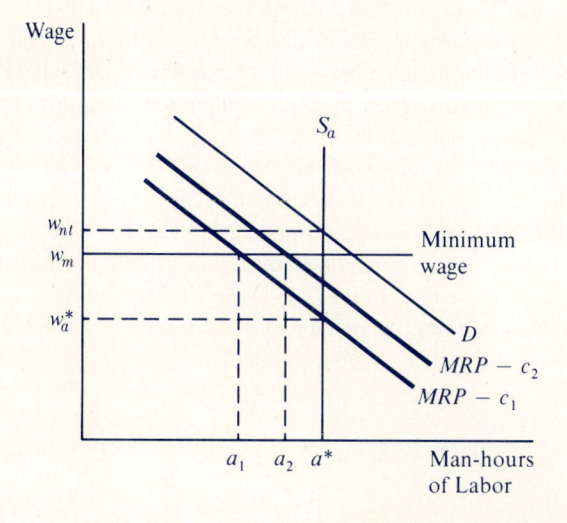

ceive no training can expect to earn a wage of w_{nt}, which equates the marginal revenue product and the marginal factor cost under these circumstances. In this case c_t in the wage rate expression above will be zero; hence, w_a will equal MRP_a.

However, recognizing that training will provide access to more productive and therefore better-paying jobs in the future, workers may choose to take advantage of on-the-job training provided by employers, even though it will lower their current wages. If this training costs the employer c_1 per unit of labor hired, the money wage must fall to w_a^*. Now let a minimum wage of w_m be imposed. This will increase the marginal factor cost by the difference between w_m and w_a^*, and employers will respond by choosing that quantity of labor which equates the higher marginal factor cost $w_m + c_1$ to marginal revenue product, that is, a_1. This leaves a part of this labor force unemployed, as a^* are seeking employment but only a_1 are hired.

Unemployed workers have two unhappy alternatives under these circumstances. They may remain unemployed, or they may accept employment with less training. Some will undoubtedly choose the latter. If the firm may reduce training costs to c_2, for example, it may hire a_2 workers at the minimum wage. However, the affected workers will not obtain this employment without cost. For by accepting employment on these terms, young workers may be accepting "dead-end" jobs with little hope for future improvement in wages or in the scope of their later careers. The net effect of such a minimum wage is a rise in the money wage for some workers combined with less training and a residual unemployment effect (shown in the figure as the difference between a^* and a_2). Note too that the value of the **full wage** (money wages plus the value of training supplied) may actually decline for those workers who remain employed. If there are important economies of scale in the provision of training, each worker may end up receiving less training per dollar of wages given up at the lower level c_2 than at the original level c_1. In such a scenario *all* workers in this category are worse off as a result.

Considerable evidence of the adverse effects of minimum wage legislation has been produced in recent years. Lazear[13] has estimated that 40 percent of the earnings of young white males comes in the form of on-the-job-training and 36 percent of the earnings of nonwhite males is received in this form. The scope for reduction in this component of compensation in response to increases in the minimum wage is therefore large. Hashimoto has estimated this impact and finds the response substantial.[14] According to his estimates a 1-percent increase in the minimum wage reduces the investment in on-the-job training by between 2.5 and 2.7 percent for young white males. Accordingly, he estimates that the 1967 revisions of this law resulted in a reduction in the value of on-the-job training for this group by from 26 to 31 percent. He attributes the failure to identify a corresponding effect for young black males to "unreliable data." His estimates also suggest a decline in the full wage in response to minimum wage increases for young white males.

---

[13] E. Lazear, "The Narrowing of Black-White Wage Differentials is Illusory," *American Economic Review* 69 (September 1979): 559.

[14] Masanori Hashimoto, *Minimum Wages and On-the-Job Training* (Washington: The American Enterprise Institute, 1981).

The employment effect has been widely documented. A recent study by Welch and Cunningham[15] suggests that in 1970 minimum wage laws had increased the costs of hiring 18 to 19 year olds by 11.3 percent, with a corresponding reduction of employment of 15.2 percent. Estimated employment effects for younger workers were considerably larger.

Supply Restrictions

Those workers unemployed as a result of minimum wage legislation are at the bottom of the economic ladder and are helpless to improve their situation. There are other workers who are unemployed because they are seeking *better* employment. This occurs where there are barriers to entry into particular types of employment so that the wages exceed the equilibrium levels. Examples of such barriers are licenses to perform certain types of work and restrictions on union membership. A similar effect is produced by wage scales for certain jobs, typically in the government sector, that are insensitive to market conditions. This effect operates in two different ways to produce unemployment. First, would-be workers in these markets may remain unemployed while seeking the license or the membership. Second, once these workers have made their entrance, the amount of work available may be inadequate to keep all of them fully employed.

Consider the first of these effects. Assume that workers have a choice of selecting jobs in an unrestricted market where they may obtain employment immediately or of attempting to gain access to other jobs where wages are kept high through licensure or restrictions on union membership. Assume further that access to the restricted market is based on a first-come, first-served basis. As access to the higher-paying market is worth something to such applicants, they will be willing to give up something, even current wages in some other employment, to obtain it. As in the case of underpriced goods discussed in Chapter 2, such a situation can give rise to queues. In this case, however, the queues of workers waiting for their turn at the restricted jobs are counted as unemployed.

The second case occurs almost exclusively in the unionized sector, where the union has not only the power to determine the *number* of workers available to perform the work but can negotiate the *wage rate* with employers at the same time. Under these circumstances the wage rate set may not be that which clears the market among those authorized to supply the restricted services. On the contrary, it is easy to show that this is typically not the case. Consider Figure 12.15. Let the supply of union labor available be S and the demand curve for this labor from employers be D. The market-clearing wage among union members would in this case be w^*. If, however, the demand for labor at w^* is inelastic, total wages paid may be increased by increasing the wage rate. Income to the membership will be maximized by selecting wage rate w_1, where the elasticity of demand is just equal to -1.

---

[15] Finis Welch and James Cunningham, "Effects of Minimum Wages on the Level and Age Composition of Employment," *Review of Economics and Statistics* 60 (February 1978): 140–145. For a survey of recent evidence on these effects and others see Finis Welch, *Minimum Wages: Issues and Evidence* (Washington: The American Enterprise Institute, 1978).

Figure 12.15 *Unions and Unemployment*

The market-clearing wage in this figure is w^*, at which the fixed supply a^* is fully employed. If demand for labor is inelastic at this equilibrium wage, total spending on labor (total wage income) will increase when the wage is increased. Wage income is maximized at w_1, at which demand elasticity is unitary. Raising the wage to this level will cause unemployment equal to the difference between a^* and a_1, the quantity of labor demanded at w_1.

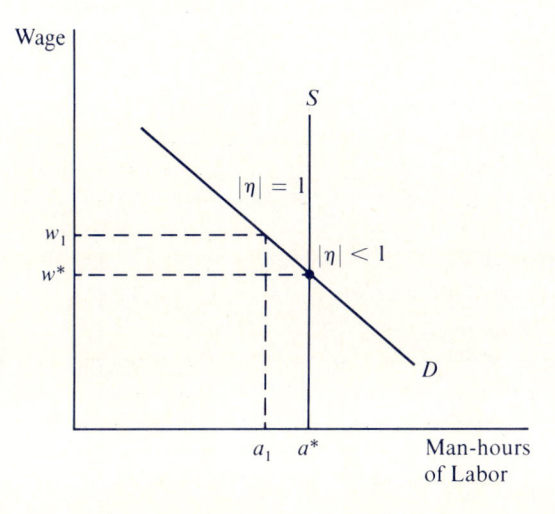

In this case, the union will typically establish some method of rationing the existing jobs among the membership, since fewer than a^* are demanded at wage w_1. Those workers who have not been assigned a job are technically unemployed and counted so by the Labor Department, in spite of the fact that their incomes are higher than they would be were the union to set a wage that kept them all fully employed.

Seasonal and Cyclical Unemployment

A third category of unemployment is not really unemployment at all in the sense of the two we have discussed thus far. In those cases more labor was supplied to perform the jobs sought at prevailing wages than was demanded. In this category we observe the *appearance* of unemployment while markets actually clear.

Consider first the case of so-called **seasonal unemployment**. In certain labor markets the demand for labor is greater during certain parts of the year than others. When demand is high, it draws workers into the labor force who are unwilling to work at wages paid during the slow season. Although counted as unemployed, these workers will not accept work at prevailing wages and hence are not technically unemployed.

This problem is illustrated in Figure 12.16. We assume that the workforce in this industry is composed of two types of workers. On the one hand we have "per-

Figure 12.16 *Seasonal Unemployment*

Panel (c) of this figure contains two demand curves reflecting demand for labor during different seasons. Demand curve D_1 depicts demand during periods of high demand, while demand curve D_2 reflects demand during off-peak months. Supply in this panel is made up of the combined quantities supplied at each wage by permanent workers (those in panel [b]) and transitory workers (those in panel [c]). During off-peak months demand falls to D_2 and with it the wage to w_2. At this wage all transitory workers leave the workforce and only permanent workers remain. Transitory workers may nevertheless consider themselves unemployed and collect unemployment benefits. They would accept work at the high demand equilibrium wage w_1 but not at the low demand wage. Technically, however, they are not unemployed.

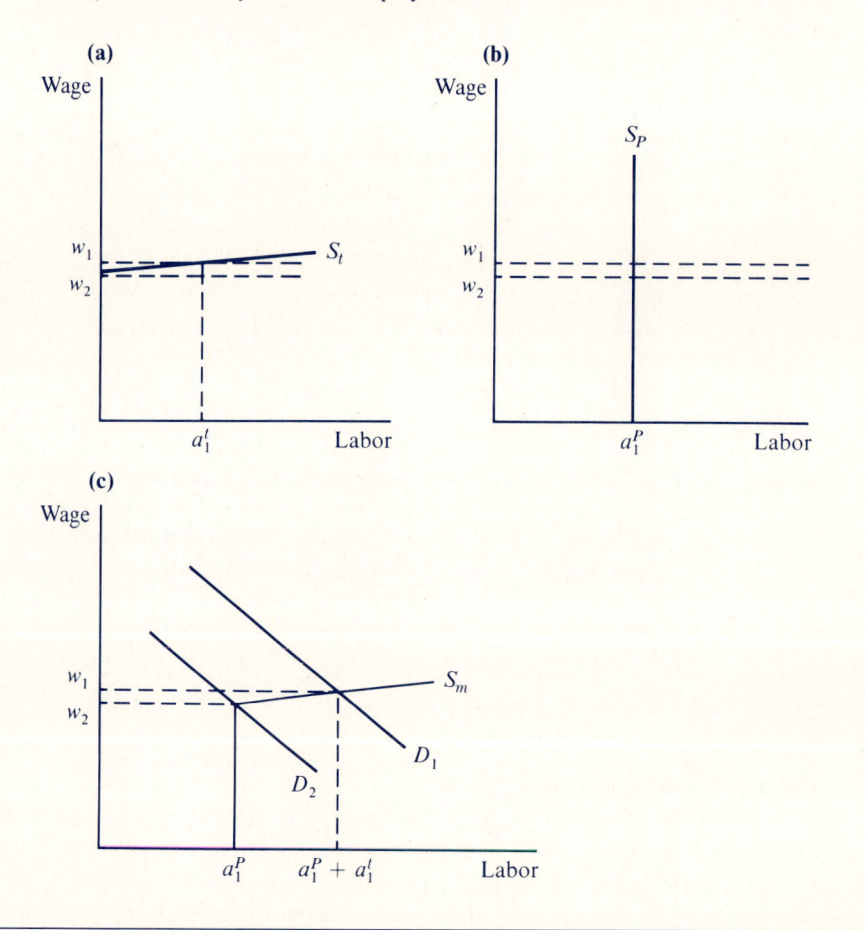

manent" workers, who are interested in full-time work regardless of the wage. These are shown in panel (b) of the figure. They are willing to supply a_1^P units of labor at any wage. On the other hand, there is a group of "transitory" workers, who will supply labor to this industry so long as the wage exceeds some minimum, w_2, but are unwilling to work at wages below this level. These may be married housewives, retired workers, students, or even some of those waiting for the restricted opportunities discussed in the previous section. The combined supplies from these two groups are shown in panel (c).

Demand is also shown in panel (c). As demand in this figure varies from season to season, we show two possible demand curves: D_1, which prevails during high demand months, and D_2, which prevails during low demand months. During the most active periods, quantity demanded equals quantity supplied at a wage of w_1, which, in addition to employing all of the permanent workers, draws into the market a_1^t of the transitory workers. During slack periods, however, demand falls and with it the equilibrium wage. The market now clears at wage w_2, with all transitory workers now having left the market. A number of these transitory workers will nevertheless represent themselves as unemployed and even claim unemployment insurance—indeed, they would certainly accept work at the peak wage of w_1 if they could find it. This is, of course, irrelevant to the question of whether they are legitimately unemployed at the prevailing wage. The fact is that the market clears at w_2, and all who are willing to accept work at this wage are employed.

An example of such a seasonal employer is the Internal Revenue Service, which employs thousands of workers during the peak period from January to July when income tax returns are filed and processed. Demand for extra clerical workers is greatly diminished for the balance of the year, and many of these employees are laid off. Some of them claim unemployment compensation for having lost their jobs in spite of the fact that few would remain working at a wage that cleared the market for their services during the off season.

A similar phenomenon occurs in connection with the business cycle. The demand for such products as steel and automobiles is closely related to the state of the economy. When times are good, demand for these products is high; hence, demand for workers in these industries is also high. When times are lean, however, auto and steel production is cut back and with it employment. As it takes time and considerable expense to train steelworkers and machinists, it is useful to have an inventory of experienced workers around to employ during peak periods. One way to achieve this result is to retain on the payroll during slow periods more workers than can be gainfully employed. The same result can be achieved, however, by paying these workers a sufficiently high wage during peaks that they will not seek other work when laid off. Instead, they will merely bide their time until being recalled to work. This method has the advantage that a part of the support for these workers when they are not needed will be paid through unemployment compensation rather than out of the firm's coffers.

Unemployment as Job Information Search

Markets function best when the item exchanged is simple in design so that all its features may be readily observed. They also work best where buyer and seller are frequently active in the market, obtaining in the process a fund of knowledge that allows them to evaluate certain offers in terms of others potentially available. The labor market exhibits neither of these features. The individual worker offers only himself or herself—a veritable Pandora's box of unknowns to prospective employers. Is this worker lazy or energetic, dull or imaginative and resourceful, bumbling or proficient, irresponsible or conscientious, honest or a crook? The employer cannot simply hire the worker who offers his or her services at the lowest wage but must sift through the available labor supply and determine what wages to pay to obtain the combination of talents and attributes sought.

Nor does the worker automatically accept the highest wage offer he or she is offered. Employers and conditions of employment vary from job to job. Even the wage is difficult to evaluate, for there are varying fringe benefits, such as vacations, retirement and health plans, available overtime work, and expectations of advancement, all of which must be factored into the calculations before the worker can be certain that one employer is more attractive than another. And unlike employers, who seek new workers with sufficient regularity that they know what they are looking for, most workers change jobs infrequently, so that few know for certain what they are worth on the market.

Under these circumstances it is not surprising that, once laid off, employees will not necessarily be made an offer by the first employer they visit, nor that they may decline the first offer they receive. On the contrary, many unemployed workers are really *employing themselves* to obtain job market information. The collection of such information is costly; wages from employment must be forgone. The information obtained may nevertheless be worth these costs to the workers. Acceptance of a job early in the search process is deterred by consideration of the possibility that the offer is untypically low relative to others yet uninvestigated. The accumulation of information, like the gathering of a sample, narrows the variance around the expectation formed, so that eventually it will pay to discontinue the search and accept an offer.

Workers are likely to enter into such a **job information search** with a bias concerning conditions. Their expectations about the jobs they seek are initially framed by those that they left. These expectations are then modified as workers collect information during their search for a new job. Even when conditions are improving, their perceptions of this improvement will be imperfectly perceived. They are more likely to accept a job that is better than their previous one but less attractive than the one that they would seek with better information about alternatives. For this reason periods of unemployment are unusually low during economic expansion. Similarly, when conditions are worsening, workers will continue this search longer than they would with better information. In these times they will seek a job more similar to their last than real conditions in the market suggest is likely to be found. Unemployment (search) during periods of stagnation or recession will therefore be unusually long.

Lucas and Rapping[16] incorporated such an "unemployment as employment at job search" approach to the study of the unemployment rate from the depression years through 1965. Using the simplest possible model of adaptive expectations in order to obtain the best possible results from their limited data, they were able to track the unemployment rate with surprising accuracy. A recent article by Darby[17] using corrected unemployment data and an alternative wage rate series goes even further toward explaining the high unemployment rates of the 1930s and subsequent year-to-year variations.

---

[16] R. E. Lucas, Jr., and L. A. Rapping, "Real Wages, Employment and Inflation," *Journal of Political Economy* 77 (September/October 1969): 721–754.

[17] Michael R. Darby, "Three-and-a-Half Million U. S. Employees Have Been Mislaid: Or, an Explanation of Unemployment, 1934–41," *Journal of Political Economy* 84 (February 1976): 1–16.

The reader is cautioned not to interpret this discussion as "explaining" in any sense the business cycle itself or the causes of depressions. That is a topic with which economists have so far failed to make much headway. Our claim here is much more modest—that is, that the presence of a business cycle does not in and of itself explain cycles in unemployment. The business cycle at most will produce shifts in the demand for labor. If prices adjusted readily to these shifts in demand, then business cycles would produce variations in worker income but no variation in unemployment. The "search" model of unemployment provides a useful bridge over the troublesome gap between price theory and the more bluntly posed issues dealt with in macroeconomics.

Summary

In this chapter we treated the theory of demand for factors of production along with two topics derived from that theory: factor productivity and unemployment. Changes in the use of a factor of production were shown to influence both sides of the income statements of firms, revenues and costs, and each was considered in detail. Increased factor use affects revenues through its effect on output. The rate at which revenues change per unit change in the use of a factor is defined as the marginal revenue product. This was shown to equal the product of the marginal physical product of the factor and marginal revenue. Increased factor use affects costs through its influence on expenditure on that factor. The rate at which cost changes per unit change in the use of the factor is defined as the marginal factor cost. Where the factor is supplied to firms at a constant price (perfectly elastically), the marginal factor cost is simply that factor price itself. Profit maximization requires that factors be used up to the point at which marginal revenue product is equal to marginal factor cost.

The demand for factors relates changes in factor prices to changes in the quantity of that factor which a firm will choose. The response of firms to factor price changes was broken down into two effects: a substitution effect and an output effect. Both effects were analyzed for the case of the normal factor and the case of the inferior factor. In each case it was shown that both substitution effects and output effects will operate in the opposite direction to a price change. Unlike the household demand curves for goods, it is therefore provable that demand curves for factors **must** *slope downward to the right. There can be no Giffen paradox where the demand for inputs is concerned.*

We considered the topic of labor productivity at length and discussed the empirical observation that suggests short-run increasing returns to labor. We derived this inference from the observation that labor productivity varies procyclically—that is, labor productivity is lower in recessions than in prosperous times. We considered several explanations for such an apparent paradox. Output may be incorrectly measured in ways that lead to underreporting during recessions relative to boom periods. Worker effort may vary procyclically, leading to underreporting of labor inputs during booms relative to recessions. And capital employment may vary over the cycle more widely than labor employment, in which case procyclical productivity change is **implied** *by diminishing returns.*

We also discussed the relationship of capital accumulation to labor productivity. A growing labor force requires increased savings and capital accumulation merely to maintain a given level of productivity and wages. Unfunded income maintenance programs such as social security were shown to have a serious impact on the savings rate and therefore on productivity and wages. A similar effect of the existing tax structure that discriminates against income paid to capital was discussed in detail.

Technical change may also affect productivity, though some disagreement exists concerning its importance in postwar growth. Discriminatory taxation of capital income can influence the level of research and development and thus the rate of technical change. Regulation intended to protect the environment or improve worker safety adversely affects measured productivity.

Unemployment is defined as a situation in which the wage rate fails to clear the labor market. Two "institutional" sources of such unemployment were discussed: wage restrictions and supply restrictions. Wage restrictions, such as the minimum wage, prevent low productivity workers from finding employment in numbers sufficient to clear the market for their services. They also diminish the amount of training undertaken by young and inexperienced workers. Supply restrictions, on the other hand, keep wages in certain occupations higher than they would be otherwise, with the effect that some workers remain unemployed trying to enter these industries. At the same time, the amount of work available for those qualified to supply it may be inadequate to keep them fully employed. Workers who leave the labor force when seasonal demand drops wages below reservation levels are incorrectly counted as unemployed.

These explanations may account for a certain amount of permanent or "normal" unemployment, but they cannot explain variations in the level of unemployment over the business cycle. Two explanations may account for the procyclical movement of measured unemployment. On the one hand, firms whose products are in greater demand in boom periods than in recessions may offer wages that compensate workers for periods of unemployment, inducing them to await recall rather than seek alternative employment. Firms prefer this to merely keeping these workers on the payroll, because government unemployment compensation will bear a portion of the cost. Cyclical unemployment may also be explained in terms of job search. Workers seeking new jobs will search longer than normal during recessions, when jobs are less attractive than they expect. During boom periods, on the other hand, they will accept employment more readily, since the jobs they find are more attractive than they expect.

Key Concepts

marginal revenue product
expansion revenue product curve (MRP_{exp})
marginal revenue product curve (MRP)
marginal factor cost
output effect of factor price change

substitution effect of factor price change
productivity
number of jobs
full wage
seasonal unemployment
job information search

Questions

1. *Easy* Explain why the marginal revenue product curve, MRP_a, slopes downward. Must it slope downward if the demand for the firm's output is perfectly elastic? Why?

Hard Under what circumstances will the expansion revenue product curve, MRP_{exp}, slope downward? Assuming that the inputs are all normal, which slope will be steeper, the MRP_a or the MRP_{exp}? Explain.

2. *Easy* The marginal factor cost is the rate of change in expenditure on a factor per unit increase in its use. Why is this sometimes different from the market price of that factor?

Hard If the units in which factor *b* are measured are defined to be of a size such that the price of one of these units is precisely $1.00, the vertical intercept of the isocost curve is always equal to total cost. Explain why this is true. How then might increasing *marginal* cost be represented geometrically?

3. *Easy* If only one factor of production is variable, the demand curve for that factor is simply the marginal revenue product curve. What does the demand curve for a factor of production tell us? Why is this the demand curve in this case?

Hard Where both factors are variable, and both are normal inputs, both the output and the substitution effects of a factor price change will be in the opposite direction of the price change. Explain why this is true, illustrating both effects in a diagram and explaining the logic of their direction of change.

4. *Easy* The productivity of labor as measured by the Bureau of Labor Statistics is simply total output divided by the total man-hours of labor employed. What serious difficulty is encountered in attempting to base policy on increasing productivity measured in this way?

Hard Labor productivity *seems* to increase more rapidly during periods of business expansion than during recessions. What principle of production theory does this seem to violate? Explain. Which of the "explanations" for this paradox discussed in this chapter do you find most attractive? Why?

5. *Easy* If technology is unchanging while the labor force is growing, it is necessary for the capital stock to grow merely to prevent the wage rate from falling. Explain. How does the social security system discourage capital accumulation?

Hard Labor unions in Europe are much more hostile to business than are most unions in the United States. They favor high taxation of income from capital and strictly regulate the introduction of new technology, while American unions are more tolerant of profits and technical innovation. Which attitude is likely to yield higher wages for workers? Why?

6. *Easy* Politicians are widely observed to seek policies that create jobs. What determines the number of jobs, and why is it fruitless for the government to pursue this objective?

Hard The minimum wage has two adverse consequences. It can cause a permanent excess supply of labor for workers with low productivity and also discourage on-the-job training for these same workers that might ultimately increase their productivity. Explain both of these results.

7. *Easy* Workers who are laid off by major employers during recessions are often observed to exert very little effort to find new jobs. For example, during the 1979 recession a mini scandal of sorts was produced when the press reported that many unemployed workers were depositing their unemployment checks in Florida. In a sense, such workers are not truly unemployed at all. The high wages that they receive in boom periods compensate them for the periods of no wages during recessions. Explain.

Hard Some of the variation in unemployment over the business cycle can be explained as increased job search during business slowdowns. Why would workers decline to accept employment more often during recessions than during boom periods?

Chapter 12 Appendix

Demand for an Inferior Factor

Inferior factors are those factors whose use diminishes as output expands holding constant the RTS. The reader will recall that inferiority in a consumer good raised the possibility of the Giffen paradox in the theory of household demand. Interestingly, though certain parallels exist between that theory and the present analysis of factor demand, there can be no such thing as a "Giffen input." Demand for inferior factors must be negatively related to price.

The source of this result may be simply stated, though its presentation will involve us in some digression. We can be certain that the demand for inferior inputs will be negatively related to price *because the output effect on their demand also operates in the opposite direction of the price change*. As the substitution effect is identified holding output constant, the inferiority of an input has no impact on this part of the response. Substitution effects will invariably lead to substitution *away* from the factor that has become relatively more costly. The combined influence of the substitution and output effects must therefore be negatively related to price.

It is in the output effect of a factor price change that inferiority in a factor might seem to introduce problems. Therefore, it is this effect on which we will focus the attention of our analysis. Recall that the output effect is the result of the change in marginal cost due to the factor price change. An increase in the price of a normal input increases marginal cost at each output, leading the firm to adjust output downward. This output adjustment leads to diminished employment of a normal input. A similar adjustment of output in the case of inferior inputs would seem to produce *increased* use of these factors, an effect that would offset the reduction in employment due to the substitution effect. How can it be that this output effect operates in the opposite direction of a factor price change and therefore reduces employment of inferior factors when their prices rise? *This occurs because an increase in the price of an inferior factor reduces marginal cost and thus influences the firm to increase output!*

There is no theoretical result in all of economics that is more counterintuitive than the assertion that an increase in a factor price can lower costs of any kind—yet, this assertion is true. Its proof is far too technical for inclusion here, but we may sketch some outlines of the underlying theory. Figure 12A.1 presents two isoquants in which factor a is inferior. This may be confirmed by noting that the quantity of factor a employed diminishes as output expands along output expansion paths RTS_1 and RTS_2. Now recall from our discussion earlier in this chapter that we may select units of measure for factor b that its price is \$1.00. In this case the vertical intercept of each isocost curve is equal to total expenditure along that curve. The change in total expenditure associated with the increase in output from q_1 to q_2 can therefore be measured by the difference in the heights of the vertical intercepts of the two isocost curves. Thus, along RTS_1 the increase in cost is $c_2 - c_1$, and along RTS_2 the cost increase is $c_4 - c_3$.

An increase in the price of factor a will imply choice of technologies associated with higher RTSs. At a lower price of factor a, for example, the cost-minimizing technology might be that which equates the factor price ratio to RTS_1 at each output. At a higher price of factor a, the price ratio will necessarily in-

Figure 12A.1 **Marginal Cost with Inferior Inputs**

The incremental cost of raising output from q_1 to q_2 depends on the output expansion path. Raising the price of an inferior input can be shown to *lower* this incremental cost. Units of factor b are defined in such a way that the vertical intercepts of isocost curves measure total cost, as was shown in Figure 12.6. At the lower price of factor a the price ratio is given by minus the slope of the isocost curve tangent to isoquant q_1 at its intersection with RTS_1. The increase in total cost associated with the increase in output at this lower price of factor a is therefore $b_2 - b_1$. At the higher price of factor a, input combinations used at each output are identified along RTS_2. Isocost intercepts associated with these combinations must therefore be used to identify the total cost of each output. The total cost of both q_1 and q_2 is higher at this higher price for a. The increase in cost associated with the increase in output from q_1 to q_2 is nevertheless smaller in this case. The incremental cost at the high price of a is $b_4 - b_3$, which is lower than $b_2 - b_1$.

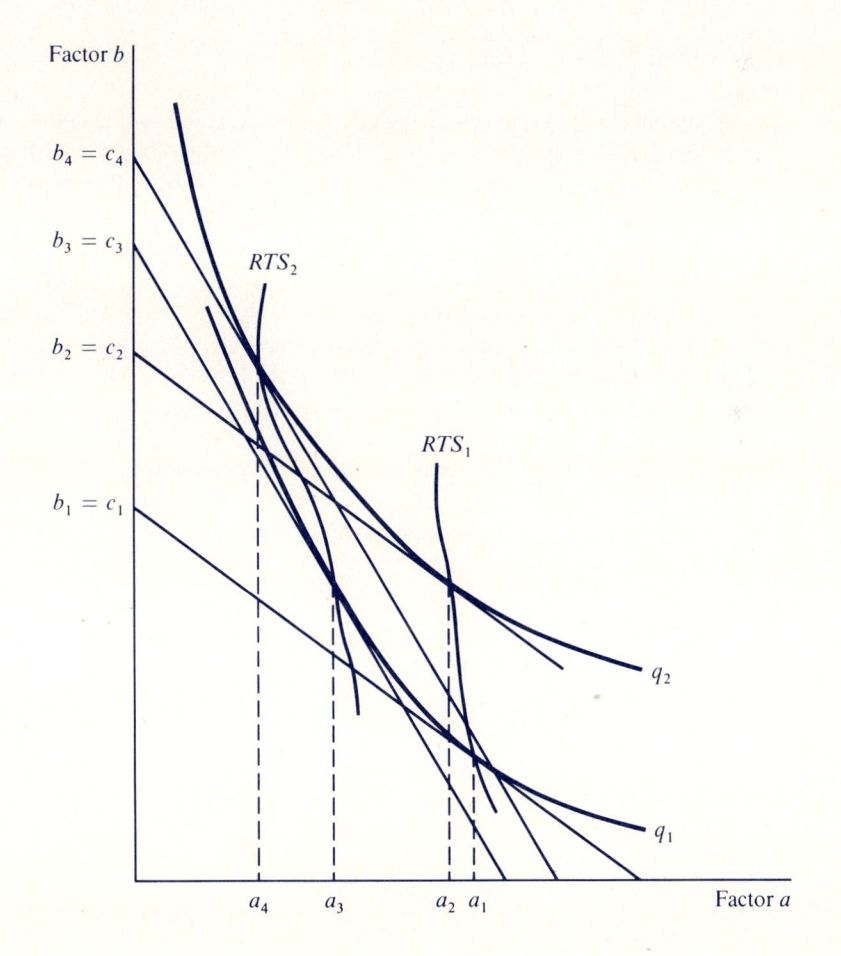

crease, implying the use of factor combinations associated with higher RTSs—for example, RTS_2. Marginal cost associated with the lower price of factor a will therefore be measured along expansion path RTS_1, while marginal cost associated with the higher price for factor a will be measured along expansion path RTS_2.

As we observe the cost changes required to increase output from q_1 to q_2, however, we note that a smaller increase is necessary along RTS_2 than along RTS_1. As the output change is the same in each case, it must be true that marginal cost is lower in the former case than in the latter; that is,

$$\text{Marginal cost} = \frac{\Delta c}{\Delta q} = \frac{\Delta b}{\Delta q},$$

and

$$\frac{b_4 - b_3}{\Delta q} < \frac{b_2 - b_1}{\Delta q}.$$

Marginal cost is lower where the price of the inferior input is higher! This results, of course, because the isoquants "bunch up" and get closer together as they become steeper. We cannot prove here that this will always be true of isoquants involving inferior factors. However, I have often promised my students that I would give an "A" to anyone who could draw a set of isoquants where this did not occur—and I have never had to pay off!

The output effect of a factor price increase also operates in the opposite direction from the price change for an inferior factor, as well. For these factors the price increase lowers marginal cost influencing the firm to expand its output. But since an inferior factor's use is itself negatively related to output, this output expansion leads to *less* of the input being used. The mechanics of the two cases differ, but the bottom line remains the same. For both normal and inferior inputs, both substitution and output effects operate in the opposite direction from price changes. Demand curves for factors must slope downward to the right.

Chapter 13

The Demand for Factors: Other Market Structures

Connections   *In this chapter we extend the analysis of the demand for factors of production to cases in which factors are purchased by firms with market power in the sale of their output and in their purchase of factors of production. This chapter makes extensive use of production theory developed in Chapter 11; it also relies heavily on the discussion of the sources of market power discussed in Chapter 10. Managers of firms operating under regulatory profit restriction are observed to engage in a form of shirking reminiscent of the discussion in Chapter 7. This chapter also considers the popular topic of exploitation and considers a framework that attempts to give it some scientific content. We raise the possibility of increasing wages and employment through regulatory intervention in one of these market settings.*

Chapter 12 treated the demand for factors of production under a single set of market structures. In deriving the demand for labor we assumed that firms were price takers in both the output and input markets. Recall that in Chapter 10, however, we reviewed several market conditions confronting the seller of output with a downward-sloping demand curve. The implications of this market power for factor demand must be considered here. It is also possible for a firm to face an upward- (or occasionally downward-) sloping supply of productive resources. This chapter will consider the sources of market power in the input market and their implications for the demand for factors.

We shall see that market power in the sale of output modifies little of the analysis of factor demand presented in Chapter 12. It makes no difference whether the firm is a price taker or a price searcher in the output market, at least so long as the firm is free to select that output and price. Price searchers who are free to maximize profits will seek the cost-minimizing technology for the selected output just as ardently as will price takers. As we shall see, this result is somewhat modified under profit controls. More difficult problems are posed by the condition of market power over the price of inputs. We will find that such a condition plays havoc with the theory of factor demand—indeed, all of our neatly derived implications for factor markets, which depend on reliably downward-sloping demand curves, are upset when the supply of factors is not perfectly elastic.

We will relate this discussion to a second topic, the various interpretations of the concept of "exploitation." This is clearly a normative—some would say an explosive—term. When people say that someone is being exploited, they are expressing a *belief* that that person is being treated unfairly. Often they are implying that the person is underpaid and should be paid more. If that were all that anyone ever meant by the word *exploitation*, we might bypass the topic altogether; economics sheds little light on the subject of "fairness." Our concern with the topic of exploitation is chiefly motivated by whether it says anything else. In this chapter we will discuss the more objective economic interpretations given to this term.

13.1 Market Power in the Output Market

The response to a factor price change for a firm that is an unregulated price searcher in the output market is in effect the same as that for a price taker considered in Chapter 12. The details of this response are illustrated in Figure 13.1. Panels (a) and (b) depict response in the two dimensions, output and technology, that we explored in the theory of price taker demand. The original equilibrium is associated with marginal cost curve MC_1 in panel (b) and isocost curve c_1 in panel (a). Given output demand D in panel (b), the firm will select output q_1, at which marginal revenue is just equal to marginal cost. The cost-minimizing technology for this output is combination K in panel (a), where the RTS along isoquant q_1 is just equal to the factor price ratio (that is, minus the slope of the isocost curve).

A change in the price of factor a has an impact on both dimensions of this equilibrium. There is again a substitution effect and an output effect. A rise in the price of a, for example, leads the firm to substitute b for a in the input combination, which is now relatively less costly. The cost-minimizing combination for the

Figure 13.1 Input Demand of an Output Price Searcher

Input choice is depicted in panel (a), and output choice is shown in panel (b). At the original price for factor a, marginal cost in the panel (b) is shown as MC_1, which intersects marginal revenue at output q_1. The cost-minimizing combination for producing this output is K in panel (a), where the RTS is equal to the original price ratio. An increase in the supply price of a shifts marginal cost upward to MC_2, lowering optimal output to q_2. In panel (a) this price change produces a substitution effect, shifting the cost-minimizing input combination from K to H, and an output effect due to the output reduction, shifting the combination employed from H to T.

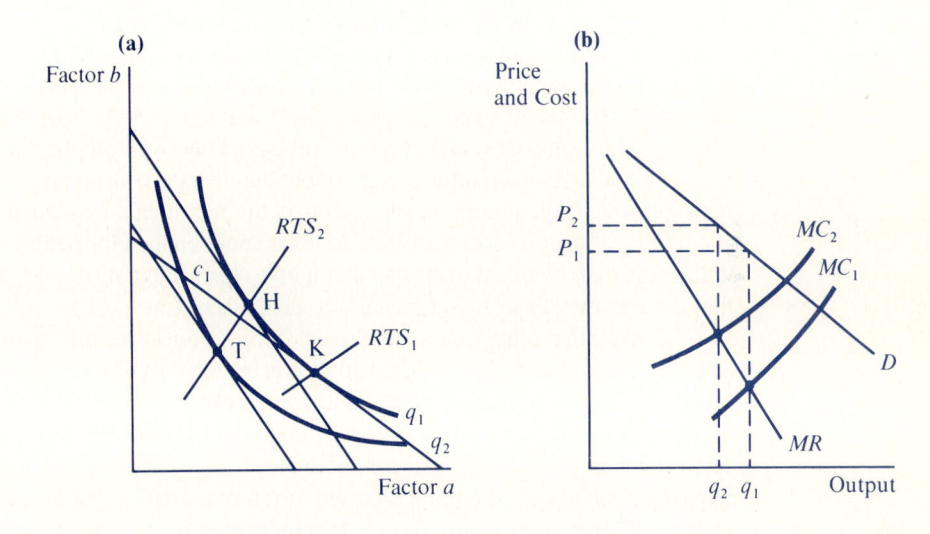

production of q_1 at the higher price of factor a is now combination H. From the slopes of output expansion paths RTS_1 and RTS_2 we can see that both inputs are normal. The increase in the price of factor a therefore increases marginal cost. The output effect of the factor price increase therefore operates through a decrease in the profit-maximizing output to q_2. We may identify the technology chosen by finding the combination on isoquant q_2, which also lies on output expansion path RTS_2. This combination is the cost-minimizing technology for the production of output q_2, since only at this point does the rate of technical substitution equal the new factor price ratio.

Clearly, the only difference between the analysis presented here and that offered in Chapter 12 lies in the output choice in panel (b). Marginal revenue is less than price at every output, and both demand and marginal revenue slope downward to the right. As a practical matter, however, this makes no difference. An upward shift in marginal cost must reduce the optimal output in both cases. This is true whether the marginal revenue curve of the firm is horizontal or downward sloping to the right. Similarly, a downward shift in marginal cost leads to an increase in output in both cases.

There is nothing very surprising in this when we think about it. A firm that is free to maximize profits will seek to minimize the cost of producing whatever output it selects. If relative input prices change, the firm will modify that input combination so that costs are minimized again. This is true whether the firm is a price taker or a price searcher in the output market. However, this analysis must be modified in some cases. As we pointed out in Chapter 10, many firms that are price searchers are natural monopolies and subject to a variety of regulatory constraints on their behavior. Such regulation on price and profit can radically affect the choice of technology of such firms and therefore the demand for inputs.

Profit Restrictions

The importance of **profit restrictions** to the choice of production technology was vividly pointed out in a classic paper by Alchian and Kessel.[1] They pointed out that the use of some inputs adds not only to output but to the satisfaction and enjoyment of the owners and managers. Such features as large and stylish offices, thick carpets, limosines, and attractive (as contrasted with merely capable) secretaries do not have much influence on output but do have consumption value for top management. Expenditure on such items is limited in an unregulated firm by the preference of the owners for money. A dollar spent on the proprietor's office is one dollar less than he or she may spend at home. Such spending comes out of profits that are the owner's to spend in any way he or she wishes.

Consider the influence on this choice of regulations that limit profits of a firm. This regulation has the result of greatly lowering the cost of such utility-producing inputs to the firm's management. Under such circumstances, we should expect firms to respond to the lower cost by employing more of these inputs. Price is often regulated so that the residual left over after all other factors have been reimbursed does not exceed a particular rate of return on the capital invested. We will say a good deal more about rate of return regulation later; here let us consider only its effect on the decision to use such utility-producing inputs.

With a given amount of capital in use, the maximum allowed size of the residual (the owner's income) is fixed. Price is set so that the difference in total revenue and expenditure on everything but capital yields this amount. Consider the cost to the owners of spending marginal dollars on a new limosine. Expenditures go up, and the residual goes down. At this point less than the allowed rate of return is earned and the price is raised, restoring the residual to its former level. Expenditures for a new limosine, new carpet, or travel to a trade meeting in Paris no longer reduce the profits of the firm on a dollar-for-dollar basis. These expenditures are offset by permitted increases in the regulated price of the firm. Permitted profits are unaffected by such expenditures—these "frills" are free!

These observations led Alchian and Kessel to suggest a number of implications concerning the use of such inputs:

> *Public utility managements . . . will engage in activities that raise costs even if they eat up profits. Management will be rational . . . if it uses company funds to hire pleasant and congenial employees and to buy its supplies from salesmen who have these same virtues. They cost more, of course, but how does the regulatory*

---

[1] Armen A. Alchian and Reuben A. Kessel, "Competition, Monopoly, and the Pursuit of Money," in National Bureau of Economic Research, *Aspects of Labor Economics* (Princeton, N.J.: Princeton University Press, 1962), 157–175.

commission decide that these are unjustifiable expenditures—even though stockholders would prefer larger profits (which they aren't allowed to have) and customers would prefer lower product prices? Office furniture and equipment will be of higher quality than otherwise. Fringe benefits will be greater and working conditions more pleasant. The managers will be able to devote a greater part of their business time to community and civic programs. They will reap the prestige rewards given to the "statesman-businessman" class of employers. Vacations will be longer and more expensive. Time off for sick leave and for civic duties will be greater. Buildings and equipment will be more beautiful. Public utility advertising will be found more often in magazines and papers appealing to the intellectual or the culturally elite, because this is a low "cost" way of enhancing the social status of the managers and owners. Larger contributions out of company resources to education, science, and charity will be forthcoming—not because private competitors are less appreciative of these things, but because they cost monopolists less.[2]

A theory of the demand for factors of production that posits cost-minimizing behavior by firms clearly suffers from a lack of realism when applied to these sorts of price searcher markets. The demands for these utility-producing inputs will certainly be greater at any price among regulated price searchers than among similar price taker firms and probably will be less sensitive to price as well.

Utility-producing inputs are not the only factors whose demand can be influenced by regulation. Rate of return regulation can bias the use of inputs, leading a firm to use input combinations that fail to minimize cost. This will occur even when no inputs yield utility to top management. Consider how rate of return regulation works in practice. The value of the capital invested in the regulated firm is estimated; this amount forms the **rate base** upon which the allowed residual is computed. This allowed residual is computed as percentage or allowed rate of return on the rate base.[3] However, the full amount of this allowed residual is not profit. The use of capital in the enterprise has an opportunity cost, which is the return that might be earned by investing it elsewhere. **Permissible profit** is therefore defined as the difference between the allowed residual and the opportunity cost of the capital invested. The firm, therefore, is led to employ the input combination that yields the highest permissible profit. This choice will under certain circumstances lead the firm to use excessive capital in the production technology chosen.

This will not occur if the permitted rate of return is also the competitive rate that capital earns in other firms. However, as choice of an allowed rate of return lower than the market rate will result in a failure to attract any new capital, conservative regulators may allow an excess return to avoid such an embarrassment. It can be shown that in these circumstances the technology chosen will be excessively capital intensive. This result is widely referred to as the **Averch-Johnson effect**, in honor of the economists who first identified it.[4]

---

[2] Ibid., 167.
[3] We will ignore the complications posed by capital depreciation in this discussion.
[4] H. Averch and L. L. Johnson, "Behavior of the Firm under Regulatory Constraints," *American Economic Review* 52 (December 1962): 1053–1069.

Isoprofit Curves

To demonstrate this point we must introduce another analytical device, the **isoprofit curve**.[5] An isoprofit curve connects all factor combinations that produce a given amount of profit. We can relate input combinations to profit in the following way. Each input combination is associated with a unique output and therefore a unique total revenue. Each also costs a certain amount to purchase; hence, these combinations are related to total cost. As profit is the difference between total revenue and total cost, each input combination is related to a unique profit level. An unregulated price searcher selects a profit-maximizing output and a cost-minimizing technology for producing that output.

Consider Figure 13.2. Let the input combination producing the profit-maximizing output be that identified by point π_m. The output itself is q_1, associated with isoquant q_1. That this is a cost-minimizing combination is indicated by the tangency of q_1 with isocost curve I_1 at π_m. This is the only input combination that produces the highest possible profit, but there are others that earn lower profits.

As long as factor prices do not change, the cost-minimizing combination of factors to produce each output will lie along the output expansion path RTS_1. The output at which marginal cost equals price might be q_2, which would be produced at least cost with combination H, also lying on RTS_1. Clearly, this combination of inputs would be associated with lower profits than π_m—say, π_4. Unlike π_m, however, there are many input combinations that will produce π_4 of profit—indeed, the full set of combinations producing π_4 form the oval labeled π_4 in the figure. Any combination inside this oval yields higher profits than π_4, while input combinations outside π_4 are less profitable. All combinations on the oval π_3 earn the same profit, which is higher than π_4, all combinations on π_2 earn the same profit, which is higher than π_3, and so on. Each of these curves is an isoprofit curve.

The Averch-Johnson Effect

We may now examine the Averch-Johnson effect specifically. In Chapter 10 we noted that a natural monopolist could be influenced to expand output toward the level at which price equals marginal cost with regulated interunit price discrimination. This form of intervention is rarely employed. Regulators of utilities favor limits on the rate of return that may be earned on a firm's invested capital. The firm is permitted to raise its prices so long as the profits earned do not exceed an allowable percentage of the value of the firm's capital (the rate base). While it may seem innocent enough, this practice will bias the choice of the technology employed by the firm. We will show that if the rate permitted is higher than the rate normally paid to capital, the firm will select a combination below RTS_1 in Figure 13.2 employing more capital and less labor than the cost-minimizing combination

---

[5]This diagrammatic presentation of the Averch-Johnson effect is adapted from Roger Sherman, *The Economics of Industry* (Boston: Little, Brown and Company, 1974), 386ff, and E. E. Zajac, "A Geometric Treatment of Averch-Johnson's Behavior of the Firm Model," *American Economic Review* 60 (March 1970): 117–125.

Figure 13.2 *Isoprofit Curves*

Each of the oval curves connects combinations of inputs that produce a given profit level. Output q_1 is the profit-maximizing level in the absence of regulation. Combination π_m is the cost-minimizing combination of inputs that produces q_1. Other combinations along isoquant q_1 produce this same output at higher cost and therefore lower profit. The output expansion path RTS_1 identifies the cost-minimizing factor combinations as output expands. At output q_2 along RTS_1, marginal cost equals price.

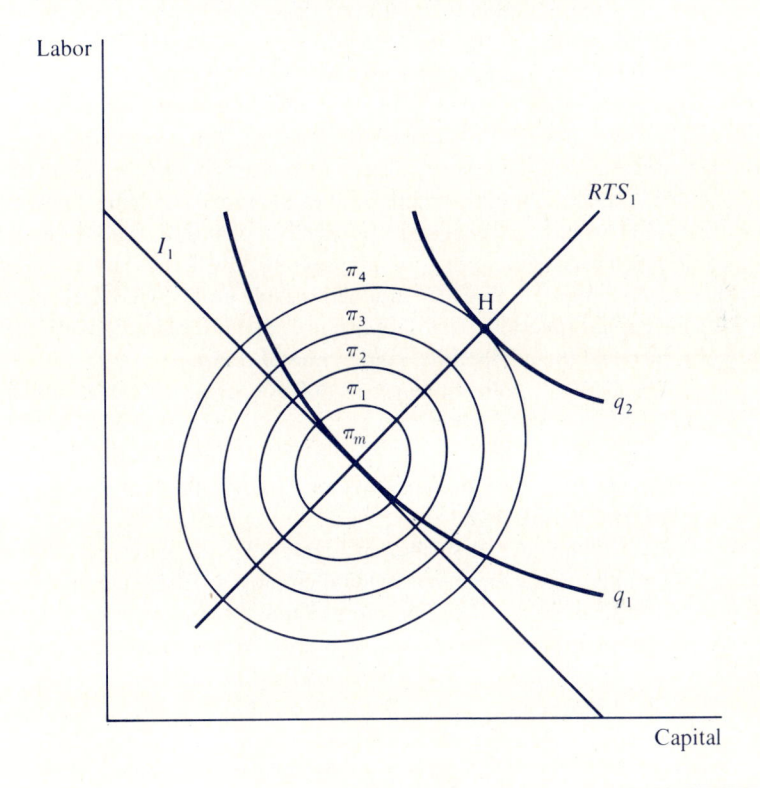

for the chosen output. The firm will choose a higher than minimum cost technology for producing that output.

Consider panel (a) of Figure 13.3. Only portions of the isoprofit curves are presented in this diagram. The combination at π_m remains the highest possible profit output and technology, and combinations along output expansion path RTS_1 identify the cost-minimizing technologies for successively higher outputs. As output expands along RTS_1, the input combinations are associated with successively lower profit levels; this is reflected in the lower isoprofit curves encountered. Where the rate of return on capital is regulated, however, it is necessary to make a distinction between *feasible profit* levels and *permissible profit* levels. **Feasible profits** are profits that can be earned by the price taker in the absence of regulation. Feasible profits are therefore those associated with input combinations along the isoprofit curves. These curves are thus labeled with subscripted fs to reflect the fact that, though they are technologically feasible, they may be unattainable due to regulation.

Permissible profits are profits that are sanctioned by rate of return regulation. As noted earlier, permissible profits represent the difference between the allowed residual that the firm is permitted to retain and the opportunity cost of the capital invested. In this simple form of regulation permissible profits are proportional to the capital employed. If the permitted rate of return is 10 percent and the firm has $1,000,000 invested in capital, the firm will be permitted to set a price that yields a residual of $100,000 after all other resource suppliers have been paid. If the market rate of return on capital is 8 percent, however, the opportunity cost of keeping that capital in the regulated enterprise is only $80,000. Permissible profits in this case are $20,000, or 2 percent of the rate base. A firm with only $900,000 in capital would be permitted a residual of $90,000, whose opportunity cost is $72,000. Permissible profits in this case are $18,000, which again is 2 percent of the capital invested. In every case permissible profits will be a constant proportion of the capital invested. That proportion is the difference between the allowed rate of return and the competitive market rate of return.

The fact that profits of, say, $18,000 are permissible does not ensure that they are feasible. On the contrary, the best that a particular firm with $900,000 in capital might do in this enterprise is earn $10,000. In each case, the firm's problem is therefore to find the input combination yielding the highest profits that are both feasible and permissible.

Such a choice is described in Figure 13.3. In panel (a), permissible profits depend only on the amount of capital employed. Thus, all combinations of labor and capital on the vertical line representing quantity of capital K_3 are associated with the *same* level of permissible profits. However, the firm will not be indifferent among all these combinations offering the same permissible profits. For any level of permissible profits, the input combination most preferred will be that which earns the highest feasible profits. For the level of permissible profits associated with K_3, the combination that actually earns the highest profits is combination S. All other combinations lie on lower isoprofit curves. For the lower level of permissible profits associated with K_2, combination T is preferred on these grounds; for permissible profits associated with K_1, combination M is preferred. For any level of capital the preferred input combination will be that identified by a tangency between an isoprofit curve and a vertical line linking all combinations for which the same profits are permitted. Schedule R in panel (a) connects all such tangency combinations.

The firm will wish to employ the input combination that lies as far to the left as possible along schedule R. It is constrained in this choice, however, by the limits of rate of return regulation. As the firm moves leftward along schedule R, feasible profits increase but permissible profits fall. We may identify the combination chosen with the aid of panel (b), which depicts both the maximum feasible profit and the maximum permissible profit associated with each quantity of capital. In this panel maximum feasible profits are identified by curve R'. These profit levels are simply read off the isoprofit curves at their intersections with schedule R in panel (a). Maximum permissible profit at each quantity of capital is the diagonal

Chapter 13 *The Demand for Factors: Other Market Structures* 411

Figure 13.3 *Averch-Johnson Effect*

Panel (a) includes segments of isoprofit curves labeled π_f^1, π_f^2, and so on, and the output expansion path RTS_1. The isoprofit curves identify the feasible profit levels associated with different combinations. The vertical lines identify the permissible profit levels that expand with capital employment. Schedule R identifies the combinations offering the maximum feasible profit for each level of capital usage. In panel (b) these profit levels from R are plotted on capital employment as schedule R'. Permissible profit levels are shown as diagonal line OK. The quantity of capital offering the highest feasible profit that is also permissible is K_2, corresponding to combination T along R in panel (a).

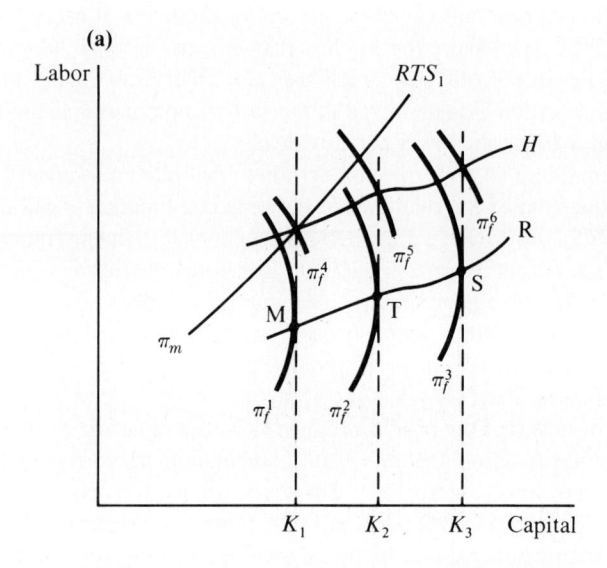

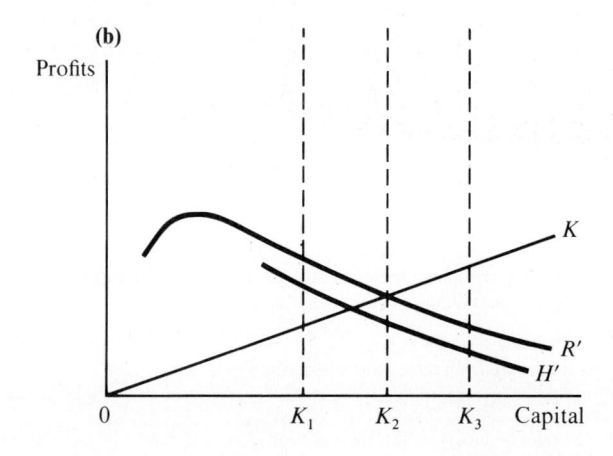

line from the origin, OK.[6] Regulation permits the earning of any profit below line OK; technology and demand permit the firm to earn any profit under curve R'. The quantity of capital that produces the highest profit while satisfying both constraints is therefore K_2. This corresponds to combination T in panel (a).

Consider combination T in panel (a). We know from panel (b) that at this combination maximum feasible profit is just equal to maximum permissible profit. No combination to the left of T along R offers a higher permissible profit, and no combination to the right of T along R earns a higher feasible profit; nor do points off curve R in panel (a) offer higher profits. Combinations above and below T offer lower feasible profits at the same level of capital usage. Curve H in panel (a), for example, connects all combinations of inputs associated with the same (negative) slope for the isoprofit curves. These are uniformly lower at every level of capital use. Profit π_f^4 is less than π_f^1, π_f^5 is less than π_f^2, and so forth. Curve H' in panel (b) relates feasible profits to capital use along curve H in the manner of R'. Clearly, combination T is preferred to the factor combination associated with the intersection of OK in the lower panel with H'.

Combination T is preferred to any other combination in panel (a). There remains the question of the relationship between combination T and output expansion path RTS_1. As we have drawn RTS_1 and curve R in the figure, combination T lies below the output expansion path and therefore contains too much capital. So far, however, we have not explained why curve RTS_1 does not lie below schedule R and result in too little capital or right on top of R implying an efficient result. This will be discussed in terms of Figure 13.4, which depicts the former possibility.

We will show that the result in Figure 13.4 cannot occur; curve RTS_1 must lie above schedule R. Combination T and combination π_m correspond to the same points in panel (a) of Figure 13.3. The vertical line at K_T connects all combinations offering the same level of permissible profits as combination T. No isoprofit curves are included here, but the figure includes an isoquant connecting all input combinations that may be used to produce output q_t, the output produced with combination T. The implied relationships of profits at combinations T, S, and H are mutually exclusive.

---

[6]The slope of line OK is the difference between the permitted rate of return on capital and the market rate that reflects its real cost. This may be confirmed by noting that profits are equal to total revenue minus total expenditure on labor and capital:

$$\pi = P_q q - P_l L - P_K K.$$

Assume that the permissible rate of return, P_K^*, exceeds the market return on capital, P_K. The regulation provides that the total residual remaining after all other factors (in this case, labor) have been paid may not exceed the permissible rate on the capital invested; that is:

$$P_K^* K \geq P_q q - P_l L.$$

Subtracting this inequality from the expression above yields:

$$\pi \geq (P_K^* - P_K) \cdot K.$$

The slope of the upper boundary of this inequality may be determined by making it an equality; thus, $\Delta \pi / \Delta K = P_K^* - P_K$, the difference between the permissible rate and the market cost of capital.

Note than when the regulators set P_K^* equal to the market rate, permissible profits are zero at every level of capital usage. In this case the input combination chosen is indeterminate. The firm is permitted to make no greater profits with any one factor combination than with any other.

Figure 13.4 The Impossible Case of Too Little Capital

Output expansion path RTS_1 cannot lie below schedule R, containing all combinations of inputs for which the slopes of the isoprofit curves are vertical. According to proposition 1, $\pi_S > \pi_H$, and according to proposition 2, $\pi_H > \pi_T$. This should imply that $\pi_S > \pi_T$, but proposition 3 states that $\pi_T > \pi_S$. If, however, curve RTS_1 passes above point T—as, for example, through K' and S'—no such inconsistency is implied. The three propositions together imply simply that $\pi_{K'} > \pi_T > \pi_{S'}$.

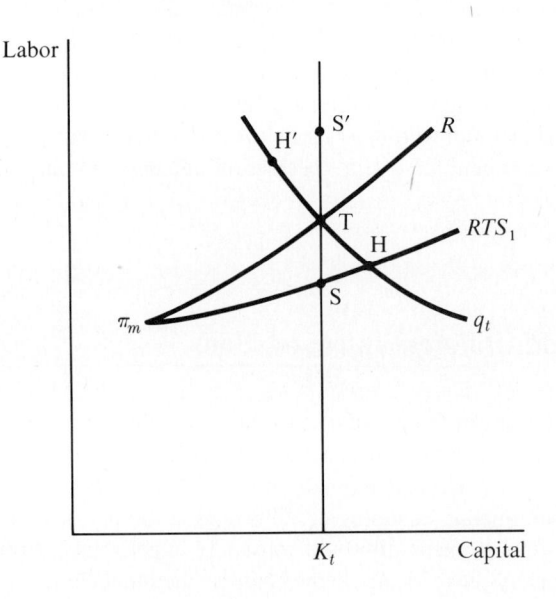

Consider the following three propositions.

1. As output expands along RTS_1, feasible profit must decline. As marginal cost exceeds marginal revenue at each output greater than π_m, profit itself must be lower at higher outputs. Thus, profit at S must be greater than profit at H: $\pi_S > \pi_H$.

2. As combination H lies on RTS_1, the cost of producing output q_t is lower at combination H than at combination T. Feasible profits must therefore be greater at combination H than at combination T: $\pi_H > \pi_T$.

3. Combination T was identified in Figure 13.3 by a tangency of an isoprofit curve and the vertical line passing through T. All other combinations on this vertical line, including S, must therefore lie on isoprofit curves offering lower profits. Profits at T must therefore exceed profits at S: $\pi_T > \pi_S$.

It cannot be the case that the three relationships thus identified hold simultaneously. Proposition 1 holds that $\pi_S > \pi_H$, while proposition 2 holds that $\pi_H > \pi_T$. This must imply that $\pi_S > \pi_T$, but proposition 3 implies exactly the opposite: $\pi_T > \pi_S$. Our three combinations may not lie in this relationship to one another.

Note, however, that no inconsistency is implied if the output expansion path passes above combination T, as it was shown to do in Figure 13.3. Consider a hypothetical output expansion path passing through combinations H' and S'. Proposition 1 would maintain in this case that $\pi_{H'} > \pi_{S'}$. Proposition 2 would hold that $\pi_{H'} > \pi_T$. Neither of these propositions is inconsistent with proposition 3, which states that $\pi_T > \pi_{S'}$. On the contrary, proposition 3 in this case merely completes the implied ordering, $\pi_{H'} > \pi_T > \pi_{S'}$.

Although feasible profits at H' are greater than those at T, they are not permissible with the smaller quantity of capital used at H'. Although combination S' produces the output associated with it at lowest cost, profits may be increased by reducing output through a withdrawal of labor, employing combination T instead. The combination employed must lie below the output expansion path; it thus contains excessive capital relative to the cost-minimizing combination for the chosen output.

13.2 Exploitation: Different Interpretations

The bias discussed in the previous section is an unintended result of government regulation of price searcher firms. In the absence of regulation (or with a different form of regulation) no such anomaly in the use of inputs occurs; firms are led to select cost-minimizing technologies. This does not imply that the input choices of these types of firms are no different from those of price-taker firms, nor that these choices are in any sense ideal. On the contrary the input choices of price searchers differ in important ways from those of price-taker firms, and some economists have found a basis for leveling the charge of exploitation in these differences.

Perhaps the first attempt to state a scientific case for **exploitation** is found in the work of Karl Marx. Marx, for all his innovativeness as a philosopher and his ingenuity as an interpreter of history, never really understood the true revolution in economic thinking that was taking place around him. His thinking was rooted in the classics: Smith, Ricardo, and Malthus. These writers had not clearly formulated the ideas of supply and demand and the importance of conditions *at the margin* for determining price; instead, they relied, rather unenthusiastically, on a labor-based theory of value. Price was determined by cost, and cost was chiefly wages. Wages were ultimately bounded from below by the amount necessary for survival. The more labor required to produce a good, the higher would be the price of that good, and vice versa. This theory sounds quite plausible even today and doubtless appeared even more so in that less complicated century.

Certain features of market economics are inconsistent with this simple view of price determination. How is it, for example, that wages vary widely from occupation to occupation and that wages on average have risen in many industrial countries to levels far above subsistence? If labor cost varies from worker to worker and from time to time, then the correspondence between cost and labor inputs (that is, man-hours of labor) is lost. More importantly, employers quite frequently find themselves in the unhappy situation of having financed the employment of vast numbers of labor man-hours on projects for which the market price is far below cost. The employment of labor does not magically bestow value upon goods. As the reader should understand quite well by now, the price (value) of goods in the market depends on their perceived usefulness by prospective purchasers *and* on the quantity available. This is true both of goods that require great quantities of labor to produce (like lace) and of goods that require little labor (like fruit).

According to Marx, however, it was labor that gave value to goods, and therefore labor was entitled to the full value of that for which it was responsible. The fact that labor's share of the revenues it produced was typically less than the total presented a clear case of exploitation. Marx developed a theory that purported to show what labor's share ought to be.

This theory was destined to fare poorly with economists, for even before publication of the first volume of Marx's *Capital* the neoclassical era had begun. The labor theory of value was jettisoned in favor of modern demand theory—and without this labor theory of value, Marx's neat demonstration of exploitation collapses. If labor does not give goods their value, then by what yardstick are we to measure labor's share? It is not surprising therefore that adherents to Marx's system on university campuses are typically found in history and sociology departments where economic understanding is rare.

The neoclassical economists were not without a theory of "just" wages. The new theory of price and distribution made it impossible to assign responsibility for portions of the *total* value of output. Who was to say that the loom or the textile worker was the more important to the production of cloth? Without both, no cloth would be produced. On the other hand, the theory directed attention to measurement in another dimension. The prices of goods were determined by value *at the margin*; output was determined by consideration of revenue and cost *at the margin*. In the midst of this "marginal revolution" it is no surprise that attention focused on the contribution of factors of production *at the margin*. The inevitable conclusion was reached that labor's fair share involved a wage equal to the value of its *marginal* products.

The **value of the marginal product (VMP)** of a factor is calculated in the same way we calculate the value of anything else—that is, quantity times price. The rate of change in output per unit change in the use of a factor (again, we will use factor *a*) is the marginal physical product. This rate of output times the market price of that output, P_x, gives us the value of this marginal physical product; that is:

$$VMP_a = MPP_a \cdot P_x.$$

Certain neoclassical economists took great satisfaction in observing that under competitive conditions a market economy pays labor exactly the wage it deserves. Profit maximization requires that firms employ each input up to the point at which its marginal revenue product equals its marginal factor cost; that is,

$$MPP_a \cdot P_x\left(1 + \frac{1}{\eta}\right) = P_a\left(1 + \frac{1}{\varepsilon}\right).$$

Where the firm is a price taker in both the input and output markets, both elasticity of demand for the firm's output, η, and the elasticity of supply for the input, ε, are infinite. The second term in the parentheses on both sides of the equation vanishes, and we are left with:

$$MPP_a \cdot P_x = P_a.$$

Each input is therefore paid exactly its VMP, or what neoclassical economists liked to call the factor's *contribution* to the value of output at the margin.

It is not difficult to take issue with such a "justification" of the distributional results of markets, and we may reasonably conclude that few were converted with this argument. Workers do not fully control their VMPs, and if the quantity of capital (typically controlled by the firm's owners) is reduced, the productivity of labor falls and with it labor's "fair" share. If the labor force is increased more rapidly than the capital stock, the same result is predicted. Technical change may render workers' skills obsolete, or barriers to employment may prevent certain members of the labor force from obtaining skills that would increase their productivity. We may ultimately judge it expedient and fair for labor to bear the risks of these and other events that affect its wages in a market economy. It is unlikely, however, that our judgment in this matter will be strongly influenced by the implied justice in distribution based on the marginal products of the factors of production.

In fact, soon after the adoption of VMP by the neoclassical economists, a new generation of economists began looking at the distribution of income as an issue completely separable from production. The arguments of the *welfare economists* will be treated extensively in a later chapter, so we will merely sketch the outlines of their work here. They believed (and many still maintain) that the function of an economy is to obtain through the activities of production and income distribution the maximum welfare for society as a whole. Wages are to be related to production only to the extent necessary to provide incentives to further production. A large body of normative theory has been developed on these premises, to which modern economists continue to contribute.

Although many influential economists embraced these ideas, others continued to attempt to forge a link between productivity and "fairness." The development in the 1930s of various theories of output under less than perfectly competitive conditions led to a revival of VMP as a viable yardstick for measuring labor's fair share. This time, however, the shoe was on the other foot: Competition was regarded to be everywhere imperfect, and imperfectly competitive firms "exploited" their workers.

Exploitation by Price Searchers

Results with imperfect competition, or what we have chosen to designate as *price searching*, in the output market differ from those of the competitive model. Assume that a price-searching firm has market power in the output market but is a price taker in the market for inputs. Assume further that the firm is not regulated, so that factor demand may be derived as it was in section 13.1. Firms in this market environment will hire labor up to the point at which MRP equals a constant MFC:

$$MPP_a \cdot P_x\left(1 + \frac{1}{\eta}\right) = P_a.$$

More simply:

$$VMP_a\left(1 + \frac{1}{\eta}\right) = P_a.$$

(13.1) $$VMP_a + \frac{VMP_a}{\eta} = P_a$$

From this expression it is clear that the price paid to factor a must be less than its VMP. Demand elasticity is negative and, from our discussion in Chapter 9, we know that at the chosen output it must have an absolute value greater than unity. The sum inside the parentheses must therefore be positive but less than 1. The factor price, P_a, must therefore be less than its VMP because it is equal to its VMP *times* a number between zero and 1.

This may be made clearer with the aid of Figure 13.5. The demand curve for this factor slopes downward, indicating the marginal revenue product of factor a for each quantity employed; this is the curve labeled $MRP_a = D_a$. For any quantity of the factor employed, however, the VMP must be higher by the amount of the second term on the left side of equation (13.1). Thus, the VMP curve is higher at each quantity of a than the demand curve. The supply curve, S, is horizontal at price P_a, indicating that factor a is supplied perfectly elastically at that price. As discussed in the previous chapter, the firm will choose to employ a_1 units of this factor, at which MRP_a equals MFC_a. Under these circumstances exploitation, according to the marginalists' definition, occurs. The "contribution" of factor a to the value of output at the margin is equal to the height of curve VMP_a at quantity a_1. The price paid to this factor is P_a. So long as the elasticity of demand facing the firm is less than infinite, the wage rate will be less than the VMP of this factor. However, in addition to the other difficulties encountered in making a case for the fairness of payment in terms of marginal contributions, we confront others here.

In the first place, the result applies generally to all factors of production used by such a firm—indeed, the underpayment will be in the same proportion for all of the factors hired by the firm. To be sure, firms own a great deal of the capital they employ and may not exploit themselves; but to the extent that capital is leased, it too will be paid less than its VMP. The idea therefore loses a bit of the edge that elements of "class" conflict always add to discussions of exploitation.

More importantly, the concept of exploitation has always carried with it the corollary implication that removing the source of the exploitation will result in higher wages. This clearly is not true for the case of exploitation due to less than perfectly elastic demand for output. Consider the case presented in Figure 13.5. Perfecting competition would have the effect of eliminating the difference between MRP and VMP. This difference, as noted, is equal to VMP/η. As competition is perfected, elasticity of demand becomes infinite; hence, the value of this ratio di-

Figure 13.5 *Monopolistic Exploitation*

As marginal revenue product is defined to be $MPP_a \cdot MR_x$, there will be a difference between this amount and the VMP_a at each quantity of factor a. Since VMP_a is defined as $MPP_a \cdot P_x$, this difference will be the difference between price and marginal revenue times MPP_a. As price is greater than marginal revenue at every quantity, this difference must be positive. The amount of the difference is $MPP_a \cdot P_x/\eta_x$. At a supply price of P_a, the firm will hire a_1 units at which the price paid will be less than VMP_a.

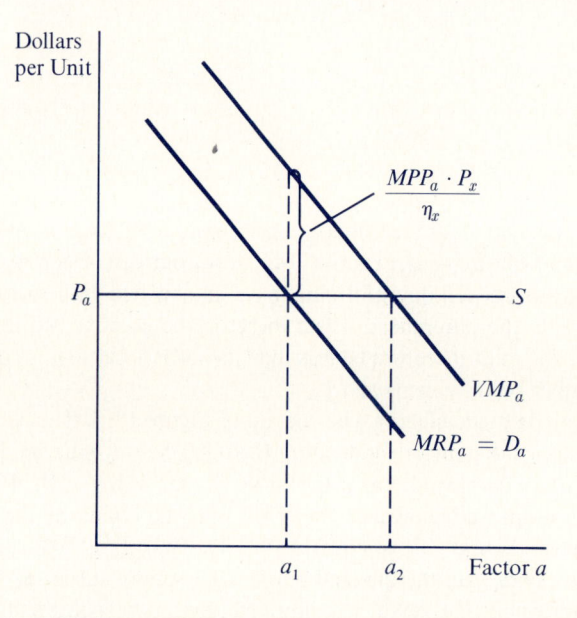

minishes toward zero. The result is that demand shifts upward until it occupies the position of curve VMP_a. Instead of hiring a_1 workers, the firm will now hire a_2. But because labor is supplied to such a firm at a constant market wage P_a, this change has no effect on wages. Equality of the wage rate and labor's VMP is ultimately accomplished by lowering VMP_a to the level of market wages rather than doing the reverse. Exploitation that can be eliminated in this way is difficult to take seriously.

13.3 Market Power in the Input Market

Exploitation of a more resonant variety occurs in connection with firms that face upward-sloping factor supplies. Even when such firms sell their output competitively, the wage received by these factors will be less than VMP and quite possibly less than the factors receive elsewhere. One of the principal sources of such market power is lack of competition from other demanders of the factor supplied. If market supply is a rising function of price, then the supply to a single demander will also slope upward. This type of market is called a **monopsony**. This translates from Greek into "one buyer," in neat opposition to its counterpart in the output market, monopoly. In the less enlightened colonial era, one of the aims of administration was to achieve such a monopsony position with respect to the resources offered by the colonies. Trade was carefully regulated to minimize the extent of competition for these resources. The colonists' perception of the resulting exploitation may have been an important factor in their unhappiness with governmental arrangements.

Where supply of a resource is less than infinitely elastic, the extent of monopsonistic exploitation can be measured in terms of our familiar profit maximization condition. Let us assume that the output market is competitive so that MRP_a becomes simply $MPP_a \cdot P_x$. However, supply is less than perfectly elastic, such that the elasticity of factor supply ε is less than infinity. Setting MRP_a equal to MFC_a yields the following:

$$MPP_a \cdot P_x = P_a\left(1 + \frac{1}{\varepsilon}\right).$$

The left side of this equation reflects something we have already noted. When the firm is a price taker in the output market, marginal revenue product will always equal the factor's VMP. Making this substitution and solving for the factor price gives:

$$\frac{VMP_a}{\left(1 + \frac{1}{\varepsilon}\right)} = P_a.$$

By assumption, ε is positive but less than infinite. In the ratio on the left side of this equation, VMP_a is therefore divided by a number larger than 1; thus, the factor price must be less than VMP_a.

Rising and Falling Supply

The analysis of demand for factors under these conditions is sufficiently differentiated from that of the other market structures already discussed to warrant a separate presentation here. The chief difference lies on the supply side of such markets. In deriving demand for factors in the cases considered thus far, we simply varied the factor price and observed the responses (in output and technology) to such factor price changes. Here that cannot be done. In this case, demanders themselves have control over price. If they employ little of the factor the price will be less than if they employ more. It therefore makes no sense to vary the price to the demander, since it is the demander who determines the price by choosing a quantity.

Alert readers will note the similarity of this problem and that posed by the supply of output by monopolies. Just as monopolies determine price in choosing output, monopsonists determine price by choosing the level of employment. The former characteristic detracts from our discussion of the supply behavior of monopolists; the latter does the same for the demand behavior of monopsonist employers. Although we may *describe* the choice of the quantity they will employ, we have difficulty in deriving the sort of comparative static results that make the competitive model such a fountainhead of empirical implications.

Before actually coming to grips with the problem, let us digress for a few paragraphs on supply curves themselves. The supply function of a factor of production identifies the quantity that is available for employment by the firm at each price. Factor **supply elasticity** is defined, as are all other elasticities, as a ratio of percentage changes:

$$\text{Elasticity of supply} = \varepsilon = \frac{\% \text{ change in quantity supplied}}{\% \text{ change in factor price}}$$

$$\varepsilon = \frac{\Delta a/a}{\Delta P_a/P_a}.$$

This may be rewritten as

(13.2)
$$\varepsilon = \frac{P_a}{a} \cdot \frac{\Delta a}{\Delta P_a}$$

This supply elasticity, like the other elasticities, may be expressed as the product of a ratio and a slope term. In this case the slope term is the inverse of the slope of the supply curve. The steeper the supply curve, the flatter is the inverse of that slope, hence, the lower is the supply elasticity.

Unlike demand elasticity, this measure of the responsiveness of supply does not conform neatly to a single set of rules relating position along the curve to elasticity. Supply curves may slope upward or downward, implying, of course, that the elasticity may be either positive or negative. For the less typical case of downward-sloping supply, the same rules governing elasticity and position on the curve applied earlier to demand may be used. For linear supply curves of negative slope, supply elasticity varies from negative infinity to zero at the vertical and horizontal intercepts, respectively. An elasticity of -1 occurs at a quantity precisely halfway out to the horizontal intercept.

Most supply curves are positively sloped, however, and here the relationship is more subtle. For a linear supply curve (in which the slope term does not vary), changes in elasticity are determined by changes in the ratio P_a/a. As both numerator and denominator increase as we move up the supply curve, the elasticity in this case is positive. We can show that any linear supply curve passing through the origin will have an elasticity of unity. We can show further that a linear curve with a negative vertical intercept has an elasticity everywhere of less than unity, while a linear curve with a positive vertical intercept has an elasticity everywhere of greater than unity.

This result is easily verified with the aid of Figure 13.6. From equation (13.2) we know that the supply elasticity may be expressed as the product of a ratio (P_a/a) and a slope $(\Delta a/\Delta P_a)$. Note, however, that the ratio term is also a slope. In panel (a) of Figure 13.6 the ratio P_a/a is the slope of a ray from the origin to the supply curve at quantity $0B$ of the factor. Let the slope of such a ray be denoted s_r.

Figure 13.6   *Supply Elasticity for Linear Supply Curves*

In panel (a) the supply curve S_a has a negative vertical intercept. Since the slope of the line *OP* is less than the slope of the supply curve itself, the elasticity at quantity *OB* is less than unity. In panel (b) the supply curve S_b has a positive vertical intercept. The slope of the ray *OP* in this case exceeds the slope of the supply curve itself, so the elasticity at quantity *OB* is greater than unity. As quantity increases along both supply curves, the elasticity approaches unity.

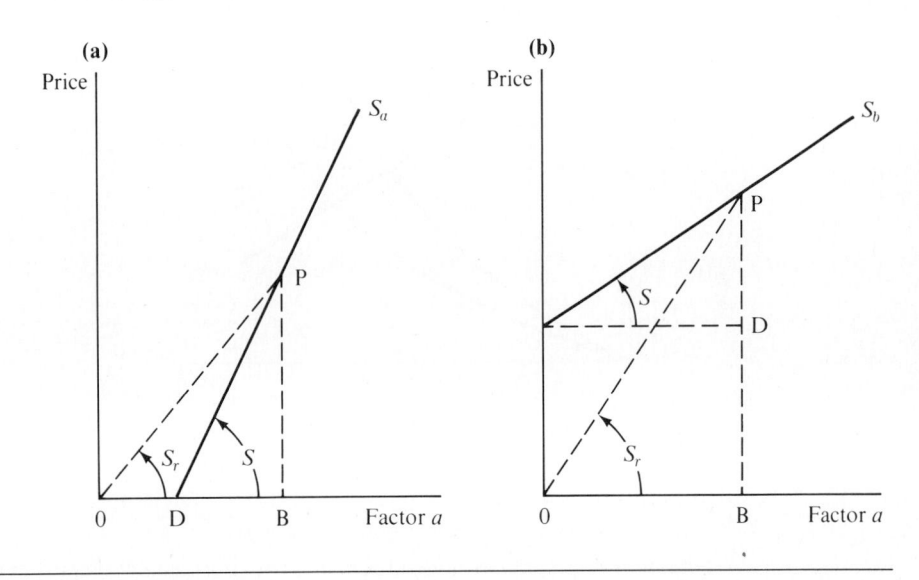

Let the slope of the supply curve be denoted s, so that the inverse of this slope, $\Delta a/\Delta P_a$, is $1/s$. The elasticity of supply is therefore equal to s_r/s. If the supply curve is a ray from the origin, then $s_r = s$ and the supply elasticity is unity. If the supply curve is steeper than the ray, as in panel (a), then s is greater than s_r and the elasticity must be less than unity. If the supply curve is less steep, as in panel (b), then s_r is greater than s and the elasticity is greater than unity.

Marginal Factor Cost with Rising Supply

Having developed some useful rules for assessing elasticity over supply curves, we may turn again to the question of demand for factors under conditions of rising supply. To keep the analysis as simple as possible, we will continue to assume that the elasticity of *demand* for the firm's output is infinite so that MRP_a is everywhere equal to $MPP_a \cdot P_x$. Were the factor in question supplied to the firm perfectly elastically at every price, the curve MRP_a would be the demand curve for factor *a*. Assume further, however, that the supply curve rises with quantity employed, as shown in Figure 13.7.

Under such circumstances MFC_a must lie above the supply curve at every quantity. This has a common-sense explanation. Marginal factor cost is the rate of

Figure 13.7 *Monopsonistic Exploitation*

For a positively sloped factor supply curve the marginal factor cost must exceed the price at every quantity. The profit-maximizing quantity of this factor is a_1, at which MRP_a is equal to MFC_a. As MRP_a here must be equal to VMP_a at each quantity, the factor price paid, P_a, is less than VMP_a.

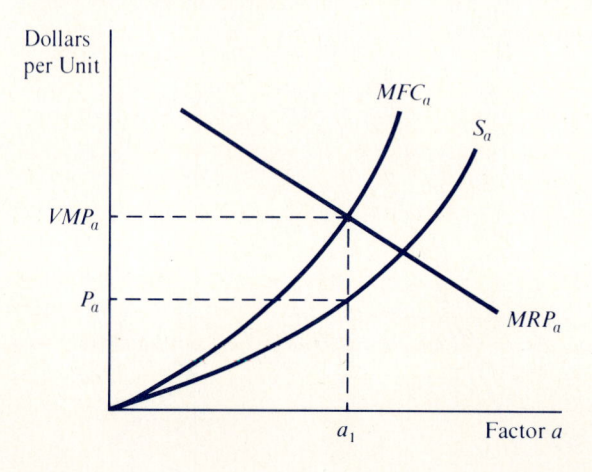

increase in expenditure on a per unit increase in its employment. Let that expenditure be E_a. Let the price be given by the function of the quantity of a employed, $P(a)$, so that the relationship between expenditure and employment may be written:

$$E_a = a \cdot P(a).$$

The **marginal factor cost** is the rate of change in E_a per unit change in a, or:

$$MFC_a = \frac{\Delta E_a}{\Delta a} = P(a) + a \cdot \frac{\Delta P_a}{\Delta a}.$$

When a monopsonist employs more of the factor, expenditure increases for two reasons, each of which corresponds to one of the terms on the right side of this expression. First, the monopsonist must pay the market price of these extra units. Thus, MFC_a includes $P(a)$ per unit employed. Second, hiring more units increases the price the monopsonist must pay for those already purchased. It is this second element, not present when the demander is a price taker in this market, that raises MFC_a above price.

It is clear, furthermore, that the difference between price and MFC_a is related to the quantity employed. Subtracting $P(a)$ from both sides gives:

$$MFC_a - P(a) = a \cdot \frac{\Delta P_a}{\Delta a}.$$

The term $\Delta P_a/\Delta a$ is the slope of the supply curve of factor a. If this is constant (that is, if the supply curve is linear), the difference between the height of the MFC curve and the supply curve must increase at a constant rate with the level of a used. The difference between MFC and price is proportional to the employment of factor a. If the curve is concave upward, as is the supply curve in Figure 13.7, this distance will increase more rapidly than employment, because the slope itself, $\Delta P_a/\Delta a$, increases with a. In the convex case, the opposite occurs.

The profit-maximizing quantity of factor a is that which equates MRP_a and MFC_a. Thus, in Figure 13.7 the firm will choose to employ a_1 units of this factor, at which MRP_a and MFC_a intersect. Because we assume that the firm sells its output competitively, we know that VMP_a is equal to the height of curve MRP_a at this quantity, that is, $MPP_a \cdot P_x$. The price paid to the factor is given by the height of the supply curve at this quantity, that is, P_a. The difference in these two amounts measures the extent of monopsonistic exploitation.

As we will have frequent occasion to employ MFC curves, it is useful to derive an explicit geometric relationship between these curves and factor supply curves. This is easily done for linear supply curves. Let price P_a be a linear function of factor a:

$$P_a = k + va.$$

Expenditure on a will be quantity times price:

$$E_a = aP_a = a(k + va).$$

Hence, MFC_a for such a supply curve is:

$$MFC_a = \frac{\Delta E_a}{\Delta a} = k + 2va.$$

The two curves have the same intercept, k, but the slope of MFC_a has exactly twice the slope of the supply curve.

For those students who (like the author) are not very adept at judging angles, it is useful to develop a relationship between the two curves in terms of distances. We can derive an implied relationship between quantities of a along these two curves at points of equal height. Let the quantity of a on the supply curve be denoted a_S and the quantity of a on curve MFC_a be denoted a_{MFC}. We wish to find the relationship between a_S and a_{MFC} at points at which the price on supply curve P_a equals MFC_a on that curve. Setting price equal to MFC_a yields the following:

$$P_a = MFC_a$$
$$k + va_S = k + 2va_{MFC}$$
$$a_S = 2a_{MFC}.$$

The supply curve must lie exactly twice the distance from the vertical axis, as does curve MFC_a for points of equal heights on the two curves. The analogy of monopsony demand with monopoly supply therefore extends to the relationship between these two curves. Just as the marginal revenue curve lies halfway between the monopolist's demand curve and the vertical axis, the monopsonist's MFC_a curve lies halfway between the factor supply curve and the vertical axis. Be sure to remember, however, that demand and marginal revenue slope downward to the right while the supply curve and MFC_a have positive slopes.

Monopsony Demand

While we may in this way derive the optimal level of employment of factors supplied under these conditions, there can be no such thing as a firm's demand curve for such factors. The quantity demanded depends not only on the price of these factors but on the elasticity of supply at each price. Price changes are the result of shifts in the supply curve, and unless we know whether such shifts make the supply curves more or less elastic we cannot predict the effect on quantity demanded.

Consider these effects on the prices and quantities demanded in Figure 13.8. Let the original price–quantity combinations chosen by the firm be that identified by point T in the figure. (This original supply curve is not shown.) The marginal revenue product curve, MRP_a, is assumed to remain stationary during the changes

Figure 13.8 *The Ambiguity in Demand for Factors*

Combination T identifies the price–quantity choice along the original supply curve (not shown here). If supply shifts to position S_1, quantity a_1 will be purchased at a price of P_1. If supply shifts to S_2, quantity a_2 will be purchased at the same price. The quantity demanded at any price depends not only on the price but on the *position* of the supply curve. There is therefore no systematic relationship between a price change and the change in the quantity a firm will demand.

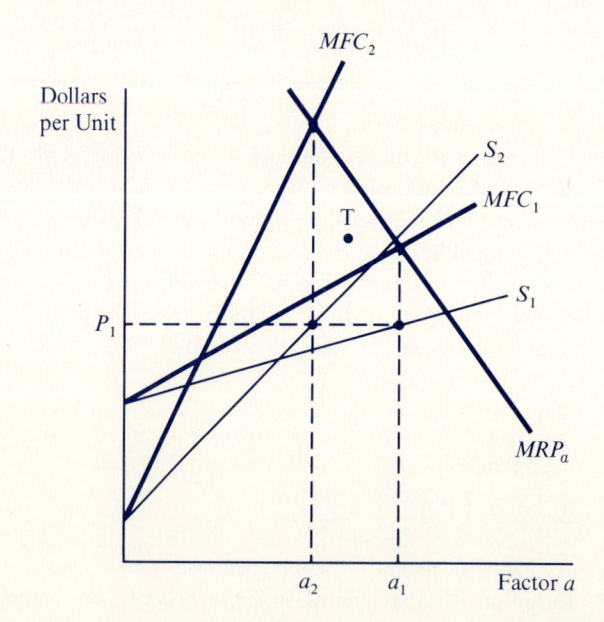

analyzed, but let the supply curve shift either to position S_1 or S_2. Both hypothesized changes may be called expansions of supply, since more is supplied at the original price, given either S_1 or S_2, than was available originally. As these curves are both linear, their respective MFC curves may be positioned as described in the previous section. They lie halfway between the supply curve and the vertical axis at every price. These supply curves have been drawn so that the same price, P_1, results in either case. Note that this price is lower than the original price. This particular price change is associated with an expansion of quantity demanded in the one case (S_1) but a contraction in quantity demanded on the other (S_2).

There cannot be a "demand curve" as such for a factor under these circumstances. Two different quantities are shown to be demanded at the same price, and over the price interval considered quantity demanded expands with the price decrease in one case and contracts in the other. It is possible, in fact, given the appropriate supply of the factor, to present circumstances in which almost any quantity is demanded at almost any price. We may not, therefore, rely on the demand curve relationship to predict effects on employment of policies or events that influence price. On the other hand, we are not absolutely rudderless in our attempts to circumnavigate these problems.

We may still use comparative statics in a limited way when analyzing a monopsonistic market. We may often predict the response of a firm in this market setting to changes in its economic environment based on more detailed knowledge of the nature of this change. We may, for example, be able to predict a shift in the MFC_a curve or the MRP_a that has unambiguous implications for the quantity of the factor demanded. Although not nearly as useful for the purposes of policy analysis as more precise demand curve estimations, these qualitative inferences concerning the behavior of monopsonists are of some value.

Anticompetitive Arrangements

Anticompetitive arrangements are best discussed in terms of market situations likely to present individual employers with market power over the factor prices they must pay. The most obvious case involves resources specialized to the production of a particular product that is itself sold under price-searching conditions. Professional sports offer a preeminent example of this situation. Baseball, football, basketball, and hockey players are less valuable in any employment other than a professional team in a league of that particular sport. The special skills that these players use are thus specific to a single industry. Furthermore, each of these leagues is for the most part a monopoly in the sale of its particular brand of sports entertainment. The individual teams may be thought of as members of a cartel that limits the size of teams, determines the number of games played, and in other ways establishes rules that enhance and protect the profits of its owners. The league commissioner is granted broad enforcement powers, because the opportunities for chiseling here are unusually attractive.

One of the most important features of such a cartel arrangement is the provision that limits competition for individual players. Traditionally, each player has been "drafted" by a single team, which has enjoyed the exclusive right to employ him. These teams have thus established themselves as effective monopsonists over a pool of athletes. These athletes may sell their services to only one employer, who

Figure 13.9 *Failure of Anticompetitive Arrangements*

Panel (a) depicts conditions in which some feature like the "player draft" is in force. As individual labor suppliers may deal with only one demander each, their supply to each demander is less than perfectly elastic. These firms hire quantities like a_1 and pay wages of P_1. A breakdown of these arrangements, such as the institution of "free agency," causes the supply curve to shift as shown in panel (b) from S_1 to S_2. Both wages and quantity of labor hired may expand with such a shift.

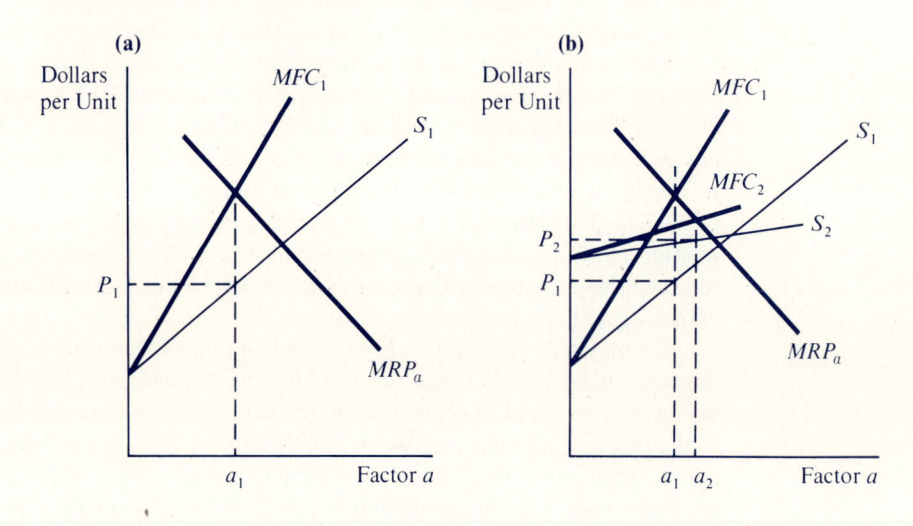

in turn faces an upward-sloping supply of this resource. The employment equilibrium for each team under these circumstances is shown in panel (a) of Figure 13.9, with a_1 players employed at a salary of P_1.[7]

Now let us consider the effect of a failure of these anticompetitive arrangements. This occurs through the formation of a new league, which itself competes for the players of the original league, as happened with the formation of the American Football League, the World Football League, and, most recently, the USFL. The American Basketball Association and the World Hockey League also arose in response to sports cartels. Strikes, or threatened strikes, by organizations of athletes (as in the case of the strike by members of the Baseball Players Association in 1981 and the Football Players Association in 1982) effectively disrupted the arrangements that prevented competition among teams for players. In panel (a) of Figure 13.9 the productivity of players at the margin is given by the height of MRP_a curve at a_1. Team organizations are now free to hire more players at higher wages without having to consider the effect of such a policy on the wages of their other players. The competition for these players by other teams can be counted on to increase wages anyway.

---

[7] A more detailed analysis of this market would recognize that there are actually markets for individual positions on teams, each of which will have its own wage and quantity.

The failure of anticompetitive arrangements is therefore predicted to have two effects in such markets: (1) Factor prices will increase, and (2) employment will expand. These results are shown in panel (b) of Figure 13.9. The original supply curve and MFC_a curve are indicated by S_1 and MFC_1, respectively. The introduction of competition for players shifts the supply curve upward and makes supply more elastic. The price must rise, because players are "worth" more (MRP_a is higher) than the wages they were originally paid at P_1. Supply to any team must be more elastic, because players who are not paid a wage equal to that worth will leave that team for another. The new equilibrium will therefore resemble that depicted by S_2 and MFC_2. Each team will employ a_2 players and pay a wage equal to P_2. Were competition for players to be made "perfect," of course, supply curves to teams would be horizontal at the market wage, and the analysis of factor demand in Chapter 12 would apply.

These implications are amply supported by recent experience with such sports organizations. The entry of new leagues and the ensuing competition for players in each case had a dramatic effect on player earnings. The merger of the National Football League with the American Football League was principally motivated by a desire on the part of team owners to put an end to the violent bidding wars for players that had been occurring. Existing league monopolies typically hope to avoid such mergers, since they expand industry output beyond the profit-maximizing level and therefore reduce profits relative to the precompetitive levels. Furthermore, the encouragement offered by the successful entry of one new league can induce others to attempt to enter these cartels through this approach.

Many examples of market conditions producing upward-sloping supply curves are observed in connection with government activity. Government is the sole employer of soldiers, firemen, air traffic controllers, and prison wardens, not to mention politicians. Unfortunately, economists have yet to develop a theory to replace the derived demand approach just used in studying factor use by government. Government does not seek profits; hence, profit maximization does not guide output or employment decisions. What does determine these factors is a hotly debated topic among today's economists. Until such a theory is presented, however, we cannot conclude that competition in these activities would necessarily lead to higher wages and expanded employment.

Locational and Contractual Advantages

Market structure is not the only feature of the economic environment that can give the firm power over factor prices. **Locational advantages** and **contractual advantages** can also have implications for the elasticity of supply, particularly for the factor labor.

In large cities workers of many types face a broad range of employment opportunities. Conditions here must closely approximate those of the price taker environment discussed in Chapter 12. In small towns, however, employment opportunities are much more limited. There may be only one firm in such a community requiring the services of machinists, metal workers, or computer programmers. Suppliers of these services therefore have three choices: working for the wage offered by the local employer, working at some other job, or seeking work in another town. University faculty almost invariably find themselves in this situation; changing jobs nearly always means moving to another town or city.

The supply of labor to such employers is clearly not perfectly elastic. Lowering the wage rate slightly will induce a few to try new occupations and a few others to depart for jobs elsewhere. Less labor will be supplied at this lower wage than at the higher one, but the quantity supplied does not go to zero with any wage reduction. These employers face an upward-sloping supply curve; hence, they pay a wage that is less than MRP_a in the previous examples. The greater the cost of moving and the more difficult it is to find suitable alternative employment, the more inelastic will be the supply and the greater will be such a divergence.

Even without locational advantages such as these, firms may affect the elasticity of supply of their workforces through contractual arrangements of their employment. Employers frequently defer a part of the workers' compensation so that it is received only after the workers have been employed for a stipulated period of time. For example, they make contributions to retirement funds, which become "vested" in the employees only after they have been employed with the company for several years. Many other advantages of seniority, such as being the last to be laid off or the first to be considered for advancement, may be thought of as methods of deferring compensation. All such practices have the effect of making the supply of labor to the employer less elastic. These advantages will be lost if the employee leaves one firm to work for another. For this reason, workers will not readily change employers if their wages are lowered. They will do so only after consideration of the cost in deferred compensation lost by leaving their present employer. Supply curves for labor slope upward for this reason.

Minimum Wage Restrictions with Rising Supply

There remains one more important divergence between the implications of price searcher and price taker demand for factors of production. This has to do with the response of the firm to price regulation. The analysis of minimum wages for firms that are price takers in the market for labor was presented in Chapter 12. The implications of that analysis are repeated in panel (a) of Figure 13.10. In the absence of restrictions on price, the equilibrium price, P^*, is paid by all employers. This price clears the market of all labor that seeks employment at this price. A minimum wage set, let us say, at P_r prevents such an equilibrium from occurring. The quantity a_d finds employment at this wage, but a_s workers seek employment. The difference in these two quantities represents the amount of labor that is unemployed as a result of these regulations. Increases in that minimum wage must increase unemployment.

In panel (b) of Figure 13.10 we present results that differ markedly from those in panel (a) for firms facing rising supply curves for labor. The standard optimum without regulation is depicted with employment of a^* units of labor employed at the intersection of the firm's MRP_a and MFC_a curves. The firm pays a wage of P^* for this quantity. It has no demand curve for this factor, however, so that the quantity hired at a higher regulated price cannot simply be read off such a curve. We must, as always, determine the effect of such a change on the position of the MFC_a curve.

Figure 13.10 A Minimum Wage

In panel (a) the results of a minimum wage are examined in a market in which the demanders are price takers in the labor market. As wages below P_r are not permitted, employment falls from a^* demanded at the equilibrium wage to a_D. The quantity supplied increases to a_S, and unemployment in the amount $a_S - a_D$ is the result. In panel (b), the demander of labor is a firm with market power in this market. If free to set price, the firm will hire a^* at a wage of P^*. At a minimum wage of P_r, the firm will hire a_1 workers.

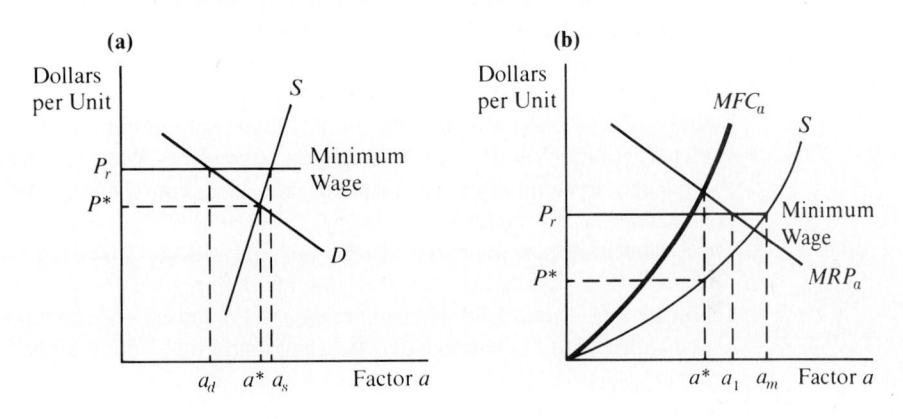

This is easily done for a minimum wage restriction. These restrictions prevent workers from offering any labor at a wage below the restricted level P_r. At this wage, however, the firm may hire up to a_m units, the quantity that the supply curve indicates is available for hire at this wage. Should the firm wish to employ any quantity up to this amount, it need pay no more than P_r but is prevented by the minimum wage from paying any less. Recall now that the marginal factor cost of a factor may be expressed as:

$$MFC_a = P(a) + \frac{\Delta P_a}{\Delta a} \cdot a.$$

Under normal circumstances, marginal factor cost will exceed price with rising supply curves because of the second term on the right side of this expression. With these price restrictions, however, the second term has a value of zero. The price does not increase with additional purchases of factor a. Price remains P_r regardless of whether the firm purchases one unit, a^* units, or a_m units. The supply curve becomes horizontal at price P_r; hence, the slope term $\Delta P_a/\Delta a$ has a value of zero over the entire range. Marginal factor cost is therefore equal to the regulated price P_r at each quantity up to a_m.

The new optimum level of employment for the firm is therefore a_1. Marginal revenue product falls to equal marginal factor cost (constant at P_r) at this quantity of labor. Unlike the case of the price taker in this market, minimum wages have the effect of raising wages and *increasing* employment.

This is potentially a very important result. Analysis based on the competitive derived demand model informs us that a minimum wage may increase the wages of some workers, but only at the cost of some unemployment. In this case, however, a different model suggests that wage increases obtained through such restrictions are costless; they not only increase wages but also increase employment. Were this analysis applicable to a broad range of employment situations, it would make a much stronger case for active intervention in the labor relations area than we currently hear. Unfortunately, on closer examination the promising case for strict wage regulation—and for any minimum wage regulation—is weakened.

The result just described does not obtain for *any* wage restriction but only for restrictions that are neither too high nor too low. Consider Figure 13.11, where the limits of this result are outlined. In the absence of a minimum wage, the firm depicted will employ a^* units of labor at a wage of P^*. Wage restrictions below P^* obviously have no effect on anything, since they constrain the choices of neither demanders nor suppliers.

The minimum wage may also be too high, yielding a reduced level of employment. These results obtain for all minimum wages set above P_m. A wage set at precisely P_m would lead the firm to demand exactly a^* units of labor, the quantity demanded with no restrictions. As a horizontal line from a higher vertical inter-

Figure 13.11 *Employment Effects of Minimum Wages*

Minimum wages can increase employment only within a certain range. Wage P_1 achieves the highest possible employment level of a_1. Minimum wages above P_m reduce employment below the quantity demanded without any regulation.

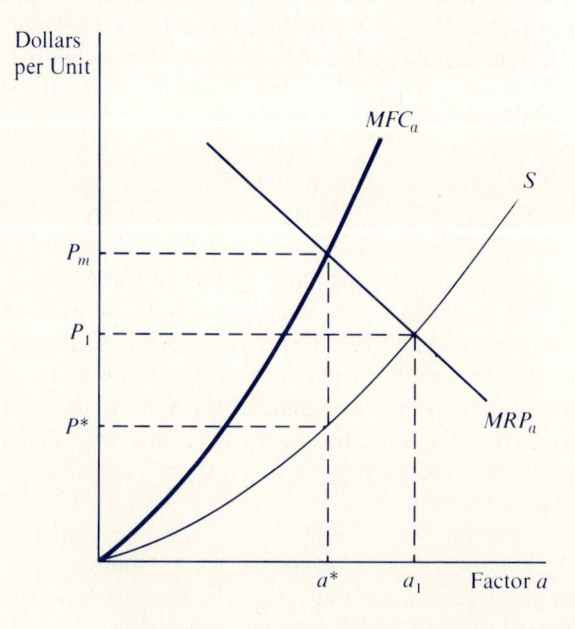

cept would intersect curve MRP_a to the left of a^*, higher minimum wages than P_m would reduce the quantity of labor demanded below that demanded with unrestricted wages.

Difficulties of Wage Regulation

This analysis offers little if policymakers are not concerned with the level of employment. They will be willing to accept a reduced number of jobs and substantial unemployment to raise the wages of some workers. As this set of options is available even in a price taker setting, they will not find much of interest in the analysis of demand with rising supply. However, for those who also place importance on employment itself, the analysis presented here offers an escape from a perplexing dilemma. For these employers wage rates may be raised without reducing the number of jobs—indeed, it appears that a truly attractive range of opportunities is opened up by this market setting. Wages may be raised as high as P_m without reducing employment. Employment may be expanded to a_1 by accepting a smaller wage increase. Unfortunately, while such policy options are available in principle, realizing them in a real-world setting is likely to be an extremely difficult task.

If this analysis is to have broad applicability, the rising supply conditions upon which it rests must result from the more typical factors producing them—that is, locational and contractual advantages. Recall that these factors are the product of moving costs on the one hand and deferred income on the other. Economists who have studied the economics of labor migration find that workers do move readily in order to obtain higher wages.[8] On the other hand, deferred income features of employment contracts must be agreed to by the workers themselves. As employees in making early career decisions typically select from a broad range of alternatives, it seems unlikely that they will choose one that is observed to severely exploit them through contractual arrangements. At this stage competition would be expected to insure that employees get only the amount of deferred income in the form of pension contributions and seniority advantages that they seek. Both locational advantages and contractual arrangements are thus expected to be sources of rather modest market power for the employer wielding them. Gains available from regulating wages in these markets thus promise to be similarly modest.

Modest gains are nevertheless gains, and should not policymakers seek to exploit them where they find them? The answer to this question is a rather frustrating "yes"—for finding such gains may be a far more difficult task than our discussion would imply. For the most part, we have treated the factor labor as a homogeneous resource that the firm employs in varying quantities. This wildly unrealistic assumption was made merely to focus our attention on the essential elements of this analysis. In the real world, each firm employs many different types of labor, and even within a particular occupation group skill levels vary. Each firm therefore faces not a single supply curve of labor that may be rising or perfectly elastic, but rather a host of different supply curves for each occupational group it employs and

---

[8] See, for example, Richard Cebula, *The Determinants of Human Migration* (Lexington, Mass.: D. C. Heath and Company, 1983).

each skill level within each group. To complicate matters further, workers are not merely paid wages of a certain level but are compensated with packages of benefits that may include paid vacations, health and life insurance, retirement plans, and discounts on the goods produced, to name only a few. Wage restrictions that apply only to money wages will typically produce a compensating reduction in such fringe benefits so that the value of full benefits earned per hour is unchanged by the restrictions.

Putting aside these problems, however, more important difficulties are created by the heterogeneity of the labor supply itself. A minimum wage that is ideal for one group of workers will be too low for another and too high for still another. For example, a wage that satisfies the objective for engineers in a particular firm will clearly create severe employment problems for custodians and clerks and may even hamper employment of engineers at other firms. It is precisely this problem that has led Congress to avoid wage regulations for middle- and upper-level wage earners (except for temporary freezes) in favor of a minimum wage policy that affects only those on the lower-wage fringe of the labor force. Wage restrictions that achieved their desired results for middle-level wage employees would have to be occupation and skill specific and, to the extent that supply elasticities vary from employer to employer, firm specific as well. The complications that would be encountered in attempting to implement such a regulatory scheme would be overwhelming.

This leaves us with the minimum wage Congress did enact and has periodically increased since that time. How do we reconcile the high estimates of reduced employment produced with these wage restrictions (discussed in Chapter 12) with the analysis of this chapter, which suggests that minimum wages may increase employment? We can do this by considering the factors that influence elasticity of supply. If a group of workers affected by a minimum wage supply labor to their respective employers highly elastically, then it is likely that wage increases will reduce employment. It is only in cases where labor is supplied under conditions of relatively low elasticity that wage increases together with employment increases are possible. Those workers with low productivity are precisely the ones expected to have the highest elasticity of supply.

Consider again the factors responsible for low elasticity of supply to a particular employer: moving costs and deferred compensation. Workers with low productivity are for the most part young and inexperienced. They have low productivity because they have had insufficient time to develop marketable skills and knowledge. Because of their youth, their cost of moving in the process of changing employers is low; because of their short tenure with their current employer, they also have little in the way of deferred compensation to make them reluctant to leave. The advantages of seniority are typically granted at their expense and thus offer little inducement for them to remain.

It is ironic that the one group for which minimum wages are administratively feasible is precisely that group who is disadvantaged by them. Older workers with large families and strong community ties, for whom moving costs are great, typically earn middle- and upper-range incomes; hence, they are out of reach of a policy that cannot put a floor under their wages without displacing a large part of the labor force. Similarly, those workers with the greatest experience and most seniority are also the most skilled and most productive. A minimum wage may increase wage rates without reducing employment only for those workers with low elasticity of supply to their current employers. Those workers currently affected by the minimum wage have supply elasticities that are so high that demanders of their services may realistically be treated as price takers in this market.

Summary

This chapter was concerned with results in factor markets where the demanding firm is a price searcher in either the input or the output market. The demand for factors by the former type of price searcher differs little from that of the perfect competitor. A price change for the factor initiates both substitution and output effects, both of which must operate in the direction opposite to the price change. If unconstrained, price searchers in the output market will use cost-minimizing technologies to produce the output chosen.

Ironically, regulation introduced to keep prices down has the unintended effect of influencing firms to produce with inefficient technologies. First, limits on profits lower the cost of utility-producing inputs, and firms will employ more of these inputs than is warranted on the basis of their marginal revenue products. Second, rate of return regulation leads firms to employ excessive amounts of capital. Firms regulated on this basis will not choose the cost-minimizing combination of inputs for the output selected. Combinations off the relevant output expansion path offer higher feasible profits that are also permissible.

Economists have from time to time attempted to develop theories of fair factor payments. We presented here a brief discussion of these efforts and their limitations. Differences between wages and the chosen benchmark is a less vacuous interpretation of the concept of exploitation than one usually encounters. This sort of exploitation is shown to occur in both market settings discussed in this chapter. Where fair compensation is defined as the value of the factor's marginal product (VMP), exploitation will occur in both cases. Also in both cases, the factor will be employed up to the point at which its marginal revenue product (MRP) is equal to its marginal factor cost (MFC). In the case of a price searcher in the output market, the MRP is equal to the wage rate but less than the VMP. In the case of a price searcher in the input market, the factor is used up to the point at which its MFC is equal to its VMP, but here the MFC exceeds the wage.

Demand for factors under price-searching conditions in the input market was considered in detail. As much of this material hinged on factor supply conditions, the theory of supply was developed more fully to include discussions of the relationship of curve shape and slope to elasticity of supply. It was shown that for linear supply curves passing through the origin the supply elasticity will be unity at every point. For linear supply through the origin, the supply elasticity will be unity at every point. For linear supply curves with a positive vertical intercept, the elasticity is greater than 1. For linear supply at zero price), the opposite is true.

A firm that employs a factor that is supplied with rising supply price will find that the factor's MFC also rises with the quantity supplied and is everywhere greater than the factor price itself. In the case of linear supply curves, the slope of the MFC curve will have precisely twice the slope of the supply curve and lie halfway between the supply curve and the vertical axis at every price. We cannot identify a demand curve for a firm facing these supply conditions, because the quantity demanded depends not only on price but on the elasticity of demand at each price. We may nevertheless predict the qualitative effect of changes in supply conditions on the quantity demanded for a broad range of such changes.

Rising supply is sometimes the result of a combination of conditions in both the input and output markets. If resources are specialized in the production of a good that is itself produced by a single firm, that producer will face a rising supply curve for these resources. The entry of competing firms in this output will lead to a rise in the factor's price along with an expansion of employment. Rising supply more commonly results from locational or contractual advantages of the employing firm. Moving costs often deter some suppliers of labor from shifting to alternative demanders of their services when wages are lowered. This implies a less than perfectly elastic supply of labor to these firms. Similarly, it will be found advantageous for workers to enter into agreements with employers in which the latter retain a part of the workers' compensation for later payment conditional upon their continued employment. The very presence of such contractual arrangements also reduces the elasticity of labor supply.

Wage restrictions that fall within certain ranges can under these conditions lead to both an increase in wages and an expansion of employment. This occurs because such restrictions render the supply of the factor perfectly elastic at the restricted wage up to the quantity available from suppliers at that wage. However, the scope for effective use of restrictions to obtain these results is severely limited. Supply elasticity is certainly less than infinite, in many cases. However, in most cases it is high enough, particularly in the long run, to limit the wage increases permissible without seriously diminishing employment. Implementation of this policy is hampered further by the heterogeneity of the workforce itself. As some workers have a higher productivity than others, minimum wages for higher-paid employees are difficult to administer without affecting employment conditions for those who earn less.

This analysis attempted to shed some light on the effect of existing minimum wage legislation. Current wage restrictions are designated to affect only those at the bottom of the economic ladder. They therefore encounter few of the complications of administration that would burden minimum wages for middle-range workers. Still, they cannot have the positive employment effects shown in this chapter to be analytically possible. For this group the costs of moving and the costs of forgone seniority are lowest. Their elasticity of supply to current employers is therefore very high; hence, the permissible range of wage increases for this group is too low to permit the large wage increases mandated by this legislation without reducing employment for this group.

Key Concepts

profit restrictions
rate base
permissible profit
Averch-Johnson effect
isoprofit curve
feasible profit
exploitation

value of the marginal product (VMP)
monopsony
supply elasticity
marginal factor cost
anticompetitive arrangements
locational advantages
contractual advantages

Questions

1. *Easy* A firm that is a price searcher in the output market but faces a perfectly elastic supply of the factors of production will have a downward-sloping demand curve for each of those factors. The derivation of this result differs only in the output effect, and there only slightly. Explain this difference.

Hard The marginal revenue product curve for a firm in this situation is not simply $MPP_a \cdot P_x$ but something else. Explain the difference and show how this difference changes in magnitude as the quantity of factor *a* changes.

2. *Easy* Profit restrictions can influence firms to use excessive amounts of factors offering consumption value to management. Will they also use less of factors that exhibit unpleasant "side effects?" Explain.

Hard Rate of return regulation can influence firms to use overly capital-intensive technologies in production. Other, less costly factor combinations might be used to produce the chosen outputs at lower cost. Why does a profit-seeking firm fail to adopt these less costly, and therefore more profitable, technologies?

3. *Easy* A price-searching firm in the output market may be said to "exploit" the factors of production that it hires because the price paid to each factor is lower than the value of that factor's marginal product. What is a factor's VMP, and why is the price paid lower than this?

Hard Is the capital supplied by the firm itself exploited in the same sense? That is, will the residual retained by the firm after everything else has been paid be less that capital's VMP times the quantity of capital used?

4. *Easy* The function $P = -20 + 2q_S$ is a supply curve. What is the elasticity of supply at 20 units?

Hard All linear supply curves with the same horizontal intercept have the same elasticity at each quantity regardless of their slopes. Explain.

5. *Easy* Draw the marginal factor cost curve for the supply curve in Question 4. What is the effect on the marginal factor cost at a quantity of 30 units of a downward shift of the vertical intercept of this supply curve to -30 (leaving the slope unchanged)?

Hard What is the shape of a supply curve with a constant supply elasticity? What relationship will the MFC curve have to such a supply curve?

6. *Easy* Function $MRP_a = 160 - 2q$ identifies the marginal revenue product of factor a at each quantity. Assume that the firm faces the supply curve in Question 4. What quantity will the firm hire under these circumstances?

Hard Although we may identify the quantity that a firm will hire given its supply and marginal revenue product curves at each quantity, we cannot derive a demand curve for a firm that is a price searcher in the input market. Explain why.

7. *Easy* "Free agency" for professional baseball players has led to substantial increases in their wages because it allows them to negotiate with a number of teams simultaneously for the best contract. However, this provision also permits each team to negotiate with a larger number of players. Why is it that this has not resulted in a fall in wages?

Hard "Free agency" for football players has not had the same result. One widely given reason is that each team in the National Football League shares most of the revenues earned by all teams on an equal basis. In what important ways does this modify the analysis in the first part of this question?

8. *Easy* Explain how a minimum wage in markets in which demanders of labor are price searchers can increase wages and employment simultaneously.

Hard If the elasticity of supply is 5, the maximum wage increase that may be obtained with a minimum wage provision without reducing employment is 20 percent. Explain why minimum wages set more than 20 percent above existing wages in the above market will result in less employment.

Part Five

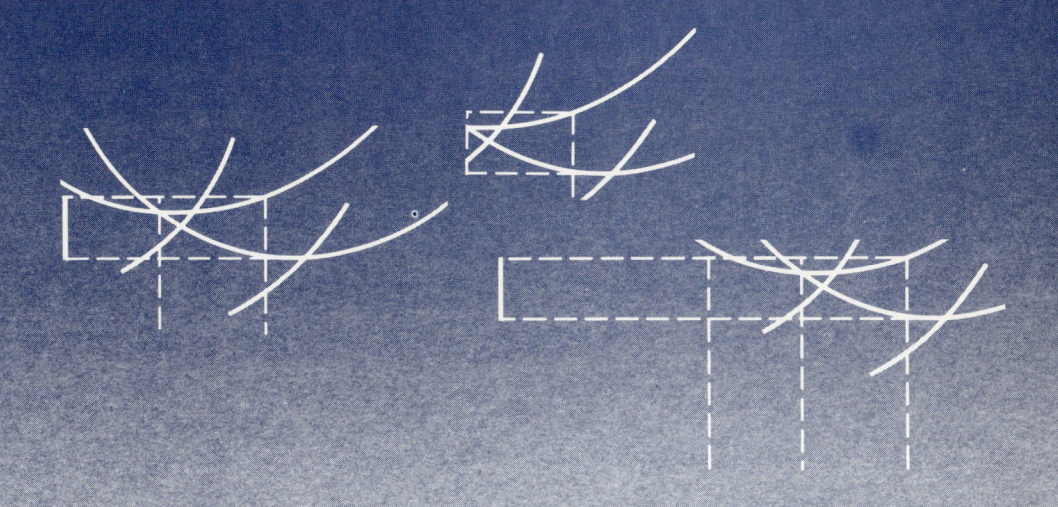

The Choice of Resource Supply

Chapter 14

The Supply of Labor

Connections Although this chapter deals chiefly with the supply of labor, our analysis of this topic more closely resembles the theory of household demand! You will want to look over Chapters 3 and 4 very carefully, paying close attention to the derivation of the opportunity sets and the ways in which they shift in response to changes in their underlying variables. On the other hand, the decision of workers to enter the labor force resembles the decision of firms to enter an industry, a topic that we discussed in Chapter 8. It is suggested that some restrictions on labor supply reflect cartel-like behavior on the part of workers and that restrictions on working conditions may reflect efforts to restrict output by existing firms in an industry. A careful rereading of the material on cartels in Chapter 10 is therefore a must. Some textbooks put labor supply in the same chapter with household demand. By placing it here, however, we can pull all these various strings together and say some interesting things about labor relations.

The previous two chapters considered markets for resources from the point of view of demand. Although our attention has occasionally been focused on conditions in one particular market, such as the supply of capital under unfavorable tax treatment or the effect of minimum wage legislation on the employment of labor, nothing in the theory developed so far makes any distinction between these two factors. The demand for factors of production is a general theory and applies with equal force to any resource employed by a firm engaged in production for profit. The extent to which results in markets for labor and capital differ is therefore determined by distinctions on the supply side of the market.

In this and the next chapter we shall lay down the foundations of the supply of labor and the supply of capital so that such phenomena can be analyzed. In this chapter we shall consider the individual's decision to supply labor. That decision can be usefully viewed in the context of the theory of household choice used earlier in our theory of demand for goods and services. In this case, however, the opportunity set is not determined by household income and prices. Income itself will vary as the quantity of labor supplied to the market varies. Here as in the treatment of consumption time in Chapter 4, the household has an endowment of time. That time may be employed alternatively in selling services in the market or in nonmarket activities, such as work in the home or leisure. As the relative productivity of that time in alternative activities changes due, for example, to a rise in the capital stock, we observe how such a shift affects the opportunity sets of households and, ultimately, the supply of labor. The rank-ordering process, as in the theory of demand, is the familiar household utility function. The starting point in such analysis is therefore a detailed development of the opportunity set from the given time endowment.

14.1 The Opportunity Set

Most of us have no difficulty making a clear-cut conceptual distinction between activities we regard as work and those we regard as leisure. Work is the time we devote to making our leisure time more pleasurable. This is not to say that people in general do not enjoy the work they do—indeed, for many people work is one of the most important things in their lives. Friends, families, and social esteem are sacrificed daily on a vast scale at the alter of career advancement. Work is nevertheless "unpleasant" at the margin. Few of us would work as much or as intensively if we might do less without suffering a reduction in income. In this sense we do not give up leisure in order to work. Rather we give it up in order to obtain the income received from work. Our problem here is therefore to take an endowment expressed in units of time and to develop from it a constraint reflecting available combinations of leisure time and income.

This problem is complicated at the start by the obvious fact that all time spent "at work" is not work and that all time spent away from the place of employment is not leisure. On the contrary, as we discussed in Chapter 7, a great deal of production takes place in the home, and it is by virtue of the considerations raised there that any part of our time is supplied to the market. There is therefore a very poor correspondence at best between work and leisure on the one hand and time spent on the job (**market time**) and time spent away from the job (**nonmarket time**) on the other. Labor economists have employed this distinction with great success in recent years to study such diverse choices as marriage, the number and spacing of children, the allocation of time of housewives, the location of housing, retirement, and sharecropping.[1] Space limitations prevent us from surveying these interesting developments here in this text. Instead we must employ here the convenient fiction that the correspondence between work and market time is perfect.

The Time Endowment

Let us begin with an expression for the **time endowment**. The length of the time endowment depends, of course, on the type of allocative decision being made. Employment contracts typically specify the length of the workday, the length of the workweek, and the amount of vacation that is, the length of the work year. Some specify a retirement year. This suggests, that as many as four distinct choices concerning the allocation of time are made in most labor supply decisions. Since they are essentially similar in their analytical aspects, we shall consider only one. Let this total endowment of time, whether hours, days, weeks, or years, be denoted as T. We allow the chooser two mutually exclusive applications of time: work (a) and nonmarket activity (n). We may therefore express this endowment as:

$$T = a + n.$$

There are many forms of contracts for the reimbursement of labor. Workers may be on an annual salary, or they may be paid on commission or on a piece rate basis. They often get bonuses and are occasionally penalized a part of their pay. We will have occasion to discuss some of these contracts and the economic basis for their popularity in Chapter 16. Here we will begin with the simplest form of reimbursement: pay at a fixed hourly basis. Income (I) is thus related to the hours worked (a) and the wage rate (P_a) in the following expression:

$$I = P_a a.$$

Solving the time endowment for the quantity of work supplied gives $a = T - n$, which, when substituted into the expression for income, yields:

$$I = P_a T - P_a n.$$

---

[1] Many fine papers devoted to related topics may be found in Gary S. Becker, *Essays in Labor Economics in Honor of H. Gregg Lewis*, a supplementary issue of *Journal of Political Economy* 84 (August 1976). A brief glance at the combined references at the end of this volume will impress the reader with the richness and scope of this literature.

Figure 14.1 *Opportunity Set for Leisure and Income*

The vertical intercept of the opportunity set identifies the amount of income that can be earned if the full time endowment T is devoted to work and the number of hours of leisure chosen is zero. Each additional hour of leisure chosen reduces income by the wage rate. Thus, the slope of the opportunity set is $-P_a$.

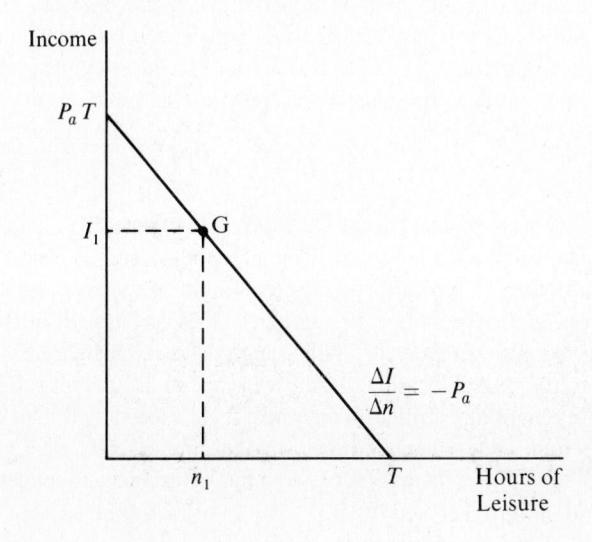

Examining this expression, we find that it contains only two variables under the control of the chooser: income and nonmarket activity. The remaining terms, the wage rate and the length of the week, are constant so far as the chooser's decision is concerned. Our constraint here is an expression relating the one good, income, to its alternative, nonmarket time. Furthermore, this opportunity set can be seen to have a familiar shape. The first term is the product of two positive constants. The second term contains a choice variable, n, multiplied by a constant coefficient, minus the wage rate. We may draw this constraint as depicted in Figure 14.1, with an intercept of $P_a T$ and a slope, $\Delta I/\Delta n$, of $-P_a$.

Any combination along this opportunity set may be chosen by the worker. For example, combination G offers the worker an income of I_1 together with n_1 hours of leisure. The vertical intercept $P_a T$ is the market value of the total time endowment and is referred to as the **full income** of the worker—although, of course, the requirements of sleep, eating, and rest prevent the worker from supplying this quantity of time to the market for more than very short intervals. The horizontal intercept is the total amount of time available, T, and the horizontal distance from n_1 to T measures the amount of work supplied. As with other opportunity sets we have analyzed, the slope of this constraint gives us the opportunity cost of one good in terms of the other. An extra hour of leisure can be obtained only at the sacrifice of income at a rate equal to $\Delta I/\Delta n$.

Shifting the Opportunity Set

Consider now the effects of changes in the environment in which work is supplied. Figure 14.2 depicts a wage increase. We observe from our constraint expression that the wage rate appears in both right-hand terms; hence, it affects both the slope and the intercept of the opportunity set. An increase in the wage rate from P_1 to P_2 will increase full income from P_1T to P_2T, shifting the intercept upward. As the slope of the constraint is equal to minus the wage rate, an increase in wages makes the slope more steeply negative. The opportunity cost of leisure is thus increased by an increase in the wage rate. However, changes in the wage rate have no effect on income if no work is done, so the horizontal intercept is unaffected by these changes. A worker may consume no more than 24 hours per day of leisure, regardless of the wage rate. For any amount of leisure of less than the full time endowment, such as n_1, higher wages imply higher income.

There are other sources of income besides earnings, and a complete treatment of labor supply must consider the influences of changes in nonwage income. Since these will not be influenced by variations in the amount of labor supplied, total income available may be expressed as the sum of earnings and the constant non-wage income (I_0):

$$I + I_0 = P_aT + I_0 - P_an.$$

Figure 14.2   *A Change in the Wage Rate*

An increase in the wage rate increases the magnitude of the slope of the opportunity set. It also implies that, for any given amount of leisure selected like n_1, more income may be enjoyed with that leisure.

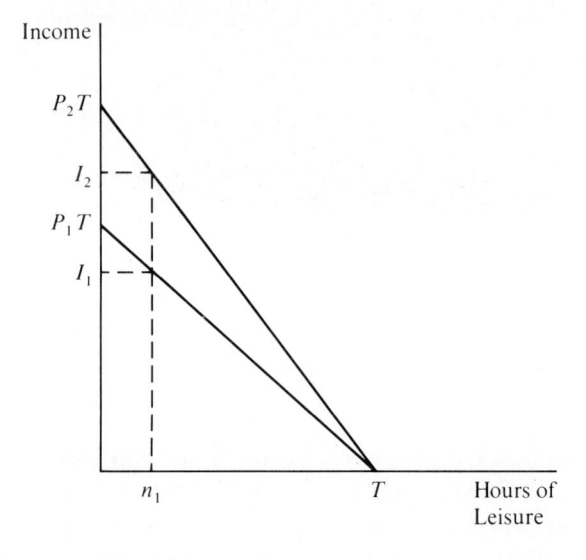

Figure 14.3   *A Change in Nonwage Income*

Total income is the sum of wage and nonwage income. Nonwage income does not vary with leisure. If the amount of nonwage income is increased from zero to I_0, the opportunity set will shift vertically by the amount I_0 at each quantity of leisure.

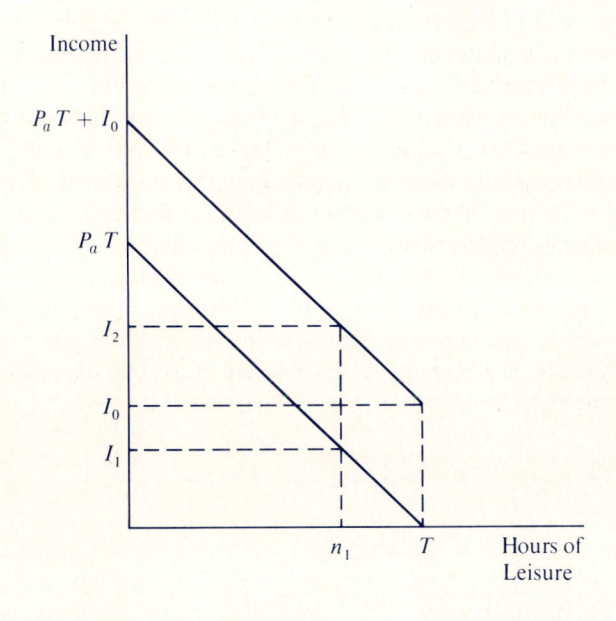

The presence of nonwage income therefore shifts the opportunity set upward as depicted in Figure 14.3. The addition to our constraint expression of the constant I_0 merely increases the value of the vertical intercept to $P_aT + I_0$; the slope is unaffected by receipt of nonwage income. Changes in the amount of income from this source will therefore shift the constraint upward or downward to a position parallel with the constraint expressed in terms of labor earnings alone. For any given amount of leisure, receipt of nonlabor income increases total income by this amount, I_0. Thus, in Figure 14.3 the difference in income received at n_1 hours of leisure, $I_2 - I_1$, is precisely I_0.

14.2   Choosing the Quantity Supplied

The choice between income and leisure suffers the same ambiguity as that which exists between green beans and black-eyed peas. It is shaped to a large degree by the tastes of the choosers, and these are observed to differ widely from household to household. There are nevertheless some characteristics of worker utility functions concerning these items that all are assumed to share in common. All the postulates stated in connection with the theory of consumer choice are assumed to apply here. The handy device of indifference curve analysis may be marshalled to our task of determining quantity supplied.

These assumptions permit us to characterize the combination chosen as an optimum, as in Figure 14.4. In this figure we present three indifference curves, each of which connects combinations of income and leisure over which the chooser is indifferent. The combinations connected by curve U_3 are preferred to those on U_2, which in turn are preferred to those on U_1. The labor supplier will choose the combination that permits him or her to reach the highest possible indifference curve. In this case that combination is T. This combination contains I^* of income and n^* of leisure, implying the supply of $T - n^*$ hours of labor per period.

This utility function assigns a rank ordering to all combinations of income and leisure. It is thus expressed as:

$$U = f(n, I).$$

The slopes of the indifference curves derived from such utility functions are equal to minus the marginal rates of substitution of one good for the other. They measure

Figure 14.4   *Leisure Can be a Bad*

Not everyone's MRS of leisure for income is positive. A person can have too much time on his hands. At combination K, for example, the value of leisure in terms of the amount of income that would be given up per additional hour is negative. This poses no problem for our theory. At the combination chosen (G in this figure), the MRS will be positive.

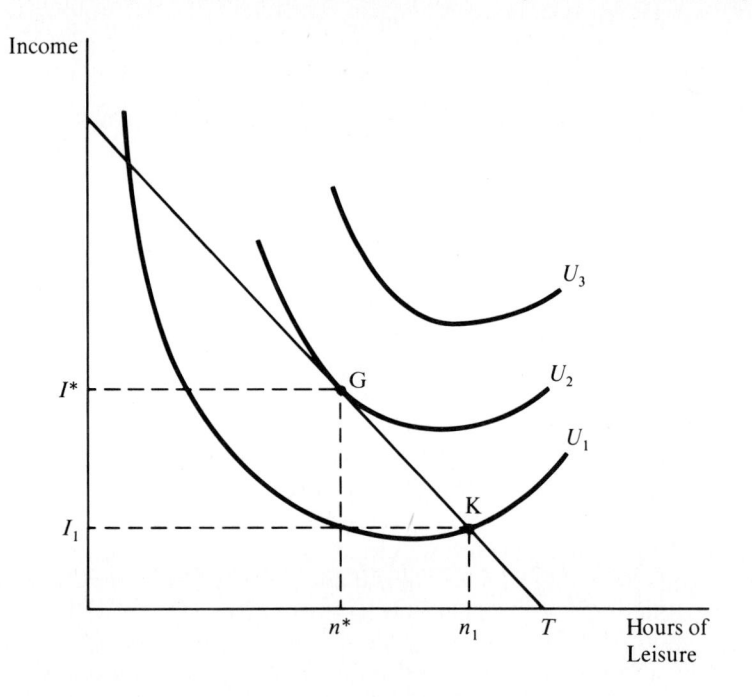

the value of one good in terms of the amount of the other that will be given up to obtain it. At the combination chosen the indifference curve and the opportunity set have the same slope. The slope of the latter is everywhere equal to minus the wage rate. It must be true at this optimum that the value of leisure in terms of the income for which it will be exchanged (MRS) will be just equal to the wage rate, P_a.

Figure 14.4 also helps clarify the assertions concerning the enjoyment of work discussed in the previous section. Note that each of the indifference curves turns upward at a quantity of leisure less than the full time endowment. A person with tastes such as these would, under certain circumstances, pay to work! As we have just seen, the slope of the indifference curve reflects the value that the individual places on the good leisure at the margin. This slope is equal to *minus* the MRS for that good. Thus, along portions of the indifference curves where the slope is positive, the value of leisure in terms of the income the chooser is willing to give up for an extra unit is *negative*. Beyond some point idleness becomes burdensome; work is preferred to leisure in this range.

The existence of these upward-sloping portions of indifference curves pose no difficulties for our theory of labor supply. For as long as opportunities exist to sell labor for a positive wage, the optima chosen will always occur along the negatively sloped portions of indifference curves. Indifference curve U_1, for example, intersects the opportunity set with a positive slope. At combination K on this opportunity set, the value of additional leisure is negative. However, a chooser who is free to select the amount of work he or she will supply will never choose this combination containing so much leisure. It produces less utility for him or her than other combinations to the northwest of K. The utility-maximizing combination will be that which is tangent to the opportunity set, and the opportunity set has a negative slope. It does not matter, therefore, that some people may enjoy work and prefer some amount of it to doing nothing. The opportunity to sell labor at a positive price insures that people will choose combinations at which the value of leisure is equal to its opportunity cost, which is positive under these conditions. Work at the margin must therefore be a "bad."

The Income Effect on Labor Supply

We can make even stronger assumptions about the utility function of labor and leisure than we could for the more general bundle of consumer goods. We assume that both leisure and income are normal goods. As income itself composes one of these goods, however, some further elaboration is clearly necessary concerning the concept of the "income elasticity of income." Recall that in the theory of consumer demand an income consumption curve was generated by connecting combinations of goods purchased at successively higher incomes holding the prices of the goods constant. The MRS for each combination on this curve, being equal to a constant price ratio, was therefore itself constant. As income is *chosen* as a part of this analysis, however, we cannot generate these curves in this way. We cannot simultaneously vary income and observe the effect of this variation on the level of income chosen. Income must be either endogenous or exogenous to the analysis. Nevertheless, a curve connecting combinations of leisure and income with the same MRS on successively higher indifference curves does play an important role in the theory of labor supply.

The correct interpretation of such a curve requires that we make a careful distinction between changes in nominal income on the one hand and changes in real income on the other. Increases in real income represent expanded consumption options holding constant the prices of all goods being chosen. One of the goods being chosen here is leisure, whose value at the margin we have ascertained to be the wage rate P_a. A correct measure of the *real* income enjoyed here is therefore the value of all goods purchased plus the value of the *leisure* chosen as a part of that combination. Nominal income, on the other hand, is merely the income earned from the sale of labor services plus other money income.

Income consumption curves in leisure and income thus link combinations of these two goods along which MRS is constant as real income rises. Thus, the ICC curve in Figure 14.5 passes through points G and K. We may now correctly interpret our statement concerning the income elasticities of these two goods. The assumption that income is a normal good refers to nominal income or, more precisely, to goods purchased with this income. At higher levels of real income more

Figure 14.5 *Leisure and Nonwage Income*

Both leisure and the goods that are purchased with income are normal goods. Thus, as real income rises, holding the opportunity cost of leisure constant, more of both are chosen.

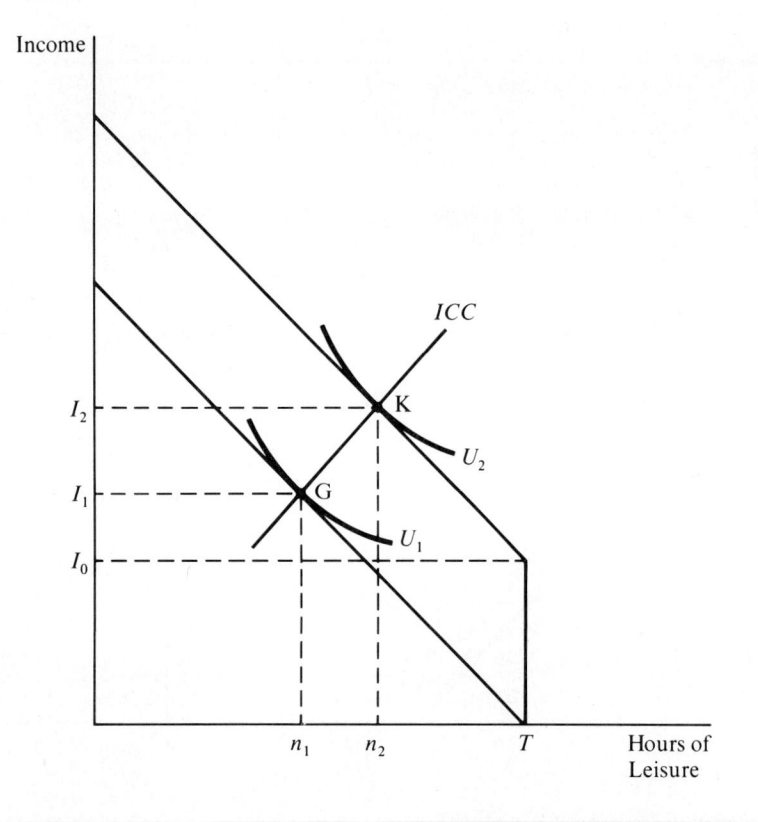

of these goods will be purchased. The assumption that leisure is also a normal good implies that more hours of leisure will also be chosen. As is the case in the theory of household demand, when both goods are normal, the ICC curve must have a positive slope.

A Change in the Wage Rate

We are now equipped to analyze the effect on labor supply of changes in the wage rate. The supply curve of an individual worker must be either positively or negatively sloped. This is illustrated in the two panels of Figure 14.6. Let the initial wage rate be P_1 so that in both panels the worker chooses a combination of leisure and income along the opportunity set extending from T to P_1T. In each case combination T is chosen. A rise in the wage rate rotates the opportunity set clockwise around the horizontal intercept T, as illustrated earlier. In panel (a) the new combination chosen, K, lies to the right of the original choice, G, reflecting the choice of more leisure. This worker therefore supplies less work at the higher wage. In panel (b), however, the combination chosen at the higher wage contains less leisure. This worker therefore supplies more hours of work at the higher wage. Even the more restrictive assumptions concerning the utility function of choosers made in this case are insufficient to rule out either of these possibilities.

We may nevertheless break down the response to wage changes into separate effects whose directions may be predicted for any case. Estimation of the magni-

Figure 14.6 *Wage Rates and the Supply of Labor*

The individual supply curve for labor may have either a positive or a negative slope. In panel (a) the higher wage rate leads to an increase in leisure and a decrease in the labor supplied. In panel (b) the higher wage rate is associated with less leisure and an increase in the supply of labor. Neither panel conflicts with the assumptions of choice theory, so neither can be ruled out.

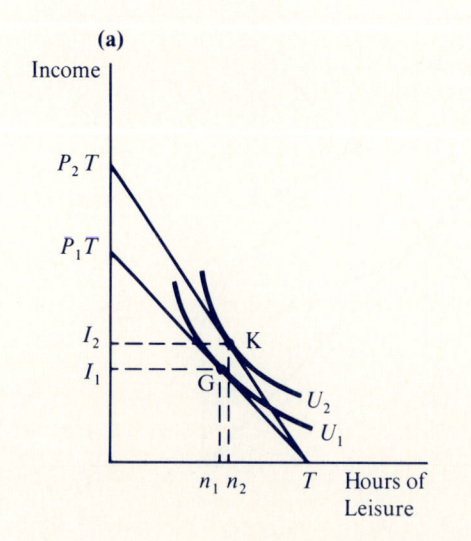

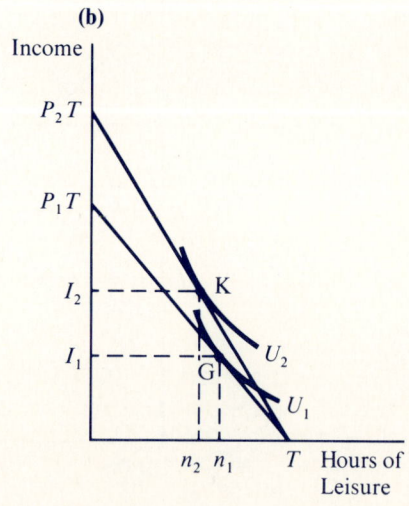

tude of these effects permits us to determine the resulting net change in quantity supplied. The response of a change in labor supply to wage rate changes results from two offsetting effects. On the one hand, an increase in the wage rate increases real income, and changes in real income affect the allocation of time between work and leisure. On the other hand, the wage rate reflects the opportunity cost of leisure. At any level of real income a worker will seek to select the quantity of leisure whose value is just equal to its opportunity cost—that is, the quantity at which the worker's MRS is just equal to the wage rate. A change in that opportunity cost also has an effect on the quantity of leisure chosen.

These effects are depicted diagrammatically in Figure 14.7. Let the initial wage be P_1 so that the original opportunity set extends from T to P_1T. The worker

Figure 14.7 *Substitution and Income Effects of Wage Changes*

Holding real income constant at U_1, the substitution effect of the wage increase results in combination K being chosen rather than initial combination G. At the higher opportunity cost of leisure, goods purchased with income are substituted for leisure. The effect of the increase in real income, holding opportunity cost constant, measures the portion of the response resulting from the income effect. This is the change from combination K to combination H. The substitution effect of the wage increase increases the labor supplied. The income effect reduces the labor supplied. The net effect depends on the relative magnitudes of these two effects.

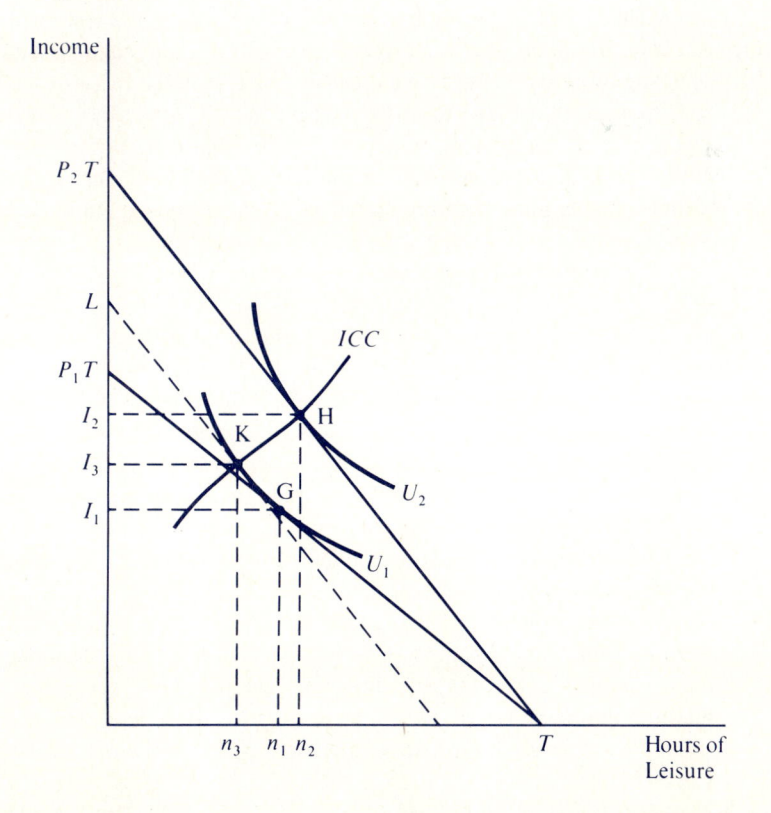

chooses combination G offering n_1 hours of leisure and I_1 dollars of income. A wage increase rotates the opportunity set in a clockwise direction to its new position with a vertical intercept at P_2T. Given these new opportunities, the worker will select combination H, in this case supplying less labor at the higher wage. In order to sort out these two effects, however, we must find a third point in the diagram, the combination that the worker would choose facing the new, higher opportunity cost of leisure but holding to his or her original real income.

We may do this in the following way. Recall that an ICC curve links all combinations of leisure and income for which the labor supplier's MRS is the same as real income varies. The ICC curve depicted in Figure 14.7 therefore connects all combinations yielding the same MRS as combination H, the one purchased at the higher wage rate. Indifference curve U_1, on the other hand, links all combinations that produce the same utility (that is, the same real income) as original combination G. The intersection of these two curves, point K, is therefore the point we seek. At this point real income is the same as that which the worker enjoyed before the wage increase. However, the worker's MRS at this combination is equal to the higher wage rate P_2, indicating the combination that he or she would choose at this higher opportunity cost of leisure.

The **substitution effect** of this wage increase is the change in leisure chosen in response to that good's higher opportunity cost, holding real income constant. In Figure 14.7 this increase is measured from n_1 to n_3. Note that because combination K must be associated with a higher MRS than combination G, K must lie to the northwest of G on the indifference curve, U_1. As is true of the substitution effect of any good, the substitution effect of the good leisure must operate in the opposite direction of the price change. The rise in the price of leisure leads to a reduction in its use due to this effect; the substitution effect of a wage reduction would reduce the amount of leisure chosen. That reduction in leisure produces a corresponding increase in the amount of labor supplied. The substitution effect of a wage change may therefore be said to produce a change in labor supplied in the *same* direction as the wage change.

The **income effect** of a wage rate change will always offset the substitution effect. This effect is the result of the expanded opportunities to consume both income and leisure due to the wage increase. A measure of this change in real income produced by the wage increase depicted in Figure 14.7 is the change in nonwage income, which would yield the same utility change. A reduction in nonwage income equal to $P_2T - L$ after such a wage increase would reduce real income by exactly the amount by which it was increased by the wage change itself. The wage change may thus be said to have increased real income by this amount.

Leisure is a normal good, and wage changes such as those depicted here increasing real income will influence the worker to choose more leisure. If we hold the opportunity cost of leisure constant at the new wage rate P_2, the increase in real income produced by the higher wage increases the quantity of leisure chosen from n_3 to n_2. Any change in leisure is associated with a corresponding change in labor supplied in the opposite direction. The income effect of the wage increase therefore produces a *reduction* in labor supplied. In general, the income effect of a wage change results in a change in labor supplied in the *opposite* direction of the wage change.

The net effect of wage changes on labor supply therefore depends on the magnitudes of these two offsetting effects. In Figure 14.7 the income effect dominates. As it is the quantitatively larger of the effects, the resulting change in labor supply is negative. However, there is no reason to believe that this will invariably occur. On the contrary, as we have already seen, it is possible to construct a similar diagram in which higher wages are associated with an increase in labor supply. The reader may readily see that in such cases the substitution effect is quantitatively larger and therefore dominates the direction of response.

We have little to guide us in predicting the magnitudes of substitution and income effects in individual cases. It does seem plausible, however, that at some point higher wages will be associated with consistently dominant income effects leading to a **backward-bending supply curve**, such as the one depicted in Figure 14.8. The reasoning behind such a conjecture is that consumption of income itself is time consuming. (The importance of consumption time for household choice and its relationship to wage rates was discussed in Chapter 4.) Clearly, as the wage rate, and with it the opportunity cost of nonmarket time rises, workers will shift to the consumption of goods that economize on that time. They will spend their income on goods that produce high utility per hour of time devoted to their consumption. They will fly to their holiday destinations rather than drive or take a train. They will eat in restaurants or hire cooks rather than prepare their own meals.

Figure 14.8   *The Backward-Bending Supply Curve for Labor*

It is possible that the individual labor supply curves of some individuals have this shape. This would be true if substitution effects had dominated at low wages but income effects were larger in magnitude at higher wages.

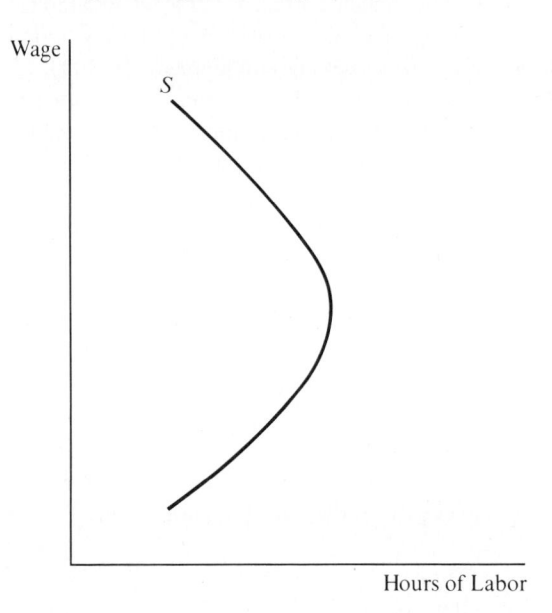

They will eat gourmet dinners rather than hamburgers. Beyond some point, however, the scope for continued shifts of this type seems likely to diminish. Once the family cook learns to prepare one's favorite dish exactly the way one wants it, one must shorten the dinner hour in order to have time to consume something besides dinner. At this point additional income will perhaps be less valuable than additional time with which to spend the income already earned.

The substitution effects of higher wage rates under such circumstances would seem to be meager compared to the income effects. This argument is purely hypothetical, however, and there is little evidence for making this claim for a backward-bending labor supply curve. On the contrary, surveys of high-income people suggest that they work longer hours than does the average American worker.[2] A fuller discussion of this evidence must be deferred to Chapter 16, when we may take up a discussion of the bases of wage rate differences themselves.

14.3 The Market Supply of Labor

Although individual labor supply curves may be backward bending, the market supply of labor has been widely observed to be positively responsive to changes in the wage rate. This is possible because changes in the supply of labor are influenced not only by changes in the quantities offered by members of the labor force but by the entrance of new suppliers at higher wages. The market supply of labor is the aggregate of all the quantities supplied by individual workers. Although a particular wage increase may lead all those presently supplying labor to reduce the quantities offered, it will almost certainly attract new suppliers into the labor force. At any time the population contains many more people capable of work than are actively employed or seeking employment. Millions of pensioners, students, homemakers, and thieves devote their full time endowments to nonmarket activities at existing wage rates but would enter the labor force if wages rose sufficiently. The entrance of new workers, therefore, offsets the reductions in supply of those already working.

This is illustrated in Figure 14.9. Panels (a) and (b) contain the supply curves of two individuals, depicting the quantities of labor that each would supply at varying wage rates. Panel (c) contains the market supply curve that is the *sum* of the quantities supplied by the two workers at each wage. Worker B supplies no work at any wage below P_1, so the market supply curve below P_1 contains only the labor supplied by worker A. At wage P_1, the market supply is H_1^m, equal to H_1^A + 0. Wage increases at any wage above P_1 influence worker A to reduce his or her supply of work. At these wages this worker is on the backward-bending portion of his or her supply curve. The market supply curve nevertheless slopes upward to the right in this case because of the added quantity offered by worker B, who is

---

[2] See Barlow, Brazer, and Morgan, *The Economic Behavior of the Affluent* (Washington: The Brookings Institution, 1966).

Chapter 14 *The Supply of Labor* 453

Figure 14.9 **The Market Supply of Labor**

Even if individual supply curves for labor are backward bending, the market supply curve for labor may have a positive slope. This will result where higher wages attract new people into the labor force. Between P_1 and P_2 the supplier in panel (a) reduces the quantity of labor supplied. The wage increase over the same interval leads the supplier in panel (b) to enter the labor force and supply H_2^B hours. The sum of these two changes leads to an increase in the market supply in panel (c).

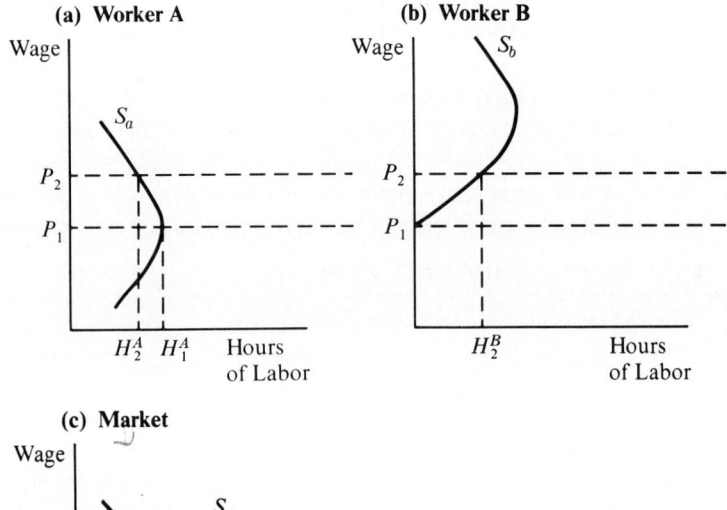

induced to join the labor force at these higher wages. At wage P_2, for example, the market supply is H_2^m, which is equal to H_2^A plus H_2^B.

The wage rate influencing a member of the population to enter the labor force is defined as that person's **reservation wage**. For worker B in Figure 14.9, this reservation wage is P_1. The reservation wage varies widely for different members of the population, depending on each person's value of the time spent on non-market activities. For this reason, at any wage rate there are many potential new entrants to the labor force who stand ready to become active suppliers should wages increase. Analysis of the market supply of labor must therefore consider not only the response of individual suppliers of labor to wage rate changes but also their very decision to become a supplier.

Choosing to Supply: Labor Force Participation

The percentage of the population actively supplying labor is defined as the **labor force participation rate**. As the wage rate increases, some of those devoting full time to nonmarket activities will find the wage rate above their reservation wage and enter the labor force. The labor force participation rate must therefore increase with wages. Analysis of the decision to supply labor must therefore focus on the determinants of the reservation wage.

The choice to supply labor and the influence of the wage rate on this decision are depicted graphically in Figure 14.10. Few households are so self-sufficient that they may get along without any income with which to buy things in the market. It therefore makes sense to assume that a person who chooses not to supply

---

Figure 14.10 *The Decision to Join the Labor Force*

At wage P_1 the full time endowment is devoted to nonmarket activity (leisure). The MRS at combination G exceeds the wage rate, and combination G is preferred to any combination on this opportunity set. At the higher wage rate P_2, an interior combination is chosen. Combination H is preferred to combination G.

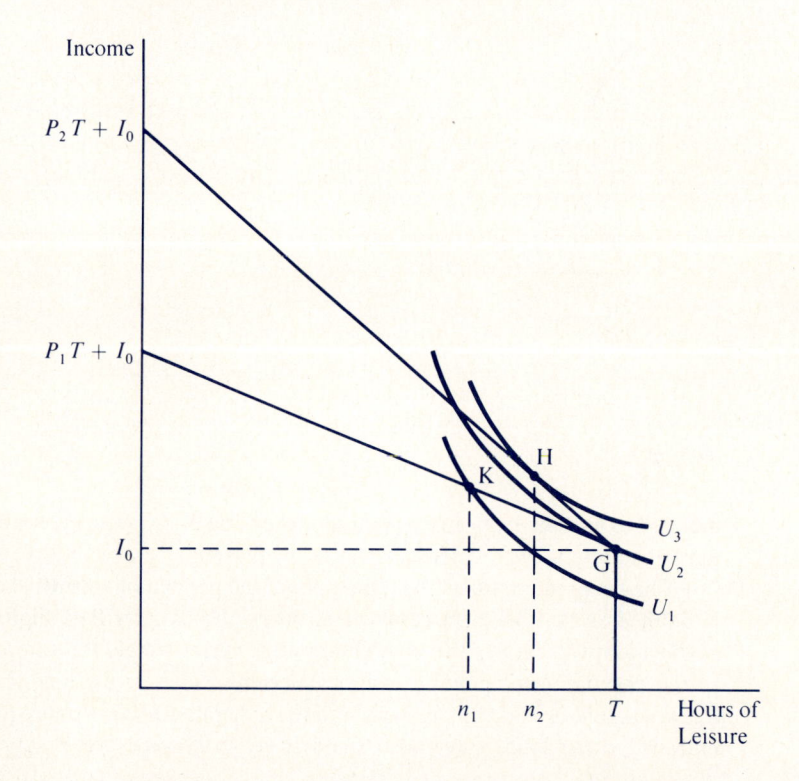

labor has some nonwage income. This income may come from the person's own capital assets, or it may come from earnings of other family members. In the figure this nonwage income is shown as I_0. Let the initial wage rate be P_1 so that the opportunity set available at this wage is that which has a vertical intercept at $P_1 T + I_0$. The individual may elect to devote his or her full time endowment to nonmarket activity and receive an income of I_0. By working, however, he or she may add to this income at a rate of P_1 per hour of work supplied. Given the preferences depicted by indifference curves U_1, U_2, and U_3, however, this person will supply none. Any combination along the opportunity set containing less than the maximum possible amount of leisure, such as combination K offering only n_1 hours, produces less utility than combination G offering the full time endowment of leisure.

Note that this combination is a **corner solution**. The person's MRS at this combination is not equal to the wage rate, because the slope of the indifference curve at this point is greater than the slope of the opportunity set. The individual would choose more than the full time endowment of leisure, but, of course, combinations to the right of T are unattainable. It is worth remembering, however, that the value of this time to such individuals exceeds the wage rate.

At some higher wage rate, the opportunity cost of leisure will exceed its value at this margin. Assume, for example, that the wage rate rises to P_2. The slope of the opportunity set now exceeds that of indifference curve U_2 at combination G. The individual will now select an interior combination in which less than the full time endowment is devoted to leisure. The most favored combination along this opportunity set is H, which contains only n_2 hours of leisure. Under these circumstances the person will enter the labor force supplying $T - n_2$ hours of work.

For any member of society, there must, in principle, be *some* wage that will induce him or her to enter the labor force. However, this threshold wage differs among individuals, so that as wages rise and fall there will always be many on the margin ready to enter or to leave. At higher wages the opportunity cost of leisure will exceed its value for more people than will be true at lower wages. The labor force participation rate will therefore be positively related to the wage rate.

What other factors influence the labor force participation rate? These can best be discussed in terms of the two factors already examined, the value of time in market and time in nonmarket activities, respectively. The value of time in the home is clearly related to the number of children who must be cared for there. The presence of children will make it more likely that time devoted to this type of nonmarket activity (child rearing) will exceed its value in the market in any individual case. Changes in the birth rate are therefore predicted to have a direct effect on labor force participation, and this implication is supported by recent observation. The declining birth rate in the United States in the postwar period has been accompanied by a steadily rising trend in the labor force participation rate, particularly among young women.

The extent of specialization in an economy and its employment of large-scale technology can also influence the labor force participation rate. These features increase the productivity of labor in firms relative to their value in household production and make supplying labor in the market relatively more attractive. When one's alternatives are limited to planting five rows of potatoes for one's household or hiring oneself out to someone else to plant five rows of potatoes, the scope for economies due to market activity are limited. It is for this reason that the reported labor force participation rates of most developing countries are very low.

Another important influence on labor force participation is income from nonwage sources. It can be shown that increases in nonwage income will decrease labor force participation. Countries with a high ratio of capital income to labor income should therefore have lower labor force participation rates than countries with similar wage rates but lower income shares going to capital.

The influence of nonwage income on the decision to supply labor is presented in Figure 14.11. Here we depict the choice of income and leisure for an individual facing a given wage rate but with varying amounts of nonwage income. The combinations chosen will trace out an income consumption curve. Given the assumption of normality in both these goods, the ICC curve slopes upward to the right. At the point at which this curve reaches the value of T hours of leisure, however, the chooser will leave the labor force; this occurs with nonwage income I_2. At higher levels of nonwage income, this person will choose not to work. At nonwage incomes below I_2, the person will elect to join the labor force.

Figure 14.11   *Nonwage Income and Labor Force Participation*

At high levels of nonwage income, a potential labor supplier is less likely to supply labor than if nonwage income is lower. With nonwage income equal to I_3, the MRS of leisure for goods purchased with income exceeds the wage rate at every quantity of leisure. No labor will be supplied by this person under these circumstances. At lower levels of nonwage income an interior combination is chosen, implying that this person will join the labor force.

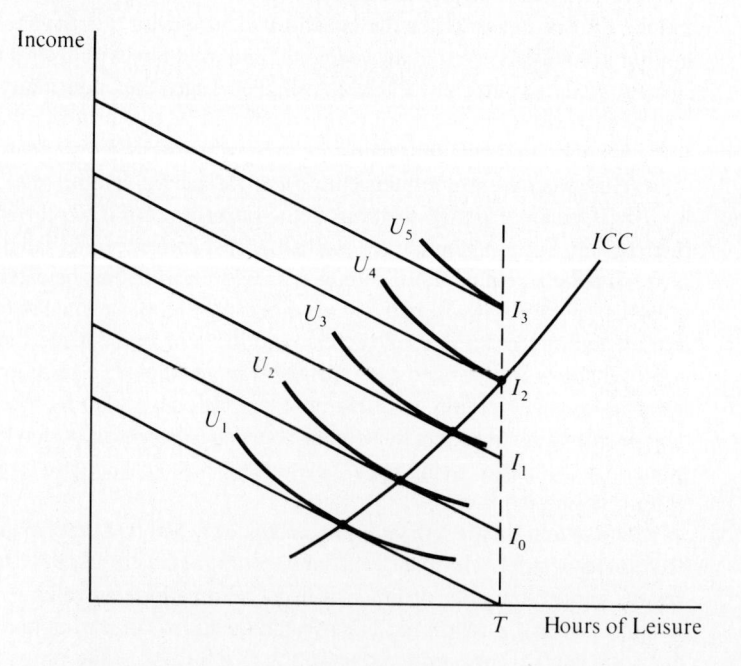

An obvious application of this result is the influence of marriage on labor force participation. An important source of nonwage income for married people is, of course, the earnings of their spouses. Economies of scale in the performance of both household and market tasks make it more economical for one partner or the other to specialize in each of these activities than for both to divide their time between them. Similarly qualified single people without a working spouse lack the income required to finance such specialization in nonmarket activity. Single people will therefore have far greater labor force participation than married people with similar characteristics.

Income Conditional Grants

Another significant influence on labor force participation is the practice of making entitlement to government grants conditional upon applicants' earnings. Social security benefits and welfare payments are the most important examples of such **income conditional grants**. Currently a retired worker may earn only $6,600 per year without becoming ineligible for social security benefits. Entitlement to welfare varies from state to state, but nowhere are they made without income tests. Such a practice can severely inhibit active labor force supply.

The effects of such restrictions are depicted in Figure 14.12. Let the amount of the grant be I_0 and the maximum allowable income be I_1. Applicants earning more than I_1 per year are no longer entitled to the grant and receive only their earnings. The opportunity set is therefore as depicted by the bold line extending upward to the right to point G with a slope of minus the wage rate P_a, then dropping vertically downward to point D, at which it turns upward to the right again with the same slope. Point G offers a total income of $I_0 + I_1$ together with n_1 hours of leisure. The position of this point (that is, the amount of work the supplier may legitimately sell) will depend upon the wage rate. A higher-wage worker will be allowed to supply fewer hours before reaching the maximum income than will the lower-wage worker.

Potential workers confronting these conditional grants are therefore forced to make a choice between combinations like G and those like K. It is quite possible that the choice will be combination G, offering less total income than combination K because of the high opportunity cost in leisure that must be sacrificed in order to obtain the additional income. Note that the reimbursement per additional hour worked over this interval from n_1 to n_2 is far lower than the wage rate. That reimbursement rate, $-\Delta I/\Delta n$, will equal minus the slope of the line extending from point G to point K, which is clearly less than the wage rate (minus the slope of the opportunity set). Under such circumstances, many will find that such a low hourly rate is less than their reservation wage. The value of this time in nonmarket activity, though less than the wage rate (see point G), is greater than the net reimbursement rate for additional work.

This is a strange policy, particularly for retired workers. Why should not those who wish to continue working be able to do so without losing their entitlement to these benefits? Benefit levels and permissible incomes are presently set so that few choose to continue working beyond age 65. Eliminating the income test will therefore add few to the entitlement roles who are not already receiving these

Figure 14.12 *Income Conditional Grants*

A grant of nonwage income equal to I_0 is received conditional upon less than I_1 in wage income being earned. This presents the worker with the opportunity set indicated by the bold line containing corners at D and G. Combination G is favored over any other on this opportunity set. A slightly smaller unconditional grant of I_0' would be favored over the conditional grant. The unconditional grant would permit the selection of combination H, which is favored over combination G.

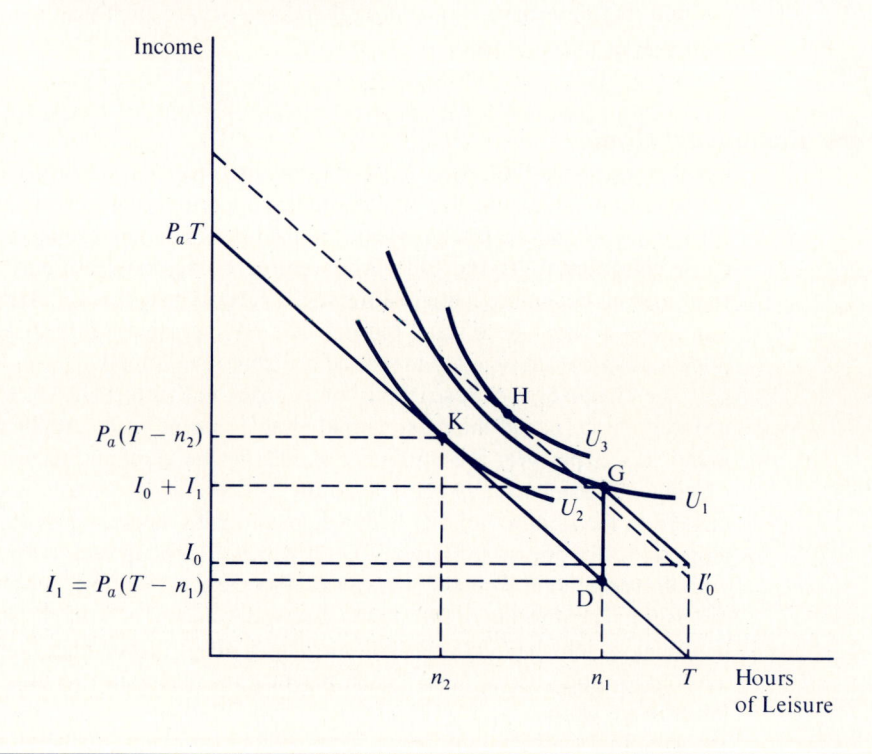

benefits. If necessary, a small reduction might be made in the benefits of those who continue to work in order to protect the integrity of the fund. The results of such a reduction in these benefits from I_0 to I_0' are shown in Figure 14.12. Under these conditions the choice of combination H is made possible, which seems to offer something for everyone. The affected households earn more income in both nominal and real terms, more labor is available for the economy, and the cost to the government of these benefits has not increased.

Why does this policy survive? Governments rarely adopt policies that do not have at least a few noisy beneficiaries, and a closer examination reveals a few clues to the answer to this question. Pursuit of these clues must be postponed, however, to a later section of this chapter, where we discuss the effect of aggregate labor supply on labor earnings.

The Negative Income Tax

While extending unconditional benefits to social security recipients can be done at low cost to the government budget, the same cannot be said of income maintenance programs. These programs are intended to transfer income from those who earn more to those who earn less. The government cannot give income to everyone; it owns few resources, and these it always seems to lose money on. In order to make income grants to some, it must take income away from others. It would therefore appear that income maintenance programs *must* have income tests in order to limit the group receiving benefits under them.

While the validity of this argument is undeniable, it is nevertheless true that welfare programs can be redesigned in ways that lessen the work-inhibiting effects of the present programs. One such method, which has received considerable attention in recent years, is the **negative income tax**. This unusual name can best be explained in terms of the two panels in Figure 14.13. The present income tax system relates taxable income to disposable (after-tax) income, as shown in panel (a). Up to I_0^t dollars of income may be earned without income tax, but beyond this point taxable and disposable income diverge. At I_1^t, for example, the taxpayer retains only I_1^d dollars and pays the difference to the government. Proponents of the negative income tax propose to push the disposable income curve across the 45° line in the diagram as shown in panel (b). Those with higher incomes would be

Figure 14.13 *Negative Income Taxes*

The effect of the present income tax is depicted in panel (a). The vertical axis measures both total and disposable (after-tax) income, while the horizontal axis measures total (taxable) income. At income below I_0^t no tax is levied, so that taxable and disposable incomes are the same. At incomes above I_0^t positive taxes are levied, reducing the proportion of taxable income represented by disposable income. Panel (b) illustrates the negative income tax. A negative tax (grant) is provided at incomes below I_0^t. However, this grant diminishes as taxable income approaches this level. At incomes above I_0^t the grant becomes a tax.

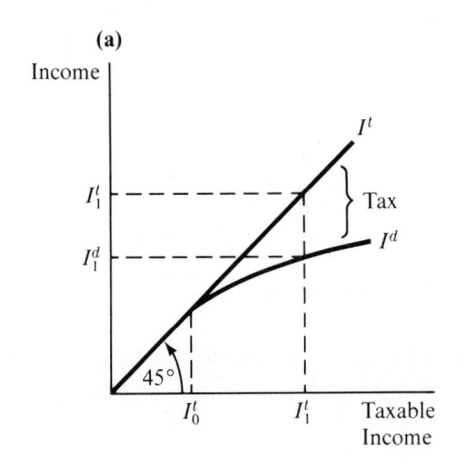

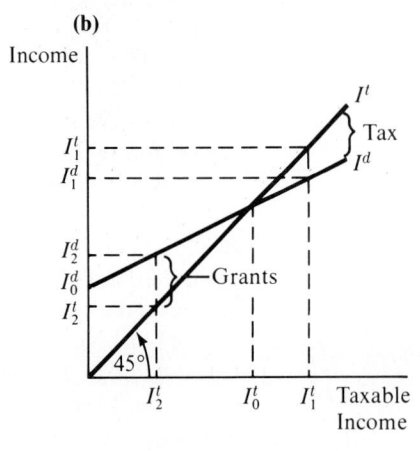

treated no differently than before. However, those with incomes below I_0^t would now receive a grant or negative tax, which itself is income related. A person with no income would receive a grant of I_0^d, while one with a higher income would receive a smaller grant. A person with taxable income I_2^t, for example, would receive only $I_2^d - I_2^t$.

The present welfare plans operate exactly like the social security system to discourage labor supply. Receipt of benefits is contingent upon the applicant's earning less than a stipulated amount. This places many recipients in the situation depicted earlier in Figure 14.12. In that figure the favored combination is a corner solution like point T, at which the value of leisure to the recipients is less than its opportunity cost. Workers will nevertheless refrain from working more and earning more, because to do so would disqualify them from receiving the grant.

Contrast these results with those of the negative income tax presented in Figure 14.14. The effect of the negative income tax on each of three workers (A, B, and C) with different wage rates is presented in the three panels of this figure. Grants under this proposal diminish as income rises but are not arbitrarily withdrawn at some minimum income. If any of the three chooses not to work, he or she receives a grant of I_0 under this program. As more labor is supplied the amount of the grant for which the worker qualifies diminishes. But since the size of the grant is tied to income, the grant diminishes more rapidly as the wage rate of this worker increases. Thus, the lowest-wage worker in panel (a) chooses n_1 hours of leisure and therefore works $T - n_1$ hours. For supplying this work he or she earns I_1^A dollars in income and receives a grant of g dollars. The other two workers would receive the same grant with these earnings, but because their wage rates are higher, the grant falls to this amount with less work. The worker in panel (b) receives the same grant with $T - n_1^B$ hours of work, and the grant falls to this amount with only $T - n_1^C$ hours of work for the highest-wage worker in panel (c).

Each worker, therefore, will likely receive a different grant, which diminishes with his or her potential wage rate. Worker B would choose n_2^B hours of leisure and $T - n_2^B$ hours of work, receiving wages of I_2^B and thus the smaller grant g'. Worker C would receive no grant at all, because the income leisure combination chosen would place his or her income above the threshold level at which a positive income tax must be paid. This worker's earnings are I_2^C, from which would be deducted a tax of t dollars, leaving him or her with a disposable income of $I_2^C - t$.

The advantages of such a program over the present welfare system are numerous and significant. Each worker is free to supply the quantity of work that he or she wishes without the severe disincentives of low or negative compensation for additional work performed at the margin. The combinations of work and leisure chosen by each will be much closer to those that equate the value of nonmarket time to its true opportunity cost at the margin. In addition, this system can be administered through the existing income tax machinery at the state or federal level. The large and costly welfare bureaucracy necessary to administer and police the existing income maintenance system could therefore be dismantled. Social workers could be free to perform the tasks of counseling and training without the barrier presently posed between them and their clients by their dual role of confidante and policeman.

Figure 14.14 *Negative Income Taxes and Labor Supply*

At different wage rates the influences of the negative income tax on the opportunity set of leisure and income differ. At low wage rates in panel (a), the grant diminishes slowly as more labor is supplied. At the somewhat higher wages shown in panel (b), the grant diminishes more rapidly, and the grant received at the chosen combination is smaller. At the still higher wage in panel (c), the grant disappears altogether at low levels of labor supply. The combination chosen on this opportunity set results in tax rather than receipt of a grant.

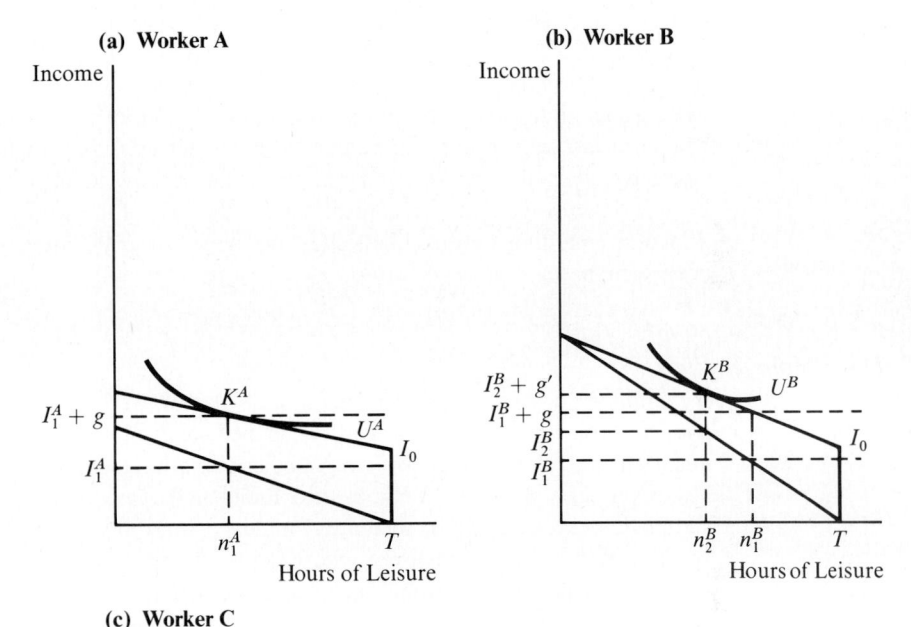

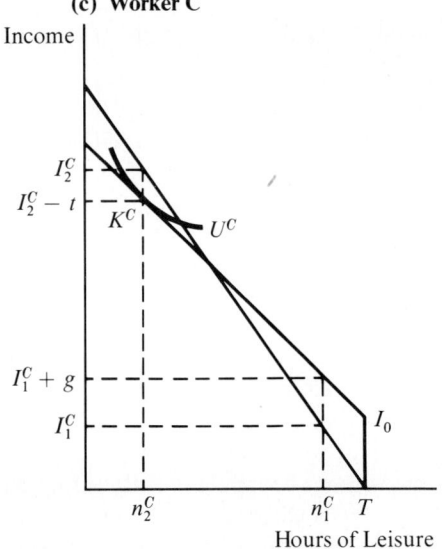

(a) Worker A

(b) Worker B

(c) Worker C

14.4 Direct Constraints on Supply

Thus far in this chapter the topics we have considered have involved a labor market in which suppliers were free to offer as much labor as they chose at each wage. Market supply curves were constructed by aggregating individual supply curves identifying the results of those choices. However, we cannot leave the topic of labor supply without considering the impact of direct constraints on these supply decisions. The labor market, after all, exhibits a great proliferation of such constraints. Child labor laws prevent underage people from offering their services to firms (but, interestingly, do not prevent them from becoming "independent contractors"). The Fair Labor Standards Act, which was passed in 1938, has established a maximum workweek preventing workers from offering their services at the contracted wage rate for more than 40 hours per week (originally 44). Union contracts universally impose similar limits on the work its members may supply at the negotiated wage. And, of course, there is the case of the strong disincentives of income conditional grants like welfare and social security, discussed in the previous section.

The Employer View

The employer has often been depicted as the villain in work arrangements. Legislation to limit hours worked is widely justified, as it protects workers from the predations of factory owners who might otherwise grind them down from dawn to dusk seven days per week. Without strict limits on the length of the workweek, it is argued, workers would be forced by employers to supply more hours than they would wish or than is consistent with good health and citizenship. These arguments may make good copy, but their economics is faulty.

Even though legislation may be justified on the basis of protecting workers, it is from themselves, as suppliers, that workers really need protection. Typically they are the only parties to employment contracts that have any interest in the length of the workweek. In fact, in the few cases in which employers have a stake in the amount of labor they purchase per employee, employers seek fewer labor hours than workers would like to supply.

Consider first the case of firms that are perfect price takers in the labor market. These firms face a perfectly elastic supply of labor at the market equilibrium wage. If the productivity of labor is unaffected by the length of the workweek, these firms will not care whether they buy 30 hours per week from each worker or 60 per week from half the number of workers. They will obtain the same amount of output from the employed labor in either case and bear the same costs. Firms in this situation are completely indifferent concerning the amount of work obtained from each worker.

If, on the other hand, productivity diminishes as hours worked per employee increases, demanding firms will not be indifferent. By hiring more workers and employing them for shorter periods per week, total output for a given number of man-hours hired will be greater. If the same price is paid per man-hour, profits will be greater with shorter workweeks than with longer ones. This will be true whether or not workers would like to supply more labor at these wages. Realistically, however, we can probably discount the influence of firms on this decision. Productivity per man-hour seems to vary little over the broad ranges of the workweek typically supplied. Firms are therefore unlikely to insist on hours of work that are widely at variance with the wishes of their employees.

Workers, on the other hand, do have an interest in the length of the workweek. They have competing uses for the time they supply, and the combinations they choose are those that will make them better off (at least in their own eyes) than any other in the opportunity set. This seems to pose a paradox concerning restrictions on the hours they may supply. It appears that these restrictions preventing them from offering as much labor as they would like to supply at the market wage leave firms neither better nor worse off but do harm workers. This appearance is deceiving.

The Maximum Workweek as a Supply Restriction

Restrictions on workweeks are most advantageously viewed as devices that limit the supply of labor and increase its price in the same way that cartel arrangements achieve a similar objective from rival firms in an industry. Just as it is in the interest of individual firms to collectively reduce output from the level that is optimum when each acts independently, it is in the interest of individual labor suppliers to collectively restrict the quantity supplied below the level each would choose on his or her own. This is shown in Figure 14.15. Given the demand curve D and unrestricted supply curve S, the equilibrium quantity supplied will be H_1 and the

Figure 14.15 *Labor Supply with and without a 40-Hour Week*

The supply curve S identifies the quantity of labor that is supplied at each wage rate with unrestricted labor supply. If workers may not offer more than 40 hours of labor at each wage, the total supply available at each wage will be reduced, shifting the supply curve from S to S'. This restriction on supply increases the wage rate from P_1 to P_2.

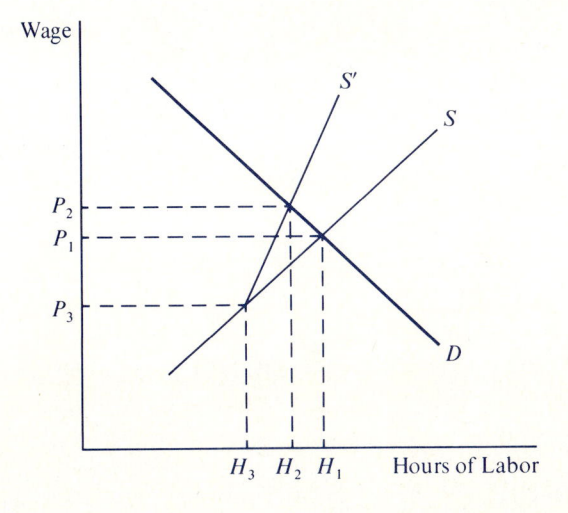

equilibrium price will be P_1. A restriction on hours worked will shift the supply curve (or at least a portion of it) leftward to some position like S'. Assume that at price P_3 the hours restriction becomes effective. Those who at price above P_3 would have supplied more than 40 hours per week will now be able to supply only 40 hours and no more. Market supply above price P_3 with these restrictions will therefore lie to the left of S at every price. If all potential workers are already in the labor force at wage P_3, then the new supply curve S' will be vertical at quantity H_3 above this wage. These workers would be unable to supply more than the permitted 40 hours regardless of the wage rate, so supply would be unresponsive to wages above this level. However, the fact that typically many who are capable of supplying labor are not doing so implies that higher wages may attract more workers into the labor force, thus increasing the labor force participation rate. This will increase the total supply of labor at wages beyond those at which the supply restrictions become effective. New supply curve S' is therefore shown to be positively sloped above wage P_3. The new equilibrium wage rate, P_2, must therefore be above the rate that prevailed in the absence of the restrictions.

Restrictions on the amount of labor that individual workers may supply increase the welfare of workers in a wide variety of cases—indeed, this seems the only plausible reason for the broad political support that policies like child labor laws, maximum workweek, and income conditional government support have always enjoyed among labor groups. As we argued earlier, in the absence of such restrictions individual employers should be indifferent concerning the amount of time per week their employees devote to work; firms should care only how many man-hours they hire, not who supplies them. It is the workers who have the interest in supplying a particular quantity, and restrictions that limit their ability to choose this quantity would otherwise operate to their disadvantage. Therefore, we can conclude only that the wage effects produced by these restrictions on supply are the ultimate objectives of these policies.

Union Contracts

A similar analysis may be applied to union contracts. These contracts typically specify both an hourly wage and a maximum workweek. Workers employed for more than the specified workweek must be paid "time and a half" for the extra hours. The shortening of some of these negotiated workweeks in the past two decades—to as few as 25 hours per week in some cases—has led to considerable comment concerning the apparent failure of the "work ethic" and growing indolence of American workers.

However, economists need not fall back on such "noneconomic" influences to explain these developments. On the contrary, these new labor conditions merely reflect the success of unions in raising the wage above the market-clearing level. Consider Figure 14.16, which contains the demand curve for labor of an employer. Two supply curves are also presented. Curve S_m is the unrestricted supply of labor to the firm. If the firm is free to hire anyone, it may hire from the unlimited supply available in the market at the market wage P_1. Under these conditions it will hire H_1 hours of labor. If this firm is unionized, it will be able to hire only union members, and the supply from this source will not be infinitely elastic. Let us assume that this union labor supply is the curve S_u. The market-clearing

Figure 14.16 *Unions and the Workweek*

Supply curve S_m reflects the supply of labor to a firm that is a price taker in the labor market. If the firm is successfully unionized, the firm must select its workers from the pool of available union members. Assume that the supply from this source is S_u. The price will not necessarily be P_2 at the intersection of these two curves, because there is a single seller (the union) and a single buyer (the firm) in such a market. The wage will depend on the relative bargaining strengths of the two parties. If the wage resulting from this bargaining is P_3, more labor will be supplied than the firm is willing to hire. A maximum negotiated workweek serves to ration the work among the union members. The firm is indifferent over how long each worker works.

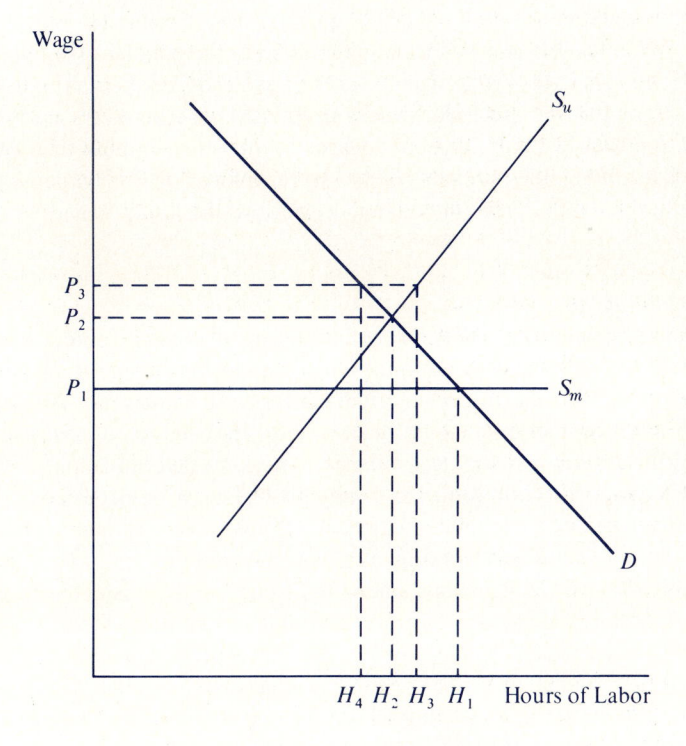

price for this supply curve is P_2, but there is no reason to expect that the union and the employer will settle on precisely this wage.

Competitive forces are absent from both demand and supply sides of this market. There is a single buyer (the firm) and a single seller (the union), and the negotiated wage will depend on the relative bargaining strengths of these two parties. The stronger the union, the larger will be the difference between the negotiated wage and P_2. Let us assume that a wage of P_3 is chosen. At this wage union members will choose to supply H_3 hours of labor, but the employer will seek only H_4 hours. There is an excess supply of labor at this wage rate, and the available employment must be rationed among those offering to supply labor. The negotiated workweek serves this purpose.

Were workers free to set their own hours there would not be enough work to go around. The workweek is therefore included in these contracts not to protect workers from being worked excessively by their employers but to allocate the available work among the membership of the union on an even basis and to prevent the wasteful queuing behavior normally associated with nonclearing prices. This seems to be the best explanation for this provision in union contracts. Again, we must point out that employers will not typically have an interest in the length of the workweek; they will be concerned only with the wage rate and the quantity of man-hours they employ. Such restrictions impose restraints chiefly on the workers themselves. Were there no rationing problem, it would make sense for the union to permit workers to supply whatever quantity they chose at the negotiated wage.

We offer this analysis as an alternative to the popular assumption that workers, and particularly organized workers, have changed their attitude toward work. We argue that the short workweeks negotiated in recent years are a manifestation of the power of unions to obtain wages far higher than those that would clear the market among their memberships. Were unions to lose bargaining power, we would predict that negotiated hours of work would return to earlier, higher levels.

Conditions of Employment

Just as employers have been blamed for the long hours of workers in the absence of restrictive workweek regulation, so have they been blamed for uncomfortable, unhealthy, and unsafe working conditions for their employees. This opprobrium is also to a considerable degree misdirected. The analysis of the determination of working conditions is quite similar to that of the determination of the workweek and leads us essentially to the same conclusions. Competitive conditions in the labor market leave employers little stake in this choice. Failure to provide the combination of wages and working conditions favored by those whose labor is sought leads to wholesale defections among these employees. It is in the employer's interest, therefore, to provide the working environment demanded by his employees.

Thus far, when we have asserted that firms using labor will employ that quantity which equates marginal revenue product with marginal factor cost, we have treated the latter as consisting wholly of wages. However, the cost of an hour of labor is clearly not limited merely to wages paid nor even to wages plus paid vacations, retirement, health benefits, and other forms of reimbursement. Many of these costs are borne by the firm merely to create a more pleasant working environment for employees.

Some of these expenditures can be at least partially justified on the basis of improving worker productivity; assembly workers, for example, will perform much less effectively in a plant that lacks adequate lighting and ventilation. However, a substantial part of the budget of many firms is devoted to expenditure on items and services that seem to bear little connection to productivity. Offices are heated in winter and cooled in summer. Walls are painted, often tastefully decorated, and floors are carpeted. Parking is frequently provided free or below cost. Buildings are equipped with elevators rather than stairs. Employees are often provided with lounges where they may relax (instead of work). In some cases, such expenditures may actually *reduce* productivity. For example, many safety features on machinery lower the speed with which it can be used, thus *decreasing* output.

Expenditure on these items is often justified in terms of building and maintaining worker morale—but that merely raises the question of why profit-seeking firms bother with morale. Some great fortunes were built in the last century in spite of less than harmonious labor relations. Andrew Carnegie and George M. Pullman, for example, occasionally fought pitched battles with their employees. In some cases morale may increase output per worker, but in others (particularly those associated with worker health and safety) such a connection is implausible. The pads and helmets worn by professional football players have a positive influence on player morale, but they clearly impair the speed and maneuverability of the players. The prevention of injuries is not a concern of team owners, for injured players, like injured factory workers, may simply be replaced. Firms do make expenditures and adopt work rules aimed at fostering the well-being of their employees that are impossible to justify in terms of increased output per worker. It can be shown, however, that firms are chiefly guided in these decisions by the demands of their workers.

This can be illustrated with the aid of Figure 14.17. In practice, firms and workers are concerned with many possible policies and expenditures, but here we shall simplify the choice by assuming that there is only one alternative to paying workers directly, and that is to spend on worker safety. We shall further simplify

Figure 14.17 *Determining Working Conditions*

Marginal revenue product is P^*. The firm is therefore willing to pay wages of P^*a for a hours of work, and no more. The firm is indifferent between paying this in wages and offering a combination of wages and working conditions that costs this amount. The combinations of money income and safety that may be offered at a cost of P^*a determine an opportunity set from which the workers ultimately choose. Workers will leave a firm that offers combination K for another that offers combination T at the same cost per worker.

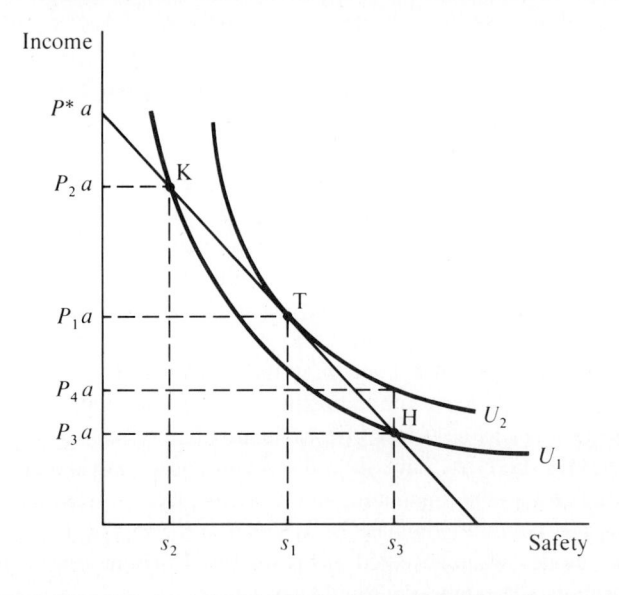

by assuming that safety may be obtained by the purchase of devices whose quantity is indicated by s and whose price is P_s. Productivity is unaffected by the quantity of s purchased by the firm.

The firm is assumed to operate in a competitive market for labor. If it does not offer a compensation package that is as attractive as those offered by competing employers, it will be unable to maintain its workforce. Workers will leave and seek employment with other firms offering superior packages. Competition among workers, on the other hand, will insure that the cost of these packages per hour of labor will be the same to all employers. Firms will be willing to spend on this factor no more than its marginal revenue product per unit employed, and competition among workers will insure that labor cost per unit to each firm is the same. Just as occurs when factor compensation involves only wages, in this market an equilibrium is established that is characterized by a common marginal revenue product for each employing firm.

Let that common marginal revenue product of labor be P^*. For a worker supplying a hours of labor, total wage income may not exceed P^*a. This particular package of P^*a income and no expenditure on safety may not be as attractive as a different package offered by a competing employer. In order to develop the full range of options available to employers, let the money wage paid by the employer be P_a so that money income to each employee is $P_a a$. The total cost of a hours of labor cannot exceed P^*a, so the implied constraint may be expressed as:

$$P^*a = P_a a + P_s s.$$

For money income, this can be solved as:

$$P_a a = P^*a - P_s s.$$

This expression provides the opportunity set of income and safety. The vertical intercept in Figure 14.17 indicates the income that workers could receive if the firm spent nothing on safety. If units of safety are purchased, however, money wages must diminish, for total expenditure per unit on this factor cannot exceed its marginal revenue product. The slope of this opportunity set, $\Delta P_a a/\Delta s$, is simply minus the unit price of the safety devices, $-P_s$.

Just as is the case with the choice of income and leisure made by each employee, the employer is indifferent concerning which combination of income and safety is chosen; each will cost the employer the same amount per hour worked. It is the employee who has an interest in the combination chosen, and the employer will seek to accommodate those wishes. He or she will seek to offer combination T containing s_1 units of safety and the lower income P_1^*a. Were this employer to offer instead combination K containing more income but only s_2 units of safety, the employees would leave for competing firms offering more favored compensation packages. The same is true of combination H.

Employers therefore have little discretion concerning the conditions of employment. Through the functioning of the competitive process, workers determine the extent of expenditure on these items *and* bear the cost by accepting lower wage rates. The money wage accepted in Figure 14.17 may be determined by solving the opportunity set expression for P_a; that is:

$$P_a = P^* - \frac{P_s s}{a}$$

The money wage diverges from the firm's marginal revenue product of labor by an amount that exactly equals the hourly cost of safety.

Regulation of Working Conditions

This analysis calls into question another regulatory practice of government: the setting by regulatory bodies, such as the Occupational Safety and Health Administration (OSHA), of standards affecting the conditions of employment. In Figure 14.17, if the standard set requires too little safety (say, requiring the purchase of only s_2 units), then the regulation is simply ineffective. Competition will force employers to adopt the more stringent standard demanded by workers—that is, combination T, containing s_1 units of safety. If, on the other hand, regulations require too *much* safety (say, the purchase of s_3 units), the analysis gets more complicated. A regulation requiring employers to accept combination H would be harmful to workers. With this combination of safety and income, the value of safety at the margin (minus the MRS of workers at this quantity) would be lower than its opportunity cost in income (minus the slope of the opportunity set).

Let us assume further, however, that the regulation affects only a small number of the demanders of labor—say, a single industry. Workers will not accept a compensation package from this set of employers that is less attractive than that offered by others. The cost of the added safety will have to be borne by the affected firms, at least in the short run. Only by offering income of $P_4 a$ with s_3 units of safety does employment in the regulated industry remain as attractive as alternative employment. In order to fully understand the effect of these regulations, we must determine the effect of these added costs on the output of the firm.

The purchase of additional safety will increase both marginal and average cost for each firm in the regulated industry. This increase in costs might be thought to lead directly to a reduction in profits for these firms, but that need not necessarily occur. On the contrary, it is quite possible that an imposition of these costs on all firms in the industry can lead to *increased* profits! It is in fact possible to interpret regulation of employment conditions as a conspiracy on the part of the regulators and the regulated to restrict output—in other words, to cartelize the industry. What the Civil Aeronautics Board did for commercial aviation before it was disbanded OSHA is now doing for many industries.

This is illustrated in Figure 14.18. In panel (b) we depict the industry demand curve D and two supply curves. Let S_1 be unregulated short-run industry supply in long-run equilibrium. Thus, in panel (a) a representative firm's average total cost, AC_1, is just tangent to the firm's demand curve (horizontal at price P_1, the equilibrium market price) so that no profits are earned. The imposition of these regulations increases *both* average and marginal cost. This shift in each firm's marginal cost curve likewise shifts each firm's supply curve leftward, producing a similar shift in market supply. Let the new marginal and average cost curves for each firm be MC_2 and AC_2, respectively, in panel (a), yielding a new short-run supply curve, S_2, in panel (b). The market price will now be P_2, with each firm electing to produce output q_2 so that n firms in the industry now together produce nq_2 units.

Figure 14.18 *Output Restriction through Cost-Increasing Regulation*

Panel (a) reflects the output choice of each firm in an industry under two cost and price conditions. Price P_1 represents long-run zero profit equilibrium, with each firm producing output q_1. This corresponds to the intersection of the market demand curve D and supply curve S_1 in panel (b). In panel (a), cost-increasing regulation shifts the average and marginal cost curves for each firm to positions AC_2 and MC_2, respectively. This reduces the quantity that each firm is willing to supply at each price, shifting the supply curve in panel (b) to S_2. At this price, however, each firm now earns positive profits equal to $(P_2 - AC_2)q_2$.

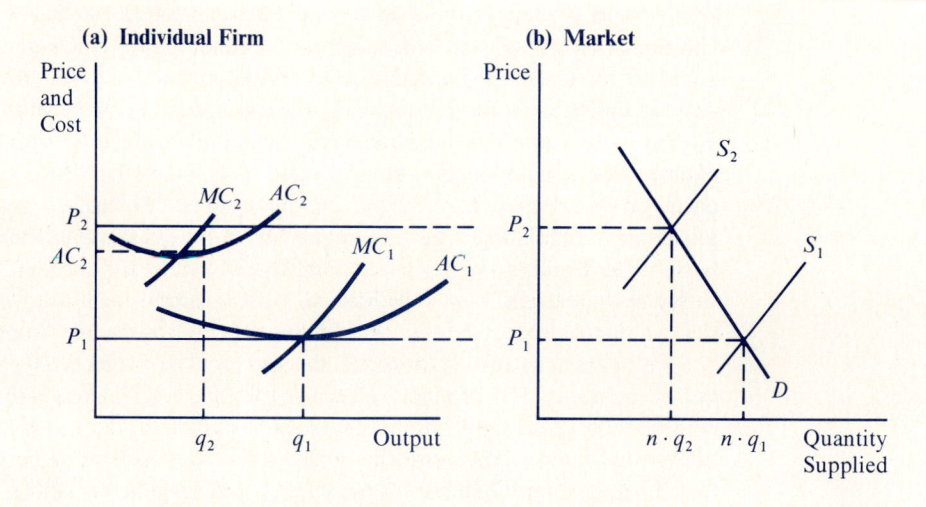

As price exceeds average cost for each firm under regulation, each earns profits equal to $(P_2 - AC_2)q_2$. Thus, although the mandated expenditure on safety has increased costs for each firm, the reduction in output has produced an even larger increase in price. The regulation has had the effect of increasing profits.

This result will not occur invariably. It is certainly possible for mandated cost increases of the type discussed to reduce profits. A sufficiently large expenditure on safety can clearly drive each firm into receivership. However, the possibility that a correctly calculated cost increase of this type *can* increase profits forces us to view this regulation in a different light.

As is the case when analyzing any government initiative, it is useful to inquire into the source of political support for the regulation discussed here. Workers themselves are unlikely to gain from the added safety mandated under this regulation. As we have just demonstrated, competition in the market by itself will yield the favored combination of wages and working conditions for workers. Any beneficiaries of a particular regulatory plan (other than suppliers of bureaucratic services) are likely to be firms seeking cartel profits of the type described. Who else would find it worthwhile to devote the resources necessary to get such a proposal passed by Congress? We must therefore cast a wary eye toward proposed extensions of this type of regulation.

Evidence that regulation of working conditions has been used for such cartelizing purposes has been developed in a recent paper by Maloney and McCormick.[3] They studied the impact of a 1974 announcement by the Department of Labor, made on the basis of a finding by OSHA, that cotton dust in American textile plants posed a potential health hazard that would be curbed by severe and binding new restrictions on working conditions in these plants. These restrictions were expected to increase the cost of cotton production and otherwise adversely affect the financial position of firms affected by the regulation. However, this was not what these authors found. By employing financial market analysis of the behavior of a portfolio of stocks of the 14 textile firms traded on the New York Stock Exchange, they were able to gauge the effect of the announcement of this regulation on the expected profit performance of these firms. They found that, far from depressing the value of textile stocks in the chosen portfolio, this announcement substantially increased their value relative to other stocks traded on the exchange. They estimated that the announcement increased the value of these firms's stocks by roughly $500 million!

What are the economic arguments in favor of government regulation of working conditions? There is only one: that individual workers are inadequately informed concerning the real health or safety risks of their employment in a particular firm or industry. They may thus be attracted by higher wages than they could earn elsewhere without considering hazards that they would otherwise avoid with full information. Government regulators have the resources to investigate thoroughly the possibility of such risks and to establish standards closer to those that fully informed workers would demand.

While plausible on the surface, this argument is less convincing when given careful analysis. In the first place, while it is true that individual workers cannot devote as many resources to the identification of health and safety risks of alternative employers as can the government, this is not true of the unions that represent them. Negotiation of working conditions under such circumstances is a vital function of organized labor, and there is no evidence that unions have been ineffective in this role. Secondly, firms competing with one another for workers themselves have important incentives to publicize the advantageous working conditions they offer and the shortcomings of competing firms in these regards. Given these two sources of information, workers undoubtedly are far less ignorant of health and safety hazards than proponents of strict regulation would have us believe.

Summary

In this chapter we developed the theory of the supply of labor. We illuminated several topics by analyzing the choices of whether to supply labor and how much labor to supply to the market. We began, as in other analyses of behavior in the market, with an exposi-

---

[3] M. T. Maloney and R. E. McCormick, "A Positive Theory of Environmental Quality Regulation," *The Journal of Law and Economics* 25 (April 1982): 99–124.

tion of the opportunity set and the rank-ordering process pertinent to the choices studied. Labor suppliers are assumed to have an interest in income and in leisure. An opportunity set in these two "goods" may be derived from a given time endowment and the wage rate. The opportunity cost of leisure in terms of income given up is the wage rate itself. The rank-ordering process adopted here, as in the theory of household demand, is utility theory with the added proviso that both income and leisure are normal goods. Individual optimization in this case leads to the conclusion that a quantity of leisure will be chosen at which its value at the margin is just equal to its opportunity cost.

The response of individual supply choices to changes in the wage rate cannot be predicted. Individual labor supply curves may have either positive or negative slopes. Wage rate changes will have substitution effects on labor supply in the same direction as the change in wage, but income effects on labor supply operate in the opposite direction. The slope of the individual's supply curve will thus be determined by the relative magnitudes of the two effects.

Although individual labor supply curves may be negatively sloped (backward bending), market supply curves in the neighborhood of existing wage rates will nevertheless be positively sloped. We draw this conclusion on the basis of a second choice typically made by many members of the population: the decision to *become* a supplier of labor. This was shown to be positively associated with the wage rate. Higher wages lead more individuals to enter the labor force. Other factors influencing the labor force participation rate are productivity of nonmarket activity, the extent of specialization in production, and the amount of nonwage income earned in the economy.

Income conditional grants, such as social security retirement benefits and welfare, adversely affect labor force participation. Both of these programs as presently structured provide strong disincentives to work. Alternative policies are offered that cost less and would be preferred to present programs by their beneficiaries.

We showed that while individual workers or relatively small groups of workers are made worse off by restrictions on the quantity of labor they may offer in the market, restrictions that appreciably reduce the market supply of labor may make the typical worker better off. Employers have little to gain or lose through such restrictions, but the gains to labor suppliers may be substantial. We suggested here that political support for maximum-hour legislation and other restrictions on labor supply have their basis in gains of this type. In a related discussion, we showed that union negotiations, which impose a limit on the amount of work any member may supply at the negotiated wage, are necessary for rationing work among members at higher than market-clearing wages.

In competitive labor markets, workers themselves choose the conditions of employment. Workers may not obtain a compensation package whose value exceeds their marginal revenue products. They can and do, however, determine how the full value of their compensation will be divided between wage income and firm expenditures on making the working environment more attractive. Workers will typically choose the quantities of safety, healthfulness, and other amenities of the workplace that equate their value and the wage income forgone to obtain them. Regulations mandating larger than the competitively determined quantities of such factors will, if applied universally, make workers worse off. Wages will be sacrificed that would be of greater value to these workers than the improvement in working conditions.

In practice, such regulations are applied only to small groups of labor demanders, so the full cost of these factors cannot be deducted from worker wages. Competition among firms for workers prevents the affected employers from offering a less attractive package than those offered by other, unregulated firms. Competition among workers also prevents employees of the affected firms from capturing any benefits from the improved working conditions. Costs must therefore be increased for the regulated firms, but *this need not imply lower profits for them. On the contrary, it is possible that this cost-increasing regulation may actually increase their profits. Regulation of working conditions in American textile firms was cited as evidence that employers may use this lever in the manner of cartels to restrict industry output and obtain profits.*

Key Concepts

market time
nonmarket time
time endowment
full income
substitution effect
income effect

backward-bending supply curve
reservation wage
labor force participation rate
corner solution
income conditional grants
negative income tax

Questions

1. *Easy* The opportunity set of income and leisure combinations faced by a potential labor supplier depends on the time endowment, the wage rate, and nonwage income. Construct a diagrammatic representation of such an opportunity set. Illustrate the effect of a change in the wage rate on this opportunity set. Do the same for a change in nonwage income.

Hard Assume that an income tax is imposed that taxes away a constant proportion of income. What effect will this have on the opportunity set of leisure and after-tax income? What will be the effect of such a tax on the slope of this opportunity set?

2. *Easy* Although some people enjoy their work, we may assert that work at the margin is a "bad"—that is, no worker would willingly give up any amount of leisure in order to work an extra hour without compensation. Explain.

Hard An increase in the wage rate may lead to an increase or a decrease in the quantity of labor supplied by a single individual. Explain why this is true, describing the importance of the substitution and income effects of such a wage change to the quantity supplied at the higher wage.

3. *Easy* Even if individual supply curves for labor are backward bending, it is still possible for the market supply curve for labor to have a positive slope. Explain why.

Hard Those not currently in the labor force may be said to have chosen a combination of leisure and income that is a "corner solution." Describe this choice, and show how there must be some wage that will induce those not currently in the labor force to join.

4. *Easy* Income conditional grants, such as welfare payments, discourage labor force participation by lowering net compensation for extra hours worked to below the wage rate. Explain.

Hard A negative income tax is not free of adverse work incentive effects (lowering the opportunity cost of leisure below the wage rate), but it does provide less of a work disincentive than the existing welfare system. Explain.

5. *Easy* The 40-hour week if applied to one individual alone would make that worker worse off, but it would leave his or her employer indifferent. Explain.

Hard If workers are harmed by constraints on the amount of labor they can supply, and employers are indifferent, how do you explain the existence of these constraints? Why does the AFL–CIO support lowering the maximum workweek?

6. *Easy* Employers who are price takers in the labor market cannot offer employment to workers that will be less attractive than terms offered elsewhere. What will happen to a firm that offers a less attractive combination of wages and working conditions than is offered elsewhere at the same cost per man-hour? What does this imply about the choice of working conditions offered by these firms?

Hard How can occupational safety regulation, which raises costs to employers, actually increase their profits? Will these profits continue to be earned in the long run? On what will this depend?

Chapter 15

The Supply of Capital: Savings and Investment

Connections Capital is supplied only indirectly by households. Households save, and the purchasing power freed by this saving is borrowed by investors to purchase capital. This chapter must therefore concern itself with these two critical groups within the economy. The behavior of savers is analyzed by observing the influence of the interest rate on the opportunity set of consumption combinations over time. The shape of this opportunity set is determined by the income endowments of households in each period and the interest rate that determines the rate at which purchasing power may be exchanged between periods in the financial sector. The behavior of investors is profit motivated, and profits on investments are also influenced by the interest rate. Like the theory of labor supply, this aspect of the supply of capital resembles more the theory of household demand for goods and services developed in Chapters 4 and 5 than it does the theory of the supply of manufactured goods discussed in Part III. An important distinction is made here between the supply of capital on the one hand and the supply of capital services on the other. It is best to think of firms as demanding capital services that are supplied by investors who specialize in purchasing and leasing the services of assets to them. A firm that owns the capital it uses can then be thought of as a special case in which the demanding and supplying function are combined under one roof. Chapter 7 offered some reasons why these functions are so frequently combined in practice.

As stressed in earlier chapters, the theory of the demand for factors of production is general. The demand curves of firms for capital are downward sloping for essentially the same reasons that govern the slopes of demand curves for labor. The aspects of this factor market that differentiate it from labor markets are therefore to be found on its supply side. The capital of an economy represents the machines, buildings, tools, and other assets produced for the purpose of production rather than for consumption. In one sense, we have already discussed the supply of these capital goods. To the extent that they are manufactured by firms, the supply of these items is no different than the supply of consumption goods. Producing firms will supply them up to the point at which marginal revenue equals marginal cost. In another sense, however, the supply of capital is more complex than this. As a factor of production it is the supply of the *services* of capital that is of chief concern to us, not their production. The supply of these services depends critically on the willingness of some members of society to own these assets and make their services available for production.

Most of the capital in the U. S. economy is owned by firms. However, this is not always the case. Many firms rent capital from other firms; there are some that do nothing but purchase capital goods for the purpose of leasing those goods to other firms. Car rental companies purchase automobiles on a large scale for renting to individuals and firms. Many shipholding companies purchase tankers and other ships for leasing to shipping companies. Even the federal government has found it expedient to place the ownership and management of most of its buildings, vehicles, and communications equipment in the hands of a specialized organization, the General Services Administration, that leases the services of these assets to other government agencies. Whether a firm owns the capital that it employs or leases the services of that capital is a subsidiary question not directly related to its supply. We have already raised this question in Chapter 7 and need not cover this ground again. We may treat the fact that many producing firms are also in the business of supplying capital as a coincidence. It will be convenient here to treat all suppliers of capital services as if that were their exclusive function. This will permit us to focus our attention on the factors that influence their willingness to hold and add to the stock of capital whose services they will supply to the market.

15.1 The Measurement Problem

Discussing the supply of capital presents particularly messy problems of aggregation. The supply of labor is not free of these problems; Vladimir Horowitz and Pete Rose supply services that are quite dissimilar, and it is unlikely that either would serve as an adequate substitute for the other. However, both are human beings, regardless of the specialized nature of their services; both are counted as members of the labor force and suppliers of labor services. Capital goods, on the other hand, are typically far more specialized. The list of goods supplying capital services includes the high-speed dentist's drill and the jackhammer, the SST and the Goodyear blimp, the Empire State Building and the El Toro Taco Stand. Capital goods perform dissimilar tasks and are made of dissimilar materials. They may be large and comparatively cheap, like an inventory of gravel, or small and precious, like a diamond-edged gem cutter's tool. Economists are indeed heroic in their attempt to treat all these items as a single factor of production.

There are two approaches to the measurement of capital in the aggregate; both present difficulties. One method is to count capital on the basis of its production cost. The other is to count it on the basis of the value of its productivity. Ideally, both approaches should yield the same result. In equilibrium under competitive conditions, the supply price will equal marginal cost and the demand price will reflect its marginal value in production. As a practical matter, however, these measures will typically diverge. By their very nature capital assets continue to be used over several periods. If costs rise or fall during the life of these goods, do we use current production cost or historical production cost in counting their quantity? Similarly, the demand for this capital may itself rise or fall, thus increasing or decreasing the value of its productivity. Do we use its current value in production or its value when it was produced as this measure? Do we permit our measure of the quantity of capital to change when the stock of physical items remains constant but demand changes? Certainly, we do not say that the quantity of labor has increased every time the wage rate rises.

There seems to be no easy way around these problems. The aggregate stock of capital is an abstract concept that defies straightforward interpretation. Efforts to estimate production functions for sectors or whole economies employing broad ranges of capital will invariably be complicated by this ambiguity. The fact remains, however, that markets for capital services all behave similarly regardless of the type of capital supplied. We may therefore confidently lay out the theory of this supply without concern for the dissimilarity of one type of capital from another. We will show that the long-run supply of the *services* of any capital asset is inversely related to the interest rate—in fact, given the production cost of capital goods, their expected life, their depreciation rate, and their rate of interest, we can predict the long-run supply price of capital services. It is chiefly because of this similarity in analytical treatment that capital goods are treated as a single factor of production. Students are cautioned to treat studies that rely more heavily on the aggregatability of capital (such as estimates of economywide production functions) with care and a certain amount of skepticism.

15.2 The Supply of Capital and the Interest Rate

Having made the necessary caveats against the dangers of treating capital as homogeneous, we shall now proceed to do precisely this. Let us assume that all capital takes the form of a single, prototype machine. At any time the number of these machines is given so that the supply of machine services is fixed. In Figure 15.1 we depict the demand curve for these services, labeled D, and their supply, K_1. The equilibrium service price is therefore P^*. The supply of these machines, and thus the supply of their services in the next period (t) is determined by two factors:

Figure 15.1 The Price of Capital Services

With any given number of machines such as K_1, the rental price of the machine services is the market-clearing price.

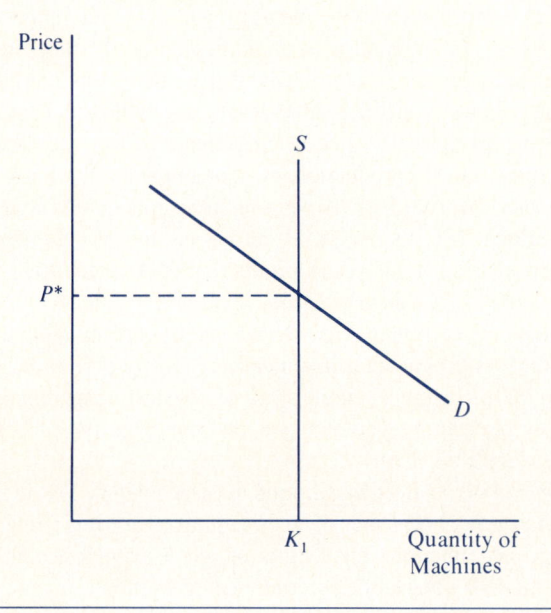

the rate of depreciation of this capital and the level of gross investment. We may express the relationship between capital in period t and depreciation D and investment N in the previous period quite simply as

$$K_t = K_{t-1} - D_{t-1} + N_{t-1}.$$

Obviously, the capital stock will expand over time only if gross investment exceeds depreciation.

There is little that can be done about the depreciation of capital. Most capital wears out with use, and the only way to limit depreciation is to limit use, which is self-defeating. We will have more to say on the topic of depreciation later in this chapter. For now, we will focus on the determinants of investment itself, since it is here that most of the "action" in the analysis of the supply of capital is to be found. The determination of the level of investment is illustrated in Figure 15.2. This figure depicts not the demand for capital but the demand for loanable funds, labeled D, and their supply, labeled S. The former is shown to be negatively related to the interest rate, while the supply is shown to have a positive slope. We will explain the slopes of these curves later. For our purposes now, we will accept them as given in determining the market interest rate, r^*, and the level of investment, I^*.

Figure 15.2 The Determination of the Market Interest Rate

The interest rate is determined in the financial market by the demand and supply of loanable funds. The demand for loanable funds slopes downward to the right. The supply of loanable funds is related to people's willingness to save. For most analyses with which we will be concerned, the supply curve must slope upward. These two curves determine the equilibrium interest rate and the quantity of saving and investment. The level of investment determines the change in the stock of capital.

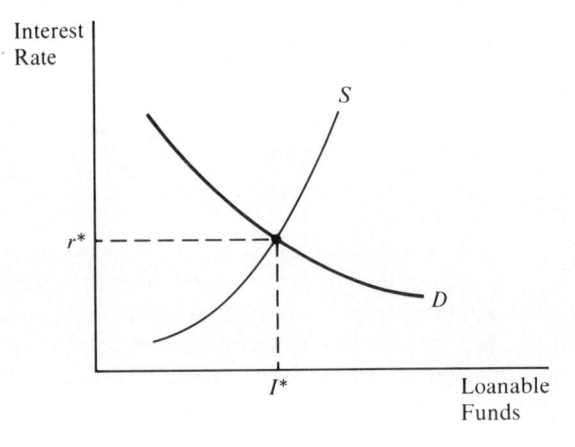

We may relate the information here to Figure 15.1 by converting these funds into machines. Let the cost of these machines be c per unit so that the number purchased is I^*/c; the value of N in any period is thus I^*/c. Whether investment in capital goods is sufficient to offset depreciation and increase the capital stock will therefore depend on the demand and supply of loanable funds and the equilibrium rate of interest.

An analysis of interest rate determination and the level of investment must consider both sides of this market. We shall do this in the customary manner, observing how the parties on each side respond to changes in the interest rate, then putting the two groups together to determine conditions at equilibrium. We begin in this case with the supply of loanable funds.

Saving: The Supply of Loanable Funds

We begin, as usual, with some definitions and some simplifying assumptions. **Saving** is defined here as the act of *deferring* consumption. In our earlier discussion of the theory of consumer demand, we assumed that the household budget was exhausted by consumption spending in each period. We may now relax that assumption and permit people to save. We will furthermore assume that saving is synonymous with supplying loanable funds—in other words, that all savings are placed in the hands of financial intermediaries, such as banks and thrift institutions. This is not, of course, literally true. Some people still hoard cash, and many simultaneously save and invest in household capital goods like refrigerators and other "consumer durables." This activity, like household production in the theory of supply, will be ignored in the interest of simplifying the analysis.

We will further simplify initially by assuming a two-period model; there is a present and a future. Each individual has income in each period. Because that person may save or dissave (consume more than his or her income in a period) by lending to or borrowing from a financial intermediary, his or her consumption opportunities in each period are not limited to this combination of incomes. In order to analyze the choice of consumption in each period, we must develop an algebraic expression for the opportunity set of consumption combinations. This is done as follows.

In the first period, income Y_0 is either consumed, C_0, or saved, S_0, so that:

$$Y_0 = C_0 + S_0.$$

For simplicity, let us assume that the person dies at the end of the next period and has no estate motive, so that there is no saving in that period. Consumption in the second period, Y_1, therefore consists of that person's income in that period, Y_1 plus the principal and accumulated interest on his or her first-period savings:

(15.1) $$C_1 = Y_1 + (1 + r)S_0.$$

We wish to express consumption opportunities in the first period in terms of consumption opportunities in the second. We may do this by solving for S_0 in equation (15.1) and substituting its equivalent into the second expression; thus:

$$C_1 = Y_1 + (1 + r)(Y_0 - C_0).$$

This is the expression for the opportunity set of consumption combinations. Note that it contains only two choice variables, C_0 and C_1. The remaining terms in this expression are in this case beyond the control of the chooser. These terms are that person's income in each period (**income endowment**) and the interest rate.

It will be convenient to have first-period consumption as the left-hand variable expressed in terms of second-period consumption, the income endowment and the interest rate. Solving for C_0 yields:

$$C_0 = Y_0 + \frac{1}{1+r} \cdot Y_1 - \frac{1}{1+r} \cdot C_1.$$

Graphing this expression, as in Figure 15.3, provides some useful interpretations. Examination of the opportunity set expression in this form reveals that it is a simple linear expression of C_0 in terms of C_1. The first two terms combine to form a constant, the vertical intercept. This intercept is the sum of income in the first and income times $1/1 + r$ in the second. We refer to this sum as the individual's **wealth**. The third term contains our choice variable C_1, the coefficient of which, $-1/1 + r$, is the slope of the opportunity set. As the interest rate is always positive, this opportunity set must slope downward to the right.

Figure 15.3   The Opportunity Set of Consumption Combinations

The position of the opportunity set of present and future consumption combinations is determined by the income endowment in each period (combination T) and the interest rate. The slope of this opportunity set is $-1/1 + r$. The vertical intercept measures the present value of the income endowment, $Y_0 + (1/1 + r)Y_1$.

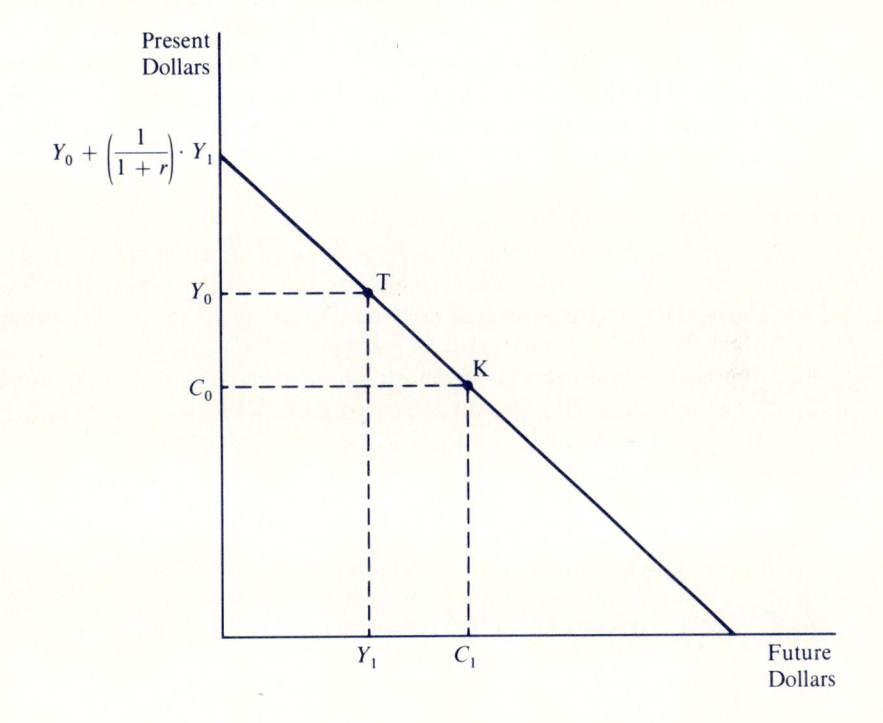

Although the income endowment is a single point, T, in this consumption space, the individual need not consume that combination. By borrowing or lending, he or she may consume any combination along the diagonal opportunity set. The choice of combinations to the southeast of T, like combination K involve saving. Consumption in the first period is less than the full amount of income in that period; amount C_0 is less than Y_0. The choice of combinations to the northwest of T along the opportunity set involves dissaving. Consumption of these combinations would require that the individual spend *more* than he or she earned in the first period. For example, he or she might choose to consume all of his or her wealth, $Y_0 + 1/1 + r \cdot Y_1$, in the first period. Such a foolish choice would leave this person no money for consumption in the second period. The income received would be just sufficient to repay his or her borrowings.

The slope of this opportunity set, $-1/1 + r$, reflects the opportunity cost of consuming an extra dollar's worth in the future. So long as the interest rate is greater than zero, this opportunity cost will be less than one dollar. The exchange rate of future dollars for present dollars in the financial sector is less than one for one. When we wish to compare or combine purchasing power in different periods, we must take account of the fact that dollars in each period exchange at different rates. We do this by converting dollars at different dates into dollars of the *same* date using the exchange rates derived in the manner just described. The process of converting dollar claims in future periods into present dollars is described as calculating the **present value** of those future claims. In calculating the wealth of the individual in Figure 15.3, we must combine income received in two periods. We do this, as we can see from the intercept term of the opportunity set, by expressing this wealth as the sum of Y_0 dollars received currently and the *present value* of Y_1 dollars to be received next year.

Preferences for Time-Specific Consumption

Combinations of consumption along the opportunity set are assumed to be ranked by a utility function that exhibits the standard properties. Indifference curves based on this function slope downward to the right, are convex downward, and do not intersect. In this case it seems plausible to assume that consumption in each period is a normal good. By this we mean that as *wealth* increases ceteris paribus, an individual will choose to consume more in *every* period. Figure 15.4 depicts

Figure 15.4 *Consumption and Wealth*

Holding the interest rate constant, an increase in wealth leads to greater consumption in each period. Income endowments K^a, K^b, and K^c yield successively greater wealth (that is, W^a, W^b, W^c). The consumption combinations chosen contain successively larger amounts of consumption in both present and future: T^a, T^b, and T^c.

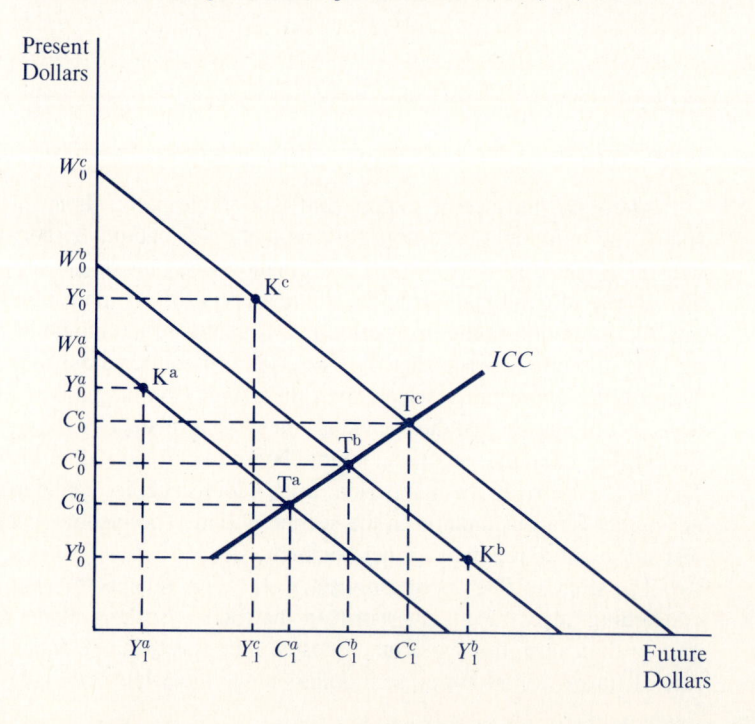

consumption choices consistent with this assumption. Income endowments are identified by combinations K^a, K^b, and K^c. Note that although current income diminishes in combination K^b relative to combination K^a, the larger future income in the former more than compensates for this reduction. Wealth identified by vertical intercept W_0^b (associated with endowment K^b) is therefore greater than wealth associated with intercept W_0^a (associated with endowment K^a). The consumption combinations associated with these three income endowments are shown by T^a, T^b, and T^c. Since wealth increases as we move outward to higher opportunity sets, the assumption of normal consumption implies that consumption in each period increases as shown.

Changing the Interest Rate

Having developed the ground rules for positioning the opportunity set and the shape of the utility function, we may now proceed to the effect of a change in the interest rate on the rate of saving. This is discussed with the aid of Figure 15.5. Let the individual's income endowment be combination K, and let the interest rate be r such that the slope of the opportunity set passing through K is $-1/1 + r_1$ with a vertical intercept of W_1. Given the indifference curves depicted, this individual would choose to consume combination T^a providing present consumption spending of C_0^a and future spending of C_1^a. In choosing this combination, he or she therefore elects to save $Y_0 - C_0^a$ at this interest rate.

The slope of the supply of saving (the supply of loanable funds) for this individual can be determined by observing whether an increase in the interest rate increases or decreases saving. Increased saving at higher interest rates would indicate that the supply of loanable funds from this individual was positively sloped, while reduced saving would indicate a negatively sloped supply curve. Note first the effect of a change in the interest rate on the position of the opportunity set. At the higher interest rate r_2 the slope becomes $-1/1 + r_2$, which is less steep because of the larger denominator. *This opportunity set must also pass through combination K*. The change in the interest rate does not affect the individual's consumption possibilities if he or she neither saves nor lends in the initial period. This person may always consume his or her income endowment in each period regardless of the rate of interest. The opportunity set at the higher interest rate is therefore shown by the flatter curve passing through K with an intercept of W_2.

Note also the effect of the interest rate on real income. This individual, whose preferences are indicated by the indifference curves shown, is a saver, and the higher interest rate increases his or her utility. Any amount saved earns more interest at the higher rate and permits him or her greater future consumption for given amounts of saving. This is confirmed by the fact that the new opportunity set lies to the right of the old for first-period consumption of less than Y_0 (involving positive saving). However, if this person were a borrower at the initial interest rate, the increased interest rate would decrease his or her real income. At higher rates, he or she would have to give up *more* future income in exchange for given amounts of borrowing. These new opportunities as a borrower are indicated by the fact that the opportunity set at interest rate r_2 lies to the left of the original opportunity set for consumption in the first period in excess of Y_0 (involving dissaving).

In the case depicted, the individual chooses to save *more* at the higher interest rate. His or her supply curve is therefore positively sloped. Saving at the lower

Figure 15.5 *A Change in the Interest Rate*

A change in the interest rate rotates the opportunity set around the income endowment point K. This rise in the rate from r_1 to r_2 has two offsetting effects on saving. Saving is the difference between current income and consumption. Original saving is $Y_1 - C_1^a$. The substitution effect of the interest rate change reflects that the opportunity cost of future consumption falls with increases in the interest rate. Thus, lowering the opportunity cost but holding real income constant, saving increases to $Y_1 - C_1^c$. The income effect operates in the opposite direction. The increase in the interest rate makes the saver better off. Holding the opportunity cost constant while allowing real income to rise from U_1 to U_2 decreases saving from $Y_1 - C_1^c$ to $Y_1 - C_1^b$. The net effect of an interest rate change on the saving rate is thus ambiguous. The direction of change depends on which of the two effects is larger.

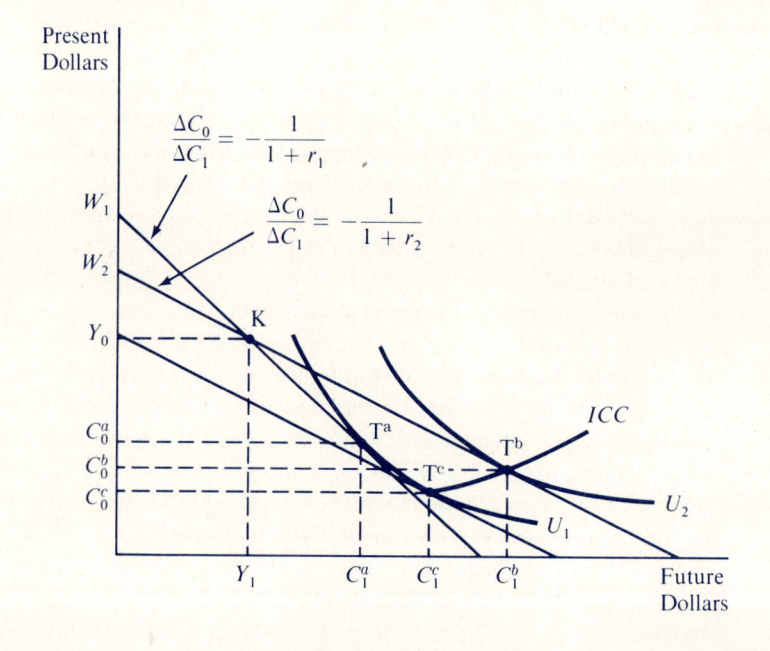

interest rate was $Y_0 - C_0^a$; saving at the higher interest rate is the larger amount $Y_0 - C_0^b$. However, we cannot conclude that this will always be the case. We cannot rule out the possibility of negatively sloped supply curves for savings (and therefore for loanable funds) because of our old problem: substitution effects and offsetting income effects. It will be useful for analytical purposes to explore these countervailing forces on the supply of saving.

Substitution and Income Effects

An increase in the interest rate has two influences on the rate of saving. Higher rates lower the exchange rate of present purchasing power for future purchasing power, lowering the opportunity cost of future consumption. As future consumption is relatively less costly at the higher rates, we expect, *other things equal*, that people will substitute future for present consumption, increasing saving in the process. However, higher interest rates increase real income for savers. Since consumption in each period is a normal good, we would expect this increase in real income to lead to higher consumption in the future and, in the present, that is, to *reduced* saving.

This is illustrated graphically in Figure 15.5. The substitution effect may be identified by finding the combination on the original indifference curve that exhibits a MRS equal to the new opportunity cost of future consumption. That combination is T^c, at which the MRS (minus the slope of the indifference curve) is just equal to the new opportunity cost of future consumption, $1/1 + r_2$. This is the combination the saver would select were his or her real income held constant as the exchange rate changed. The effect of this substitution effect is clearly in the same direction as the interest rate change. An increase in this rate must lower the opportunity cost of future consumption, and the only combinations on the original indifference curve with lower MRSs are to the southeast of the initial combination T^a. The substitution effect of this interest rate increase must therefore lead to a substitution *away* from current consumption and thus to greater saving. In the case depicted, saving increases due to the substitution effect by the amount $C_0^a - C_0^c$. A decrease in the interest rate would clearly increase the opportunity cost of future consumption, leading to a substitution toward current consumption and consequently a decrease in saving.

Income effects are identified by tracing combinations chosen along an income consumption curve. These effects are the result of changing real income alone, so they must be identified holding the opportunity cost of present consumption constant. In Figure 15.5, as real income expands from U_1 to U_2 we may trace such an ICC through combinations T^c to T^b. The effect on present consumption of this increase in real income is the increase equal to $C_0^b - C_0^c$.

The two effects must therefore be offsetting. The substitution effect will always operate in the same direction as the interest rate (on saving), while the income effect will operate in the opposite direction. We have no a priori basis for assessing the relative magnitudes of these two effects. In the case depicted, the substitution effect was larger; hence, it dominated the smaller income effect so that the interest rate increase resulted in more saving. Since it would be equally easy to construct a different set of indifference curves yielding the opposite result, we cannot rule out the possibility of negatively sloped individual supply curves for loanable funds.

Two Supply Curves for Loanable Funds

The preceding analysis suggests a further parallel with the theory of household demand for goods. In Chapter 5 it was pointed out that the presence of income effects in the analysis of individual household demand required the development of two types of market demand curves. While some changes in market prices reflect income-increasing developments in the economy (such as technical change), others do not. It was therefore necessary in that chapter to distinguish two types of demand curves, compensated and uncompensated demand curves, to permit analysis of each of these situations. This same problem confronts us here.

The market supply of loanable funds is the sum of the savings of all households in the economy at different interest rates. Whether all households who are savers can in fact be made better off by an interest rate change depends on the source of the change itself. There are two possibilities. The rise in interest rates may reflect an increase in the demand for loanable funds due to changing technology. New discoveries may make possible expanded output in both the present and the future. These higher interest rates may reflect increased consumption opportunities in both periods for everyone, just as they shifted the opportunity set outward for the saver depicted in Figure 15.5. The analysis of the supply response to changes in interest rates of this type is the **uncompensated supply curve for loanable funds**, which incorporates both substitution and income effects. Being the sum of individual supply curves containing both effects, these market supply curves may have either a positive or a negative slope. Although the substitution effects of higher interest rates influence all households to consume less and save more, the income effects have exactly the opposite influence. The net result on the supply of saving will therefore depend on whether the sum of all substitution effects is greater than the sum of all income effects.

Of perhaps greater importance to many policy decisions, however, is the response of the supply of loanable funds to interest rate changes that have no income effects. Interest rates are influenced by many government policies whose effects on the feasible combinations of present and future income are negligible. Of particular interest is the tax treatment of income from capital. For example, interest rates may rise due to an increase in demand for loanable funds resulting from a change in tax policy, like the investment tax credit.[1] Policies like these have a negligible effect on the feasible combinations of current and future income for the economy as a whole. They may encourage investment and thus expand consumption opportunities in the future, but only at the expense of greater saving and thus a lower rate of current consumption. An investment tax credit is a subsidy to investors "paid for" by other taxpayers. Since the government must obtain revenue from taxpayers to finance this subsidy, the higher interest rates will not benefit everyone—indeed, on average real incomes must remain about the same. Savers will get higher interest rates, but taxes will rise, implying less after-tax income to finance current consumption.

Such policies have no income effects; hence, the use of an uncompensated supply curve that incorporates these effects is inappropriate. Increased taxes or other fiscal changes compensate for the increase in income produced by the interest rate change. A **compensated supply curve for loanable funds** is therefore appropriate for the analysis of this and similar policies. A compensated supply curve is made up of the summed responses of all savers to changes in the interest rate holding real income constant. It contains only substitution effects. However, the fact that interest rate changes due to these policies have no income effects does not imply that saving choices will be unaffected. These policies affect the interest rate and therefore the opportunity cost of future consumption. Recall that this opportunity cost is $1/1 + r$, which varies inversely with the interest rate. Households will respond to increases in this rate by substituting future consumption for present consumption—by saving more and consuming less in the current period. These compensated supply curves for loanable funds must therefore slope upward.

---

[1] An investment tax credit gives businesses a tax reduction for qualifying investments in new capital.

Taxes need not operate directly on the interest rate in order to affect the rate of saving and thus the supply of loanable funds. The direct taxation of income from capital has similar effects and may be analyzed with the tools developed here. Taxing interest and dividend income increases the opportunity cost of future consumption above $1/1 + r$ because the household obtains only the net of tax interest or dividends on the forgone consumption. The imposition of such a tax or a change in the tax rate can be shown to shift the opportunity set of present and future consumption just as does an interest rate change.[2] This taxation, like the investment tax credit, has no appreciable effect on real income. The revenue from the tax may simply be distributed, other taxes may be lowered, or the money may be spent on goods that households might otherwise purchase themselves. Real income on average is unaffected by these alternative uses of the revenues. However, because the opportunity cost of future consumption has been changed by these taxes, they will have substitution effects. A tax on the income from capital clearly increases the opportunity cost of future consumption and reduces the supply of loanable funds.

15.3 Investment Opportunities: The Demand for Loanable Funds

So far we have treated the income endowment as given. Households have been assumed in each period to have claims to purchasing power originating from the sale of the services of assets that they own and supply to the market. These may include their own labor services as well as any land, buildings, and equipment that they own outright. They may also include the services of assets indirectly owned through equity in businesses that own and supply capital services to themselves and other firms. In our analysis of the supply of net saving we treated the quantity of this capital, and thus the income endowment, in each period as constant. However, the investment demand for loanable funds arises out of plans to increase and modify that stock of capital. In order to analyze the decision to demand loanable funds for this purpose we must now lay a foundation of distinctions and assumptions.

It is important to make a sharp distinction between the **real assets**, useful in production, and **financial assets**, such as bonds, certificates of deposit, and sav-

---

[2]This may be shown by subtracting the tax $tS_1 r$ (letting t be the tax rate) from the expression for future income, equation (15.1). Doing so gives:

$$C_1 = Y_1 + (1 + r)S_0 - tS_0 r$$
$$= Y_1 + (1 + r - tr)S_0.$$

Substituting for S_0 again and solving for present consumption, C_0, gives:

$$C_0 = Y_0 + \frac{1}{1 + (1 - t)r} \cdot Y_1 - \frac{1}{1 + (1 - t)r} \cdot C_1.$$

As long as the tax rate t is between zero and unity, an increase in the tax rate increases the vertical intercept and makes the slope steeper (more negative). Whether the portion of this new opportunity set to the northwest of the income endowment may be chosen depends on the government's tax treatment of negative savings. To the extent that interest payments are deductible, this portion of the curve may be chosen.

ings and checking accounts. Only expenditure on the former qualifies as **investment** in the sense employed here. The latter are assumed to be traded with financial intermediaries at exchange rates *determined by* the market interest rate. They are further distinguished by information conditions in the two markets. Information in the financial markets is assumed to be "perfect"; there is no risk of default. Only one exchange rate, and therefore only one interest rate, may prevail. On the other hand, information in the investment sector is assumed to be "imperfect." We assume that individual investors are privy to information concerning conditions in their market that is not generally available. Since perfect information would imply widespread knowledge of every possible production technique, as well as of all future scientific innovations, the assumption that investment information is imperfect is realistic. There will always be opportunities to make money through discovery and innovation. It is the search for such undiscovered opportunities that motivates investors to engage in this activity instead of merely "clipping coupons."

Opportunities to invest profitably have two effects on the market for current period purchasing power. On the one hand, these opportunities increase the real income of investors, leading them to seek increased consumption in each period including the present. On the other hand, the finance of investment also requires current purchasing power. It is the demand for loanable funds for both these purposes that together with supply produces a market equilibrium equating saving and investment.

A Change in the Income Endowment

In order to analyze this demand for loanable funds we must develop a method of representing investment in our choice model. This may be done by treating investment as a shift in the income endowment. Consider Figure 15.6, which depicts the situation of the "average" investor. As income *on average* must equal consumption in each period, the individual is shown just choosing to consume his or her initial endowment, K^a. This endowment is made up of Y_0^a income in the current period and Y_1^a in the future. The value of this endowment expressed in present value terms is W_0. Now let this average investor discover an investment possibility that permits the purchase of a machine that may be leased in the next period to produce income. Let the cost of this machine be ΔY_0 and the rental income in the next period be ΔY_1. The investor's endowment after making this investment will be K^b. This new endowment, if consumed, would be less preferred than the initial endowment. The theory of investment informs us concerning the conditions under which the investment may nevertheless be undertaken.

The Decision to Invest

A very useful property of the theory of investment is that we do not need to know anything about an investor's preferences (other than that they conform to the principles already stated) to know whether he or she will choose to make an investment. This is demonstrated in Figure 15.7. The investor will benefit from the investment depicted regardless of the position of his indifference curves in the figure. If he declines the investment, his consumption combinations are limited to the opportunity set OS_1. Making the investment provides the investor with income

Chapter 15 The Supply of Capital: Savings and Investment

Figure 15.6 Investment as a Change in the Income Endowment

The original income endowment is K^a, which is also consumed. By giving up ΔY_0 of income in the current period, income in the future may be increased by ΔY_1. This provides the household with a new endowment combination, K^b.

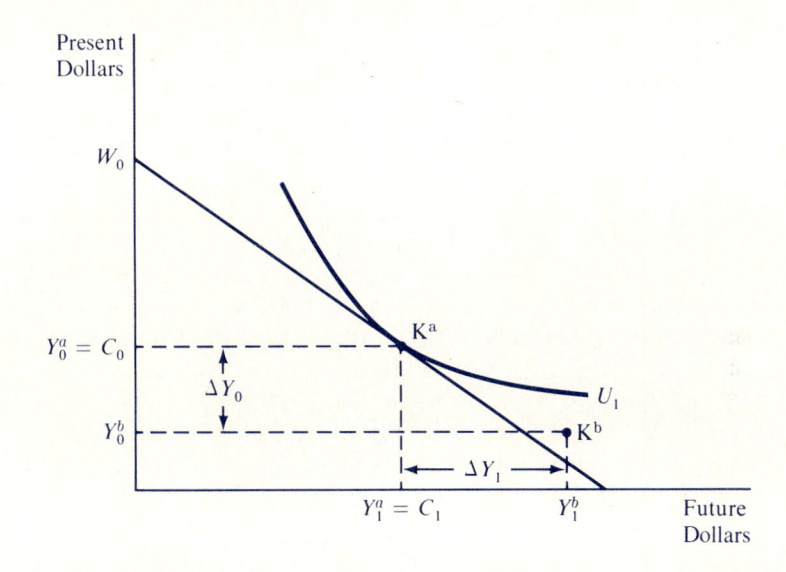

claims in each period represented by combination K^b. By borrowing and lending in the financial sector against *this* endowment, he or she may in this case select a consumption combination from the higher opportunity set OS_2. Because OS_2 is higher, for any most preferred combination along OS_1, there must be a combination on OS_2 containing more consumption in each period which is preferred to it. For example, here the most preferred combination on OS_1 is K^a. The investment makes possible the choice of consumption combination T which contains more current and more future consumption than K^a.

The investor will therefore choose to make this investment regardless of the position of the indifference curves in the diagram. Note that were the individual required to *consume* the income endowment in each period, the investment would leave him or her on a lower indifference curve. As long as this investor may borrow and lend at the market interest rate, however, he or she is not restricted to consuming combination K^b, which is less preferred than combination K^a. He or she may borrow to finance combination T, which is preferred to *any* combination along the original opportunity set.

Note the effect of the discovery of this investment opportunity on the demand for loanable funds. This investor consumes his or her income endowment if no investment opportunity is presented, therefore demanding no loanable funds at this discount rate. However, the purchase of the machine makes necessary a trip to the bank. Desired consumption after the investment is made is C_0, but the investor

Figure 15.7 *Investment and Demand for Loanable Funds*

If the household is restricted to income endowment K^a, it will consume this endowment and borrow nothing. If, however, it may exchange ΔY_0 for ΔY_1, obtaining endowment K^b, access to the financial sector will be sought. Consumption combination T is most favored along OS_2, implying a need to borrow amount $C_0 - Y_0^b$.

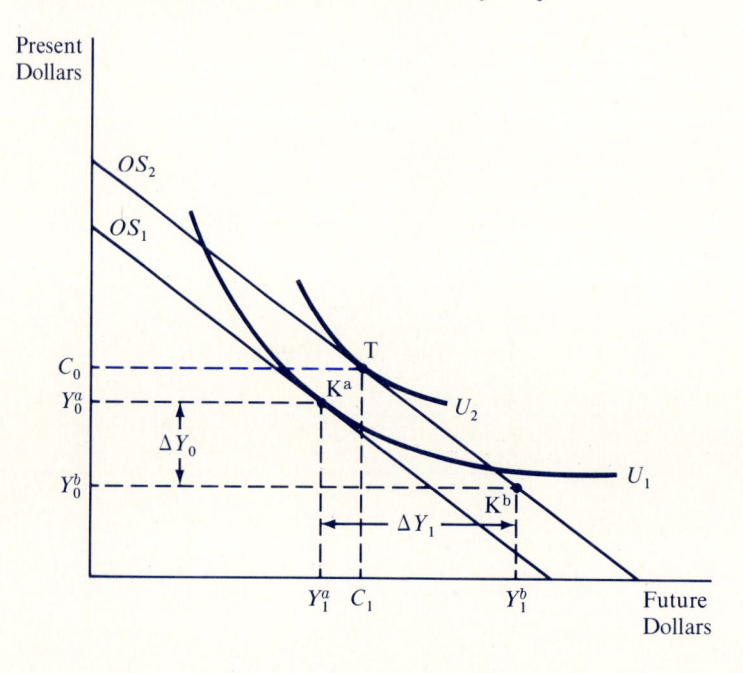

has only Y_0^b left over after purchasing the machine. Potential investments generate demand for loanable funds in this way. A portion of the borrowings may be said to finance the machine—but not all. Part of the demand for loanable funds originates in the increased planned consumption due to the change in wealth produced by the investment. The machine, after all, costs only ΔY_0. Total borrowings amount to $C_0 - Y_0^b$.

Note that the investment need only lift the opportunity set upward to make it desirable as described. An investment such as that depicted in Figure 15.8 would leave the individual on a lower opportunity set offering consumption opportunities less attractive than some available on the initial opportunity set. Households confronted by such investment opportunities can be expected to decline them. A necessary and sufficient condition for investments to be viewed favorably, therefore, is that the investment increase the vertical intercept of the opportunity set. Recall that we defined this vertical intercept as the wealth of the household, and that it was shown to be equal to

$$W_0 = Y_0 + \frac{1}{1+r} \cdot Y_1.$$

Figure 15.8 *Unprofitable Investment*

The fact that the yield on an investment is greater than the investment itself does not alone indicate that the investment is profitable. Here ΔY_1 exceeds ΔY_0, but wealth declines. This is because the opportunity cost of a dollar invested is more than a dollar next period. That dollar might have been placed in the financial sector, where it could have returned both principal and interest.

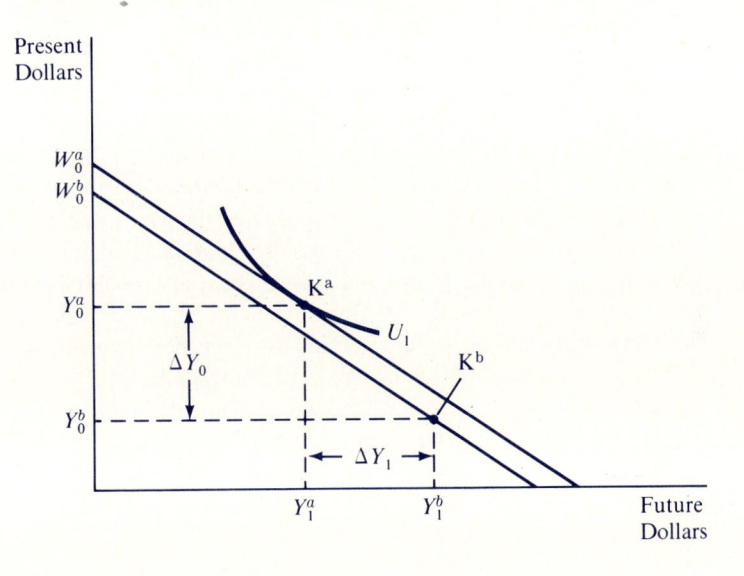

Attractive investments must *increase* wealth, implying the following condition for those viewed favorably by potential investors:

$$\Delta W_0 = \Delta Y_0 + \frac{1}{1+r} \cdot \Delta Y_1 > 0.$$

We further define such wealth increases as the **profits on investments**—indeed, so long as the interest rate remains unchanged, all investment behavior is consistent with the assumption of **wealth maximization**. This empirically more tractable maximand governing investment decisions is itself implied by utility maximization, as we have just seen.

The Present Value Rule

From this discussion we may derive a normative rule governing investment decisions by households and firms. According to the formula just derived, any potential investment offering a positive ΔW_0 increases wealth and must therefore increase the potential real income of the investor. This **present value rule** is the fundamental principle underlying the theory of finance. Investors should be guided in their selection of projects by this rule. Let us state this rule in terms of the more common language of finance. Typically, the value of ΔY_0 is negative, representing the outlay for the asset, and is commonly referred to as the **cost of the investment**. The term ΔY_1, the earnings of the asset in the future, is positive in these cases and is referred to as the **return on the investment**. The return is multiplied by the exchange rate in order to express its value in terms of present dollars. The exchange rate, $1/1 + r$, is referred to as the **discount factor**, and the product of the discount factor and the return is called the *present value* of the return. When the whole expression for ΔW_0 is evaluated, we refer to it as both the **net return** on the investment and as the *profits* earned.

Although we normally think of investment as following this pattern, it is possible to invest profitably in the other direction. Consider those investors who "sell short," that is, sell a security (or asset) for future delivery without presently owning the asset. In such cases, ΔY_0 is positive and ΔY_1 is negative. Sellers of such short contracts expect prices of the assets sold to fall so that they may buy them at the lower price in the future and deliver them at a positive profit. However, as these transactions typically are observed in the financial market rather than in the investment market, as we have treated the terms here, we will have few occasions to discuss short contracts here. We shall return to the topic of present values later in the chapter, when we extend these developments to the far more common case of investments yielding multiperiod returns.

Varying the Interest Rate to Demanders

At any date investors see before them an array of investment possibilities and apply to each the wealth-maximizing calculus just discussed. Those projects whose net returns are positive will be adopted; those having negative net returns will be rejected. Let us therefore observe the effect of changing interest rates on the adoption of projects. It can easily be shown that a rise in the interest rate will make all such projects less attractive. Some will continue to be undertaken. Others that were adopted at lower rates will be viewed as no longer profitable and will be rejected at higher rates. The effect of a rise in interest rates on the demand for loanable funds will thus be shown to be negative.

Consider Figure 15.9, the two panels of which depict the opportunity sets of two investors with identical income endowments. These endowments are represented in each panel by combination K^a. At the initial lower interest rates, these endowments represent wealth of W_0^a for each. The investment in panel (a) offers new endowment combination K^b. For the investment of ΔY_0 in the present this investor obtains ΔY_1^a in the future, increasing his or her wealth to W_0^b. The investor in panel (b) would make a different investment, offering combination K^c, which for the same outlay would provide the smaller return ΔY_1^b. This increases that individual's wealth to W_0^c at the initial interest rate. At this rate both investments are profitable, and both will be adopted by these investors. Demand for loanable funds for investment from these two investors is $2\Delta Y_0$.

An increase in the interest rate will diminish the attractiveness of all investments, discouraging some investors from making them. At the higher interest rate the opportunity sets passing through the initial income endowments and the income combinations made possible by the investments have flatter slopes. The in-

Figure 15.9   *Investment Profitability and the Interest Rate*

At the original interest rate the investments in both panels are profitable. Wealth in panel (a) increases from W_0^a to W_0^b, while profits in panel (b) are $W_0^c - W_0^a$. At the higher interest rate, however, both profits are reduced, and those in panel (b) become negative. The wealth increase associated with the investment in panel (a) falls to $W_1^b - W_1^a$. Profits in panel (b) become negative, equal to $W_1^c - W_1^a$. Demand for loanable funds is diminished by this increase in the interest rate.

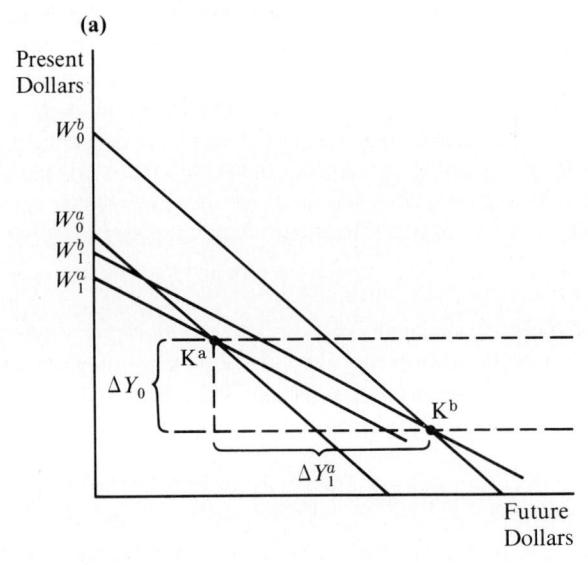

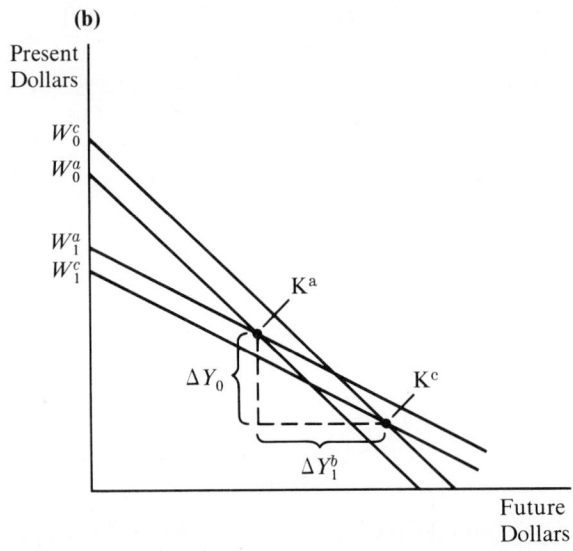

vestment in panel (a) remains profitable; though the wealth change is smaller in this case, it remains positive. The investment in panel (b) is no longer profitable at the higher interest rate. Adopting it actually decreases wealth, from W_1^a to W_1^c. Potential investors will therefore decline to make this investment.

The effect of an increase in the interest rate on investors must therefore be to reduce demand for loanable funds for investment. Some investments that were attractive at lower rates will become unattractive at higher ones. In our example, demand for loanable funds for investment at the lower interest rate was $2\Delta Y_1$. At the higher interest rate only one investor found the investment profitable, so demand for current funds for this purpose falls to ΔY_1. In an economy with many possible investments offering varying yields, increasing interest rates can be expected to discourage investors from adopting some of them. At successively higher interest rates increasing numbers of such investments will become unattractive, and the quantity of loanable funds demanded for these purposes will diminish. The demand for loanable funds for investment must therefore be negatively sloped.

The Equilibrium Interest Rate

The interest rate that clears the market will equate the supply and demand for loanable funds. Such an equilibrium is presented in Figure 15.10. At any date we may assume that technology, and therefore the capability of the economy to produce

Figure 15.10 *Market Demand and Supply for Loanable Funds*

Market demand for loanable funds slopes downward to the right, while the compensated supply slopes upward. The equilibrium interest rate is r^*, which clears the market for loanable funds. At lower interest rates, borrowers seek to secure more loans than the financial sector can offer. At higher interest rates, savers supply more funds than the financial sector can lend.

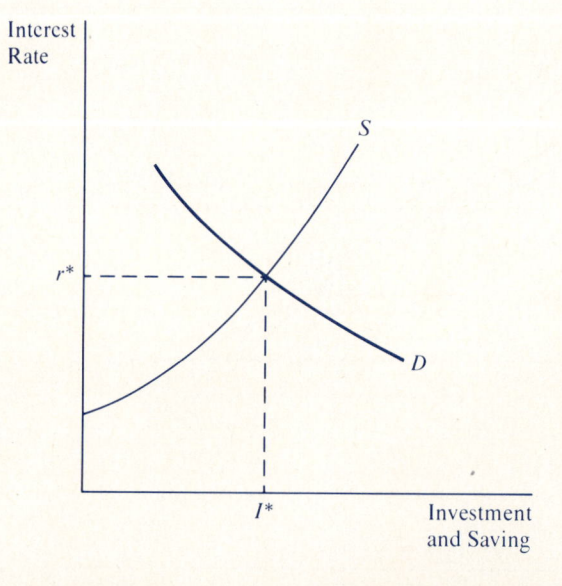

combinations of present and future income, is fixed. Under such circumstances, as we have seen, changes in interest rates to suppliers of loanable funds (savers) cannot have income effects for the economy as a whole. Though demand for loanable funds may vary in such a static economy, interest rate changes will have only substitution effects for savers. Any income effects must be compensated for by tax increases or shifts if the changes are the result of government policy. A compensated supply curve for loanable funds is therefore appropriate for the analysis of the determination of an equilibrium interest rate on a given date. As we noted earlier, compensated supply curves for saving slope upward to the right.

The demand curve for loanable funds slopes downward, reflecting the fact that all investment projects are made less attractive by an increase in interest rates. At higher rates the yield on the investment in some projects will fall below the financial market exchange rate and thus be wealth reducing. Such projects will not be undertaken at these rates; others that remain attractive at this point will become unattractive at still higher rates. The equilibrium rate of interest is that at which desired borrowings equal the amount saved—that is, the rate at which the demand and supply of loanable funds are equal.

15.4 Multiperiod Analysis

Practical application of the theory of saving and investment requires that the analysis be extended to deal with more than two periods. Most planners may look forward to more than two years' consumption before he or she disappears from the scene, and the service life of many capital goods, like buildings and heavy equipment, may extend for decades. Luckily, the analysis of multiperiod consumption planning and investment may be readily developed from the two-period model. Although the helpful geometric presentations cannot accommodate choice in more than two dimensions, the similarity of the algebraic notation in the two cases will provide the student with sufficient intuition that the analysis may be understood without graphs.

The opportunity set in the two-period case was developed by noting that consumption in the final period was equal to income in that period plus the principal and accumulated interest on savings from the former period. As savings in the former period were equal to income minus consumption in that period, second-period consumption was shown as:

$$C_1 = Y_1 + (1 + r)(Y_0 - C_0).$$

To extend this analysis to a third period, we simply repeat this process. We assume that the planning horizon extends to a third period in which all remaining resources are consumed. Consumption in this period will be equal to third-period income plus principal and interest on saving from the second period. We obtain saving in the second period by reducing consumption in the above expression by the amount saved, S_1:

$$C_1 = Y_1 + (1 + r)(Y_0 - C_0) - S_1.$$

Solving this expression in turn for second-period saving yields:

$$S_1 = Y_1 + (1 + r)(Y_0 - C_0) - C_1.$$

Consumption in the third period is thus

$$C_2 = (1 + r)S_1 + Y_2,$$

which, when we substitute from the previous equation the equivalent expression for S_1, becomes:

$$C_2 = (1 + r)Y_1 + (1 + r)^2 Y_0 - (1 + r)^2 C_0 - (1 + r)C_1 + Y_2.$$

Again it is more useful to express this opportunity set as a function of present consumption in terms of consumption in the remaining periods. Solving for C_0 and rearranging terms, we therefore obtain the following:

$$C_0 = Y_0 + \frac{1}{1 + r} \cdot Y_1 + \frac{1}{(1 + r)^2} \cdot Y_2 - \frac{1}{1 + r} \cdot C_1 - \frac{1}{(1 + r)^2} \cdot C_2.$$

Just as in the two-period model, this opportunity set is linear in the choice variables C_1 and C_2. The slope terms $\Delta C_0/\Delta C_1$ and $\Delta C_0/\Delta C_2$ are the negative constants $-1/1 + r$ and $-1/(1 + r)^2$, respectively. They reflect the rate at which future dollars may be exchanged for present dollars with some intermediary. The intercept expression now contains three terms and has the same interpretation as the two-period model intercept. It measures the wealth of the household, the sum of the exchange value of all income claims in all periods for present dollars. It is:

$$W_0 = Y_0 + \frac{1}{1 + r} \cdot Y_1 + \frac{1}{(1 + r)^2} \cdot Y_2.$$

Although the algebra gets increasingly tedious with the addition of each period, it is possible to continue adding periods in the manner described and solving for the opportunity set for time periods as large as we choose. It is hoped, however, that this extension into three periods is sufficient to reveal the pattern of this process.

Recalling that for any positive interest rate $(1 + r)^0 = 1$ and $(1 + r)^1 = 1 + r$, the expression for wealth may be rewritten as:

$$W_0 = \frac{1}{(1 + r)^0} \cdot Y_0 + \frac{1}{(1 + r)^1} \cdot Y_1 + \frac{1}{(1 + r)^2} \cdot Y_2$$

$$= \sum_{i=0}^{2} \frac{1}{(1 + r)^i} \cdot Y_i.$$

Since the same progression may be observed in the consumption terms, the opportunity set generally may be written as:

$$\sum_{i=0}^{n} \frac{1}{(1+r)^i} \cdot C_i = \sum_{i=0}^{n} \frac{1}{(1+r)^i} \cdot Y_i.$$

The present value of consumption over time must equal the present value of income (wealth).

Investment in Multiperiod Analysis

All of the results developed in the previous section concerning investment extend to this analysis. Investments should be undertaken if they increase household wealth. Wealth-increasing investments make possible the choice of consumption combinations that were unattainable at lower wealth. Any project for which the wealth change, expressed as

$$\Delta W = \sum_{i=0}^{n} \frac{1}{(1+r)^i} \cdot \Delta Y_i,$$

is greater than zero should be adopted. There are many varieties of such investment programs. The type that leaps most readily to mind involves a single, negative ΔY in the first period followed by a series of positive ΔYs representing the yield on the investment. The construction of a building or the purchase of a machine presents such an income profile. Many investments involve a continuous stream of negative ΔYs followed by another stream of positive ΔYs. For example, research into the development of new pharmaceutical products requires years of investment before the products are perfected and certified as safe by the Food and Drug Administration. Investments involving a series of negative ΔYs followed by a single positive ΔY are not unheard of. Perhaps the most familiar of these is the intense investment in the development of rocketry and outer space life support systems that was made throughout the 1960s for the express purpose of getting a man to the moon before the Russians did.

All such investments may be evaluted similarly by calculating the value of ΔW in each case. Those for which a positive change in wealth is revealed should be adopted; those for which the change is negative should be rejected. Because the analysis is so similar in each case, we will restrict ourselves to consideration of a special case of investment for which a shortcut method of performing this calculation may be developed. This case will also be useful for explaining the relationship between the asset prices and the service prices of certain capital goods.

Constant Yield Assets

The case we wish to consider in detail involves a single-period investment that produces a continuous stream of income in the future for a stipulated period—a **constant yield asset**. We may return to our original example of a firm that purchases machines and leases them out to users. By applying the investment calculus developed for that case, we may derive the determinants of the supply of these capital goods to demanders.

Let us rewrite the expression for ΔW by taking the first ΔY out of the summation, so that it becomes:

$$\Delta W = \Delta Y_0 + \sum_{i=1}^{n} \frac{1}{(1+r)^i} \cdot \Delta Y_i.$$

The first term on the right side of this expression is the negative income change representing the investment in the asset. This will be the purchase price of the machines. We will assume that these machines are supplied by producers at constant cost, c. The asset purchased is assumed to yield a rental price, R, in each future period that does not vary. The term ΔY_i is therefore the same in each year. We will assume further that the service life of such machines is known to be n years, at the end of which the machines have no scrap value and are discarded. Because R is a constant it may be factored out of the summation, and our expression for ΔW becomes:

$$\Delta W = -c + R \cdot \sum_{i=1}^{n} \frac{1}{(1+r)^i}.$$

The present value of the return stream of any such project may be evaluated by multiplying the annual return R by the value of the summation term, which varies only with the interest rate and the length of the period the return is received. This summation is called the **annuity factor**. Tables of these factors are widely published for differing values of r and n; many pocket calculators are programmed with routines for computation of the annuity factor for any values of these two variables.

Computation of these factors can be tedious if such tables or computers are unavailable. There is a shortcut method that may be useful on such occasions. Let us denote the value of the annuity factor as A so that:

$$A = \frac{1}{1+r} + \frac{1}{(1+r)^2} + \frac{1}{(1+r)^3} + \ldots + \frac{1}{(1+r)^n}.$$

Next, we factor the term $1/1 + r$ out of this expression:

$$A = \frac{1}{1+r}\left[1 + \frac{1}{1+r} + \frac{1}{(1+r)^2} + \frac{1}{(1+r)^3} + \ldots + \frac{1}{(1+r)^{n-1}}\right].$$

Note, however, that the expression inside the brackets lacks only the final term $1/(1+r)^n$ to equal $1 + A$. The expression for A may therefore be written as:

$$A = \frac{1}{1+r}\left[1 + A - \frac{1}{(1+r)^n}\right].$$

Thus:

$$A(1+r) = 1 + A - \frac{1}{(1+r)^n}$$

Chapter 15 The Supply of Capital: Savings and Investment

(15.2) $$A(1 + r) - A = 1 - \frac{1}{(1 + r)^n}.$$

Performing the indicated multiplication on the left side of this expression and seeking a common denominator on the right yields:

$$A + Ar - A = \frac{(1 + r)^n - 1}{(1 + r)^n}.$$

This may be solved for A as:

$$A = \frac{(1 + r)^n - 1}{r(1 + r)^n}.$$

The investment producing rentals of R per year for n years at interest rate r may therefore be evaluated using the above expression for A:

(15.3) $$\Delta W = -c + RA.$$

Those opportunities for which ΔW is positive are wealth increasing and should be adopted; those for which ΔW is negative are wealth diminishing and should be declined.

Infinitely Lived Assets

Occasionally it is necessary to evaluate assets that have infinite service lives—**infinitely lived assets**. The purchase of land or the drilling of a tunnel will continue to yield benefits indefinitely. It is somewhat surprising to discover that the sum of an infinite stream of positive values (the present values of those benefits) is not itself infinite. On the other hand, this discovery is economically reassuring, because these assets do not command a price of infinity in the market. We may not use the expression just derived to compute the annuity factor, because that would require evaluation of

$$A = \frac{(1 + r)^\infty - 1}{r(1 + r)^\infty},$$

which is difficult to do even with a computer. However, returning to equation (15.2) we note that A may also be expressed as:

$$A = \frac{1}{r} - \frac{1}{r(1 + r)^n}.$$

Clearly, for any positive interest rate the denominator of the second term on the right side approaches infinity as n itself approaches infinity. One over infinity is zero; hence, the second term will vanish for infinitely lived return streams, leaving:

$$A = \frac{1}{r}.$$

The Supply of Capital Services

Thus far our analysis has been confined to factors influencing the decision to invest. However, we began this chapter with a discussion of the **supply of capital services**, and we must now return to this topic. Unless we can identify a supply function for capital services we will be unable to describe conditions at the equilibrium in this market. This is most easily done for assets producing a constant service stream, so we shall confine our discussion to identifying the supply of capital services for these assets. The reader who masters this section should have a reasonable intuition into the mechanics of the supply of services of assets yielding more irregular service streams.

Let us consider Figure 15.11, which depicts the demand curve for capital *services* and two supply curves. Let the initial supply be S_1 so that the market-clearing rental price for the capital is R_1. Whether or not this is an equilibrium depends on whether or not investments equal to the cost of these assets are wealth increasing at this rental price. Let us assume that when substituted into equation (15.3) the values pertinent to this investment yield a positive ΔW. Investing in these assets is therefore profitable, and we should expect investors to take advantage of these opportunities. However, as they do so the new assets produced and made available in the market will shift the supply curve to the right. This rightward shift, in turn, will cause the market-clearing rental price to fall to R_2, as shown in the figure.

How far will the price fall? We may determine this by studying equation (15.3). Let us assume that this increased supply of these assets affects only R in this expression. Increased production is assumed to have no effect on the asset

Figure 15.11 *The Service Price of Capital*

The demand for capital services is simply the demand curve for a factor of production derived in Chapter 12. The service price is determined by the quantity of capital supplying these services. If q_1 is supplied, the rental price is R_1. If the quantity of capital is expanded to q_2, the rental price falls to R_2.

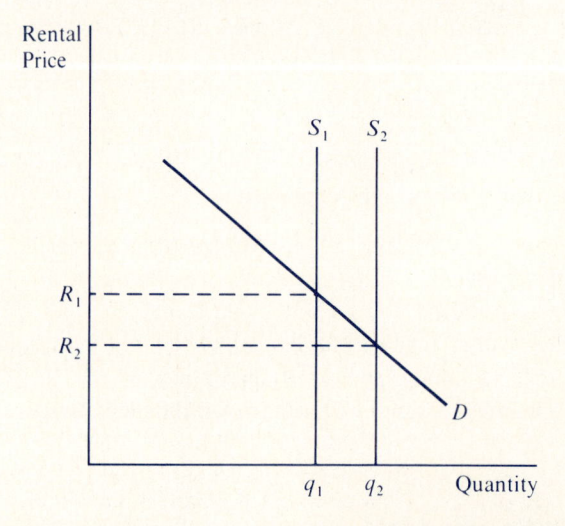

cost, c, the service life of the asset, n, or the interest rate r (the latter two variables determining A). Under these circumstances decreases in R must decrease ΔW. At some point, therefore, expansion of the supply of the services of these capital goods will reduce the profitability of this investment to zero. Once this supply is in place, profits may no longer be earned. Investment will cease, and the quantity supplied will stabilize.

We may identify this equilibrium rental price by finding that value of R in equation (15.3) which yields a zero value for ΔW. Let that equilibrium rental price be R^*. Clearly, by setting ΔW in expression (15.3) equal to zero, we obtain the following:

(15.4) $$R^* = \frac{1}{A} c.$$

This expression tells us that regardless of demand conditions in the market for the services of these assets, the rental price must invariably move toward R^*, which itself depends only on three factors: the purchase price of the asset, the service life, and the interest rate. From this we may derive a very useful conclusion concerning the supply of capital services. If production of these assets exhibits constant returns (so that c is constant), the supply of the services of these assets will be perfectly elastic at rental price R^*.

Consider Figure 15.12. Let initial demand be given by D_1 and initial supply by S_0. This is clearly not an equilibrium, because the market-clearing price under these conditions is R_1, which is greater than R^*. Positive profits will be earned at this price, leading investors to expand supply until price falls to R^* when supply reaches S_1. This price–quantity combination identifies one point on the long-run supply curve for the services of these assets. Now let demand expand out to D_2. If this expansion is unanticipated, supply will remain S_1, and the market-clearing price of these asset services will rise to R_2. At this price investment becomes profitable again (R_2 is greater than R^*), so additional investment will be undertaken. Supply will thus shift rightward again until the rental price again falls to R^*—indeed, for any shift in demand, supply will adjust so as to provide the quantity at which the demand price equals R^*. We may therefore draw a long-run supply curve for the services of these machines. This curve, labeled S_L, is horizontal at rental price R^*.

How long is the long run? That depends on whether demand shifts are predictable or unpredictable, on whether demand is growing or declining, and on the service life of these assets. Clearly, if demand is expanding at a predictable rate per year, investors will be aware of the profit opportunities likely to emerge in that industry and will invest in anticipation of future demand growth. Investment in anticipation of such growth should accelerate convergence to equilibrium. In the limiting case, where investors may forecast perfectly, the quantity of these assets supplied in each year will be exactly that which will clear the market at a rental price of R^*. If demand is unpredictable, on the other hand, price changes themselves must signal the availability of profitable opportunities. In these cases, convergence to long-run equilibrium will necessarily take longer.

If demand is growing, full adjustment depends on the recognition lag just described as well as on the time needed to produce and install the items. If the assets are "off-the-shelf" items which may be instantly installed, the adjustment will be

Figure 15.12 *Long-Run Supply of Capital Services*

The long-run supply price of capital is R^*, which is equal to the purchase price of the capital times the reciprocal of the annuity factor. The supply of these assets will adjust until the equilibrium rental rate falls to R^*. Given demand D_1 supply will expand to S_1, at which the market-clearing rate is equal to R^*. If demand expands to D_2, the market-clearing rate rises to R_2, at which profits are earned on these assets. This leads to expansion of supply to S_2, where the rental rate falls again to R^*. A horizontal long-run supply curve at R^* is traced out by these adjustments.

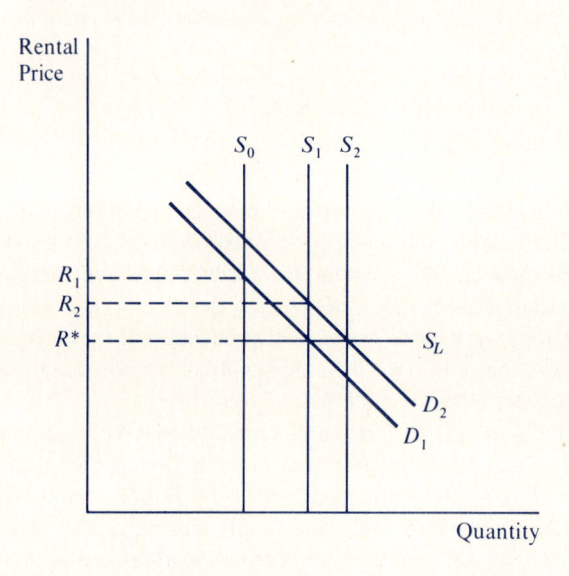

faster than where the capital item is one of a kind and installation takes months. If demand is falling, full adjustment requires a recognition lag, but production and installation time is not an important factor. Falling demand implies a declining long-run optimal stock of these assets, but that does not mean that it will pay to "scrap" existing capital items. On the contrary, as long as anything at all may be obtained for renting them it will pay to continue to operate them even though it does not pay to invest in new ones. Adjustment to long-run equilibrium therefore depends on the service life of the equipment. Existing machines will continue to be used so long as they may be operated, but unless the machines wear out faster than the rate at which the optimal stock diminishes it will not pay to produce any new ones.

Declining Industries: The Case of Passenger Rail Travel

Our description of the adjustment to falling demand suggests a not uncommon vignette in American industry: the **declining industry**. This phenomenon is characterized by two conditions: falling revenue and aging capital base. Revenues fall because the price paid to (or earned on) capital owned by the firms in that industry falls below R^*. The average age of the capital itself rises because those assets that wear out are infrequently replaced. Lost customers, as well as outsiders, on observing conditions in such an industry, have been known to declare that if these firms modernized their facilities and/or equipment, they would return as customers and business would return to normal. It is not uncommon to hear these people inveigh against the "stupidity" and "shortsightedness" of the management of the firms in question. Occasionally such comments may be on target. However, we must not lose sight of the fact that if demand is declining for reasons beyond the control of the company management, the observed behavior is not shortsighted at all but the best that can be done.

Consider the case of passenger rail travel in the United States during the postwar period. As the technology of both air and highway travel advanced impressively during this period, increasing numbers of passengers were attracted away from rail travel. For example, in 1950 American railroads provided 31 billion passenger miles to their customers. By 1970, this output had fallen to 10 billion passenger miles. Sleeping-car passenger miles over this period fell from 9.3 billion to 765 million, and the number of passenger train cars in service fell from roughly 37,000 to 11,000.

It may well have been true that fewer people were riding trains in the 1960s than would have had the trains been in better condition. On the other hand, when considering the rate at which demand was diminishing, it is not difficult to sympathize with the railroad management's decisions to invest little in new and modernized passenger cars.

A similar analysis of governmental efforts to shore up passenger rail travel may be given. Although gasoline prices were rising sharply during the 1970s, Amtrak experienced a steady decline in demand during that decade. In spite of the large subsidies made to Amtrak every year ($975 million in 1981), that decline has continued relentlessly. The fact remains that it was not shortsighted management that produced this decline but the changing technology of air and automobile travel that made the latter more efficient (if not more romantic) modes of transportation. Continued large expenditures by the railroads on new equipment and installations will not appreciably affect demand and are unwarranted on the basis of the criteria for investment developed in this chapter.

Depreciation and the Opportunity Cost of Capital

Equation (15.4) identifies the equilibrium rental price of capital as the purchase price of the asset times the reciprocal of the annuity factor. The latter term, $1/A$, has an important economic interpretation of its own. It is often called the **capital recovery factor** and may be interpreted as the opportunity cost per year of a dollar invested. For an asset having no scrap value at the end of its service life, the opportunity cost of the investment represents both the principal invested and the interest that might have been earned and accumulated over the life of the asset. The capital recovery factor is the amount that, if received for n years at interest rate r, would have a present value of $1. The product of $c \cdot 1/A$ therefore yields the amount that, if received for the same period at the same interest rate, would have a present value of c. If one cannot obtain at least $c \cdot 1/A$ each year over the life of the asset, then the present value of the rental stream is less than the cost of the asset.

Such an investment is wealth decreasing and should not be made. It is in this sense that the capital recovery factor measures the opportunity cost per year of capital invested.

Accounting statements of businesses typically will understate the real cost of capital assets to the firm. These statements list as cost only the **depreciation** of capital owned by the firm. It is easy to show that this understates the real opportunity cost of owning these capital assets. Assume that an asset has an expected life of 10 years and may be purchased for $100. Straight line depreciation would cost out one tenth of the purchase price in each of the ten years. The depreciation cost in each year would therefore be recorded as $10. Compare this with the correct measure of that cost, which includes not only the depreciation but the interest that might have been earned and accumulated. For $r = 10\%$, this yields $\$100 \cdot 1/A = \$16.30$.[3]

The understatement of depreciation as a measure of the opportunity cost of investing in capital is even more obvious for the case of assets that do not depreciate. Is holding land costless simply because it is not partially used up in each period? Of course not! The present purchasing power tied up in the land might be exchanged for future dollars at a premium. The land might be sold and the proceeds deposited in a bank at interest. We may easily compute the opportunity cost of capital in this case. By definition such a nondepreciating asset has a service life of infinity. The value of A for such an infinite service stream was shown earlier to be $1/r$. The opportunity cost of capital invested per dollar per year is therefore $1/A = r$. The opportunity cost of a nondepreciating asset is simply the interest that might have been earned on the asset price.

Asset Prices and Capitalization

One way to profit from investments is to purchase assets that may be leased out (or used by the owning firm) when the present values of the expected rentals exceed the purchase prices of the assets themselves. So long as one is quick enough to take advantage of such opportunities while they remain profitable, these investments will be wealth increasing.

There is another way to profit from investment, without having to hold and manage the use of an inventory of real assets like machines, buildings, and trucks. This process is called **capitalization**. It concerns the tendency of asset prices to move toward an equilibrium that reflects the present value of the return stream.

Earlier we were concerned with the theory of the supply of capital services. Since it is the services of these assets that are demanded in the productive process, they thus represent the unit of analysis appropriate to the theory of derived demand developed in Chapters 12 and 13. In that analysis it was useful to assume that the assets themselves were produced and sold competitively at prices equal to (constant) marginal cost. As capital goods by definition have a service life of more than a single year, however, there are many instances in which one has the option of purchasing a new asset in the manner described or purchasing an existing asset from someone else. The latter possibility raises the question of how such asset

---

[3] Note from our formula that for $r = .10$ and $n = 10$, $A = 6.14$, and thus $1/A = 0.163$.

prices themselves are determined and also introduces the possibility of profitable transactions due to changes in these prices.

Here, as in all discussions of opportunities for profit, information conditions in the market are important. If all buyers and sellers are perfectly informed concerning all market opportunities, the prices of assets will at all times reflect their equilibrium values, and gains to asset traders will be impossible. While many markets may approach this condition (as do major stock exchanges and commodity exchanges), markets in individual capital assets clearly do not. These markets are frequently too "thin" to support widespread investment in information concerning the expected future yields and supply conditions for every capital good. Individual investors may discover new little-known opportunities to employ such assets or locate owners who are unaware of other potential buyers. In either case, the purchaser may turn his or her information into a profit.

It will be convenient for our purposes here to assume that such assets are not produced at all but exist in an unchanging quantity. An example of such an asset is land in a particular location. Let us assume further that the potential purchaser knows of the demand for this asset and predicts correctly that it will yield an equilibrium rental price of R^* per year. From equation (15.3), we know that for any purchase price c less than R^*A the owner may obtain a profit. However, he or she need not hold the asset for its entire service life in order to obtain this profit. The owner may simply sell it to someone else who is also knowledgeable about its true rental value. In doing so, he or she may capture the full profits obtainable.

Let us define c^* as the asset purchase price at which ΔW is exactly equal to zero, that is, $c^* = R^*A$. At a purchase price of c^* an investor acquiring the asset neither gains nor loses wealth. Other investors aware of the asset's expected yield of R^* per year will thus be willing to pay c^* to obtain it. The initial purchaser, who obtains this asset at a price, c, less than c^* and sells it for c^*, earns $c^* - c$ on the transaction. Clearly, the investor's gain on the purchase and sale of the asset is the same ΔW that he or she would have obtained had it been held for its entire service life. We can see this by simply substituting c^* for R^*A in equation (15.3); this yields:

$$\Delta W = c^* - c.$$

As the discovery of such underpriced assets yields immediate profits to those who find them, we can expect that investors will exert great effort to uncover such assets. This will have the beneficial effect of withdrawing capital from activities where it is less valuable and shifting it to activities of greater value. This process itself will drive capital asset prices toward c^*—that is, toward the value of their capitalized service stream.

Property Taxes and Tax Relief

In the latter half of the 1970s, Americans experienced a phenomenon referred to by both the media and academic circles as the "Tax Revolt." Citizens' groups, despondent over continually rising taxes and their apparent inability to obtain relief through traditional state legislative processes, began to seek tax reductions through statewide referenda. The most publicized of the few real successes of this movement was the adoption by California of its Proposition 13 in 1977, which placed a cap on state and local property taxes, lowering them in some cases by as much as 75 percent.

One of the most frequently heard—and therefore presumably most persuasive—arguments in favor of this proposition was that property taxes had increased to such an extent that individual families could no longer afford to purchase housing. A large number of citizens who lived in rental housing also supported the proposition, believing that the high taxes also contributed to the high cost of renting. While such arguments sound quite plausible, it can be shown that both are false. Taxes, at least in the reasonably short run, affect the cost of neither owner-occupied nor rental housing. The passage of such property tax reductions provided a wealth increase to those investors (including individual homeowners) who held these capital assets at the time the measures were adopted. These measures provided nothing that in the short run would be expected to lower housing costs to either owners or renters.

The supply of housing is constrained by the available land in a particular community and changes only as new housing is constructed. In large metropolitan areas land use is very intensive, so that new housing must often be built on the site of old housing, which in turn must be removed. As the stock of existing housing is large relative to new building even where older housing is not displaced to accommodate it, the supply is very inelastic and in the short run may be treated as fixed. The demand for housing slopes downward for all the usual reasons. Conditions in a representative market are therefore as shown in Figure 15.13, which exhibits such demand and supply curves. The market-clearing price of housing services in such a market is R_1, and this is the value that consumers of these services place on them at the margin when q_1 are supplied.

Let us treat the case of rentals first, since that is the easier to dispose of. If the supply is reasonably fixed in the short run, then changes in the level of property taxation will not affect the quantity supplied. There is also no reason to expect a reduction in taxes affecting property owners to influence the demand for rental housing. If neither demand nor supply is affected by the change in taxation, there is no reason for the market-clearing rental price to change. On the contrary, one would predict no effect, and that is precisely what happens.

Even in the long run, the only effect on rental prices comes through the influence of taxes on the attractiveness of building additional housing and maintaining the old. If taxes rise sufficiently to actually discourage this activity, then property tax relief may in the long run expand supply and lower rental prices. However, property tax rates in most communities are too low to have much effect on the supply of housing. While the size of a property tax is often impressive, this is usually because the property itself is so valuable. As these prices reflect what people are willing to pay to obtain this real estate (along with its implicit tax liabilities), plenty of scope remains in most places for profitable investment in housing.

The case of owner-occupied housing is only superficially different. One may think of this case as one of real estate owners renting to themselves. As owners they will insist on getting as much value as they can for their houses. The value they derive from living in their homes must therefore be at least as much as the market rental price. Let that rental price (which is also the value placed on these

Figure 15.13 The Rental Rate for Housing

The demand for rental housing is given by D. This demand is unaffected by changes in the taxation of housing. The supply of rental housing is shown by the vertical supply curve S. In the short run, this curve will also be unaffected by changes in the taxation of housing. The rents charged by landlords will remain R_1 so long as this supply is unchanged.

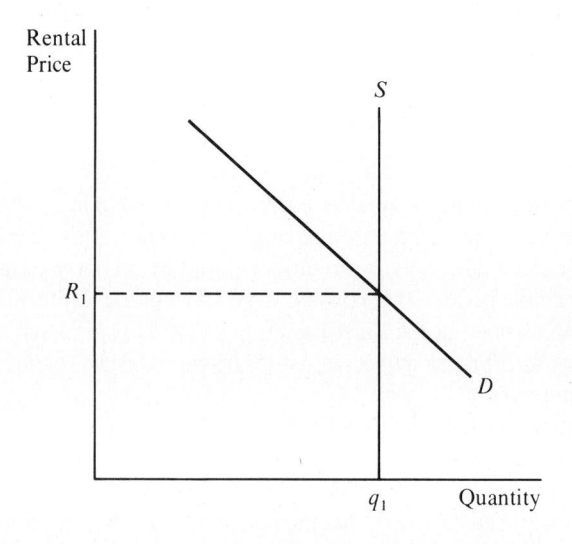

housing services) be R. As renters, on the other hand, they will insist that the housing services they receive at this price be at least as good as those they might obtain from other landlords. The effect of a reduction in tax will have no more effect on their demand for housing services than it will for any other renters. It is slightly more complicated to show that a tax reduction does not change the cost of renting to oneself.

Since the owners of the houses must pay the taxes, they therefore enjoy as a net return on their investment only what is left over after paying the taxes. For simplicity, let us assume that the tax itself, T, is unrelated to the value of the house. This simplifying assumption makes no difference to the point we are addressing here. Let the *net gain* on the ownership of this house be N, so that:

$$N + T = R.$$

Hence:

$$N = R - T.$$

Since R is unaffected by a change in tax,

$$\Delta N = -\Delta T.$$

The asset price of such a house will reflect only the net gain from ownership. In equilibrium, this asset will be worth the present value of these net returns. Let the house price be P, which will thus be equal to $N \cdot A$. Changes in the expected net return stream will bear the following relationship to house prices:

$$P + \Delta P = (N + \Delta N)A.$$

Thus:

$$\Delta P = \Delta N \cdot A$$

(15.5)
$$\Delta P = -\Delta T \cdot A.$$

Earlier we argued that capital asset prices move to that level which reflects the expected present value of the return stream of the assets. This change in the property tax on housing affects the net returns enjoyed by property owners and is thus capitalized into the price of that housing. One effect of the California tax reduction is clear: Homeowners, at the time that Proposition 13 was passed, earned profits on their status as property owners equal to the capitalized value of the tax reduction in all future years.

Since the tax nevertheless declined, and property tax is clearly a part of the cost of owning a home, how is it that this did not lower the cost of home ownership? As the asset price of a house rises, the opportunity cost of holding that house rises, and it can be shown that the rise in the opportunity cost will just offset the property tax reduction. *The net effect is therefore no change in the total cost of home ownership.*

In our previous discussion we saw that this opportunity cost per year per dollar of capital is equal to $1/A$. Let this opportunity cost of owning a house be designated c, so that:

$$c = P \cdot 1/A.$$

Thus:

$$c + \Delta c = (P + \Delta P) \cdot 1/A.$$

Hence:

$$\Delta c = \Delta P \cdot 1/A.$$

Substituting for ΔP from equation (15.5), we see that:

$$\Delta c = -\Delta T.$$

Consider the meaning of this result carefully. Lowering the taxes on property lowers the tax cost of these services without reducing their value to the market or in owner use. The value of these services net of taxes (the net return) is therefore increased. This increase in the net return will be capitalized into higher house prices. Increases in asset prices increase the opportunity cost of holding wealth in this form. As the expression we just derived makes clear, the increase in this opportunity cost per year turns out to be precisely equal to the tax reduction. Lowering the tax does *not*, therefore, lower the cost of home ownership; it merely shifts the relative importance of the two ways in which that cost is borne.

Those of us who were homeowners in California during the Proposition 13 campaign were, of course, delighted by its passage. Developments in the Los Angeles real estate market was a topic that few around the economics lunch table at UCLA never tired of discussing. As the prices of our houses increased, we all began to feel very wise for having invested in this real estate. We also felt wealthier. Although the opportunity cost of remaining in our homes had not decreased, our wealth had increased. We could look forward to a stream of reduced tax payments into the future, implying more purchasing power in each year could be devoted to other goods. The capitalized value of this reduced taxation in each year was reflected in the higher house prices; hence, these profits could be realized into current purchasing power by selling one's house. The problem with doing this and remaining in Los Angeles was that it left one with nowhere to live. As all house prices there had risen, selling one house at a high price merely made it necessary to purchase another at a high price. The only way that these wealth increases due to the tax reduction could be converted into current purchasing power was to leave the state. Some did.

Summary

In this chapter we analyzed choice within an intertemporal context. We first posited a financial sector in which claims to purchasing power were exchanged. By assuming that these claims were exchanged costlessly, we were able to derive opportunity sets permitting each household to select a consumption pattern over time that equated the marginal rate of substitution of consumption in each period with its opportunity cost in terms of present consumption. We defined wealth as the present exchange value of claims in all periods for claims to present purchasing power.

We defined saving as present income minus consumption. We developed an individual supply of saving function by observing the change in saving associated with shifts in the opportunity set due to changes in the interest rate. We showed that the slope of this individual savings function depends on the relative magnitudes of the substitution effect and the income effect of the interest rate change. The total supply of saving available for investment is the difference between total income in each period and total consumption.

We discussed two types of savings functions, the compensated and uncompensated supply curves for loanable funds. The former contains only substitution effects that yield greater savings, hence a larger supply of loanable funds, at higher interest rates. These curves are appropriate for the analysis of most policy considerations. Taxes and other policies that affect the opportunity cost of deferring consumption do not typically affect the ability of the economy to produce alternative combinations of present and future consumption. However, they do affect the particular combination chosen. The apparent increases in the real income of savers obtained from higher interest rates associated with such policies are compensated for by increases in taxes or other resource withdrawals. Real incomes are largely unaffected by interest rate changes resulting from such policies.

The uncompensated supply of savings reflects both the substitution and the income effects of interest rate changes, and these curves may have either slope. They are typically the result not of policy but of changes in technology, which increase the productivity of capital and make possible the production of more present **and** *future consumption. Changes in the saving rate observed in the past reflect a combination of these types of influences as well as changing fiscal policy.*

We analyzed the demand for loanable funds by permitting individuals to exchange portions of their income endowments in each period. We defined wealth as the present value of the entire income endowment of the household. Exchanges of present and future claims to income can increase wealth, and we saw that increased wealth is clearly welfare increasing for investors, leading to the present value rule governing investment choice. Higher interest rates make all potential investments less attractive and in some cases discourage investment entirely. The demand for loanable funds is therefore negatively sloped. The market interest rate is that which equates the quantities of loanable funds demanded and supplied.

Investment in assets that last more than two periods may be evaluated just like investments in two-period analysis. This is done by calculating the effect of such investments on household wealth. The present value of the return stream for investments yielding a constant expected return may be calculated by using the annuity factor. The inverse of the annuity factor measures the opportunity cost of investment per dollar per year. The long-run supply price of the services of capital assets may thus be computed as the supply price of the asset times the appropriate opportunity cost factor. In declining industries, the service price may remain below this long-run equilibrium value for long periods. In such cases we expect to see a diminished rate of capital replacement with a consequent aging capital stock.

The theory we developed also provides insights into the pricing of capital assets. These should be priced to reflect the present value of their lifetime service streams. Profits may be earned by purchasing these assets where the value of their services is low and shifting them to higher-valued uses. Shifting the employment of capital in this way permits a higher-valued service stream to be capitalized in the asset price. These profits may be obtained either by holding the asset and accepting the higher return or by selling the asset to someone else. The change in wealth associated with the transaction will be the same in either case.

Changes in property taxes affect the net gain from owning real estate and thus affect property values. Reductions in property taxes will therefore affect the prices of real estate. As taxation of property has no effect on demand and only a negligible effect on supply in the short run, changes in these taxes will have no effect on rental prices of housing. Changes in property taxes also have little effect on the cost of owner-occupied housing. The chief effect of property tax reduction is therefore to increase the wealth of those who presently own real estate, both landlords and individual homeowners. In no way does it lower the cost of housing to members of the community.

Key Concepts

saving
income endowment
wealth
present value
uncompensated supply curve for
   loanable funds
compensated supply curve for loanable
   funds

cost of the investment
return on the investment
discount factor
the present value rule
net return
constant yield asset
annuity factor
infinitely lived assets

real assets
financial assets
investment
profits on investments
wealth maximization

supply of capital services
declining industry
capital recovery factor
depreciation
capitalization

Questions

1. *Easy* Show diagrammatically the effect of an increase in the interest rate on the opportunity set of present and future consumption for a two-period model. Show how the income effect of this increase raises the consumption of persons who have been saving at the original interest rate.

Hard Show how someone who was a net borrower at the original interest rate is made worse off by the above interest rate change. What will be the effect of interest rate increases on the consumption of those who would be borrowers at the initial rate?

2. *Easy* Martha Maloney is wondering how to finance her new home computer. She can (a) pay $1000 now, (b) pay $139 per year for 10 years, or (c) make three payments of $400 each: one now, another at the end of the fifth, and the third at the end of the tenth year. The interest rate is 8 percent. Using Table 15.1 at the end of these questions determine which option will minimize Martha's cost.

Hard An asset that yields valuable services for an infinite length of time (like a well or a scientific discovery) does not have infinite value. Explain.

3. *Easy* The demand for loanable funds must slope downward. Show why investment projects that are attractive at low interest rates can be made less attractive—and even absolutely unattractive—by increasing the interest rate.

Hard An increase in wealth associated with an investment is called the profit on that investment as well as the net return. Explain how we can assert that a wealth-increasing investment will invariably leave the investor better off regardless of the combination of income that it provides. Explain why wealth-decreasing investments invariably harm him or her.

4. *Easy* A patent protects the rights of the holder to be the monopoly supplier of a product for 17 years. However, the developer of a new drug must obtain approval from the Food and Drug Administration in order to market it, requiring lengthy testing of its safety and efficacy. This testing may require many years before approval after the patent is issued. What will be the effect on the profitability of investment in the research on new drugs of regulatory changes requiring even more lengthy testing?

Hard In the United States, medical school and residency for physician specialists consume at least seven years of a potential entrant's working life—that is, it delays entrance into the labor force for at least seven years. By not choosing a medical career, the qualified applicant can expect to earn $24,000 per year in another career for the next 47 years.

    a. Assuming that the appropriate discount rate is 8 percent and retirement ages for both careers are the same, would you expect earnings of medical specialists earning $40,000 per year to rise or fall? (Hint: Consult Table 15.1.)

b. What would you predict the long-run equilibrium earnings of these physicians to be?

5. *Easy* What is meant by the phrase *declining industry*? It has been argued that capital assets in declining industries will typically be older, less well maintained, and infrequently replaced when they wear out. Explain.

Hard Machine A was originally priced at $800,000. It will last indefinitely and requires no maintenance. This machine requires a crew of four workers to operate it at a total wage cost of $100,000 per year. Machine B is introduced at a lower purchase price of only $700,000. It also will last indefinitely and requires no maintenance, but it can be operated with a crew of two lower-wage workers at an annual total wage cost of only $40,000 per year. The interest rate is 10 percent.

a. It will not pay a present owner to "scrap" machine A and replace it with machine B even though both the purchase price and the operating cost for machine B are lower. Explain.

b. Ignoring moving and installation costs, we can predict the long-run equilibrium secondhand price of machine A in a market where machine B is available to all at the $700,000 price. That resale price for machine A will be $100,000. Explain. (Hint: Remember that firms will earn zero profits in long-run equilibrium.)

6. *Easy* Earl Thompson is considering a business venture. He wants to open a chain of commercial basketball courts around the country that may be rented by the hour. He calculates that he can build each court for $28,000 and that operating costs will be $65,000 per installation. The courts would have to be "scrapped" after 25 years. If the interest rate is 8 percent, what will Thompson have to gross per year to break even?

Hard Property taxes may be said to reduce the wealth of homeowners but leave the cost of housing unchanged. Under what circumstances is this true?

Table 15.1 Future Value, Present Value, Annuity and Capital Recovery Factors for Interest Rate of 8 Percent

Year	$(1 + r)^n$	$1/(1 + r)^n$	Annuity Factor	Capital Recovery Factor
1	1.08	.93	.93	1.08
2	1.17	.86	1.78	.56
3	1.26	.79	2.58	.39
4	1.36	.74	3.31	.30
5	1.47	.68	3.99	.25
6	1.59	.63	4.62	.22
7	1.71	.58	5.21	.19
8	1.85	.54	5.74	.17
9	2.00	.50	6.25	.16
10	2.16	.46	6.71	.15
11	2.33	.43	7.14	.14
12	2.52	.40	7.54	.13
13	2.72	.37	7.90	.13
14	2.94	.34	8.24	.12
15	3.17	.32	8.56	.12
16	3.43	.29	8.85	.11
17	3.70	.27	9.12	.11
18	4.00	.25	9.37	.11
19	4.32	.23	9.60	.10
20	4.66	.21	9.82	.10
25	6.85	.20	10.67	.09
30	10.06	.18	11.26	.09
35	14.79	.17	11.65	.09
40	21.72	.16	11.92	.08
45	31.92	.15	12.11	.08
50	46.90	.14	12.23	.08
∞	∞	0	12.50	.08

Part Six

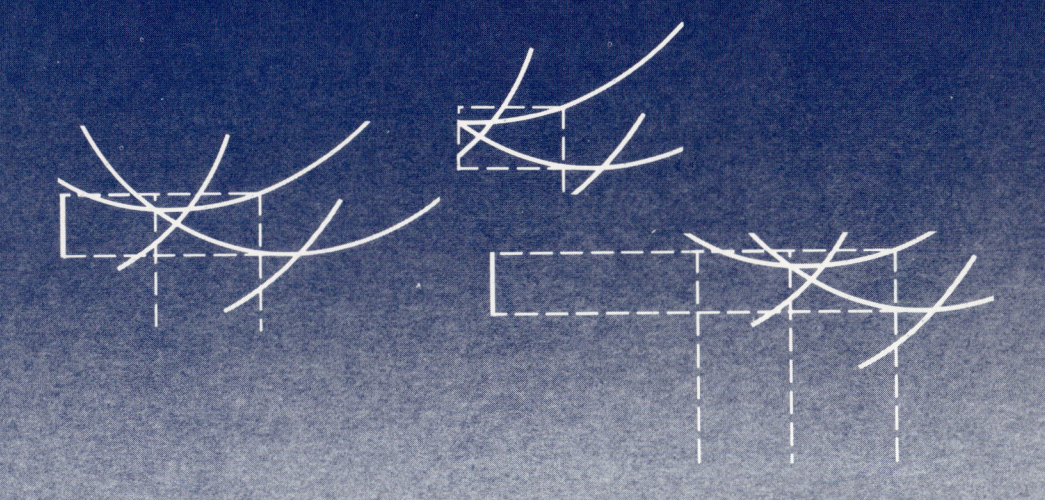

The Big Picture

Chapter 16

The Distribution of Income

Connections   Many readers will find this the most interesting and useful chapter in the book. Few economic issues are pondered more searchingly than the question of why others so obviously less deserving make more money than we do. Economic theory cannot promise to provide a fully satisfying answer to this question.

This chapter explores the sources of income variation in considerable detail. Since more than three fourths of all income is wages, most of our discussion here concerns itself with variation in wage rates. We can go a considerable distance in this discussion with the simple demand and supply analysis presented in Chapter 2. Surprisingly, the theory of labor supply plays a smaller, though important, role in the discussion of wage rate variation than does the theory of the supply of capital. The reason for this is that people invest in their productivity as workers. A familiarity with the basic ideas in Chapter 15 is therefore essential preparation for this chapter. The observed correlation between earnings and level of education has several competing explanations in economic theory that have yet to be empirically resolved. These are given equal time in this chapter.

The chapter ends on a note of discord. In the final section we examine the impact of prejudice and discrimination on wage disparity. This material relies quite heavily on the theory of factor demand developed in Chapter 12.

In a market economy household income represents the revenues from the sale of the services of resources supplied by the household. In the preceding chapters we developed the analysis of the determination of the market prices commanded by those services. Firms require them for production, and the quantities they are willing to purchase depend on factor productivity and prices offered. On the other hand, the quantities households are willing to supply depend on the prices they are offered and the opportunity cost of those resources in the home. These forces determine an equilibrium market price for each resource. Household income in each market is therefore determined by these prices and by the endowments of the resources. In a competitive market all prices paid for the same resource must be equal. Variation in income within a single market must therefore be directly related to variation in endowments. This chapter will analyze the extent to which household incomes vary due to variation in wealth.

All income variation is not explained in these terms. As we shall see in the analysis to follow, economic theory is consistent with varying equilibrium prices for the same resource across markets. To a certain extent, then, variation in income is also due to variation in the prices that resources in each household command in the market in which they supply them. The sources of intermarket price variation and its implications for the distribution of income in the American economy are also explored here.

16.1 The Distribution of Total Family Income

In 1979, mean family income was $22,376. Individual income varied considerably around this mean. Table 16.1 presents the percentage of families earning incomes in each income interval in that year. To a certain degree this table understates the extent of income variation, for federal census statistics include as income government transfers such as social security benefits and welfare payments. These totaled $294.2 billion in 1980, roughly 14 percent of total income in that year. As these income transfers are not payments for factor services, their inclusion in Table 16.1

Table 16.1   *Distribution of Family Income, 1979*

Family Income	% of Families
Under $5,000	7.0
5,000– 9,999	13.6
10,000–14,999	15.6
15,000–19,999	15.0
20,000–24,999	14.4
25,000–34,999	19.2
35,000–49,999	10.3
50,000 and over	5.2

Source: *U. S. Statistical Abstract, 1982.*

Chapter 16 The Distribution of Income   519

overstates the income of many, such as the retired and disabled at the lower end of the income spectrum.

Even ignoring this potential bias, the variation in income revealed in the table is considerable. Nearly 35 percent of the population earns at least $25,000 per year and therefore at least five times more than the lowest 7 percent. Before attempting to assess the appropriateness of such a distribution or the advisability of policies aimed at altering it, we must consider its sources.

The Distribution of Wealth

As noted earlier, one important source of income variation is variation in household endowments of productive resources. If the distribution of these resources is uneven among the population, then the distribution of total income, including payments for these resources, will clearly vary from household to household. Even if the wage rate for labor were equal everywhere, variation in wealth would produce unequal total incomes. The distribution of wealth for 1970 is presented in Table 16.2 along with the income distribution for that year. Included in this measure of wealth are such items as corporate stock, short-term debt, real estate, business equity, and consumer durables. This measure is an imperfect reflection of this distribution, because it fails to include wealth held in the form of life insurance and pension funds, which accounted for roughly $200 billion or 6 percent of all wealth in 1970. Their inclusion would have reduced the dispersion of wealth among the population.[1]

From Table 16.2 it is nevertheless clear that wealth is even more unevenly dispersed than income. The 22.3 percent with incomes over $15,000 in 1970 pos-

Table 16.2 *Distribution of Wealth and Income, 1970*

Income Group	% Distribution of Families	% Distribution of Wealth
Under $2,000	4.6	2.68
2,000– 2,999	4.3	2.92
3,000– 3,999	5.1	2.93
4,000– 4,999	5.3	3.04
5,000– 5,999	5.8	3.26
6,000– 6,999	6.0	3.18
7,000– 9,999	19.9	11.65
10,000–14,999	26.8	18.97
15,000–24,999	17.7	22.96
25,000 and over	4.6	28.41

Median income = $9867

Sources: *U. S. Statistical Abstract, 1976*, and Stanley Lebergott, *The American Economy: Income, Wealth and Want* (Princeton, N.J.: Princeton University Press, 1967), 246.

---

[1]Stanley Lebergott, *The American Economy: Income, Wealth and Want* (Princeton, N.J.: Princeton University Press, 1976), 238.

Table 16.3 *Percentage of Personal Income by Source*

	1950	1960	1970	1980
Labor Income	70.1	73.9	76.6	75.8
Wages and Salaries	68.4	71.0	72.3	68.8
Private Sector	57.9	58.2	56.9	55.8
Government	10.5	12.9	15.4	13.0
Other Labor Income	1.7	2.9	4.3	7.0
Nonlabor Income	29.9	26.1	23.3	24.2
Proprietors' Income	18.0	12.3	8.7	6.7
Farm	6.4	3.1	1.9	1.2
Nonfarm	11.6	9.3	6.8	5.5
Rental Income	3.3	3.8	2.6	1.6
Dividend Income	4.1	3.5	2.9	2.8
Personal Interest	4.5	6.5	9.1	13.1
Personal Income*	100.0	100.0	100.0	100.0

*Pre-tax, pre-transfer.
Source: *U. S. Statistical Abstract, 1982*, and author's computations.

sessed more than half of the personal wealth of the population. The 25 percent who had incomes of less than $7000 controlled only 18 percent of the wealth.

What can we make of these statistics? One fact that stands out boldly is that there are other factors besides these capital claims that produce variation in family income. If all other sources of income did not vary, the distribution of family income would exactly mirror that of the distribution of wealth. In equilibrium all assets would earn an equal rate of return; hence, income from capital holdings would be roughly equal to the rate of return times the value of the household portfolio. The fact that the two distributions are so dissimilar suggests that variations in other sources of income—in particular, wage earnings—have an important influence on the distribution of income.

This conclusion is supported by the data in Table 16.3. In this table we find the proportion of personal income accounted for by human and nonhuman resources. Personal income figures have been adjusted for these computations. As already noted, standard government accounts include income transfers in official measures of personal income. These transfers have been deleted from the base figure in computing these percentages. Contributions to social insurance are also deducted in standard reporting. As we are chiefly interested in the distribution of factor earnings prior to their disposition, these deletions have been restored to the base figure of personal income. Other labor income represents contributions by employers to social insurance plans.

The share going to labor is large and seems to have risen during the thirty years of observation represented in Table 16.3. This rise would have been more pronounced had it not been for the large increase in the share going to interest payments in the 1960s and 1970s. This increase exaggerates the importance of interest payments as a source of income during those years. This is due to the high rates of inflation in that period. Recall that inflation diminishes the real value of claims denominated in money values. The high interest rates in more recent years do not therefore imply a larger return on capital invested; they are high in order both to pay returns to suppliers and to compensate them for the lost purchasing power of the dollars they have loaned.

Reflection on these figures also makes clear why the distribution of wealth failed to explain the whole picture of the distribution of income. Nonlabor income accounts for only about one fourth of all income received in this country. Rental income, which popular 19th-century economics amateur Henry George hoped would finance the entire public sector, would today hardly make a dent in the government payroll, not to mention its purchases of other resources. If nonlabor income accounts for only one fourth of total household income, even substantial variation in the shares of wealth producing it will clearly have a far less dramatic overall impact.

A far more important factor than the distribution of wealth influencing the distribution of income is the age of the wage earners. Young people entering the labor force do not expect to earn the same wages over their entire careers. They expect their earnings to rise over time as they gain experience and are moved to jobs of greater responsibility. Once their families are self-sufficient and have accumulated household assets like homes and automobiles, most plan to retire on a smaller income than they earned in their 40s and 50s. The life cycle of earnings for the typical worker forms a curve that is convex upward, reaching a peak at about 50 years and declining thereafter. Median family income by age of the head of household for 1970 is shown in Table 16.4, together with the number of families in each grouping.

A comparison of information in Tables 16.2 and 16.4 is instructive. Both tables reflect income received in 1970. Clearly, a large number of the families in the former table earning low incomes are either very young or very old. The income inequality observed in Table 16.2 reflects to a substantial degree variation in the age of the income earners. Since at any time society contains large numbers of people from all age categories, the degree to which a given distribution of income among families reflects a permanent disparity in economic well-being is greatly exaggerated.

Table 16.4 *Median Family Income by Age of Head of Household, 1970*

Age Group of Head of Household	Number (1000s)	% Total Families	Median Income
14–24	3,190	7.2	$ 7,630
25–34	9,291	21.0	10,359
35–44	9,342	21.1	12,086
45–54	9,396	21.2	12,941
55–64	7,313	16.5	10,723
65–over	5,797	13.1	4,990

Source: *U. S. Statistical Abstract, 1976.*

Morton Paglin has examined the influence of age on the distribution of income and found that about one third of the income inequality in recent years is attributable to age alone.[2] Conventional measures of inequality that ignore the age factor overstate it by roughly 50 percent. Paglin also developed a measure of income inequality exclusive of variation due to age and computed this measure for most years from 1947 to 1972. These estimates revealed a steady and substantial decline in the extent of income inequality over this period. According to Paglin, income inequality has declined over this quarter of the century by more than one fifth.

We turn now to an analysis of the factors that give rise to variation in wage rates. Much of the difference in income due to age results from wage rate variation over the life cycle. As will be seen in the next section, occupation, region, sex, and race also play important roles in the distribution of income via their influence on wages. A complete understanding of the forces giving rise to income inequality must therefore confront the underlying economic explanation for wage rate variation among workers in these groups.

16.2 The Distribution of Earnings

Even if we restrict our range of observation to males, we observe a great deal of variation in earnings from occupation to occupation and region to region. Consider Table 16.5, which presents *means* of the earnings of men by broad classes of occupations and sections of the country. Women and minority workers earn less than men in every class and section, and even within such groupings earnings vary considerably. This variation raises a serious challenge to economic theory.

In our analysis of the market for labor in Chapter 14 we treated workers and jobs as perfectly homogeneous. This approach clearly must be modified if we are to deal with markets that are characterized by persistent and extensive wage variation. Consider Figure 16.1, which depicts the demand curves for labor in two sectors. At this point different sectors may represent different parts of the country, different occupations, different shifts, or any other aspect of employment chosen by suppliers of labor. For simplicity we will assume that individual supply curves are perfectly inelastic so that one unit of labor is supplied by each worker. Supply curve S_A in panel (a) therefore shows the number of workers supplying labor to that sector, while S_B reveals the same information for the alternative sector. Given this distribution of workers between the two sectors, wage rates will be P_A and P_B, respectively.

Clearly, this is not an equilibrium under the assumptions we have been employing. As P_A exceeds P_B we should expect some workers to "migrate" from sector B to sector A. As this shift of workers progresses, wage rates will fall in sector A and rise in sector B, reflecting the shift in the supply curves in each panel. Only when the supply curves have shifted to positions S'_A and S'_B, at which wages are

---

[2] Morton Paglin, "The Measurement and Trend of Inequality: A Basic Revision," *American Economic Review* 65 (September 1975): 598–699.

Chapter 16 The Distribution of Income

Table 16.5   Median Earnings of Full-Time Employed Male Workers in 1969 by Region and Occupation

	Northeast	Central	South	West
Experienced Civilian Labor Force	$ 8,856	$ 8,864	$ 7,365	$ 9,276
Professional/Technical	12,156	11,538	11,053	12,280
Managers/Administrators (nonfarm)	12,585	11,961	10,427	12,164
Craftsmen	8,921	9,370	7,536	9,387
Operatives (nontransport)	7,502	8,082	6,148	8,048
Nonfarm Laborers	6,683	6,870	4,721	7,002
Farmers/Farm Managers	5,415	5,366	4,049	5,919
Farm Laborers and Foremen	4,108	3,523	3,096	4,843

Source: U. S. Department of Commerce, Bureau of the Census, 1970 *Census of Population*.

Figure 16.1   Equilibrium in the Distribution of Labor

Demand curves D_A and D_B reflect the demands for labor in the two sectors considered. The two vertical supply surves, S_A and S_B, reflect the number of workers supplying labor in the two sectors. The market-clearing wages P_A and P_B are not equilibrium wages. Differing wages lead some workers in the low-wage sector to shift to the high-wage sector. This continues until wages in the two sectors are equal.

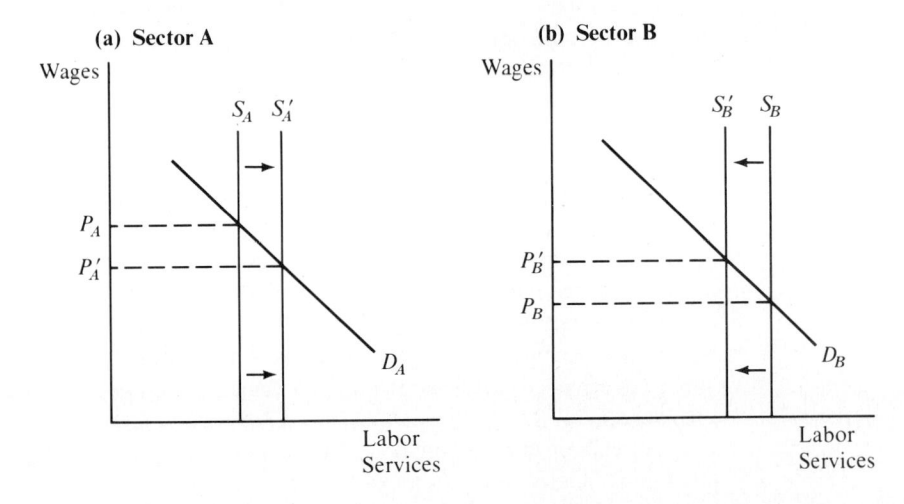

equal between sectors, is the model in equilibrium. So long as workers are identical and thus interchangeable in production, each will have the same productivity and thus the same demand price as any other worker from either sector. And so long as all workers are free to choose and all jobs are regarded by all workers as identical, no worker will remain in one sector when he or she could obtain a higher wage in another. No employers will be willing to pay one worker more than another, and no worker will work for less in one job than another. Our assumptions lead unequivocally to the conclusion that there should be no variation in wages in the long run.

Sources of Wage Variation

We can derive some interesting implications by relaxing the assumptions made in Figure 16.1. Workers are not homogeneous, nor are all jobs regarded as equally rewarding by workers. However, we may go further—for there are specific aspects of occupational choice that may be developed into powerful theories of income distribution. We will begin with the most obvious deviation from the equilibrium just described—the case in which workers are not free to choose.

Coercion

Assume that in the initial situation shown in Figure 16.1 workers are *not* free to move from sector B to sector A. The wage differential existing between the sectors would be permanent. Supply curves would not shift; thus, the market-clearing wage in each sector would remain the same. Examples of such barriers are immigration controls, licensure, and union contracts. The Union of South Africa patrols its borders vigorously to prevent the covert immigration of citizens of its neighboring countries to the north. As it seems highly implausible that these refugees are seeking a more liberal political climate, we must conclude that the chief motive for their migration is economic: These would-be immigrants are seeking the higher wages offered in the South. We may assume that in the absence of border restrictions wages in South Africa would fall toward their level in the north.

Union dealings with employers have much the same effect. Let the two sectors in Figure 16.1 be union and nonunion, respectively. The only way that the union may protect the high wages that it obtains from employers is to prevent lower-paid nonunion workers from moving into their sector. These workers from sector B (called "scabs" by the higher-paid workers of sector A) would otherwise offer to work for less than the wage demanded by the unionized workers. This migration is prevented by **coercion**. The union makes it clear to nonunion workers that the wages net of the costs that they are capable of imposing on stubborn strike breakers are not likely to be higher than their wages in sector B. They also warn employers that dealings with nonunion workers are not likely to be as profitable as might appear once the costs of possible damage to property and equipment are considered.

As much of this intimidation of worker and employer is illegal, unions have often found it expedient to seek government support for barriers to worker migration. One method is, of course, licensure. If cab drivers, barbers, butchers, and bakers must obtain licenses to practice these trades, then control of the number of licenses issued will control the supply of workers in these sectors.

Another, more subtle, method is the minimum wage. Most union workers earn far more than the minimum wage; hence, there seems little reason (other than concern for fair play, of course) for unions to support increases in the minimum wage. Yet the first successful federal labor legislation achieved by the labor movement was a wage and hour law passed long before Roosevelt and the New Deal. In Chapter 14 we discussed how the minimum wage discouraged training and the acquisition of skills, therefore discouraging entry into markets in competition with other skilled suppliers. Employees cannot reimburse employers for investing in their training by accepting a wage less than their marginal revenue product. Strict enforcement of minimum wage laws therefore limits entry into skilled trades earning far higher wages than those stipulated by the legislation.

Variation in Ability

People are different, and not so simply because they have acquired different bundles of skills and talents. On the contrary, Mozart was remarkably musical before he could read and write language, and Joseph Haydn as a child had to conceal his musical aspirations (as well as his practice) from his father. Few dedicated musicians with a lifetime of work and study behind them, not to mention fellowships and instruction at prestigious music academies, have accomplished what these two artists achieved before they reached the age of 25. The author occasionally fantasizes that with more determination, better training and fewer attractive alternative career opportunities he might have been able to shoot a basketball like Doctor J and pass like the Bird. However, no one who has ever seen him with a basketball in his hands agrees. Likewise, few of us will ever be able to sing like Pavarotti, dance like Nureyev, catch like Johnny Bench or ride like Willie the Shoe, even with expert coaching and true grit. The variation in native ability is unquestionably huge.

Fortunately for most of us, earnings do not vary nearly as widely as does, say, the ability to strike out a major league batter. Variation in **ability** does not translate directly into variation in wage rates; the connection is much more subtle. Few people are good at everything and, more importantly, most people are reasonably good at something. The influence of ability on earnings is limited to variation in the performance of people who have chosen that activity as an occupation—and most people choose to do what they are best at. Great singers earn more than moderately good ones, but not necessarily more than brain surgeons. Great salesmen earn more than less effective ones, but not necessarily more than airline pilots. There are many lawyers who cannot throw a football or sing a note who earn more than very good quarterbacks or sensational baritones. The relationship between the average earnings of singers and lawyers is influenced less by ability differences than by demand and other considerations.

Tastes for Work of Different Types

Just as employers do not regard all workers as homogeneous, workers do not regard all jobs as equivalent. Some involve the risk of injury or death. Others involve unpleasant or demeaning working conditions. Still others subject the worker to insecurity of income or foreshortened career. Workers will not choose to become test pilots for the same salary they might earn flying commercial airliners.

They will not install roofing for the same wages they might earn as house painters. They will not work as morticians for the same pay as butchers, or as commercial songwriters for the same expected pay as orchestra musicians. Universal **tastes**, such as the aversion toward pain and suffering, the attractiveness of fame and social position, or the avoidance of risk have straightforward implications for the wage rate structure.

These job attributes may be thought of as goods. Just as workers are willing to give up income to obtain food and clothing, so will they sacrifice income to obtain jobs with desired characteristics. If the good aspects of a job are worth more than the existing wage differential between that job and the next most attractive position, the worker will accept it even though it implies less pay. Under such circumstances, the equilibrium depicted in Figure 16.1 will be modified. Assume that jobs in sector B are more attractive to workers than jobs in sector A. At equal wages such as P'_A and P'_B workers will migrate to the more attractive sector. This migration will shift supply leftward in sector A and rightward in sector B until the wage difference between the two sectors is exactly equal to the value that workers place on the preferred attributes of sector B.

Note that the observed wage difference in such circumstances does not imply that the higher-wage workers are in any sense better off than their lower-wage counterparts. The free mobility of workers between sectors insures they are equally well off—otherwise, they would relocate. The observed wage difference therefore merely reflects the willingness of some workers to purchase more pleasant working conditions out of income they might earn in less desirable occupations.

It is possible to squeeze some additional implications out of this approach. Let us assume that such attributes are normal goods and that increases in wealth increase the amount that workers are willing to pay for given amounts of them. Wage income can have little effect on this decision, since all workers confront the same wage rate opportunities. However, nonwage income has a predictable effect. Those workers with more nonwage income will be willing to give up more in wages to obtain attractive jobs than workers with less. This will lead to a stratification of workers with the wealthier ones filling the attractive but lower-paying jobs and those with less nonwage income opting for the less attractive but higher-paying ones.

This is illustrated in Figure 16.2. Assume that worker tastes for occupations are identical but that nonwage income varies from worker to worker. In panel (c) of this figure we depict a demand curve for the jobs in sector B relative to sector A. Because each worker consumes the same "quantity" of the attractive attributes in B, the demand curve may be thought of as an array of workers arranged from the worker willing to pay the most to the worker willing to pay the least. Assume too that there are h workers in total. Furthermore, because we have assumed that these job characteristics are normal goods, the worker at the left end of the array, who is willing to give up d_1 in wages for employment in sector B, has the highest nonwage income. The worker at the opposite end of the array has the lowest nonwage income and is therefore willing to give up only d_2 in wages to work in sector B.

The demand curves for labor in the two sectors are shown in panels (a) and (b). Consider how wages get determined in these two sectors. Assume that all workers were initially employed in sector B. This would imply a supply of h work-

Figure 16.2 *Equilibrium with Different Preferences for Sectors*

Each worker supplies one unit of work per period. In panel (c) the amount that each worker would give up in wages to work in sector B forms a demand curve for jobs in that sector. If all workers were in sector B, the wage rate there would be P_B. A worker who left this sector to work in sector A could earn P_A, a wage differential that is greater than anyone would accept to remain in sector B. Workers shift to sector A until the supply curve there has position S_A and the supply curve in sector B has position S_B. In panel (c) all workers to the left of h_B work in sector B, because they are willing to give up a wage differential of d_3 or more to remain there. Those to the right of h_B will work in sector A, because they value jobs in sector B less than this amount.

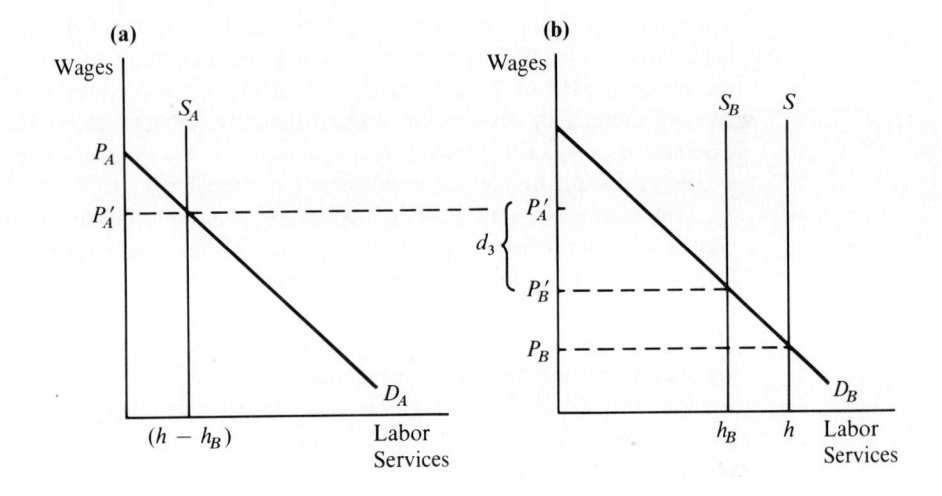

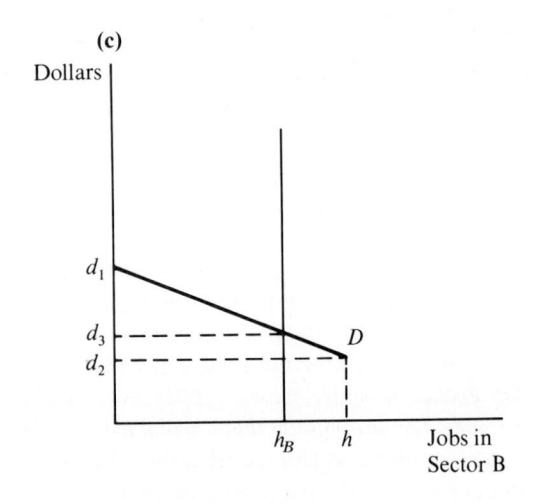

ers to this sector at a market-clearing wage of P_B, yielding a differential far greater than anyone would be willing to give up to remain in this more attractive sector. Assume that those willing to give up the least are the first to migrate. As this migration continues, the supply of labor to sector B shifts leftward while that to sector A shifts rightward, producing a rise in B's wages and a fall in A's wages. Equilibrium will be established when the supply curves to each sector take the positions S_A and S_B so that h_B workers are supplied to sector B and $h - h_B$ workers are supplied to sector A.

We may identify this as an equilibrium by noting the relationship of the amounts supplied to the array in panel (c). Such an equilibrium must satisfy the condition that no worker be influenced to change sectors. This will be true of the situation depicted by S_A and S_B. The wage differential $P'_A - P'_B$ is just equal to d_3 in panel (c). Under these circumstances exactly h_B workers will elect to remain in sector B and be willing to give up d_3 or more in earnings to do so. None of the workers to the left of h_B in the array will shift to sector A, since all are willing to give up more than the existing wage differential to work in B. The remaining workers, $h - h_B$, will prefer to work in sector A; the existing wage differential exceeds the value they place on the attractive characteristics of sector B.

The author is aware of no studies relating nonwage income to occupational choice, though this implication seems consistent with a bit of socioeconomic folklore. There it is maintained that a disproportionate number of successful entrepreneurs and risk takers have come from modest backgrounds while the products of more prosperous households have flown in disproportionate numbers into the secure and satisfying but less remunerative fields of education, government service, and the cloth. Such predictions suggest a far more pleasing social dynamic than the gloomy Darwinist depictions of capitalism popular in the last century.

Data on the turnover among the richest families in America in fact lend support to this view. Economic historian Stanley Lebergott has carefully studied lists of the wealthiest families from decade to decade since 1828 with the following rather startling conclusions:

(1) Of the families who make up the top 1 percent of the wealth distribution in one U. S. generation, about 40 percent fail to have heirs who appear in the next generation's top group.

(2) The share of U. S. personal wealth owned by the top 1 percent of the U. S. wealth distribution has neither clearly increased, nor decreased, over the past century.

(3) . . . the top 1 percent of wealth holders in recent generations has been heavily recruited from lower wealth classes. Given a minimum 40 percent attrition rate among established wealth holders, the nouveau riche will constitute over one-third of the top group, and may make up as much as two-thirds of the top group.

(4) The probability that anyone will rise from the lower 99 percent to the top 1 percent of the wealth distribution is less than 0.0002—or about as great as the chance of winning a top prize in the typical state lottery.[3]

---

[3] Stanley Lebergott, op. cit., 161ff.

Income Growth and Relative Wages

Consider the influence of secular increases in income for everyone on relative wages between sectors. In Figure 16.2 rises in income for all workers will shift the demand curve for desired working conditions in panel (c) upward. This implies that those workers formerly indifferent between working in either sector—that is, those workers at the margin—will no longer be indifferent at existing wage differentials. Along with everyone else they will now insist on a larger differential to remain in sector A. Unless this rise in income is accompanied by differentially large increases in productivity in sector A, we should expect a larger and larger proportion of workers to choose work in sector B. This in turn will be accompanied by increases in the equilibrium wage differential between sectors.

This implication also seems consistent with some stylized facts about labor markets in the postwar period. The author's generation grew up listening to complaints from its elders that "no one was willing to work anymore," which may be loosely interpreted to mean that the wages demanded for such tedious and laborious household jobs as nursemaids, cooks, washerwomen, and handymen were now beyond the means of most of their employers. Likewise, wages in many blue collar jobs, such as plumbers, painters, bus drivers, and stagehands, today compare much more favorably with white collar jobs than was true in earlier times. It is even possible that at least some of the momentum behind the recent movement to improve job safety through regulation and other means has its origins in the willingness of increasingly affluent American workers to give up larger amounts of income to obtain such a desirable job characteristic.

It Pays to be Different

This approach must be modified slightly where tastes differ among workers. Some workers prefer warm climates; some prefer cold. Some would rather work behind a desk, and some prefer to work outdoors. Some would rather give orders, and others are more comfortable being told what to do. These differences may not be related to income or to any other identifiable socioeconomic variable. To incorporate these variations in taste into our analysis, we will simply drop our demand curve for job attributes in sector B to a position at which it crosses the horizontal axis. We do this in Figure 16.3.

The arrangement of workers along the horizontal axis in panel (c) does not conform to any ordering such as income or wealth. Nevertheless, those at the left end of the demand curve are willing to give up the most earnings to work in sector B, while those further to the right are willing to give up less. Those on the extreme right, on the other hand, prefer to work in sector A. They must be compensated by the amount of the negative prices reflected on this part of the demand curve to accept employment in sector B. Alternatively, they would be willing to pay the amounts indicated to work in sector A.

Panels (a) and (b) again depict the demand curves for labor in the two sectors. Let the respective supply curves be given by S_A and S_B so that the same wage, P, is paid in each sector. This involves the supply of h_B workers to sector B and h_A workers—that is, $h - h_B$—to sector A. This clearly is not an equilibrium, because an equilibrium must leave all workers with no incentive to shift sectors. Those workers in panel (c) to the left of h_B have no incentive to shift sectors. They are

Figure 16.3   *It Pays to Be Different*

As in Figure 16.2, panel (c) depicts the amount workers will give up in lower wages to work in sector B. Some workers here prefer sector A, so this demand curve extends below the horizontal axis. With workers distributed between sectors so that wages are equal, some are led to migrate to sector B. With h_B workers in this sector, the marginal worker in sector A would give up some wages to have a job in sector B. A shift of the supply curve in sector B to S'_B with a corresponding shift in sector A to S'_A yields an equilibrium differential of d^*. Some workers in sector B would give up a great deal more to be there. Some in sector A would actually pay to be there but earn a premium instead.

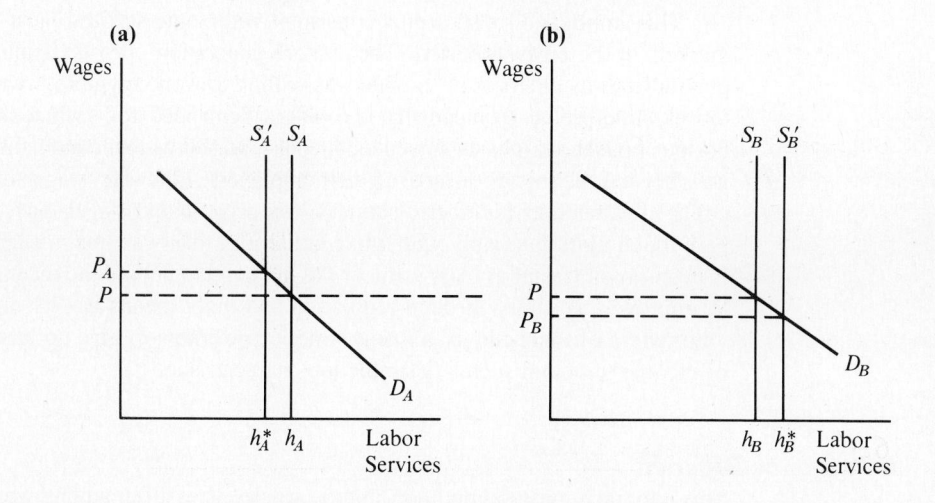

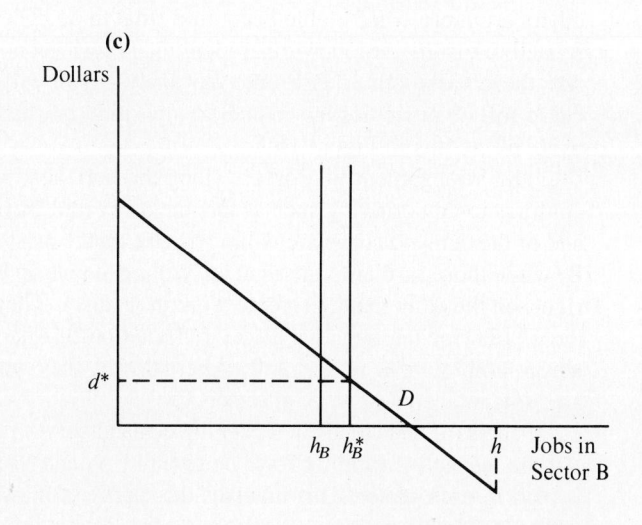

willing to accept lower earnings to have jobs in sector B, but in fact they are paying nothing for the job characteristics they desire. However, some workers to the right of h_B will wish to shift sectors. Among those working in sector A are some—those between h_B and the horizontal intercept of the demand curve—who would give up income to work in that sector. These workers prefer to work in sector B when both sectors pay the same. Again, however, a shift in workers from one sector to the other changes the wages paid. As workers shift to sector B the supply of workers there will shift to the right, causing wages to fall. The migration of workers from sector A, on the other hand, causes the supply there to shift leftward, raising wages.

This will be reflected in panel (c) by a rightward shift in h_B as increasing numbers of the total workforce, h, shift to sector B. Equilibrium is depicted by the distribution h_A^* and h_B^* in panels (a) and (b), producing wages P_A and P_B whose difference is d^* in panel (c). With this distribution and wage structure no worker will be influenced to shift sectors. In panel (c) all workers in sector B (those to the left of h_B^*) are willing to give up an earnings differential of at least d^* to work in that sector. All workers in sector A (to the right of h_B^*) are willing to give up less than d^* to obtain employment in sector B. As the earnings differential is d^*, these workers will not wish to change sectors—in fact, some of those working in sector A would give up income to work there but instead are paid a premium. It does indeed pay to be different!

16.3 Human Capital

Another element important in the decision to enter one occupation rather than another is the cost of obtaining the requisite qualifications to perform the work. One need not be a graduate of a haute cuisine academy to obtain employment as a cook, but a certain amount of training is required for employment even in the most unpretentious eatery. Carpenters, bricklayers, tennis players, musicians, and even business forecasters require training to obtain the skills necessary to perform their jobs, and training is a costly activity. The worker himself must bear the cost of this training even when, as is often the case, the employer provides it. The marginal factor cost of an employee cannot exceed his or her marginal revenue product, and if the employer offers costly training, the wages paid must be correspondingly reduced.

In choosing a job a worker will therefore consider not only the wages offered in each occupation but the cost of the training necessary to qualify. How are these two elements combined to influence the decision? Economists maintain that workers treat such decisions in the same way that they treat investments in physical capital. Job training costs are viewed as investments in **human capital**, whose yield is the higher earnings received only if the training is obtained. Entry into occupations requiring training may therefore be treated as an investment decision. If the present value of the wage premium received in each future year exceeds the cost of the training, people will enter the occupation and make the investment. If the present value of the wage premium is insufficient, however, the investment in

Figure 16.4 *Wage Differences Due to Human Capital Investment*

Panels (a) and (b) reflect market demand and supply in two occupations. Panel (c) depicts the age-earning profile of workers in the two occupations. Occupation B requires forgoing t years of work. The present value of earnings in occupation A (at an interest rate of zero) is the number of years worked times the income earned in each year. The present value of earnings in sector B is the same, but the number of years worked is lower. Equal incomes in each occupation do not constitute an equilibrium, because the present values of the earnings streams will not be the same. At equilibrium the cost of the investment in training, $t_1 P_A$, must just equal the value of the return, $(P_B - P_A)(T - t_1)$.

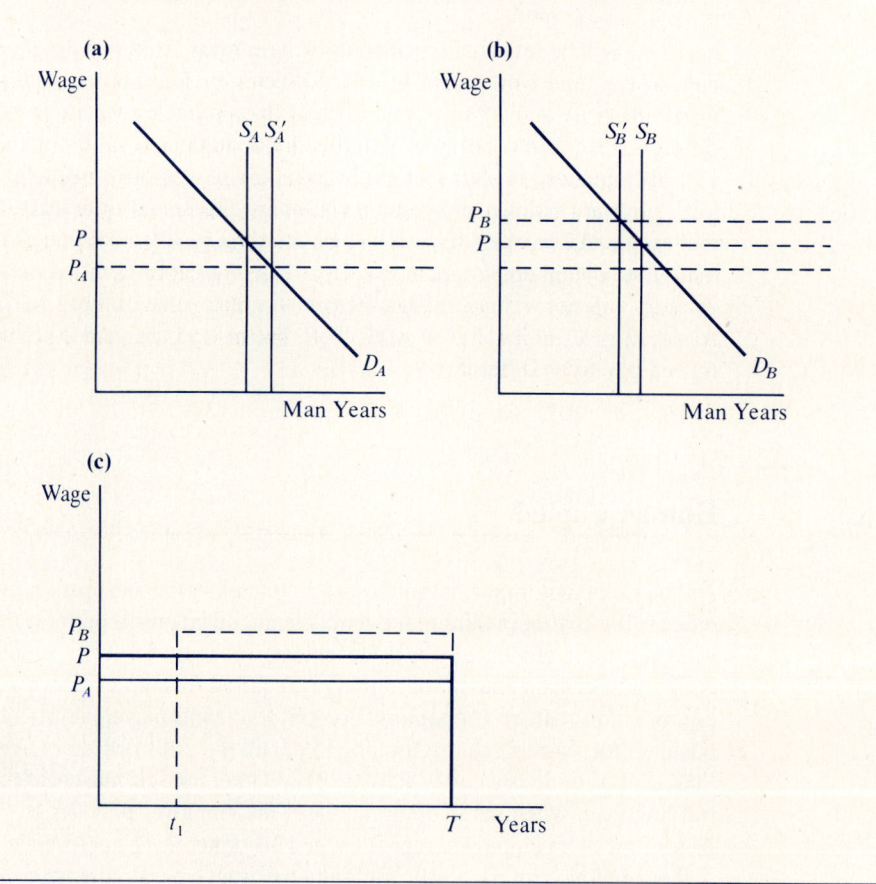

training will be regarded as unattractive, and workers will decline to enter the occupation.

A highly simplified version of this model is presented in Figure 16.4. Here we assume that there are only two occupations: sector A, which requires no training, and sector B, for which some investment in skills is essential. For simplicity we also assume that the interest rate is zero. The present value of future income in this case is simply the sum of all amounts received in each year.[4] In panel (c) of the figure the wage rate (per year) is measured on the vertical axis, and the year is indicated along the horizontal axis beginning with the worker's entry into the labor force. Year T marks the date of retirement. The present value of career earnings is thus given by the area under the curve, that is, T times the yearly wage rate.

Let workers initially be distributed as shown by S_A and S_B so that the same wage rate, P, is earned in each occupation. Assume further that training for sector B work requires t_1 years during which the worker receives no wages. Clearly, such a situation cannot be an equilibrium. The present value of career earnings in sector B is the rectangle in panel (c) of area PT, while the present value of career earnings in sector A is $P(T - t_1)$. Career A will be preferred. New entrants into the labor force will choose that sector, and the supply of workers there will shift rightward. Retirement and attrition will at the same time shift the supply of workers in sector B leftward. Wages will fall in sector A and rise in sector B.

As wages change, however, the attractiveness of the two careers also changes. The rectangle reflecting the present value of earnings in sector A gets shorter, while that indicating the present value of earnings in B grows taller. This process continues until both careers are equally attractive. Once the present values of the earnings in the two careers have equalized, entry into *both* will resume, and the supply curves to each will stop shifting. Such an equilibrium is shown by S'_A and S'_B, yielding wages P_A and P_B, respectively. The present values of career earnings in the two sectors are equal, expressed thus:

$$P_A T = P_B (T - t_1).$$

For T on the left side we may substitute $t_1 + (T - t_1)$, which yields:

$$P_A t_1 + P_A (T - t_1) = P_B (T - t_1)$$

$$P_A t_1 = (P_B - P_A)(T - t_1).$$

The left side of this expression is the present value of the opportunity cost of the training for career B—that is, the total wages that might have been earned in career A while the training was being obtained. The right side reflects the return on this investment in training, the present value of the increase in wages obtained. In equilibrium here as in other investment markets, the present value of the investment is just equal to the present value of the return.

Of course, where the discount rate is not zero, the geometry is not quite so neat. The analytics are nevertheless straightforward. The earnings in each career must be related by the following simple formula. Recall from Chapter 15 that the capital recovery factor gives the amount that must be received in each of n years for the stream to have a present value of \$1 at interest rate r. For the income dif-

[4] $\sum_{i=0}^{n} Y_i \cdot \dfrac{1}{(1+0)^i} = \sum_{i=0}^{n} Y_i.$

ference to have a present value equal to any training cost, K, an amount equal to $CRF_{n,r} \cdot K$ must be received in each year; that is:

$$P_B - P_A = CRF_{n,r} \cdot K$$
$$P_B = P_A + CRF_{n,r} \cdot K.$$

Discount rates do not vary much from person to person for reasons discussed in the last chapter. Because amounts received far into the future have a negligible present value, capital recovery factors for long periods of time vary very little as the time period n changes by a few years. For rule-of-thumb purposes we may therefore treat the capital recovery factor as constant across careers. Where this is true the equilibrium income difference between any two careers will be roughly proportional to the differences in human capital invested in those careers.

Education as Human Capital

There can be little doubt that attendance at a medical school creates human capital. The same can be said for engineering school, law school, or business school. The training imparted at these schools has a direct effect on the productivity of students later employed in the field. The connection between higher education in general, or even a great deal of secondary and primary education, and worker productivity is less obvious. Yet some economists maintain that all schooling is human capital, and in the 1960s and early 1970s it was fashionable to promote education as productivity-increasing investment. Indeed, even some influential educators became impressively conversant in the parlance of labor economics.

Rather surprisingly, a good deal of empirical evidence supports this view. Education has been shown to earn a reasonable return in scores of studies based on correlations of earnings with years of schooling. Freeman[5] has produced convincing evidence that the demand for higher education is itself influenced by the expected profits earned on such human capital. However, many remain skeptical. It is difficult to see how even an exceptional knowledge of the works of Latin poets or details of the Hundred Years War can influence the performance of workers in most jobs. Every spring this author faces the severe frustration of counseling graduating seniors on the types of careers their economics training has equipped them for. The bald truth is that economics, like most fields in the liberal arts, has little practical value, though perhaps more than most. As Oscar Wilde put it, "Art is perfectly useless." It must be appreciated for its own sake. Perhaps the same may be said for training in the liberal arts.

In behalf of the human capitalists, it may be argued that it is not the knowledge imparted by education but the process of obtaining it that affects eventual productivity. Students are repeatedly drilled in the routine of accepting assignments, completing them, and being held accountable for the results. They must learn to interpret directions, which are often rather vague, since the subject to be studied is frequently poorly understood by both teacher and student. Students

---

[5] Richard B. Freeman, *The Overeducated American* (New York: Academic Press, 1976).

must learn to budget their time and resources, allocating to each project sufficient time and effort to secure the best possible results. These are techniques with obvious applicability to many jobs. Schooling that develops these skills through intensive practice in a variety of tasks can conceivably improve the productivity of the students receiving it.

Economists who take issue with the treatment of general education as human capital must confront the empirical findings just discussed. Why does education appear to earn positive returns, and why does demand for education seem to respond to the level of these returns? One explanation is that education acts as a proxy for some environmental characteristic favorable to earnings. Some home situations may stimulate children to greater achievement in both the classroom and the boardroom. Others may leave the child both a poor student and an indifferent worker. A similar but more cynical interpretation maintains that wealthy parents both purchase more education for their children and provide the connections that launch them into more successful jobs. Both are consistent with a positive relationship between earnings and level of education attained.

While these alternative explanations of the returns to education are themselves convincing, there are other findings that are less easily explained. Freeman's results indicating a positive sensitivity of college enrollments to expected returns are based on changing total enrollments over time. There seems little scope for education to act as a proxy for environmental characteristics in this type of setup. Furthermore, Paul Taubman[6] has analyzed the returns to education based on differential schooling and earnings among a sample of identical twins. This permits him to control for home-based environmental as well as inheritable influences on earnings. When this is done, Taubman finds a smaller than normal but nevertheless positive relationship between age-adjusted earnings and years of education.

It is possible, of course, to raise questions about the interpretation of Taubman's results. Some have asked why identical twins would have different levels of education. The answers to that question might be factors that would also influence earnings, for example, injuries or personality problems. It is therefore still quite possible that even Taubman's results are spurious and that there is no real link between education and earnings. The persistence of findings favorable to the human capital hypothesis in the face of widespread skepticism has led predictably to the development of alternative theories consistent with the same observations. One of the more interesting of these is the so-called **signaling** or **screening model**.

The Signaling Explanation

Imagine two polar extremes in the characterization of the market for labor. In both cases worker productivity is assumed to vary due to environmental and genetic backgrounds that are unknown to employers. At one extreme, worker productivity is directly and costlessly observed; competition among workers insures that each

---

[6] Paul Taubman, "Earnings, Education, Genetics and Environment," *Journal of Human Resources* 11 (Fall 1976): 447–461.

will receive a wage equal to his or her marginal revenue product. At the other extreme, information concerning the productivity of individual workers is prohibitively costly. Firms that employ many workers may, by simply observing the relationship between output and labor inputs, estimate the average productivity of all workers in the firm. However, they may not determine which workers are more productive than average and which are less productive. If individual workers are indistinguishable, competition for labor will insure that each worker receives a wage equal to the average marginal revenue product of all workers.

The signaling model[7] assumes a "hybrid" environment, midway between these two extremes. Information on individual productivity may be obtained, but it is costly. In such a situation the ability to sort can be profitable. A single employer who can economically identify high-productivity workers and pay them a wage equal to the average productivity of all workers obtains more output per worker for the same cost. Of course, if more than one employer can sort, competition for high-productivity workers will raise their wage above the average of the remainder. In this situation it pays the high-productivity workers themselves to bear the cost of revealing their superiority. If they can convince employers that they are unusually productive, they will obtain higher wages.

It is possible to describe an equilibrium within such a framework that has potentially important features. One of the most startling aspects is that it is possible for all workers—those with high and those with low productivity—to be made worse off by signaling their productivity in this way.

An equilibrium in a model in which people form probabilistic beliefs is reached when, among other things, there is no longer a tendency for beliefs to change. If expectations formed on the basis of signals produced by potential employees are not supported by the performance observed, they and the process by which they were formed will be modified. If, on the other hand, experience confirms the expectations, neither they nor the process upon which they are formed will be changed.

For a signal to be produced in equilibrium it must provide information. If college diplomas were offered to everyone for a payment of $20,000 and the present value of wages paid to college graduates exceeded those of non-diploma holders by significantly more than this, such a situation would not be an equilibrium. All workers would buy diplomas. Employers would find that the average productivity of workforces made up exclusively of college graduates would be no greater than the productivity of those employed before diplomas went on sale. Employers would modify their expectations about the productivity of college graduates and decline to pay them the original premium. Without the higher wages workers would fail to buy the diplomas, and the signal would no longer be produced.

Imagine a slightly different situation, however. Assume that the signal must be produced by the workers themselves and that the cost to each worker varies inversely with his or her productivity in the market. It is quite possible that expec-

---

[7] This model was developed by Michael Spence in *Market Signaling: Information Transfer in Hiring and Related Screening Processes* (Cambridge, Mass.: Harvard University Press, 1974). For a simpler geometric presentation, see Michael Spence, "Job Market Signaling," *Quarterly Journal of Economics* 87 (August 1973): 55–374.

tations about worker productivity based on these signals will be confirmed. It may be worth the cost of producing the signal to the low-cost (and high-productivity) group but not to the high-cost (and low-productivity) workers. Those who invest in the signal will turn out to be the high-productivity workers, and those who do not will turn out to be the low-productivity workers. Thus, a firm that hires exclusively those workers who signal will find that its output is higher than another firm that hires only the nonsignalers. The signal conveys information in this case, and it will be regenerated in successive periods. This situation thus conforms to our definition of equilibrium. The fact that it may convey some incorrect information at the same time will not disturb the equilibrium.

Thus, it may seem that the process itself of producing the signal affects productivity positively. Assume the signal is higher education. Employers and even employees may actually believe that the process of obtaining higher education increases the productivity of workers. This belief will not be shattered by observation. Workers with education will be observed to have higher productivity than those without it even though education has not affected anyone's productivity.

Spence has developed a geometric example of such an equilibrium.[8] Assume that there are n workers, half of whom have a "lifetime" marginal revenue product of P_1 and half of whom have a marginal revenue product of $P_2 = 2P_1$. Assume the discount rate is zero. Employers cannot, without the signal, distinguish the high-productivity workers from the low. However, workers may produce signals that can be interpreted by employers as conveying information about productivity. Assume that employers acquire the following set of beliefs. Those workers who have produced less than e^* have a productivity of P_1, and those who have produced e^* or more have a productivity of P_2. The wage rage may be related to the amount of signal produced, as shown in Figure 16.5 by curve $P(e)$. This curve is horizontal at P_1 up to amount e^*, at which it shifts to a horizontal position at P_2.

The cost of producing the signal varies between the two groups. The cost of signaling for the low-productivity group is given by $c^a(e)$, and the cost to the high-productivity group is $c^b(e)$, which is lower for any value of e. The cost curves are so labeled in the figure.

Workers will invest in e^* of the signal or none at all. Thus, it is the cost of producing this amount alone that is pertinent to the decision to signal or not to signal. A worker who invested in less than e^* would be assumed by all employers to have a productivity of P_1, so any such investment would yield nothing. Similarly, a worker who invested more than e^* would earn no more than he or she would producing only e^*. The marginal gain from producing the signal is zero everywhere but at amount e^*.

Each worker will compare his or her earnings net of the cost of producing e^* of the signal with earnings associated with no signal. He or she will choose to signal if the former (denoted R) exceeds the latter—that is, a worker will signal if:

$$R = P_2 - c^i(e^*) \geq P_1.$$

---

[8] Michael Spence, "Job Market Signaling," op. cit.

Figure 16.5 *Signaling Equilibrium*

High-productivity workers produce an output per hour of P_2, while low-productivity workers produce an output per hour of P_1. Employers sort and pay workers according to whether they have invested e^* or more in the signal. Cost varies with the level of e at different rates for these two groups. At the given position of e^* low-productivity workers will decline to invest, while high-productivity workers, who can produce the signal at lower cost, will invest in the signal. Expectations that signalers are high-productivity workers will be confirmed, and the signal will be regenerated.

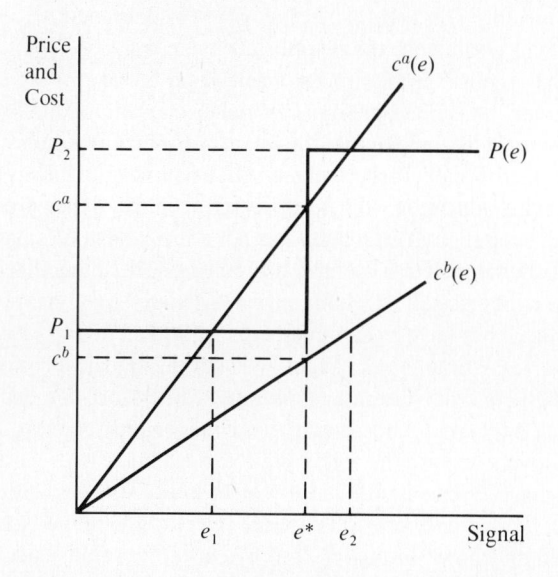

Given the construction of Figure 16.5, the high-productivity workers clearly will signal while the low-productivity workers will not. When we evaluate R for the former group we find that it exceeds P_1. $P_2 - c^b$ must be greater than P_1 because c^b is less than P_1 and P_2 is equal to $2P_1$. Evaluating R for the latter group produces the opposite result. Net earnings R in this case must be less than P_1. Since c^a exceeds P_1, $2P_1 - c^a$ must be less than P_1.

The expectations of employers based on the signal will thus be confirmed. They will believe that workers who have invested in the requisite amount of signal will have a productivity of P_2 while those who have not made such an investment will have a productivity of P_1. These expectations will be confirmed, because those whose signaling cost is sufficiently low to make signaling attractive happen also to be high-productivity workers. They will invest in the signal, while low-productivity workers will not. Expectations will not be disappointed, and the signal will be regenerated.

There are several important results in this equilibrium that must be noted. First, e^* is not unique. The requisite level of investment might be reduced to as low as e_1 before low-productivity workers would find it attractive to signal. Amount e_1 is the lower limit for e^*. At signaling levels below e_1, where $c^a(e_1) =$

Figure 16.6 *Two Disequilibrium Signals*

The position of e^* relative to the intersection of the signaling cost curves with the horizontal line at P_1 determines whether the signal will be regenerated. If the cost curve for the low-productivity workers intersects this horizontal line to the right of e^*, all workers will invest in the signal, and it will convey no information. If the cost curve for the high-productivity workers intersects this horizontal line to the left of e^*, no workers will signal.

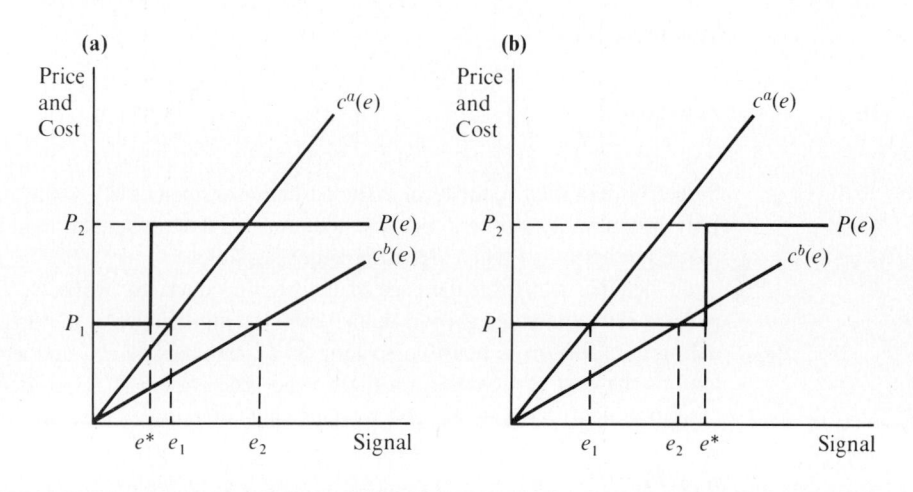

P_1, net earnings R exceed P_1. In this case, shown in panel (a) of Figure 16.6, all workers would signal, a result that will not regenerate itself for the reasons just stated. The upper limit is given by e_2. For requisite levels of signal above e_2, where $c^b(e_2) = P_1$, even the high-productivity workers will not find signaling attractive. In this case, shown in panel (b), net earnings with signaling are less than P_1 for both groups. No signal will be produced, so the signaling result will not regenerate itself. However, for any value of e^* between these two extremes, the signaling result is an equilibrium. Should such a signal get established at any value greater than e_1 but lower than e_2, it will regenerate itself.

Second, for equilibria between e_1 and e_2, the higher e^* happens to be, the worse off will be the high-productivity group. Increases in e^* do not result in increased wages. As the signal does not affect productivity, increases in signaling cost merely serve to reduce net income for this group. The low-productivity workers are not affected by changes in the equilibrium level of e^*; they receive P_1 regardless.

Third, the low-productivity group, and possibly even the high-productivity workers, are harmed by the possibility of signaling. This is easily shown for the former group. In the absence of signaling each worker receives a wage equal to the average product of the group. Let there be n workers in all and b members of the low-productivity group. Total output for the low-productivity group will be bP_1, and output of the high-productivity group will be $(n - b)P_2$. Each worker will therefore receive:

$$P = \frac{bP_1 + (n - b)P_2}{n}.$$

As $P_2 = 2P_1$, we may substitute for P_2, obtaining:

$$P = \frac{bP_1 + (n - b)2P_1}{n}.$$

This reduces to:

(16.1) $$P = P_1\left(\frac{2n - b}{n}\right).$$

Since b is less than n, the term in the parentheses must have a value greater than 1. Low-productivity workers, because they receive a wage greater than their productivity, are better off when signaling is not possible.

Consider, however, the case of the high-productivity workers. They too will receive the same wage greater than P_1 without signaling. As we have seen, a signaling equilibrium is possible so long as e^* lies between e_1 and e_2—that is, so long as the cost of signaling for them is no greater than P_1. Consider the limiting case in which $c^b(e^*) = P_1$. The workers' net wage in this case is:

$$R = P_2 - c^b(e^*)$$
$$R = P_2 - P_1 = P_1.$$

They also receive P_1, which is less than an equal share of total wages paid without signaling.

From equation (16.1) we see that the difference between P_1 and the no-signaling share P depends on the relative sizes of the two groups. The smaller the proportion of low-productivity to high-productivity workers, the greater will be the difference between P and P_1. High-productivity workers are thus more likely to be made worse off by signaling the more numerous they are relative to their low-productivity fellow workers. This result is also more likely the more costly the signaling activity. It is nevertheless possible that education, a very costly and sought-after activity, is such a signal, absorbing such a large proportion of the economy's resources that all workers, both educated and uneducated, are made worse off than if no (or at least less) education were available to all.

Some Unanswered Questions

There are some conceptual problems with the signaling model. Perhaps the most troublesome is the assumption that worker productivity is assumed as given regardless of circumstance. A worker is either a high-productivity worker or a low-productivity worker, and his or her productivity is assumed to be invariant to the nature of the environment in which the work is performed. It might be more plausible to assume that worker productivity itself is influenced by the nature of the reimbursement process. If each worker is reimbursed at a rate equal to the average product of all workers because the employer is unable to monitor his or her performance individually, we might expect to see the productivity of all the workers, potentially high- and low-output, fall far lower than the level at which any are capable.[9] This is certainly the observation of many scholars studying the performance of collective farms in communist countries where workers are paid on this basis for ideological reasons.[10] It is difficult to imagine how any output at all could be expected from a system in which individual worker productivity may be varied by the worker himself or herself without penalty. This casts doubt on the realism of the assumptions driving the signaling model.

It is nevertheless a provocative idea and is being fruitfully pursued by research economists. At present, policymakers are confronted with an interesting paradox. On the one hand, education may be a valuable resource, enhancing the productivity of workers in a broad range of career activities and generally earning reasonably high returns. On the other, it may represent nothing more than a signal, consuming vast amounts of resources with no productive result. It may contribute to income disparity in our society while leaving all workers less well off than they would be were such an investment unavailable. To date, the issue is far from resolved.

16.4 Discrimination and Wages

The Tastes of Demanders

Tastes may also play a role in determining wages by their effects on demand. Perhaps the most important case to consider here is the influence of **prejudice**. Prejudice in employment takes the form of systematic preferences for workers of a particular sex or race over others. It may be due to a belief that the expected productivity of the favored workers will be superior or simply to a preference for association with the favored group. As the analyses of both forms of prejudice is essentially the same, we will cast our discussion in terms of the latter.

This type of prejudice may influence market decisions through one or more of the following three channels: (1) Firm owners may be prejudiced and give employment preference to favored races or sexes, (2) workers themselves may be prejudiced, preferring to work only with others like themselves, and (3) customers may be prejudiced and prefer doing business with people of the same race or sex. The effect on demand for the unfavored workers is the same in all three cases.

We will illustrate the influence of prejudice on demand by examining results of case (2). We will also confine our discussion to sex prejudice (although, of course, the same principles apply to racial prejudice). Both men and women are assumed to be perfect substitutes in the work performed. Let the number of hours

---

[9] This point is forcefully argued by Yoram Barzel in "Some Fallacies in the Interpretation of Information Costs," *The Journal of Law and Economics* 20 (October 1977): 291–308.

[10] See, for example, John H. Moore, "Agency Costs, Technological Change, and Soviet Central Planning," *The Journal of Law and Economics* 24 (October 1981): 189–214.

worked by men be m and the number of hours worked by women be w. Total hours worked are thus $h = m + w$. Let labor be the only input so that the production function is $q = f(h)$. Assume that the firm is a price taker in the input market so that output price is a constant P_q.

Consider case (2). Here we assume that men prefer to work only among other men. They can be persuaded to overcome this prejudice only by receiving higher wages. We may represent this by expressing the wage for men as a function of the number of women employed—that is, $P_m = P_m(w)$. We assume initially that the supply prices of men and women workers are otherwise unaffected by the quantity employed. We also assume that women are not prejudiced.

Profits for this firm are, as always, equal to total revenue (output times price) minus total cost (summed expenditure on the wages of men and women):

$$\pi = f(h)P_q - P_w w - P_m(w)m.$$

Profits are maximized by using the labor input up to the point at which $\Delta\pi/\Delta h = 0$. As men and women are perfect substitutes, $\Delta f/\Delta w = \Delta f/\Delta m = MPP_h$. The profit-maximizing conditions for these two inputs may therefore be written:

(16.2) $$\frac{\Delta\pi}{\Delta m} = MPP_h P_q - P_m = 0.$$

(16.3) $$\frac{\Delta\pi}{\Delta w} = MPP_h P_q - P_w - m \cdot \frac{\Delta P_m}{\Delta w} = 0.$$

Solving for $MPP_h P_q$ in each expression and setting the results equal to each other gives the following unhappy conclusion:

$$P_m = P_w + m \cdot \frac{\Delta P_m}{\Delta w}.$$

The wages for men and women must differ. As the effect of women on the wages of men, $\Delta P_m/\Delta w$, is positive, men will be paid more than women in this firm.

Another way of viewing this is illustrated with the aid of Figure 16.7. The diagonal curve labeled $MPP_h P_q$ is marginal revenue product. As in our earlier discussion, we assume that workers are perfectly mobile among employers; hence, the firm behaves as a price taker in the labor market. Assume that a combined total of h man-hours are supplied to the firm so that the MRP of labor is equal to P_m. From equation (16.2) we see that this will be the wage paid to men workers; they will receive a wage equal to their marginal revenue product.

The women workers will receive less. Solving for the women's wages from equation (16.3) we obtain:

$$P_w = MPP_h P_q - \frac{m\Delta P_m}{\Delta w}.$$

This tells us that for any quantity of labor *in total*, the wages paid to women by this firm must be less than the marginal revenue product of labor by the amount of the

Figure 16.7 **Fellow Employee Prejudice**

Marginal revenue product of labor is given by $MPP_h P_q$. Prejudiced male workers will receive this wage from their employers depending on the quantity of labor employed in total (h). As the prejudiced men will insist on a wage premium to work with women, the demand price for women workers will discount the cost of this premium. Depending on the total man-hours used, their demand price will be as shown by the lower curve, $MPP_h P_q - m \Delta P_m / \Delta w$.

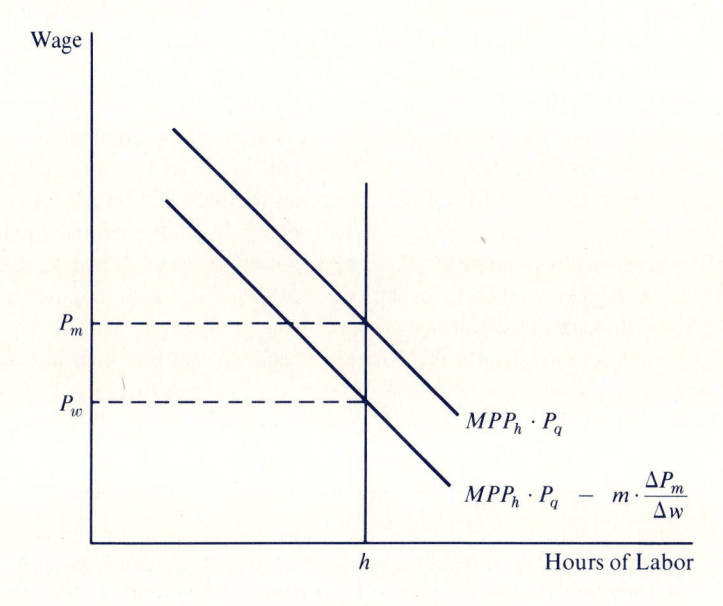

term $m \Delta P_m / \Delta w$. Thus, as the total quantity of labor varies to the firm and the short-run supply curve h shifts leftward and rightward, the wages of men are determined by the height of curve $MPP_h P_q$ while the wages of women are determined by the height of the lower curve. If the total quantity of labor supplied is h, then all men workers will receive a wage of P_m while all women workers will receive the lower wage P_w.

Response to Prejudice

The same result obtains for cases of customer and owner prejudice. Regardless of its source, prejudice influences the demand price that firms will be willing to pay workers of different sexes. We have not finished the story yet, however. Surprisingly, the presence of one or all of the types of prejudice described is insufficient to produce wage differences between the sexes. For though prejudice influences the behavior of demanders of labor in the manner described, it also affects the *supply* of labor to each employer. We shall see that so long as women may respond to the presence of prejudice in a firm by withholding their services and offering them elsewhere, no wage disparity will occur at equilibrium. Only when there is literally nowhere else to go and women must accept employment from prejudiced firms will this prejudice actually have wage rate effects.

Full equilibrium is depicted in Figure 16.8. As in our discussion of other factors producing wage differences, our point here may be illustrated by describing the migration of suppliers between two sectors. As the geometry of the effect on demand prices offered by firms is essentially the same in all three cases, we shall ignore for the present the source of prejudice and speak only of "prejudiced firms." Assume that no firms show prejudice initially but firms in sector A will exhibit prejudice in the future. Workers, unaware of this impending event, will distribute themselves among firms in these two sectors in conformance with our earlier discussion. Let us further assume that women comprise one third of the labor force and that sector A and sector B are roughly equivalent in size. Demand curves for labor aggregated across all firms in the two sectors are given by MRP_h. As all workers are indifferent concerning the sector in which they are employed, they will supply themselves to the two sectors in quantities that equate wage rates. That will result in quantity S_A being supplied to sector A and S_B to sector B, producing wages equal to P_h in the two markets. Both men and women will be employed in each market at equal wage rates.

Now let us consider the effect of prejudice. Assume that the equilibrium just described places equal numbers of workers of each sex in each sector—that is, one third of the workers in sector A are women. As we have just seen, prejudice has

Figure 16.8 *Supply Response to Discrimination*

Originally there is no prejudice in either sector. Supply in each sector is given by S_A and S_B, respectively, yielding a wage of P_h for both men and women employees. If the firms in panel (a) become prejudiced, women must discount this discrimination in their wages. This will lower their wages below those earned in the unprejudiced sector, and women will leave for sector B. This will raise wages of the men in sector A above the wages of men in sector B, and men workers from sector B will shift to sector A, replacing the women. Equilibrium will be characterized by an all-male workforce in sector A earning wages equal to the mixed workforce in sector B.

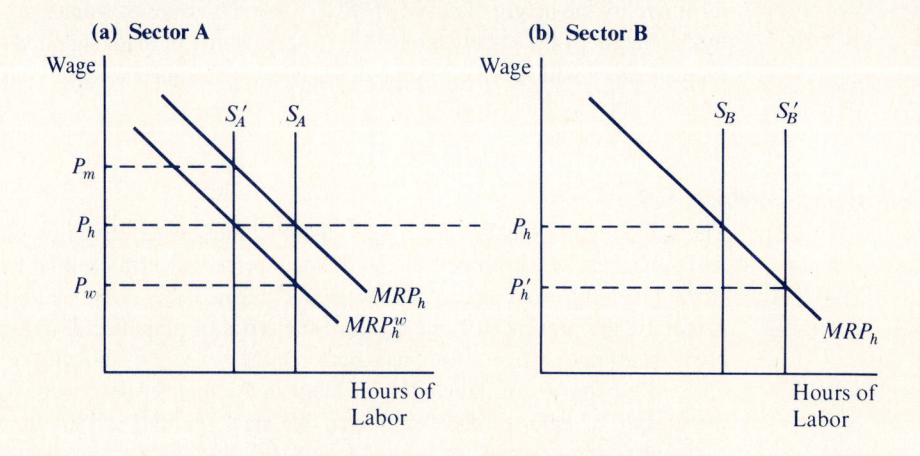

the effect of shifting the demand price for women downward. Firms will no longer be willing to pay them a wage equal to the marginal revenue product of labor. For any quantity of labor supplied to sector A the demand price for women is given by the lower curve, MRP_h^w, in panel (a). At the initial supply of labor to this sector, the prejudiced firms will be willing to pay women only P_w, while continuing to pay men the full value of MRP_h. Meanwhile, in the unprejudiced sector B both men and women continue to earn P_h.

Clearly this is not an equilibrium. Our equilibrium condition for supply to multiple markets is not satisfied. Demand prices to women are not equal in all markets. Women in sector A may under these circumstances earn a higher wage by migrating to sector B. Let us assume that all do so. This will shift S_A leftward by one third and shift S_B rightward by the same amount. Only men workers are left in sector A, and their wage rises to P_m. Both men and women in sector B earn P_h', which is less than P_m. This is still not an equilibrium, for the demand price of men is now unequal in the two markets. Men workers from sector B will thus migrate to sector A until their wages are equalized between the two sectors.

When this is achieved, the market will be in full equilibrium. No worker can gain by shifting from one market to the other. Men will earn the same in both markets, and women will earn the same as men in the unprejudiced sector. Events set in motion by prejudice result in exactly the same number of men shifting to sector A as women leaving that sector. The final equilibrium wages will be P_h in the unprejudiced sector, equal to P_h earned by men alone in the prejudiced sector. Under these circumstances prejudice will influence the pattern of employment but not wage rates. All men and women will earn exactly the same wages they earned under conditions of no prejudice, but some will now simply earn them in different places.

Two assumptions are required for full equilibrium to have no wage rate effects. First, workers must be mobile enough to adjust in the manner described. If women are not mobile enough to change employers (or, more practically, to avoid certain employers) when prejudice is present, and if men are not mobile enough to be "crowded out" of employment in prejudice-free firms by women seeking better-paying jobs, then wage effects of prejudice will be observed. Second, if prejudice is so pervasive that there are more women (or minority group members) seeking employment than there are jobs available at equal wage rates, then wages for the victims of prejudice will be lower.

Necessary Conditions for Wage Rate Disparity

Regardless of the mechanics producing wage disparity, a condition necessary for these effects to be realized in equilibrium is that the number of **sensitive jobs** be a large proportion of the total number of jobs women might fill. By "sensitive" here we mean likely to be influenced by prejudice. As this distinction is important in assessing the empirical significance of prejudice-based wage disparity, it is worthwhile discussing it in some detail.

All jobs are not sensitive to prejudice. This is apparent in certain obvious cases. Employers of models of women's fashions are unlikely to be willing to pay more for men than for women models. Likewise, producers of ballet or opera are unlikely to give preference to men for the title roles in *Giselle* or *Aida*. A return to the sources of prejudice gives us a feeling for the scope of such sensitive jobs.

Recall that prejudice is an expression of the tastes of either customers, fellow employees, or owners. The range of jobs likely to be sensitive due to the first form of prejudice is therefore limited by the extent of customer contact. If some customers prefer dealing with male representatives, then jobs in sales, promotion, customer service, and the like will be sensitive, while jobs in internal administration, planning, and other staff- and production-type work will not. To the extent that some customers are free of this prejudice and male employees may be directed to prejudiced customers the scope for jobs to be sensitive due to customer prejudice is even more circumscribed.

The number of jobs likely to be sensitive due to the prejudice of fellow workers is also smaller than might be perceived at first glance. Here prejudice operates only through the association of women employees with prejudiced men employees. In many cases where prejudice threatens to produce the results described, it will be more profitable to replace the prejudiced men than the women employees. To the extent that equally skilled women are available at lower wages than men, such substitution will lower cost and raise profits. Equilibrium in markets characterized by fellow-employee prejudice is thus predicted to result in worker segregation and equal wages, as was described in Figure 16.8.

Finally, we must consider the scope of the influence of owner prejudice. As pointed out above, an owner who is willing to bear the cost may hire an exclusively male workforce. If there are few unprejudiced firms, women will merely crowd out men in the unprejudiced sector, and wages will equalize. If there are many, on the other hand, women will be crowded into the unprejudiced firms, producing a wage differential. In this case, however, prejudiced employers will operate at a cost disadvantage due to the employment of higher priced labor, and profits suffer accordingly.

Even in this situation market forces act to limit the extent of sensitive jobs. Here it is the market for ownership itself that operates against wage disparity. In essence, ownership prejudice that results in the hiring of men at wages in excess of those earned by equally qualified women is inefficient; higher profits would be obtained by replacing men with lower-cost female employees. Such firms are therefore worth more to unprejudiced owners than prejudiced owners. Equilibrium in the market for ownership will thus be characterized by a replacement of sufficient numbers of prejudiced owners to eliminate wage disparity.

Evidence on Wage Disparity

The theory just discussed has a great deal of explaining to do. The impression gathered from it is that there is little scope for prejudice to have effects on wage rates. For prejudice to have substantial effects on wage rates, the number of sensitive jobs must be large relative to the total number of jobs women might fill. Casual empiricism suggests the opposite: The number of sensitive jobs will be too small to produce substantial wage rate disparity between men and women workers. However, data on earnings of each sex reveal substantial differences. Mean earnings of full-time employed men exceed those of women by 58 percent. Even when such factors as education, race, location, and experience are factored into the analysis, a substantial unexplained residual difference remains.[11]

Economists have offered a number of hypotheses to explain these findings. One approach has been to abandon the competitive marginal productivity model of factor demand altogether. According to this view, competition for workers exists only at entry levels and for "secondary segments" involving little skill, ineffective unionization, and high job turnover. Jobs in "primary segments," on the other hand, are shielded from the forces of competition by lack of worker mobility and information on job alternatives. The wage structures in this latter segment are held to have little correspondence to worker productivity but rather are influenced by a variety of employer and worker motives, including prejudice.[12]

This approach raises more questions than it answers. Worker mobility and the accumulation of market information are the results of economic choices by the affected workers. Similarly, the promotion itself of workforce stability by employers, an activity that plays a large role in these writings, has an obvious and direct influence on firm profits. If the economic influences described in the preceding chapters do not affect these decisions, what does? If they influence these decisions only within limits, what determines these limits? In its present state of development this approach fails to present a convincing set of answers to such questions. A theory of labor markets must do more than simply assert that competition does not work; it must explain why and buttress its explanation with evidence. The institutionalist view is certainly consistent with the observation of wage disparity between sexes. The problem is that it is also consistent with the lack of such disparity.

Several writers have sought to explain wage disparity within the framework of the standard competitive model with moderate success. Mincer and Polachek[13] have considered the impact of the higher rate of entry and exit of women from the labor force as an explanation. They note that even women college graduates spend less than 60 percent of their working lives in the active labor force. This affects not only their total experience but the rate of accumulation of skills while working. Women planning to spend a small portion of their lives in their current careers will be influenced to devote fewer resources to the accumulation of human capital useful to those careers. When they control for this effect, Mincer and Polachek are able to explain roughly half of the earnings differential. In a similar paper, Elizabeth Landes[14] focusing on the higher rates of turnover among women employees, explains an even larger share of the difference.

---

[11] Ronald Oaxaca, in a very thorough empirical analysis incorporating 40 variables reflecting labor markets and worker characteristics, still finds an unexplained residual difference between men's and women's wages of between 20 to 30 percent, in "Male-Female Wage Differentials in Urban Labor Markets," *International Economic Review* 14 (October 1973): 693–709.

[12] See Donald J. Treiman and Heidi I. Hartmann, eds., *Women, Work and Wages: Equal Pay for Jobs of Equal Value* (Washington: National Academy Press, 1981), Chapter 3.

[13] J. Mincer and S. W. Polachek, "Family Investments in Human Capital: Earnings of Women," *Journal of Political Economy* 82 (March/April 1974): S76–S108.

[14] Elizabeth M. Landes, "Sex Differences in Wages and Employment: A Test of the Specific Capital Hypothesis," *Economic Inquiry* 15 (October 1977): 523–538.

Gwartney and Stroup[15] pursue an alternative explanation. They argue that marital status is a key variable, maintaining that marriage has an important influence on the occupational choice of men and women. Married women with primary responsibility for children will seek jobs with flexible hours and jobs involving skills that are transportable from community to community. They will also specialize to a greater extent than married men in performing household-productive activities. Married men, on the other hand, will specialize in market activity, performing few household tasks.

These differences in occupational preferences of married workers of each sex are alleged to be responsible for the disparity in wage rates earned. Gwartney and Stroup go on to argue that the tastes for occupations and mix of household and career activity are far more similar between single men and women. They maintain that comparisons of wage rates among unmarried workers of each sex are a better gauge of the existence of wage effects of discrimination than are comparisons of all male and female workers. When they examine wage rates of single men and women, virtually the entire wage difference between men and women disappears. While the mean of all men and women workers in their sample differs by 44 percent, the ratio of the wages of single women to those of single men were found to be between 0.91 and 0.96.

None of these findings may be regarded as conclusive; the issue of the extent to which the large and surprisingly stable differences in wages of men and women may be attributed to prejudice is far from settled. Other studies have found less explanatory power in differential turnover rates,[16] and Gwartney and Stroup's findings are open to alternative interpretation. It may be argued, for example, that the factors influencing women to remain single are likely to make them untypically high earners while the opposite may be true of single men. Until such questions may be definitively answered, this large sex-related portion of the variation in the distribution of earnings must be considered unresolved.

Summary

Income represents revenues to households for the sale of resource services. In this chapter we examined the distribution of that income from two perspectives: the distribution of nonhuman endowments and variation in the prices paid for labor. As income in wages and salaries represents by far the greater share of total income, the latter source of variation is the dominant influence on the distribution of total income. The larger part of this chapter was concerned with analyzing the distribution of earnings.

It is useful to categorize the sources of variation in wage rates into two compartments. On the one hand, there are those influences which produce real variation in wel-

---

[15] J. Gwartney and R. Stroup, "Measurement of Employment Discrimination According to Sex," *Southern Economic Journal* 39 (April 1973): 575–587.

[16] See, for example, M. Corcoran and G. J. Duncan, "Work History, Labor Force Attainment and Earnings Differences Between the Races and Sexes," *Journal of Human Resources* 14 (Winter 1970): 3–20.

fare in society. Included in this group is the influence of inborn abilities, which are distributed unevenly in each generation and result in variation in productivity. Also included are such influences as coercion, which prevents the flow of workers out of low-wage and into higher-wage activities, and prejudice, which exacts a wage penalty for sex or race.

In the other compartment we place those influences on the distribution of earnings that compensate for particular features of the markets in which labor is supplied. Included here are variations in wages due to workers' tastes for work of different types. Also included here is variation due to human capital. According to this view, the higher earnings of those workers with keenly developed skills merely compensate for the cost of obtaining those skills. In equilibrium there can be no rents so long as there is free entry, because investment in such skills can be counted upon to take place until they have been eliminated.

One of the most important factors producing income inequality is age. The rising and falling income profile of the average worker over his or her life cycle accounts for one third of the inequality of income in society as a whole. This cycle itself has an explanation rooted in human capital. In the early years of a worker's career, he or she is provided valuable training by the employer, for which the worker pays by accepting a wage that is less than his or her marginal revenue product. This training increases his or her productivity in the next period, in which the worker continues to receive more training. This worker's observed income rises over time due to the influence of age.

However, human capital, like physical capital, depreciates. As technology changes certain skills become obsolete, and things learned years before are forgotten. As the worker ages, two things occur. First, the period over which human capital will have to be amortized gets shorter; as the worker approaches retirement age, it becomes very short indeed. Second, the stock of human capital has grown year by year so that total depreciation per year becomes a large magnitude. Due to the first influence, the worker invests less in additional training. Due to the second, this smaller investment is likely to fall short of the total depreciation in each year. The combined effect is therefore a net reduction of human capital in the latter years of the life cycle and an actual fall in earnings.

Certain types of education are clearly skill producing. In this chapter we explored some of the arguments and evidence concerning the issue of whether general education is human capital in the sense of being productivity improving. Although skeptics seem to have the force of logic on their side, it is difficult to fault the evidence in support of the hypothesis of education as human capital. We also surveyed an alternative explanation for the observed correlation of earnings and education. According to this intriguing theoretical development, education performs a screening function, sorting workers who are congenitally more productive from those who are less so, but in itself it adds nothing to the productivity of anyone. As high-productivity workers may obtain education at lower cost, they will find it advantageous to make this investment and signal their superiority. Lower-productivity workers will eschew this investment, insuring that the signal conveys correct information and that it will continue in use.

The signaling model has two troublesome implications. First, as resources devoted to signaling do not affect productivity, investment in this activity is a waste of resources. Resources used for signaling might be devoted to production of goods valued in consumption with no net loss of output. Second, it is possible that all are made worse off in signaling equilibrium than they would be were signaling impossible. As signaling by definition does not increase output, it is purely redistributional. High-productivity workers obtain increased wages at the expense of low-productivity workers. It is possible, however, that resources devoted to signaling may exceed in value the income transfer achieved in this way. Under such circumstances both high- and low-productivity workers are harmed by the presence of signaling.

In this chapter we included a rather detailed discussion of wage discrimination. This lengthy treatment was warranted on the basis of the economic importance of this phenomenon. Women account for 40 percent of the labor force, and blacks account for 11 percent. If the large income disparities associated with sex and race are the result of prejudice, then their magnitude implies an injustice of staggering proportions. Our analysis raised some doubts about the interpretation of these income disparities. The theory of labor markets suggests that the influence of prejudice will be chiefly observed in the distribution of employment. Wage rate effects of prejudice are limited in theory to special cases that do not seem to have widespread counterparts in the real world.

Finally, we examined some attempts to reconcile theory with observed income disparity. These explanations focused on a variety of factors arising out of the typical role of the wife as having primary responsibility for children and household activities. While empirical estimates of the influences of these factors are encouraging to this line of explanation, the issue remains unresolved and is likely to for some time.

Key Concepts

coercion
ability
tastes
human capital
human capital returns

signaling or screening model
prejudice
restricted mobility
crowding hypothesis
sensitive jobs

Questions

1. *Easy* Morticians earn higher wages than butchers although both occupations require roughly the same amounts of training. Explain why competition for jobs in these two occupations fails to equalize wages.

Hard Some workers enjoy the outdoors and choose to be cowboys. Others prefer office work and become clerks. Explain how the relative wages of clerks and cowboys are determined with free entry into both. Explain why it "pays" to be different.

2. *Easy* A minimum wage can increase the extent of income disparity even though it increases the money wages of many workers at the lower end of the income scale. Explain.

Hard A great tenor makes more money than a promising tenor, and a great tennis player makes more than a promising tennis player. What determines whether tennis players or tenors earn more on average? In what ways is the answer to this question similar to the answer to the second part of Question 1?

3. *Easy* Applicants for licenses to enter certain occupations are frequently required to pass examinations which include questions of arcane subject matter unrelated to the skillful performance of the jobs in question. For example, barbers are frequently required to exhibit detailed knowledge of the anatomy of the skull, and optometrists must answer questions about diseases of the eye. What is the effect of the inclusion of such requirements for licensure on wages in these occupations?

Hard Tightening requirements (by adding more questions of this type) is frequently done with a "grandfather clause" which exempts present license holders from satisfying the added requirements. Who gains more from such tightening of requirements, present license holders or new applicants for licenses? Explain.

4. *Easy* What explanations can be given for the observed significant positive correlation of wages with years of education other than the hypothesis that education increases worker productivity?

Hard One of the chief difficulties with the signaling model of investment in education is the assumption that productivity is given. An individual worker is assumed to be either a high-productivity worker or a low-productivity worker. This assumption is difficult to credit, because it suggests that productivity is beyond the control of the worker. Explain.

5. *Easy* If an employer's workforce is made up of prejudiced men, he or she may decline to employ an equally qualified woman except at a lower wage even though he or she as an employer is unprejudiced. Explain.

Hard The presence of a large number of prejudiced male workers in the workforce is insufficient to result in wage disparity among men and women workers. Explain. What other factors must be present in order for discrimination to produce differences in wages of equally qualified men and women?

6. *Easy* Wages are not equal over the life cycle. They typically rise with age until the worker reaches roughly 50 years, after which they decline. What accounts for this rise and decline?

Hard All human capital does not depreciate at the same rate. McDowell[17] has estimated the rate of decay in knowledge of academics in various fields by observing the rate at which professional articles are cited in new works. He finds, for example, that the citation rate falls at 18.3 percent per year for physics articles but at only 2.7 percent per year for English scholarship. Assume that many women academics leave the labor force in mid-career to have children. Would you be surprised to learn that women pursuing an academic career are twice as likely as men to enter the humanities but are only one third as likely to choose one of the physical sciences? Explain why or why not.

[17] J. M. McDowell, "Obsolescence of Knowledge and Career Publication Profiles: Some Evidence of Differences among Fields in Costs of Interrupted Careers," *American Economic Review* 72 (September 1982): 752–768.

Chapter 17

Welfare Economics: Defining Efficiency

Connections   This is the first of two chapters concerned with economic efficiency and its implications for economic organization. These chapters develop a system of prescriptions for organizing the economy. In this sense they represent normative theory rather than the purely descriptive or positive theory that has occupied us up to this point. A review of the discussion of this distinction in Chapter 1 may thus prove helpful. The concept of efficiency applies with equal force to any form of economic organization. In developing the conditions necessary for efficiency we must therefore suppress any reference to particular types of economic institutions, like markets, prices, firms, and costs. The norms developed in this chapter can then be applied to these institutions as well as to others for evaluating their efficiency-fostering or subverting properties. That is done in Chapter 18. The building blocks for this theory thus consist of utility theory as presented in Chapter 3 and production theory as developed in Chapter 11.

Virtually all of the theory in the preceding chapters has been descriptive. In the language of philosophers, it has been **positive theory**. It has provided us with a forecasting kit enabling us to predict the behavior of economic agents in response to changes in their economic environment. Economic theory is therefore useful in assessing the results of government policies. Positive economic theory takes no position on the appropriateness of these policies; it merely describes their results. On the other hand, there is a long tradition of **normative** theory by economists seeking to derive policy guidance directly from price theory. Adam Smith's *The Wealth of Nations* is to a large extent a book of advocacy. It seeks to demonstrate the folly of contemporary merchantilist policies and the advantages of *laissez-faire* both in international trade and in broad areas of domestic activity. Although the sense in which results of free market organization were better than other policies was not to be rigorously stated for more than a century, its implicit truth has become widely accepted among economists and, to a lesser extent, a potent force in guiding policy.

In the 20th century considerable effort has been devoted to clarification of what economic theory has to say about the appropriateness of government policy as well as to developing particular policy statements in terms of this norm. The term **economic efficiency** has been carefully examined. The theory's interpretation of the relationships between individual and social welfare has been rigorously developed and its implications for economic organization subjected to repeated modification. It seems fair to summarize the state of modern welfare economics as simultaneously splendid in aspect but vacuous in content. The policymakers looking for guidance from up-to-date versions of this theory will find its message hopelessly vague in interpretation, equivocal in application, and almost void of normative force.

Yet it is necessary to learn this theory, if only to protect oneself from its misuse. A little knowledge can be dangerous, and ill-informed economists proliferate both the marble halls of Washington and the granite towers of Wall Street. Old ideas die slowly, particularly if they can be stretched to buttress the case for someone's favorite program. In this sense welfare economics seems infinitely elastic. It has been used in recent times to break up large firms in the guise of promoting competition as well as to consolidate firms into cartels in the service of market stability. It has been used to promote the elimination of taxes and subsidies as well as to support the extension of taxes and subsidies. It has been used in support of expanding the role of government in the economy as well as to justify limiting such growth. Serious students will therefore wish to study this and the following chapter carefully.

17.1 Efficiency Defined

The concept of efficiency can be neatly stated in the abstract. Figure 17.1 presents both the problem economists confront and their carefully evolved solution. Let us assume that different states of the world (resulting from different methods of economic organization, different methods of resolving conflict, different policies,

Chapter 17 *Welfare Economics: Defining Efficiency* 555

Figure 17.1 *The Utility Possibility Frontier*

Orville's utility is measured along the vertical axis, and Wilbur's utility is measured along the horizontal axis. Those combinations on or below the utility possibility frontier, passing through combinations B, C, and D, are feasible given the resources in the economy. A policy that yields combination B rather than combination A produces an efficiency gain. A policy that yields combination C rather than combination A also yields an efficiency gain. The states of the world B, C, and D are all efficient; yet a change from state A to state D may not be said to yield an efficiency gain.

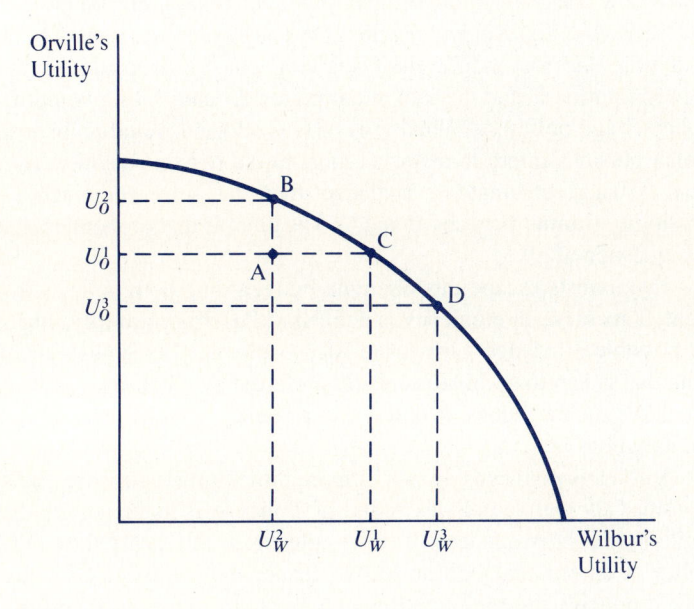

etc.) yield different combinations of utility to different citizens in the community. Here we shall assume a very small community containing only two people, Orville and Wilbur. Wilbur's utility is measured along the horizontal axis, while Orville's is measured along the vertical axis. However, the possibility of providing utility to either or both is limited by the resources in the community. The limits of the productivity of the resource base, however organized, are shown by the diagonal curve containing points B, C, and D. By ignoring Orville's interests altogether, we might confer upon Wilbur the utility indicated by the horizontal intercept of this curve. Under the opposite set of circumstances, Orville might obtain the utility indicated by its vertical intercept.

At a sufficiently abstract level, this presents the nature of the policy options concerning which economists might offer advice. Assume that policy A yields utility combination A while policy B yields utility combination B. This is the easy problem which dominates most economic discussion of policy in spite of its limitations. By choosing policy B in preference to policy A, Orville's situation is improved, and Wilbur is made no worse off. Economists claim that adoption of policy B offers an **efficiency gain**. This gain is defined as an increase in someone's welfare achieved with no offsetting decrease in the wellbeing of anyone else. Once policy B is in force—or policy C or policy D, for that matter—no further efficiency gains are possible. However, so long as the existing regime results in a utility combination below the frontier, the situation is inefficient. A welfare-improving policy awaits discovery.

Normative Limits of Efficiency

Let us now consider a more difficult problem. What if the policy options are A, B, and C? Both policies B and C offer efficiency gains over policy A, but Orville and Wilbur are far from indifferent concerning which is adopted. Orville is indifferent between policy C and the inefficient policy A, and Wilbur is indifferent between policy B and policy A. Whether B or C is adopted would realistically depend on which person's interests mattered most to the person or entity making this decision. A fair result might be neither of these but some combination on the utility possibility frontier between B and C. The point is that economics sheds no light on this question at all.

Economists escape this dilemma by regarding both policies B and C as efficient. This sense of efficiency is defined as **Pareto optimality**,[1] the state in which all possible efficiency gains have been exploited. Economists maintain that any state that is Pareto optimal is equally preferred by efficiency criteria and that other standards such as ethics or political expediency must be applied to rank any such combinations.

But let us now consider a still more difficult (though more realistic) problem. Consider alternative policies A and D. Policy A is inefficient by these standards, while policy D is efficient. Can we infer from this that policy D is preferred to policy A on efficiency grounds? We cannot. Policy D is clearly preferred to unnamed policies resulting in utility combinations to the southwest of D, but policy A is not among these. Policy A is inferior on efficiency grounds to other policies that lie above and to the right of A, but D is not among these even though it is Pareto optimal. This standard of efficiency is therefore of limited usefulness in practical applications. Policies may be ranked according to this norm only when there are no losers but only gainers and nonlosers. It seems hardly likely that, should Congress ever discover a program offering benefits to many and harm to none, it will find it necessary to seek economists' blessings before adopting such a proposal.

Measuring Utility

The problem depicted in this section may be more formally described as incompleteness in the rank-ordering process of the efficiency standard. Definite orderings among continuous sets of alternatives can be developed with efficiency

---

[1] This term was named for its originator, Vilfredo Pareto (1848–1923), who was born in Paris, trained and worked for many years as an engineer in Italy, taught economics at the distinguished University of Lausanne, and ultimately resigned his chair there to devote the remainder of his life to sociology, where his contributions are also substantial.

criteria only along lines in the opportunity set having slopes of zero or greater. Alternatives that lie along negatively sloped lines cannot be ranked. As political choices almost invariably involve the harming of some for the benefit of others, they involve the comparison of combinations lying along negatively sloped lines; hence, they are uninformed by the efficiency standard.

This raises the question of why economists have felt constrained to limit their normative apparatus so severely. Why not simply declare that policy D is preferred to policy A and be done with it? The answer to this question must be sought by asking another. In what sense is society's aggregate welfare improved by a shift from policy A to policy D? In fact, what do we mean by "society's aggregate welfare?"

Earlier generations of economists were committed to the idea that social welfare was identical with total utility, that is, the sum of the utility of all members of the community. Clearly, such an approach avoids the ambiguities inherent in the present formulation. It permits the ranking of points along the **utility possibility frontier**—indeed, an explicit ranking of *all* conceivable policies. This can easily be shown in Figure 17.2.

The utility possibility frontier expresses the utility enjoyed by Orville as a function of Wilbur's utility, $U_O = U_O(U_W)$. Total welfare is the sum of the utility of both; that is:

Total welfare = $U_T(U_W) = U_O(U_W) + U_W$.

We find conditions for the maximization of this sum by calculating the slope of this expression and setting it equal to zero. This yields:

$$\frac{\Delta U_T}{\Delta U_S} = \frac{\Delta U_O}{\Delta U_W} + 1 = 0$$

$$\frac{\Delta U_O}{\Delta U_W} = -1.$$

Maximum utility for society is identified by combination T, at which the slope of the utility possibility frontier has a value of precisely minus one. As combination T provides more total utility than any other combination on the frontier, policies that yield this combination are regarded as preferred—that is, more efficient—than any other policy.

The Weighting Problem

There are two major problems with such an approach. The first concerns the **weighting of individual utilities**. According to this formulation, the utility of each person "counts" equally. While such an assumption might appear superficially innocent, there is certainly no logical basis in economics for making it. Any argument we might advance for such a weighting scheme must have a basis in ethics and cultural tradition. Our present treatment of criminals and the mentally incompetent are merely the most obvious cases of unequal weights in our own society today.

Alternative weights change the solution. Let us return to Figure 17.2. If we assign a weight of 0.6 to Orville's utility and 0.4 to Wilbur's, social welfare, properly measured, is given by:

$$U_T(U_W) = 0.6 U_O(U_W) + 0.4 U_W.$$

Setting the slope of this expression equal to zero yields:

$$\frac{\Delta U_T}{\Delta U_W} = 0.6 \cdot \frac{\Delta U_O}{\Delta U_W} + 0.4 \cdot U_W = 0.$$

$$\frac{\Delta U_O}{\Delta U_W} = -\frac{2}{3}.$$

Maximum social welfare is now given by combination K, which is preferred to combination T. The ranking of all other policies will likewise be disturbed. If we cannot assign a set of weights to individual utilities, then we are forced into the incomplete scheme of modern welfare economics. Weights are unnecessary in that scheme, because it ranks only combinations that would be welfare increasing according to any set of weights.

The Measurement Problem

A second and no less critical problem with the earlier formulation is the difficulty of its implementation. It is one thing to gaze at Figure 17.2 and discuss the efficiency-related merits of policy T and policy K. It is quite another problem to translate real policy options into coordinates in this utility space. **Measurement of utility levels** cannot be done directly. The only contact that utility theory has with economic theory in positive economics is in the expression of *relative* welfare states, such as Wilbur being *happier* with one bundle of goods than he is with another. If we cannot measure the utility levels of members of the community, this raises serious questions indeed about the usefulness of a norm expressed in these terms.

It is occasionally argued that we know enough about the relationship of income to utility to make welfare-maximizing judgements on this basis. By holding the hypothesized relationship before us, we supposedly may evaluate policies based on their influence on income, which we can measure, and therefore come close to satisfying criteria expressed in terms of utility, which we cannot. The closeness of such an approximation itself can be gauged only by concerted spiritual endeavor.

Consider how this approach has been used to design policy in the area of income distribution. For analytical simplicity we will make the wildly unrealistic assumption that total income, $\hat{Y}$, is insensitive to redistributional policy. We will assume further that the utility level of our two citizens is directly related to their own income so that $U_O = U_O(Y_O)$ and $U_W = U_W(Y_W)$. Since total income is fixed, $\hat{Y} = Y_O + Y_W$. An extra dollar enjoyed by Wilbur therefore reduces the dollars available for Orville by exactly 1. Orville's dollars may thus be expressed as a function of Wilbur's. This function is linear with a slope of -1; that is:

Figure 17.2 **Maximum Total Welfare**

The sum of the utilities of the two individuals Orville and Wilbur is maximized at combination T, at which the slope of the utility possibility frontier is minus unity. If utilities are weighted unequally, however, the combination which maximizes social welfare will be some other combination like K.

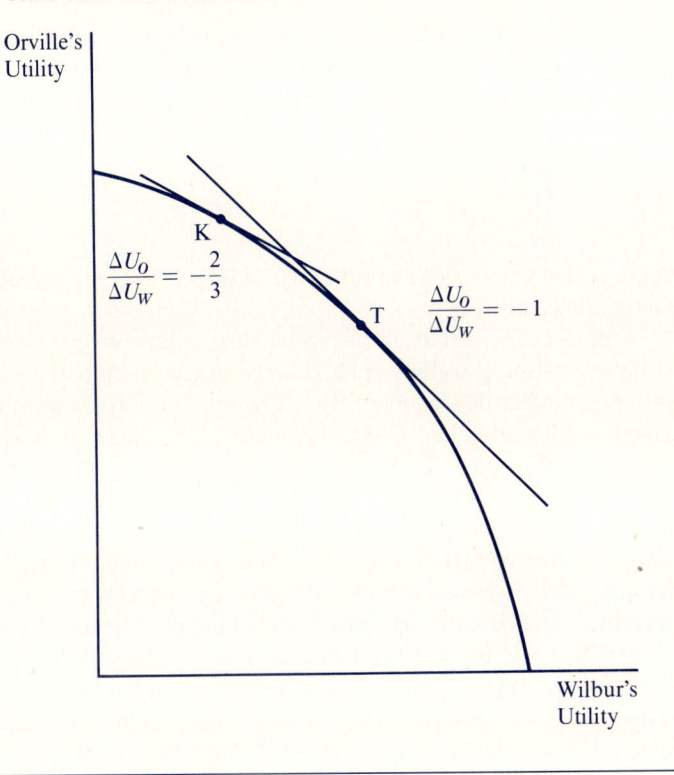

$$Y_O = \hat{Y} - Y_W.$$

$$\frac{\Delta Y_O}{\Delta Y_W} = -1.$$

Social welfare may now be expressed as a function of the income enjoyed by each:

$$U_T = U_O(Y_O) + U_W(Y_W).$$

The rate of change in social welfare per dollar of extra income awarded to Wilbur is given by:

$$\frac{\Delta U_T}{\Delta U_W} = \frac{\Delta U_O}{\Delta Y_O} \cdot \frac{\Delta Y_O}{\Delta Y_W} + \frac{\Delta U_W}{\Delta Y_W}$$

$$\frac{\Delta U_T}{\Delta U_W} = \frac{\Delta U_O}{\Delta Y_O} \cdot (-1) + \frac{\Delta U_W}{\Delta Y_W}.$$

We may identify the welfare-maximizing combination by setting this expression equal to zero. Doing so provides us with some guidance—not much but some:

$$\frac{\Delta U_O}{\Delta Y_O} = \frac{\Delta U_W}{\Delta Y_W}.$$

Welfare is maximized by distributing income in such a way that the marginal utility of income is equal for each member of the community. We may confirm that this is consistent with our earlier result by cross-multiplying here:

$$\frac{\Delta U_O}{\Delta U_W} = \frac{\Delta Y_O}{\Delta Y_W} = -1.$$

Such a policy does indeed result in the slope of the utility possibility frontier of exactly minus unity.

What does this tell us about income distribution policy? Does it suggest, for example, that social welfare is likely to be improved by policies resulting in one distribution rather than another? This depends on the outcome of the spiritual endeavor mentioned earlier. Consider Figure 17.3, where the width of the graph measures total income, $\hat{Y}$. Any point along the horizontal axis, therefore, identifies a distribution of income among our two citizens. As each distribution exhausts the total income available, a point like Y_W^1 identifies both shares, this amount going to Wilbur and the remainder, measured from right to left, going to Orville. The vertical axes measure marginal utility, and the two curves associate the income of each citizen with his own marginal utility of income.

It is assumed that both individuals experience diminishing marginal utility as income rises. There is no way to verify this assumption either, but there are enough problems without raising others. Thus, both curves fall as income increases, Wilbur's from left to right and Orville's from right to left. Wilbur's curve MU_W^1 is drawn as the mirror image of Orville's MU_O. Thus, if we are willing to accept that everyone's utility function with respect to income is the same, we get a very clean result. This result would be very satisfying to some, because it suggests that the distribution of income that maximizes social welfare is absolute **egalitarianism**. If the two marginal utility curves are mirror images of each other, it must be the case that Y_W^2, where marginal utilities of income are equal, lies exactly in the middle: $Y_W^2 = Y - Y_W^2$.

Some are willing to accept such an assumption, and others are not. The great welfare economist A. C. Pigou expressed the views of the more tolerant to this notion as follows.

In the ordinary affairs of life, while recognizing the existence of individual idiosyncrasies, racial differences, differences due to habit and training and so on, we always assume that groups of **prima facie** *similar men will be mentally affected by similar situations in much the same way; that they will get roughly equal enjoyment from a dish of ham and eggs and will suffer a roughly similar sacrifice from surrendering their seat in a railway carriage. We* **expect** *similar*

Figure 17.3   *Efficient Division of Income*

Total income in the economy is $\hat{Y}$. Any value for Y_W therefore determines both Y_W and Y_O. Wilbur's marginal utility of income diminishes from left to right; Orville's marginal utility of income diminishes from right to left. Total utility is maximized at the division indicated by the intersection of the marginal utility of income curves. If the utility functions are the same, the two curves will be mirror images of each other and will intersect at precisely $Y_W^2 = \hat{Y}/2$. If the utility functions differ, the division of income yielding maximum total utility will be unequal.

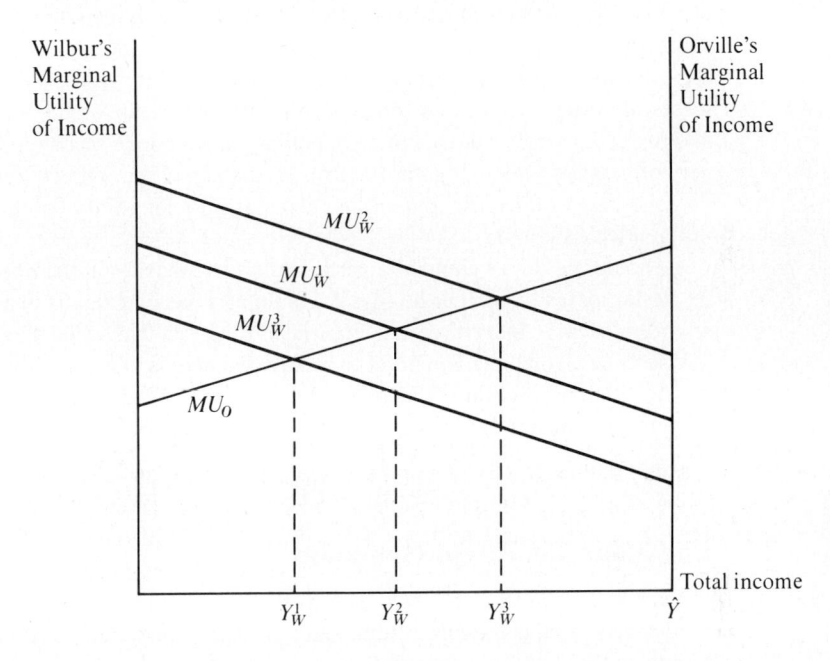

situations to produce similar mental effects, and it is only when they seem not to do so in normal non-philosophic moods that we think there is something to explain.[2]

Less sympathetic views have been expressed by many others, including Stamp:

[I]t is very difficult for a man to say quantitatively that one boot pinches three times as much as the other, even when both are his own, and how much more difficult is it for one man to say that his boot pinches twice as much as another's![3]

---

[2] A. C. Pigou, *A Study in Public Finance*, 3d ed. (London: Macmillan, 1951), 41–42. See footnote 3.
[3] Stamp, *Fundamental Principles of Taxation*, 1921, 53–54. This and the previous quotation were found in the classic essay of W. J. Blum and Harry Kalven, Jr., *The Uneasy Case for Progressive Taxation* (Chicago: University of Chicago Press, 1953).

The author will limit the injection of his own views into this debate of titans to the observation that, though he loathes ham and eggs, he believes his enjoyment of income to be at least on a par with others of his acquaintance who devour them with gusto.

Without this assumption of identical utility functions in income we are rudderless again. Suppose Wilbur's marginal utility of income schedule in Figure 17.3 is really MU_W^2. The optimal distribution of income in this case is for Wilbur to be awarded an income of Y_W^3 and Orville to get the remainder. With marginal utility curve MU_W^3, Wilbur should get only Y_W^1 while Orville gets the larger share. In short, unless we are willing to make very strong assumptions on the basis of introspection alone, we cannot rank alternative policies that involve gains to some and losses to others. Even if, as sometimes is true, we are able to convert these gains and losses into dollar terms, there is nothing in economic theory to assure us that net dollar gains yield net gains in terms of social welfare. Direct income transfers may increase or decrease total utility, depending on the utility functions in income of the affected people.

Should the dollar gains of a particular project be substantial to one group and the dollar losses to another be trivial, common sense may tell us that it is a worthwhile endeavor—indeed, casual empiricism suggests that social choices often follow such an algorithm. The point to be stressed here is that common sense is in no way fortified by economic theory in such a process. Whether such a policy is efficient in a social welfare framework is a matter of guesswork, not of social science.

17.2 Conditions for Pareto Optimality

Of what use is the concept of efficiency or Pareto optimality if it cannot be employed in the day-to-day evaluation of government policy? One important application is that it represents a formidable weapon in the arsenal of economists. While there are many issues one may raise concerning the results of market organization (and we shall discuss some of these in this section), modern welfare economics serves a useful function in shaping and defining these issues. It therefore forms a reasonable vehicle for the pursuit of hypothetical results under various assumed states of the world.

It would be impossible to survey all imaginable sets of assumptions for their implications concerning efficiency. Such a project would fill many books, and we at present have only two chapters at our disposal. Choices must be made concerning which scenarios to present and which to leave out. As realism can hardly form a standard for the assessment of theory (whose chief purpose is abstraction from reality), some other guide must be sought. The examples included here have thus been chosen on the basis of their apparent importance to more specialized fields of economics.

The history of discourse on economic organization is filled with assertions about the inherent defects of capitalism and market-based allocations of resources. One of the more resilient of these ideas is the notion that without some sort of central direction a market economy will produce less output than it is capable of yielding with its resources and/or too few of the "right" type of goods and too many of the "wrong" ones. A logical starting point for a discussion of the merits of this theoretical view would be a description of the conditions necessary for maximization of output from given resources and for the assortment of goods produced to be that most desired by consumers. It turns out that the set of such conditions describes a Pareto optimum. In the next chapter we shall discuss markets in which these conditions are satisfied and others in which they are not.

Models of the economy come in various sizes and shapes. They may be dazzlingly elaborate, or they may be so simple as to convey no information at all. We shall attempt to set a course of moderation between these two extremes.

Results with pairs of variables are the easiest for readers to generalize without straining their credibility. We will therefore reduce our representation of the world to a sort of Noah's Ark, containing two of everything: resources, goods, and people. As a further concession to simplicity we will assume that the resource base is given, though the reader is encouraged to speculate on the additional results necessary to bring forth efficient quantities of labor and capital. We will also assume that technology is independent of institutions and economic settings, an issue of grave importance but analytical intractableness for both the author and his readers.

Early essays in welfare economics were challenged on the grounds that their conclusions were limited in scope to a market-organized economy. A finding that within a market economy society achieves the best results obtainable in a market economy may tell us something about people but very little about the desirability of this form of economic organization. We are more interested in the question of whether people are likely to do better under some other economic regime. It is therefore important to derive our necessary conditions for this social optimum with a minimum of built-in institutional backdrop. We therefore will include no market behavior in our derivation of these conditions and will assume only that individual welfare is related to the combinations of goods each consumes and that output of each good is related to the combination of resources used in its production. The assumptions embodied in our discussion of utility functions and production functions in earlier chapters will govern these relationships.

Three Conditions

Pareto optimality was defined earlier as a state in which it is impossible to make any member of society better off without making someone else worse off. We may give this idea substance in the present framework by considering three decisions governing individual and social welfare.

1. What resources are to be used to produce which goods?

2. How is output to be distributed among persons?

3. What combination of goods will be produced?

These questions must be answered simultaneously. One cannot divide output without knowing how much of each good there is to divide, and one may not know this without also knowing how resources are allocated in production. It is nevertheless possible to derive conditions concerning each of these decisions that must hold if their results are to represent a Pareto optimum.

We may pose the problem in terms of an economy that produces only shoes. If it is possible to increase the output of left shoes without reducing the output of right shoes by reassigning resources from the production of one to the other, the original allocation of resources to production cannot be efficient. The extra shoes might be given to someone increasing their welfare while reducing no one's shoe consumption. We define **technological efficiency** as a situation in which increases in the output of one good that do not reduce the output of another are technically unachievable.

An economy in which half the people had only left shoes and the remaining half had only right shoes would likewise be inefficient. If some redistribution of shoes among the populace were effected, it is quite plausible that some—perhaps all—could be made better off without harming anyone. A second condition for Pareto optimality, therefore, is that all such potential gains from redistributing goods be exhausted. We define this condition as **distributional efficiency**. An economy is distributionally efficient if it is impossible to make anyone better off without making someone else worse off through a reassignment of the goods produced.

Finally, there is the question of what is to be produced. An economy may be producing as many left shoes as is technically feasible without reducing the output of right shoes *and* distributing all shoes produced in ways that permit no gain though reassignment and still be inefficient. Such an economy might be *producing* nothing but left shoes. Under such circumstances it is easy to imagine a reallocation of resources from left to right shoes coupled with a well-calculated distribution of output that would leave some—again, perhaps all—better off without harming anyone. We therefore define **allocative efficiency** as the condition in which no such gains due to a change in the output combination of the economy are achievable. An economy is allocatively efficient if it is impossible to improve the welfare of anyone without reducing the welfare of someone else through a change in the output combination.

In the next three sections we will derive expressions that embody each of these conditions. They are useful in that they are expressed in economic terms and thus may be compared under a variety of conditions to the results of market organization—or any other form of organization, for that matter. They may be used, at least in hypothetical terms, to evaluate the performance of different modes of economic organization in achieving economic efficiency.

Technological Efficiency

Discussion in this and the next section will be developed in terms of a very convenient, if intimidating, device called an **Edgeworth box**.[4] It has the valuable property of representing *pairs* of combinations by a single point in a two-dimensional space. Figure 17.4 is such a box. Let us assume that the total quantity of each resource is fixed and equal to its length and height. As in all of our previous dis-

---

[4]This was named for the inventor of the indifference curve, Francis Y. Edgeworth (1845–1926), an Irish-born economist who spent most of his career at Oxford University.

Figure 17.4 The Edgeworth Box

The total amounts of two resources are given by a and b, the horizontal and vertical dimensions of this rectangle. The isoquant labeled x identifies all combinations of inputs that produce the same output of good x as that produced by combination T. Combination T also identifies the quantities of a and b left over after the use of this combination to produce good x. Let these remaining quantities be used to produce good y. At points to the left of combination T, less a will be left over for the production of y; at points above T, less b will be left over for the production of y. The isoquants for good y production therefore have their origin in the upper right-hand corner and are convex downward.

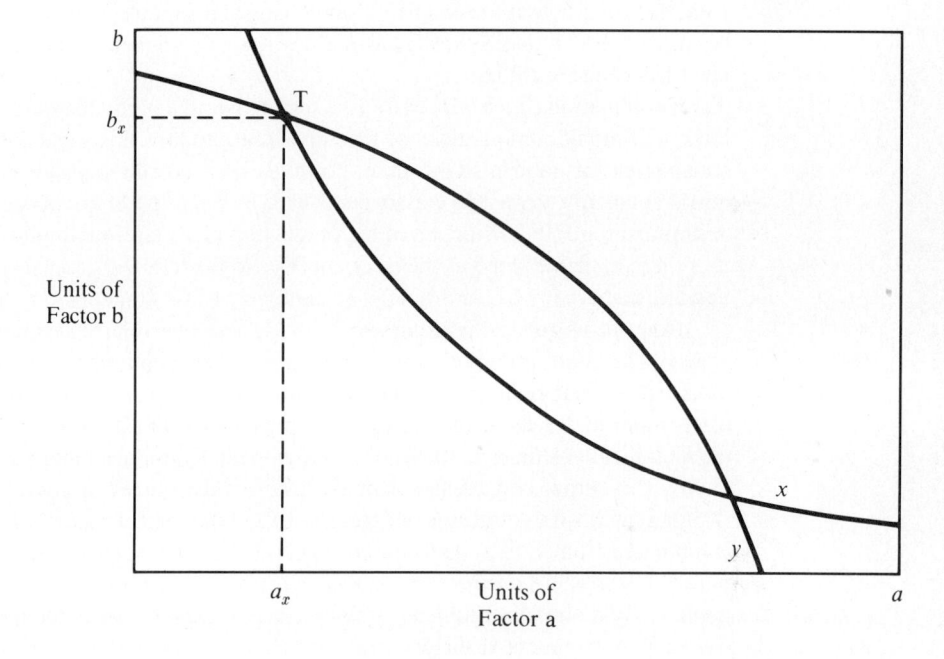

cussions a point like T represents a combination of quantities of these resources, in this case combination (a_x, b_x). However, since the *total* quantities of both resources are fixed, combination T also identifies a second combination: the remainder of these resources once these quantities have been deducted from the total endowments. Let us define these as $a_y = a - a_x$ and $b_y = b - b_x$. Point T thus may be thought of as representing both combinations (a_x, b_x) and (a_y, b_y). For the latter combination, however, the pair of quantities represents coordinates of point T measured from right to left $(a - a_x)$ and from top to bottom $(b - b_x)$. Thus, an increase in b_y would be represented by a *downward* movement of point T, and an increase in a_y would involve a *leftward* shift of this point. Combination $(0_x, 0_x)$ lies in the lower left-hand corner, while combination $(0_y, 0_y)$ lies in the upper right-hand corner. Furthermore, a movement of point T from the left side of the box to the right side identifies every possible division of resource a into two exhaustive quantities, while a movement of point T from top to bottom identifies every possible division of resource b. It therefore follows that every possible pair of combinations of the two resources may be represented by some point in the diagram.

This last observation is most important. Let x be one good and y be the other produced by the economy. Through the production function for each good the combinations of resources associated with each point may be related to the outputs of the two goods. Every point in the diagram thus identifies a specific combination of outputs. Consider point T again. Combination (a_x, b_x) produces a given quantity of good x. We may link all other points associated with combinations that yield the same output to construct a single isoquant for this good. Let that isoquant be the curve x in the figure. It has the downwardly convex shape implied by the law of diminishing RTS.

Combination (a_y, b_y) likewise is associated with a particular output of good y. We may link all combinations of resources that produce this same output to form an isoquant for good y. In this case, however, the isoquant is upside down, points to the southeast along it are associated with less of input a and more of input b. A diminishing RTS for input a in the production of y therefore implies an increasingly *less* negative slope as the isoquant rises to the left. This explains its convex-upward shape.

Now let us relate this Edgeworth box to our question of technological efficiency. That state is defined as one in which higher output of one good cannot be obtained without reducing the output of the other good. Clearly, in this sense an assignment of inputs to production as depicted by point T in Figure 17.5 is not technologically efficient. Alternative assignment K produces more x without reducing the output of y; assignment H increases the output of good y relative to assignment T with no sacrifice of output of x. In the former case, output of good x is increased from x_1 to x_2 while output of good y is unchanged. We see this because points T and K lie on the same isoquant for good y but on higher isoquants for good x. By a similar argument, assignment H represents an efficiency gain relative to T. Assignment H yields y_2 rather than y_1, yet lies on the same isoquant for good x.

According to our definition both assignment H and assignment J are technologically efficient. It can easily be verified that no reassignments away from either of these points can be performed without reducing the output of at least one good. Reassignments that increase the output of good x uniformly lower the output of good y; reassignments that expand y reduce the output x. Cleverly calculated reassignments can reduce both outputs.

We may conclude two things from this exercise. First, any assignment of inputs to production yielding a tangency between the two isoquants passing through it is technologically efficient. Should the isoquants have different slopes, as do the two passing through T, superior points like H and K will invariably exist, implying the possibility of increasing the output of one good without sacrificing the other.

Second, our standard of technological efficiency is satisfied by numerous—indeed, infinite—combinations of goods. Neither H nor K is preferred on efficiency grounds. Both satisfy the criteria defining this condition, as does combination J identified by the tangency of isoquants x_3 and y_3. In fact, tangencies between isoquants undrawn identify a curve passing through H, K, and J connecting all the various assignments of inputs to production that are technologically efficient.

Figure 17.5 Technological Efficiency

Combination T is not efficient. By reassigning inputs to the production of goods x and y, it is possible to increase the output of one good without reducing the output of the other. Reassignment to point H increases the output of y without reducing the output of x; reassignment to K increases the output of x without reducing the output of y. There are an infinite number of assignments that are technologically efficient. These are indicated by the curve connecting H, K, and J.

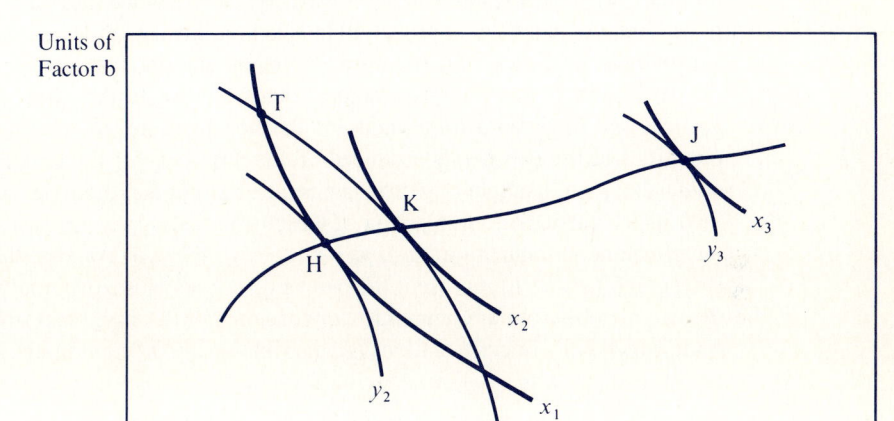

In theory, by knowing the two production functions and the resource endowments of society we could solve such a model for the combinations lying along this technological efficiency locus. Fortunately, for our purposes, no such arithmetical feats are required. We may instead develop from the analysis a set of conditions that may be compared with hypothetical results of market organization to determine if such results are technologically efficient. Our analysis has suggested that technological efficiency requires an assignment involving a tangency of isoquants. Unfortunately, nothing in our analyses of the theory of the firm or the theory of production says anything about isoquants being tangent to each other. However, tangency in the Edgeworth box merely implies that the slopes of the isoquants (minus the RTSs) are equal. From this we may derive a condition for technological efficiency that applies to any community regardless of the form of economic organization: Rates of technical substitution among inputs must be the same for all outputs.

Condition 1: Technological Efficiency

$$RTS^x_{a\ for\ b} = RTS^y_{a\ for\ b}.$$

Distributional Efficiency

Any point along the technologically efficient locus of Figure 17.5 identifies two quantities of goods. A Pareto optimum requires that any such output combination be distributed so that no different distribution makes one consumer better off without harming the other. We must take quantities of two goods and represent them as *pairs* of combinations of the two goods in ways that permit us to evaluate them as such. This sounds very much like what was done with the technological efficiency problem. In that case, quantities of resources were divided into pairs of combinations, and the analytical approach to be taken in this case is almost identical. Not surprisingly, an Edgeworth box may be used here to good effect.

In Figure 17.6 we depict another such diagram. In this case, however, the vertical and horizontal dimensions of the box measure not resources but total quantities of the two goods produced. Total output of x is the length of the horizontal axis, while output of y determines the height of the rectangle. A point like T identifies a particular combination of these two goods—say, (x_O, y_O)—as well as the remainder combination, $(x_W, y_W) = (x - x_O, y - y_O)$. We may therefore allow such combinations to represent the pair of quantities of the two goods assigned to the two members of our community for consumption. Our problem is then to determine which pairs of combinations are distributionally efficient in the sense defined above.

Figure 17.6 *Distributional Efficiency*

This Edgeworth Box identifies pairs of combinations of goods consumed by two individuals. Assignment T is not distributionally efficient. Assignment K increases Orville's utility without lowering Wilbur's, and assignment H increases Wilbur's utility without lowering Orville's. The curve connecting assignments H, K, J, and F identifies all assignments that are distributionally efficient.

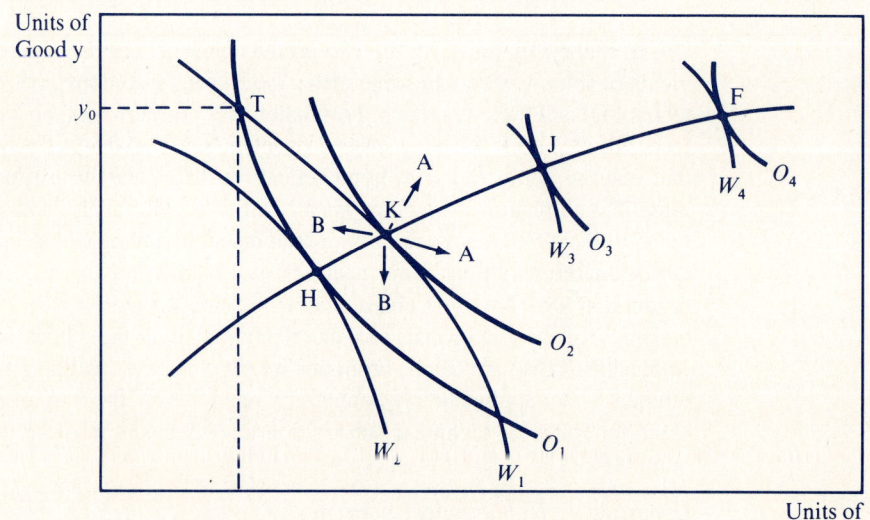

Let us give these two citizens names so that we may keep their consumption activity distinct. Let Orville consume the combination measured in the conventional manner and Wilbur consume the remainder combination. Combination (x_O, y_O) produces a utility for Orville determined by his utility function. From this utility function we may determine all combinations of goods x and y that yield the same utility level and connect them, forming indifference curve O_1. Assuming the property of diminishing MRS gives this curve its convex-downward shape. If Orville consumes (x_O, y_O), Wilbur must consume (x_W, y_W); thus his utility is also determined by point T. We may connect all combinations of x and y yielding the same utility for Wilbur, recalling that these quantities of each good are measured from right to left and top to bottom. Wilbur's indifference curve under these circumstances must be convex upward, reflecting that his MRS diminishes as good x is consumed increasingly along the indifference curve in a northwesterly direction.

The pair of consumption combinations identified by point T cannot be distributionally efficient. A reassignment of goods from the pair of combinations at T is definitely inferior to that represented by both points H and K. The reassignment to K, for example, gives Orville more x and less y than he received at T, and Wilbur's holdings are subtracted from and added to in the same quantities. Such a reassignment increases Orville's welfare, enabling him to reach indifference curve O_2. Wilbur is made no worse off, however, because his new combination containing less x and more y lies on the same indifference curve as (x_W, y_W) at point T. Similarly, the different reassignment to point H is also superior to that of T. In this case, Orville gets a smaller increase in his holdings of x and gives up more y. Wilbur is therefore made better off, enjoying utility W_2 while Orville remains on his initial indifference curve.

Again, two conclusions may be reached from this exercise. First, the condition of distributional efficiency requires that the indifference curves passing through the point identifying the pair of consumption combinations be tangent at that point. Point T, where this is not the case, has been shown to be distributionally inefficient. It is easily shown that point K, where such a tangency does occur, conforms to the definition of distributional efficiency. Reassignments away from K that improve Orville's welfare (those illustrated by the arrows labeled A) reduce Wilbur's. Reassignments that make Wilbur better off (that is, reassignments in directions illustrated by the arrows labeled B) harm Orville. Still other reassignments can reduce the welfare of both. As it is impossible through reassignment to improve the welfare of either citizen without harming the other, point K must be distributionally efficient.

Second, we note that point K is not unique in this respect. Point H also conforms to the definition of distributional efficiency. Reassignments that benefit Orville harm Wilbur, and vice versa. The same applies to points J and F, and to all points along the line joining these and other tangencies between indifference curves not shown in the figure. Although at point F Orville is much better off than he is at point H, while the opposite is true for Wilbur, each of these points is distributionally efficient—not in terms of the distribution of utilities but in terms of the distribution of the output of goods x and y.

If we knew the utility function of each person and the total quantities of the goods to be distributed, we could solve for the set of distributionally efficient pairs of consumption combinations. We could then, at least in principle, observe whether the assignments resulting from hypothetical models of alternative organizations were among the efficient set. Luckily, we need not do this. Again, it is much simpler merely to develop conditions corresponding to these distributions, which may then be compared with hypothetical results under the various institutional forms that might be used to organize them. A tangency between indifference curves implies that the slopes of the curves are the same at the point of tangency. The slope of an indifference curve is equal to minus the consumer's MRS. The condition of equal slopes therefore implies equal MRSs. From this we may state a condition for distributional efficiency: Marginal rates of substitution among goods must be the same for all consumers.

Condition 2: Distributional Efficiency

$$MRS^O_{x \text{ for } y} = MRS^W_{x \text{ for } y}.$$

Allocative Efficiency

We must now confront the problem of identifying efficient combinations of goods for the economy to produce. The opportunity set of such goods has already been identified in Figure 17.5. Each point along the technologically efficient locus is associated with a pair of input combinations that will produce a given output of each good. Combination H, for example, is associated with x_1 units of good x and y_2 units of good y. By moving upward to the right along this line we thus identify increasing quantities of x and diminishing quantities of y that may be produced together. These pairs of outputs may be treated as coordinates of a function relating the quantity of y that may be produced in association with each quantity of x.

Panel (a) of Figure 17.7 depicts such a function, which has been given the name of **production possibility frontier (PPF)**. By definition, points along this curve are technologically efficient. Those lying below it are technologically inefficient, and those above it are technologically unattainable. The economy simply cannot produce the latter. Our problem here is to identify, from among those that can be produced, the combination or combinations that satisfy our definition of allocative efficiency.

For a combination of goods to be allocatively efficient, it must be impossible, by changing that combination, to make anyone better off without harming someone else. We will approach this problem by holding Orville's welfare constant and allowing Wilbur to maximize his. We do this by constraining Orville to consume some combination along his indifference curve, U_O, in panel (a), then permitting Wilbur to select among all combinations left available by this constraint.

The nature of Wilbur's opportunities are depicted in panel (b) of Figure 17.7. This process is made cumbersome by the fact that we must choose for Wilbur both an opportunity set and a favored combination along it. This is necessary because the consumption opportunities available to Wilbur are themselves affected by the combination we make available to Orville. Consider Orville's combination, T, in panel (a), containing x_1^O of good x and y_1^O of good y. We may supply Orville with this bundle from any combination along *PPF* from point T_1 to T_2. Doing so, of course, changes the combination that Wilbur obtains. If we select T_1, Wilbur gets

Figure 17.7 *Allocative Efficiency*

Panel (a) contains a production possibility frontier and one of Orville's indifference curves. If we restrict Orville's utility level to that associated with the indifference curve in this panel, he must consume some combination on the indifference curve. Consumption by Orville of a combination like T implies that Wilbur may consume any combination along opportunity set T in panel (b). If Orville is provided with H instead, the opportunity set for Wilbur changes to that indicated by curve H in panel (b). Whatever combination Orville is provided with, Wilbur will prefer a combination like K in panel (b), at which his MRS is equal to the RPT.

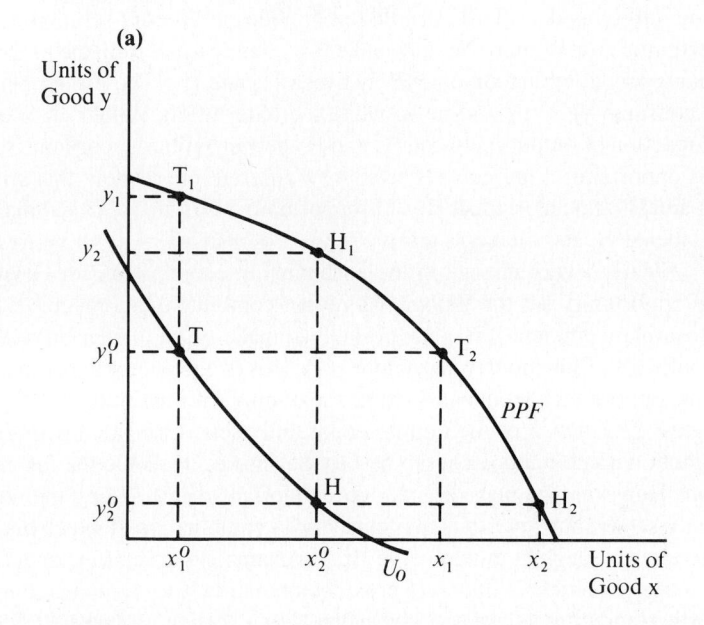

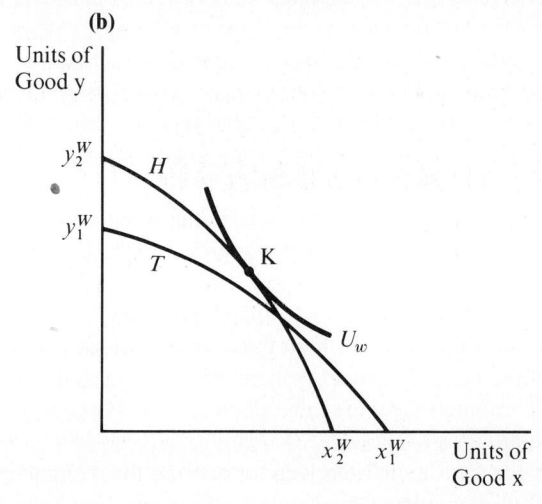

$y_1 - y_1^O$ units of y and none of x; if we select T_2, he gets $x_1 - x_1^O$ units of x and no y. Selection of a point between T_1 and T_2 provides varying amounts of both. Close inspection of panel (a) will reveal that Wilbur's opportunity set under these circumstances consists of the pie-shaped piece cut from the opportunity set with corners at T_1 and T_2 and an origin at T. This opportunity set is shown in panel (b) as the curve labeled T. The vertical intercept is $y_1^W = y_1 - y_1^O$, and the horizontal intercept is $x_1^W = x_1 - x_1^O$.

Now observe how the opportunities change when Orville is permitted to consume an alternative combination, H. This combination, (x_2^O, y_2^O), produces the same utility as does T for Orville but provides a different set of consumption opportunities for Wilbur. We may make this combination available to Orville by producing any combination on PPF between H_1 and H_2. The former permits Wilbur to consume $y_2 - y_2^O$ and no x, while the latter offers Wilbur $x_2 - x_2^O$ and no y. Production of outputs between H_1 and H_2 permit Wilbur to consume some of both. His opportunities are now reflected by a different pie section, that with corners at H_1 and H_2 and an origin at H. This opportunity set is also depicted in panel (b) and is labeled H. Its intercepts are $y_2^W = y_2 - y_2^O$ and $x_2^W = x_2 - x_2^O$, respectively.

Clearly, every change in the consumption combination for Orville will shift the opportunity set for Wilbur. An output combination along curve PPF will be allocatively efficient if it is not possible to make Wilbur better off without moving Orville off of his indifference curve, U_O. This is equivalent to finding the point on some opportunity set in panel (b) that maximizes Wilbur's utility. We cannot see in Figure 17.7 *which* of the infinite opportunity sets (associated with different consumption combinations chosen by Orville) makes available the favored combination. However, we may discover one important result. Along the chosen opportunity set Wilbur's utility is maximized by a combination at which his indifference curve is just tangent to that curve. If, for example, curve H in panel (b) offers the best opportunities, Wilbur will prefer combination K to any other along this curve. Furthermore, since curve H corresponds to a section of curve PPF in panel (a), the slope at point K must be equal to the slope of PPF at the point identifying the total output of goods x and y that makes this choice possible.

This can be seen in Figure 17.8. In panel (b) of this figure we have reproduced the opportunity set for Wilbur (curve H) associated with Orville's combination H in panel (a). Wilbur's favored combination among those available in panel (b) is K, containing y^W of good y and x^W of good x. This corresponds to total output combination K in panel (a). This total output combination yields just enough of the two goods to provide each consumer with the quantity identified by his combination: $y_3 = y_2^O + y^W$ and $x_3 = x_2^O + x^W$. Since K lies exactly x^W units to the right of x_2^O and y^W units above y_2^O, the slope of PPF at that point must be exactly equal to the slope at point K in panel (b). A necessary condition for the output combination to be allocatively efficient is that the indifference curve of at least one of the consumers have the same slope through his consumption combination as the slope of PPF.

We may invoke Condition 2, derived for distributional efficiency, to complete the development of conditions for allocative efficiency. That condition stated that distributional efficiency requires that total output be assigned to consumers so as to equate the MRSs of each. Since allocative efficiency requires that minus the

Figure 17.8 *Consumption Combinations and Allocative Efficiency*

The consumption combination K chosen by Wilbur in panel (b) corresponds to output combination K in panel (a). Orville receives combination H in panel (a), providing Wilbur with the opportunity set labeled H in panel (b). Wilbur selects combination K in panel (b), which contains x^W of good x and y^W of good y. The amounts of each of these goods added to Orville's quantities of each add up to the coordinates of combination K in panel (a).

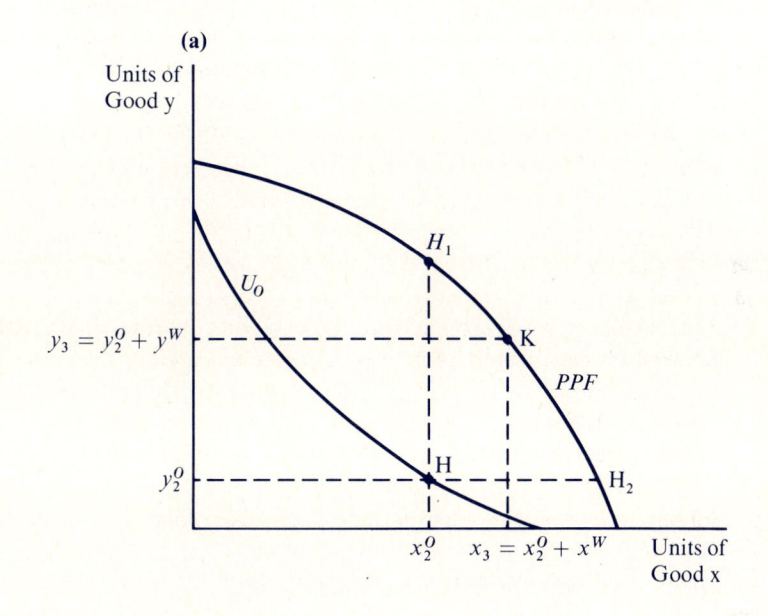

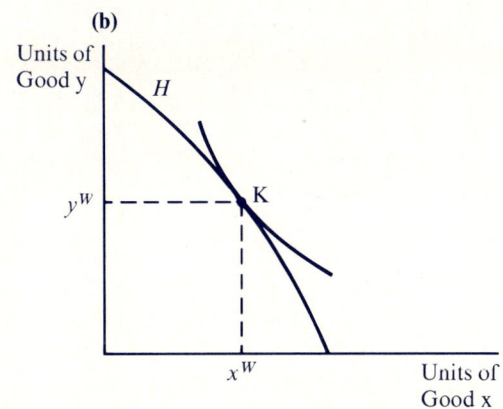

MRS of at least one consumer be equal to the slope of the PPF at the effective output combination, both conditions together require that *all* MRSs conform in this regard.

The Rate of Product Transformation (RPT)

It is useful to express the slope of the PPF in terms of recognizable economic variables. For this purpose we define another economic ratio, the ratio of the marginal physical product of a single factor in the production of two separate goods, that is MPP_a^y/MPP_a^x, as the **rate of product transformation (RPT)**. Here we will show that the slope of the PPF is equal to minus the RPT.

We begin with Condition 1 for efficiency, which states that rates of technical substitution must be equal for all goods:

$$\frac{MPP_a^x}{MPP_b^x} = \frac{MPP_a^y}{MPP_b^y}.$$

By cross-multiplying, we see that this condition requires that the RPT (labeled ρ) be equal for each factor:

$$\frac{MPP_a^y}{MPP_a^x} = \frac{MPP_b^y}{MPP_b^x} = \rho.$$

Solving for two marginal physical products, we obtain:

(17.1) $\qquad MPP_a^y = \rho \cdot MPP_a^x; \quad MPP_b^y = \rho \cdot MPP_b^x.$

Consider now the production functions for good x and good y. As the output of x depends on the quantity of a and b used in its production—that is, $x = x(a, b)$ —we may write an expression for the change in *x* produced as:

$$\Delta x = \frac{\Delta x}{\Delta a} \cdot \Delta a_x + \frac{\Delta x}{\Delta b} \cdot \Delta b_x$$

$$\Delta x = MPP_a^x \Delta a_x + MPP_b^x \Delta b_x.$$

As the output of good y is also a function of the quantity of a and b used in its production—$y = y(a, b)$, we may also express changes in the output of this good as:

$$\Delta y = MPP_a^y \Delta a_y + MPP_b^y \Delta b_y.$$

Substituting into this expression from (17.1) yields:

$$\Delta y = \rho MPP_a^x \Delta a_y + \rho MPP_b^x \Delta b_y$$

$$\Delta y = \rho (MPP_a^x \Delta a_y + MPP_b^x \Delta b_y).$$

Now we wish to derive from these materials the slope of the PPF. In other words we wish to evaluate $\Delta y/\Delta x$ under specific circumstances: that all of the resources a and b are used in the production of either one good or the other. As the slope is measured for positive changes in x, this implies that $\Delta a_y = -\Delta a_x$ and $\Delta b_y = -\Delta b_x$. Making these substitutions in equation (17.2) and dividing one differential by the other establishes the theorem. The slope of the PPF is equal to minus the RPT:

$$\frac{\Delta y}{\Delta x} = \frac{-\rho(MPP_a^x \Delta a_x + MPP_b^x \Delta b_x)}{(MPP_a^x \Delta a_x + MPP_b^x \Delta b_x)}$$

$$\frac{\Delta y}{\Delta x} = -\rho = -RPT.$$

Returning to the condition for allocative efficiency, we may now state this condition in terms of the ratio just developed. Previously it was shown that the slope of the indifference curves of all consumers must equal the slope of the PPF at the combination of x and y produced for the economy as a whole. As the slopes of indifference curves are equal to minus the consumer's MRSs and the slope of the PPF is equal to minus the RPT, a condition for allocative efficiency is given by the following:

Condition 3: Allocative Efficiency

$$MRS^O_{x\ for\ y} = MRS^W_{x\ for\ y} = RPT_{y\ into\ x}.$$

The marginal rate of substitution of each consumer between any pair of goods must equal the economy's rate of product transformation between the two goods.

17.3 Pareto Optimality with Public Goods

Public Goods

The three conditions developed in the previous section are sufficient to insure Pareto optimality in the simple world that we have been discussing. We must now complicate that world a bit in order to deal with a special type of good that has been ignored in earlier chapters. The goods with which we have been concerned up to this point may be consumed only by a single person or household; their use must be rationed. If you eat a peach, the amount of peaches available for others to consume is reduced by one unit. If you are using an automobile, there is one less automobile available for use by others. There are some goods, however, that may be used by everyone simultaneously and whose quantity available at any moment provides services to all simultaneously. Consumption of these goods has been described as *nonrival*, because making them available to some users does not diminish the quantity available to others. These goods are called collective consumption goods, or, more commonly, **public goods**. Their use need not be rationed.

There are many goods that seem to qualify as public goods. Examples are inventions and scientific discoveries, songs, mathematical theorems, television signals, and economic forecasts. Your use of the Pythagorean theorem does not imply that you have used up some of this knowledge, precluding its employment by others. Just as much knowledge concerning the relationship among the sides of right triangles exists after your application of the theorem as existed before. You do not have to compete with other demanders for the services of this public good. The same is true of television broadcasts; when you tune in, no one else need tune out.

Allocative Efficiency with Public Goods

The existence of public goods does not alter the conditions we derived. Allocation of resources in production, as well as the choice and distribution of output combinations for conventional or **private goods**, must conform to these conditions even where public goods are present. We must simply add a fourth condition describing efficient resource allocation pertaining to these goods. This is developed in connection with Figure 17.9. This figure resembles Figure 17.8 in which allocative efficiency conditions were described for two private goods. In this case, however, we let good x be a public good and good y be a private good. As good x is a public good, *both* Orville and Wilbur may use whatever quantity of that good is produced. The curve labeled *PPF* again describes the combinations of the two goods that are technically feasible to produce with the resources that are available in the community.

Here as in the earlier figure we approach the problem of achieving a Pareto optimum by holding Orville's utility constant and maximizing Wilbur's utility over the remaining set of combinations. Two constraints operate to determine the opportunity set available to Wilbur: (1) Total consumption by both individuals must be technically feasible—that is, all x and y consumed by the community must be a combination on the PPF—and (2) Orville's consumption combination must lie on the indifference curve associated with his given utility level.

The two curves associated with these two constraints are depicted in the figure. Feasible production combinations are identified by curve *PPF*, and Orville's indifference curve is labeled U_O. These two curves represent functions of good y in terms of the public good, x. *PPF* identifies quantities of y that may be produced together with chosen quantities of x. Let us identify this function as $y_t = t(x)$. Orville's indifference curve associates quantities of each good that together produce the given utility level. Let this function be described as $y_o = U_o(x)$. Wilbur's quantity of the private good can therefore be related directly to the quantity of the public good x produced. It too is a function of x—indeed, it may be shown to be the difference in the two functions just described.

Consider the y intercept of Orville's indifference curve. Here Orville uses no public good at all. He achieves the given utility level by consuming y_1^o of the private good and no x. If Orville consumes no public good, then neither will Wilbur, since both consume all the public good that is produced. The total quantity of y that may be produced with zero public goods is y_1, identified by the vertical intercept of *PPF*, quantity $t(O)$. The quantity of good y available to Wilbur may thus

Figure 17.9   *Allocative Efficiency with Public Goods*

Here we have a production possibility frontier for a public good and a private good. An indifference curve for Orville is labeled U_O. Wilbur's opportunity set may be included in this figure, since both consume the same quantities of the public good. The vertical dimension of this opportunity set identifies the quantity of private good y left over after Orville is provided with enough to keep him on indifference curve U_O at each quantity of public good x produced. The best Wilbur can do along this opportunity set is combination K. This identifies x^* as the efficient quantity of the public good and T as the allocatively efficient combination to produce.

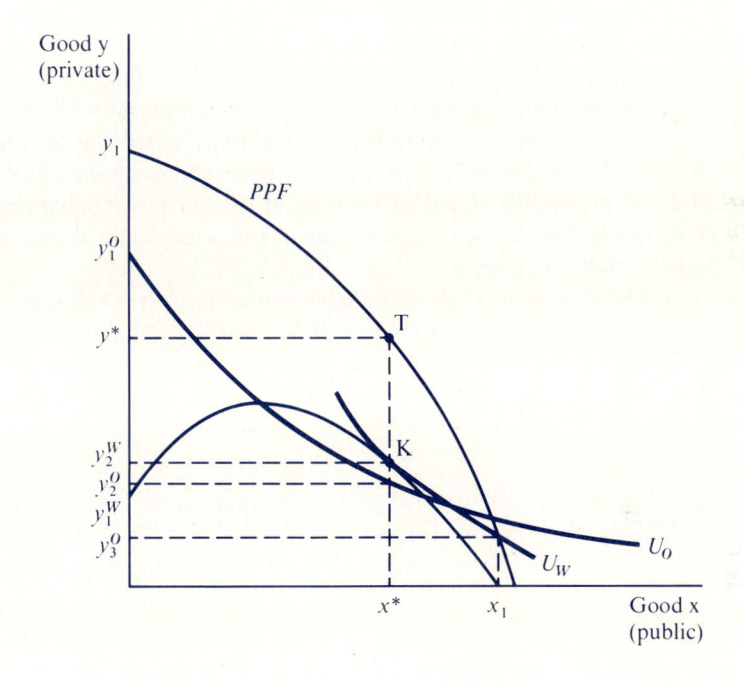

be identified by subtracting $y_1^O = U_O(O)$ from $y_1 = t(O)$. Thus, we have one point on Wilbur's opportunity set, (O, y_1^W), where $y_1^W = y_1 - y_1^O$.

When positive amounts of the public good are produced, the amount of good y available to Wilbur at each quantity of x is also determined by the difference in the heights of the two curves. Let quantity x^* of the public good be produced. Combination T identifies the maximum quantity of the private good, y, that may be produced with this quantity of the public good. Orville must be provided with y_2^O units to keep him on indifference curve U_O, leaving $y_2^W = y^* - y_2^O = t(x^*) - y_O(x^*)$ for Wilbur. Let us therefore define Wilbur's opportunity set as the function of private good y in terms of public good x as follows:

$$y_W(x) = t(x) - y_O(x).$$

The reader may verify that the height of this curve at each value of x is equal to the difference between the height of the PPF and Orville's indifference curve at that quantity. Note that this curve has a height of zero at x_1 where these two curves intersect, and the difference in their heights is zero—$t(x_1) - y_O(x_1) = y_W(x_1) = 0$.

Wilbur's utility is maximized along such an opportunity set by combination K, at which one of his indifference curves is just tangent to $y_W(x)$. Note that there is no presumption that both Wilbur and Orville have the same tastes. It is possible that the indifference curves of these two individuals may intersect as shown in the figure. This solution to the efficiency problem implies both an optimal combination of outputs and an optimal distribution of the private good among the two consumers. Combination T will be produced containing x^* of the public good and y^* of the private good. Both will consume this quantity of the public good. The private good will be distributed with y_2^O going to Orville and y_2^W going to Wilbur.

As a tangency between Wilbur's indifference curve and his opportunity set identifies this optimum, we may conclude that a necessary condition for allocative efficiency is that the slopes of the two curves be equal. Giving economic interpretations to these curves therefore provides us with conditions that must be satisfied for Pareto optimality.

Consider first the slope of Wilbur's opportunity set. This slope must be equal to the difference between the slopes of $t(x)$ and $y_O(x)$; that is:

$$\frac{\Delta y}{\Delta x} = \frac{\Delta t}{\Delta x} - \frac{\Delta y_O}{\Delta x}.$$

Consider the terms on the right side of this expression. The first term is the slope of the PPF, which is minus the RTS; the second is the slope of Orville's indifference curve, which is minus his MRS. This slope may thus be rewritten:

$$\frac{\Delta y_W}{\Delta x} = -RPT + MRS^O.$$

Now note that efficiency requires that Wilbur's indifference curve have the same slope as his opportunity set. At the efficient allocation, in other words, the slope of the opportunity set must be equal to minus Wilbur's MRS, and:

$$\frac{\Delta y_W}{\Delta x} = -MRS^W = -RPT + MRS^O.$$

This, by rearranging terms, yields:

$$RPT = MRS^O + MRS^W.$$

By analogy, we may generalize this result to the case of many *(n)* individuals in the community. For that case Pareto optimality requires the following:

Condition 4: Allocative Efficiency with Public Goods

$$RPT_{y \text{ into } x} = \sum_{i=1}^{n} MRS^i_{x \text{ for } y}.$$

The rate of product transformation of private into public goods must equal the *sum* of the marginal rates of substitution of all who value the public good.

Again, the optimum illustrated by this process need not be unique. Had we held Orville's utility constant at a different level, it is quite possible that the optimum derived would have been achieved at a different combination than T. It certainly would have resulted in a different distribution of the private good y. Combination (x^*, y_2^o), which Orville receives at this optimum, lies on indifference curve U_O and no other. The *condition* derived must hold regardless. Allowing Orville more or less utility modifies Wilbur's opportunity set, but the optimum allocation will under any circumstances be identified by a tangency between one of the latter's indifference curves and an opportunity set derived in the manner described.

Two things are noteworthy concerning this result. First, we see that for public goods, unlike private goods, efficiency requires that the RPT be greater than any single individual's MRS. Second, the MRSs of individuals for public goods need not be equal; Condition 2 need not hold for these goods. In the figure the slope of Orville's indifference curve is steeper than Wilbur's at quantity x^*. Wilbur's MRS therefore exceeds Orville's at this optimum.

Pareto Optimality Again

In a world containing both public and private goods, satisfaction of these four conditions may be sufficient to achieve Pareto optimality. We could complicate this world further with corner solutions, non-convexities, and any number of such technical difficulties requiring modifications or extensions of these conditions, but these are left for more advanced theory courses; in a "well-behaved" world, these four are enough. However, it must be stressed that in deriving these four conditions we have in no way solved the efficiency problem. The theory leads us neither to a unique combination of goods for the economy to produce nor to a unique combination of utilities among citizens. Changes in the latter typically imply changes in the former, and we have neither sidestepped nor extricated ourselves from the problem of combining and comparing utilities discussed at the beginning of this chapter. A particular allocation may be Pareto optimal and yet be grossly unfair. We offer here no economic method for choosing among the various possible Pareto optima.

Our purpose in presenting this material was to illustrate circumstances under which certain institutional settings do and do not yield allocations that are hypothetically efficient. This can provide a potentially important lesson. News analysts and folk singers are fond of pie-in-the-sky. They see the world as an elaborate riddle that can be made to yield up an endless stream of satisfying solutions to the problems they discover. According to these visionaries we might have invisible air, crystal water, safe automobiles, and world peace, not to mention low-cost food, clothing, housing, education, and dental care, if only people listened. The latter items might, of course, be paid for out of a "guaranteed" wage that would not be permitted to fall below the "poverty" level. Utopia is only a few bold steps away.

The lesson that welfare economics teaches is that the existing allocation of goods may be fairly close to a Pareto optimum, at least if we remain vague concerning the units in which that proximity is measured. The market system can be shown to approach this result under certain hypothetical characterizations. If this is true, however, then society must make painful decisions offering scant inspiration for song and dance, not obvious and easy ones. In such a world there are no solutions to problems; social change requires subverting the interests of some citizens to serve the interests of others. One man's solution is another man's problem. This is not to say that such change is not desirable or should not be undertaken. It is merely another way of repeating that dismal platitude, "There's no such thing as a free lunch."

Summary

In this chapter we sought to do three things. First, we attempted to define economic efficiency in a way that is both analytically useful and logically correct. Second, we tried to alert the reader to the extremely limited range of welfare economics in the analysis of policy. Third, we used our definition of efficiency to derive a set of economic conditions that are necessary if efficiency is to be achieved.

The first of these involved an excursion into the history of economic analysis. We discussed early attempts to aggregate community welfare and demonstrated the impossibility of moving analytically from individual welfare levels to some exact measure of social welfare. Efforts to do this are confounded by the impossibility of utility measurement on the one hand and the assignment of weights to individual welfares on the other. Common sense may suggest methods of dealing with both of these problems, but economics offers no substitute solutions.

Efficiency can therefore be defined only in an incomplete and extremely limited form. No particular allocation of resources is more efficient than all others. Efficiency is defined as an allocation that leaves no opportunity for improvement in anyone's welfare without reducing the welfare of someone else. Such a state is said to be Pareto optimal, and an infinite number of such states are possible. Different states of the world may be identified as either efficient or inefficient, but we cannot say that all efficient states are better than any inefficient state. We are limited to the far less useful proposition that for any inefficient state there must be some efficient state preferred to it on welfare grounds. The scope for welfare economics to illuminate policy is therefore extremely limited. Only those changes which improve the welfare of some without harming others can be described as clearly welfare improving.

Welfare economics is chiefly useful as an aid in abstracting results of economic organization. We can develop from our definition of efficiency various conditions that are necessary for its achievement. Several forms of economic organization may thus be evaluated at an abstract level in terms of the satisfaction of these conditions. For that purpose we developed four conditions governing the assignment of inputs to outputs, the assignment of goods to individuals, the determination of efficient combinations of output of private goods, and the determination of efficient quantities of public goods.

Chapter 17 Welfare Economics: Defining Efficiency

There remain the questions of whether markets or other forms of economic organization satisfy some or all these conditions and under what circumstances. These issues are treated in the next chapter.

Key Concepts

positive theory
normative theory
economic efficiency
efficiency gain
Pareto optimality
utility possibility frontier
weighting of individual utilities
measurement of utility levels
egalitarianism

technological efficiency
distributional efficiency
allocative efficiency
Edgeworth box
production possibility frontier (PPF)
rate of product transformation (RPT)
public goods
private goods

Questions

1. *Easy* Explain the difference between an efficiency gain and an efficient state of the world, that is, a state of the world that is Pareto optimal.

Hard The ranking of states of the world in terms of efficiency gains is said to suffer from incompleteness. Describe this problem and explain how it might be eliminated by the invention of a utility meter that could measure individual utilities in each state of the world.

2. *Easy* The sum of two people's utilities is maximized at the point at which the slope of the utility possibility frontier is exactly minus unity. Explain.

Hard The sum of utilities may be maximized by relating utility levels to the distribution of income. By distributing income so as to equate each person's marginal utility, maximum social welfare may be achieved. Demonstrate this result and explain the circumstances under which it suggests equalizing all income. How would this conclusion have to be modified if output in the economy were related to individual incomes?

3. *Easy* In what sense are input assignments H and K in Figure 17.5 more efficient than assignment T?

Hard Can we say conclusively that a shift from assignment T to assignment J in Figure 17.5 will offer efficiency gains? Why or why not?

4. *Easy* What is the relationship between the line passing through combinations H, K, and F in Figure 17.5 and the production possibility frontier in Figure 17.7?

Hard The slope of the production possibility frontier is equal to minus the rate of product transformation, MPP_A^y/MPP_A^x. Bearing the interpretation of the marginal physical product of a factor in mind, give a common-sense explanation for this equality.

5. *Easy* The production of an extra unit of a public good has an opportunity cost in terms of the reduction in the quantities of other goods that might be produced with the same resources. However, the opportunity cost of making such a good available for consumption by an additional person is zero. Explain.

Hard It is sometimes argued that theatrical productions are public goods because an additional patron may view the performances without increasing production cost (as long as there are empty seats). A similar argument can be made about highways and universities. This incorrect argument is based on an excessively short-run view; the cost of making these goods available to additional users is not zero in the long run. Explain.

6. *Easy* Achieving allocative efficiency with respect to the production of public goods does not require that all consumers' marginal rates of substitution be equal. Explain.

Hard A particular allocation may be Pareto optimal and yet be unfair. Give some examples of hypothetical allocations to which this statement applies in your view. State as explicitly as you can your reasons for regarding these allocations as unfair in language that applies generally (that is, to many cases, not simply a few specific instances).

Chapter 18

Markets, Governments, and Efficiency

Connections   *This final chapter applies the efficiency conditions developed in Chapter 17 to alternative characterizations of the real world. In general, where markets contain price-taking buyers and sellers the conditions are satisfied. Where one or the other has power over price, the conditions are violated. However, market failure is not the only source of inefficiency. Many activities of government also inhibit efficient resource use; examples of these are price controls, rationing, taxation, and regulation. As efficiency concerns itself with production, technology, and distribution, our discussion here draws bits and pieces of analysis from almost every chapter of this book. Of particular note are the discussions of transaction costs in Chapter 7 and cartel behavior in Chapter 10. In a world of no transaction costs there is little scope for inefficiency. Transaction costs therefore shape the efficiency problems with which we deal here. This chapter also contains an extensive discussion of the problems of market organization of the production of public goods. Readers will identify significant parallels between the analysis of colluding firms from Chapter 10 and that of public good users.*

There is little disagreement among economists on the requirements for efficiency discussed in the previous chapter. Those conditions are sufficiently abstract to make disagreement difficult. Few economists disagree over the interpretation of tangency conditions. The real world, on the other hand, is an infinitely malleable clay in the hands of its various portrayers. According to some, there are scarcely any markets that function as we have described them in the earlier chapters of this book. Big business joins with big labor to administer prices and wages. The consumer is seen to be awash in a sea of fraudulent claims for useless and unhealthy merchandise, lacking any semblance of the information necessary to make intelligent purchases. Employment and mobility through the corporate hierarchy are seen as less a matter of merit and productivity than of profitable connections and cunning duplicity.

On the other hand, some economists see the world as highly competitive at every margin. Information is cheap and resource mobility highly responsive to prices. Such a world conforms in most details to the competitive version of the market economy described by economic theory. Monopoly is a rare and fleeting condition vitiated by the inherent instability of collusive arrangements and the absence of important scale economies in production.

It is not our purpose here to weigh the merits of these or other less extreme characterizations of the American economy. The correct description of the world is the function of positive economics: theory, hypothesis, and verification. It is a continuing task of economists to articulate a clearer view of the nature of that world, and we have only scratched the surface. This task may in fact never be completed, for the world changes too. When we do welfare economics, we are therefore very obviously playing at what was described as "What if?" in the last chapter. It is a game in which the answers depend to a distressingly large extent on the "ifs" posited.

18.1 The Competitive Model

We begin by describing a world in which all economic agents are price takers. Markets for all goods and resources are competitive, and prices are determined by supply and demand. Consider the case of firms organizing production. In Chapter 12 it was shown that any cost-minimizing firm will hire the combination of resources to produce its chosen output that equates its RTS with the ratio of the prices of these resources. If this is true for producers of every good, and factor prices are the same for all firms, then:

$$RTS^x_{a \text{ for } b} = \frac{P_a}{P_b} = RTS^y_{a \text{ for } b}.$$

Condition 1 is satisfied. The competitive market organizes production in a technologically efficient way.

Similarly, in Chapter 4 it was shown that consumers maximize their welfare subject to a constraint expressed in terms of income and constant prices by choosing combinations of goods that equate their MRSs to the price ratios of those goods. If this is true of every consumer and goods are priced the same to all, then:

$$MRS^O_{x\text{ for }y} = \frac{P_x}{P_y} = MRS^W_{x\text{ for }y}.$$

MRSs are equated among consumers, and Condition 2 holds as well. The assignment of goods to individuals by competitive markets is distributionally efficient.

It may also be shown that competitive markets will satisfy Condition 3, though this argument requires a bit more foundation. Once more we begin with the cost minimization condition requiring that the RTS of producers equal the ratio of the factor prices:

$$RTS^x_{a\text{ for }b} = \frac{MPP^x_a}{MPP^x_b} = \frac{P_a}{P_b}.$$

Cross-multiplying in this case yields the conclusion that the ratio of input prices to marginal physical products must be the same for all inputs:

$$\frac{P_a}{MPP^x_a} = \frac{P_b}{MPP^x_b} = \lambda_x.$$

Solving for these prices yields:

(18.1) $$P_a = \lambda_x MPP^x_a; \quad P_b = \lambda_x MPP^x_b.$$

Now we will show that λ_x must equal marginal cost. Total cost will equal the sum of expenditure on factor a, which varies with the amount employed, $P_a a$ and expenditure on factor b, which also varies with the quantity employed, $P_b b$. Thus, total cost is:

$$c = P_a a + P_b b.$$

The change in cost is given by:

$$\Delta c = P_a \Delta A + P_b \Delta b.$$

Substituting for the factor prices from equation (18.1) gives:

$$\Delta c = \lambda_x MPP^x_a \Delta A + \lambda_x MPP^x_b \Delta b$$

$$\Delta c = \lambda_x (MPP^x_a \Delta A + MPP^x_b \Delta b).$$

Now consider output. For any good such as x, the firm's output of that good depends on the quantities of the factors used. Since $x = x(a, b)$, changes in that output may be represented as:

$$\Delta x = \frac{\Delta x}{\Delta a} \cdot \Delta a + \frac{\Delta x}{\Delta b} \cdot \Delta b.$$

$$\Delta x = MPP_a^x \Delta a + MPP_b^x \Delta b.$$

Dividing one change by the other gives the promised result. Marginal cost (*MC*) is equal to λ, which itself is equal to the ratio of the factor price to its marginal physical product for any input:

$$MC_x = \frac{\Delta c}{\Delta x} = \frac{\lambda_x(MPP_a^x \Delta a + MPP_b^x \Delta b)}{MPP_a^x \Delta a + MPP_b^x \Delta b} = \lambda_x.$$

We are now equipped to deal with Condition 17.3. Competitive firms maximize profits by selecting outputs at which marginal cost equals price. For producers of goods x and y, this implies that:

$$P_x = MC_x = \lambda_x; \, P_y = MC_y = \lambda_y.$$

Dividing one equality by the other yields for any factor, *i*:

$$\frac{P_x}{P_y} = \frac{\lambda_x}{\lambda_y} = \frac{P_i/MPP_i^x}{P_i/MPP_i^y} = \frac{MPP_i^y}{MPP_i^x} = RPT.$$

Firms selecting output on the basis of price equal to marginal cost thereby insure that the price ratio will be equal to the rate of product transformation.

To close the circle we need only recall that consumers choose combinations of goods that equate their MRSs to the market price ratios:

$$MRS_{x \, for \, y} = \frac{P_x}{P_y} = RPT_{y \, into \, x}.$$

Price taking in input and output markets satisfies Condition 3. Each consumer buys the combination that equates his or her MRS to the ratio of the prices of the goods he or she buys. On the other side of the market, suppliers produce quantities of these goods that equate their marginal costs to their prices. The ratio of marginal costs will equal the RPT for each pair of goods, so this behavior insures that the RPT will also equal the price ratio. Equilibrium between the buyers and sellers of goods therefore produces a selection of goods that is allocatively efficient.

18.2 Market Failure

In this simple description of a market economy, the resulting allocation of resources is not inconsistent with Pareto optimality. Market results satisfy each of the necessary conditions for economic efficiency in private good allocation. To the extent that the real world mirrors the assumption of price-taking behavior in all private good markets, allocation of resources may also be Pareto optimal. However, students are cautioned against a facile acceptance of these heady conclusions. Before adopting such a stance, it will profit the reader to consider the efficiency properties of other characterizations of market results.

Price Searching

Chapter 10 described the forces likely to interfere with price taking in the output market. We need not rehearse here the arguments presented, which concluded that economies of scale, transportation costs, and information costs can give a seller market power. In each of these cases profits are maximized at an output at which price exceeds marginal cost. The incorporation of a price-searching sector into our model of the real world inserts a sobering inequality into the congenial chain discussed in the previous section. Consumers continue to purchase combinations at which their MRSs equal the price ratio, but the price ratio no longer reflects the RPT.

Let good x represent the price searching sector, and let the elasticity of demand faced by its producers be η. Here profits are maximized at outputs at which marginal cost is equal to marginal revenue given by $P_x(1 + 1/\eta)$. Assuming that demanders and suppliers of good y are price takers, price will continue to equal marginal cost in that sector. In this case we are left with:

(18.2) $$MRS_{x\,for\,y} = \frac{P_x}{P_y} > \frac{P_x\left(1 + \frac{1}{\eta}\right)}{P_y} = \frac{MC_x}{MC_y} = RPT_{y\,into\,x}.$$

This clearly does not satisfy Condition 3.

It may be helpful to attempt a graphical presentation of this efficiency problem. This is done in Figure 18.1, which is a simplified version of Figure 17.8. Simplification is essential here, for we must attempt to compress the behaviors of buyers, producers, factor suppliers, and demanders, as well as the entire paraphernalia, of a market economy into a single picture. Figure 18.1 depicts this attempt. The organization of production and the distribution of income have been suppressed. The economy will produce one of the combinations depicted by the production possibility frontier in this figure, and there is a single consumer who receives all the income generated by the economy, hence will consume the entire output. The problem posed by Figure 18.1 is therefore to determine which output combination will be chosen and consumed and to compare this combination with that which is efficient.

Combination T is the efficient output. This may be easily confirmed by observation as well as by comparing results here with those prescribed by Condition 3. Clearly, no other combination along the PPF permits our single consumer to enjoy as high a utility as that made possible by combination T; all other combinations along it lie on lower indifference curves. At combination T we also observe that this consumer's MRS is equal to the RPT for the economy. The consumption of x_1 units of this good and y_1 units of the other will satisfy the condition necessary for allocative efficiency.

If one good happens to be supplied by a price searcher, however, combination T will not be offered by the economy. Assume that good y is supplied to our consumer competitively but that good x is supplied by a price searcher. Under these conditions market behavior of producers and our consumer leads to an equilibrium like K, at which too little of good X and too much of good Y are produced. In this equilibrium the consumer will purchase the combination for which his or her MRS is equal to the price ratio. This ratio cannot be observed in the diagram, but we know that it will *not* be equal to minus the slope of the PPF at combination T.

Figure 18.1   *Price Searching and Allocative Inefficiency*

Allocative efficiency requires the production of combination T, at which the marginal rate of substitution of the consumer is just equal to the rate of product transformation. If good x is supplied by a price searcher, however, the price of that good will exceed its marginal cost. The consumer will choose a combination at which his or her MRS is equal to the ratio of the prices of x and y. That ratio will exceed the ratio of marginal costs and thus the rate of product transformation. This result corresponds to points like K, involving too little x and too much y.

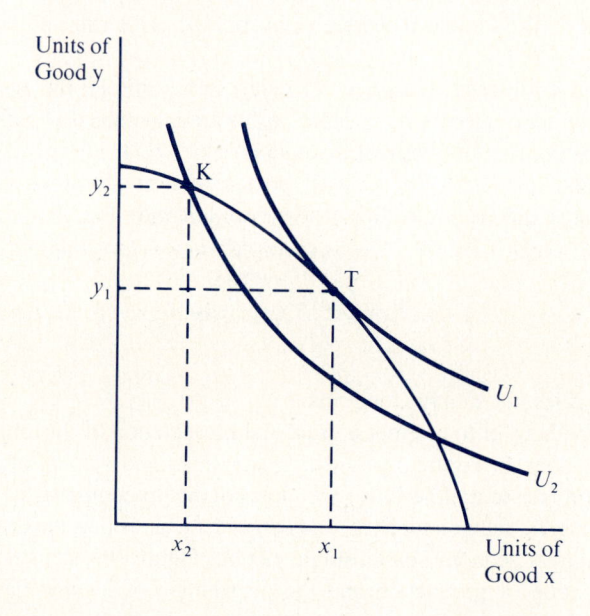

Recall that minus this slope is equal to the ratio of the marginal costs of x and y. If the price of y is equal to MC_y (as is implied by the theory of price taker output) and the price of x is greater than MC_x (as is implied by the theory of price searcher output), then the price ratio must be greater than the ratio of marginal costs.

This must imply an equilibrium at a point like K to the northwest of the optimum point, T. Our consumer's MRS must be equal to the price ratio that is greater than the RPT. Only for combinations along the PPF containing fewer than x_1 units of x and more than y_1 units of y is it true that the consumer's MRS exceeds the RPT. Equation (18.2) may be solved for the conditions at the equilibrium, K. The output produced is identified by the following condition:

$$MRS_{x\ for\ y} = \frac{RPT_{y\ into\ x}}{1 + \frac{1}{\eta}}.$$

Price searching in the output market can therefore cause an economy to produce an inefficient combination of goods. It is important to understand the source of this inefficiency. It has nothing to do with the fact that price searchers may earn monopoly profits. Although good x is produced and sold monopolistically, all income is returned to the consumer, including any monopoly gain. Our consumer after all receives combination K, which lies on the PPF. All existing resources are used to produce K. The inefficiency arises because it would be possible to use these resources to produce a different combination (such as T) that would improve the consumer's welfare. In this case this would clearly occur at no one else's expense, since no other consumer exists. Combination K is not a Pareto optimum.

Price Discrimination

Conditions giving rise to price searching can also yield another source of inefficiency. Recall that under some conditions a price-searching firm may price discriminate. It may charge different customers different prices and may charge the same customer a different price for each unit purchased. Interperson price discrimination invariably produces inefficiency. Interunit price discrimination may yield a price for the last unit to each consumer equal to marginal cost, hence satisfying both distributive and allocative conditions.

Consider that the supplier of good x price discriminates among customers but that the supplier of good y does not. Assume too that Orville's elasticity of demand for x exceeds that of Wilbur. The firm that supplies x will therefore price its product to Wilbur higher than it makes it available to Orville. Each of these two consumers maximizes his utility in the market by purchasing the combination that equates his MRS to the ratio of the prices of the goods he seeks. Under these circumstances the assignment of goods will be distributively inefficient. As each equates his MRS to a *different* price ratio the MRSs of our two consumers will themselves differ; thus,

(18.3) $$MRS^O_{x \text{ for } y} = \frac{P^O_x}{P_y} < \frac{P^W_x}{P_y} = MRS^W_{x \text{ for } y}.$$

In the case of interunit discrimination, the producer may charge a different price for each unit sold. As was shown in Chapter 9, revenue from inframarginal units is not affected by additional sales. Under these conditions the price of the last unit sold *is* marginal revenue. Price-discriminating sellers therefore will sell the quantity at which this last price (equal to marginal revenue) is equal to marginal cost. Although consumers will pay more *in total* for the good under these circumstances, they will purchase the same quantity as they would were it offered at a uniform price equal to this last price. Suppliers will therefore offer and consumers will purchase the same quantities as under competitive conditions.

Consider Figure 18.2. Here we have the demand curve of a single consumer of good x, which, as we know, identifies quantities of x at which his or her MRS is equal to the ratio P_x/P_y as P_x varies vertically. Thus, we know that for quantity x_1 this consumer's MRS is equal to P^1_x/P_y, the demand curve being defined for constant prices of good y. For the seller who may employ interunit price discrimination this demand curve is his or her marginal revenue curve. The seller will therefore maximize profits by producing output x_1. The consumer has no choice but to accept this quantity at the price schedule offered.

Clearly, this result is both allocatively and distributively efficient. Assuming that good y is produced and sold competitively, its price equals its marginal cost.

Figure 18.2 *Interunit Price Discrimination and Efficiency*

The demand curve, D, identifies quantities of good x for which the MRS equals the price ratio at different prices of good x, holding constant the price of good y. If it can practice interunit price discrimination, the price-searching firm's demand curve is also its marginal revenue curve. Such a firm will choose to supply x_1 units of x. At this quantity the consumer's MRS is equal to the price ratio. Because the marginal cost of x_1 is P_x^1, the price ratio will also equal the RPT; hence, the result will be efficient.

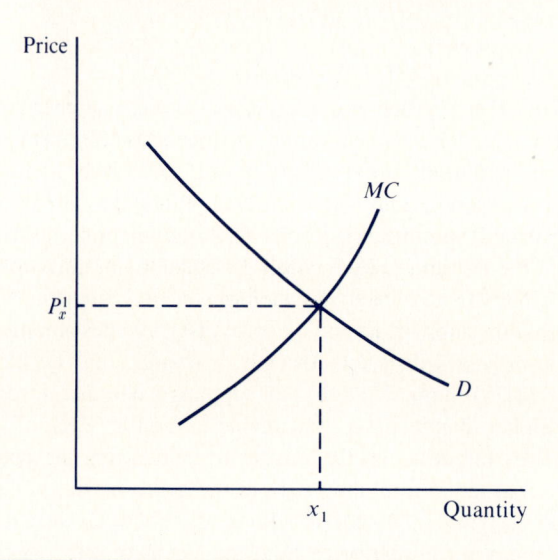

The ratio of prices will thus equal the ratio of marginal costs and the RPT. At the same time, consumers are provided with combinations of goods for which their MRSs are equal to the ratios of these last prices. Their MRSs are thus all equal to the RPT (satisfying conditions for allocative efficiency) and also to one another (satisfying conditions for distributional efficiency).

Price Searching for Inputs

Efficiency problems are also present when there is price searching in the market for inputs. Let factor a be supplied to producers under these conditions, with an elasticity of ε_a^x to producers of good x and ε_a^y to producers of good y. Marginal revenue product is equated with marginal factor cost for these two sets of users under the following conditions:

$$MPP_a^x P_x = P_a^x\left(1 + \frac{1}{\varepsilon_a^x}\right); \; P_a^y\left(1 + \frac{1}{\varepsilon_a^y}\right) = MPP_a^y P_y.$$

Let factor B be supplied to both producers competitively so that quantities employed are identified by these conditions:

$$MPP_b^x P_x = P_b; \; P_b = MPP_b^y P_y.$$

Dividing each set of equalities by the other yields:

(18.4)
$$\frac{MPP_a^x}{MPP_b^x} = \frac{P_a^x\left(1 + \frac{1}{\varepsilon_a^x}\right)}{P_y} \; ; \; \frac{P_a^y\left(1 + \frac{1}{\varepsilon_a^y}\right)}{P_y} = \frac{MPP_a^y}{MPP_b^y}.$$

The ratio on the extreme left is, of course, the RTS of these two inputs in the production of good x, while the ratio on the extreme right is the RTS in the production of good y. In the event that the two prices and elasticities have values that equate the numerators of the two middle ratios, production would be technologically efficient; rates of technical substitution would be the same between these two inputs for both goods. However, there seems little reason for this to be true. Factors influencing the elasticity of supply to a particular producer seem most plausibly firm, or at least region, specific. To the extent that factors are sufficiently immobile to give employers market power over their prices each producer will face its own supply curve with a given elasticity and determine its own price. Price searching in the input market will therefore produce technological inefficiency.

18.3   Government Failure

Price Controls and Rationing

In earlier chapters we had numerous occasions to discuss the implied results of price controls for output and market behavior. Price controls also have efficiency implications, and these will be explored here. Consider Figure 18.3. Panel (a) contains the market demand and supply curves for good x. The equilibrium price in this market is P^*, and output x^* is produced in the absence of government intervention. If good x is supplied by price taker firms, marginal cost will equal P^* for each supplier at this output. If good y is also produced by price takers, the equilibrium price in that market will equal the marginal cost of good y. Under these conditions the ratio of output prices will equal the rate of product transformation, and the resulting output combination will be allocatively efficient, as described earlier. Let combination T on the production possibility frontier in panel (b) represent this efficient result.

Price controls affect output and disturb this efficient output combination. A price ceiling on good x of P, for example, reduces the equilibrium output to x_1. This might suggest the production of combination K, which is clearly allocatively inefficient. However, results of price controls do not stop there. To complete the description we must stipulate how the output produced is rationed among the competing demanders.

One method of accomplishing such nonprice rationing is simply to permit demanders to form queues. This process was described in Chapter 2. As the waiting time lengthens, the value of good x to each demander falls. This will continue until demand in panel (a) shifts to D', at which a money price of P clears the market. In the queuing process resources are used that might have been employed to produce one of the goods consumed. This withdrawal of resources from produc-

Figure 18.3 *Efficiency Implications of Price Controls and Rationing*

Panel (a) depicts the demand and supply curves for good x, labeled D and S, respectively. The equilibrium price in this market is P^*, at which x^* is produced in conjunction with y^* in panel (b). If suppliers of both goods x and y are price takers, this combination, T, is efficient. Price controls without rationing violate all three conditions. Too little of good x and too much of good y are produced. Resources are wasted, and queuing occurs, so production is technologically inefficient. This method of assigning goods to consumers fails to equate their MRSs. The introduction of rationing may eliminate the technological inefficiency but will worsen the distributional inefficiency problem.

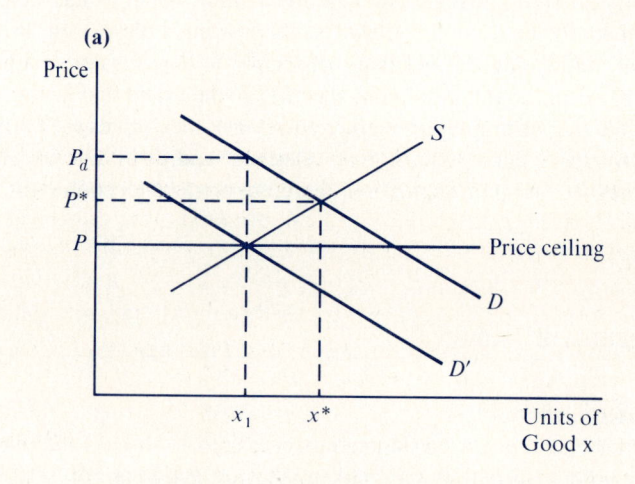

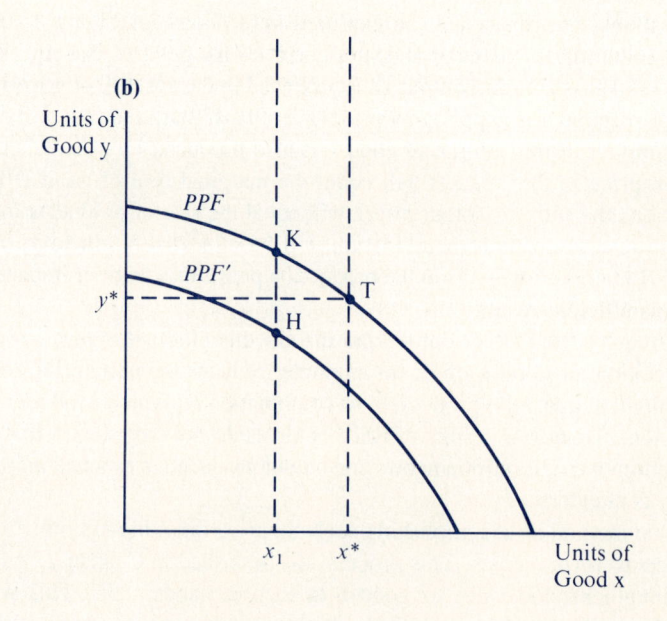

tion is represented in panel (b) by a shifting inward of the production possibility frontier to PPF'.

Under these conditions there is clearly a failure of Condition 1; production is not technologically efficient. Labor is employed seeking the right to consume good x. This resource might have been used to increase the output of good x without decreasing the output of good y, or vice versa. It is used instead for an activity that contributes nothing to the economy's output. Labor is wasted.

Typically this result is distributionally inefficient as well. In such a queuing equilibrium the waiting time is the same for all, but time has different value to different people. This implies that the cost of obtaining good x will differ among demanders. Those whose time is more valuable must bear a higher cost per unit (including the value of their time) than those whose time is less valuable. Marginal rates of substitution are not equal among all consumers, and Condition 2 will not be satisfied. In common-sense terms, those who ultimately receive good x are not those for whom it is most valuable. Some who receive good x by waiting in a queue could and would, if free to do so, gainfully sell their share to others.

Rationing can reduce some of these inefficiencies—but only by making others worse off. Assume that instead of being required to wait in line each consumer is rationed an allotment entitling him or her to an equal share of good x. These allotments can, in principle, be calculated to precisely exhaust output x_1. In this case no lines form; hence, output may be technologically efficient. There is no resource withdrawal to shift the PPF inward as in the previous case. In this case production of a combination like K results, which is technologically efficient but allocatively inefficient. However this does not suggest, as it seems to, that combining rationing with price controls necessarily makes things better. The distribution of good x, when rationed, is almost certainly less efficient than the assignment resulting from queuing. Those who wait in line to qualify for some of the good are willing to give up something to obtain it; their MRSs are not zero. With rationing we have no assurance that this is true. The values placed on the good by those who receive it will vary more widely with rationing than with queuing.

Excise Taxes

Taxes on goods exchanged in the market will affect the quantity of those goods produced. As the real world contains many taxes, it is interesting to observe their effects on the efficiency of the resulting allocation of resources. This may be done by observing the effects of taxes levied on price-taking suppliers of these goods. From Chapter 8 we learned that the supply curve for a competitive firm is its marginal cost curve. The height of the supply curve for any output is the firm's supply price for that quantity. Observe the effects of a tax of amount T levied on each unit sold. Profits may be expressed as total revenue, Px, minus the sum of production costs, $c(x)$, and taxes, Tx:

$$\pi(x) = Px - c(x) - Tx.$$

Profits are therefore at a maximum at the output at which the slope of this profit function is zero:

$$\frac{\Delta \pi}{\Delta x} = P - \frac{\Delta c}{\Delta x} - T = 0.$$

The term $\Delta c/\Delta x$ is marginal cost. Solving for the supply price under these circumstances yields:

$$P = MC(x) + T.$$

The supply price is for every quantity equal to marginal cost plus the unit tax T. The effect of this tax, therefore, is to shift the supply curve of the firm upward by an amount equal to this tax. As we obtain a market supply curve by simply summing quantities supplied at each price, that curve is itself shifted upward by the amount of this tax. Two firms originally willing to supply a sum of 100 units at a price of $3 will, after a tax, be willing to supply the same quantity at a price of $3 *plus* the tax.

Figure 18.4 presents market equilibria before and after the imposition of such a tax. The demand curve for good x is shown by the curve D, and the original supply curve by S. The imposition of this tax shifts the supply curve vertically by the amount T. Prior to the tax, the equilibrium quantity supplied was x_1 at a market price of P. After the tax, the quantity sold falls to x_2, for which demanders pay a price of P^d. The supplier must pay the government T out of the revenues ob-

---

Figure 18.4 **Excise Taxation**

A constant per-unit excise tax, if paid by producers, increases the marginal cost of each unit. This causes the supply curve to shift upward vertically by the amount of the tax. If the original equilibrium price and quantity are P and x_1, a tax of T per unit shifts supply to the position indicated by the curve labeled $S + T$. This yields a new price and quantity of P^d and x_2. The marginal production cost of this quantity (equal to the price net of the tax received by the suppliers) is P^s. The price paid by demanders is thus greater than marginal cost.

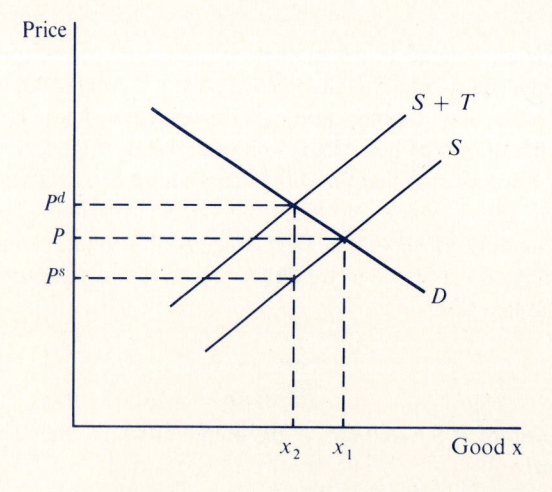

tained for each unit, leaving it with net proceeds per unit of P^s, the marginal cost of that quantity.

Our chief concern here is not with prices but rather with output. It can be shown that such taxes will influence the economy to produce an output combination that is allocatively inefficient. Assume that good x has been singled out for such a tax, but that good y is untaxed. Consumers will face prices for x and y, respectively, of P_x^d and P_y and choose combinations of these goods that equate their MRSs to the ratio of these prices. If both markets are competitive, firms will supply quantities at which the marginal cost of good y is equal to its price, P_y, and quantities of good x at which its marginal cost is P_x^s, which differs from P_x^d by the amount of tax. This introduces another inequality between MRS and RPT:

$$MRS_{x \text{ for } y} = \frac{P_x^d}{P_y} > \frac{P_x^s}{P_y} = \frac{MC_x}{MC_y} = RPT_{y \text{ into } x}.$$

Taxation products a result similar to monopoly. The equilibrium in such an economy must occur at a point like K in Figure 18.1. Consumer MRSs are greater than the RPT, suggesting that the combination produced contains excessive amounts of the untaxed good and too little of the taxed good.

Income and Other Taxes

In Chapter 17 efficiency conditions were derived under the assumption that quantities of resources available for production were fixed. This approach offers the advantage of shortening the list of efficiency conditions that we had to derive in Chapter 17. However, this simplification has not been achieved costlessly. As we saw in Chapters 14 and 15, the quantities available of these two resources are responsive to their prices, and income taxes can affect these prices. Without explicitly derived conditions for efficient quantities, it is difficult to discuss *deviations* from efficient quantities. We shall nevertheless discuss the sources of these distortions in general terms.

Consider the supply of labor. Efficient use of labor requires that it be equally useful in work and nonwork (leisure) activities at the margin. It must be the case that at the margin the value of leisure just equals its opportunity cost in forgone earnings. Recall from Chapter 13 that the value of work time per unit is labor's VMP ($VMP_a = MPP_a \cdot P_x$). The value of leisure is reflected in the worker's MRS for leisure in terms of income. With no tax on wages each worker chooses the correct combination. As we saw in Chapter 14, labor suppliers will select the combination of labor and leisure that equates their MRSs with the wage rate. If labor and output are both supplied to individual demanders perfectly elastically, then the wage rate correctly measures worker productivity (that is, the wage equals labor's VMP), and this efficiency condition is satisfied.

Now let us assume a tax. In exchange for leisure, workers now obtain *after-tax* wages and select work/leisure combinations at which MRSs equal after-tax wage rates. Worker productivity is still measured by the pretax wage rate, however, introducing an inequality into what might otherwise indicate "efficiency as usual" in competitive market results. Let the wage rate be given by P_a and the tax *rate* be given by t. Profit maximization in price-taking markets insures that

$VMP_a = P_a$ while labor supply in the presence of an income tax results in $MRS = (1 - t)P_a$. Putting these two conditions together yields:

$$VMP_a = P_a > (1 - t)P_a = MRS.$$

Efficiency is not achieved. The presence of the tax influences workers to choose combinations of work and leisure in which the value of work time at the margin exceeds the value of leisure.

A similar result can be shown to hold for taxation of income from interest and income from capital assets. Efficiency in the capital market requires that each person's MRS for consumption in different periods equal the RPT among those periods. The RPT for present into future consumption is equal to the discount factor $1/1 + r$, where r is the interest rate. This is the amount of present dollars that must be saved in order to produce one dollar's worth of income next period. In the absence of taxation, individual savers will select the combination of consumption and saving that equates their MRSs to this discount factor, as described in Chapter 15. When interest income is taxed, however, savers will consider interest *net of tax* when making such a choice. In equilibrium each MRS will equal $1/[1 + (1 - t)r]$, where t is the tax rate. This will clearly exceed the RPT. In this situation, the value of future consumption as revealed by individual MRSs exceeds its opportunity cost in terms of the present consumption that would have to be forgone to obtain it at the margin.

Regulation

Government affects resource allocation in other ways besides price controls and taxation. It may directly or indirectly affect resource use through regulation. Regulations affect the quantity of labor (through the Wage and Hour Act), who may work (through child labor legislation), the conditions of employment (various labor relations laws), and conditions of the work itself (through the Occupational Safety Act). They affect how resources will be used (for example, the granting of routes to airlines by the CAB and to truckers by the ICC) and by whom (for example, the banning of certain discharges into waterways by the EPA, thereby effectively reserving the use of waterways for other purposes). The government has from time to time banned the use of certain products (alcoholic beverages during Prohibition and James Joyce's *Ulysses* at about the same time) and controlled the design of others (aspirin containers and automobile bumpers). Drugs must now be shown to be "efficacious" as well as safe before they may be sold. Any day we may expect legislation requiring that education be "improving," newspapers be "informative," and television be "entertaining."

As this list makes clear, the influence of government on both the technology of production and the economy's output is pervasive. While instances of this regulation may occasionally foster efficiency, many of its acknowledged aims are typically directed toward other objectives. The minimum wage was never set with the idea of eliciting the optimal quantity of labor, nor was the Volstead Act adopted with consumer appreciation of the well-put-together martini uppermost in mind. The 55 mph speed limit was originally passed, it would seem, to save oil regardless of cost. Now we are told that its purpose is to save lives regardless of cost.

There are, in other words, countless occasions of failure by government to conform its behavior to the strictures laid down in Chapter 17. Market failure is not the sole source of inefficiency in any economy; it may not even be the most important source. These market and government failures are only the errors of commission, however. A fuller view of the efficiency with which market economies operate may be obtained by considering as well those activities that are essentially governmental—that is, the definition and enforcement of property rights and the adjudication of claims. Government's behavior in these spheres also has important efficiency implications which will occupy us in the next section.

18.4 Transaction Costs and Property Rights

The Coase Theorem

In most of our previous analyses we have assumed that transactions involving mutually advantageous exchanges can be costlessly arranged. In the real world, of course, almost nothing is costless, and the **transaction costs**, too, have implications for efficient use of resources. Consider the case in which some aspect of production by one firm affects the costs of production of another. A wheat farm located next to a dairy provides an example of this interaction. The cows from the dairy may stray onto the land of the adjacent farm, trampling and perhaps eating the crops grown there. The efficiency question involves whether a fence will be erected between the two farms. The answer to this question is not obvious. Fence building consumes resources, and the cows' grazing on the wheat farmer's land has value as well. It will be efficient to build a fence only if the cost of the damage done to the wheat farmer's crop exceeds the cost of the fence *and* the cost of the damage prevented by the fence. *It can be shown that in a market where transactions between the two farmers may be costlessly undertaken, an efficient arrangement will be worked out regardless of how property rights are assigned between the two farmers in activities related to grazing.*

Let us assume that building the fence is efficient. The value of the trampled wheat exceeds the cost of the fence and the cost of the reduced pasturage for the cows. Where this is true, the fence will be built regardless of how property rights to the use of the land are originally assigned. If the dairy farmer has these rights, it will be in the interests of the wheat farmer to build the fence. The latter will compare the damage to crops with the cost of building the fence and compensating the dairy farmer for the lost grazing rights and find that costs are minimized by adopting the fencing alternative. If the wheat farmer has the rights, the dairy farmer will build the fence. He or she will compare the costs of building the fence and forgoing the added pasturage with the cost of compensating the wheat farmer for the crop damage. Since the latter exceed the former, the dairy farmer will build the fence.

On the other hand, if building the fence is inefficient, it will not be done. In this case the cost of the trampled wheat is less than the cost of building the fence together with the added value of pasturage on the wheat farmer's land. If the dairy farmer has the rights to an "open range," it will not benefit the wheat farmer to compensate the dairy farmer for the loss of these rights by building the fence. On the other hand, if the wheat farmer has the property rights to these uses of the land, it will profit the dairyman to compensate the wheat farmer for the damage done rather than build a fence.

The **assignment of property rights** makes no difference in either case. When it is allocatively efficient to build the fence, it gets built; when it is inefficient to do so, no fence is built. This example illustrates a fundamental principle of economics. In the absence of transaction costs, the allocation of resources is both (1) allocatively efficient, and (2) insensitive to the distribution of property rights in the community. This principle is referred to as the **Coase theorem** in honor of its discoverer.[1] However, it is a rule that is more important in its violations than in its compliance.

Consider some cases in which transactions between the two neighbors are prohibitively costly. Let the fence be efficient; total damage to the wheat farmer's crops exceeds the combined costs of fence construction and reduced pasturage. If the wheat farmer has the right to collect damages, the fence will be built as in the former case. The dairy owner will find it cost effective to build a fence rather than pay these damages. In the opposite case, however, no fence will be built. If the dairy owner has the right to an open range, neither of the two farmers will build the fence. The dairy owner has no incentive to do so; he or she is not responsible for damage to the wheat farmer's crop, and has no reason to bear the costs of building the fence. The wheat farmer, on the other hand has no right to limit the grazing of the cows, and so may not construct a fence either. He or she would buy these rights from the dairy owner—but transaction costs prevent it.

Similar results occur when the fence is inefficient. So long as the damage covers the construction costs of the fence, the wheat farmer—if he or she has the right to do so—will build the fence. This is true even if the total cost of the fence, including the reduced pasturage, exceeds the gain in protected crops. The dairy owner in this case would be willing to pay the wheat farmer enough to persuade him or her not to do so, but such transactions are by assumption excessively costly. If, on the other hand, the dairyman has rights to an open range, the allocatively efficient result will obtain: No fence will be built.

The lesson is clear. Where transaction costs prevent markets from functioning, both pleasing aspects of the Coase theorem no longer apply. Allocative results depend on the assignment of property rights. The fence will be built in some cases and not in others depending on the assignment of property rights—and since this is true regardless of whether the activity (fence building) is efficient, there is no presumption that the results will themselves be efficient. Scholars in the new economic field of *Law and Economics* have seen in these results important implications for the legal system. In the real world, where transaction costs are frequently important, judicial determination of rights can have important allocative implications.

The reader may object that our farm example is unrealistic. The transaction costs between neighboring farmers would in real life be trivial. It is difficult to

---

[1] Ronald H. Coase, "The Problem of Social Cost," *The Journal of Law and Economics* 3 (October 1960): 1–44.

imagine circumstances involving pairs of individuals in a community in which the costs of reaching mutually beneficial arrangements was high enough to deter allocatively important transactions. However, we cannot leap to the conclusion that this is an unimportant problem in general. In many cases the appropriate transactions involve not two people but many, and the costs of organizing efficient arrangements in the market are staggering.

In place of the dairy farmer with "open range" rights to land use imagine thousands of automobile owners with "open range" rights to emit noxious pollutants into the air. On the other side of these potential transactions imagine thousands of air breathers (including, of course, all drivers). If transaction costs were zero, breathers might negotiate a payment to drivers to equip their cars with pollution abatement equipment that would emit efficient amounts of pollutants into the air. Of course, this would be impossible; the costs of organizing such a transaction among all breathers and all drivers would simply be too high. The same might be said of industrial plants located along a river or drivers on a crowded highway. If plants have the right to discharge waste into the river, this need not insure that the river will be polluted. In principle, river users who value clean water can pay these plants to refrain from discharging their wastes—and will, if such transactions are not too costly. Drivers who place a higher value on the use of highways could pay other drivers to stay off the roads, insuring efficient use of these resources. In all of these cases, however, the transaction required to achieve efficiency involves many people and complicated terms. It is certainly possible that in many such cases the costs of transacting outweigh the gains and that the resulting allocation of resources is inefficient.

External Costs and Benefits

In some cases an activity by one individual imposes costs on another, but transactions are deterred that might affect the level of that activity. There is a difference between the cost of that activity perceived by the actor and the total cost of that activity to all members of society. We must make a distinction between the marginal cost to the decision maker, the **marginal private cost (MPC)**, and the cost to the full community, the **marginal social cost (MSC)**. Where there is a difference between these two costs, a portion of the total cost is said to be an **external cost** to the decision; inefficiency results. There may also be cases in which an activity produces **external benefits**. In this section we will develop an explicit model illustrating the nature of the inefficiency in each case.

In order to simplify the analysis, we will assume that the market prices of our two goods are fixed. We can think of our community as a small part of a larger economy supplying goods as price takers to this "global" market. The problem for these suppliers therefore translates into a search for the combination of output that will maximize the total value of their output of these two goods net of their production costs. Combined total revenue (TR) is therefore given by:

$$TR = P_x x + P_y y.$$

Let the cost of good x depend only on the quantity produced, $c_x = c_x(x)$. However, let the cost of good y be affected by both the quantity of y and the quantity of x—that is, $c_y = c_y(x, y)$. The production of x may therefore be said to yield external effects. Total cost (TC) of both outputs is therefore:

$$TC = c_x + c_y = c_x(x) + c_y(x, y).$$

The net value (NV) of community output is given by total revenue minus total cost:

$$NV = TR - TC = P_x x + P_y y - c_x(x) - c_y(x, y).$$

Discovering the combination of output that maximizes this net value involves finding the quantity of each good that *simultaneously* maximizes the net value with respect to each. We find this by setting the slope of NV with respect to each output equal to zero:

$$\frac{\Delta NV}{\Delta x} = P_x - \frac{\Delta c_x}{\Delta x} - \frac{\Delta c_y}{\Delta x} = 0;$$

$$\frac{\Delta NV}{\Delta y} = P_y - \frac{\Delta c_y}{\Delta y} = 0.$$

Solving for the prices in both equations yields:

$$P_x = \frac{\Delta c_x}{\Delta x} + \frac{\Delta c_y}{\Delta x};$$

$$P_y = \frac{\Delta c_y}{\Delta y}.$$

The right sides of these expressions may be thought of as the MSCs of their respective outputs. The second term on the right side of the first expression, $\Delta c_y/\Delta x$, measures the external effect of good x. If production of x increases the cost of y, this term will have a positive sign. Production of x yields external costs in this case. However, it may reduce the cost of y. In that case the term will have a negative sign, and production of x will be said to yield external benefits.

Dividing one equality by the other produces:

(18.5)
$$\frac{P_x}{P_y} = \frac{\Delta c_x/\Delta x + \Delta c_y/\Delta x}{\Delta c_y/\Delta y}.$$

This expression may be used to illustrate the efficiency problem caused by these external effects. The right side now contains the ratio of marginal social costs. As we saw earlier, the ratio of marginal costs is equal to the rate of product transformation, which is equal to minus the slope of the production possibility frontier. Such a PPF is illustrated in Figure 18.5, and minus the slope of this curve at every point is given by the ratio of MSCs just shown.

As output prices are fixed, any given amount of revenue may be earned by selling combinations of goods x and y along a diagonal line with a slope equal to

Figure 18.5   *External Costs and Benefits*

The slope of the production possibility frontier is equal to minus the ratio of the marginal social costs of good x and good y. If some portion of the social cost of good x is not borne by its producers, market prices will equal the ratio of marginal private costs, and a combination like H will be produced. If production of good x yields external benefits, the slope of *PPF* must be less than minus the ratio of the equilibrium prices. In this case production of a combination like K will be the result.

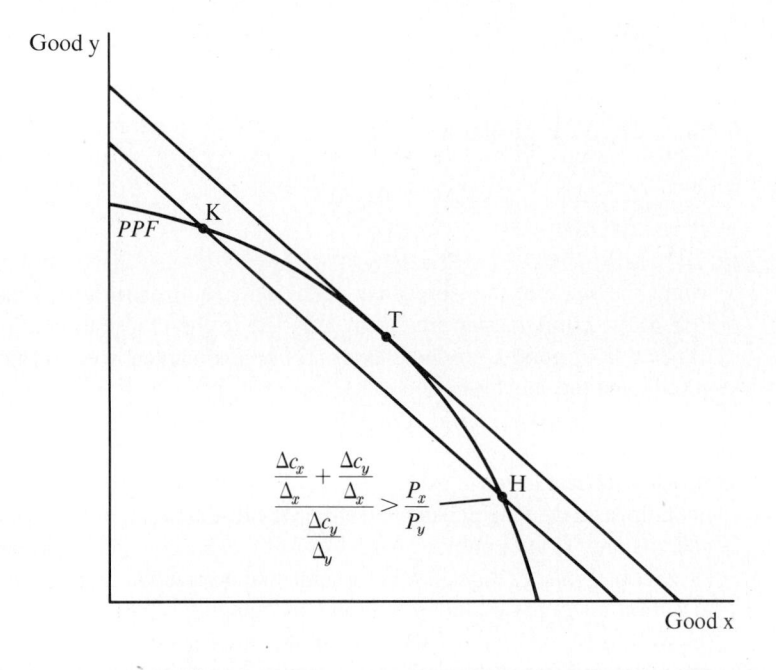

$$\frac{\frac{\Delta c_x}{\Delta_x} + \frac{\Delta c_y}{\Delta_x}}{\frac{\Delta c_y}{\Delta_y}} > \frac{P_x}{P_y}$$

---

minus the price ratio. For example, amount $TR_1 = P_x x + P_y y$ may be obtained by any combination given by the expression:

$$y = \frac{TR_1}{P_y} - \frac{P_x}{P_y} \cdot x.$$

The vertical intercept of this **isorevenue curve** indexes total revenue. Higher revenue is associated with higher isorevenue curves, each having a slope equal to minus the output prices. As the community is constrained to produce a combination along the PPF, peak efficiency is achieved by producing combination T. This combination, identified by the tangency between the isorevenue curve and the PPF, yields the highest possible total revenue. Efficiency requires, as in equation (18.5), that the RPT equal the price ratio.

However, a market economy may not produce this combination. Assume that production of good x yields external costs—$\Delta c_y/\Delta x$ is positive. The producers of x do not bear these costs, hence will not consider them in choosing the profit-maximizing outputs. Their profits are maximized by selecting outputs at which marginal revenue (in this case, price) equals marginal private costs—that is, $P_x = \Delta c_x/\Delta x$. Production of good y involves no external costs; producers of that good will select outputs at which $P_y = \Delta c_y/\Delta y$. The combination produced by the market for example, combination H—will therefore contain too much of good x and too little of good y. It must lie on PPF to the southeast of combination T, because profit maximization of producers assures us that:

$$\frac{P_x}{P_y} = \frac{\Delta c_x/\Delta x}{\Delta c_y/\Delta y}.$$

Since $\Delta c_y/\Delta x$ is greater than zero,

(18.6) $$\frac{P_x}{P_y} = \frac{\Delta c_x/\Delta x}{\Delta c_y/\Delta y} < \frac{\Delta c_x/\Delta x + \Delta c_y/\Delta x}{\Delta c_y/\Delta y}.$$

Minus the slope of the isorevenue curve must be less than minus the slope of the PPF at the combination produced. It is left to the reader to confirm that where production of good x produces external *benefits* markets will produce too little of good x and too much of good y.

Market Provision of Public Goods

Economists have long debated the efficiency results where markets are left to organize the provision of public goods. Most of the disagreement concerns the characterization of market results. If we assume that transaction costs are sufficiently low to permit negotiation among all users and suppliers, then this efficiency problem (as well as all others) vanishes. If, on the other hand, transaction costs are high enough to prevent such complicated deals from being put together, then efficiency fails. An exhaustive discussion of these issues is far beyond the scope of the portion of this chapter assigned to public goods. We shall therefore limit our comments here to a simple demonstration of the sources of the transaction cost problems and a restatement of the efficiency question itself.

The nature of the problem is depicted in Figure 18.6.[2] Here we have a community of two people (let them be Orville and Wilbur again) who both consume and produce one private and one public good. Each person's production possibility curve for the two goods is given by curve PPF. We assume that Orville and Wilbur are identical in both their production capabilities and their tastes so that each may produce any combination along PPF and the indifference curves apply to both. The income consumption curve labeled ICC identifies all combinations of the two goods for which the MRSs of each person are equal to minus the slope of PPF, which, as we know, is equal to the RPT. Each person consumes the amount of the private good (measured on the vertical axis) that he produces. However, because x is a public good, each consumes the total amount of this good produced by both.

---

[2] This figure is adapted from a model developed by J. M. Buchanan in *The Demand and Supply of Public Goods* (Chicago: Rand McNally, 1968), Chapter 2.

Chapter 18 *Markets, Governments, and Efficiency* 603

Figure 18.6 *Public Goods and the Individual Adjustment Equilibrium*

Individual production possibility frontiers are given by curve *PPF*. If each individual produces combination G, he or she will be provided with combination H. In attempting to secure combination F, each will produce B and be provided with combination D. This process of adjustment and response will reach an equilibrium in which each produces combination K and receives combination T. As the MRS of each at T is equal to his or her own RPT, neither will modify his or her production combination away from this equilibrium. This result is the individual adjustment equilibrium.

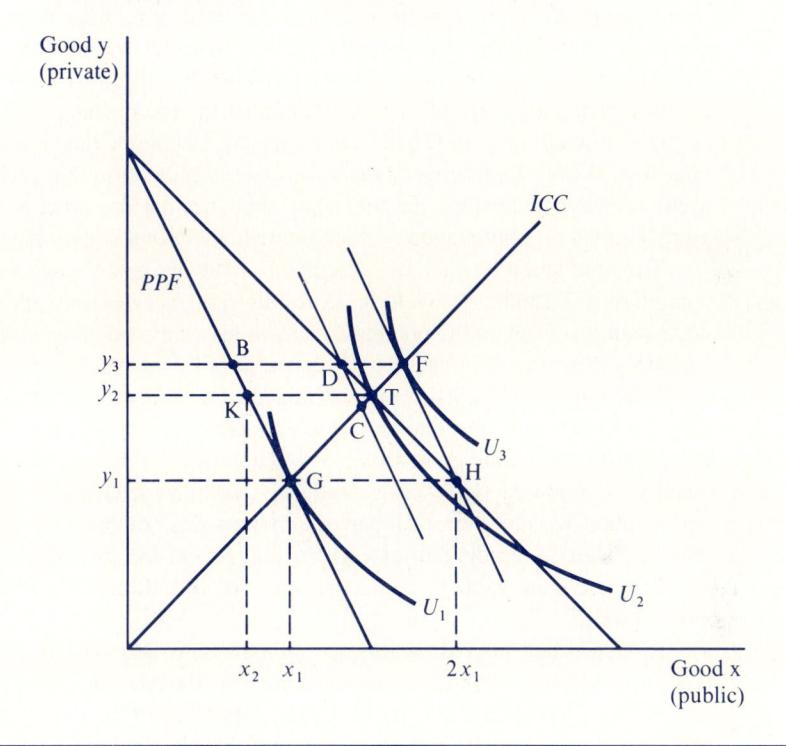

The Individual Adjustment Equilibrium

It can be shown that in the absence of transactions between Orville and Wilbur in Figure 18.6 each will, in equilibrium, produce combination K, yielding a consumption combination for each of T. Let us begin by assuming that both perceive their respective PPFs and seek to produce the utility-maximizing combination along this curve, each being unaware of the production plans of the other. Each will therefore produce combination G, which is the best one obtainable under these circumstances. As both have produced x_1 units of the public good, however, each finds himself provided with twice as much public good as he produced and may now consume combination H instead. This is not an equilibrium situation. Aware now that the other is producing x_1 units of the public good, each calculates that by reallocating his resources to the production of the private good he may obtain combination F. This combination may be obtained by one person producing combination B while the other continues to produce combination G. If both seek to do this, however, and both produce B, each obtains combination D instead of F. Now each perceives that he is underprovided with the public good. Each consumer's MRS now exceeds the opportunity cost of the public good given by the slope of his PPF, and each will seek to compensate by adjustment along the thin line passing through combination D.

The movement toward equilibrium will continue to follow this process. When both Orville and Wilbur produce the same combination MRSs will differ from the RPT, leading both to modify their production combinations. Each modifies his combination, assuming that the other will continue to produce the existing quantity of the public good. As this assumption is in each case found to be incorrect, each fails to obtain the combination sought. Note, however, that in the several iterations depicted the range of oscillation diminished. The planned expansion in public good production from D to C was smaller in magnitude than the earlier reduction from H to F. Experimentation with a ruler will confirm that each subsequent oscillation is smaller than the preceding one and that the process converges to point T, involving production by each individual of combination K.

The production by each of combination K involving consumption by each of combination T can be shown to be an equilibrium. Each expects the other to produce x_2 units of the public good and chooses his own production combination accordingly. But since combination T lies on the ICC, the MRS of each person will equal the opportunity cost of the public good for this consumption combination. Each will not be influenced to modify his production, and expectations concerning the quantities of public good produced by the other will be confirmed. Uncoordinated production by both yields production combinations that converge toward combination K, and once each person produces this combination he is not motivated to alter it. Production of combination K and the associated consumption by each of combination T is referred to as the **individual adjustment equilibrium (IAE)**.

It is clear that the IAE is allocatively inefficient. The RPT in this example is constant and equal to minus the slope of the PPF. Each consumer enjoys combination T where his MRS is also equal to minus the slope of the PPF. If *each person's* MRS is equal to the RPT, it is impossible for this allocation to satisfy Condition 4 from Chapter 17. The sum of all MRSs cannot equal the RPT under these circumstances. Clearly, it must be possible to make at least one of the parties better off without making the other worse off.

Transaction Costs in Public Good Allocation

One possible allocation that is Pareto optimal is shown in Figure 18.7. This figure is identical to Figure 18.6 in the construction of most of its features. Production combination K and consumption combination T correspond to the same points in that figure; these identify the IAE. If instead of K each individual produced combination B along the PPF, both would be able to consume combination H, which is preferred to T. This combination is allocatively efficient, which may be verified by noting that the indifference curve of each individual at that combination is just tangent to the line labeled *CCF*. This curve, called the **common consumption frontier (CCF)**, identifies all the combinations that both consumers could possibly enjoy *simultaneously*. By its construction this curve must lie exactly twice the

Figure 18.7 *Inefficiency of the Individual Adjustment Equilibrium*

Since the MRS of each at the IEA combination T is equal to the RPT, it cannot be the case that the RPT is equal to the sum of both MRSs. Efficiency requires production of a combination like combination H, at which the sum of both MRSs is less. At combination H each MRS is equal to $RPT/2$; hence, the sum of the MRSs is equal to the RPT. Achievement of combination H requires that each produce combination B, which is not the IEA.

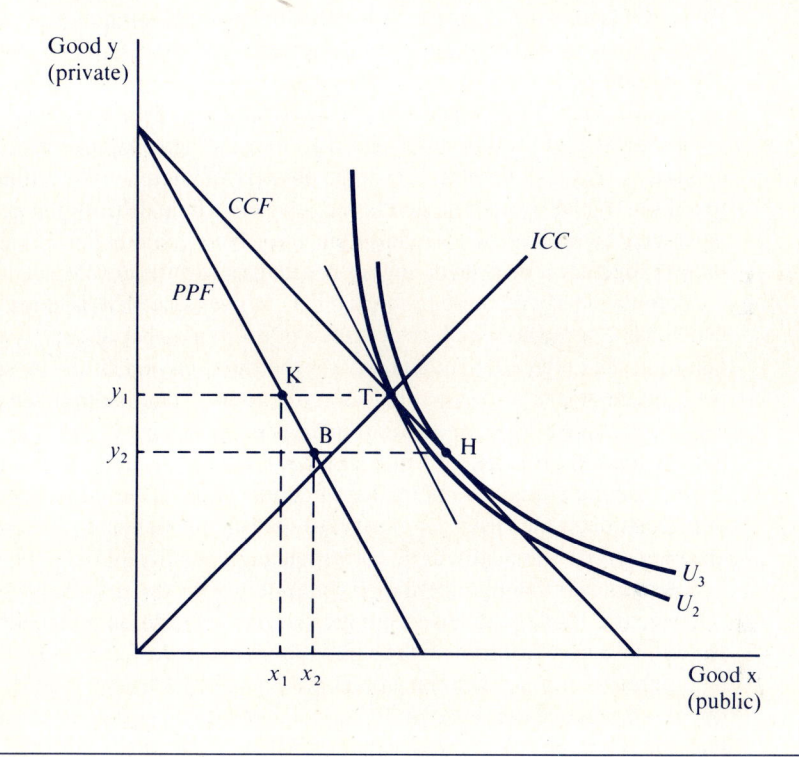

distance from the vertical axis as does the PPF. As the PPF is linear in this example, so must be the CCF—indeed, the slope of the CCF must be one half the slope of the PPF. Since the indifference curve of each is tangent to the CCF at combination H, we may conclude that:

$$MRS^O = \frac{-\Delta y_{CCF}}{\Delta x} = \frac{1}{2} RPT;$$

$$MRS^W = \frac{-\Delta y_{CCF}}{\Delta x} = \frac{1}{2} RPT.$$

By adding one equality to the other, we get:

$$MRS^O + MRS^W = RPT.$$

The summed MRSs of Orville and Wilbur equal the RPT, and Condition 4 is satisfied.

In principle, so long as each (or, in the general case, all) potential user is aware of the production possibilities of the other, both may conclude a transaction involving the agreement to produce combination B rather than K, obtaining for consumption combination H rather than T. By extension, this conclusion is not restricted to cases of household production. If that good is produced and sold by firms, consumers need only agree among one another to purchase the amounts of public goods corresponding to those provided in combination B rather than the IAE amounts.

While such arrangements are theoretically possible, there are a number of **public good transaction costs** that may forestall agreement to produce efficient quantities of these goods. The most obvious of these is the **communications problem**. While two public good users may have little difficulty in negotiating an agreement in which each would produce (or buy) combination B rather than K, putting together a deal involving all beneficiaries of the development of a cancer cure would clearly be more problematical. As everyone alive is at least a potential beneficiary, agreement and participation of every member of society might be required to obtain an efficient amount. As the expected benefit to any single person is not large, the cost of communicating the terms from one individual to another could conceivably deter most from involving themselves in such negotiations. If the two parties in Figure 18.6 cannot communicate, they will produce the IAE rather than the efficient combination of goods. In the general case, if communications costs deter the larger set of users of realistic public goods from making other arrangements, the result will be correspondingly inefficient.

A similar difficulty emerges in connection with the enforcement of these arrangements. Having agreed to produce combination B, both Orville and Wilbur have an incentive to chisel on the agreement. This is illustrated in Figure 18.8. Let both agree to produce combination B rather than K. Clearly, if either expects the other will produce combination B, he can do better by producing a different combination. Consider the choice each must make. Assume that each expects the other to honor the agreement and produce combination B. By producing B, he may consume H and derive utility U_3. By producing combination D instead, however, he may consume combination F, which yields utility U_4. If each expects the other to honor the agreement, he is better off producing less than the efficient amount of the public good. However, if each expects the other to chisel, we return to the IAE. This problem is commonly referred to by economists as the **free-rider problem**. Each user seeks to obtain a "free ride" on the public good provided by the other.

This problem is not limited to public goods. It occurs because it is often difficult to prevent others from using public goods once they have been produced. In our example, it is only by using the public goods produced by his "honest" counterpart that the chiseler may consume combination F. If the honest user could exclude the potential chiseler from using his public good when the latter chiseled, producing combination D would be far less attractive. The same might be said of many private goods. If you could not prevent others from using the automobile that you purchased, you would probably be less inclined to automobile ownership than otherwise. The enforcement of contracts and property rights has important

Chapter 18 Markets, Governments, and Efficiency 607

Figure 18.8   The Free-Rider Problem

Agreement by each user to produce combination B rather than the IEA combination, K, yields utility gains to both. Utility for each is increased from U_2 to U_3. However, if each expects the other to honor the agreement, each is influenced to produce combination D instead, securing combination F and utility U_4. The presence of this influence to chisel on agreements to produce efficient quantities of public goods is the free-rider problem.

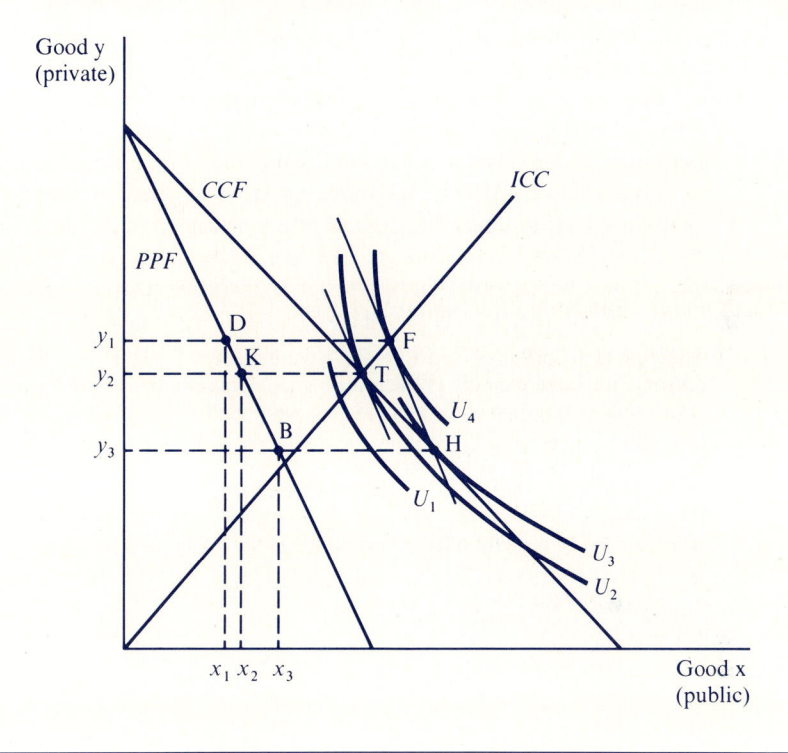

efficiency implications for the allocation of resources in production of both public and private goods.

It is therefore not surprising that we see unusual property rights structures in connection with public goods. Patent law protects the investors in the public good technology from free-riding by others for a period of 17 years. Copyright laws similarly protect investors in such public goods as songs, plays, novels, and economics textbooks. Here we observe the apparent trading off of one inefficiency for another. Once a public good is produced, consumption of the available amount by an additional person is by definition costless. Excluding users who refuse to pay the royalty fee is therefore inefficient. Some (the excluded users) could be made better off without harming anyone if this royalty price were reduced to zero, permitting universal access. However, to do so would invite free-riding and thus the predicted underinvestment. By giving to investors these exclusionary rights, the extent of free-riding is reduced at the cost of less than universal access.

The third and final problem confronting market provision of public goods concerns not the enforcement of agreements to produce optimal amounts but rather the negotiation of these agreements. As we have just seen, it is possible for some users to benefit at the expense of others by failing to honor agreements to produce appropriate quantities of public goods. It is also possible for some users to benefit at the expense of other users by persuading the latter to bear a larger portion of the cost of these goods. Consider Figure 18.9. Here again each user may benefit by producing combination B rather than K, permitting each to consume combination H rather than T.

However, other agreements might be negotiated involving the production of *different* combinations. A limiting case is also presented in this figure. Here one user agrees to produce combination F while the other produces C. This results in the same total quantity of the public good being produced as was contained in combination H. Individual quantities of the private good produced and consumed

---

Figure 18.9 *Public Goods and Bargaining Behavior*

Although both consumers must use the same quantity of the public good, both need not consume the same quantity of the private good. Consumption by each is not limited to those combinations along the common consumption frontier (*CCF*). It is possible through bargaining for one person to produce combination C and enjoy consumption of combination G while the other is persuaded to produce combination F and consume only D. Such a solution can be efficient, but it offers differential gains to the successful bargainer. Efforts to secure these gains from bargaining can prevent the negotiators from reaching an agreement to produce efficient quantities of the public good.

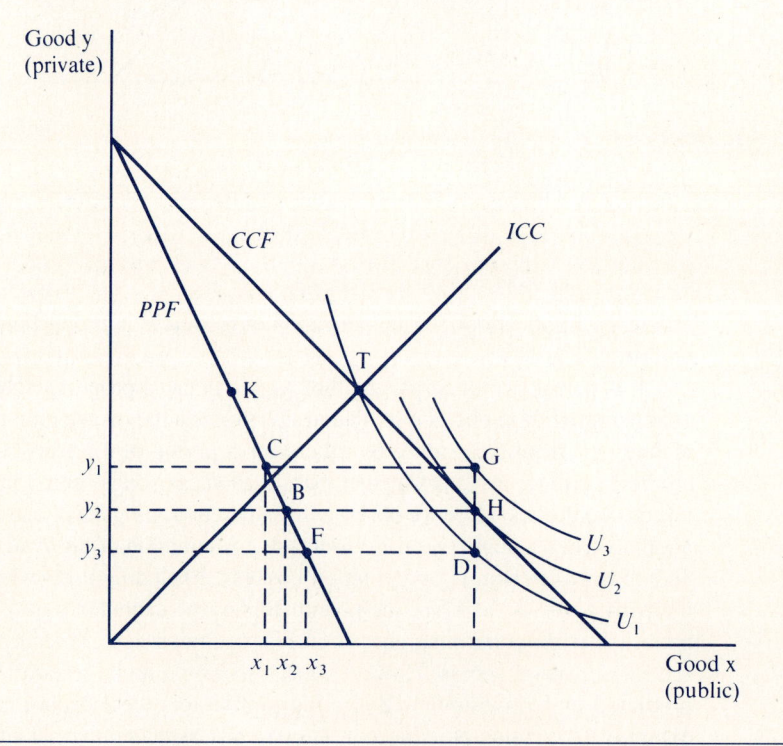

differ. Thus, one obtains combination G while the other consumes combination D. Clearly, users of public goods will not be indifferent concerning which combination of goods they get. The one who invests most heavily in the public good ends up worse off. We can expect **bargaining behavior** by public good users seeking to obtain the public good on the best terms. This may include, but is not limited to, concealing demands for the public good in the same way that buyers in flea markets conceal their valuations of the goods offered. The difference between the two examples merely involves the roles played by the bargainers. In the case of flea market negotiations, bargaining takes place between buyer and seller. In the case of public goods negotiations, bargaining takes place among joint users of the public good. The objective is the same in both cases: to obtain the good sought on the most favorable terms.

The possibility of bargaining raises efficiency questions. If all users bargain by concealing their demands for these goods, offers involving efficient quantities may never be considered. Imagine that both bargainers in Figure 18.9 insist that they attach low values to the use of the public good and thus are willing to produce no more than x_1 units (combination C). Will offers involving efficient quantities ever be generated or accepted under these circumstances? To date, theorists have failed to resolve this issue. It has been shown that under very restrictive circumstances public good users can be influenced to reveal their true valuations of these goods,[3] but no real-world counterparts of these demand-revealing conditions have yet been identified.

18.5 The Government Alternative

Optimal Intervention

In theory, for every market failure to produce efficiency there exists a government solution. Where price searching results in underallocation, price ceilings appropriately set at marginal cost coupled with subsidies where necessary to insure firm survival can restore the equality that fails in equation (18.2). This technique for eliciting expanded output from such firms was discussed in Chapter 9; a regulatory requirement that prevents firms from charging different prices to different customers can eliminate the inefficiency caused by price discrimination revealed in equation (18.3). In Chapter 13, on the other hand, it was shown that regulations setting minimum prices in factor markets can influence the use of resources there. In theory, this tool may be used to eliminate the inefficiency produced by price searching in input markets, insuring that technological efficiency in production is achieved.

Taxes and subsidies may also be used to restore efficiency in the presence of external costs or benefits. Assume that a tax equal to $\Delta c_y/\Delta x$ in equation (18.6) is levied on producers of good x. The value of this external cost would then enter the profit calculations of these producers, leading them to select the output at which

---

[3] See T. N. Tideman and Gordon Tullock, "A New and Superior Process for Making Social Choices," *Journal of Political Economy* 84 (December 1976): 1145–1160.

price equals the full marginal social cost, and efficiency would be restored. A subsidy would achieve the same results where production of x yielded external benefits. Finally, government itself might simply organize the production of public goods, financing their provision and making them available to users at zero price.

Policies such as these may, if correctly implemented, move the economy from an inefficient allocation to one that is Pareto optimal. However, there is no assurance that in doing so the government would actually increase social welfare. In Chapter 17 we described the problems of attempting to deploy welfare theory to policy, and these apply here with considerable force. Owners of monopolies are harmed by the loss of their rights to charge what the market will bear and to price discriminate. Price-searching employers of factors of production lose profits when prices of these resources are raised. Profits of firms whose production yields external costs are reduced by government taxes equal to the marginal external damage they must pay. For the reasons discussed in Chapter 17, we have no assurance that the welfare losses suffered as a result of these policies are fully compensated for in the welfare gains enjoyed by beneficiaries. All we can say is that sufficient additional output ought to be produced to *make possible* the compensation of the injured parties. As compensation is rarely a part of realistic policy proposals, this point offers scant reassurance.

Similarly, we have no assurance that government production of public goods, financed through the levy of taxes on its citizens, will leave everyone a net beneficiary, even if the choice of public good output is efficient. We cannot say that the combination of public and private goods made available to every citizen through such a government scheme will be preferred to that obtained without it. Some citizens more adept at bargaining may quite conceivably lose through such an arrangement. Gains to those who benefit need not necessarily be greater than losses to others.

Which Way is Up?

The objections raised in the previous section are purely theoretical. Of at least equal importance to the usefulness of welfare economics in policy are more practical difficulties. As was pointed out in Chapter 10, the "literal" price taker firm facing a perfectly elastic demand for its output is likely an extremely rare species. Although natural monopoly is probably not a very common phenomenon, the advantage of location and the market power it confers is likely to be almost universal. Similarly, uncertainty concerning product quality can also be expected to produce attachment to branded products, which translates into downward-sloping demand curves. Are all these prices to be regulated?

In order to know the correct price to set in each case the government must know the marginal cost and the elasticity of demand facing each firm. In addition, as both costs and demand are constantly responding to changes in the economic environment, effective price regulation requires that this information be constantly updated. Furthermore, since individual firms are likely to be harmed by the price regulations actually set, the government can expect little cooperation from them in acquiring this information. On the contrary, these firms will do everything in their power to convince government regulators that the marginal costs and demand elasticities they face are both sky-high. The experience of rate-setting commissions in determining the prices of public utilities discussed in Chapter 13 gives one little confidence in the ability of government price regulation to achieve Pareto optimality.

Similar difficulties beset the government in attempting to regulate factor prices in markets where demanding firms are price searchers. The elasticity of supply of factors to these firms will vary from firm to firm. Efficient regulation requires knowledge of each firm's production function and the supply functions of the various factors—and, as we know, the supply of factors facing individual employers is rarely perfectly elastic. Such influences as locational preference, occupational advantages, and dual-income opportunities for households may imply a limited selection of jobs for particular workers and a low elasticity of supply to employers. How is the government to obtain such information in each case? Experience with the government's sole effort to set wages to date, the minimum wage law, suggests that political rather than efficiency considerations are likely to dominate deliberations involving this form of regulation, even where correct information is available.

The informational requirements for optimal intervention in the case of external effects are similarly discouraging. Earlier in this chapter we outlined the circumstances in which external effects are likely to pose an efficiency problem. There we saw that cases where activities impose costs (or offer benefits) that are not internalized through market transactions are those involving substantial transaction costs. One of the most important of these costs is that of determining the total value of these effects and arranging measures to modify the level of the activity. However, these are precisely the costs that can be expected to deter the government from achieving an optimal intervention. In order to determine the appropriate tax or subsidy for each producer of an external effect, it is necessary to know the extent of the *marginal damage or benefit to each person from each individual producer*. Were this information costless to assemble market transactions might be expected to eliminate the external effect. In some cases the transaction costs that make such market adjustments infeasible also hinder government efforts to achieve efficient allocation.

Nor is government provision of public goods likely to move us effortlessly to the utility possibility frontier. Again, the transaction costs that impair efficient market arrangements do the same to government intervention. Efficiency requires that the government provide the quantity of these goods that equates the sum of individual MRSs with the RPT. How is the government to identify the former of these magnitudes? Communication costs will inhibit the assembly of this information, and contact with individual users, once established, will yield information of limited usefulness.

Assume that the government seeks to determine the appropriate quantity of a particular public good by simply polling the population. Responses to such a poll will be influenced by the **gaming behavior** of the users. Depending on whether the users expect their information to be used in determining their tax liability or in the quantity of the good to be provided, they will respond in one of two ways, each of which will be misleading. If they expect that their responses will be used for both purposes, they will proclaim that the public good has no value for them— their taxes would contribute to the production of a negligible amount of public good compared to the total provided by all taxpayers. By responding in such a deceptive way, such users may escape paying any tax for the public good. If *all* users respond in this way, however, the government will conclude—incorrectly— that *no* user values the public good.

Now assume that these same users are assured that their own taxes will not be influenced by their responses. In this case, they will certainly *inflate* their valuation. As larger amounts of the public good will in effect cost them nothing, they will eagerly insist on more of it than they are willing to pay for.

The Problem of "Second Best"

The difficulties of achieving Pareto optimality through government intervention related thus far should convince all but the most credulous that even the most well-intentioned and best-informed government will fail to satisfy our four efficiency conditions for all goods. Some corrective measures will overshoot or fall short of their marks, and some failures will go overlooked. Intuition seems to suggest that in such cases it is best for the government to attempt to satisfy these conditions for as many goods and resources as it can. It should, according to this intuition, promote as much efficiency as it can by seeking a **second-best allocation of resources** if a "first-best" is not feasible. Intuition is incorrect in this case—indeed, it has been shown that when one efficiency condition cannot be satisfied it is *not* desirable in general to satisfy all others.[4]

The proof of this result would require technical skills beyond those possessed by many readers of this text. However, with Figure 18.10 we can indicate the nature of the problem posed by the search for such a second-best optimum. For our purposes here we resort to the simplified world of Robinson Crusoe, in which he is the only consumer and must select a consumption combination from those available on or below the PPF. In this case, unlike our previous example of a single-consumer world, some efficiency conditions in the economy cannot be satisfied. We may represent this failure to satisfy all conditions as an added constraint on the opportunity set of Crusoe, ruling out the attainment of combinations lying above the diagonal line labeled C in the figure.

The first-best combination, T, is therefore unattainable. Strict adherence to other efficiency conditions, such as the satisfaction of technological efficiency in Condition 1, might therefore drive the economy to produce combination H lying on indifference curve U_1. However, Crusoe prefers combination K, which is not on the PPF. Making Crusoe as well off as he can be given the productive capabilities of the economy and the constraints imposed by the failure of certain efficiency conditions requires that additional efficiency conditions be violated as well.

Consider the following example. If governments are to finance their activities, including the pursuit of efficiency through the production of public goods and the subsidy of activities generating external benefits, it is quite likely that taxes must be levied. However, as we have already seen, taxes themselves can generate inefficiencies. These taxes may interfere with the satisfaction of Condition 3. Under

---

[4]This rather startling conclusion was first presented by R. G. Lipsey and Kevin Lancaster in "The General Theory of Second Best," *Review of Economic Studies* 14 (1956–1957): 11–32. A more accessible treatment is provided in P. R. G. Layard and A. A. Walters, *Microeconomic Theory* (New York: McGraw-Hill, 1978), 180–188. The diagrammatic treatment here is based on that developed in Walter Nicholson, *Microeconomic Theory*, 2d ed. (Hinsdale, IL.: Dryden Press, 1978), 571–573.

Figure 18.10 *The Problem of Second-Best Efficiency*

Combination T is Pareto optimal in the sense that all efficiency conditions are satisfied. This result may be ruled out by a failure of one or more conditions that may not be corrected. Such a situation is represented here by the addition of constraint C, which prevents the economy from producing combinations above this curve. Requiring that the condition of technological efficiency be satisfied may force the production of combination H, which yields less utility to the consumer than combination K, which violates the technological efficiency condition.

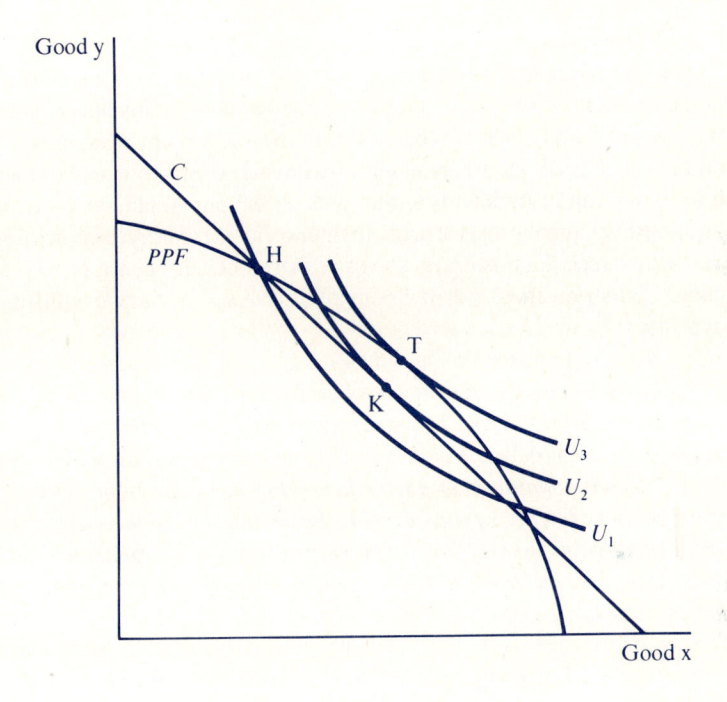

such circumstances it is quite possible that efficiency could be improved by some departure from the competitive result equating price and the firm's marginal cost. If good x is taxed and good y is not, for example, too little of the former and too much of the latter will be produced. Permitting producers of good y to collude to restrain output under these circumstances might improve the allocation of resources by guiding those diverted from good x by the tax back toward production of that good.

In recent years economic theorists have developed a large body of theory concerning optimal taxation under such second-best conditions. These studies seek to develop schemes of taxation that correct for the failure of efficiency due to imperfect taxation and other problems.[5] To date, however, these studies are chiefly useful only in pointing out the pitfalls of relying on intuition to guide such efforts.

---

[5] The technically equipped reader will find a thorough survey of this work in A. B. Atkinson and J. E. Stiglitz, *Lectures on Public Economics* (New York: McGraw-Hill, 1980).

The informational requirements necessary for implementation of such a set of taxes rule out their use in the day-to-day choice of government policy. An optimal tax scheme requires information on an even broader scope than that described here to insure a first-best optimum for a market economy. It is therefore not unrealistic to describe these efforts in their current state as offering a "cure" more costly than the "disease."

The Politics of Efficiency

Thus far we have for the most part treated government as a benevolent mechanism that would seek tirelessly to maximize social welfare if it could only obtain the proper guidance. We cannot close our discussion of policy analysis without pointing out the pitfalls of this view. From the vantage point of economic theory government is merely an organization of men and women bound together by a structure of rules and agreements within which each pursues his or her own interest. In this sense it is much like a firm. Economists have rarely been willing to assume that firms seek to maximize social welfare. On the contrary, one of the most quoted passages from Adam Smith's *The Wealth of Nations* affirms exactly the opposite:

But man has almost constant occasion for the assistance of his brethren, and it is in vain for him to expect it from their benevolence only. He will be more likely to prevail if he can interest their self-love in his favor, and show them that it is for their own advantage to do for him what he requires of them. . . . It is not from the benevolence of the butcher, the brewer, or the baker, that we expect our dinner, but from their regard to their own interest. We address ourselves, not to their humanity but their self-love, and never talk to them of our own necessities but of their advantages.

A good portion of this book has been devoted to the analysis of the behavior of firms, seeking to develop an understanding of when such convergences of interests will occur and when they will not. Why do we simply assume that government organizations respond to motives that we rule out as implausible guides to the behavior of different forms of organization?

In the last few decades economists have begun to apply to the behavior of government the sort of rigorous economic analysis formerly reserved for proprietary firms. Officeholders and bureaucrats have been treated in this analysis as suppliers of services to the government organization, not as seekers of Pareto optimality. The objectives sought by these government agents are similar to those sought by employees of any firm: high wages, job security, pleasant working conditions, and tax shelters.

The products of these organizations are services, albeit occasionally unusual ones. Politicians supply laws, and bureaucrats administer them. In some aspects this behavior is barely distinguishable from the supply of similar services by private firms. Passenger train travel originally was supplied by firms; now it is supplied by Amtrak. The mail was once delivered by a government agency; now it is supplied by an at least quasi-private corporation. Hospital services are provided by several types of organization. Most are nonprofit private firms, but many are government owned and operated, and a rapidly growing number are organized to make money.

The behavior of these alternative forms of organization is not indistinguishable. Some of these differences were discussed in Chapter 7. Here we wish to direct our attention to the other, more differentiated services offered by governments; we wish to focus on those powers that the government has because it is the government and not a private firm. One of the most important of these powers is its ability to reassign property rights and to redistribute income. Government may tax and it may alter the rights that individuals hold to their property. Politicians wield this power, and economists who wish to understand this government behavior must look to the incentives that these particular agents face in making those decisions. It is far from obvious that these incentives direct behavior toward efficiency-related objectives.

The current state of this theory is far too underdeveloped to enable us to present a complete model of the use of these powers. We can only sketch some outlines of the basic directions in which these studies have progressed. One of the most important is interest group theory. In a democracy, a politician obtains power by attracting sufficient votes to be elected. However, only a majority of votes need be obtained to secure office, implying that a politician who attracts just over one half of the voters may ignore the remainder. Under these circumstances coalitions may form to win political power, then exploit this power by redistributing wealth from the minority to itself. This may take the form of seizing property or certain uses of property, as when a California majority voted to seize the rights of coastal landowners, preventing them from developing that property in profitable ways. It may take the form of using government fiscal apparatus to finance benefits and services to specific groups of people, as when the elderly and voters sympathetic to their situation obtained government funding for their medical care needs.

Interest groups may use the government to redistribute wealth to themselves through mechanisms other than simple seizure or taxation and spending. One aspect of this behavior that has attracted the most attention recently is the use of government police power to cartelize the supply of goods and services. As we observed in Chapter 10, cartels are inherently unstable. Marginal revenue to any member of the cartel exceeds marginal cost, and typically this divergence is directly related to the number of cartel members. In the absence of some mechanism to police the output behavior of individual members, we would predict that each firm would be influenced to expand output beyond the agreed-upon level, leading to a collapse of such arrangements. If, however, government itself policed the output of each member and had the power to punish offenders, no such collapse would be predicted. The cartel output could thus be stabilized.

Merely to state this possibility leaves many questions unanswered, and few have been satisfactorily answered by economists seeking to develop predictive models of government behavior. Why are not all industries regulated and cartelized, and if all are, which would be the most likely candidates? Some answers to these questions have been offered by Sam Peltzman.[6] He poses the ques-

---

[6] Sam Peltzman, "Toward a More General Theory of Regulation," *The Journal of Law and Economics* 19 (August 1976): 211–240.

tion in the following way: Who are the suppliers of this regulation, and what is its cost to them? He identifies policitians as the suppliers of regulation, who supply it in exchange for votes. Regulation increases prices and therefore profits, securing electoral support among members of the affected industry. However, higher prices also affect consumers, breeding discontent and therefore costing votes among this group. Efficient regulation (in terms of the regulator's objective of obtaining the maximum majority) requires that prices be raised only to the point where votes gained per dollar of price increase are just equal to the votes lost among consumers at this margin.

The politician's choice of the optimal regulated price is illustrated in Figure 18.11. Potential profit is related to price by the curve labeled PP. Given the under-

---

Figure 18.11 *Vote Maximization and Government Choice*

Government regulators selecting price affect the numbers of votes they receive. By increasing price they gain support from suppliers, who obtain higher profits but lose support from consumers, who must pay the higher prices. The curves M_1, M_2, and M_3 identify sets of combinations of prices and profits that yield equal numbers of votes. Curve M_1 is associated with a larger number of votes than M_2, which represents more votes than M_3. Each has a positive slope, reflecting the assumption that the votes lost through a price increase can be recouped through a sufficiently large increase in profits. The potential profit curve, PP, connects the combinations that are feasible given demand and the costs of suppliers. Combination T is chosen by a vote-maximizing regulator. It is associated with price P_2, which is between the monopoly price, P^*, and the efficient price, P_1. A shift in the potential profit curve to $P'P'$ would lead regulators to select combination K, associated with lower price P_3.

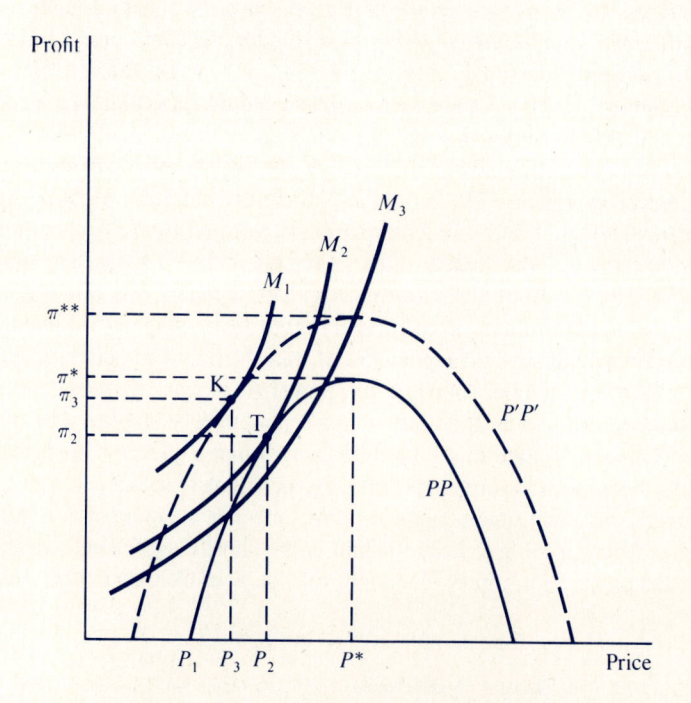

lying demand and cost functions of firms in this industry, profits can be zero at outputs yielding prices sufficiently high or low. These extreme prices bracket the cartel profit-maximizing price, $P*$. This curve therefore forms the opportunity set for the regulator, whose problem is to select the combination along it that will maximize his or her votes. He or she therefore ranks these combinations according to the total number of votes produced by each combination.

These rankings are revealed by the *iso-vote curves*, labeled M_1, M_2, and M_3. Each of these curves identifies combinations of price and profit that will yield the same number of votes. Each must have a positive slope, reflecting the fact that higher prices lose votes from consumers that may be recouped only by higher profits, and thus more political support, from the supplier group. Their convex shape reflects Peltzman's assumption that such support is gained from either group at diminishing rates from policies favorable to their interests.

So long as higher prices discourage some political support the regulated price will not be the profit-maximizing cartel price, $P*$. To adopt this price would be to ignore the political costs (including possible loss of the election) due to the impact of these prices on consumer voting. Nor will the price be the zero profit price, P_1, expected to result from long-run competitive equilibrium. Assuming that regulators choose such efficient outcomes is equivalent to assuming that desirable results can be obtained costlessly, a position that by now all readers of this text should be suspicious of adopting rashly. The political optimum will lie somewhere between these two extremes, such as price P_2 in Figure 18.11. This combination is identified by a tangency between the opportunity set PP and the highest attainable iso-vote curve, M_2.

In some of its aspects such behavior by politician-regulators can appear benign. Consider the result of a change in technology that lowers costs at every output, hence increases the potential profits earned at every price. This will have the effect of shifting the opportunity set upward to the dashed line $P'P'$. The regulator may under these circumstances choose a lower price even though the cartel optimum price is not reduced.

Nor should the reader interpret the language in which this discussion has been cast too narrowly. Peltzman's model applies with a few superficial modifications to almost any government program. Let tax rates in Figure 18.11 be measured along the horizontal axis and programs offering benefits to an interest group be measured along the vertical. Increased benefits can be financed only by higher taxes; hence, the opportunity set will have a positive slope, at least over a certain range.[7] Higher taxes discourage some voters whose political support can be restored only by offering benefits to others. Politicians confronting such an opportunity set will therefore seek a combination of tax rates and benefits corresponding to the tangency solution offered by point T. As it is votes gained and lost by the politician that is weighed in choosing this combination, all we can say is that at point T the

---

[7]The negatively sloped portion has an interesting interpretation as well. Some readers will remember the widely discussed "Laffer curve" that figured prominently in the presidential campaign of 1980. It was the contention of some economists and politicians at that time that increased benefits could be financed by *lowering* tax rates. As the analysis here indicates, even if such a negatively sloped portion of this opportunity set existed, we would not predict that politicians would ever find themselves on that portion of the curve.

political cost of higher taxes at the margin is equal to the political gain from increased spending. There is no reason to expect that this result also corresponds to an efficient equating of marginal social costs and benefits.

Summary

In this chapter we were chiefly concerned with market success and market failure where success is measured only against the standard of satisfying the necessary conditions for Pareto optimality developed in Chapter 17. We saw, for example, that market organization will produce Pareto optimality in a world lacking public goods and exhibiting perfect price taking in all output and input markets. This refulgent conclusion is somewhat dimmed by the recognition that price searching is very common in daily life, both in our demand for goods and services as consumers and in our supply of resources to firms. The former is likely to imply a failure of Condition 3, while the latter suggests failure of Condition 1. The practice of price discrimination, employed so usefully in Chapter 9 to explain whole ranges of seemingly peculiar business practices, was found to be a source of failure of Condition 2.

Nor does a realistic view of government behavior suggest that existing practice in this sector satisfies these conditions. Ideally, government should finance its activities by a series of lump-sum taxes that have no allocative effects. Instead, government taxes goods, a practice that distorts relative prices; it taxes wage income, which distorts work leisure choices; and it taxes interest income, which distorts consumption versus savings decisions. Regulation, price controls, and rationing are other government activities that have efficiency implications.

The importance of transaction costs to the allocation of resources was also discussed. In the absence of transaction costs, all activities affecting other parties will be internalized through a transaction. Under such circumstances there can be no divergence between private and social costs. This result is referred to as the Coase theorem. When transactions are costly, however, some will not be worth the cost. Two conclusions emerged from this discussion. First, since the assignment of property rights in this case will affect the allocative outcome, attention should be paid to these alternative results in the assignment process itself. Second, the possibility of divergences between social and private costs may be a source of allocative inefficiency.

In Chapter 17 public goods were defined as those goods whose consumption by some fails to reduce the quantity available for others. Several transaction costs impair the efficient provision of these goods. An individual adjustment equilibrium was identified that suggests results where there is no communication among public good users. All public good users must be involved in negotiations if efficient quantities are to be produced. If there are vast numbers of beneficiaries, the cost of communication can clearly deter such arrangements. A second problem in achieving efficient allocation is the problem of agreement enforcement. Like members of a cartel, each party to an agreement has the incentive to violate that agreement for private gain. The final problem experienced by private efforts to provide public goods is bargaining. The provision of public goods provides net benefits to users in direct proportion to the support of these goods by others and in inverse proportion to the support provided by the individual user. Each user is therefore influenced to minimize his or her own contribution by feigning disinterest, among other tactics. If all users dissimulate in this fashion, society's true valuation of the public good may never be known.

To know these problems of resource allocation by markets is not necessarily to have an agenda for government action. Although theoretical correctives may be derived for each of the market and government failures, practical issues concerning implementation of such policies raise doubts about the implicit role of government in such action. The information requirements for optimal intervention are quite often exactly the same as those for efficient market organization. If this information is available for government use, it must be available for private use as well. When it is unavailable, government is forced to "shoot in the dark" and possibly miss the desired target.

Also troublesome for the design of optimal intervention is the problem posed by the theory of second-best efficiency. If all marginal efficiency conditions cannot be satisfied for all goods, then in general it is not desirable to satisfy as many as possible. Efforts to promote marginal cost pricing or taxation of activities generating external costs may move us further away from the utility possibility frontier rather than closer.

Finally, this chapter raised the question of whether government as an economic organization is likely to respond to efficiency-directed advice. Much policy discussion is carried on under the implicit assumption that economists need merely to name optimal interventions to insure that efficient policies will be implemented. Firms behave efficiently, when they do, not from altruistic motives but because doing so is to their private advantage. The questions naturally arise of whether and when a similar convergence of interests occurs in the decisions and behavior of government. Economists have developed only the fragments of an economic theory of government organization, some of which were outlined here. These preliminary developments are not encouraging to the idea that democratic governments are led toward efficiency in broad ranges of public choice by the force of competition for votes. Where this competition does lead is as of today unresolved. There are many theories, quasi-theories, and conjectures, all of which imply too little government, too much government, or the wrong kind. Some economists have suggested that until we gain more confidence in our models of how government behaves, offering advice on how to achieve Pareto optimality may be a waste of economic resources.

Key Concepts

transaction costs
assignment of property rights
Coase theorem
marginal private cost (MPC)
marginal social cost (MSC)
external cost
external benefit
isorevenue curve

individual adjustment equilibrium (IEA)
common consumption frontier (CCF)
public good transaction costs
communications problem
free-rider problem
bargaining behavior
gaming behavior
second-best allocation of resources

Questions

1. *Easy* Price taking by all demanders of inputs will result in the satisfaction of Condition 1 from Chapter 17, which requires that the rates of technical substitution be equal for all pairs of inputs in the production of every output. Explain.

Hard The military draft, when used, allows the Defense Department to forcibly enroll conscripts into military service at wages below the market-clearing level. Explain how the use of the draft can be interpreted as a form of tax on draftees that forces them to bear a portion of the cost of defense not borne through taxation. What difficulty does this present to the Defense Department in seeking to organize this activity in a technologically efficient manner?

2. *Easy* Marginal cost pricing of all goods is necessary to achieve both distributional efficiency and allocative efficiency. Explain why.

Hard Price controls with no rationing result in failures of both distributional and allocative efficiency conditions. Explain this failure in each case. Is the result improved if rationing accompanies the price controls? The discussion of the efficiency implications of price controls in this chapter was limited to price ceilings. Develop your own analysis of the effects of price floors.

3. *Easy* Interperson price discrimination results in a failure of the necessary condition for distributional efficiency. Explain why.

Hard It is possible for firms to practice interunit price discrimination without interfering with the achievement of distributional efficiency. However, doing so requires that the firm price discriminate "perfectly." What is meant by this, and why is this important?

4. *Easy* Interstate trucking regulation establishes rates over particular routes and forbids competition for service over those routes. What types of inefficiency are likely to result from this regulation? Can you name other forms of regulation that seem to interfere with market efficiency? What is the basis for each of the regulations you named? Do these objectives seem reasonable?

Hard The Coase theorem maintains that without transaction costs the allocation of resources will be both efficient and invariant with respect to the assignment of property rights. Our discussion of external benefits and costs suggests, on the other hand, that we may have excessively dirty air, congested streets, crowded parks, and vanishing wildlife in terms of the efficiency standard. Identify the transaction that might internalize all costs in each of these examples, and explain its role in deterring the market from achieving efficiency.

5. *Easy* One important transaction cost that prevents markets from achieving efficient levels of public good provision is the cost of communicating. Communication among consumers of private goods is not necessary to obtain production of efficient quantities of these goods. Why cannot consumers of public goods reach efficiency without communicating with one another? What is the difference?

Hard The discovery of new knowledge is a public good. Explain why. In the United States an inventor is given a patent that establishes a monopoly protected by law for 17 years. In what sense does the granting of patents serve efficiency? In what ways does it interfere with efficiency? Can you suggest a different arrangement for the rewarding of producers of this public good that will not produce inefficiency of some sort? Remember that taxes also have allocative effects.

6. *Easy* In an economy with two monopolies it may be more efficient to do nothing than to eliminate one and leave the other. Explain.

Hard It has been argued that voters are more likely to support candidates who espouse inefficient programs that provide them with large direct benefits than candidates who support efficient programs whose benefits are difficult to perceive and small by comparison. If this statement is true, what is its implication for government's ability to correct inefficiencies arising from market failure?

Index

Ability, 525
Advertising,
    and demand, 203–206
Aggregation problem, 174–175
Agricultural Adjustment Administration, 57
Agricultural Marketing Act, 56
Airline Deregulation Act, 266, 267
Airlines,
    and market separation, 293–294
Akerlof, George, 201n
Alchian, Armen A., 219n, 220, 220n, 406–407, 406n
Annuity factor, 498
Anticompetitive agreements, 425–427
Antitrust law,
    and labor unions, 322
    and vertical integration, 324
Arbitrage, 53–56
    definition, 55
Arc elasticity, 159
Asset prices, 504–505
Assets,
    constant yield, 497–499
    financial, 487–488
    infinitely lived, 499
    real, 487
Atkinson, A. B., 613n
Automobiles, 114–115
Averch, H., 407n
Averch-Johnson effect, 407, 408–414

Bain, Joe S., 320, 320n
Bargaining behavior, 609
Barlow, Robin, 452n
Barzel, Yoram, 541n
Battalio, Raymond, 8n
Becker, Gary S., 441n
Benefits,
    external, 599–602
Benson, Ezra Taft, 57
Berg, A. Scott, 47
Berndt, Ernst R., 386, 386n
Bid rent curves, 123–128
    definition, 128
Binding price regulation, 56
Blum, W. J., 561n
Boskin, Michael J., 387n
Brand loyalty, 201–202
    definition, 311
Brazer, H., 452n
Buchanan, James M., 88n, 602n
Budget constraints, 98
    definition, 97
    slopes of, 107
Buy or make, 216

California,
    and rent controls, 59
Capital,
    human, 531–541
        education as, 534–535

621

Capital (*continued*)
   signaling models, 535-541
   —labor ratio 385–387
   opportunity costs of, 503–504
   supply of, 475–509
      changing interest rates, 483–484
      and interest rates, 477–487
      investment opportunities and demand for loanable funds, 487–495
      loanable funds, 479–482
      measurement problem, 476–477
      multiperiod analysis, 495–509
      preferences for time-specific consumption, 482–483
      substitution and income effects, 484–485
      supply curves for loanable funds, 485–487
Capitalization, 504–505
Capital recovery factor, 503
Capital services, 500–502
Carnegie, Andrew, 467
Cartels, 425–427
   definition, 315
   stability of, 316–320
Cebula, Richard, 431*n*
Ceteris paribus, 35, 38, 41
   definition, 33
Chain rule, 27–28
Changes,
   compensating, 120–122
      definition, 120
   factor technical, 360
   technical, 349–350, 387–388
      definition, 349
      and employment, 358–360
   in technology, 349
China,
   and monopolies, 282
Chiseling, 316
Choice,
   analysis of, 66
   and bundled goods, 114–130
      bid rent curves, 123–128
      compensated changes, 120–122
      consumption optima and wages, 118–120
      rapid transit, 128–130
      time cost of consumption, 115–118
   consistency, 83–84
   corner solutions, 82–83
   describing, 78–86
   and economic theory, 66–67
   folly of priorities, 86–87
   with imperfect information, 190–206
      advertising and demand, 203–206
      brand loyalty, 201–202
      informal markets for insurance, 197–199
      lemon principle, 200–201
      the opportunity set, 195–197
      property rights and information, 202–203
      ranking wtih uncertainty, 192–195
      risk and insurance, 191–192
      transaction costs, 199–200
   more vs. less, 84–86
   opportunity cost,
      with continuous opportunities, 81–82
   and opportunity sets, 66
      continuous, 78–81
   political, 87–90
   public, 88–90
   purposeful, 17–18
   and rank ordering, 66, 103
   rational, 87
   and relatively time intensive goods, 122–123
   social, 86–90
   theory of,
      describing choice, 78–86
      opportunity sets, 67–69
      rank ordering, 69–78
      social choice, 86–90
Choice theory, 96
Civil Aeronautics Act, 267
Civil Aeronautics Board, 266–267, 469
Clarkson, Kenneth W., 223, 223*n*, 224*n*
Coase, Ronald H., 214–219, 214*n*, 220, 324, 598*n*
Coase theorem, 597–599
Collection of attributes, 226
Collusion, 314–322
   augmented, 322
   cartels, 315–316
      stability of, 316–320
   definition, 314
   and entry, 320–321
Communications problems, 606
Comparative statistics, 33
Competition, 230–232
Competitive models, 584–586
   definition, 239
Complements, 36, 37
Consistency, 37, 83–84
Constant-scale operations, 249
Consumer behavior, 40–41
Consumer consumption frontier, 604–605
Consumer surplus, 288
Consumption,
   opportunity cost of, 105
   preferences for time-specific, 482–483
   time cost of, 96, 115–118, 122–123
Consumption optimum,
   conditions at, 104–105
   definition, 103–104
   with different wages rates, 118–120
   interpreting conditions, 105
Continuous opportunities,
   ranking with, 71–72

Index

opportunity cost with, 81–82
Contractual advantages, 427–428
Convexity, 76–78
    and rational choice, 87
Corcoran, M., 548n
Corner solutions, 82–83, 455
    definition, 82
Cost advantages, 321
Cost curves,
    long-run average, 256
    positioning, 244–247
    shape of total, 247–249
Cost minimization, 215
Costs,
    average, 242–244
    external, 599–602
    and inputs, 369–373
    of investments, 492
    marginal, 242
    marginal factor, 371
    marginal private, 599
    marginal social, 599
    operating, 240–242
        definition, 240
    and optimization, 215–219
    of output in terms of inputs, 371–373
    and outputs, 240–256
        choice of scale, 251–252
        economies and diseconomies of scale, 254–256
        envelope curves, 252–254
        positioning cost curves, 244–247
        rates of, 242
        shape of total cost curves, 247–249
    overhead, 240–242
        definition, 240
    and returns to scale, 338–341
    short and long run, 249–251
Coupons,
    and market separation, 294–296
Cunningham, James, 392n
Customers,
    price discrimination among, 289–292

Darby, Michael R., 396, 396n
Demand,
    and advertising, 203–206
    aggregating, 151–155
        altering distribution of goods, 152–153
        economics of hoarding, 153–155
    with all factors variable, 276–277
    compensated, 144–149
    definition, 33
    effects of price changes on, 144
    elastic, 163
    first law of, 33–34, 138, 141
    with fixed supply, 33–41

    and income, 37–40
    inelastic, 163
    influence of time, 40–41
    for normal factors, 377–380
    other prices, 34–37
    second law of, 41
    theory of, 20
    and time, 50
    uncompensated, 144–149
Demand curves,
    compensated, 144–149
        definition, 144
    constant elasticity, 165–167
    linear, 161–163
    nonlinear, 164
    with one variable factor, 374–376
    uncompensated, 144–149
        definition, 144
Demand elasticities, 155–167
    arc elasticity, 159
    constant, 164–167
    elasticity and nonlinear demand curves, 164
    income elasticity, 157–158
    linear demand curves, 161–163
    point elasticity, 160–161
    price elasticity, 158–159
Demand variables, 33
Demsetz, Harold, 220, 220n
Denison, Edward F., 338n, 386n, 388
Depreciation, 503–504
Differentials,
    definition, 11
    total, 12–13, 194
Diminishing returns, 337
Discount factor, 492
Discrimination,
    and wages, 541–548
        evidence on wage disparity, 546–548
        conditions for wage disparity, 545–546
        responses to prejudice, 543–545
        tastes of demanders, 541–543
Duality, 340
Dumping, 293
Duncan, G. J., 548n

Earnings,
    distribution of, 522–531
        coercion, 524–525
        income growth and relative wages, 529
        sources of wage variation, 523
        tastes for different work, 525–528
        variation in ability, 525
Economic efficiency, 554. *See also* Efficiency
Economics,
    equilibrium, 18
    of hoarding, 153–155

Economics (*continued*)
  purposeful choice, 17–18
  as social science, 5, 17–18, 21
Economic theory,
  and social behavior, 5
  and choice, 66–67
Edgeworth boxes, 564–567
Edgeworth, Francis Y., 564n
Egalitarianism, 560
Efficiency,
  allocative, 564, 570–574
    with public goods, 576–579
  defined, 554–562
  distributional, 564, 568–570
  and markets and government.
    See Markets, and government and efficiency
  measuring utility, 556–557
  measuring utility levels, 558–562
  normative limits, 556
  politics of, 614–618
  technological, 564–567
  weighting individual utilities, 557–558
Efficiency gain, 555–556
Elasticity, 15–16

  and marginal revenue, 274–276
  of substitution, 355–356
    definition, 355
    and factor income shares, 357–358
Employers,
  constraints on supply of labor, 462–463
Employment, 383–397
  capital-labor ratio, 385–387
  conditions of, 466–469
  technical changes, 358–360, 387–388
Endowments, 106–108
Entry, 266
  barriers to, 320–321
  collusion and, 320–321
  regulation of, 266–267
Envelope curves, 252–254
  definition, 254
Equilibrium 20–21
  conditions, 50–52
  determining, 41–46
  first condition, 44
  free-for-all system, 43–45
  full, 52
  nonprice rationing systems, 45–46
  second condition, 50
Exchange,
  gifts, 109–110
  value of, 105–110
Expansion revenue product curves, 367
Exploitation, 404, 414–418
  by price searchers, 416–418

Factor cost,
  marginal,
    definition, 422
    with rising supply, 421–424
Factor income shares, 357–358
  and elasticity of substitution, 357–358
Factor price changes,
  output effect of, 377, 379–380
  substitution effect of, 377–379
Factors,
  choosing level of one, 373–374
  demand curves with one variable, 374–376
  demand for, 363–397, 404–433
    costs and inputs, 369–373
    demand for labor and number of jobs, 389–397
    exploitation, 414–418
    market power in input markets, 418–433
    market power in output markets, 404–414
    productivity in theory and practice, 380–388
    revenue effects and marginal revenue products, 364–369
  demand for inferior, 400–402
  demand for normal, 377–380
  demand with all variable, 376–377
  varying fixed, 377
Farm policy, 56–58
Federal Communications Commission, 266
Feldstein, Martin, 386n
Firms,
  as metering devices, 220–223
  profits, 226
  proprietary, 49, 223
  theory of, 374–376
Food and Drug Act, 388
Foreclosure, 324
Free-for-all rationing, 43–45, 46
Freeman, Richard B., 534, 534n
Free-rider problems, 606
Full price, 307
Functions,
  definition, 8–9
  demand, 134
  deriving demand, 134–151
    changes in goods' prices, 138–141
    changes in income, 135–136
    compensated and uncompensated demand, 144–149
    effects of price changes on demand, 144
    Giffen paradox, 149–151
    income effects of price changes, 141–143
    real and nominal income, 137–138
    substitution effects of price changes, 143–144
  differential, 11
  elasticity, 15–16

Index

and graphs, 8–16
linear, 12
maxima and minima, 13–15
multivariate, 12–13
nonlinear,
   definition, 23
   slopes of, 23–25
slopes of, 10–12

Gains from trade, 105–108
   value of, 107–108
Game theory, 318–319
Gaming behavior, 611
Giffen, Robert, 140
Giffen paradox, 149–151
   definition, 139–140
Gifts, 109–110
Goldman, Marshall I., 202n
Goods,
   altering distribution, 152–153
   bundled,
      bid rent curves, 123–128
      and choice, 114–130
      compensated changes, 120–122
      consumption optima with wages, 118–120
      rapid transit, 128–130
      time cost of consumption, 115–118
   changes in price, 138–141
   free, 67–68
   inferior, 38–39, 136
   normal, 39, 136
   relatively time intensive, 122–123
      definition, 118
Goods space,
   and income consumption curves, 136
   and indifference curves, 103–104
Government alternatives, 609–618
   optimal intervention, 609–612
   politics of efficiency, 614–618
   second-best allocation of resources, 612–614
Government failure, 591–597
   excise taxes, 593–595
   income and other taxes, 595–596
   price controls and rationing, 591–593
   regulation, 596–597
Governments,
   and markets and efficiency. See Markets, and governments and efficiency
   organization, 224–227
      and profits, 226–227
      and quality, 227–230
Graphs,
   and functions, 8–16
   importance of, 9
Great Britain,
   and nationalized medicine, 60–61
   and rent control, 59–60
Gwartney, J., 548, 548n

Hartman, Heridi, I., 547n
Hashimoto, Masanori, 391, 391n
Hilton, George W., 129n
Hoarding, 152
   economics of, 153–155
Household budgets,
   effects of income changes, 100–101
   effects of price changes, 101–102
   opportunity costs of purchasing, 99
   as opportunity set, 96–102
Household choices, 95–130
   choice involving bundled goods, 114–130
   and choice theory, 96
   conditions at consumption optimum, 104–105
   household budget as opportunity set, 96–102
   indifference curves in goods space, 103–104
   inefficiency and welfare loss, 111–114
   value of exchange, 105–110
Housing,
   public, 112–114

Income,
   changes in, 135–136
   changes in wages, 448–452
   choosing the quantity supplied, 444–452
   definition, 174
   and demand, 37–40
   distribution of, 517–548
      discrimination and wages, 541–548
      human capital, 531–541
   distribution of earnings, 522–531
   distribution of total family, 518–522
   distribution of wealth, 519–522
   effect of changes on household budgets, 100–101
   full, 442
   and indifference curves, 194
   nominal, 137–138, 177
   real, 137–138
      definition, 174
      measuring, 176–177
   relation to prices, 96–99
Income-compensating measure of welfare change, 108
Income conditional grants, 457–458
Income consumption curves, 136
Income effects,
   capital supply and interest rates, 484–485
   definition, 141
   of price changes, 141–143
   of wage changes, 450
   on labor supply, 446–448
Income elasticity, 157–158
Income endowments, 480
   changes in, 488
Income growth,
   and relative wages, 529

Income measurement, 173–190
Index numbers, 174–190
  converting changes to indexes, 184–186
  measuring real income, 176–177
  Laspeyres measures, 177–186
  Paasche measures, 177–186
  practical considerations, 189–190
  price indexes, 186–189
  purchasing power of money, 186
  weights and measures, 174–175
Indexes,
  converting changes to, 184–186
  definition, 184
Indifference curves,
  convexity, 76–78
  definition, 73
  in goods space, 103–104
  and income, 194
  marginal rate of substitution, 75–78
  properties of, 72–78
  slope of, 104
Individual adjustment equilibrium, 603–604
Individual behavior, 69–70
Industries,
  declining, 502–503
Industry supply, 264–267
  regulation of entry, 266–267
Inefficiency,
  and welfare loss, 111–114
    of public housing, 112–114
Inflation, 521
Information,
  choice with imperfect, 190–206
    advertising and demand, 203–206
    brand loyalty, 201–202
    informal markets for insurance, 197–199
    lemon principle, 200–201
    opportunity sets, 195–197
    property rights and information, 202–203
    ranking with uncertainty, 192–195
    risk and insurance, 191–192
    transaction costs, 199–200
  costs of, 307, 311
    equilibrium with, 311–314
    as source of market power, 311–314
Input markets,
  market power in, 418–433
    anticompetitive agreements, 425–427
    difficulties of wage regulation, 431–433
    locational and contractual advantages, 427–428
    marginal factor cost with rising supply, 421–424
    minimum wage restrictions with rising supply, 428–431
    monopsony demand, 424–425
    rising and falling supply, 419–421

Inputs,
  cost of output in terms of, 371–373
  and costs, 369–373
  inferior, 354, 400
  output as function of, 364
Insurance,
  complete, 199
  informal markets for, 197–199
  and opportunity sets, 195–197
  and risk, 191–192
Interest rates, 521
  and capital supply, 477–487
  changing, 483–484
  equilibrium, 494–495
  preferences for time-specific consumption, 482–483
  substitution and income effects, 484–485
  supply curves for loanable funds, 485–487
  supply of loanable funds, 479–482
  varying to demanders, 492–494
Interior combinations, 82, 86
Interstate Commerce Commission, 266
Investment opportunities, 487–495
  changes in income endowments, 488
  decision to invest, 488–491
  equilibrium interest rates, 494–495
  present value rule, 491–492
  varying interest rates to demanders, 492–494
Investments,
  costs of, 492
  in multiperiod analysis, 497
  profits on, 491
  return on, 492
  See also Savings and investments
Isocost curves, 351
Isoprofit curves, 408
Isoquants, 351
  definition, 341
  and returns to scale, 346–349
Isorevenue curves, 228

Job information searches, 396
Jobs,
  number of, 389–397
    minimum wage, 389–392
    seasonal and cyclical unemployment, 393–395
    sources of unemployment, 389
    supply restrictions, 392–393
  sensitive, 545–546
  unemployment as information search, 395–397
Johnson, L. L. 407n
Justice Department, 323, 324

Kagel, John, 8n
Kalven, Harry, Jr., 561n

Index

Kessel, Reuben A., 406–407, 406n
Khaled, Mohammed S., 386, 386n
Kraft, John, 114, 114n

Labor,
—capital ratio, 385–387
demand for, 389–397
minimum wage, 389–392
seasonal and cyclical unemployment, 393–395
sources of unemployment, 389
supply restrictions, 392–393
unemployment as job information search, 395–397
direct constraints on supply, 463–471
conditions of employment, 466–469
employer view, 462–463
maximum workweek as supply restriction, 463–464
regulation of working conditions, 469–471
union contracts, 464–466
market supply of, 452–460
income conditional grants, 457–458
labor force participation, 454–457
negative income tax, 459–460
paradox of increasing returns to, 383–385
productivity, 382–383
supply of, 439–471
choosing the quantity supplied, 444–452
income effects on, 446–448
opportunity sets, 440–444
Labor force participation, 454–457
Labor unions, 392–393
and collusion, 322
contracts, 464–466
and coercion, 524–525
Laffer curve, 617n
Lancaster, Kevin, 612n
Landes, Elizabeth M., 547, 547n
Laspeyres measures, 117–186
definition, 177
items included, 190
of price level change, 187, 189
when used, 189
Law of diminishing rate of substitution, 345
Law of diminishing returns, 337
Layard, P. R. G., 612n
Lazear, E., 391, 391n
Lebergott, Stanley, 519n, 528, 528n
Leisure,
changes in wages, 448–452
choosing the quantity supplied, 444–452
income effect on labor supply, 446–448
opportunity sets, 440–444
Lemon principle, 200–201
Lindsay, C. M., 60n, 230n
Linear regression, 157

Lipsey, R. G., 612n
Loanable funds,
demand for, 487–495
changes in income endowments, 488
decision to invest, 488–491
equilibrium interest rates, 494–495
present value rule, 491–492
varying interest rates to demanders, 492–494
supply curves for, 485–487
Location,
advantages of, 307–311
as source of market power, 307–314
Locational advantages, 427–428
Lotteries,
as rationing system, 45, 46
Lucas, R. E., Jr., 396, 396n

Mafia, 319–320
Maloney, M. T., 322, 322n, 471, 471n
Malthus, Thomas Robert, 332, 414
Marginal,
definition, 15
Marginal rate of substitution.
See Substitution, marginal rate of,
Market-clearing conditions, 44
Market demand,
definition, 152
theory of, 133–167
aggregating demand, 151–155
demand elasticities, 155–167
deriving demand functions, 134–151
Market demand curves, 152
Market equilibrium, 31–61
controlled prices, 56–61
demand with fixed supply, 33–41
determining equilibrium with zero price, 41–46
price as rationing device, 46–49
simultaneous systems, 32–33
supply side of market, 49–56
Market failure, 586–591
price discrimination, 589–590
price searching, 587–589
for inputs, 590–591
Market power,
definition, 274
in input markets, 418–433
anticompetitive agreements, 425–427
difficulties of wage regulation, 431–433
locational and contractual advantages, 427–428
marginal factor cost with rising supply, 421–424
minimum wage restrictions with rising supply, 428–431
monopsony demand, 424–425

Market Power (*continued*)
    rising and falling supply, 419–421
    in output markets, 404–414
        Averch-Johnson effect, 408–414
        isoprofit curves, 408
        profit restrictions, 406–407
    sources of, 301–324
        collusion, 314–322
        location and information, 307–314
        monopoly, 302–304
        tactics that don't work, 323–324
Markets,
    factors determined in, 31
    and governments and efficiency, 583–618
        competitive model, 584–586
        government alternatives, 609–618
        government failure, 591–597
        market failure, 586–591
        transaction costs and property rights, 597–609
    informal, 197–199
    separation of, 293–296
    supply side of, 49–56
        arbitrage and speculation, 53–56
        cobweb models, 52
        equilibrium conditions, 50–52
Market structures, 403–433
    exploitation, 414–418
    market power in input markets, 418–433
    market power in output markets, 404–414
    and organization, 230–232
Market time, 441
Marshall, Alfred, 140, 140n
Martin, D. L., 224n
Marx, Karl, 332, 414–415
Maxima and minima, 13–15
Maximum, 14
McCormick, R. E., 322, 322n, 471, 471n
McDowell, J. M., 551, 551n
McGee, John S., 323, 323n
McLuhan, Marshall, 206
Medicine,
    and price controls, 60–61
Middlemen,
    and arbitrage and speculation, 53–56
Mincer, J., 547, 547n
Minimum, 14
Models,
    cobweb, 52
    definition, 4
    systems of equations, 8
Money,
    purchasing power of, 174, 186
Monitors, 222
Monopoly, 47, 281–283, 302–304
    government-sanctioned, 302
    natural, 302–304
        definition, 303
        regulation of, 304–307
Monopsony, 419–420
    definition, 419
Monopsony demand, 424–425
Moore, John H., 541n
Morgan, J., 452n
Multiperiod analysis, 495–509
    asset prices and capitalization, 504–505
    constant yield assets, 497–499
    declining industries, 502–503
    depreciation and opportunity costs of capital, 503–504
    infinitely lived assets, 499
    investment in, 497
    property taxes and tax relief, 505–509
    supply of capital services, 500–502

Nicholson, Walter, 612n
Nonbinding price regulations, 56
Nonmarket time, 441
Nove, Alec, 175n

Oaxaca, Ronald, 547n
Ockham's razor, 7
Occupational Safety and Health Administration, 469
OEP. See Output expansion paths
Okun, Arthur M., 384n
Olsen, Edgar, 114, 114n
Operations,
    and costs, 249–251
Opportunity costs, 67–69, 82, 85
    capital, 503–504
    consuming, 105
    with continuous opportunities, 81–82
    purchasing, 99
Opportunity sets, 67–69, 71, 82, 85
    and choice, 66
    continuous, 78–81
    definition, 67
    and demand function, 134
    of goods and services, 96–102
    household budgets as, 96–102
    and insurance, 195–197
    of labor and leisure, 440–444
    opportunity cost, 67–69
    shifting, 443–444
    slopes of, 107
    time endowments, 441–442
    and utility function, 103
Optimization,
    and costs, 215–219
    and choice, 66

Index

Order,
  in ranking, 70
Organization,
  choice of, 211–232
  limits of, 212–215
  and market structure, 230–232
  nonprofit, 223–230
    government, 224–230
    private, 223–224
  theory of, 212–223
    costs and optimization, 215–219
    firms as metering devices, 220–223
Organization of Petroleum Exporting Countries, 319
Organized crime, 319–320
Output,
  choice of, 235–267, 271–296
    components of profit, 238–239
    industry supply, 264–267
    price discrimination, 284–296
    supply for price takers, 256–264
  choice of scale and, 276–277
  cost of, 371–373
  and costs, 240–256
    average, 242–244
    choice of scale, 251–252
    economies and diseconomies of scale, 254–255
    envelope curves, 252–254
    operating and overhead, 240–242
    positioning cost curves, 244–247
    rising, of constant-scale operations, 249
    shape of total cost curves, 247–249
  as function of inputs, 364
  maximum feasible, 333
  and price for price searchers, 272–284
    marginal revenue and elasticity, 274–276
    price searcher supply, 283–284
    revenue for price searchers, 272–274
  price searcher, 278–283
  rates of, 242
    definition, 240
  and revenue, 238–239
  theory of, 20
Output effect,
  of factor price changes, 377, 379–380
Output expansion paths, 353–355
Output markets,
  market power in, 404–414
    Averch-Johnson effect, 408–414
    isoprofit curves, 408
    profit restrictions, 406–407

Paasche measures, 177–186
  definition, 177
  items included, 190
  of price level changes, 187, 188
  when used, 189
Paglin, Morton, 522, 522n
Pareto optimality, 579–580
  allocative efficiency, 570–574
    with public goods, 576–579
  conditions for, 562–574
  definition, 556
  distributional efficiency, 568–570
  technological efficiency, 564–567
  with public goods, 575–580
  rates of product transformation, 574–575
Pareto, Vilfredo, 556
Passes,
  as rationing system, 45
Patents, 302
Peltzman, Sam, 388, 388n, 615, 615n, 617
Pigou, A. C., 560–561, 561n
Plott, Charles, 8n
Point elasticity, 160–161
Polachek, S. W., 547, 547n
Predatory pricing, 323
Preferredness, 70
Prejudice, 541
  responses to, 543–545
Present value, 482
  rule, 491–492
Price ceilings, 278–283
Price controls, 591–593
Price discrimination, 285–296
  conditions for, 292–293
  among customers, 289–292
  definition, 285
  interperson, 285
  interunit, 285–289
  market failure, 589–590
  separation of markets, 293–296
Price elasticity, 158–159
Price expectations, 50–52
Price indexes, 186–189
Price levels, 186
Prices, 415
  advantages of system, 46–47
  changes in goods', 138–141
  controlled, 56–61
    definition, 56
    farm policy, 56–58
    nationalized medicine, 60–61
    rent controls, 58–69
  determining, 32, 33, 41–46, 47–49
  effect of changes on demand, 144
  effect of changes on household budgets, 101–102
  income effects of changes, 141–143
  other, 34–37
  output, 364–365

Prices (*continued*)
   and output for price searchers, 272–284
      choice of output and scale, 276–277
      marginal revenue and elasticity, 274–276
      price searcher output with price ceilings, 278–283
      revenue for price searchers, 272–274
      price searcher supply, 283–284
   as rationing device, 46–49
   relations to income, 96–99
   and scale, 262–263
   substitution effects of changes, 143–144
   and supply and profits, 236
   supported, 56
Price searchers, 271–296
   definition, 238
   exploitation by, 416–418
   output and price for, 272–284
      choice of output and scale, 276–277
      marginal revenue and elasticity, 274–276
   output with price ceilings, 278–283
   price discrimination, 284–296
   revenue for, 272–274
   supply, 283–284
Price searching,
   definition, 272
   for inputs, 590–591
   market failure, 587–589
Price spread, 292–293
Price takers,
   definition, 238, 277
Price taking, 235–267
   components of profit, 238–239
   costs and outputs, 240–256
   definition, 272
   industry supply, 264–267
   price and scale, 262–263
   supply for, 256–264
   supply price elasticity and time, 263–264
   supply response for firms of given scale, 259–261
Priorities, 86–87
Private goods, 576
Product,
   average, 334–337
   marginal, 335
   marginal physical, 335
   total, 333–335
   total curve, 333
Product differentiation, 321
Product rule, 28–29
Production functions, 332–341, 356
   average product, 335–337
   definition, 332
   diminishing returns, 337
   marginal product, 335
   returns to scale and cost, 338–341
   total product, 333–335
   varying fixed factors, 337
Production theory, 331–360
   choosing technology, 350–360
   fixed proportions, 341–342
   isoquants, 341
      and returns to scale, 346–349
   perfect substitutes, 342–343
   production function, 332–341
   rate of technical substitution, 343–346
   technical changes, 349–350
Productivity, 363–388
   capital-labor ratio, 385–387
   costs and inputs, 369–373
   demand for factors, 373–380
   growth and statistics, 382–383
   revenue effects and marginal revenue products, 364–369
   technical changes, 387–388
   in theory and practice, 380–388
      paradox of increasing returns to labor, 383–385
Products,
   marginal revenue, 364–369
      definition, 365–366
   value of the marginal, 415–416
Profit restrictions, 406–407
Profits,
   components of, 238–239
      revenue and output, 238–239
   definition, 238
   feasible, 409–410
   firms, 226
   government organizations, 226–227
   on investments, 491
   permissible, 407, 410
   and supply and price, 236
Property rights,
   assignment of, 598
   and information, 202–203
   and tax relief, 505–509
   and transaction costs, 597–609
      Coase theorem, 597–599
      external costs and benefits, 599–602
      individual adjustment equilibrium, 603–604
      market provision of public goods, 602
      in public goods allocation, 604–609
Proportions,
   fixed, 341–242
Public goods,
   allocative efficiency with, 576–579
   definition, 575–576
   market provision of, 602
   Pareto optimality with, 575–580
   transaction costs in allocation, 604–609
Pullman, George M., 467

Index

Purchasing,
  opportunity cost of, 99

Quality,
  expected, 200
  and government, 227–230
Quantity, 49

Rail travel, 502–503
Ranking,
  with continuous opportunities, 71–72
  with uncertainty, 192–195
Rank ordering, 69–78
  and choice, 103
  convexity, 76–78
  and demand functions, 134
  and individual behavior, 69–70
  marginal rate of substitution, 75–76
  properties of indifference curves, 72–78
  ranking with continuous opportunities, 71–72
  utility, 70–71
Rapid transit, 128–130
Rappling, L. A., 396, 396n
Rate base, 407, 408
Rates of product transformation, 574–575
Rates of technical substitution, 343–346, 355–356, 400–402
  definition, 345
  law of diminishing, 345
Rates of return,
  regulation, 406–407, 410
Rationing, 43
  definition, 152
  nonprice, 43–46
  price as device, 46–49
  and price controls, 591–593
Regulations, 596–597, 615–618
  of business, 387–388
Rent controls, 58–60
Residual claimants, 222, 223
Responsiveness, 15–16
Return, 492
Returns to scale, 356
  constant, 339
  the cost, 338–341
  decreasing, 338–339
  increasing, 338
  and isoquants, 346–349
Revealed preference,
  theory of, 181–182
Revenue,
  marginal, 273–274, 365
    definition, 238
    and elasticity, 274–276
    and output, 238–239
    for price searchers, 272–274
  total, 272–273, 365
Revenue effects, 364–369
Ricardo, David, 332, 414
Risk, 191–192
Risk pooling, 198
Robinson, E. A. G., 255, 255n

Sanctions, 319
Savings,
  definition, 470
Savings and investment, 475–509
  capital supply and interest rates, 477–487
  decision to invest, 488–491
  investment opportunities and demand for loanable funds, 487–495
  measurement problem, 476–477
  multiperiod analysis, 495–509
  supply of loanable funds, 479–482
Scale,
  choice of, 251–252
  choice of output and, 276–277
  definition, 240
  economies and diseconomies of, 254–256
  and price, 262–263
  returns to,
    and cost, 338–341
    and isoquants, 346–349
  supply response for firms of given, 259–261
Schumpeter, Joseph A., 282, 282n
Screening models, 535
Second-best allocation of resources, 612–614
Senior, Nassau, 332
Sherman, Roger, 408n
Shirking, 220–222
Signaling models, 535–541
Sims, Christopher A., 385n
Simultaneous systems, 32–33
Slopes, 12, 65
  of budget constraints, 107
  definition, 10
  determining,
    chain rule, 27–28
    product rule, 28–29
  of indifference curves, 104
  of nonlinear functions, 23–25
  of opportunity set, 107
Smith, Adam, 414, 554
Smith, Vernon, 8n
Soil Bank, 57
South Africa,
  and coercion, 524
Soviet Union,
  and aggregation problem, 175
  and monopolies, 282
Speculation,
  arbitrage, 53–56
  definition, 55

Spence, Michael, 536n, 537, 537n
Spreads, 55
Stamp,   , 561, 561n
Standard Oil, 323
Stiglitz, J. E., 613n
Stroup, R., 548, 548n
Substitutability, 77, 83
Substitutes, 37
   definition, 36
   perfect, 342–343
Substitution,
   diminishing marginal rate of, 76
   elasticity of, 355–356
   marginal rate of, 75–76, 83, 87
      definition, 76
      and income consumption curves, 136, 137
Substitution effects,
   capital supply and interest rates, 484–485
   definition, 141
   of factor price changes, 377, 379
   of price changes, 143–144
   of wage increases, 450
Sunk costs, 240
Suppliers, 50–52
Supply,
   first law of, 263
   industry, 264–267
      regulation of entry, 266-267
   of labor, 392–393
   marginal factor cost with rising, 421–424
   minimum wage restrictions with rising, 428–431
   price searcher, 283–284
   for price takers, 256–264
   and profits and price, 236
   response for firms of given scale, 259–261
   rising and falling, 419–421
   second law of, 263
   theory of, 20, 212
Supply curves,
   backward-bending, 451
   compensated, 486
   for loanable funds, 485–487
   uncompensated, 486
Supply elasticity, 263
   definition, 420
Supply price elasticity, 263–264
Supply side,
   of markets, 49–56
      arbitrage and speculation, 53–56
      cobweb models, 52
      equilibrium conditions, 50–52
Surplus, 56
Survival, 219
Systems of equations, 8

Tangents, 11
Tastes,
   of demanders, 541–543
   for different work, 525–528, 529–531
Tatom, John A., 384–385, 384n
Taubman, Paul, 535, 535n
Tautologies, 6
Taxes,
   excise, 593–595
   income and other, 595–596
   negative income, 459–460
Tax relief,
   and property taxes, 505–509
Teams, 220
Technology,
   choice of, 331–360
      fixed proportions, 341–342
      isoquants, 341
      isoquants and return to scale, 346–349
      perfect substitutes, 342–343
      production function, 332–341
      rate of technical substitution, 343–346
      technical changes, 349–350
   choosing, 350–360
      elasticity of substitution, 355–356
      elasticity of substitution and factor income shares, 357–358
      optimum conditions, 352–353
      output expansion paths, 353–355
      technical changes and employment, 358–360
Theory,
   definition, 4–8
   empty, 6
   and information, 6
   as metaphor, 4–5
   normative, 554
   Ockham's razor, 7
   and prediction, 6–7
   positive, 554
   and verification, 7–8
Thompson, Earl, 224, 224n
Tideman, T. N. 609n
Time,
   demand, 40–41, 50
   and supply price elasticity, 236–264
Time cost,
   of consumption, 96, 115–118
   theory of, 126
Time endowments, 441–442
Tollison, R. D., 322, 322n
Transaction costs, 109–110
   definition, 214, 216
   and imperfect information, 199–200
   and property rights, 597–609
      Coase theorem, 597–599
      external costs and benefits, 599–602
      individual adjustment equilibrium, 603–604
      market provision of public goods, 602

Index

public good, 606
  in public good allocation, 604–609
Transferability, 292
Transitivity, 88
  definition, 74
  and intransitivity, 90
Transportation costs, 307–314
  equilibrium with, 311–314
Treiman, Donald J., 547n
Tullock, Gordon, 609n

Uncertainty, 173, 190–206
  choice with imperfect information, 190–206
  ranking with, 192–195
Unemployment,
  as job information search, 395–397
  seasonal and cyclical, 393–395
  sources of, 389
Unit change, 25
United Mine Workers, 322
Unit increase, 25
Utility,
  expected, 193–194
  measuring, 556–557
  and rank ordering, 70–71
  weighting of individual, 557–558
Utility functions, 70, 71–72
  and opportunity sets, 103
Utility levels,
  measuring, 558–562
Utility possibility frontiers, 557
Utility theory, 96

Value,
  expected, 191, 193
Vertical integration, 324
  definition, 216
Vertical intercepts, 12
  definition, 9

Wages, 414–415
  changes in, 448–452
  and consumption optima, 118–120
  difficulties of regulation, 431–433
  and discrimination, 541–548
    evidence on wage disparity, 546–548
    necessary conditions for wage disparity, 545–546
    responses to prejudice, 543–545
    tastes of demanders, 541–543
  full, 391
  minimum, 389–392
    and coercion, 525
    restrictions with rising supply, 428–431
  relative, 529
  reservation, 453–454
  sources of variations, 524
Walters, A. A., 612n
Wealth, 480
  distribution of, 519–522
  maximization, 491
Weights and measures, 174–175
Welch, Finis, 392n
Welfare economics, 553–580
  conditions for Pareto optimality, 562–575
  efficiency defined, 554–562
  Pareto optimality,
    with public goods, 575–580
Welfare loss,
  definition, 112
  and inefficiency, 111–114
  of public housing, 112–114
Working conditions,
  regulation of, 469–471
Workweeks, 463–464

Zajac, E. E., 408n